fourth edition

Writing Arguments

A Rhetoric with Readings

John D. Ramage
Arizona State University

John C. Bean
Seattle University

Allyn and Bacon

Boston ▪ London ▪ Toronto ▪ Sydney ▪ Tokyo ▪ Singapore

Vice President: Eben W. Ludlow
Editorial Assistant: Linda M. D'Angelo
Marketing Manager: Lisa Kimball
Editorial Production Administrator: Susan Brown
Editorial-Production Service: Matrix Productions
Text Designer: Denise Hoffman
Composition Buyer: Linda Cox
Manufacturing Buyer: Suzanne Lareau
Compositor: Omegatype Typography, Inc.
Cover Administrator: Linda Knowles
Cover Designer: Susan Paradise

Library of Congress Cataloging-in-Publication Data

Ramage, John D.
    Writing arguments : a rhetoric with readings / John D. Ramage,
John C. Bean. — 4th ed.
        p.   cm.
    Includes index.
    ISBN 0-205-26917-6
    1. English language—Rhetoric.   2. Persuasion (Rhetoric)
3. College readers.   4. Report writing.   I. Bean, John C.
II. Title.
PE1431.R33   1997
808'.0427—dc21   97–18531
                                                                     CIP

Printed in the United States of America

10 9 8 7 6 5 4 3 2 1   RRDV   01 00 99 98 97

brief contents

PART I   OVERVIEW OF ARGUMENT   1

CHAPTER 1   Argument: An Introduction   3

CHAPTER 2   Reading Arguments   24

CHAPTER 3   Writing Arguments   52

PART II   PRINCIPLES OF ARGUMENT   79

CHAPTER 4   The Core of an Argument:
A Claim with Reasons   81

CHAPTER 5   The Logical Structure of Arguments   95

CHAPTER 6   Evidence in Argument   113

CHAPTER 7   Moving Your Audience:
Audience-Based Reasons, *Ethos,* and *Pathos*   145

CHAPTER 8   Accommodating Your Audience:
Treating Differing Views   166

PART III   ARGUMENTS IN DEPTH:
FIVE CATEGORIES OF CLAIMS   189

CHAPTER 9   Using the Categories of Claims to Generate Ideas   191

CHAPTER 10   Definition Arguments: X Is/Is Not a Y   198

CHAPTER 11   Causal Arguments: X Causes/Does Not Cause Y   228

CHAPTER 12   Resemblance Arguments: X Is/Is Not Like Y   264

CHAPTER 13   Evaluation Arguments: X Is/Is Not a Good Y   281

CHAPTER 14   Proposal Arguments:
"We Should/Should Not Do X"   304

CHAPTER 15   Ethical Arguments   339

PART IV   WRITING FROM SOURCES:
THE ARGUMENT AS A FORMAL RESEARCH PAPER   355

CHAPTER 16   Finding and Selecting Sources:
The Library and the Internet   357

CHAPTER 17   Using and Documenting Sources   380

APPENDIXES   421

APPENDIX 1   Logical Fallacies   421

APPENDIX 2   The Writing Community: Working in Groups   435

PART V   AN ANTHOLOGY OF ARGUMENTS   453

CREDITS   709

INDEX   713

contents

Preface   xxv

PART I
OVERVIEW OF ARGUMENT   1

CHAPTER 1   Argument: An Introduction   3

What Do We Mean by Argument?   3
  Argument Is Not a Fight or a Quarrel   3
  Argument Is Not Pro-Con Debate   4
  Arguments Can Be Explicit or Implicit   4
The Defining Features of Argument   7
  Argument Requires Justification of Its Claims   7
  Argument Is Both a Process and a Product   9
  Argument Combines Truth Seeking and Persuasion   10
Argument and the Problem of Truth   12
  When Does Argument Become Propaganda?
  The Debate Between Socrates and Callicles   12
  What Is Truth? The Place of Argument in Contemporary Life   13
A Successful Process of Argumentation: The Well-Functioning Committee   17
"Petition to Waive the University Math Requirement"—Gordon Adams   19
Conclusion   23

CHAPTER 2   Reading Arguments   24

Why Reading Arguments Is Important for Writers of Argument   24
Suggestions for Improving Your Reading Process   24
Strategies for Reading Arguments: An Overview   26

Strategy 1: Reading as a Believer   26

"The Coming White Underclass"—Charles Murray   27

    Summary Writing as a Way of Reading to Believe   31

    Incorporating Summaries into Your Writing   37

    Suspending Doubt: Willing Your Own Belief in the Writer's Views   38

Strategy 2: Reading as a Doubter   39

Strategy 3: Seeking Out Alternative Views and Analyzing Sources of Disagreement   42

    Disagreement about Facts or Truth   42

    Disagreement about Values, Beliefs, or Assumptions   42

"Letter to the Editor" in Response to Charles Murray—Patricia Bucalo   44

"Letter to the Editor" in Response to Charles Murray—Pamela J. Maraldo   45

Excerpt from "New Cultural Conscience Shifts the Welfare Debate"—John Leo   46

"Wrong Way to Reform Welfare"—Dorothy Gilliam   46

    Writing an Analysis of a Disagreement   48

"An Analysis of the Sources of Disagreement between Murray and Gilliam" (A Sample Analysis Essay)   48

Strategy 4: Evaluating the Conflicting Positions   50

Conclusion   51

CHAPTER 3   Writing Arguments   52

A Brief Description of Writers' Process   52

Strategies for Improving Your Writing Process   54

Using Expressive Writing for Discovery and Exploration   56

    Freewriting   56

    Idea-mapping   58

    Playing the Believing and Doubting Game   58

    Brainstorming for Pro and Con *Because* Clauses   61

    Brainstorming a Network of Related Issues   62

Shaping Your Argument   63

    Classical Argument as an Initial Guide   63

    The Power of Tree Diagrams   66

Using Expressive Writing to Discover and Explore Ideas:
Two Sets of Exploratory Tasks   71

    Set 1: Starting Points   71

    Set 2: Exploration and Rehearsal   73

 Writing Assignments for Chapters 1–3   75

 PART II
PRINCIPLES OF ARGUMENT   79

CHAPTER 4   The Core of an Argument:
A Claim with Reasons   81

The Rhetorical Triangle   81

Issue Questions as the Origins of Argument   83

    Difference Between an Issue Question and an Information Question   83

Difference Between a Genuine Argument and a Pseudo-argument   85

    Pseudo-Arguments: Fanatics and Skeptics   85

    Another Source of Pseudo-Arguments:
    Lack of Shared Assumptions   86

Frame of an Argument: A Claim Supported by Reasons   88

    What Is a Reason?   88

    Advantages of Expressing Reasons in Because Statements   90

Application of this Chapter's Principles to Your Own Writing   92

Application of this Chapter's Principles to the Reading of Arguments   93

Conclusion   94

CHAPTER 5   The Logical Structure of Arguments   95

Overview to *Logos:* What Do We Mean by the "Logical Structure"
of an Argument   95

Adopting a Language for Describing Arguments: The Toulmin System   99

Using Toulmin's Schema to Determine a Strategy of Support   106

    Evidence as Support   107

    Chain of Reasons as Support   110

Conclusion   112

CHAPTER 6   Evidence in Argument   113

Using Evidence from Personal Experience   113
    Using Personal Experience Data Collected from Memory   113
    Using Personal Experience Data Collected from Observations   114

Using Evidence from Interviews, Surveys, and Questionnaires   115
    Conducting Interviews   115
    Using Surveys or Questionnaires   116

Using Evidence from Reading   117
    Facts and Examples   117
    Summaries of Research   118
    Testimony   118

Using Numerical Data and Statistics   118
    Representing Numbers in Tables, Graphs, and Charts   119
        Line Graphs   121
        Bar Graphs   122
        Pie Charts   124
    Using Graphics for Effect   124
    Using Numbers Strategically   127

What to Do When the Experts Disagree   128
    Coping with Uncertainty   131

Writing Your Own Argument: Using Evidence Persuasively   133
    When Possible, Select Your Data from Sources Your Reader Trusts   133
    Increase Persuasiveness of Factual Data by Ensuring Recency, Representativeness, and Sufficiency   134
    In Citing Evidence, Distinguish Fact from Inference or Opinion   135
    To Use Evidence Persuasively, Position It Effectively   136

Conclusion   137

❧ Writing Assignments for Chapters 4–6   138

"Choose Life"—Dao Do (student)   143

CHAPTER 7   Moving Your Audience: Audience-Based Reasons, *Ethos*, and *Pathos*   145

Starting from Your Readers' Beliefs: The Power of Audience-Based Reasons   145
    Difference Between Writer- and Audience-Based Reasons   146
    Finding Audience-Based Reasons: Asking Questions about Your Audience   149

Ethos and *Pathos* as Persuasive Appeals: An Overview   151

How to Create an Effective *Ethos:* The Appeal to Credibility   153
    Be Knowledgeable about Your Issue   153
    Be Fair   153
    Build a Bridge to Your Audience   154

How to Create *Pathos:* The Appeal to Beliefs and Emotions   154
    Use Concrete Language   155
    Use Specific Examples and Illustrations   155
    Use Narratives   156
    Choose Words, Metaphors, and Analogies with Appropriate Connotations   158

The InterRelatedness of *Logos, Ethos,* and *Pathos:*
Where Should I Reveal My Thesis?   159

"Minneapolis Pornography Ordinance"—Ellen Goodman   160

Our Rewrite of the Same Essay into the Classical Argument Structure   162

Conclusion   165

CHAPTER 8   Accommodating Your Audience:
                    Treating Differing Views   166

Opening Exercise   166

One-Sided Versus Multisided Arguments   169

Determining Your Audience's Resistance to Your Views   170

Appealing to a Supportive Audience: One-Sided Argument   172

Appealing to a Neutral or Undecided Audience: Classical Argument   173
    Summarizing Opposing Views   173
    Refuting Opposing Views   174
    Strategies for Rebutting Evidence   178

"Abstract Versus Representational Art" (student essay)   179
    Conceding to Opposing Views   181

Appealing to a Resistant Audience: Delayed Thesis or Rogerian Argument   182
    Delayed Thesis Argument   182
    Rogerian Argument   183

"Letter to Beth Downey" (student essay)   185

Conclusion   186

❖ Writing Assignments for Chapters 7 and 8   187

❧ PART III
ARGUMENTS IN DEPTH:
FIVE CATEGORIES OF CLAIMS   189

CHAPTER 9   Using the Categories of Claims
to Generate Ideas   191

What Is a Truth Argument?   191

What Is a Values Argument?   192

Three-Step Strategy for Developing Values Arguments   193
  An Argument from Definition or Principle   194
  An Argument from Consequence   195
  An Argument from Resemblance   195

CHAPTER 10   Definition Arguments: X Is/Is Not a Y   198

The Special Nature of a Definitional Issue   199

❧ Writing Assignment for Chapter 10
  Extended Definition/Borderline Case: Is This X a Y?   200

The Criteria-Match Structure of Definitional Arguments   201

Conceptual Problems of Definition   203
  Language as a Way of Ordering the World   203
  Why Can't We Just Look in the Dictionary?   203
  Definitions and the Rule of Justice:
  At What Point Does X Quit Being a Y?   204

Conducting a Criteria-Match Argument   206

Defining the Y Term (Establishing Criteria for Y)   206
  Aristotelian Definition   206
  Effect of Rhetorical Context on Aristotelian Definitions   208
  Operational Definitions   209

Conducting the Match Part of a Definitional Argument   209

Writing Your Definitional Argument   210
  Starting Points: Finding a Definitional Controversy   210
  Exploration Stage I: Developing Criteria for Your Y Term   212

Exploration Stage II: Exploring Your Match Argument   214

Writing the Discovery Draft—A Possible Organizational Structure
for Your Essay   215

Revision Stage   215

Conditions for Rebuttal: Testing a Definitional Argument   217

Attacking the Criteria   217

Attacking the Match   218

"Oncore, Obscenity, and the Liquor Control Board"—Kathy Sullivan (student)   220
A series of photographs in a gay bar should not be considered obscene because they
do not violate the community standards of the patrons of the bar, because they do
not appeal to prurient interests, because children are not apt to be exposed to them,
and because they promote an important social purpose of safe sex to prevent AIDS.

"How to Save the Homeless Mentally Ill"—Charles Krauthammer   221
The United States should rebuild its system of asylums to care for the mentally
ill homeless, who need to be involuntarily institutionalized if necessary. The
criteria should include the conditions of being degraded or made helpless by
mental illness.

CHAPTER 11   Causal Arguments: X Causes/Does Not Cause Y   228

The Frequency of Causal Arguments   229

The Nature of Causal Arguing   230

Describing the Logical Structure of a Causal Argument:
Because Clauses and the Toulmin Schema   233

❦ Writing Assignment for Chapter 11:
An Argument Involving Surprising or Disputed Causes   236

Three Methods for Arguing that One Event Causes Another   237

First Method: Explain the Causal Mechanism Directly   237

Second Method: Use Various Inductive Methods to Establish
a High Probability of a Causal Link   239

Third Method: Argue by Analogy or Precedent   243

Glossary of Terms Encountered in Causal Arguments   244

Writing Your Causal Argument   247

The Starting Point: Finding a Causal Issue   247

Make a List of People's Unusual Likes and Dislikes   247

Make Lists of Trends and Other Puzzling Phenomena   247

Exploration Stage   248

Writing the Discovery Draft:
Typical Ways of Organizing a Causal Argument   248

Revision: Seeing Your Argument Afresh   250

Conditions for Rebuttal: Critiquing Causal Arguments   250

If You Described Each Link in a Causal Chain, Would Skeptics
Point Out Weaknesses in Any of the Links?   250

If Your Argument Is Based on a Scientific Experiment, Could Skeptics
Question the Validity of the Experiment?   251

If You Have Used Correlation Data, Could Skeptics Argue that
the Correlation Is Much Weaker than You Claim or that You Haven't
Sufficiently Demonstrated Causality?   252

If You Have Used an Analogy Argument, Could Skeptics
Point Out Disanalogies?   252

Could a Skeptic Cast Doubt on Your Argument by Reordering
Your Priority of Causes?   252

"The Warming of the World"—Carl Sagan   253
A global catastrophe is inevitable unless the world's nations act cooperatively to
combat the greenhouse effect.

"What Drugs I Take Is None of Your Business—The Consequences of Drug Testing"
—Mary Lou Torpey (student)   257
A sufferer from narcolepsy, Mary Lou Torpey shows how mandatory drug testing
may lead to job discrimination against persons with chronic diseases treatable with
controlled substance drugs.

"Why Married Mothers Work"—Victor Fuchs   259
Rejecting the hypothesis that the increase in the number of working mothers has
been caused primarily by feminism, by affirmative action, or by economic necessity,
Fuchs proposes a different causal hypothesis: More mothers work because of
increased wages and increased numbers of jobs in the service sector of the economy.

"Students Who Push Burgers"—Walter S. Minot   262
What is wrong with American education? Although many critics blame drugs or
television or the decline of the family, perhaps the chief cause is the desire of
teenagers to hold part-time jobs.

CHAPTER 12   Resemblance Arguments:
X Is/Is Not Like Y   264

The Difference Between Resemblance Arguments
and Definition Arguments   265

❧ Writing Assignments for Chapter 12   267

First Type of Resemblance Argument: Arguments by Analogy   268

Using Undeveloped Analogies   268

Using Extended Analogies   269

Second Type of Resemblance Argument: Arguments by Precedent   271

Writing Your Resemblance Argument   274

Conditions for Rebuttal: Testing a Resemblance Argument   274

Will My Audience Say I Am Trying to Prove Too Much
with My Analogy or Precedent?   274

Will My Audience Point Out Disanalogies in My Resemblance Argument?   274

Will My Audience Propose a Counteranalogy?   276

From "Against Our Will: Men, Women and Rape"—Susan Brownmiller   278
Feminist writer Susan Brownmiller argues that pornography is analogous to racist
propaganda. Liberals need to fight the degrading and dehumanizing images of
women in pornography just as they have fought the racism implicit in *Little Black
Sambo* or the *Frito Bandito.*

CHAPTER 13   Evaluation Arguments: X Is/Is Not a Good Y   281

❦ Writing Assignment for Chapter 13: Evaluate a "Controversial" X   283

Criteria-Match Structure of Evaluation Arguments   284

General Strategy for Evaluation Arguments   286

The Problem of Standards: What's Normal or What's Ideal?   286

The Problem of Mitigating Circumstances   287

The Problem of Choosing Between Two Goods or Two Bads   287

The Problem of Seductive Empirical Measures   287

The Problem of Cost   288

How to Determine Criteria for Your Argument   288

Step 1: Determine the Category in Which the Object
Being Evaluated Belongs   288

Step 2: Determine the Purpose or Function of This Class   289

Step 3: Determine Criteria Based on the Purposes or Function
of the Class to Which X Belongs   290

Step 4: Give Relative Weightings to the Criteria   291

Determining Whether X Meets the Criteria   291

Writing Your Evaluation Argument   294

Starting Point: Finding and Exploring an Evaluation Issue   294

Writing a Discovery Draft: Some Suggestions for Organizing
Your Evaluation Argument Revision   294

Revision   295

Conditions for Rebuttal: Testing Your Evaluation Argument   295

   Will My Audience Accept My Criteria?   295

   Are My Criteria Based on the "Smallest Applicable Class" for X?   295

   Will Readers Accept My General Weighting of Criteria?   295

   Will Readers Question My Standard of Reference?   296

   Will Readers Criticize My Use of Empirical Measures?   296

   Will Readers Accept My Criteria but Reject My Match Argument?   296

"How to Reform the Federal Tax System: Just the Basics, Please"
—Murray Weidenbaum   297

   Professor Weidenbaum of the Center for the Study of American Business
   enumerates a set of six criteria by which any tax reform can be judged.

"Clinton Can Show Courage by Vetoing Bad Welfare Bill"—Terry Tang   298

   Columnist Terry Tang urges President Clinton to veto the proposed welfare reform
   package on the grounds that it hits hardest at those least able to help themselves,
   particularly children. (Clinton subsequently signed the bill into law.)

"Would Legalization of Gay Marriage Be Good for the Gay Community?"
—Sam Isaacson (student)   300

   Student writer Sam Isaacson, addressing a gay audience, evaluates the potential
   impact of gay marriage on the gay community.

"Beauty Pageant Fallacies"—Debra Goodwin (student)   302

   Beauty pageants harm society by damaging women's self-esteem, by reducing
   women to pornographic objects, and by exploiting women through stereotyping
   of female sexuality and devaluing older women.

CHAPTER 14   Proposal Arguments: "We Should/Should Not Do X"   304

The Nature of Proposal Arguments   305

The General Structure and Strategy of Proposal Arguments   306

Special Requirements of Proposal Arguments   306

   Adding "Presence" to Your Argument   307

   Overcoming the Natural Conservatism of People   308

   The Difficulty of Predicting Future Consequences   308

   The Problem of Evaluating Consequences   309

❦ Writing Assignment for Chapter 14:
   Options for Proposal Arguments   309

Developing a Proposal Argument   311

   Convincing Your Readers That a Problem Exists   311

Showing the Specifics of Your Proposal   312

The Justification: Convincing Your Reader That Your Proposal
Should Be Enacted   312

Touching the Right Pressure Points   314

Using the "Stock Issues" Strategy to Develop a Proposal Argument   314

Using the Toulmin Schema to Develop a Proposal Argument   315

Writing the Proposal Argument   318

Starting Points: Finding a Proposal Issue   318

Exploration Stage   319

Writing the Discovery Draft:
Some Ways to Organize a Proposal Argument   319

Revision Stage   320

Conditions for Rebuttal: Testing Your Proposal Argument   320

Will My Audience Deny That My Problem Is Really a Problem?   320

Will My Audience Doubt the Effectiveness of My Solution?   321

Will My Audience Think My Proposal Costs Too Much?   321

Will My Audience Suggest Counterproposals?   322

"A Proposal to Save Bernie's Blintzes Restaurant"—Jeffrey Cain (student)   324
Faced with competition from fast-food chains and battling the public's growing
preference for low-fat health foods, Matzoh Momma, an ethnic Jewish restaurant,
faces bankruptcy. Jeffrey Cain offers an innovative advertising campaign as a
possible solution.

"What Should Be Done about the Mentally Ill Homeless?"
—Stephen Bean (student)   330
Opposing Charles Krauthammer's proposal for massive rebuilding of the nation's
mental asylums, Stephen Bean argues that homelessness among the mentally ill is
primarily a social and economic problem rather than a psychiatric problem and that
the mentally ill homeless would be better served through community-based care.

CHAPTER 15   Ethical Arguments   339

Special Difficulties of Ethical Arguments   339

An Overview of Major Ethical Systems   340

Naive Egoism   341

Consequences as the Grounds of Ethics   343

Principles as the Grounds of Ethics   344

The Two Systems Compared   344

Some Compromise Positions Between Consequences and Principles   345

Developing an Ethical Argument   346

Testing Ethical Arguments   348

*"The Ones Who Walk Away from Omelas (Variations
on a Theme by William James)"*—Ursula Le Guin   349

> The happiness of the mythical city of Omelas depends on the misery of one
> unfortunate child. There is nothing the people can do. "If the child were brought
> into the sunlight . . . in that day and hour all the prosperity and beauty and delight
> of Omelas would wither and be destroyed. These are the terms."

PART IV
WRITING FROM SOURCES:
THE ARGUMENT AS A FORMAL RESEARCH PAPER   355

CHAPTER 16   Finding and Selecting Sources:
The Library and the Internet   357

Formulating a Research Question   358

Exploring on the Internet   360
  Listserv Discussions   360
  Usenet Newsgroups   362
  Real-Time Discussion or Chat   364

Locating Sources in the Library or Online   366
  Using the Card Catalog   367
  Using Periodical and Newspaper Indexes   369
  Using Online and Electronic Databases   372
  Using the World Wide Web and Gopher   375
  Using Other Library Sources   377

Using Your Sources: Sitting Down to Read   379

CHAPTER 17   Using and Documenting Sources   380

Clarifying Your Own Thinking: The Case of Lynnea   380

Developing a Good System of Note Taking   382

Incorporating Sources into Your Argument: Some General Principles   382

"Reading, Writing, and (Ugh!) You Know What"—Science '86   382

    Citing Information   383

    Summarizing an Argument: Different Contexts Demand
Different Summaries   384

    Article Summaries as a Note-Taking Tool   386

    Paraphrasing Portions of an Argument   386

    Quoting   386

Incorporating Sources into Your Argument: Technical Advice
on Summarizing, Paraphrasing, and Quoting   387

"The Case for Torture"—Michael Levin   387

    Although most people think of torture as an outdated, barbaric practice, under
certain conditions torture is not "merely permissible but morally mandatory."

    Summary   389

    Paraphrase   390

    Block Quotation   390

    Inserted Quotation   391

    Shortening or Modifying Quotations   391

    Using Quotations within Quotations   392

    An Extended Illustration: Martha's Argument   393

    Signaling Directions: The Use of Attributive Tags   394

Avoiding Plagiarism   395

    Note Taking to Avoid Plagiarism   396

Documenting Your Sources   396

    When to Cite Sources   396

    What Format to Use   397

Overview of the MLA and APA Systems of Documentation   397

    Feature 1: Place a Complete Bibliographic List at the End of the Text   397

    Feature 2: Cite Sources in the Text by Putting Brief References
in Parentheses   398

    Form for Entries in "Works Cited" (MLA) and "References" (APA)   400

Conclusion   410

Example of a Student Research Paper as an Argument (APA style) *"Women Police
Officers: Should Size and Strength Be Criteria for Patrol Duty?"*—Lynnea Clark   414

    Examining available data on women police officers, student writer Lynnea Clark
concludes that police departments should establish rigorous strength and size
requirements for police on patrol.

❧ APPENDIXES   421

APPENDIX 1   Logical Fallacies   421

The Problem of Conclusiveness in an Argument   421

An Overview of Informal Fallacies   422

APPENDIX 2   The Writing Community:
Working in Groups   435

From Conflict to Consensus:
How to Get the Most Out of the Writing Community   435

Forming Writing Communities: Skills and Roles   437

A Several-Days' Group Project: Defining "Good Argumentative Writing"   442

A Classroom Debate   451

❧ PART V
AN ANTHOLOGY OF ARGUMENTS   453

Overview of the Anthology   453

Guide Questions for the Analysis and Evaluation of Arguments   455

Questions for Analyzing and Evaluating a Conversation   455

Questions for Analyzing and Evaluating an Individual Argument   455

Immigration Policy   457

"The Case for Greatly Increased Immigration"—Julian L. Simon   457
Noted economist Julian Simon argues that the United States would benefit
substantially from increased immigration. In the long run, argues Simon, immigrants
create new jobs rather than produce unemployment and pay more in taxes than they
use in public services. For these and other reasons, increased immigration will boost
U.S. productivity and benefit the whole nation.

"Huddled Excesses"—Michael Lind   467
Arguing on the basis of "social justice," liberal social commentator Michael Lind
favors limits on the number of legal immigrants allowed into the United States.
While many conservatives nominally support such limitations, they do so half-
heartedly knowing that the influx of immigrants creates a pool of cheap labor. Such
labor in turn drives many poor Americans out of work and taxes the welfare system.

"Timeout: The United States Needs a Moratorium on Immigration"—Dan Stein   469
Dan Stein argues that the recent influx of immigrants into the United States exceeds
our ability to assimilate them into mainstream culture and prevents our developing
policies to stop illegal immigration.

Mercy Killing and the Right to Die   472

"Active and Passive Euthanasia"—James Rachels   472
In a classic essay from the *New England Journal of Medicine,* medical ethicist James
Rachels argues against the traditional legal and moral distinction between active and
passive euthanasia. "Letting" someone die, Rachels argues, is not a "passive act";
moreover, passive euthanasia is often crueler than active euthanasia.

"Saying What We Mean"—David B. McCurdy   477
Christian writer David McCurdy calls attention to a "disturbing" language shift
in recent discussions about euthanasia. According to McCurdy, euthanasia was
traditionally defended as an act of mercy and compassion, a warrant consonant
with Christian values. But increasingly, pro-euthanasia arguments have characterized
it as a mode of "rationing" medical care that is justifiable largely on economic
grounds. McCurdy abhors this shift, which he sees as inimical to Christian belief.

"Rising to the Occasion of Our Death"—William F. May   479
Legalizing active euthanasia to eliminate suffering may blind us to the value of
suffering. "The community . . . may need its aged and dependent, its sick and its
dying, and the virtues they sometimes evince."

What Responsibility of the Rich for the Poor?   481

"Lifeboat Ethics: The Case Against Aid that Harms"—Garrett Hardin   481
Hardin argues that rich nations are like lifeboats and that impoverished people are
like swimmers in the sea clamoring to climb aboard the lifeboat. If we allow all the
swimmers to come aboard, the lifeboat sinks. "Complete justice; complete catastrophe."

"Rich and Poor"—Peter Singer   489
We have a moral obligation to help those living in "absolute poverty." "Helping is
not, as conventionally thought, a charitable act which is praiseworthy to do, but not
wrong to omit; it is something that everyone ought to do."

Civil Disobedience   497

*"Letter from Birmingham Jail" in Response to "Public Statement by Eight Alabama
Clergymen"*—Martin Luther King, Jr.   497
On April 12, 1963, eight Alabama clergymen signed a public statement urging
"outsiders" to halt the racial demonstrations they had instigated. Writing from the
Birmingham jail, Martin Luther King, Jr., gives a compelling justification for his
actions. "I am in Birmingham because injustice is here."

"Civil Disobedience: Destroyer of Democracy"—Lewis H. Van Dusen, Jr.   510
Attorney Lewis H. Van Dusen, Jr., a Rhodes scholar and graduate of Harvard Law
School, distinguishes between "conscientious disobedience"—in which one willingly
accepts punishment in order to make a moral protest—and active group disobedience
aimed at changing laws. "[C]ivil disobedience [e.g., the kind practiced by Martin Luther
King, Jr.], whatever the ethical rationalization, is still an assault on our democratic
society, an affront to our legal order, and an attack on our constitutional government."

From *The Crito*—Plato   514

> Socrates, who was himself ill-served by the state, here argues in favor of a citizen's absolute obligation to obey the rules of the state. He has been unjustly sentenced to die, and his friend Crito urges him to escape from prison. Socrates declines on ethical grounds.

Censorship on the Internet   519

"In Defense of Decency"—Mike Romano   519

> Writer Mike Romano argues against extending special exemptions from censorship to the Internet. While Internet proponents see the Net as an especially egalitarian medium of communication, Romano argues that it's largely controlled by two corporate giants, and hence deserves no greater claim to censorship exemption than other media.

"Net Benefit"—Kathleen Durkan   522

> Media producer Kathleen Durkan worries that in our concern to control pornography on the Net, we will lose sight of far more significant issues involving control of ideas. She is more concerned to protect the Net against television and "the present media monopolies on serious information" than to compromise the free flow of ideas by some sort of central control.

"The Net Doesn't Need Thought Police"—Marc Rothenberg   523

> Science historian Marc Rothenberg argues that censoring online discussion is akin to telling telephone users "which words they can use." Noting also that the Communications Decency Act allows officials to open private e-mail and to punish people for "offensive language," Rothenberg rejects the notion that "bad stuff" can be eliminated without impairing users' ability to share important ideas.

"Only the Force of Law Can Deter Pornographers"—James Exon   525

> Senator James Exon of Nebraska, cosponsor of the controversial Communications Decency Act, denies that the act will have any dampening effect on free speech between consenting adults. According to Exon, the bill's sole concern is the protection of children against pornography, and he sees no reason why First Amendment protections covering print, television, radio, and telephonic media should be extended any more generously to online communication.

"This Is Safe Sex?"—James Gleick   527

> Well-known science writer James Gleick calls Internet censorship on a national scale, "anomalous" in the context of existing censorship legislation's concern for violations of community, not national, standards. Gleick also sees such censorship as misplaced, insofar as there is less objectionable material on the Net than is popularly believed, and unenforceable because the Net has no single controllable "source."

The Legalization of Drugs   530

"The Federal Drugstore"—an interview with Michael S. Gazzaniga   530

> In this interview, Michael S. Gazzaniga, professor of neuroscience at Dartmouth Medical School, provides a scientific perspective on drugs and abuse. Gazzaniga's own stance is a scientifically cautious belief that the benefits of legalizing drugs outweigh the costs.

"Biting the Bullet: The Case for Legalizing Drugs"—Walter Wink   539

Theologian Walter Wink examines the arguments for and against legalization of drugs and concludes that it is wrong to fight evil with evil. "Legalization offers a nonviolent, nonreactive, creative alternative that will let the drug menace collapse of its own deadly weight."

"The Economics of Legalizing Drugs"—Richard J. Dennis   544

Conducting a cost-benefit analysis of drug legalization, Dennis concludes that "[t]o the pragmatist, the choice is clear: legalization is the best bet." It seems doubtful that making most drugs legal would significantly increase the number of addicts but certain that it would reduce crime and save society money.

"Against the Legalization of Drugs"—James Q. Wilson   552

Noted professor and former member of the National Council for Drug Abuse Prevention James Q. Wilson compares contemporary arguments for cocaine legalization to earlier arguments for heroin legalization. Focusing on the disquieting consequences, he rejects drug legalization as costly and dehumanizing, leading to huge increases in crime, addiction, and violence.

"Drug Use by U.S. Army Enlisted Men in Vietnam: A Follow-Up on Their Return Home"—Lee N. Robins, Darlene H. Davis, and Donald W. Goodwin   563

This frequently cited research study has been interpreted in different ways (see the conflicting interpretations by Gazzaniga and Wilson in this section). "The results of this study indicate that, contrary to conventional belief, the occasional use of narcotics without becoming addicted appears possible even for men who have previously been dependent on narcotics."

Sexual Harassment: When Is Offensiveness a Civil Offense?   581

"Gender Dilemmas in Sexual Harassment Policies and Procedures"
—Stephanie Riger   581

Psychology professor Riger analyzes reasons for the paucity of sexual harassment complaints. She concludes that a gender bias is built into the way sexual harassment policies are written.

"Harassment Blues"—Naomi Munson   596

Munson questions present definitions of sexual harassment and confusion between harassing remarks and innuendo. The writer blames "feminist rage" for much of the failure to distinguish between harassment and normal insensitivity in the workplace.

"Fear of Flirting"—Erica Jong   599

Erica Jong, while deploring the actions of many recently noted sexual harassers, argues for more tolerance toward a special class of harassers who can't "bring [their] intellect and [their] emotions into the same century," who support women's issues with their heads but can't find it in their hearts to quit trying to exploit them.

"Watch That Leer, Stifle That Joke"—Gretchen Morgenson   602

Forbes writer Morgenson argues that "the alleged increase in sexual harassment [is] more a product of propaganda from self-interested parties" than from substantive cases.

"A Wink Here, a Leer There: It's Costly"—Susan Crawford   606

  Attorney Susan Crawford offers a pragmatic defense of sexual harassment laws
  based on lost employee work time, inefficient use of the work day, and costly
  lawsuits growing out of sexual harassment issues.

"Universal Truth and Multiple Perspectives: Controversies on Sexual Harassment"
—Martha Chamallas   607

  Law professor Chamallas argues that the burden of proof in sex discrimination cases
  ought not to be on the putative victim but on the accuser; antidiscrimination laws,
  she contends, ought to take the "victim's perspective."

Recycling and Garbage   612

"America's 'Garbage Crisis': A Toxic Myth"—Patricia Poore   612

  Environmental writer Patricia Poore calls on the environmental movement to quit
  focusing so much attention on garbage as a problem and on recycling as its only
  solution. She asks instead that we refocus our attention on environmental issues that
  pose more immediate threats to life and quit pretending that recycling assures a net
  economic gain.

"Time to Dump Recycling?"
—Chris Hendrickson, Lester Lave, and Francis McMichael   614

  Drawing largely on data from their own area of Pittsburgh, academics Hendrickson,
  Lave, and McMichael reject the arguments for the economic viability of recycling. In
  turn, they underscore the often-overlooked environmental costs of recycling
  programs.

"Don't Dump Recycling"—Robert Steuteville   620

  Robert Steuteville, editor of *Biocycle Magazine,* challenges Hendrickson and his
  colleagues in a letter to the editor of *Issues in Science and Technology.* In particular, he
  calls attention to the authors' use of unrepresentative and out-of-date data and their
  reliance on faulty economic assumptions.

"Response to Hendrickson et al."—Reid Lifset and John Schall   622

  Planners Reid Lifset and John Schall respond to Hendrickson and his colleagues
  in a letter that draws heavily on what they contend is a superior study of
  recycling conducted by the Tellus Institute of Boston for the Regional Plan
  Association. This study found that the costs of recycling are about the same as
  the costs of disposal.

"Response to Hendrickson et al."—Brenda Platt and Neil Seldman   623

  Citing a number of examples to offset the Pittsburgh experience with recycling
  detailed by Hendrickson and his colleagues, authors Platt and Seldman point out
  ways in which costs of recycling can decline or soar depending on the mode and the
  rate of collection. Moreover, they argue that many of the benefits of recycling may
  not be immediately visible.

"Recycling: Asking the Right Questions"—Lynn Scarlett   624

  Economist Lynn Scarlett plots a middle course in the recycling debate, calling for
  selective recycling that's market driven and determined by "the material, the
  product, the process and local circumstance."

"Recycling: The Other Coast, The Other Story"—Nancy Glaser   626

> Seattle city official Nancy Glaser cites Seattle's success as an example of what can be done with a well-run recycling project. In particular, she takes issue with a claim made in a *New York Times Magazine* piece that the "environmental costs of a product are included in the price" of that product. If this were true, the market has a self-correcting mechanism—high price—for limiting the production of environmentally harmful products. Such an assumption, Glaser argues, assumes a pure market free of price distorting forces—and such a market doesn't exist.

Social Policy Toward the Mentally Ill Homeless   632

"Crazy in the Streets"—Paul S. Appelbaum   632

> A professor of psychiatry outlines the history of deinstitutionalization of the mentally ill and calls for its reversal. "Far from impinging on their autonomy, treatment of [the psychotic homeless], even coercive treatment, would not only hold out some hope of mitigating their condition but might simultaneously increase their capacity for more sophisticated autonomous choices."

"Are the Homeless Crazy?"—Jonathan Kozol   641

> The author of *Rachel and Her Children* offers a social and economic explanation of homelessness among the mentally ill. "The notion that the homeless are largely psychotics who belong in institutions, rather than victims of displacement at the hands of enterprising realtors, spares us from the need to offer realistic solutions to the deep and widening extremes of wealth and poverty in the United States."

"The Homeless Mentally Ill"—Steven Vanderstaay   644

> Freelance writer Steven Vanderstaay spent many months living among the homeless and recording their stories. In his book *Street Lives: An Oral History of Homeless Americans,* Vanderstaay interweaves homeless persons' own stories with his own interpretive commentary based on research in the literature on homelessness. The following reading is extracted from the chapter on mentally ill homeless in Vanderstaay's book.

"Who Goes Homeless?"—E. Fuller Torrey   653

> Dr. E. Fuller Torrey, a clinical and research psychiatrist and volunteer worker in a clinic for homeless mentally ill women, places the problems of the mentally ill homeless within the larger context of general homelessness. He claims that the solutions to homelessness are known. "The mystery no longer is what to do, but rather why we do not do it."

Same-Sex Marriage   659

"Here Comes the Groom: A (Conservative) Case for Gay Marriage"
—Andrew Sullivan   659

> *New Republic* editor Andrew Sullivan recommends the legalization of civil gay marriage primarily on legal and procedural grounds. The hybrid notion of "domestic partnership" that currently applies to most long-term gay relationships remains too ambiguous to resolve issues of partners' entitlement, and it promotes an inherently unstable bond. Acknowledging opposition to his proposal within the gay community, Sullivan champions gay marriage as an unabashedly conservative means of legitimating already recognized gay relationships.

"Against Gay Marriage—I: What Heterosexuality Means"—Dennis O'Brien   662
Writer Dennis O'Brien argues that the marriage bond is not primarily a civil bond so much as a religious and political one. Seeing sex as a "human artifact" rather than a purely biological phenomenon, O'Brien argues that the procreative meaning of marriage can't be embodied in a homosexual union.

"Gay Rights, Gay Marriages"—John Leo   665
Editorial writer John Leo argues against gay marriage and for continued privileging of heterosexual marriage on the grounds that marriage is designed to ensure two-gender families, which are in turn necessary for effective child-rearing.

"For Better or Worse? The Case for Gay (and Straight) Marriage"
—Jonathan Rauch   666
Author Jonathan Rauch rejects the idea that marriage is primarily a religious institution. Likening the ban on gay marriage to former interracial marriage, Rauch rejects the argument that the privileging of marriage rests on society's compelling social interest in rearing and protecting children. Marriage serves a number of other socially useful functions, according to Rauch, including the civilizing of young males and ensuring people of a caregiver late in life.

Family Values, Single Parenthood, and Welfare Reform   673

"Why I Hate 'Family Values' (Let Me Count the Ways)"—Katha Pollitt   673
Writer Katha Pollitt argues that sitcom anchor Murphy Brown's decision to have a child is defensible and unlikely to influence welfare recipients to follow suit. Pollitt pans conservative critics of Brown for using vague, contradictory, and outmoded notions of "family values" to coerce married parents into remaining in unhappy marriages.

"Abolishing Welfare Won't Stop Poverty, Illegitimacy"—Elija Anderson   679
Sociologist Elija Anderson argues against abolishing welfare as an answer to the problem of a growing "underclass." According to Anderson, the prospect of increased welfare benefits does not motivate poor women to have more children. Anderson instead attributes the growing number of single mothers to underlying economic problems.

"Dan Quayle Was Right"—Barbara Dafoe Whitehead   681
Social scientist Barbara Dafoe Whitehead, responding to the furor created by Dan Quayle's critique of Murphy Brown, argues that the dissolution of the two-parent family has harmed many children, not to mention the very social fabric of the nation. Whitehead particularly laments the shift from a concern for children's welfare to a concern for adult happiness.

Credits   709

Index   713

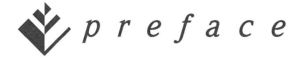
preface

Overview

Through its first three editions, *Writing Arguments* steadily emerged as the leading college textbook on the art of writing arguments. In this fourth edition, we have revised and streamlined the book to clarify and enliven its message and to reflect our own evolving understanding of the theory and practice of argumentation. In either its regular edition, which includes an anthology of readings, or in its brief edition without the anthology, *Writing Arguments* has been used successfully at every level, from freshman writing to advanced argumentation courses.

As in previous editions, our aim is to integrate a comprehensive study of argument with a process approach to writing. The text treats arguments as a means of clarification and truth seeking as well as a means of persuading audiences. In both its treatment of argumentation and its approach to teaching writing, the text is rooted in current research and theory.

The fourth edition retains the following successful features from the third edition: The text has an extensive treatment of invention that includes use of the Toulmin system of analyzing arguments combined with use of the enthymeme as a discovery and shaping tool. To aid invention, it also has explanations of *logos, pathos,* and *ethos,* and a major section treating five categories of claims. It focuses on both the reading and the writing of arguments and also includes a copious treatment of the research paper, including two student examples—one using the MLA system and one using the APA system. Among the book's distinguishing features are numerous "For Class Discussion" exercises designed for collaborative groups, a full sequence of writing assignments, and an extensive appendix on working in groups. The fourth edition contains sixteen student essays of varied length and complexity as well as sixty professional essays aimed at producing discussion, analysis, and debate. Fifteen of the professional selections appear in the rhetoric portion of the text (Parts I–IV) and forty-five in the anthology.

Improvements in the Fourth Edition

Following the recommendations of many users of the third edition at both four-year and two-year institutions, we have substantially strengthened *Writing Arguments* through the following additions and changes.

- Larger format and new design, which allow for a more open, more readable page and invite better use of annotations.

- More consistent treatment of argument as multisided conversation rather than as pro-con debate. Throughout the text we show how issues are embedded in a context of subissues, side issues, and larger issues that resist reduction to a simple pro-con focus. To this end, we have removed the pro-con pairs from the beginning of the anthology and have organized the anthology by topic areas rather than by already formulated issues. We have also eliminated such combative terms as *opponents* or *adversaries* in order to treat argument as a truth-seeking inquiry among alternative views instead of a win-lose debate between two sides.

- Extensive rewriting of Chapter 1. New to this chapter are an explanation of the difference between implicit and explicit arguments, enriched discussion of the truth-seeking dimension of argument, and clearer explanations of the tension that arguers always feel between truth seeking and persuasion.

- More interesting and substantive examples throughout the text. For instance, a hate speech example replaces the third edition's dorm room carpets example in Chapter 3, and the provocative issue of women in combat replaces the teenage job issue used for illustration in Chapters 4–6.

- Fuller explanation of how the strategies of this text can be applied to reading arguments as well as to writing arguments.

- A greatly expanded discussion of numerical and statistical evidence incorporated into Chapter 6.

- Enriched discussions of *pathos* (derived from the Greek for *suffering*) as an appeal to the imaginative sympathies of an audience rather than more narrowly as an appeal to emotions.

- Extensive rewriting of Chapter 8 to explain how writers can vary the tone and structure of an argument to accommodate audiences along a scale of resistance from sympathetic to hostile. The third edition's extended example of the "group writing controversy" has been replaced by a range of more interesting and relevant examples to explain refutation, concession, and Rogerian argument.

- Much fuller treatment of electronic databases, computerized searches, and the Internet and World Wide Web in our discussions of research writing in Part IV.

- Inclusion in the anthology of eighteen new professional arguments as well as three new topic areas: Censorship on the Internet, Recycling and Garbage, and Gay Marriage. To make room for these new topics, the third edition's Political Correctness, Gun Control, and Global Warming topics have been dropped. Throughout the anthology we have continued our policy of mixing shorter, op-ed arguments with longer, research-based arguments taken from scholarly journals or serious public affairs magazines.

Our Approaches to Argumentation

Our interest in argumentation grows out of our interest in the relationship between writing and thinking. In writing arguments, writers are forced to lay bare their thinking processes in an unparalleled way. In an effort to engage students in the kinds of critical thinking that argument demands, we draw on four major approaches to argumentation:

- *The enthymeme as a rhetorical and logical structure.* This concept, especially useful for beginning writers, helps students "nutshell" an argument as a claim with one or more supporting because clauses. It also helps them see how real-world arguments are rooted in probabilistic assumptions granted by the audience rather than in universal and unchanging principles.

- *The three classical types of appeal*—logos, ethos, *and* pathos. These concepts help students place their arguments in a rhetorical context focusing on audience-based appeals; they also help students create an effective voice and style.

- *Toulmin's system of analyzing arguments.* Toulmin's system helps students see the complete, implicit structure that underlies an enthymeme and develop appropriate grounds and backing to support the claim. It also highlights the rhetorical, social, and dialectical nature of argument.

- *Stasis theory on categories of claims.* This approach stresses the heuristic value of learning different patterns of support for different categories of claims and often leads students to make surprisingly rich and full arguments.

Throughout the text these approaches are integrated and synthesized into generative tools for both producing and analyzing arguments.

Structure of the Text

The text has five main parts plus two appendixes. Part I gives an overview of argumentation. These first three chapters present our philosophy of argument, showing how argument helps writers clarify their own thinking. Throughout we link the process of arguing—articulating issue questions, formulating propositions, examining alternative points of view, and creating structures of supporting reasons and evidence—with the processes of reading and writing.

Part II examines the principles of argument. Chapters 4 through 6 show that the core of an argument is a claim with reasons. These reasons are often stated as enthymemes, the unstated premise of which must sometimes be brought to the surface and supported. Discussion of Toulmin logic shows students how to discover both the stated and unstated premises of their arguments and to provide structures of reasons and evidence to support them. Chapters 7 and 8 focus on the rhetorical context of arguments. These chapters discuss the writer's relationship with an audience, particularly with finding audience-based reasons; with using *pathos* and *ethos* effectively and responsibly; and with accommodating arguments to different kinds of audiences, from sympathetic to neutral to hostile.

Part III discusses five different categories of argument: definitional arguments, causal arguments, resemblance arguments, evaluation arguments, and proposal arguments. These chapters introduce students to two recurring strategies of argument that cut across the different category types: *criteria-match arguing,* in which the writer establishes criteria for making a judgment and argues whether a specific case does or does not meet those criteria; and *causal arguing,* in which the writer shows that one event or phenomenon can be linked to others in a causal chain. The last chapter of Part III deals with the special complexities of moral arguments.

Part IV shows students how to incorporate research into their arguments. It explains how writers use sources, with a special focus on the skills of summary, paraphrase, and judicious quotation. Unlike standard treatments of the research paper, our discussion explains to students how the writer's meaning and purpose control the selection and shaping of source materials. Part IV explains both the MLA and the APA documentation system, which are illustrated by two student examples of researched arguments. Throughout Chapters 16 and 17, we incorporate new discussions of electronic searching and uses of the Internet.

The appendixes provide important supplemental information useful for courses in argument. Appendix 1 gives an overview of informal fallacies, and Appendix 2 shows students how to get the most out of collaborative groups in an argument class. Appendix 2 also provides a sequence of collaborative tasks that will help students learn to peer-critique their classmates' arguments in progress. The numerous "For Class Discussion" exercises within the text provide additional tasks for group collaboration.

Finally, Part V, the anthology, provides a selection of professional arguments covering eleven provocative topics. The anthology selections are now grouped by topic rather than by issue question to encourage students to see that any conversation of alternative views gives rise to numerous embedded and intertwined issues. Formulating the issue question is part of the writer's task. Additional readings—both student and professional—are placed throughout Parts I–IV to illustrate concepts and strategies under discussion. Many of the issues raised in Parts I–IV (for example, illegitimacy and single parenthood from Chapter 2, recycling and garbage from Chapter 8, the mentally ill homeless in Chapters 10 and 14, and gay marriage in Chapter 13) are treated more fully in the anthology.

Writing Assignments

The text provides a variety of sequenced writing assignments, including expressive tasks for discovering and exploring arguments, "microthemes" for practicing basic argumentative moves (for example, supporting a reason with statistical evidence), cases, and numerous other assignments calling for complete arguments. Thus, the text provides instructors with a wealth of options for writing assignments on which to build a coherent course.

ACKNOWLEDGMENTS

We are happy for this opportunity to give public thanks to the scholars, teachers, and students who have influenced our approach to composition and argument. We would especially like to thank Jeffrey Cain and Stephen Bean for their research assistance in preparing the fourth edition. We also thank the following reviewers who gave us unusually helpful and cogent advice on this revision: Linda Bensel-Meyers, University of Tennessee–Knoxville; Beth Daniell, Clemson University; Charles Watterson Davis, Kansas State University; Judith Ferster, North Carolina State University; Christy Friend, University of Texas–Austin; Mary Anne Reiss, Elizabethtown Community College; and Linda Woodson, University of Texas–San Antonio.

We would also like to thank our editor Eben Ludlow, whose unflagging good humor and faith in our approach to both composition and argument have kept us writing and revising for the better part of twelve years. Eben called forth this book and kept it going. For that we are grateful. Additional thanks go to Daniel Anderson of The University of North Carolina at Chapel Hill. Daniel Anderson contributed the chapter on electronic writing and research in our 1997 text *The Allyn & Bacon Guide to Writing,* and we have again drawn on his expertise to bring Chapters 16 and 17 up to the minute in these important areas.

Finally, we would like to thank our families. John Bean: Thanks to Kit, Matthew, Andrew, Stephen, and Sarah for their love, support, good humor, rich conversation, and willingness to discuss argument in any context at any time. John Ramage: Thanks to my siblings for their extended support—brother Steve and sisters Carol Flinders, Wendy Hawkins, and Mary Beth Smith—and to my parents Gib and Jeanne Ramage for a lifelong dialectic. May the final synthesis never be achieved.

John D. Ramage
John C. Bean

part one

Overview of Argument

CHAPTER 1   Argument: An Introduction

CHAPTER 2   Reading Arguments

CHAPTER 3   Writing Arguments

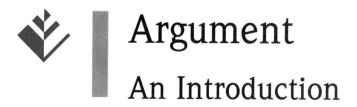

chapter 1

Argument

An Introduction

At the outset of a book on argument, we ought to explain what an argument is. Instead, we're going to explain why no simple definition is possible. Philosophers and rhetoricians have disagreed over the centuries about the meaning of the term and about the goals that arguers should set for themselves. This opening chapter introduces you to some of these controversies. Our goal is to introduce you to various ways of thinking about argument as a way of helping you become a more powerful arguer yourself.

We begin by asking what we mean by argument and then proceed to three defining features: *Argument* requires justification of its claims, it is both a product and a process, and it combines elements of truth seeking and persuasion. We then explore more deeply the relationship between truth seeking and persuasion by asking questions about the nature of "truth" that arguments seek. Finally, we give you an example of a successful arguing process.

WHAT DO WE MEAN BY ARGUMENT?

Let's begin by examining the inadequacies of two popular images of argument—fight and debate.

Argument Is Not a Fight or a Quarrel

To many, the word *argument* connotes anger and hostility, as when we say, "I just got in a huge argument with my roommate," or "My mother and I argue all the time." What we picture here is heated disagreement, rising pulse rates, and an urge to slam doors. Argument imagined as fight conjures images of shouting talk show guests, name-calling letter writers, or fist-banging speakers.

But to our way of thinking, argument doesn't imply anger. In fact, arguing is often pleasurable. It is a creative and productive activity that engages us at high levels of inquiry and critical thinking, often in conversation with persons we like and respect. For your primary image of argument, we invite you to think not of a fist-banging speaker but of a small group of reasonable persons seeking the best solution to a problem. We will return to this image throughout the chapter.

Argument Is Not Pro-Con Debate

Another popular image of argument is debate—a presidential debate, perhaps, or a high school or college debate tournament. According to one popular dictionary, debate is "a formal contest of argumentation in which two opposing teams defend and attack a given proposition." Although debate is an excellent activity for developing critical thinking, its weakness is that it can turn argument into a game of winners and losers rather than a process of cooperative inquiry.

For an illustration of this weakness, consider one of our former students, a champion high school debater, who spent his senior year debating the issue of prison reform. Throughout the year he argued for and against propositions such as "The United States should build more prisons" and "Innovative alternatives to prison should replace prison sentences for most crimes." When we asked him, "What do you personally think is the best way to reform prisons?" he replied. "I don't know. I haven't thought about what I would actually choose."

Here was a bright, articulate student who had studied prisons extensively for a year. And yet nothing in the atmosphere of pro-con debate had engaged him in truth-seeking inquiry. He could argue for and against a proposition, but he hadn't experienced the wrenching process of clarifying his own values and taking a personal stand. As we explain throughout this text, argument entails a desire for truth; it aims to find the best solutions to complex problems. We don't mean that arguers don't passionately support their own points of view or expose weaknesses in views they find faulty. It means that their goal isn't to win a game but to find and promote the best belief or course of action.

Arguments Can Be Explicit or Implicit

Before proceeding to some defining features of argument, we should note also that arguments can be either explicit or implicit. An *explicit* argument states directly a controversial claim and supports it with reasons and evidence. An *implicit* argument, in contrast, doesn't look like an argument. It may be a poem or short story, a photograph or cartoon, a personal essay, or an autobiographical narrative. But like an explicit argument, it persuades its audience toward a certain point of view. Steinbeck's *Grapes of Wrath* is an implicit argument for the unionization of farm workers, just as the following poem is an implicit argument against the premise that it is sweet and fitting to die for one's country.

Dulce et Decorum Est

Bent double, like old beggars under sacks,
Knock-kneed, coughing like hags, we cursed through sludge
Till on the haunting flares we turned our backs,
And towards our distant rest began to trudge.
Men marched asleep. Many had lost their boots,
But limped on, blood-shod. All went lame, all blind;
Drunk with fatigue; deaf even to the hoots
Of gas-shells dropping softly behind.

Gas! Gas! Quick, boys—An ecstasy of fumbling,
Fitting the clumsy helmets just in time,
But someone still was yelling out and stumbling
And flound'ring like a man in fire or lime.
Dim through the misty panes and thick green light,
As under a green sea, I saw him drowning.

In all my dreams before my helpless sight
He plunges at me, guttering, choking, drowning.

If in some smothering dreams, you too could pace
Behind the wagon that we flung him in,
And watch the white eyes writhing in his face,
His hanging face, like a devil's sick of sin,
If you could hear, at every jolt, the blood
Come gargling from the froth-corrupted lungs
Bitter as the cud
Of vile, incurable sores on innocent tongues,—
My friend, you would not tell with such high zest
To children ardent for some desperate glory,
The old lie: *Dulce et decorum est*
*Pro patria mori.**

—Wilfred Owen

Here Wilfred Owen makes a powerful case against the "old lie"—that war is honorable, that dying for one's country is sweet and fitting. But the argument is implicit: It is carried in the horrible image of a soldier drowning in his own fluids from a mustard gas attack rather than through an ordered structure of thesis, reasons, and evidence.

---

*"How sweet and fitting it is to die for one's country." Wilfred Owen (1893–1918) was killed in World War I and wrote many of his poems while in the trenches.

For another example of the distinction between explicit and implicit arguments, consider the following two pieces written by a student as an in-class exercise:

EXPLICIT ARGUMENT

In order to reduce the perpetuation of sexual stereotypes, colleges should abolish cheerleaders. Although some aspects of cheerleading require acrobatic skill, female cheerleaders still wear short skirts and tight sweaters and spend most of their time in front of the crowd as beautiful women for males to ogle. In televised football games, the camera often pans from the action on the field to dancing cheerleaders waving pompons on the sidelines. The contrast between the male football players and the miniskirted cheerleaders perpetuates stereotypes that define women as beautiful objects.

IMPLICIT ARGUMENT

I hadn't been to a basketball game in years, so when my boyfriend asked me to go I readily accepted. He and I were sitting in the front row when a group of women in short skirts and tightly fitting tops skipped in front of us on the court and started a dance routine. Some men behind us began watching this new game—the cheerleaders dancing.

"Whoa! Let's see some leg!" one of the men yelled at the cheerleaders. One of them kicked higher. The men in the first few rows yelled shouts of approval. "Look at the jiggle in that sweater," one of them snickered, punching his buddy in the arm.

My friend and I moved to seats farther back in the stands; I was suddenly reminded why I really don't care for sports.

❦ FOR CLASS DISCUSSION

1. How do the explicit and implicit arguments differ?

2. Imagine that you wanted to take a photograph that creates an implicit argument persuading (1) teenagers against smoking; (2) teenagers against becoming sexually active; (3) the general public toward banning handguns; (4) the general public against banning handguns; (5) the general public toward saving endangered species; (6) the general public toward supporting timber companies' desire to harvest old-growth forests. Working individually or in small groups, describe a photograph you might take that would create an appropriate implicit argument.

EXAMPLE: To create an implicit argument against legalizing hard drugs, you might photograph a blank-eyed, cadaverous teenager plunging a needle into her arm.

Although implicit arguments can be powerful, the predominant focus of this text is on explicit argument. We don't leave implicit arguments entirely, however, because their strategies—especially the persuasive power of stories and narratives—can often be incorporated into explicit arguments, as we discuss more fully in Chapter 7.

THE DEFINING FEATURES OF ARGUMENT

We turn now to examine argument in more detail. (From here on out, when we say "argument" we mean "explicit argument.") This section examines three defining features.

Argument Requires Justification of Its Claims

To begin defining argument, let's turn to a humble but universal site of disagreement: the conflict between a parent and a teenager over rules. In what way and in what circumstances do these conflicts constitute arguments?

Consider the following dialogue:

YOUNG PERSON (*racing for the front door while putting coat on*): Bye. See you later.

PARENT: Whoa! What time are you planning on coming home?

YOUNG PERSON (*coolly, hand still on doorknob*): I'm sure we discussed this earlier. I'll be home around 2 A.M. (*The second sentence, spoken very rapidly, is barely audible.*)

PARENT (*mouth tightening*): We did *not* discuss this earlier and you're *not* staying out till two in the morning. You'll be home at twelve.

At this point in the exchange, we have a quarrel, not an argument. Quarrelers exchange antagonistic assertions without any attempt to support them rationally. If the dialogue never gets past the "Yes-you-will/No-I-won't" stage, it either remains a quarrel or degenerates into a fight.

Let us say, however, that the dialogue takes the following turn:

YOUNG PERSON (*tragically*): But I'm *sixteen years old*!

Now we're moving toward argument. Not, to be sure, a particularly well-developed or cogent one, but an argument all the same. It's now an argument because one of the quarrelers has offered a reason for her assertion. Her choice of curfew is satisfactory, she says, *because* she is sixteen years old, an argument that depends on the unstated assumption that sixteen-year-olds are old enough to make decisions about such matters.

The parent can now respond in one of several ways that will either advance the argument or turn it back into a quarrel. The parent can simply invoke parental authority ("I don't care—you're still coming home at twelve"), in which case argument ceases, or the parent can provide a reason for his or her view ("You will be home at twelve because your dad and I pay the bills around here!"), in which case the argument takes a new turn.

So far we've established two necessary conditions that must be met before we're willing to call something an argument: (1) a set of two or more conflicting assertions, and (2) the attempt to resolve the conflict through an appeal to reason.

But good argument demands more than meeting these two formal requirements. For the argument to be effective, an arguer is obligated to clarify and support the reasons presented. For example, "But I'm sixteen years old!" is not yet a clear support for the assertion "I should be allowed to set my own curfew." On the surface, Young Person's argument seems absurd. Her parent, of all people, knows precisely how old she is. What makes it an argument is that behind her claim lies an unstated assumption—all sixteen-year-olds are old enough to set their own curfews. What Young Person needs to do now is to support that assumption.* In doing so, she must anticipate the sorts of questions the assumption will raise in the minds of her parent: What is the legal status of sixteen-year-olds? How psychologically mature, as opposed to chronologically mature, is Young Person? What is the actual track record of Young Person in being responsible? and so forth. Each of these questions will force Young Person to reexamine and clarify her assumptions about the proper degree of autonomy for sixteen-year-olds. And her response to those questions should in turn force the parents to reexamine their assumptions about the dependence of sixteen-year-olds on parental guidance and wisdom. (Likewise, the parents will need to show why "paying the bills around here" automatically gives them the right to set Young Person's curfew.)

As the argument continues, Young Person and Parent may shift to a different line of reasoning. For example, Young Person might say: "I should be allowed to stay out until 2 A.M. because all my friends get to stay out that late." (Here the unstated assumption is that the rules in this family ought to be based on the rules in other families.) The parent might in turn respond, "But I certainly never stayed out that late when I was your age"—an argument assuming that the rules in this family should follow the rules of an earlier generation.

As Young Person and Parent listen to each other's points of view (and begin realizing why their initial arguments have not persuaded their intended audience), both parties find themselves in the uncomfortable position of having to examine their own beliefs and to justify assumptions that they have taken for granted. Here we encounter one of the earliest senses of the term *to argue*, which is "to clarify." As an arguer begins to clarify her own position on an issue, she also begins to clarify her audience's position. Such clarification helps the arguer see

---

*Later in this text we will call the assumption underlying a line of reasoning its *warrant.*

how she might accommodate her audience's views, perhaps by adjusting her own position or by developing reasons that appeal to her audience's values. Thus Young Person might suggest an argument like this:

> I should be allowed to stay out until 2 on a trial basis because I need enough space to demonstrate my maturity and show you I won't get into trouble.

The assumption underlying this argument is that it is good to give teenagers freedom to demonstrate their maturity. Because this reason is apt to appeal to her parent's own values (the parent wants to see his or her daughter grow in maturity) and because it is tempered by the qualifier "on a trial basis" (which reduces some of the threat of Young Person's initial demands), it may prompt productive discussion.

Whether or not Young Person and Parent can work out a best solution, the preceding scenario illustrates how argument leads persons to clarify their reasons and provide justifications that can be examined rationally. The scenario also illustrates two specific aspects of argument that we will explore in detail in the next sections: (1) Argument is both a process and a product, and (2) arguments combine truth seeking and persuasion.

Argument Is Both a Process and a Product

As the preceding scenario revealed, argument can be viewed as a *process* in which two or more parties seek the best solution to a question or problem. Argument can also be viewed as a *product,* each product being any person's contribution to the conversation at a given moment. In an informal discussion, the products are usually short, whatever time a person uses during his or her turns in the conversation. Under more formal settings, an orally delivered product might be a short impromptu speech (say, during an open-mike discussion of a campus issue) or a longer, carefully prepared formal speech (as in an oral brief before a judge, a presentation to legislative subcommittee, or an argument at a public hearing for or against a proposed city project).

Similar conversations occur in writing. Roughly analogous to a small group discussion is an e-mail discussion of the kind that occurs regularly through informal chat groups or professional listservs. In an online discussion, participants have more thinking time to shape their messages than they do in a real-time oral discussion. Nevertheless, messages are usually short and informal, making it possible over the course of several days to see participants' ideas shift and evolve as conversants modify their initial views in response to others' views.

Roughly equivalent to a formal speech would be a formal written argument composed through multiple drafts over the course of days or weeks and submitted as a college essay assignment, a grant proposal, a guest column for the op-ed (opinion-editorial) section of a newspaper, a letter to a congressperson, a legal brief for a judge, or an article for an organizational newsletter, popular magazine, or professional journal. In each of these instances, the written argument (a product) enters a conversation (a process)—in this case, a conversation of readers, many of whom will carry on the conversation by writing their own responses or by discussing the writer's views with others. The goal of the community of writers and readers is to find the best solution to the problem or issue under discussion.

Argument Combines
Truth Seeking and Persuasion

In thinking about argument as a product, the writer will find herself continually moving back and forth between truth seeking and persuasion—that is, between questions about the subject matter (What is the best solution to this problem?) and about audience (What do my readers already believe or value? What reasons and evidence will most persuade them?). Back and forth she'll weave, alternately absorbed in the subject of her argument and in the audience for that argument.

Neither of the two focuses is ever completely out of mind, but their relative importance shifts during different phases of the development of a paper. Moreover, different rhetorical situations place different emphases on truth seeking versus persuasion. We could thus place arguments on a kind of continuum that measures the degree of attention a writer gives to subject matter versus audience. At the far truth seeking end of the continuum might be an exploratory piece that lays out several alternative approaches to a problem and weighs the strengths and weaknesses of each with no concern for persuasion. At the other end of the continuum would be outright propaganda, such as a political campaign advertisement that reduces a complex issue to sound bites and distorts an opponent's position through out-of-context quotations or misleading use of data. (At its most blatant, propaganda obliterates truth seeking; it will do anything, including the knowing use of bogus evidence, distorted assertions, and outright lies, to win over an audience.) In the middle ranges of the continuum, writers shift their focuses back and forth between truth seeking and persuasion but with varying degrees of emphasis.

As an example of a writer focusing primarily on truth seeking, consider the case of Kathleen, who, in her college argument course, addressed the definitional question "Is American Sign Language (ASL) a 'foreign language' for purposes of meeting the university's foreign language requirement?" Kathleen had taken two years of ASL at a community college. When she transferred to a four-year college, the chair of the foreign languages department at her new college would not allow her ASL proficiency to count for the foreign language requirement. ASL isn't a "language," the chair said summarily. "It's not equivalent to learning French, German, or Japanese."

Kathleen disagreed, so she immersed herself in developing her argument. While doing research, she focused almost entirely on subject matter, searching for what linguists, brain neurologists, cognitive psychologists, and sociologists had said about the language of deaf people. Immersed in her subject matter, she was only tacitly concerned with her audience, whom she thought of primarily as her classmates and the professor of her argument class—persons who were friendly to her views and interested in her experiences with the deaf community. She wrote a well-documented paper, citing several scholarly articles, that made a good case to her classmates (and the professor) that ASL was indeed a distinct language.

Proud of the big red A the professor had placed on her paper, Kathleen returned to the chair of the foreign language department with a new request to count ASL for her language requirement. The chair read her paper, congratulated her on her good writing, but said her argument was not persuasive. He disagreed with several of the linguists she cited and with the general definition of "language" that her paper assumed. He then gave her some additional (and to her fuzzy) reasons that the college would not accept ASL as a foreign language.

Spurred by what she considered the chair's too-easy dismissal of her argument, Kathleen decided, for a subsequent assignment in her argument class, to write a second paper on ASL—but this time aiming it directly at the chair of foreign languages. Now her writing task falls closer to the persuasive end of our continuum. Kathleen once again immersed herself in research, but this time it focused not on subject matter (whether ASL is a distinct language) but on audience. She researched the history of the foreign language requirement at her college and discovered some of the politics behind it (an old foreign language requirement had been dropped in the 1970s and reinstituted in the 1990s, partly—a math professor told her—to boost enrollments in foreign language courses.) She also interviewed foreign language teachers to find out what they knew and didn't know about ASL. She discovered that many teachers thought ASL was "easy to learn," so that accepting ASL would allow students a Mickey Mouse way to avoid the rigors of a real foreign language class. Additionally, she learned that foreign language teachers valued immersing students in a foreign culture; in fact, the foreign language requirement was part of her college's effort to create a multicultural curriculum.

This new understanding of her target audience helped Kathleen totally reconceptualize her argument. She condensed and abridged her original paper down to one line of reasoning in her new argument. She added sections showing the difficulty of learning ASL (to counter her audience's belief that learning ASL was easy), showing how the deaf community formed a distinct culture with its own customs and literature (to show how ASL met the goals of multiculturalism), and showing that the number of transfer students with ASL credits would be negligibly small (to allay fears that accepting ASL would threaten enrollments in language classes). She ended her argument with an appeal to her college's public emphasis (declared boldly in its mission statement) on eradicating social injustice and reaching out to the oppressed. She described the isolation of deaf people in a world where almost no hearing people learn ASL and argued that the deaf community on her campus could be integrated more fully into campus life if more students could "talk" with them. Thus, the ideas included in her new argument—the reasons selected, the evidence used, the arrangement and tone—all were determined by her primary focus on persuasion.

Our point, then, is that all along the continuum writers are concerned both to seek truth and to persuade, but not necessarily with equal balance. Kathleen could not have written her second paper, aimed specifically at persuading the chair of foreign languages, if she hadn't first immersed herself in truth-seeking research that convinced her that ASL was indeed a distinct language. Nor are we saying that her second argument was better than her first. Both fulfilled their purposes and met the needs of their intended audiences. Both involved truth seeking and persuasion, but the first focused primarily on subject matter whereas the second focused primarily on audience.

ARGUMENT AND THE PROBLEM OF TRUTH

The tension that we have just examined between truth seeking and persuasion raises one of the oldest issues in the field of argument: Is the arguer's first obligation to truth or to winning the argument? And just what is the nature of the truth to which arguers are supposed to be obligated? To this second question we now turn.

When Does Argument Become Propaganda? The Debate Between Socrates and Callicles

One of the first great debates on the issue of truth versus victory occurs in Plato's dialogue *The Gorgias,* in which the philosopher Socrates takes on the rhetorician Callicles.

By way of background to the dispute, Socrates was a great philosopher known to us today primarily through his student Plato, whose "dialogues" depict Socrates debating various friends and antagonists. Socrates' stated goal in these debates was to "rid the world of error." In dialogue after dialogue, Socrates vanquishes error by skillfully leading people through a series of questions that force them to recognize the inconsistency and implausibility of their beliefs. He was a sort of intellectual judo master who takes opponents' arguments the way they want to go until they suddenly fall over.

Callicles, on the other hand, is a shadowy figure in history. We know him only through his exchange with Socrates—hence only through Plato's eyes. But Callicles is easily recognizable to philosophers as a representative of the Sophists, a group of teachers who schooled ancient Greeks in the fine art of winning arguments. The Sophists were a favorite, if elusive, target of both Socrates and Plato. Indeed, opposition to the Sophists' approach to life lies at the core of Platonic philosophy. Having said all that, let's turn to the dialogue.

Early in the debate, Socrates is clearly in control. He easily—too easily, as it turns out—wins a couple of preliminary rounds against some less determined

Sophists before confronting Callicles. But in the long and arduous debate that follows, it's not at all clear that Socrates wins. In fact, one of the points being made in *The Gorgias* seems to be that philosophers committed to "clarifying" and discovering truth may occasionally have to sacrifice winning the debate in the name of their higher ends. Although Plato makes an eloquent case for enlightenment as the goal of argument, he may well contribute to the demise of this noble principle if he should happen to lose. Unfortunately, it appears that Socrates can't win the argument without sinning against the very principle he's defending.

The effectiveness of Callicles as a debater lies in his refusal to allow Socrates *any* assumptions. In response to Socrates' concern for virtue and justice, Callicles responds dismissively that such concepts are mere conventions, invented by the weak to protect themselves from the strong. In Callicles' world, "might makes right." The function of argument in such a world is to extend the freedom and power of the arguer, not to arrive at some vision of "truth." Indeed, the power to decide what's "true" belongs to the winner of the debate. For Callicles, a truth that never wins is no truth at all because it will soon disappear. In sum, Callicles sees the ends (winning the argument) as justifying the means (refusing to grant any assumptions, using ambiguous language, and so forth). Socrates, on the other hand, believes that no good end can come from questionable means.

Based on what we've said up to this point about our belief in argument as truth seeking, you might guess that our sympathies are with Socrates. To a great extent they are. But Socrates lived in a much simpler world than we do, if by "simple" we mean a world where the True and the Good were, if not universally agreed-upon notions, at least ones around which a clear consensus formed. For Socrates, there was one True Answer to any important question. Truth resided in the ideal world of forms, and through philosophic rigor humans could transcend the changing, shadowlike world of everyday reality to perceive the world of universals where Truth, Beauty, and Goodness resided.

Callicles, on the other hand, rejects the notion that there is only one possible truth at which all arguments will necessarily arrive. For Callicles, there are different degrees of truth and different kinds of truths for different situations or cultures. In raising the whole nettlesome question—How "true" is a "truth" that you can't get anyone to agree to?—Callicles is probably closer to the modern world than is Plato. Let's expand on Callicles' view of truth by examining some contemporary illustrations.

What Is Truth? The Place of Argument in Contemporary Life

Although the debate between Socrates and Callicles appears to end inconclusively, many readers over the centuries conceded the victory to Socrates almost by default. Callicles was seen as cheating. The term *sophistry* came to be synonymous with trickery in argument. The Sophists' relativistic beliefs were so repugnant to most people that they refused to grant any merit to the Sophists' position. In our century, however, the Sophists have found a more sympathetic readership, one that takes some of the questions they raised quite seriously.

One way of tracing this shift in attitude toward truth is by looking at a significant shift in the definition of the verb *to argue* over the centuries. As we have seen, one of the earliest meanings of *to argue* was "to clarify," a definition focusing on truth seeking. Another early meaning was "to prove"—a definition that focuses simultaneously on truth seeking and persuasion in that it implies that truth can be both known (truth seeking) and "proved" (persuasion). Argument in this sense was closely associated with mathematical demonstrations in which you move from axioms to proofs through formulae. An argument of this sort is virtually irrefutable—unless we play Callicles and reject the axioms.

Today, on the other hand, *to argue* is usually taken to mean something like "to provide grounds for inferring." The better the argument, the better the reasons and evidence one provides, the more likely the audience will infer what the arguer has inferred. Instead of "proving" one's claim, the best an arguer can hope for is to make an audience *more likely to agree with* the arguer's claim. One contemporary philosopher says that argument can hope only to "increase adherence" to ideas, not absolutely convince an audience of the necessary truth of ideas.

In the twentieth century, absolute, demonstrable truth is seen by many thinkers, from physicists to philosophers, as an illusion. Some would argue that truth is merely a product of human beings' talking and arguing with each other. These thinkers say that when considering questions of interpretation, meaning, or value one can never tell for certain whether an assertion is true—not by examining the physical universe more closely or by reasoning one's way toward some Platonic form or by receiving a mystical revelation. The closest one can come to truth is through the confirmation of one's views from others in a community of peers. "Truth" in any field of knowledge, say these thinkers, is simply an agreement of knowledgeable people in that field.

To illustrate the relevance of Callicles to contemporary society, suppose for the moment that we wanted to ask whether sexual fidelity is a virtue. A Socratic approach would assume a single, real Truth about the value of sexual fidelity, one that could be discovered through a gradual peeling away of wrong answers. Callicles, meanwhile, would assume that sexual morality is culturally relative; hence, he might point out all the societies in which monogamous fidelity for one or both sexes is not the norm. Clearly, our world is more like Callicles'. We are all exposed to multiple cultural perspectives directly and indirectly. Through television, newspapers, travel, and education we experience ways of thinking and valuing that are different from our own. It is difficult to ignore the fact that our personal values are not universally shared or even respected. Thus, we're all faced with the need to justify our views in such a diverse society.

It should be clear, then, that when we speak of the truth-seeking aim of argument, we do not mean the discovery of an absolute "right answer," but the willingness to think through the complexity of an issue and to consider respectfully a wide range of views. The process of argument allows social groups, through the thoughtful exchange of ideas, to seek the best solution to a problem. The value of argument is its ability to help social groups make decisions in a rational and humane way without resorting to violence or to other assertions of raw power.

FOR CLASS DISCUSSION

On any given day, newspapers provide evidence of the complexity of living in a pluralist culture. Issues that could be readily decided in a completely homogeneous culture raise many questions for us in a society that has few shared assumptions.

What follows are three brief news stories that appeared on recent Associated Press wires. Choose one or more of the stories and conduct a "simulation game" in which various class members role-play the points of view of the characters involved in the controversy. If you choose the first case, for example, one class member should role-play the attorney of the woman refusing the Caesarean section, another the "court-appointed representative of the woman's fetus," and another the doctor. If you wish, conduct a court hearing in which other members role-play a judge, cross-examining attorneys, and a jury. No matter which case you choose, your class's goal should be to represent each point of view as fully and sympathetically as possible to help you realize the complexity of the values in conflict.

Illinois Court Won't Hear Case
of Mom Who Refuses Surgery

CHICAGO—A complex legal battle over a Chicago woman's refusal to undergo a Caesarean section, even though it could save the life of her unborn child, essentially was settled yesterday when the state's highest court refused to hear the case.   1

The court declined to review a lower court's ruling that the woman should not be forced to submit to surgery in a case that pitted the rights of the woman, referred to in court as "Mother Doe," against those of her fetus.   2

The 22-year-old Chicago woman, now in the 37th week of her pregnancy, refused her doctors' advice to have the surgery because she believes God intended her to deliver the child naturally.   3

The woman's attorneys argued that the operation would violate her constitutional rights to privacy and the free exercise of her religious beliefs.   4

Cook County Public Guardian Patrick Murphy, the court-appointed representative of the woman's fetus, said he would file a petition with the U.S. Supreme Court asking it to hear the case. He has 90 days to file the petition, but he acknowledged future action would probably come too late.   5

6   Doctors say the fetus is not receiving enough oxygen from the placenta and will either die or be retarded unless it is delivered by Caesarean section. Despite that diagnosis, the mother has stressed her faith in God's healing powers and refused doctors' advice to submit to the operation.

Maryland Court Strikes Down State's Cross-Burning Law

1   ANNAPOLIS, Md.—Maryland's cross-burning law was struck down as unconstitutional yesterday by the state's highest court, whose judges said it interfered with free speech.

2   U.S. Supreme Court rulings make clear that burning a cross or other religious symbol qualifies as speech under the First Amendment, the Maryland Court of Appeals said in a unanimous ruling.

3   "The open and deliberate burning of religious symbols is, needless to say, odious to thoughtful members of our society," wrote Chief Judge Robert Murphy in an opinion joined by six other judges.

4   "But the Constitution does not allow the unnecessary trammeling of free expression even for the noblest of purposes."

The decision affirmed a circuit-court ruling dismissing charges in two Prince George's County cases. In one case, a cross was burned on the property of an African-American family; in the other case, on public property.

5   The Maryland law, which was adopted in 1966, made it illegal to burn a cross on private property without getting permission of the landowner and notifying the local fire department.

Homeless Hit the Streets to Protest Proposed Ban

1   SEATTLE—The homeless stood up for themselves by sitting down in a peaceful but vocal protest yesterday in Seattle's University District.

2   About 50 people met at noon to criticize a proposed set of city ordinances that would ban panhandlers from sitting on sidewalks, put them in jail for repeatedly urinating in public, and crack down on "intimidating" street behavior.

3   "Sitting is not a crime," read poster boards that feature mug shots of Seattle City Attorney Mark Sidran, who is pushing for the new laws. . . . "This is city property; the police want to tell us we can't sit here," yelled one man named R.C. as he sat cross-legged outside a pizza establishment.

4   Marsha Shaiman stood outside the University Book Store holding a poster and waving it at passing cars. She is not homeless, but was one of many activists in the crowd. "I qual-

ify as a privileged white yuppie," she said. "I'm offended that the privileged people in this country are pointing at the poor, and people of color, and say they're causing problems. They're being used as scapegoats."

Many local merchants support the ban saying that panhandlers hurt business by in-   5 timidating shoppers and fouling the area with the odor of urine, vomited wine, and sometimes even feces.

A SUCCESSFUL PROCESS OF ARGUMENTATION: THE WELL-FUNCTIONING COMMITTEE

We have said that neither the fist-banging speaker nor the college debate team represents our ideal image of argument. The best image for us, as we have implied, is a well-functioning small group seeking a solution to a problem. In professional life such small groups usually take the form of committees.

We must acknowledge that many people find committee deliberations hopelessly muddled and directionless—the very antithesis of good argumentation. Our collective suspicion of committees is manifest in the many jokes we make about them. (For example, do you know the definition of the word *committee*? It's a place where people keep minutes and waste hours. Or: What is a zebra? A horse designed by a committee.)

Our society relies on committees, however, for the same reason that Winston Churchill preferred democracy: However imperfect it may be, the alternatives are worse. A single individual making decisions may be quirky, idiosyncratic, and insensitive to the effects of a decision on different groups of people; worse yet, he or she may pursue self-interests to the detriment of an entire group. On the other hand, too large a group makes argumentative discussion impossible. Hence, people have generally found it useful to delegate many decision- and policy-making tasks to a smaller, representative group—a committee.

We use the word *committee* in its broadest sense to indicate all sorts of important work that grows out of group conversation and debate. The Declaration of Independence is essentially a committee document with Thomas Jefferson as the chair. Similarly, the U.S. Supreme Court is in effect a committee of nine judges who rely heavily, as numerous books and articles have demonstrated, on small group decision-making processes to reach their judgments and formulate their legal briefs.

To illustrate our committee model for argument, let's briefly consider the workings of a university committee on which coauthor John Ramage recently served, the University Standards Committee. The Arizona State University (ASU) Standards Committee plays a role in university life analogous to that of the Supreme Court in civic life. It's the final court of appeal for ASU students seeking exceptions to various rules that govern their academic lives (such as registering under a different catalog, waiving a required course, or being allowed to retake a course for a third time).

The Standards Committee is a large committee, comprising nearly two dozen members who represent the whole spectrum of departments and offices across campus. Every two weeks, the committee meets for two or more hours to consider between twenty and forty appeals. Several days before each meeting, committee members receive a hefty packet of materials relevant to the cases (i.e., originals of the students' appeals, including the responses of those who've heard the appeal earlier, complete transcripts of each student's grades, and any supporting material or new information the student might wish to provide). Students may, if they choose, appear before the committee personally to make their cases.

The issues that regularly come before the committee draw forth all the argumentative strategies discussed in detail throughout this text. For example, all of the argument types discussed in Part III regularly surface during committee deliberations. The committee deals with definition issues ("Is math anxiety a 'learning disability' for purposes of exempting a student from a math requirement? If so, what criteria can we establish for math anxiety?"); cause/consequence issues ("What were the causes of this student's sudden poor performance during spring semester?" "What will be the consequences of approving or denying her appeal?"); resemblance issues ("How is this case similar to an earlier case that we considered?"); evaluation issues ("Which criteria should take precedence in assessing this sort of appeal?"); and proposal issues ("Should we make it a policy to allow course X to substitute for course Y in the General Studies requirements?").

On any given day, the committee's deliberations showed how dialogue can lead to clarification of thinking. On many occasions, committee members' initial views shifted as they listened to opposing arguments. In one case, for example, a student petitioned to change the catalog under which she was supposed to graduate because the difference in requirements would let her graduate a half year sooner. Initially, most committee members opposed the petition. They reminded the committee that in several earlier cases it had denied petitions to change catalogs if the petitioner's intent was to evade the more rigorous graduation requirements imposed by a new General Studies curriculum. Moreover, the committee was reminded that letting one student change catalogs was unfair to other students who had to meet the more rigorous graduation standards.

However, after emphatic negative arguments had been presented, a few committee members began to voice support for the student's case. While acknowledging the truth of what other committee members had said, they pointed out reasons to support the petition. The young woman in question had taken most of the required General Studies courses; it was mostly changes in the requirements for her major that delayed her graduation. Moreover, she had performed quite well in what everyone acknowledged to be a demanding course of study. Although the committee had indeed turned down previous petitions of this nature, in none of those cases had the consequences of denial been so dire for the student.

After extended negotiations between the two sides on this issue, the student was allowed to change catalogs. Although the committee was reluctant to set a bad precedent (those who resisted the petition foresaw a deluge of similar petitions from less worthy candidates), it recognized unique circumstances that legitimately made this petitioner's case different. Moreover, the rigor of the student's curriculum, the primary concern of those who opposed the change, was shown to be greater than the rigor of many who graduated under the newer catalog.

As the previous illustration suggests, what allowed the committee to function as well as it did was the fundamental civility of its members and their collective concern that their decisions be just. Unlike some committees, this committee made many decisions, the consequences of which were not trivial for the people involved. Because of the significance of these outcomes, committee members were more willing than they otherwise might have been to concede a point to another member in the name of reaching a better decision and to view their deliberations as an ongoing process of negotiation rather than a series of win-lose debates.

To give you firsthand experience at using argument as a process of clarification, we conclude this chapter with an actual case that came before the University Standards Committee. We invite you to read the following letter, pretending that you are a member of the University Standards Committee, and then proceed to the exercises that follow.

Petition to Waive University Mathematics Requirement

Standards Committee Members,

I am a 43-year-old member of the Pawnee Tribe of Oklahoma and a very non-traditional student currently pursuing Justice Studies at the Arizona State University (ASU) College of Public Programs. I entered college as the first step toward completion of my goal—becoming legal counsel for my tribe, and statesman. 1

I come before this committee in good faith to request that ASU suspend, in my special case, its mathematics requirement for undergraduate degree completion so I may enter the ASU college of Law during Fall 1993. The point I wish to make to this committee is this: I do not need algebraic skills; I will never use algebra in my intended profession; and, if forced to comply with ASU's algebra requirement, I will be needlessly prevented from graduating in time to enter law school next fall and face an idle academic year before my next opportunity in 1994. I will address each of these points in turn, but a few words concerning my academic credentials are in order first. 2

Two years ago, I made a vow of moral commitment to seek out and confront injustice. In September of 1990, I enrolled in college. Although I had only the benefit of a ninth grade education, I took the General Equivalency Diploma (GED) examination and placed in the top ten percent of those, nationwide, who took the test. On the basis of this score I was accepted 3 into Scottsdale Community College (SCC). This step made me the first in my entire family, and practically in my tribe, to enter college. During my first year at SCC I maintained a 4.0 GPA, I was placed on the President's list twice, was active in the Honors Program, received the Honors Award of Merit in English Humanities, and was conferred an Honors Scholarship (see attached) for the Academic year of 1991–1992 which I declined, opting to enroll in ASU instead.

4   At the beginning of the 1991 summer semester, I transferred to ASU. I chose to graduate from ASU because of the courses offered in American Indian studies, an important field ignored by most other Universities but necessary to my commitment. At ASU I currently maintain a 3.6 GPA, although my cumulative GPA is closer to 3.9, I am a member of the Honors and Justice Colleges, was appointed to the Dean's List, and awarded ASU's prestigious Maroon and Gold Scholarship twice. My academic standing is impeccable. I will enter the ASU College of Law to study Indian and criminal law during the Fall of 1993—if this petition is approved. Upon successful completion of my juris doctorate I will return to Oklahoma to become active in the administration of Pawnee tribal affairs as tribal attorney and advisor, and vigorously prosecute our right to sovereignty before the Congress of the United States.

5   When I began my "college experience," I set a rigid time schedule for the completion of my goal. By the terms of that self-imposed schedule, founded in my belief that I have already wasted many productive years, I allowed myself thirty-five months in which to achieve my Bachelor of Science degree in Justice Studies, for indeed justice is my concern, and another thirty-six months in which to earn my juris doctorate—summa cum laude. Consistent with my approach to all endeavors, I fell upon this task with zeal. I have willingly assumed the burden of carrying substantial academic loads during fall, spring and summer semesters. My problem now lies in the fact that in order to satisfy the University's math requirement to graduate I must still take MAT-106 and MAT-117. I submit that these mathematics courses are irrelevant to my goals, and present a barrier to my fall matriculation into law school.

6   Upon consideration of my dilemma, the questions emerged: Why do I need college algebra (MAT-117)? Is college algebra necessary for studying American Indian law? Will I use college algebra in my chosen field? What will the University gain or lose, from my taking college algebra—or not? I decided I should resolve these questions.

7   I began my inquiry with the question: "Why do I need college algebra (MAT-117)?" I consulted Mr. Jim _____ of the Justice College and presented this question to him. He referred to the current ASU catalog and delineated the following answer: I need college algebra (1) for a minimum level of math competency in my chosen field, and (2) to satisfy the university math requirement in order to graduate. My reply to the first answer is this: I already possess ample math skills, both practical and academic; and, I have no need for algebra in my chosen field. How do I know this? During the spring 1992 semester at ASU I successfully completed introductory algebra (MAT-077), scoring the highest class grade on one test (see attached transcript and test). More noteworthy is the fact that I was a machine and welding contractor for fifteen years. I used geometry and algebra commonly in the design of many welded structures. I am proficient in the use of Computer Assisted Design (CAD) programs, designing and drawing all my own blueprints for jobs. My blueprints and

designs are always approved by city planning departments. For example, my most recent job consisted of the manufacture, transportation and installation of one linear mile of anodized, aluminum handrailing at a luxury resort condo on Maui, Hawaii. I applied extensive use of math to calculate the amount of raw materials to order, the logistics of mass production and transportation for both men and materials from Mesa to Maui, the job site installation itself, and cash flow. I have successfully completed many jobs of this nature—all without a mathematical hitch. As to the application of math competency in my chosen field, I can guarantee this committee that there will not be a time in my practice of Indian law that I will need algebra. If an occasion ever occurs that I need algebra, I will hire a mathematician, just as I would an engineer if I need engineering, or a surgeon if I need an operation.

I then contacted Dr. _____ of the ASU Mathematics Department and presented him   8
with the same question: "Why do I need college algebra?" He replied: (1) for a well rounded education; (2) to develop creative thinking; and (3) to satisfy the university math requirement in order to graduate. Responding to the first answer, I have a "well rounded education." My need is for a specific education in justice and American Indian law. In fact, I do not really need the degree to practice Indian law as representative of my tribe, just the knowledge. Regarding the second, I do not need to develop my creative thinking. It has been honed to a keen edge for many years. For example, as a steel contractor, I commonly create huge, beautiful and intricate structures from raw materials. Contracting is not my only experience in creative thinking. For twenty-five years I have also enjoyed the status of being one of this country's foremost designers and builders of racebikes. Machines I have designed and brought into existence from my imagination have topped some of Japan and Europe's best engineering efforts. To illustrate this point, in 1984 I rode a bike of my own design to an international victory over Honda, Suzuki, Laverda, BMW and Yamaha. I have excelled at creative thinking my entire life—I called it survival.

Expanding on the question of why I need college algebra, I contacted a few friends who   9
are practicing attorneys. All responded to my question in similar manner. One, Mr. Billy _____, Esq., whose law firm is in Tempe, answered my two questions as follows: "When you attended law school, were there any courses you took which required algebra?" His response was "no." "Have you ever needed algebra during the many years of your practice?" Again, his response was "no." All agreed there was not a single occasion when they had need for algebra in their professional careers.

Just to make sure of my position, I contacted the ASU College of Law, and among oth-   10
ers, spoke to Ms. Sierra _____. I submitted the question "What law school courses will I encounter in which I will need algebra?" The unanimous reply was, they knew of none.

I am not proposing that the number of credit hours I need for graduation be lowered.   11
In fact, I am more than willing to substitute another course or two in its place. I am not trying to get out of anything hard or distasteful, for that is certainly not my style. I am seeking only to dispose of an unnecessary item in my studies, one which will prevent me from entering law school this fall—breaking my stride. So little holds up so much.

I agree that a young adult directly out of high school may not know that he needs alge-   12
braic skills. Understandably, he does not know what his future holds—but I am not that young adult. I claim the advantage. I know precisely what my future holds and that future holds no possibility of my needing college algebra.

13   Physically confronting injustice is my end. On reservations where government apathy allows rapacious pedophiles to pose as teachers; in a country where a million and a half American Indians are held hostage as second rate human beings whose despair results in a suicide, alcohol and drug abuse rate second to no other people; in prisons where helpless inmates are beaten like dogs by sadistic guards who should be the inmates—this is the realm of my chosen field—the disenfranchised. In this netherworld, algebra and justice exist independently of one another.

14   In summary, I am convinced that I do not need college algebra for a minimum level of math competency in my chosen field. I do not need college algebra for a well rounded education, nor to develop my creative thinking. I do not need algebra to take the LSAT. I do not need algebra for any courses in law school, nor will I for any purpose in the practice of American Indian law. It remains only that I need college algebra in order to graduate.

15   I promise this committee that ASU's integrity will not be compromised in any way by approving this waiver. Moreover, I assure this committee that despite not having a formal accreditation in algebra, I will prove to be nothing less than an asset to this University and its Indian community, both to which I belong, and I will continue to set a standard for integrity, excellence and perseverance for all who follow. Therefore, I ask this committee, for all the reasons described above, to approve and initiate the waiver of my University mathematics requirement.

[Signed: Gordon Adams]

 ## FOR CLASS DISCUSSION

1. Before class discussion, decide how you would vote on this issue. Should this student be exempted from the math requirement? Write out the reasons for your decision.

2. Working in small groups or as a whole class, pretend that you are the University Standards Committee and arrive at a group decision on whether to exempt this student from the math requirement.

3. After the discussion, write for five to ten minutes in a journal or notebook describing how your thinking evolved during the discussion. Did any of your classmate's views cause you to rethink your own? Class members should share with each other their descriptions of how the process of argument led to clarification of their own thinking.

We designed this exercise to help you experience argument as a clarifying process. But we had another purpose. We also designed the exercise to stimulate thinking about a problem we introduced at the beginning of this chapter: the difference between argument as clarification and argument as persuasion. Is a good argument necessarily a persuasive argument? In our opinion, this student's letter to the committee is a good argument. The student writes well, takes a clear stand, offers good reasons for his position, and supports his reasons with effective evidence. To what extent, however, is the letter a *persuasive* argument? Did it win its case? You know how you and your classmates stand on this issue. But what do you think the University Standards Committee at ASU actually decided during its deliberations?

We will return to this case again in Chapter 7.

CONCLUSION

In this chapter we have explored some of the complexities of argument, showing you why we believe that argument is not a matter of fist-banging or of win-lose debate but of finding, through a process of rational inquiry, the best solution to a problem or issue. What is our advice for you at the close of this introductory chapter? Briefly, to see the purpose of argument as truth seeking as well as persuasion. We suggest that throughout the process of argument you seek out a wide range of views, that you especially welcome views different from your own, that you treat these views respectfully, and that you see them as intelligent and rationally defensible. (Hence you must look carefully at the reasons and evidence upon which they are based).

Our goal in this text is to help you learn skills of argument. If you choose, you can use these skills, like Callicles, to argue any side of any issue. And yet we hope you won't. We hope that, like Socrates, you will use argument for truth seeking and that you will consequently find yourselves, on at least some occasions, changing your position on an issue while writing a rough draft (a sure sign that the process of arguing has complicated your views). We believe that the skills of reason and inquiry developed through the writing of arguments can help you get a clearer sense of who you are. If our culture sets you adrift in pluralism, argument can help you take a stand, to say, "These things I believe." In this text we will not pretend to tell you what position to take on any given issue. But as responsible beings, you will often need to take a stand, to define yourself, to say, "Here are the reasons that choice A is better than choice B, not just for me but for you also." If this text helps you base your commitments on reasonable grounds, then it will have been successful.

chapter 2

Reading Arguments

WHY READING ARGUMENTS IS IMPORTANT FOR WRITERS OF ARGUMENT

In the previous chapter we explained how argument is a social phenomenon. It grows out of people's search for the best answers to questions, the best choices among alternative courses of actions. Part of the social nature of argumentation is the requirement to read arguments as well as write them.

Although this chapter focuses on reading, much of its advice applies also to listening. In fact, it is often helpful to think of reading as a conversation. We like to tell students that a college library is not so much a repository of information as a discussion frozen in time until you as reader bring it to life. Those books and articles, stacked neatly on library shelves, are arguing with each other, carrying on a great extended conversation. As you read, you bring those conversations to life. And when you write, you enter those conversations.

So writing and speaking are only half of the arguing process. The other half is careful reading and listening.

SUGGESTIONS FOR IMPROVING YOUR READING PROCESS

Before we offer specific strategies for reading arguments, let's examine some general strategies that can improve your ability to read any kind of college-level material, from complex textbooks to primary sources in a history or philosophy course.

1. Slow down: Advertisements for speedreading mislead us into believing that expert readers read rapidly. In fact, experts read difficult texts slowly, often rereading them two or three times, treating their first readings like first drafts. They hold confusing passages in mental suspension, hoping that later parts of the essay will clarify earlier parts. They "nutshell" or summarize passages in the margins. They interact with the text by asking questions, expressing disagreements, linking the text with other readings or with personal experience.

2. Get the dictionary habit: When you can't tell a word's meaning from context, get in the habit of looking it up. One strategy is to make small tick marks next to words you're unsure of; then look them up after you're done so as not to break your concentration.

3. Lose your highlighter/find your pen: Relying on those yellow highlighters makes you too passive. Next time you get the urge to highlight a passage, write in the margin why you think it's important. Is it a major new point in the argument? A significant piece of support? A summary of the opposition? A particularly strong or particularly weak point? Use the margins to summarize the text, protest vehemently, ask questions, give assent—but don't just color the pages.

4. Reconstruct the rhetorical context: Train yourself to ask questions such as these: Who is this author? What audience is he or she writing for? What occasion prompted this writing? What is the author's purpose? Any piece of writing makes more sense if you think of its author as a real person writing for some real purpose out of real historical context.

5. Join the text's conversation by exploring your views on the issues before reading: To determine the text's issues before reading it through, note the title, read the first few paragraphs carefully and skim the opening sentences of paragraphs. You can then explore your own views on the issue. This sort of personal exploration at the prereading stage both increases your readiness to understand the text and enhances your ability to enjoy it.

6. Continue the conversation after your reading: After you've read a text, try completing the following statements in a journal: "The most significant question this essay raises is. . . ." "The most important thing I learned from this essay is. . . ." "I agree with the author about. . . ." "However, I disagree about. . . ." These questions help you remember the reading and urge you to respond actively to it.

7. Try "translating" difficult passages: When you stumble over a difficult passage, try "translating" it into your own words. Converting the passage into your own language forces you to focus on the precise meanings of words. Although your translation may not be exactly what the author intended, you see more clearly where the sources of confusion lie and what the likely range of meanings might be.

STRATEGIES FOR READING ARGUMENTS: AN OVERVIEW

Whereas the preceding suggestions can be applied to all sorts of reading tasks, the rest of this chapter focuses on reading strategies specific to arguments. Because argument begins in disagreements within a social community, we recommend that you examine any argument as if it were only one voice in a larger conversation. We therefore recommend the following strategies in sequence:

1. Read as a believer.
2. Read as a doubter.
3. Seek out alternative views and analyze sources of disagreement to clarify why participants in the conversation are disagreeing with each other.
4. Evaluate the various positions.

Let's now explore each of these strategies in turn.

STRATEGY 1: READING AS A BELIEVER

When you read as a believer, you are practicing what psychologist Carl Rogers calls *empathic listening*, in which you mentally walk in the author's shoes, trying to join the author's culture and to see the world through the author's eyes. Reading as a believer helps you guard against coloring the author's ideas with your own biases and beliefs.

Because empathic listening is such a vital skill, we ask you now to try it on an influential and controversial article by conservative political writer Charles Murray. The article, published in the *Wall Street Journal* in 1993, initiated a national debate on the problem of rising illegitimacy rates. In it Murray details his proposed solution to the problem. According to syndicated political columnist John Leo (also a conservative), Murray's article "may turn out to be the most potent op-ed article in about 10 years. . . . [It] has had an explosive impact in policy discussions [at the presidential level]."* Before reading the article, reflect briefly on your own attitudes toward single parenthood. Do you think it is a problem that 30 percent of American babies are now born to unmarried mothers? Can a single parent raise a child as effectively as a married couple? What are the causes for the rise in single parenthood in our culture? If you think the 30 percent illegitimacy rate is a problem, what can be done about it?

---

*John Leo, "New Cultural Conscience Shifts the Welfare Debate," *Seattle Times* 14 Dec. 1993: B4.

The Coming White Underclass

Charles Murray

Every once in a while the sky really is falling, and this seems to be the case with the latest national figures on illegitimacy. The unadorned statistic is that, in 1991, 1.2 million children were born to unmarried mothers, within a hair of 30 percent of all live births. How high is 30 percent? About four percentage points higher than the black illegitimacy rate in the early 1960s that motivated Daniel Patrick Moynihan to write his famous memorandum on the breakdown of the black family.[1]

The 1991 story for blacks is that illegitimacy has now reached 68 percent of births to black women. In inner cities, the figure is typically in excess of 80 percent. Many of us have heard these numbers so often that we are inured. It is time to think about them as if we were back in the mid-1960s with the young Moynihan and asked to predict what would happen if the black illegitimacy rate were 68 percent.

Impossible we would have said. But if the proportion of fatherless boys in a given community were to reach such levels, surely the culture must be *Lord of the Flies* writ large,[2] the values of unsocialized male adolescents made norms—physical violence, immediate gratification and predatory sex. That is the culture now taking over the black inner city.

But the black story, however dismaying, is old news. The new trend that threatens the U.S. is white illegitimacy. Matters have not yet quite gotten out of hand, but they are on the brink. If we want to act, now is the time.

In 1991, 707,502 babies were born to single white women, representing 22 percent of white births. The elite wisdom holds that this phenomenon cuts across social classes, as if the increase in Murphy Browns[3] were pushing the trendline. Thus, a few months ago, a Census Bureau study of fertility among all American women got headlines for a few days because it showed that births to single women with college degrees doubled in the last decade to 6 percent from 3 percent. This is an interesting trend, but of minor social importance. The real news of that study is that the proportion of single mothers with less than a high school education who gave birth jumped to 48 percent from 35 percent in a single decade.

These numbers are dominated by whites. Breaking down the numbers by race (using data not available in the published version), women with college degrees contribute only 4 percent of white illegitimate babies, while women with a high school education or less contribute 82 percent. Women with family incomes of $75,000 or more contribute 1 percent

---

[1]A reference to a controversial Department of Labor study, *The Negro Family: The Case for National Action* (Office of Planning and Research, March 1965).

[2]A reference to William Golding's novel *Lord of the Flies,* in which a group of adolescent males become stranded on an island and create their own society with no adult supervision. As soon as adult "norms" begin to fade, the boys' culture gradually descends into savagery and violence.

[3]Murphy Brown, the star of a TV sitcom by the same name, became a single mother on a TV episode made famous in 1992 by then Vice President Quayle, who used her as a symbol of the breakdown of the traditional family.

of white illegitimate babies, while women with family incomes under $20,000 contribute 69 percent.

7   The National Longitudinal Study of Youth, a Labor Department study that has tracked more than 10,000 youths since 1979, shows an even more dramatic picture. For white women below the poverty line in the year prior to giving birth, 44 percent of births have been illegitimate, compared with only six percent for women above the poverty line. White illegitimacy is overwhelmingly a lower-class phenomenon.

8   This brings us to the emergence of a white underclass. In raw numbers, European-American whites are the ethnic group with the most people in poverty, most illegitimate children, most women on welfare, most unemployed men, and most arrests for serious crimes. And yet whites have not had an "underclass" as such, because the whites who might qualify have been scattered among the working class. Instead, whites have had "white trash" concentrated in a few streets on the outskirts of town, sometimes a Skid Row of unattached white men in the large cities. But these scatterings have seldom been large enough to make up a neighborhood. An underclass needs a critical mass, and white America has not had one.

9   But now the overall white illegitimacy rate is 22 percent. The figure in low-income, working-class communities may be twice that. How much illegitimacy can a community tolerate? Nobody knows, but the historical fact is that the trendlines on black crime, dropout from the labor force, and illegitimacy all shifted sharply upward as the overall black illegitimacy rate passed 25 percent.

10   The causal connection is murky—I blame the revolution in social policy during that period, while others blame the sexual revolution, broad shifts in cultural norms, or structural changes in the economy. But the white illegitimacy rate is approaching that same problematic 25 percent region at a time when social policy is more comprehensively wrongheaded than it was in the mid-1960s, and the cultural and sexual norms are still more degraded.

11   The white underclass will begin to show its face in isolated ways. Look for certain schools in white neighborhoods to get a reputation as being unteachable, with large numbers of disruptive students and indifferent parents. Talk to the police; listen for stories about white neighborhoods where the incidence of domestic disputes and casual violence has been shooting up. Look for white neighborhoods with high concentrations of drug activity and large numbers of men who have dropped out of the labor force. Some readers will recall reading the occasional news story about such places already.

12   As the spatial concentration of illegitimacy reaches critical mass, we should expect the deterioration to be as fast among low-income whites in the 1990s as it was among low-income blacks in the 1960s. My proposition is that illegitimacy is the single most important social problem of our time—more important than crime, drugs, poverty, illiteracy, welfare or homelessness because it drives everything else. Doing something about it is not just one more item on the American policy agenda, but should be at the top. Here is what to do.

13   In the calculus of illegitimacy, the constants are that boys like to sleep with girls and that girls think babies are endearing. Human societies have historically channeled these elemental forces of human behavior via thick walls of rewards and penalties that constrained the overwhelming majority of births to take place within marriage. The past 30 years have seen those walls cave in. It is time to rebuild them.

The ethical underpinning for the policies I am about to describe is this: Bringing a child into the world is the most important thing that most human beings ever do. Bringing a child into the world when one is not emotionally or financially prepared to be a parent is wrong. The child deserves society's support. The parent does not.   14

The social justification is this: A society with broad legal freedoms depends crucially on strong nongovernmental institutions to temper and restrain behavior. Of these, marriage is paramount. Either we reverse the current trends in illegitimacy—especially white illegitimacy—or America must, willy-nilly, become an unrecognizably authoritarian, socially segregated, centralized state.   15

To restore the rewards and penalties of marriage does not require social engineering. Rather, it requires that the state stop interfering with the natural forces that have done the job quite effectively for millennia. Some of the changes I will describe can occur at the federal level; others would involve state laws. For now, the important thing is to agree on what should be done.   16

I begin with the penalties, of which the most obvious are economic. Throughout human history, a single woman with a small child has not been a viable economic unit. Not being a viable economic unit, neither have the single woman and child been a legitimate social unit. In small numbers they must be a net drain on the community's resources. In large numbers, they must destroy the community's capacity to sustain itself. *Mirabile dictu,* communities everywhere have augmented the economic penalties of single parenthood with severe social stigma.   17

Restoring economic penalties translates into the first and central policy prescription: to end all economic support for single mothers. The AFDC (Aid to Families with Dependent Children) payment goes to zero. Single mothers are not eligible for subsidized housing or for food stamps. An assortment of other subsidies and in-kind benefits disappear. Since universal medical coverage appears to be an idea whose time has come, I will stipulate that all children have medical coverage. But with that exception, the signal is loud and unmistakable. From society's perspective, to have a baby that you cannot care for yourself is profoundly irresponsible, and the government will no longer subsidize it.   18

How does a poor young mother survive without government support? The same way she has since time immemorial. If she wants to keep a child, she must enlist support from her parents, boyfriend, siblings, neighbors, church or philanthropies. She must get support from somewhere, anywhere, other than the government. The objectives are threefold.   19

First, enlisting the support of others raises the probability that other mature adults are going to be involved with the upbringing of the child, and this is a great good in itself.   20

Second, the need to find support forces a self-selection process. One of the most shortsighted excuses made for current behavior is that an adolescent who is utterly unprepared to be a mother "needs someone to love." Childish yearning isn't a good enough selection device. We need to raise the probability that a young single woman who keeps her child is doing so volitionally and thoughtfully. Forcing her to find a way of supporting the child does this. It will lead many young women who shouldn't be mothers to place their babies for adoption. This is good. It will lead others, watching what happens to their sisters, to take steps not to get pregnant. This is also good. Many others will get abortions. Whether this is good depends on what one thinks of abortion.   21

22   Third, stigma will regenerate. The pressure on relatives and communities to pay for the folly of their children will make an illegitimate birth the socially horrific act it used to be, and getting a girl pregnant something boys do at the risk of facing a shotgun. Stigma and shotgun marriages may or may not be good for those on the receiving end, but their deterrent effect on others is wonderful—and indispensable.

23   What about women who can find no support but keep the baby anyway? There are laws already on the books about the right of the state to take a child from a neglectful parent. We have some 360,000 children in foster care because of them. Those laws would still apply. Society's main response, however, should be to make it as easy as possible for those mothers to place their children for adoption at infancy. To that end, state governments must strip adoption of the nonsense that has encumbered it in recent decades.

24   The first step is to make adoption easy for any married couple who can show reasonable evidence of having the resources and stability to raise a child. Lift all restrictions on interracial adoption. Ease age limitations for adoptive parents.

25   The second step is to restore the traditional legal principle that placing a child for adoption means irrevocably relinquishing all legal rights to the child. The adoptive parents are parents without qualification. Records are sealed until the child reaches adulthood, at which time they may be unsealed only with the consent of biological child and parent.

26   Given these straightforward changes—going back to the old way, which worked—there is reason to believe that some extremely large proportion of infants given up by their mothers will be adopted into good homes. This is true not just for flawless blue-eyed blond infants but for babies of all colors and conditions. The demand for infants to adopt is huge.

27   Some small proportion of infants and larger proportion of older children will not be adopted. For them, the government should spend lavishly on orphanages. I am not recommending Dickensian barracks. In 1993, we know a lot about how to provide a warm, nurturing environment for children, and getting rid of the welfare system frees up lots of money to do it. Those who find the "orphanages" objectionable may think of them as 24-hour-a-day preschools. Those who prattle about the importance of keeping children with their biological mothers may wish to spend some time in a patrol car or with a social worker seeing what the reality of life with welfare-dependent biological mothers can be like.

28   Finally, there is the matter of restoring the rewards of marriage. Here, I am pessimistic about how much government can do and optimistic about how little it needs to do. The rewards of raising children within marriage are real and deep. The main task is to shepherd children through adolescence so that they can reach adulthood—when they are likely to recognize the value of those rewards—free to take on marriage and family. The main purpose of the penalties for single parenthood is to make that task easier.

29   One of the few concrete things that the government can do to increase the rewards of marriage is make the tax code favor marriage and children. Those of us who are nervous about using the tax code for social purposes can advocate making the tax code at least neutral.

30   A more abstract but ultimately crucial step in raising the rewards of marriage is to make marriage once again the sole legal institution through which parental rights and responsibilities are defined and exercised.

31   Little boys should grow up knowing from their earliest memories that if they want to have any rights whatsoever regarding a child that they sire—more vividly, if they want

to grow up to be a daddy—they must marry. Little girls should grow up knowing from their earliest memories that if they want to have any legal claims whatsoever on the father of their children, they must marry. A marriage certificate should establish that a man and a woman have entered into a unique legal relationship. The changes in recent years that have blurred the distinctiveness of marriage are subtly but importantly destructive.

Together, these measures add up to a set of signals, some with immediate and tangible consequences, others with long-term consequences, still others symbolic. They should be supplemented by others based on a re-examination of divorce law and its consequences.   32

That these policy changes seem drastic and unrealistic is a peculiarity of our age, not of the policies themselves. With embellishments, I have endorsed the policies that were the uncontroversial law of the land as recently as John Kennedy's presidency. Then, America's elites accepted as a matter of course that a free society such as America's can sustain itself only through virtue and temperance in the people, that virtue and temperance depend centrally on the socialization of each new generation, and that the socialization of each generation depends on the matrix of care and resources fostered by marriage.   33

Three decades after that consensus disappeared, we face an emerging crisis. The long, steep climb in black illegitimacy has been calamitous in black communities and painful for the nation. The reforms I have described will work for blacks as for whites, and have been needed for years. But the brutal truth is that American society as a whole could survive when illegitimacy became epidemic within a comparably small ethnic minority. It cannot survive the same epidemic among whites.   34

Now that you have finished the article, ask yourself how well you "listened" to it. The best way to demonstrate such listening is first to restate the author's argument fairly and accurately in your own words—that is, to summarize it—and then to examine all the ways that you could agree with Murray by bringing your own experience and values to bear supportively on his message.

Summary Writing as a Way of Reading to Believe

A *summary* (also called an *abstract* or a *precis*) condenses the original by eliminating supporting data and leaving only the major points. Summaries can vary in length from one sentence to several pages (if, say, you are summarizing a book). Summaries of articles typically range from a single paragraph (containing, say, 100–250 words) to several paragraphs that reduce the original to about one-third its original length.

If you practice the following steps, you should eventually find yourself writing summaries with relative ease.

1. The first time through, read the essay for general meaning. Follow the flow of the argument without judgment or criticism, trying to see the world as the author sees it.

2. Reread the essay carefully, writing brief statements in the margins that sum up what each paragraph (or group of closely related paragraphs) says and does. A "what it says" statement summarizes a paragraph's content. A "what it does" statement identifies a paragraph's function, such as "summarizes opposition," "develops second supporting reason," "offers illustrative anecdote," "provides statistical data to support a point," and so on. Figure 2.1 shows a page from Murray's article with "says" and "does" statements intermixed in the margin.

The first few times you summarize an article, you might find it helpful to write "says" and "does" statements on a separate page to help you understand the structure and argument of the essay. To illustrate this powerful strategy, we provide paragraph-by-paragraph "says" and "does" statements for approximately two-thirds of Murray's essay (numbers in boldface refer to original paragraph numbers).

DOES/SAYS ANALYSIS OF MURRAY

Paragraphs 1–2: *Does:* Introduces problem and uses comparison of present illegitimacy birth rates with earlier rates to underscore significance of problem. *Says:* Illegitimacy birth rates have soared in recent years, far exceeding the 25 percent danger level that prompted Daniel Moynihan in the 1960s to prophesy the breakdown of the black family.

Paragraph 3: *Does:* Lends presence to his claim by drawing an analogy between communities full of fatherless adolescents and a novel about adolescent boys marooned on an island. *Says:* Like the boys in *Lord of the Flies*, contemporary illegitimate children will create a savage society.

Paragraph 4: *Does:* Provides a transition from discussion of black illegitimacy rates to white illegitimacy rates. *Says:* The white illegitimacy problem is growing but there's still time to get it under control.

Paragraphs 5–7: *Does:* Supports and limits the claim that white illegitimacy rate is growing. *Says:* Although 22 percent of white births are illegitimate, the proportions are much larger among working class whites.

Paragraph 8: *Does:* Defines the illegitimacy problem as a part of the larger problem of an "emergent white underclass." *Says:* The white underclass is now large enough to constitute a "critical mass."

Paragraphs 9 and 11: *Does:* Compares white illegitimacy rate to historical black rates and predicts bad consequences. *Says:* As white illegitimacy rates approach 25 percent, we can expect to see crime and unemployment figures rise dramatically as they did when black rates achieved a similar level.

Paragraph 10: *Does:* Claims a causal connection between illegitimacy rates and social problems. *Says:* While admitting the connection is "murky," Murray identifies "social policy"—not changes in sexual mores or cultural economic shifts—as the key to illegitimacy rates.

Paragraph 12: *Does:* Sums up and restates problem. *Says:* Illegitimacy is the "single most important social issue of our time" because it drives other social problems.

. . . .

But now the overall white illegitimacy rate is 22 percent. The figure in low-income, working-class communities may be twice that. How much illegitimacy can a community tolerate? Nobody knows, but the historical fact is that the trendlines on black crime, dropout from the labor force, and illegitimacy all shifted sharply upward as the overall black illegitimacy rate passed 25 percent.   [9]

> White illegitimacy rate approaching danger point of 25%.

The causal connection is murky—I blame the revolution in social policy during that period, while others blame the sexual revolution, broad shifts in cultural norms, or structural changes in the economy. But the white illegitimacy rate is approaching that same problematic 25 percent region at a time when social policy is more comprehensively wrong-headed than it was in the mid-1960s, and the cultural and sexual norms are still more degraded.   [10]

> What is the cause?
> Murray blames social policy   Others blame sexual revolution, shifts in culture, economy
>
> danger signs

The white underclass will begin to show its face in isolated ways. Look for certain schools in white neighborhoods to get a reputation as being unteachable, with large numbers of disruptive students and indifferent parents. Talk to the police; listen for stories about white neighborhoods where the incidence of domestic disputes and casual violence has been shooting up. Look for white neighborhoods with high concentrations of drug activity and large numbers of men who have dropped out of the labor force. Some readers will recall reading the occasional news story about such places already.   [11]

As the spatial concentration of illegitimacy reaches critical mass, we should expect the deterioration to be as fast among low-income whites in the 1990s as it was among low-income blacks in the 1960s. My proposition is that illegitimacy is the single most important social problem of our time—more important than crime, drugs, poverty, illiteracy, welfare or homelessness because it drives everything else. Doing something about it is not just one more item on the American policy agenda, but should be at the top. Here is what to do.   [12]

> Illegitimacy _single_ most important problem.

In the calculus of illegitimacy, the constants are that boys like to sleep with girls and that girls think babies are endearing. Human societies have historically channeled these elemental forces of human behavior via thick walls of rewards and penalties that constrained the overwhelming majority of births to take place within marriage. The past 30 years have seen those walls cave in. It is time to rebuild them.   [13]

> Turning point: Here is what to do.
>
> (1) We must rebuild walls that used to constrain births within marriage.

The ethical underpinning for the policies I am about to describe is this: Bringing a child into the world is the most important thing that most human beings ever do. Bringing a child into the world when one is not emotionally or financially prepared to be a parent is wrong. The child deserves society's support. The parent does not. [14]

> It is _wrong_ to have a baby unless parents are emotionally and financially prepared.

The social justification is this: A society with broad legal freedoms depends crucially on strong nongovernmental institutions to temper and restrain behavior. Of these, marriage is paramount. Either we reverse the current trends in illegitimacy—especially white illegitimacy—or America must, willy-nilly, become an unrecognizably authoritarian, socially segregated, centralized state.   [15]

> Either we restore cultural norms against illegitimacy or we will degenerate into an authoritarian state.

To restore the rewards and penalties of marriage does not require social engineering. Rather, it requires that the state stop interfering with the natural forces that have done the job quite effectively for millennia.

FIGURE 2.1   Reading-to-believe annotations on Murray text

Paragraphs 23–25: *Does:* Anticipates objection that not all mothers will find aid or place children for adoption voluntarily. *Says:* When mothers don't act responsibly, we have the legal means to remove them and place them in sound families, if we ease adoption restrictions.

Paragraphs 26–27: *Does:* Predicts large numbers of children will be given up for adoption and offers an alternative for those who are not placed. *Says:* For those illegitimate children not adopted, we need to provide "24-hour-a-day preschools" (orphanages).

Paragraphs 28–32: *Does:* Offers second prong of proposal, rewarding marriage. *Says:* In addition to penalizing illegitimacy, we need to reward marriage by favoring it in the tax code and in civil laws defining parental rights and responsibilities.

Paragraph 33: *Does:* Cites a precedent for the current proposal. *Says:* Most aspects of the current proposal were law of the land in the Kennedy era.

Paragraph 34: *Does:* Underscores significance by returning to earlier precedents. *Says:* If we don't act, we can look for the same sorts of problems in the white underclass that we've already seen in the black underclass.

 ## FOR CLASS DISCUSSION

Working individually or in groups, make "what it does" and "what it says" statements for the middle paragraphs (paragraphs 13–22) of Murray's article.

3. After you've analyzed the essay paragraph by paragraph, try locating the main divisions or parts of the argument. At the largest level, Murray's article divides into two major parts: the first part (paragraphs 1–12) describes the problem, whereas the second part (paragraphs 13–35) explains Murray's proposed solution. Subdividing the essay further, we identified the following main sections (different readers might subdivide the sections in slightly different ways):

- an introductory section describing the problem of illegitimacy among inner-city blacks and showing that the illegitimacy rate is also rising among lower-class whites (paragraphs 1–7)
- a section showing how the increase in the illegitimacy rate among lower-class whites is reaching a critical mass that will lead to the emergence of a white underclass and a dramatic increase in crime, unemployment, drug use (paragraphs 8–12)
- an overview paragraph saying that we must rebuild the "walls" that restrict childbirth to married couples (paragraph 13)
- a section giving the ethical and social justification for his proposal (paragraphs 14–16)

- a section showing the three "good" results of ending all economic aid to single mothers (paragraphs 17–27). This section also includes a subsection on improving the process of adoption (paragraphs 23–27)

- a section showing that we must reestablish the rewards for marriage (paragraphs 28–32)

- a conclusion showing the importance of the proposal and claiming that this proposal is not radical.

Instead of listing the sections as we just did, many readers might prefer to make an outline, flowchart, or diagram of the article showing its main parts and subparts. (See our diagram of Murray's article in Figure 2.2.)

4. Turn your list, outline, flowchart, or diagram into a prose summary. Typically, writers do this in one of two ways. Some start with a lengthy paragraph-by-paragraph summary and then prune it in successive drafts. Others start with a one-sentence summary of the argument's thesis and major supporting reasons and then gradually flesh it out with more supporting ideas.

5. Continue writing drafts until your summary is the desired length and is sufficiently clear, complete, and concise that someone who hasn't read the original could read your summary and explain the original to a third party.

As illustrations, consider the following three summaries of Murray's article.

ONE-SENTENCE SUMMARY

To solve the problem of illegitimacy, which has long been at crisis levels for black culture and now is reaching crisis proportions among lower-class whites, the United States should end all economic support for single mothers, thereby reawakening social stigmas against single parenthood. (45 words)

100-WORD SUMMARY

The illegitimacy rate in America, now 30 percent of all live births, has increased most dramatically among lower-class whites, where we can now predict the same kind of social breakdown that characterized black inner-city culture when illegitimacy rates soared above 25 percent. The solution is to revitalize cultural constraints against illegitimacy by ending all economic support for single mothers. Three good results will follow: (1) More family and friends will be involved in raising the child; (2) more infants will be given for adoption; and (3) social stigmas against illegitimacy will be reawakened. This approach, although seemingly drastic, returns our nation to earlier policies. (101 words)

250-WORD SUMMARY

The illegitimacy rate in America has reached 30 percent of all live births, thus exceeding the 25 percent black illegitimacy rate in the 1960s that sparked Moynihan's

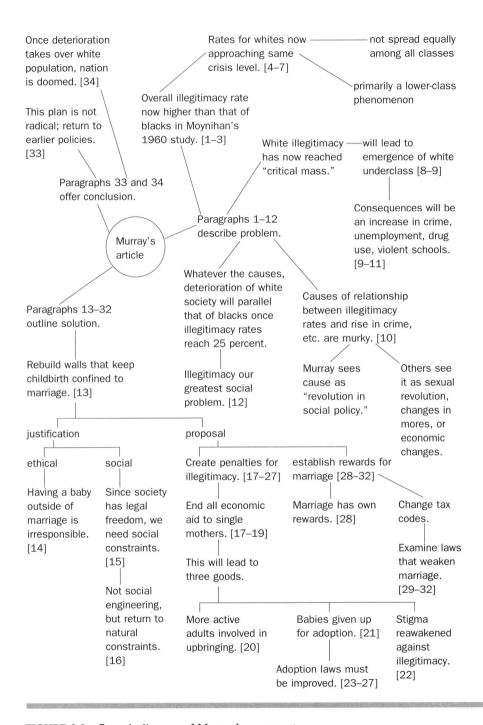

FIGURE 2.2 Branch diagram of Murray's argument

prophetic warnings about the breakdown of the black family. Illegitimate births among lower-class whites have risen so dramatically that a new white underclass is beginning to emerge. We can thus predict the same kind of social breakdown among working-class whites (increase in crime, drug abuse, unemployment, unmanageable schools) that has characterized the black inner city. The solution, which can be justified on both ethical and social grounds, is to revitalize cultural constraints against illegitimacy. We should begin by ending all economic support for single mothers, forcing them to seek assistance from family, boyfriends, or charities. Three good results will follow: (1) more adults will be involved in raising the child; (2) many single mothers will decide against keeping infants and offer them for adoption; and (3) angry families will reawaken the social stigma against illegitimacy. To make the solution workable, we must ease adoption laws and be prepared to spend lavishly on orphanages. Finally, we must increase the rewards of marriage through restructured tax codes and reexamination of divorce laws and other regulations that undermine the social importance of marriage. Although this approach seems drastic, it merely returns our nation to the policies that prevailed up through John Kennedy's presidency. Unless we return to the values of virtue and temperance, the social catastrophe that has undermined black culture will sweep through white culture also, thus destroying our nation. (253 words)

We don't want to pretend that these summaries were easy to write. They weren't. Murray's argument is quite difficult to summarize because he doesn't always make the links between parts explicit. Moreover, some readers might fault our summaries for overemphasizing some aspects of the essay while neglecting others. Such differences are to be expected in the absence of prominently stated transitions and other structural markers.

Incorporating Summaries into Your Writing

Suppose you were writing your own argument on welfare reform and wanted to incorporate a summary of Murray's views into your own essay. Any of the preceding summaries could be woven into your own essay through the use of *attributive tags,* which are phrases such as "Murray says," "according to Murray," and so forth. These tags, together with a bibliographic citation to Murray's article, indicate that you are reporting someone else's views rather than your own. If you were to copy any phrases directly from Murray's article, you would also need quotation marks around the part you copied. The following example uses the Modern Language Association (MLA) citation system.*

---

*In this example, numbers in parentheses indicate page numbers in this text where the quotations can be found. A listing of complete bibliographic information would be included on a separate page at the end of the essay under the heading "Works Cited." See Chapter 17 for further discussion of documentation systems.

SUMMARY OF MURRAY INCORPORATED INTO YOUR OWN ESSAY

The conservative social critic Charles Murray, writing in the October 29, 1993, *Wall Street Journal,* has argued that America's skyrocketing illegitimacy rate is "the single most important social problem of our time" (28). Citing extensive statistical evidence, Murray argues that the illegitimacy rate in America has reached 30 percent of all live births, thus exceeding the 25 percent black illegitimacy rate in the 1960s that sparked Daniel Patrick Moynihan's prophetic warnings about the breakdown of the black family. According to Murray, illegitimate births among lower-class whites have risen so dramatically that a new white underclass is beginning to emerge. Murray thus predicts the same kind of social breakdown among working-class whites (increase in crime, drug abuse, unemployment, unmanageable schools) that has characterized the black inner city. Murray's proposed solution, for which he gives both ethical and social justification, is to revitalize cultural constraints against illegitimacy. We should begin, he claims, by ending all economic support for single mothers, forcing them to seek assistance from family, boyfriends, or charities. He wants to send adolescents a "loud and unmistakable" (29) message. "From society's perspective, to have a baby that you cannot care for yourself is profoundly irresponsible, and the government will no longer subsidize it" (29). Murray claims that three good results will follow from the withdrawing of economic support: First, more adults will be involved in raising the child; second, many single mothers will decide against keeping infants and offer them for adoption; and third, angry families will reawaken the social stigma against illegitimacy. To make the solution workable, Murray argues that we must ease adoption laws and be prepared to spend lavishly on orphanages. Finally, Murray wants to increase the rewards of marriage through restructured tax codes and reexamination of divorce laws and other regulations that undermine the social importance of marriage. Although this approach seems drastic, Murray argues that it merely returns our nation to the policies that prevailed up through John Kennedy's presidency. Unless we return to the values of virtue and temperance, claims Murray, the social catastrophe that has undermined black culture will sweep through white culture also, thus destroying our nation.

WORKS CITED

Murray, Charles. "The Coming White Underclass." *Wall Street Journal* 29 Oct. 1993: A13. Rpt. in Ramage, John D. and John C. Bean *Writing Arguments: A Rhetoric with Readings.* 4th ed. Needham, MA: Allyn and Bacon, 1998. 27–31.

Suspending Doubt: Willing Your Own Belief in the Writer's Views

Summarizing an argument is only the first step in your effort to believe it. If the argument takes a stand that you already agree with, then it is easy to believe the author, whose views and values accord with yours. But if your tendency is to doubt the argument—if its views affront your own values—then trying to "be-lieve" the argument is a hard but valuable exercise. It is through trying to believe strange, dangerous, or unfamiliar views that we grow as learners and thinkers.

To believe an argument, search your own life for experiences that support the author's message and articulate any values or beliefs that you share with the author. Try to walk in the author's shoes. Here is how one student, whose liberal background made her hostile to Murray, tried to believe his argument. We quote from her journal:

> Murray seems unconcerned about the fate of children (I can't stand the thought of putting babies in orphanages), but I admit that I can see the problem that Murray is trying to address. I agree that a rising illegitimacy rate is a scary problem and that kids are better off with two parents who will love their children and not leave them to roam the streets. Anything that would put social pressure on families to keep their daughters from getting pregnant (and sons from seeking sex) might help. Although I don't think girls get pregnant for the welfare money, I can see how the absence of that money might lead adults to put more social pressure on teenagers to avoid sex or have safe sex. I don't know what would happen to all the babies during the transition period, but I can see how we would be sending a strong message that you shouldn't have a baby unless you can support it. If there were only some way to punish the teenagers without abandoning the babies!

STRATEGY 2: READING AS A DOUBTER

But reading as a believer is only half of being a powerful reader. You must also read as a doubter by raising objections, asking questions, expressing skepticism, and withholding assent. In the margins you add a new layer of notations de-manding more proof, doubting evidence, challenging the author's assumptions and values, and so forth. Figure 2.3 shows one reader's doubting commentary as she made marginal notations on a page from Murray's article. (For purposes of illustration, this reader's believing commentary—efforts to understand and sum-marize the argument—aren't shown. Marginal notations of a text usually inter-mingle both believing and doubting commentary.)

FOR CLASS DISCUSSION

Before we inform you of some of the doubts and queries raised by our own students, we ask you to return now to the Murray article and read it skeptically yourself. Raise questions, offer objections, express all your doubts. Then, working as a whole class or in small groups, make a list of problems you find with Mur-ray's argument.

But now the overall white illegitimacy rate is 22 percent. The figure in low-income, working-class communities may be twice that. How much illegitimacy can a community tolerate? Nobody knows, but the historical fact is that the trendlines on black crime, dropout from the labor force, and illegitimacy all shifted sharply upward as the overall black illegitimacy rate passed 25 percent.   [9]

The causal connection is murky—I blame the revolution in social policy during that period, while others blame the sexual revolution, broad shifts in cultural norms, or structural changes in the economy. But the white illegitimacy rate is approaching that same problematic 25 percent region at a time when social policy is more comprehensively wrongheaded than it was in the mid-1960s, and the cultural and sexual norms are still more degraded.   [10]

How much does Murray's "solution" depend on his analysis of the cause here? What if the primary causes are economic, or changes in sexual or cultural norms?

The white underclass will begin to show its face in isolated ways. Look for certain schools in white neighborhoods to get a reputation as being unteachable, with large numbers of disruptive students and indifferent parents. Talk to the police; listen for stories about white neighborhoods where the incidence of domestic disputes and casual violence has been shooting up. Look for white neighborhoods with high concentrations of drug activity and large numbers of men who have dropped out of the labor force. Some readers will recall reading the occasional news story about such places already.   [11]

As the spatial concentration of illegitimacy reaches critical mass, we should expect the deterioration to be as fast among low-income whites in the 1990s as it was among low-income blacks in the 1960s. My proposition is that illegitimacy is the single most important social problem of our time—more important than crime, drugs, poverty, illiteracy, welfare or homelessness because it drives everything else. Doing something about it is not just one more item on the American policy agenda, but should be at the top. Here is what to do.   [12]

Murray claims that illegitimacy drives all other social problems. But maybe he has causality reversed. Maybe there would be less illegitimacy if poor people had better jobs—they would have greater sense of self-worth and more sexual responsibility. Seems to claim that most single mothers wanted to get pregnant. What if lack of sex education has a lot to do with this problem?

In the calculus of illegitimacy, the constants are that boys like to sleep with girls and that girls think babies are endearing. Human societies have historically channeled these elemental forces of human behavior via thick walls of rewards and penalties that constrained the overwhelming majority of births to take place within marriage. The past 30 years have seen those walls cave in. It is time to rebuild them.   [13]

The ethical underpinning for the policies I am about to describe is this: Bringing a child into the world is the most important thing that most human beings ever do. Bringing a child into the world when one is not emotionally or financially prepared to be a parent is wrong. The child deserves society's support. The parent does not. [14]

But he wants to reverse this trend by punishing single mothers. Not providing economic help seems authoritarian to me.

The social justification is this: A society with broad legal freedoms depends crucially on strong nongovernmental institutions to temper and restrain behavior. Of these, marriage is paramount. Either we reverse the current trends in illegitimacy—especially white illegitimacy—or America must, willy-nilly, become an unrecognizably authoritarian, socially segregated, centralized state.   [15]

To restore the rewards and penalties of marriage does not require social engineering. Rather, it requires that the state stop interfering with the natural forces that have done the job quite effectively for millennia.

He seems to think that the middle-class, two-parent family is the "natural" way. What about other cultures where polygamy or communal child raising is the norm?

FIGURE 2.3   Reading-to-doubt annotations on Murray text

We hope that you have now done your own doubting of Murray's article. What follows is a selective list of doubts and queries raised by students in our classes:

- Murray seems to have no compassion for the individuals who would suffer from his proposal. He treats people like abstract numbers.

- Murray glosses over the question of cause, calling it "murky" (paragraph 9). He believes that the "revolution in social policy" is the primary cause, and thus he thinks that changing the social policy will reverse the trend. But what if the other factors are more important—sexual revolution, shift in cultural norms, or changes in the economy?

- Will changing welfare rules really change attitudes of sexually active teenagers or young adults? Murray seems to assume that desire for welfare money is a primary motivation for getting pregnant. Perhaps the desire of poor women to have a baby is the result of alienation and hopelessness in living a life of poverty.

- Is illegitimacy really the root cause that drives all the other social problems such as crime, drug use, unemployment, and so forth? Perhaps poverty is the root cause. What good will it do to force the boyfriend to marry the girl (shotgun wedding) if the boyfriend has no job?

- What would happen to single mothers and their children if welfare payments suddenly stopped and they were unable to get help from family and friends? How many babies would starve or be abandoned? Would these "lavish" orphanages really work?

- Our group felt the article was racist. Murray seemed to think we could tolerate illegitimacy among blacks but not among whites. He seems to have completely given up on Black America.

- Murray seems to have a sentimental attachment to the past. He assumes that all earlier cultures were modeled on 1950s two-parent nuclear families. What worked in the 50s he believes has worked "for millennia." Were the 50s really all that great?

- Murray is a sexist when it comes to sex. He assumes that boys like sex and that girls want babies. He thus puts no emphasis on birth control or safe sex. But girls like sex too and need to be taught how to have sex without getting pregnant. Perhaps we need better sex education and family planning programs rather than changes in welfare rules.

These are only some of the objections that might be raised against Murray's article. Perhaps you and your classmates have other objections that are equally important. Our point is that you should practice "doubting" an argument as well as "believing" it. Both skills are essential. Whereas believing helps you expand your view of the world or modify your arguments and beliefs in response to others, doubting helps protect you from becoming overpowered by others' arguments and teaches you to stand back, consider, and weigh carefully.

STRATEGY 3: SEEKING OUT ALTERNATIVE VIEWS AND ANALYZING SOURCES OF DISAGREEMENT

When you analyze an argument, you shouldn't isolate it from the general conversation of differing views that form its context. If you were an arbitrator, you wouldn't think of settling a dispute between A and B on the basis of A's testimony only. You would also insist on hearing B's side of the story. In analyzing an argument, therefore, you should try to seek out the views of those who disagree with the author to appreciate the full context of the issue.

As you listen to differing views, try to identify sources of disagreement, which often fall into two categories: (1) disagreement about the facts or truth of the case, and (2) disagreement about underlying beliefs, values, or assumptions, including assumptions about definitions or appropriate analogies. Let's look at each in turn.

Disagreement about Facts or Truth

Theoretically, a fact is a piece of empirical data on which everyone agrees. Often, however, what one person takes as fact another takes as a misconception or an opinionated misinterpretation. Thus in the 1996 presidential elections, Bob Dole claimed that President Clinton had pushed through "the largest tax increase in U.S. history," whereas Clinton claimed in turn that an earlier tax increase passed during President Bush's administration (and voted for by Senator Dole) was in "adjusted dollars" much higher. Here Dole and Clinton disagree about "facts"—in this case, the truth represented by raw numbers that can be cooked in a variety of ways. Other examples of disagreements about facts or truth include the following:

- In arguing whether silver-mercury amalgam tooth fillings should be banned, dental researchers disagree on the amount of mercury vapor released by older fillings; they also disagree on how much mercury vapor has to be present before it is harmful.

- In arguing about the legalization of drugs, writers disagree about the degree to which Prohibition reduced alcohol consumption; they also disagree on whether crack cocaine is "crimogenic" (has chemical properties that induce violent behavior).

- In arguing what to do about the problem of illegitimacy, disputants agree that the illegitimacy rate is rising but disagree about causes and therefore about solutions.

Disagreement about Values, Beliefs, or Assumptions

A second source of disagreement concerns differences in values, beliefs, or assumptions. Here are some examples:

- Persons A and B might agree that a huge tax on gasoline would cut down on the consumption of petroleum. They might agree further that the world's supply of petroleum will eventually run out. Thus A and B agree at the level of facts. But they might disagree about whether the United States should enact a huge gas tax. Person A might support the law in order to conserve oil whereas B might oppose it, perhaps because B believes that scientists will find alternative energy sources before the petroleum runs out or because B believes the short-term harm of such a tax outweighs distant benefits.

- Person A and Person B might agree that capital punishment deters potential murderers (an agreement on facts). Person A supports capital punishment for this reason, but Person B opposes it, believing that the taking of a human life is always wrong in principle even if the state does it legally (a disagreement about basic beliefs).

Sometimes disagreements about assumptions present themselves as disagreements about definitions or appropriate analogies.

- Person A and Person B may disagree about whether *Playboy* is pornographic—a disagreement stemming primarily from different definitions of the term *pornography*, which in turn reflect different underlying values or beliefs.

- In supporting a Texas law forbidding flag burning, Chief Justice William Rehnquist argued that desecration of a flag in the name of free speech is similar to desecrating the Washington Monument. He thus makes this analogy: Just as we would forbid desecration of a national monument, so should we forbid desecration of the flag. Opposing justices did not think the analogy was valid.

- Person A and Person B disagree on whether it is ethically acceptable to have Down's syndrome children undergo plastic surgery to correct some of the facial abnormalities associated with this genetic condition. Person A supports the surgery, arguing it is analogous to any other cosmetic surgeries done to improve appearance. Person B argues against such surgery, saying it is analogous to the racial self-hatred of some minority persons who have tried to change their ethnic appearance and become lily white. (The latter analogy argues that Down's syndrome is nothing to be ashamed of and that persons should take pride in their difference.)

❧ FOR CLASS DISCUSSION

As discussed in Chapter 1, we live in a pluralistic world wherein many differing systems of values and beliefs compete for our allegiance. It follows that one of the most frequent sources of disagreement among participants in a conversation is disagreement about values, beliefs, or basic underlying assumptions. What follows are four different responses to Charles Murray's proposal to cut off welfare support for single mothers. The first two are letters to the editor that appeared in the *Wall Street Journal* on November 15, 1993. The third is part of a newspaper editorial by conservative columnist John Leo. The fourth is an op-ed piece by columnist Dorothy Gilliam. Read the four pieces carefully. Then, working as a whole class or in small groups, answer the following questions.

1. What does each piece reveal about the underlying beliefs, assumptions, and values of its writer?

2. In what way do these writers' underlying beliefs, assumptions, and values cause them to agree or disagree with Charles Murray and with each other?

Piece 1: Letter to the Editor in Response to Charles Murray

1   Charles Murray's Oct. 29 editorial page piece "The Coming White Underclass" raises a profound moral paradox that he himself appears not to fully appreciate.

2   With considerable thoughtfulness and conservative passion over the mounting tragedy of illegitimate births in this country, Mr. Murray calls essentially for a return to the social values and policies of "as recently as John Kennedy's presidency": i.e., holding up marriage as the only socially acceptable venue for bearing and raising children and removing all government support for single women who bear and raise the children, however well or poorly, by themselves.

3   His respect for the institution of marriage is laudable. He's right to say that the optimum human environment from within which a child can become a productive, responsible, compassionate member of society is the marriage commitment. But in prescribing his bitter pills of social stigmatization and sink-or-swim governmental policy, he almost ignores the patient's most convenient remedy for this social illness—abortion.

4   At the staggering rate of 1.6 million times a year, American women and teenage girls, married and unmarried, are aborting their unborn children. The unmarried are doing it for many reasons, one of which is that an illegitimate birth is still a "socially horrific act" throughout much of society. But an increasingly more compelling reason for this profoundly destructive act is that "the old way" on the subject of abortion has also been dramatically altered since John Kennedy's presidency. It has been legal to elect abortion for any reason in this country since 1973. Even more alarmingly, it has become a "reproductive right" that virtually defines a woman's bodily and emotional integrity while it defines away the other human life involved.

5   Mr. Murray's reasoning seems either astoundingly sloppy or astoundingly "pro-choice" in this regard. In order to argue against the irresponsibility of pre-marital sex and single

motherhood, he uses language like "bringing a child into the world" and "having a baby." But after the pre-marital sex and before the single motherhood, there's another human life involved with a right to be born. Mr. Murray acknowledges that many women may have abortions when AFDC and other public supports are withdrawn as he recommends. He then casually concludes that "whether this is good depends on what one thinks of abortion."

Among socially horrific acts, abortion has to rank far above even illegitimacy.   6

Patricia Bucalo, Burlingame, Calif.

Piece 2: Letter to the Editor in Response to Charles Murray

There is no question that virtually every social problem facing our nation—in his words, "crime, drugs, poverty, illiteracy, welfare, [and] homelessness"—is vastly exacerbated by the epidemic of unintended and unwanted births. But Mr. Murray's assessment of the roots of the problem and his proposed solutions are dangerously off course.   1

Mr. Murray begins with the patronizing and treacherous premise that out-of-wedlock births happen because "boys like to sleep with girls and . . . girls think babies are endearing." He ends with a call to restore "economic penalties [and] severe social stigma" on single parents. Along the way, he makes clear that by "single parents," he really means single mothers—suggesting that women spontaneously generate not only babies, but poverty itself.   2

In sum, Mr. Murray wants to pull the plug on our nation's most vulnerable women and children. Every tub on its own bottom, he says: Able mothers will eke out a subsistence without government help; and as for the others, well, let's just cart their children off to "lavishly [funded] orphanages." This is a grotesque vision. First, it maligns the many single mothers who are doing all they can to achieve independence. Worse, it's a prescription for disaster. Already, 360,000 children languish in a child welfare system plagued by funding shortages, inadequate facilities and staffing crises. Mr. Murray's plan would crush this overburdened system, leaving more and more babies to be abandoned in alleys, Dumpsters, and public restrooms.   3

Here are some real solutions to the epidemic of teen pregnancy and its attendant cycle of hopelessness: America must provide universal access to comprehensive sexuality education and confidential, affordable contraception. We must make safe, legal abortion available to all women, with federal and state funding for those who need it. We must raise our expectations of young men, making them equal partners in preventing unintended pregnancy and in caring for the children they father; as U.S. Surgeon General Joycelyn Elders has said, "There is more to being a father than providing the sperm."   4

Above all, we must equip our young people with self-esteem and hope—through decent education, better job opportunities, and meaningful life options. In short, we must give them a future worth protecting.   5

Pamela J. Maraldo, Ph.D., R.N.
President, Planned Parenthood Federation of America

Piece 3: Excerpt from "New Cultural Conscience Shifts Welfare Debate"

John Leo

1   . . . Reflecting the current state of the argument, President Clinton seems to say things like this, over and over: "Would we be a better-off society if babies were born to married couples? You bet we would." He told ministers in Memphis, Tenn., that if the Rev. Martin Luther King Jr. were to reappear today, he would say, among other things, "I did not live and die to see the American family destroyed." We are a long way here from last year's general babble about "family diversity" and "new family forms."

2   It says a lot about the current cultural moment that a Democratic president is starting to echo conservative scholar Charles Murray. . . . Murray wants America to go cold-turkey on welfare—eliminating it completely. On Oct. 29, *The Wall Street Journal* published a piece by Murray that may turn out to be the most potent op-ed article in about 10 years. . . .

3   Murray's piece has had an explosive impact in policy discussions. He says it's like striking a spike into the earth and feeling "enormous pressure in the ground ready to explode." He feels there's a chance now for "real radical reform." That's the new cultural moment. Like it or not, President Clinton seems to feel it, too. He said in an interview with Tom Brokaw that Murray's op-ed piece is "essentially right," though he questions the prescription of eliminating welfare entirely.

4   The debate on welfare will now take place on Murray's terms, not Clinton's, a rather amazing phenomenon that nobody could have predicted a few weeks ago. Murray's analysis removes race from the welfare debate, since he sees whites and blacks going through the same process. And it calls into question all the sex programs and condom distribution schemes that sustain the highly sexualized youth culture driving the illegitimacy rate. Welcome to a new moment and a very different debate.

Piece 4: Wrong Way to Reform Welfare

Dorothy Gilliam

1   With an eye toward reducing the rate of teenage pregnancy, the White House task force on welfare reform wants to curtail additional benefits to unmarried mothers who have more children while on welfare.

2   Taking this drive to discourage out-of-wedlock births among young welfare recipients a step further, Charles Murray, a fellow at the conservative American Enterprise Institute, wants to cut off all economic support to single mothers who have additional children while on welfare—no monetary assistance, no food stamps, no subsidized housing.

3   I agree with the underlying analysis that the problem of children born to poor, single mothers is a crucial issue in welfare reform because it helps drive so many other social problems: crime, drugs, violence, poverty and illiteracy.

But the task force proposal and Murray's draconian "solutions" are not the answer.   4

Not only is there a lack of substantiated evidence linking welfare benefits to increases   5
in illegitimate births, but the task force's approach also is really a punitive, morally questionable attempt at social engineering on the backs of poor people.

President Clinton has not received the task force's final report on welfare reform,   6
which includes the aforementioned proposal and several others meant to discourage additional births among single, young mothers. But, thank God, he already has had the good
sense to question whether that alternative would be "morally right."

Meanwhile, many children and family advocacy groups are working hard to turn the   7
tide against the idea.

"Frankly, I'm sick and tired of social engineering on the backs of poor women," said   8
David S. Liederman, executive director of the Child Welfare League of America.

Citing New Jersey's current experiment with "child exclusion" provisions for mothers   9
on public assistance, Liederman said trying to stop women from having additional children
is "nonsense."

"There is no history that says these kinds of behavior-modification schemes have any   10
effect on whether or not women have children," Liederman said in an interview. "It assumes women have children for money, and that is not true. The children suffer, and the
baby who needs support doesn't get it."

Murray, writing recently in the *Wall Street Journal* that the United States is quickly de-   11
veloping a white underclass that is larger and potentially more devastating than the black
underclass, goes on to propose a myriad of solutions to reduce the rising number of births
among poor, single white women.

But the fallacy of Murray's argument is his belief that punitive action would change be-   12
havior. It's an argument that does not take into account why such behavior exists. Pamela
J. Maraldo, president of Planned Parenthood Federation of America, believes too much attention is being paid to the issue of marital status, and too little to the more crucial issue
of mutual commitment of parents to each other and their children.

"The issue is not whether a child is illegitimate, but whether that child is wanted or   13
unwanted," Maraldo said.

Though a great deal of attention has been focused on the huge cost of welfare, Lieder-   14
man notes that the budget for Aid to Families with Dependent Children equals 1 percent
of the federal budget.

"To hear some folks rail about welfare, you'd think it's the terrible monster that is caus-   15
ing all of the evils," he said. "But to care for almost 10 million children with 1 percent of
the budget is miraculous."

If Clinton is serious about "ending welfare as we know it," as he pledged in his campaign,   16
his planners must take seriously what most advocates have long said: Most women do not want
to be on welfare and would prefer jobs that position them to get off the rolls permanently.

Though welfare certainly includes a fringe of recipients who abuse the system, the focus   17
should be on the majority of poor mothers and children who earnestly want better lives.

It's a quick-fix mentality that presumes that welfare can be reformed in isolation of   18
all the root social problems that feed into it: poor housing, drug-related violence, joblessness,
lack of opportunity. It's a cowardly mentality that targets the poor because they lack clout.

19   Why not, instead, exploit the current momentum for welfare reform by offering more continuing education and job-training opportunities for people who want meaningful work? That way reform would help them and their children, not punish them because they had the bad luck to be born disadvantaged and poor.

20   It would be a sad day if this country chooses the proposed alternative: to throw poor women and their children overboard.

Writing an Analysis of a Disagreement

A common writing assignment in argument courses asks students to analyze the sources of disagreement between two or more writers who take different positions on an issue. In writing such an analysis, you need to determine whether the writers disagree primarily about truth or values (or both). Specifically, you should pose the following questions:

1. Where do the writers disagree about facts and/or the interpretation of facts?

2. Where do the writers disagree about underlying beliefs, values, or assumptions?

3. Where do they disagree about key definitions or about appropriate analogies? How do these differences imply differences in values, beliefs, or assumptions?

To illustrate how these three questions can help you write an analysis, we've constructed the following model: our own brief analysis of the sources of disagreement between Murray and Gilliam (pp. 46–48) written as a short, formal essay.

An Analysis of the Sources of Disagreement Between Murray and Gilliam

1   In their response to the problem of illegitimacy, Charles Murray and Dorothy Gilliam have one major area of agreement. Both agree that illegitimacy *is* a major social problem that drives many other social problems. A bulk of their disagreement is over how to solve the problem, a disagreement involving dissension about both truth and values.

2   Murray and Gilliam agree on the relevant statistics. Both agree that the current illegitimacy rate among lower-class whites is rising and that high illegitimacy rates drive other social problems such as crime, drugs, violence, poverty, and illiteracy. But they disagree in their analysis of causes. Whereas Murray asserts a causal relationship between welfare ben-

efits and illegitimacy, Gilliam rejects this causal connection. She states her case first in her own words: There is "a lack of substantiated evidence linking welfare benefits to increases in illegitimate births" (47). Then she cites the authority of David Liederman, executive director of the Child Welfare League of America, who said in an interview, " 'There is no history that says these kinds of behavior-modification schemes have any effect on whether or not women have children. . . . It assumes women have children for money, and that is not true' " (47). Although Gilliam denies Murray's claim, she herself provides no evidence against a causal link between welfare benefits and illegitimacy rates other than Liederman's testimony. For her own part, Gilliam attributes the rising illegitimacy rate to the more basic problems of "poor housing, drug-related violence, joblessness, [and] lack of opportunity" (47). Neither writer, however, offers empirical evidence to support his or her position on this causal issue.

As can be expected, Gilliam's disagreement with Murray about the causes of rising illegitimacy rates leads her toward dramatically different solutions as well. She argues that by providing job training and meaningful work to low-income people, we could avoid Murray's more "draconian" solution. The difference between Murray's and Gilliam's solutions indicates a substantial difference in values. For Gilliam, Murray's solution is not only unworkable, it's morally repugnant as well. She sees his solution as "punitive" (47) and part of a "cowardly mentality that targets the poor because they lack clout" (47). To Gilliam, Murray chooses to "throw poor women and their children overboard" (48) in lieu of offering them means to solve their own problems. While she doesn't directly cite Murray's "ethical underpinning" ("The child deserves society's support. The parent does not" [Murray, 29], she clearly thinks it's not possible to separate the moral interests of the child from those of the parent. All in all, Murray reveals values that we typically think of as conservative—belief that the old ways are better than the present, that we should make individuals responsible for their actions by restoring penalties and bad consequences for wrong choices, and that we should place the good of the social order above the individual happiness of each member. Gilliam, on the other hand, espouses values that we typically associate with liberalism—attributing problems to their social or economic causes rather than to individual mistakes, believing the state should help the "victims" of a bad economy or social environment, and believing that education, job training, and fuller employment will solve many social problems. 3

These values differences also give rise to some interesting disputes involving definitions or analogies. For example, is Murray's plan a form of "social engineering"? Murray takes pains to deny that his plan involves social engineering. "To restore the rewards and penalties of marriage," he says, "does not require social engineering. Rather, it requires that the state stop interfering with the natural forces that have done the job quite effectively for millennia" (29). He thus sees his proposal as a way of returning to the "natural" (and hence better) way of doing things. Gilliam, on the other hand, believes that helping poor mothers and their children is the "natural" thing to do. She therefore pointedly calls Murray's proposal an instance of "social engineering" (47) as well as a " 'behavior modification scheme' " (47). 4

Their value differences are also reflected in the meanings they attach to "illegitimacy." Gilliam wants to shift attention away from mere marital status to consider the broader issue 5 of " 'mutual commitment of parents to each other and their children' " (47). According to Gilliam, an "illegitimate" child is not by definition an "unwanted" or neglected one. Gilliam wants us to see that many illegitimate children may in fact be well loved and well nurtured while many "legitimate" children may be unwanted and abused. Thus for Gilliam, legitimacy is not a necessary condition for a functional family unit or for happy, well-adjusted children. In contrast, Murray uses illegitimacy as a statistical gauge of social health. In his abstract use of numbers, any out-of-wedlock child (no matter how loved) counts in the negative column while any in-wedlock child (no matter how neglected or abused) counts in the positive column.

6   To conclude, the disagreement between Murray and Gilliam hinges on disagreements over the causes of the rise in illegitimacy rates and the basic values that each writer brings to the debate. To accept Murray, one would have to believe that eliminating welfare benefits would lead to a dramatic drop in illegitimate births, that this reduction in illegitimacy would lead to greater family stability and a corresponding drop in crime, and that the long-range good to society would outweigh the hardships it would impose on current welfare mothers and children. To accept Gilliam, one would have to believe that eliminating welfare benefits would have little effect on reducing illegitimacy rates, that the suffering imposed on welfare recipients would outweigh whatever long-range social good might come from Murray's proposal, and that better sex education programs, job training, and employment opportunities would be more effective than Murray's proposal in solving the problems of illegitimacy.

WORKS CITED*

Gilliam, Dorothy. "Wrong Way to Reform Welfare." *Washington Post* 11 Dec. 1993: B01. Rpt. in *Writing Arguments: A Rhetoric with Readings.* John D. Ramage and John C. Bean. 4th ed. Needham, MA: Allyn and Bacon, 1998. 46–48.

Murray, Charles. "The Coming White Underclass." *Wall Street Journal* 29 Oct. 1993: A13. Rpt. in *Writing Arguments: A Rhetoric with Readings.* John D. Ramage and John C. Bean. 4th ed. Needham, MA: Allyn and Bacon, 1998. 27–31.

STRATEGY 4: EVALUATING THE CONFLICTING POSITIONS

When we ask you to evaluate an argument or a set of arguments, we aren't asking you to choose a winner. Rather, we are asking you to take stock as you make your own journey toward clarity. Which lines of reasoning seem strong to you? Which seem weak? Before you could make up your mind on the issue, what additional research would you want to pursue? What value questions do you still need to resolve? As we have seen in the dispute between Murray and Gilliam, writers don't always address neatly the questions you would like them to address.

---

*When you type your own documented essays, the "Works Cited" list begins on a separate page.

For example, neither Murray nor Gilliam satisfactorily analyzes the causes of rising illegitimacy rates. The one blames welfare benefits, the other blames hopelessness and poverty, but neither provides supporting data. Therefore, before we formulated our own position on illegitimacy and welfare reform, we would want to do more research. Specifically, we would like to address issues such as the following:

- What did Daniel Moynihan say in his 1960s study of the black family, the study that is so crucial to Murray's analogy argument?

- How does the present welfare system actually work? Who gets AFDC money and how? What percentage of single parents receive welfare payments? How has the passage of the 1996 Welfare Reform Bill affected the distribution of welfare payments?

- What evidence is there that the opportunity to receive welfare money actually motivates a girl to have a baby out of wedlock? What evidence is there that a change in welfare policy will affect social attitudes toward illegitimate pregnancy?

- Is it true that children are better off in two-parent families than in a single-parent family? What about unhappy two-parent families forced together "by shotgun"? What percentage of single parents are doing a good job raising their children?

- What other kinds of welfare reform or family policies are being considered at the federal or state level?

Our point, then, is that evaluation of opposing arguments doesn't mean picking sides. Rather, it means examining the conversation carefully to determine the lines of debate, the essential questions at issue, and the research remaining to be done. It also forces us to examine our own values because ultimately the position we take will grow out of our own beliefs, values, and underlying assumptions.

CONCLUSION

This chapter has shown you why reading arguments is crucially important to writers of argument and has offered suggestions for improving your own reading process. The chapter has explained four main strategies for reading an argument: (1) Read as a believer, (2) read as a doubter, (3) seek out alternative views and analyze the sources of disagreement, and (4) evaluate the various positions. The chapter has also shown you how to write a summary of an article and how to incorporate summaries into your own writing through the use of attributive tags.

In the next chapter we turn from the reading of arguments to the writing of arguments and suggest ways that you can improve your writing process.

c h a p t e r 3

Writing Arguments

As the opening chapters have suggested, when you write about an issue, you begin seeing it more complexly. By role-playing alternative views and by examining the logic and structure of your own position, you often discover that what you have been saying seems doubtful or requires qualification or is simply an assertion of faith without persuasive supporting reasons. It follows, then, that writing is an act of discovering your argument, of developing and clarifying your thinking.

If you accept the notion that you learn about your ideas as you write, then you will accept the notion of writing as a process. A writer's ideas evolve through stages. For many writers it is impossible to achieve an effective final product without going through a series of rambling, confusing drafts. Too often students stop the process short, turning in as a finished product something that is not yet "ready for strangers" but that is nonetheless a good draft on its way to becoming a good argument.

You should plan, then, to allow yourself plenty of time to write a formal argument—time for planning and talking, for drafting, and for extensive rethinking and revision. It sometimes helps to think of revision not as editing (cleaning up errors) but as "re-vision"—"seeing again." To be willing to "see again" is to be willing to make major changes in your draft, even to throw a draft out and recompose your ideas from beginning to end. The more your final product differs from your first draft, the more you will be engaging in deep revision as opposed to surface editing that merely cleans up problems with spelling, punctuation, or grammar. A brief description of the kinds of processes skilled writers go through will help us clarify our point.

A BRIEF DESCRIPTION OF WRITERS' PROCESSES

No two writers go through exactly the same process in composing an argument. In fact, your own writing processes will vary from essay to essay depending on circumstances. Although there are many paths to a good argument, most writers go through stages that are somewhat similar. Of course, writers do not approach each stage in the same way, nor do the stages occur in an orderly sequence. Instead, writers loop back through earlier stages whenever they encounter difficulties, and often parts of a draft will be in one stage of the process while other parts will be in different stages. Nevertheless, the stages can be described in a loose way as follows:

First Stage—Starting point: Most writers begin with a sense of a problem. In the case of argumentative writing, writers usually begin with an issue, that is, with a sense of a conversation going on "out there" in which people are disagreeing about something. Their goal is to make a contribution to that conversation. Writers sometimes begin with their point of view already decided, sometimes not.

Second Stage—Exploration and rehearsal: Writers try to find out as much as they can about the issue through reading, interviewing, and recalling personal experiences. They examine reasons and weigh evidence on all sides of the issue. Particularly, they try to understand the causes of disagreement among people on this issue, including disagreements about the facts of the case and conflicts about values, assumptions, and beliefs. Many writers do exploratory writing at this stage, either in notes or in journals, jotting down ideas or rehearsing parts of their argument through rapid drafting.

Third Stage—Writing a discovery draft: Stage 2 blends into Stage 3 when the writer's attention shifts from gathering data and exploring an issue to actually composing a draft. Writers at this stage often shut out their audiences temporarily and concentrate on getting their ideas clear for themselves. Discovery drafts are often messy, jumbled, and incoherent to others.

Fourth Stage—Revision, or "seeing again": The completion of a discovery draft often sends the writer back to earlier stages to get new ideas and to rethink the problem. At this stage, talking to others is particularly helpful. As their arguments become increasingly clarified to themselves, writers begin to reshape their essays for readers, worrying now about unity, coherence, emphasis, and all the traditional features of formal writing. Often several drafts are needed at the revision stage.

Fifth Stage—Editing: Writers now polish their drafts, worrying about the clarity of each sentence and the links between sentences. Often writers are still trying to clarify their meanings at the level of individual sentences and paragraphs. Thus, they try to make each sentence more precise—reworking structure to keep each sentence focused on intended meaning. They are also concerned about surface features such as spelling, punctuation, and grammar. Before they submit a finished product, writers proofread carefully and worry about the appearance and form of the final typed manuscript.

STRATEGIES FOR IMPROVING
YOUR WRITING PROCESSES

The stages of the writing process described here are based on observations of skilled writers actually composing. Unskilled writers, however, generally go through a quite different process, one that takes less time and is less rigorous in its demand for clarity. Many student writers, for example, compose rough drafts without sufficient exploration and rehearsal beforehand and revise without sufficient concern for the needs of readers. A good, long-range way for most college students to improve their writing, then, is to try to enrich their processes of composing. Here are some strategies you might try.

Talking about ideas in small groups: This is especially helpful in the very early stages of writing when you may have an issue in mind but not yet a claim to make or a sense of how to develop your argument. The greatest power of groups is their ability to generate ideas and present us with multiple perspectives. Listen to objections your classmates make to your arguments, trying to get a sense of what kinds of reasons and evidence succeed or fail. Appendix 2 at the end of this text suggests ways to make group work as successful as possible.

Using expressive writing for discovery and exploration: Expressive writing is writing you do for yourself rather than for others; it is like talking to yourself on paper. Its purpose is to help you think through ideas and get them recorded for later recall. At the end of this chapter we provide some expressive writing tasks that will help you discover and explore ideas for your argument essays.

Talking your draft: After you have written a draft, it's often helpful to talk through your argument with another person (classmate, roommate, tutor, instructor). Without reading from your draft or even looking at it, explain your argument orally to your listener. Be prepared for interruptions when your listener looks confused or unpersuaded. The act of talking through your argument forces you to formulate your ideas in new language. Often you will immediately see ways to improve your draft.

Inventing with research: *Invention* is a term used by the rhetoricians of ancient Greece and Rome. It is the art of finding "the best available means of persuasion"—that is, the art of generating ideas and finding arguments. One good way to do so is through reading in the library or off the Internet, where you can gather evidence related to your issue and examine the argumentative strategies used by others. Although most students know how to use a card catalog, few are experienced in using indexes to find articles appearing in magazines, journals, newspapers, or electronic sources. Yet these are often the best sources for arguers. If you don't know how to use a library or the Internet or how to incorporate sources into your arguments, read Part IV in this text, which deals with research writing.

Inventing with heuristic strategies: Another strategy for generating ideas for an argument is to use one or more structured processes called "heuristics" (derived from the Greek word *heuresis,* meaning "to discover"). In the next section we will explain several heuristic strategies in more detail. You may find them helpful as ways to think of ideas for your arguments.

Using visual techniques for brainstorming and shaping: Cognitive psychologists have conducted extensive research on the way human beings think. One of their discoveries is that verbal modes of thinking can often be enhanced when supplemented with visual modes. In our own teaching, we have had good results emphasizing visual techniques such as idea maps and tree diagrams as ways of helping writers imagine the content and shape of their emerging arguments. Later in this chapter we will explain idea maps and tree diagrams in more detail.

Seeking out alternative views: Although you will often address your arguments to a neutral audience who will be weighing arguments on all sides of the issue, you can get excellent help by discussing your ideas directly with someone skeptical of your position or downright opposed to it. Unlike friendly audiences, who will usually tell you that your argument is excellent, skeptical audiences will challenge your thinking. Skeptics may find holes in your reasoning, argue from different values, surprise you by conceding points you thought had to be developed at length, and dismay you by demanding development of points you thought could be conceded. In short, opponents will urge you to "re-see" your draft.

Extensive revision: Don't manicure your drafts, rebuild them. Make sure you leave lots of white space between lines and in the margins for rewriting. And be sure to apply some of the systematic strategies described later in this text for testing the logic and evidence of an argument. Apply these tests to your own drafts as well as to opposing arguments as a means of being more objective about the substance of your argument.

Exchanging drafts: Get other people's reactions to your work in exchange for your reactions to theirs. Exchanging drafts is a different process from conversing with someone who disagrees with you. Conversation with a dissenting audience is aimed at invention and clarification of ideas; it focuses on content. An exchange of drafts, however, is aimed at the creation of well-written arguments. In addition to content, partners in a draft exchange focus on organization, development, and style. Their concern is on the quality of the draft as product.

Saving "correctness" for last: Save your concern for sentence correctness, spelling, and punctuation for last. Focusing on it at the early stages of writing can shut down your creative processes.

USING EXPRESSIVE WRITING FOR DISCOVERY AND EXPLORATION

We have already suggested the usefulness of expressive writing as a way to talk to yourself on paper. We recommend that you keep all your expressive writings for this course in a notebook, portfolio, or journal where you will have them as a permanent record of your exploratory thinking.

What follows is a compendium of strategies to help you discover and explore ideas. Some of these strategies may not work very well for you, but many of them might work and all of them are worth trying. Each of them takes practice before you become good at it, so don't give up too soon if the strategy doesn't seem to work for you when you first try it.

Freewriting

Freewriting is an idea-generating activity useful at almost any stage of the writing process. When you freewrite, you put pen to paper and write rapidly *nonstop*, usually ten to fifteen minutes at a stretch. Don't worry about grammar, spelling, organization, transitions, or other features of edited writing. The object is to think of as many ideas as possible. Some freewriters achieve almost a stream-of-consciousness style: Their ideas flow directly onto the paper, stutters and stammers and all, without editing or rearrangement. Other freewriters record their thinking in more organized and focused chunks, but nevertheless they keep pushing ahead without worrying whether or not the chunks connect clearly to each other or whether they fully make sense to a strange reader. Many freewriters, perhaps most, find that their initial reservoir of ideas runs out in three to five minutes. When this happens, force yourself to keep your pen moving. If you can't think of anything to say, write "relax" over and over (or "this is stupid," or "I'm stuck," or whatever) until new ideas emerge.

Here is an example of a freewrite from Steve, a student writer, at the start of a research project on homelessness. (Steve eventually wrote the proposal argument on pp. 330–338 of this text). This freewrite explores his thinking on the question, "What can be done about the homeless?"

> Lets take a minute and talk about the homeless. Homeless homeless. Today on my way to work I passed a homeless guy who smiled at me and I smiled back though he smelled bad. What are the reasons he was out on the street? Perhaps an extraordinary string of bad luck. Perhaps he was pushed out onto the street. Not a background of work ethic, no place to go, no way to get someplace to live that could be afforded, alcoholism. To what extent do government assistance, social spending, etc, keep people off the street? What benefits could a person get that stops "the cycle"? How does welfare affect homelessness, drug abuse programs, family planning? To what extent does the individual have control over homelessness? This

question of course goes to the depth of the question of how community affects the individual. Relax, relax. What about the signs that I see on the way to work posted on the windows of businesses that read, "please don't give to panhandlers it only promotes drug abuse etc" a cheap way of getting homeless out of the way of business? Are homeless the natural end of unrestricted capitalism? What about the homeless people who are mentally ill? How can you maintain a living when haunted by paranoia? How do you decide if someone is mentally ill or just laughs at society? If one can't function obviously. How many mentally ill are out on the street? If you are mentally ill and have lost the connections to others who might take care of you I can see how you might end up on the street. What would it take to get treatment? To what extent can mentally ill be treated? When I see a homeless person I want to ask, How do you feel about the rest of society? When you see "us" walk by how do you think of us? Do you possibly care how we avoid you.

 FOR CLASS DISCUSSION

Individual task: Choose one of the following controversial claims (or another chosen by your instructor) and freewrite your response to it for ten to fifteen minutes. **Group task:** Working in pairs, in small groups, or as a whole class, share your freewrite with classmates. Don't feel embarrassed if your freewrite is fragmentary or disjointed. Freewrites are not supposed to be finished products; their sole purpose is to generate a flow of thought. The more you practice the technique, the better you will become.

1. A student should report a fellow student who is cheating on an exam or plagiarizing an essay.

2. States should legalize marriages between homosexuals.

3. Recycling cans, bottles, plastics, and paper does little to help the environment.

4. Spanking children should be considered child abuse.

5. State and federal governments should legalize hard drugs.

6. For grades 1–12, the school year should be extended to eleven months.

7. Certain advertisements such as the "Joe Camel" cigarette campaign are so immoral they should be made illegal.

8. Violent video games such as Mortal Kombat should be made illegal.

9. Rich people are morally obligated to give part of their wealth to the poor.

10. Women should be assigned to combat duty equally with men.

Idea Mapping

Another good technique for exploring ideas is *idea mapping,* which is more visual than freewriting and causes you to generate ideas in a different way. When you make an idea map, you draw a circle in the center of the page and write some trigger idea (usually a broad topic area, a question, or your working thesis statement) in the center of the circle. Then you record your ideas on branches and subbranches that extend from the center circle. As long as you pursue one train of thought, you keep recording your ideas on subbranches off the main branch. But as soon as that chain of ideas runs dry, you go back and start a new branch. Often your thoughts jump back and forth between one branch and another. That's a major advantage of "picturing" your thoughts. You can see them as part of an emerging design rather than as strings of unrelated ideas.

An idea map usually records more ideas than a freewrite, but these ideas are not so fully developed. Writers who practice both techniques report that they think of ideas in quite different ways, depending on which strategy they are using. Figure 3.1 is an idea map created by Steve, the student who wrote the previous freewrite on homelessness. When Steve made this idea map, he had completed approximately ten hours of research on the issue, "What should society do about the mentally ill homeless?" He found himself disagreeing with syndicated columnist Charles Krauthammer, who argued that states should place the homeless mentally ill in state-funded mental hospitals. (You can read Krauthammer's argument on pp. 221–227.) He used the idea map to try to find some order in his evolving and as yet unclarified thinking on this topic.

 FOR CLASS DISCUSSION

Choose a current national, local, or campus issue that is interesting to the class and about which members of the class are divided. The instructor will lead a class discussion on this issue, recording ideas on an idea map as they emerge. Your goal is to appreciate the fluidity of idea maps as a visual form of idea generation halfway between an outline and a list.

Playing the Believing and Doubting Game

To argue effectively, you must appreciate that positions different from your own can be reasonably defended. An excellent way to imagine alternative views is to play the "believing and doubting" game.*

---

*A term coined by Peter Elbow, *Writing Without Teachers* (Oxford University Press, 1973), pp. 147–90.

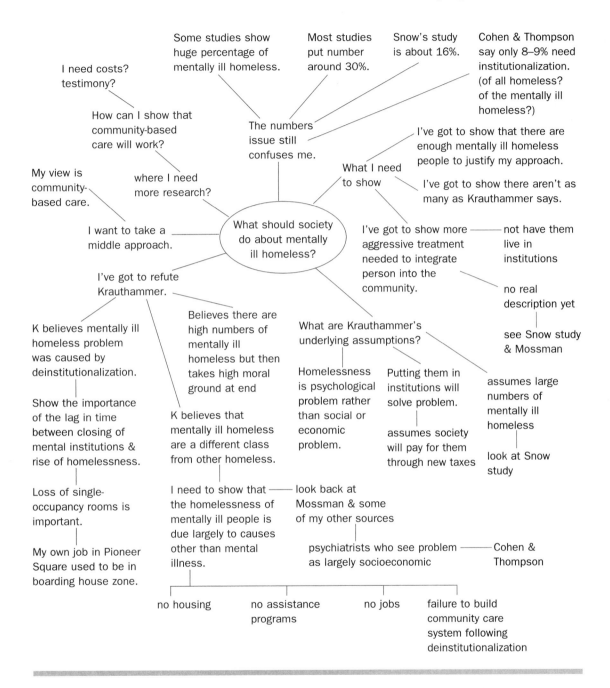

FIGURE 3.1 Steve's initial idea map on the issue of "What should society do about the mentally ill homeless?"

When you play the believing side of this game, you try to become sympathetic to an idea or point of view; you listen carefully to it, opening yourself up to the possibility of its being true. You try to appreciate why the idea has force for so many people; you try to accept the idea by discovering as many reasons as you can for believing it. It is easy to play the believing game with ideas you already believe in, but the game becomes more difficult, sometimes even frightening and dangerous, when you try believing ideas that seem untrue or disturbing to you.

The doubting game is the opposite of the believing game. It calls for you to be judgmental and critical, to find faults with an idea rather than to accept it. When you doubt a new idea, you try your best to falsify it, to find counterexamples that disprove it, to find flaws in its logic. Again, it is easy to play the doubting game with ideas you don't like, but it too can be threatening when you try to doubt ideas that are dear to your heart or central to your own world view.

Here is how one student played the believing and doubting game with the assertion "Pornography serves a useful function in society."

DOUBT

Pornography is smutty, indecent, outlandish usage of the human body. People who look at that have to be indecent nonmoralistic sexists with nothing better to do. Pornography uses the human body to gain pleasure when the human body is supposed to be like a temple that you take care of. I feel very strongly against pornography especially when they use it with young children and pets, etc. I just don't understand how people can get such a big kick out of it. It really surprised me how Dr. Jones [a guest speaker in this student's psychology course] admitted that he had bought pornographic materials, etc. I would think that it would be something that someone wouldn't readily admit to. It seems socially unacceptable to me.

BELIEVE

Pornography is something that people look at when they are feeling sexually frustrated or lonely. It is a form of escape that everyone needs at one time or another. There is always a time where one is unhappy with their sexual relationships and looking at pornography helps. Pornography is an art form. The human body is a beautiful thing and these pictures are for everyone to see the beauty of it all. People should not be afraid to be open about sex and their bodies. Everyone feels the same things. Why not share the experience with others? There is nothing dirty or smutty about being open. It is so individualistic, another way of getting out of the rut of conformity. Sex is beautiful and pornography helps share it with others that aren't quite so lucky to share these moments. (I feel this doubting game with this topic for me opens no new ideas because my mind is so set against pornography but I guess it is good to open up the new avenues of thinking.)

It is easy to see from this entry how the believing game threatens this student's moral views. Yet she does a good job of starting to get inside the head of someone who believes that pornography serves a useful purpose. Although she denies at the end of her entry that playing this game opened up new ideas, the game certainly helped her to see what the issue is and to appreciate that not all people share her values.

When you play the believing and doubting game with an assertion, simply write two different chunks, one chunk arguing for the assertion (the believing game) and one chunk opposing it (the doubting game). Freewrite both chunks, letting your ideas flow without censoring. Or, alternatively, make an idea map with believing and doubting branches.

 FOR CLASS DISCUSSION

Return to the ten controversial claims in the For Class Discussion exercise following the section on freewriting (p. 57). **Individual task:** Choose one of the claims and play the believing and doubting game with it by freewriting for five minutes trying to believe the claim and then for five minutes trying to doubt the claim. Or, if you prefer, make an idea map by creating a believing spoke and a doubting spoke off the main hub. Instead of freewriting, enter ideas onto your idea map, moving back and forth between believing and doubting. **Group task:** Share what you produced with members of your group or with the class as a whole.

Repeat the exercise with another claim.

Brainstorming for Pro and Con Because Clauses

This activity is similar to the believing and doubting game in that it asks you to brainstorm ideas for and against a controversial assertion. In the believing and doubting game, however, you simply freewrite or make an idea map on both sides of the issue. In this activity, you try to state your reasons for and against the proposition as *because clauses*. The value of doing so is discussed in depth in Chapter 4, which shows how a claim with because clauses can form the core of an argument.

Here is an example of how you might create because clauses for and against the claim, "Pornography serves a useful function in society."

PRO

Pornography serves a useful function in society

- because it provides a sexual outlet for lonely men.
- because what some people call pornography might really be an art form.
- because it helps society overcome Victorian repression.
- because many people obviously enjoy it.
- because it may relieve the sexual frustration of a person who would otherwise turn to rape or child molestation.

CON

Pornography is harmful to society

- because it is degrading and oppressive to women.
- because it depersonalizes and dehumanizes sexuality.
- because it gives teenagers many wrong concepts about loving sexuality.
- because it is linked with racketeering and crime and destroys neighborhoods.
- because it often exploits children.
- because it might incite some people to commit rape and violence (serial murderer Ted Bundy's claim).

 FOR CLASS DISCUSSION

Generating because clauses like these is an especially productive discussion activity for groups. Once again return to the ten controversial claims in the For Class Discussion exercise in the freewriting section (p. 57). Select one or more of these claims (or others provided by your instructor) and, working in small groups, generate pro and con because clauses supporting and attacking the claim. Share your group's because clauses with those of other groups.

The preceding strategies for exploring ideas should help you develop, expand, and complicate your thinking on an issue. Later in this text several additional strategies for exploring and developing arguments are introduced. They include the Toulmin system for analyzing the structure of an argument (in Chapter 5), the "principles/consequences/analogies" strategy for finding persuasive reasons (in Chapter 9), and the "stock issues" strategy for developing proposal arguments (in Chapter 14).

Brainstorming a Network of Related Issues

The previous exercise helps you see how certain issues can provoke strong pro-con stances. Occasionally in civic life, an issue is presented to the public in just such a pro-con form, as when voters are asked to approve or disapprove a referendum or when a jury must decide the guilt or innocence of a defendant.

But in most contexts, the argumentative situation is more openended and fluid. You can easily oversimplify an issue by reducing it to two opposing sides. Because most issues are embedded in a network of subissues, side issues, and larger issues, seeing an issue in pro-con terms can often blind you to other ways to join a conversation. For example, an arguer might propose a middle ground between adversarial positions, examine a subissue in more depth, connect an issue to a related side issue, or redefine an issue to place it in a new context.

Consider, for example, the previous assertion, "Pornography serves a useful function in society." Rather than arguing for or against this assertion, a writer might focus on pornography in a variety of other ways:

- How can pornography be defined?
- Should pornography be censored?
- Can violence be considered pornographic?
- Should pornography be allowed on the Internet? If so, how could children be denied access to it?
- Does pornography exploit or degrade women?
- What effect does pornography have on sexual offenders?
- Is Demi Moore's character as a stripper and single mom in the movie *Striptease* a role model for feminism or an embarrassment?

 FOR CLASS DISCUSSION

Working as a whole class or in small groups, choose one or more of the controversial assertions on page 57. Instead of arguing for or against them, brainstorm a number of related issues (subissues, side issues, or larger issues) on the same general subject. For example, brainstorm a number of issues related to the general topics of cheating, gay marriage, recycling, and so forth.

SHAPING YOUR ARGUMENT

We turn now from discovery strategies to strategies for organizing and shaping your argument. When you begin writing the first draft of an argument, you probably need some sort of plan, but how elaborate or detailed that plan is varies considerably from writer to writer. Some writers need to plan extensively before they can write; others need to write extensively before they can plan. But somewhere along the way, whether at the first draft stage or much later in the process, you need to concentrate on the shape of your argument. This section offers two strategies for helping you structure an argument: (1) Using the conventional structure of "classical argument" as an initial guide, and (2) considering tree diagrams as an alternative to traditional outlining.

Classical Argument as an Initial Guide

As you draft your essay, it helps to envision a typical argumentative structure that can guide your thinking. Perhaps the most common argument type is the *classical argument*—so called because it follows a pattern recommended by the great rhetoricians of classical Greece and Rome. In the traditional Latin terminology, a classical argument has the following parts: the *exordium* (in which the speaker gets the audience's attention); the *narratio* (which provides the needed background); the *propositio* (the speaker's proposition or thesis); the *partitio* (a forecast of the main parts of the speech); the *confirmatio* (speaker's arguments in favor of the proposition); the *confutatio* (the refutation of opposing views); and the *peroratio* (the conclusion that sums up the argument, calls for action, and leaves a strong last impression).

Let's look more closely at this structure (see Figure 3.2), this time using English vernacular rather than Latin. The classical argument typically begins with an attention grabber, which may be a startling statistic, a dramatic fact, or a real or hypothetical story or example. The attention grabber is usually followed by a section that focuses the issue (often by stating it directly and briefly summarizing alternative views) and provides needed background (perhaps historical information about the origins of the controversy, reference to the immediate context, a definition of a key term, and so forth). The introduction typically ends with the presentation of the writer's thesis, usually accompanied by some forecasting of the structure to follow.

The next major part of a classical argument—usually the longest part—presents the writer's reasons and evidence in support of the thesis. Typically each reason is developed in its own separate section. Each section opens with a statement of the reason, which is then supported with evidence or chains of other reasons. As the writer switches from one reason to the next, he or she guides the reader with an appropriate transition.

Next the writer typically summarizes and responds to opposing or alternative views. (Sometimes writers choose to place this section earlier in the argument *before* presenting their own position.) If the opposing arguments consist of several parts, the writer has two options for organizing this section: to summarize all of the opposing arguments before moving to the response, or to summarize and respond to one part at a time. Typically the writer responds to opposing views either by refuting them or by conceding to their strengths and shifting to a different field of values (see Chapter 8).

Finally, the conclusion of a classical argument creates a sense of closure. It sums up the previous argument and tries to make a strong final impression, often calling for some kind of action.

The classical argument, as we have described it here, is not always effective as a final product. In some cases, it is more persuasive to delay your thesis until the end or use other strategies for appealing to certain kinds of audiences. Even in these cases, however, the classical argument is useful for planning an initial draft. By requiring a thesis statement and a forecasting statement in the introduction, it encourages you to articulate your thesis and supporting reasons, thereby helping you see the whole of your argument in miniature. By further requiring you to summarize and refute (or concede to) opposing views, the classical argument encourages you to understand and consider alternative positions. In many contexts, the classical structure is also a powerful way to organize your final product, especially when you address a neutral or undecided audience. Even in cases where it is less

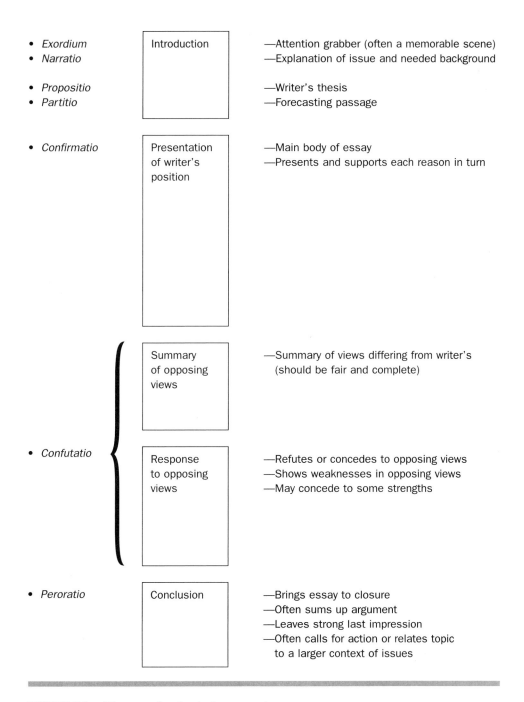

- *Exordium*
- *Narratio*

- *Propositio*
- *Partitio*

- *Confirmatio*

- *Confutatio*

- *Peroratio*

Introduction

Presentation
of writer's
position

Summary
of opposing
views

Response
to opposing
views

Conclusion

—Attention grabber (often a memorable scene)
—Explanation of issue and needed background

—Writer's thesis
—Forecasting passage

—Main body of essay
—Presents and supports each reason in turn

—Summary of views differing from writer's
  (should be fair and complete)

—Refutes or concedes to opposing views
—Shows weaknesses in opposing views
—May concede to some strengths

—Brings essay to closure
—Often sums up argument
—Leaves strong last impression
—Often calls for action or relates topic
  to a larger context of issues

FIGURE 3.2   Diagram of a classical argument

effective, such as in addressing hostile audiences, knowing the classical argument structure can help you generate and develop initial ideas at the rough draft stage. (See Chapters 7 and 8 for a fuller discussion of how to adapt structure to audience.)

The Power of Tree Diagrams

Knowing the shape of a classical argument helps you envision an effective structure, but it doesn't, in itself, help you wrestle with your own subject matter. It is one thing to know that you need one or more reasons to support your thesis. It is quite another thing to figure out what your reasons are, to articulate them clearly, and to decide what evidence supports them. The traditional tool for helping you plan a structure is the outline. For many writers, an even more powerful tool is the tree diagram.

A *tree diagram* differs from an outline in that headings and subheadings are indicated through spatial locations rather than through a system of letters and numerals. An example of a tree diagram is shown in Figure 3.3. It reveals the plan for a classical argument opposing a campus ban on hate speech. The writer's introduction is represented by the inverted triangle at the top of the tree above the claim. The main reasons appear on branches beneath the claim, and the supporting evidence and argumentation for each reason are displayed vertically underneath each reason.

The same argument displayed in outline form would look like this:

THESIS: Colleges should not try to ban hate speech.

   I. A ban on hate speech violates the First Amendment.
     II.   A ban on hate speech doesn't solve the problem of hate.
     A. It doesn't allow people to understand and hear each other's anger.
     B. It disguises hatred instead of bringing it out in the open where it can be dealt with.
     C. The ability to see both sides of an issue would be compromised.

  III. Of course, there are good arguments in support of a ban on hate speech.
     A. Banning hate speech creates a safer environment for minorities.
     B. It helps eliminate occasions for violence.
     C. It teaches good manners and people skills.
     D. It shows that ignorant hate-speech is not the same as intelligent discussion.

  IV. Although these arguments have strengths, they conceal a major flaw.
     A. I concede that a hate-speech ban might make a safer, less violent campus and might help teach good manners.
     B. But in long run, it doesn't change people's prejudices; it just drives them underground.

   V. CONCLUSION: There are better ways to deal with prejudice and hatred.
     A. Instead of repressing hate, let ugly incidents happen.
     B. Create discussions around the ugly incidents.

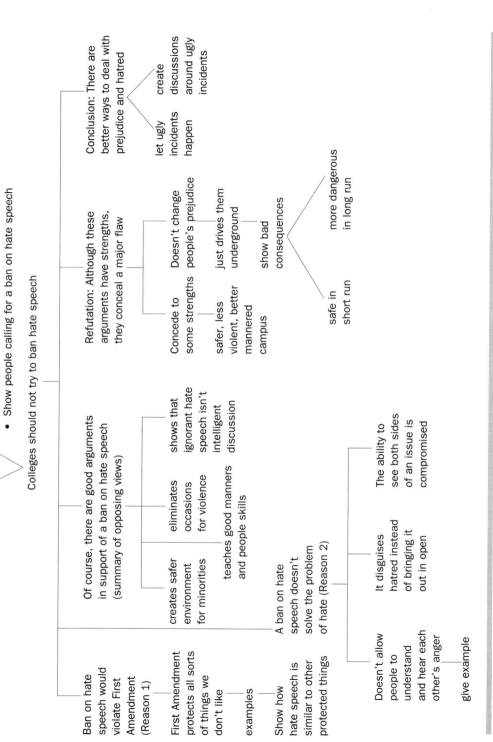

FIGURE 3.3   Tree diagram of an argument opposing a ban on hate speech

Although the traditional outline may be the more familiar way to plan an argument, tree diagrams have distinct advantages. First, they are visual. The main points of an argument are laid out horizontally, and the evidence and details supporting each point are displayed vertically. In planning the argument, a writer can move back and forth between both dimensions, working horizontally to develop the main reasons of the argument and then working vertically to find supporting data and evidence. Our own teaching experience suggests that this visual/spatial nature of tree diagrams leads writers to produce fuller, more detailed, and more logical arguments than does traditional outlining.

A second advantage is their flexibility in representing different mental operations. Traditional outlines represent the division of a whole into parts and of parts into subparts. Consequently, a rule of outlining is that you can't divide a whole into just one part (that is, if you divide something, you must have at least two pieces). Thus every A must have a B, every 1 must have a 2, and so forth. Tree diagrams can easily represent this division-into-parts operation by showing two or more lines branching off a single point.

But tree diagrams can also show a single line descending vertically from a higher-level point. Such a line might represent a sequence of step-by-step ideas as in a flowchart (in Figure 3.3, note the single line descending from the left branch headed "Hate-speech ban would violate the First Amendment"). A single descending line might also represent a movement from a generalization to a specific, as when you choose to support a point with a single example. Thus you could logically have the following structure on a tree diagram:

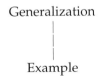

If you tried to put that same structure on an outline, however, it would look like this:

A. Generalization
　　1. example

and some stuffy traditionalist might tell you you were being illogical. (Note the amount of information on the tree diagram that could not easily be represented on the traditional outline and was hence omitted there.)

Finally, tree diagrams can be powerful aids to invention because you can put question marks anywhere on a tree to hold a space open for ideas that you haven't thought of yet. Consider the value of tree diagraming for student writer Steve as he began drafting his argument on the mentally ill homeless. His first tree diagram is shown in the dark continuous lines of Figure 3.4. As he wrote his first draft, he returned to his idea map (Figure 3.1) for more ideas, which he added to the tree (shown in the dotted lines on Figure 3.4). Note his use of question marks at places where he needs to add more ideas. His final tree diagram, produced after another draft, is shown in Figure 3.5.* The fluid, evolving nature of tree diagrams, in which branches can be added or moved around, make them particularly valuable planning tools for writers.

*If you would like to read Steve's final essay, it is reproduced in its entirety on pages 646–655.

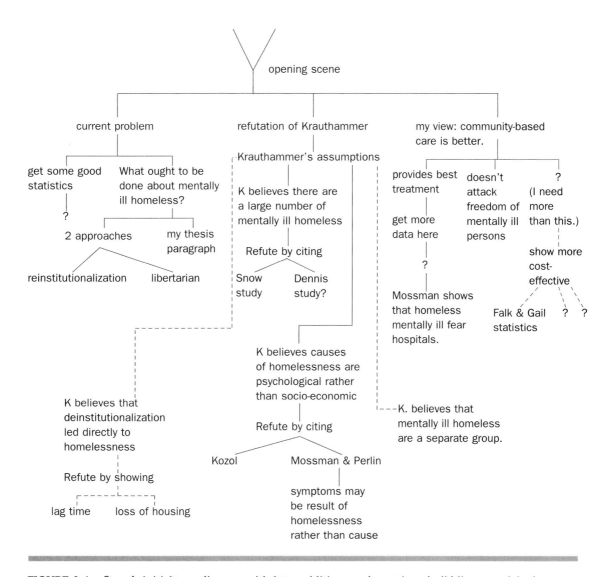

FIGURE 3.4 Steve's initial tree diagram with later additions and notations (solid lines = original tree diagram; broken lines = later additions).

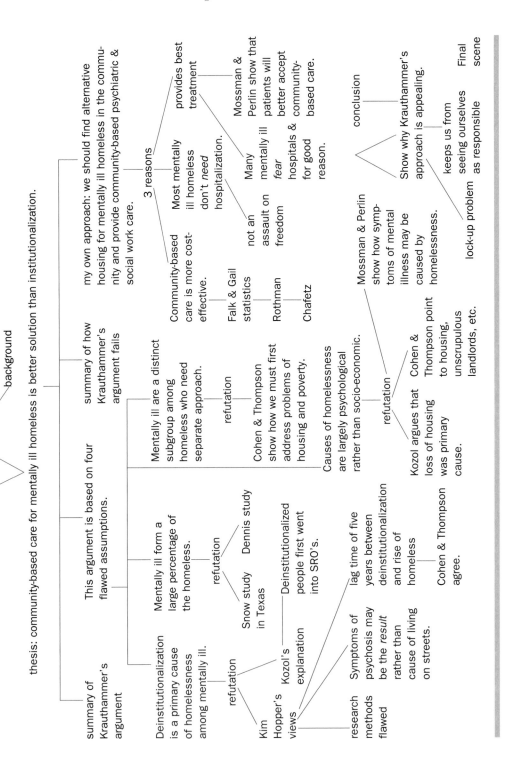

FIGURE 3.5   Steve's final tree diagram

USING EXPRESSIVE WRITING TO DISCOVER AND EXPLORE IDEAS: TWO SETS OF EXPLORATORY TASKS

The tasks that follow are intended to help you use expressive writing to generate ideas. The first set of tasks, which we call "Starting Points," helps you build a storehouse of ideas early in a writing project, either by helping you think of issues to write about (if your course gives free choice of topics) or by helping you deepen and complicate your response to readings. The second set of tasks, designed as an aid to drafting almost any kind of argument, helps you think systematically through your ideas before composing a first draft.

Set 1: Starting Points

These tasks help you take an inventory of issues that already interest you and about which you may have had personal experiences. They also give you ideas for responding to readings.

Task 1: Making an Inventory of Issues that Interest You

If your course gives you free choice of topics for some assignments, this task and the next will help you take an inventory of possible topics that interest you. Using one or more of the following "trigger questions" as a way to stimulate thinking, make a list of ten to fifteen possible issues or topic areas that you might like to write about. Share your list with classmates, adding to your list ideas from theirs.

- My friends and I disagree about . . .
- I think it is wrong when . . .
- Our campus (this city, my hometown, our state, the country) would be better if . . .
- Person X believes . . .; however, I believe . . .
- When people discuss X (plug in different possible topic areas), what do they disagree about? (For example, when people discuss money [cars, baseball, guns, cooking], what do they disagree about?)

Task 2: Choosing Several Areas of Controversy and Exploring Them

For this task, choose two or three possible areas of controversy from your previous list and explore them in your journal through freewriting or idea mapping. Try responding to the following questions:

a. What is my position on this issue and why?

b. What are opposing or alternative positions on this issue?

c. Why do people disagree about this issue? Use the same exploratory procedures suggested in Chapter 2: Do people disagree about the facts of the
case? About underlying values, assumptions, and beliefs?

d. If I were to argue my position on this issue, what evidence would I need to
gather and what research might I need to do?

Once again, share your explorations with those of classmates. Your goal is to
find issues that engage you, that are controversial, and that seem arguable. If your
topic areas are good, you should have been able to freewrite several pages in response to the previous questions.

Task 3: Identifying Issues that
Are Problematic for You

A major assignment commonly given in argument courses is to write a research-
based argument that takes a stand on a problem initially puzzling to you. Steve's
proposal argument on the homeless mentally ill (pp. 646–655) and Lynnea's argument on women police officers (pp. 414–420) are examples of arguments written for
an assignment of this type. Perhaps you don't know where you stand on an issue
because you haven't been able to study it enough (for example, global warming, legalized gambling, endangered species controversies). Or perhaps the issue draws
you uncomfortably into a conflict of values (for example, euthanasia, legalization
of drugs, noncriminal incarceration of sexual predators). This course may give you
an opportunity to clarify your views on such an issue through systematic research
and exploratory writing and talking. Your goal for this task is to identify several
such issues, preferably issues of public policy or enduring concern. Try making
an inventory of several possible topics in response to this trigger question:

I am not sure where I stand on the issue of . . .

Task 4: Exploring Your Current
Thinking on a Problematic Issue

For this task, choose one of your issues from Task 3 and explore your current
thinking about it through freewriting or idea mapping. What is your gut feeling
about the issue? What confuses you about it? Why can't you make up your mind?
What personal experiences, if any, link you to the issue? What research questions
about it do you need to try to answer?

Task 5: Deepening Your Response to Readings

Another common assignment in argument classes asks you to join an argumentative conversation. Typically, the class will read and discuss a collection of arguments on an issue and then write either analyses of these arguments or their
own position papers on the same issue. Before doing the writing for this task, read
carefully a collection of arguments assigned by your instructor, annotating the

margins with believing and doubting notes as explained in Chapter 2. Then deepen your engagement with these readings through freewriting or idea mapping by responding to one or more of the following trigger questions:

- What are the sources of disagreement in these readings? Are there disagreements about facts? About underlying values, beliefs, and assumptions?

- Review the readings and identify "hot spots"—passages that you particularly agree with or disagree with, or that make you angry, confuse you, or otherwise stick in your mind. Copy or summarize several hot spot passages into your journal. Then explore your reaction to these passages.

- Explore the evolution of your thinking as you read the essays and later reviewed them. What new questions have the readings raised for you? What changes have occurred in your own thinking? Where do you currently stand and why?

- If you could talk back to one or more of the authors (imagine meeting them in a tavern or as seatmates on a plane), what would you say to them?

Set 2: Exploration and Rehearsal

The previous set of tasks helps you explore ideas for possible argumentative topics, including deepening your response to readings. The following set of tasks is designed to help you at the exploration and rehearsal stage of writing, after you have chosen a topic for an essay and begun to clarify your thesis. Most students take two or three hours to complete the following tasks; the time pays off, however, because most of the ideas you need for your rough draft will be on paper. We recommend that you freewrite your responses to these tasks each time you are given a formal essay assignment for this course.

Task 1

What is the issue that you plan to address in this essay? Try wording the issue as a single-sentence question. Then try wording your question in several different ways. Sometimes slight changes in the way you word the question—for example, making it somewhat broader or somewhat narrower—will help you clarify the way your argument will proceed. Finally, write the question in the way that currently seems best. Put a box around it.

Task 2

For this task, explain why you think people disagree on this issue. In other words, why is this issue controversial? Is there not yet enough evidence to resolve the issue? Is the evidence controversial? Do different parties in the controversy hold different values, assumptions, or beliefs? Do they disagree about key definitions? What do people fear in each other's positions?

Task 3

What personal interests or personal experiences do you have with this issue? (By "personal experiences," we mean not only firsthand experiences but also memories from things you've read, TV news stories you've seen, lectures you've heard, and so forth.) Exploring these questions should help you clarify your personal interest in this topic as well as its relationship to concerns and values in your own life.

Task 4

What is your current position on this issue? What claim do you wish to support? Try writing your claim as a single-sentence thesis statement that gives your answer to the issue question you posed in Task 1.

Task 5

What reasons and evidence can you think of to support your position on this issue? Brainstorm for every possible point you can think of in support of your position. You might want to use an idea map here instead of freewriting. Get as many ideas as possible on paper. In this task, you will be "rehearsing" the main body of your paper, which will set forth reasons and then support them with evidence or chains of other reasons.

As you generate ideas for reasons and evidence, you are likely to find gaps in your knowledge where you need to do further research either in the library or through interviews. If your claim could be strengthened through the use of statistics, testimony of experts, and so forth, develop a plan for conducting your research.

Task 6

In this task, begin by rereading what you wrote in Task 5 and then reconsider your argument from the perspective of a neutral or opposing audience. What values, beliefs, or assumptions would your audience have to hold in order to accept your argument? Do you think your audience holds these values, assumptions, or beliefs?

Task 7

Continue your exploration of audience by assuming the role of someone who opposes your position. Writing from that person's perspective, try to construct a counterargument that opposes your own views. (In other words, play the doubting game with the argument you created in Task 5.)

Task 8

Why is this an important issue? What are its broader implications and consequences? What other issues does it relate to? Thinking of possible answers to these questions may prove useful when you write your introduction or conclusion.

❖ WRITING ASSIGNMENTS FOR CHAPTERS 1–3

OPTION 1: *A Letter to Your Instructor about Yourself as a Writer*   Write a letter to your instructor about yourself as a writer. In the first part of your letter, give your instructor a complete picture of how you go about writing. Describe the process you normally go through, using examples from recent writing experiences. Address questions such as the following:

Mechanical procedures: When and where do you like to do your writing? Do you compose your drafts by hand, by typewriter, or by word processor? If by hand, what kind of paper and pens do you use for your first drafts? Subsequent drafts? Do you single-space or double-space your early drafts? One side of the page or two? If you handwrite, do you write large or small? Big margins or little margins? Do you write rapidly or slowly? Do you use the same procedures for second and later drafts? If you use a word processor, do you compose directly at the terminal or do you write out a draft and then type it in? Do you revise at the terminal or make changes on hard copy?

Mental procedures: Do you procrastinate when you need to write? Do you suffer writer's block or anxiety? Do you write a paper the night before it is due or spread your writing time out over several days? Do you normally do exploratory writing such as freewriting and idea mapping? Do you organize your ideas before drafting or draft first and then organize? How many drafts do you typically make? What kinds of changes do you typically make as you revise? Do you discuss your ideas with friends before you write or between drafts? Do you exchange drafts with friends?

Writing preferences: Do you like to write? What kind of writing do you most like to do? Least like to do? Do you like to choose your own topics or have the teacher choose topics for you? Do you like openended assignments or assignments with clear guidelines and constraints? How much time are you willing to put into a paper?

In the second part of your letter, analyze your strengths and weaknesses as a writer. Address questions such as these:

Strengths and weaknesses in final products: What have you been praised for or criticized for in the past as a writer? How consistent are you in coming up with good ideas for your papers? In general, do you have trouble organizing your papers or is organization a strength? Are your sentences usually clear and grammatically correct? Do you have trouble with punctuation? Are you a good speller?

Strengths and weaknesses in writing process: How does your writing process compare with the typical writing processes of experienced writers as described in this chapter? If you were to improve your writing process, what would you work on most?

These questions are meant to be representative only. Use them as suggestions for the kinds of information your instructor needs to get to know you as a writer. Your goal is to give your instructor as much helpful information as possible.

OPTION 2: *An Argument Summary*   Write a 250-word summary of an argument selected by your instructor. Then write a one-sentence summary of the same argument. Use as models the summaries of Charles Murray's essay in Chapter 2 (pp. 35–37).

OPTION 3: *An Analysis of the Sources of Disagreement in Opposing Arguments* Using as a model the analysis in Chapter 2 of the Murray/Gilliam controversy over welfare reform (pp. 48–50), write an analysis and evaluation of any two arguments that take differing views on the same issue.

OPTION 4: *A Debate Essay*   Write a debate essay on an issue of your own choosing. Write your essay as a miniplay in which two or more characters argue about an issue. Create any kind of fictional setting that you like: a group of students having beers at a local tavern, two people on a date, a late-night dorm room bull session. Have the characters disagree with each other on the issue, but make your characters reasonable people who are trying to argue logically and intelligently.

The purpose of such an assignment is to free you from strict demands of organization in order to let you explore an issue from all sides. Try to have characters find weaknesses in each other's arguments as well as present their own side of the issue.

Here is a brief example of the format. Imagine that you are looking in on the middle of a debate essay on whether writing courses should be pass/fail:

JOE: Here's another thing. Pass/fail would make students a lot more creative. They wouldn't worry so much about pleasing the teacher.

ANN: Hogwash, Joe. Pass/fail would make them less creative.

JOE: Why?

ANN: They'd put less time into the course. If a course is pass/fail, students won't work as hard. They'll put their energy into the courses that will be graded. That's what happened to me when I took an art class pass/fail my freshman year. I started out really interested in it and vowed to spend a lot of time. But by midterms I was getting behind in my other classes, so I neglected art in order to get good grades where they would show up on my transcripts.

JOE: But pass/fail will make you examine your values. Maybe you would quit working just for grades. Besides, in a writing class you would have a different motivation. In a writing class you would have the motivation of knowing that your writing skills will make a big difference in other classes and in your future careers.

ANN: Yes, but students don't worry about long-range benefits. They always take the short-range benefit.

JOE: But maybe you would really get into writing for its own sake. If you don't have to follow a teacher's silly rules, writing can be really creative, like doing art. Remember how much time you spent drawing pictures when you were a little girl? You weren't motivated by grades then. You liked to draw because people are naturally creative. We would still be creative if we weren't afraid. A pass/fail course would take away the fear of failure. How long would you have painted those little kid pictures if some teacher came along and marked up your painting with red ink and said, "Shame, look at all the mistakes you made." You'd quit drawing right away. That is what has happened to writing. Students hate to write because all they get for it is criticism. A pass/fail course would allow us to get praise and to explore writing in new ways.

ANN: You have too much faith, Joe, in the natural creativity of students. You can't overcome twelve years of schooling in one pass/fail course. Look at some other consequences of a pass/fail system. First . . .

OPTION 5: *Propose a Problem for a Major Course Project*   An excellent major project for an argument course is to research an issue about which you are initially undecided. Your final essay for the course could be an argument in which you take a stand on this issue. Choose one of the issues you listed in "Starting Points," Task 3, "I am unable to take a stand on the issue of . . ." and make this issue a major research project for the course. During the term keep a log of your research activities and be ready, in class discussion or in writing, to explain what kinds of arguments or evidence turned out to be most persuasive in helping you take a stand.

For this assignment, write a short letter to your instructor identifying the issue you have chosen and explain why you are interested in it and why you can't make up your mind at this time.

p a r t   t w o

Principles of Argument

CHAPTER 4   The Core of an Argument: A Claim with Reasons

CHAPTER 5   The Logical Structure of Arguments

CHAPTER 6   Evidence in Arguments

CHAPTER 7   Moving Your Audience:
              Audience-Based Reasons, *Ethos,* and *Pathos*

CHAPTER 8   Accommodating Your Audience:
              Treating Differing Views

c h a p t e r 4

The Core of an Argument

A Claim with Reasons

THE RHETORICAL TRIANGLE

Before looking at the way arguments are structured, we should recognize that arguments occur within a social context. They are produced by writers or speakers who are addressing an audience—a relationship that can be visualized as a triangle with points labeled *message, writer/speaker,* and *audience* (see Figure 4.1). In composing an effective argument, writers must concern themselves with all three elements of this "rhetorical triangle." As we will see in later chapters, when you alter one point of the triangle (for example, you change the audience for whom you are writing or you reimagine the role you want to take as a writer—switching, say, from sarcasm to sympathy), then you may also need to restructure the message itself.

The rhetorical triangle's focus on message, speaker/writer, and audience relates also to the three kinds of persuasive appeals identified by classical rhetoricians: *logos, ethos,* and *pathos.*

Logos (Greek for "word") refers to the internal consistency of the message— the clarity of its claim, the logic of its reasons, and the effectiveness of its supporting evidence. The impact of *logos* on an audience is sometimes called the argument's *logical appeal.*

Ethos (Greek for "character") refers to the trustworthiness or credibility of the writer or speaker. *Ethos* is often conveyed through the tone and style of the message and through the way the writer or speaker refers to differing views. It can also be affected by the writer's reputation as it exists independently from the message— his or her expertise in the field, his or her previous record of integrity, and so forth. The impact of *ethos* is often called the argument's "ethical appeal" or the "appeal from credibility."

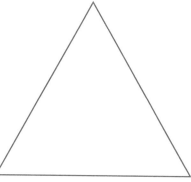

Message
(LOGOS: How can I make the argument
internally consistent and logical?
How can I find the best reasons and
support them with the best evidence?)

Audience
(PATHOS: How can I make the reader
open to my message? How can I best
appeal to my readers' values and
interests? How can I engage my
reader emotionally and imaginatively?)

Writer or Speaker
(ETHOS: How can I present myself
effectively? How can I enhance my
credibility and trustworthiness?)

FIGURE 4.1   The rhetorical triangle

Our third term, *pathos* (Greek for "suffering" or "experience"), is often associated with emotional appeal. But a better equivalent might be "appeal to the audience's sympathies and imagination." An appeal to *pathos* causes an audience not just to respond emotionally, but to identify with the writer's point of view—to feel what the writer feels. In this sense, *pathos* evokes a meaning implicit in the verb "to suffer"—to feel pain imaginatively, as in "I suffer whenever I think about the homeless." Perhaps the most common way of conveying a pathetic appeal is through narrative or story, which can turn the abstractions of logic into something palpable and present. The values, beliefs, and understandings of the writer are implicit in the story and conveyed imaginatively to the reader. *Pathos* thus refers to both the emotional and the imaginative impact of the message on an audience, the power with which the writer's message moves the audience to decision or action.

Using the rhetorical triangle, we can create a checklist of questions that can help a writer plan, draft, and revise an argument (see Figure 4.1). As the checklist suggests, writers should consider ways to make their messages as logically sound and well developed as possible, but they should also take care to link their arguments to the values and beliefs of the audience and to convey an image of themselves as credible and trustworthy.

The chapters in Part II of this text treat all three elements in the rhetorical triangle. Chapters 4–6 are concerned primarily with *logos*, whereas Chapter 7 is concerned with *pathos* and *ethos*. However, all these terms overlap so that it is impossible to make neat separations among them.

Given this background on the rhetorical triangle, we are ready now to turn to *logos*—the logic and structure of arguments.

ISSUE QUESTIONS AS THE ORIGINS OF ARGUMENT

At the heart of any argument is an issue, which we can define as a controversial topic area such as "criminal rights" or "the minimum wage," that gives rise to differing points of view. A writer can usually focus an issue by asking an issue question that invites at least two alternative answers. Within any complex issue— for example, the issue of abortion—there are usually a number of separate issue questions: Should abortions be legal? Should the federal government authorize Medicaid payments for abortions? When does a fetus become a human being (at conception? at three months? at quickening? at birth?)? What are the effects of legalizing abortion? (One person might stress that legalized abortion leads to greater freedom for women; another person might respond that it lessens a society's respect for human life.)

Difference Between an Issue Question and an Information Question

Of course, not all questions are issue questions that can be answered reasonably in two or more differing ways; thus, not all questions can lead to effective argument essays. Rhetoricians have traditionally distinguished between *explication*, which is writing that sets out to inform or explain, and *argumentation*, which sets out to change a reader's mind. On the surface, at least, this seems like a useful distinction. If a reader is interested in a writer's question mainly to gain new knowledge about a subject, then the writer's essay could be considered explication rather than argument. According to this view, the following questions about abortion might be called information questions rather than issue questions:

How does the abortion rate in the United States compare with the rate in Sweden?

If the rates are different, why?

Although both questions seem to call for information rather than for argument, we believe the latter one would be an issue question if reasonable people disagreed on the answer. Thus, two writers might agree that abortion rates in the United States and Sweden differ significantly, but they might disagree in their explanations of why. One might say that Sweden has a higher abortion rate because of the absence of a large Catholic or conservative Protestant population in the country. The other might say, "No, the real reasons are linked to the country's economic structure." Thus, underneath the surface of what looks like a simple explication of the "truth" is really a controversy.

You can generally tell whether a question is an issue question or an information question by examining your purpose in relationship to your audience. If your relationship to your audience is that of teacher to learner, so that your audience hopes to gain new information, knowledge, or understanding that you possess, then your question is probably an information question. But if your relationship to your audience is that of advocate to decision maker or jury, so that your audience needs to make up its mind on something and is weighing different points of view, then the question you address is an issue question. Often the same question can be an information question in one context and an issue question in another. Let's look at the following examples:

- How does a diesel engine work? (This is probably an information question since reasonable people who know about diesel engines will probably agree on how they work. This question would be posed by an audience of new learners.)

- Why is a diesel engine more fuel efficient than a gasoline engine? (This also seems to be an information question since all experts will probably agree on the answer. Once again, the audience seems to be new learners, perhaps students in an automotive class.)

- What is the most cost-effective way to produce diesel fuel from crude oil? (This could be an information question if experts agree and you are addressing new learners. But if you are addressing engineers and one engineer says process X is the most cost-effective and another argues for process Y, then the question is an issue question.)

- Should the present highway tax on diesel fuel be increased? (This is certainly an issue question. One person says yes; another says no; another offers a compromise.)

  FOR CLASS DISCUSSION

Working as a class or in small groups, try to decide which of the following questions are information questions and which are issue questions. Many of them could be either, depending on the rhetorical context. For such questions, create hypothetical contexts to show your reasoning.

1. What percentage of single-parent families receive welfare support?

2. What is the cause for the recent dramatic increases in the number of out-of-wedlock births in the United States?

3. Should the United States eliminate welfare support for unwed mothers?

4. What percentage of TV shows during prime-time hours depict violence?

5. What is the effect of violent TV shows on children?

6. Are chiropractors legitimate health professionals?

7. How does chiropractic treatment of illness differ from a medical doctor's treatment?

8. Is radial keratotomy for correcting nearsightedness safe?

9. Should a woman with a newly detected breast cancer opt for a radical mastectomy (complete removal of the breast and surrounding lymph tissue) or a lumpectomy (removal of the malignant lump without removal of the whole breast)?

10. Is Simone de Beauvoir correct in calling marriage an outdated, oppressive, capitalist institution?

DIFFERENCE BETWEEN A GENUINE ARGUMENT AND A PSEUDO-ARGUMENT

We have said that the heart of an argument is an issue question that invites two or more alternative answers. This does not mean, however, that every disagreement between people can lead to a rational argument. Rational arguments depend also on two additional factors: (1) reasonable participants, that is, participants who agree to operate within the conventions of reasonable behavior, and (2) potentially shareable assumptions that can serve as a starting place or foundation for the argument. You should learn to recognize the difference between genuine arguments, which proceed reasonably, and pseudo-arguments, which generate a lot of heat but are as irresolvable as a game of chess in which the players do not agree on how the pieces move.

Pseudo-Arguments: Fanatics and Skeptics

As you know, many arguments that at first seem like reasonable disputes are really shouting matches masquerading as arguments. Without really listening to each other, these disputants carry on into the night asserting as facts statements they are unsure of, citing vague authorities, moving illogically into tangential issues, and trying, in general, to rationalize a position based more on feeling and opinion than on careful thought.

Often such disputants belong to one of two classes, Fanatics and Skeptics. Fanatics are people who believe their claims are true because they say so, period. Oh, they may assure us that their claims rest on some authoritative text—the Bible, the *Communist Manifesto*, some Ph.D.'s new self-help book or child-raising guide—but in the end it's their narrow and quirky reading of the text or their faith (which others might not share) in the authority of the writer that underlies their argument. When you disagree with a Fanatic, therefore, you'll get a desk-thumping rehash of the Fanatic's preconceived convictions.

The Skeptic, on the other hand, dismisses the possibility that anything could be proven right. Because the sun has risen every day in recorded history is inadequate reason for the Skeptic to claim that it will rise tomorrow. Short of absolute proof, which never exists, Skeptics accept no proof. Skeptics, in short, do not understand that an argument cannot be a proof. We can hope that a good argument will increase its readers' adherence to a claim by making the claim more plausible, more worthy of consideration, but only rarely will it eliminate doubt or overcome the influence of alternative views. In the presence of Fanatics or Skeptics, then, genuine argument becomes impossible.

Another Source of Pseudo-Arguments: Lack of Shared Assumptions

A reasonable argument is difficult to conduct unless the participants share common assumptions on which the argument can be grounded. These assumptions are like axioms in geometry or the self-evident truths in the Declaration of Independence—starting points or foundations for the argument. Consider the following conversation in which Randall refuses to accept Rhonda's assumptions.

RHONDA: Smoking is bad because it causes cancer. (*Rhonda assumes that Randall will agree with her that cancer is bad. This is the assumption that lets her say that smoking is bad.*)

RANDALL: I agree that smoking causes cancer, but what's so bad about that? I like cancer. (*Rhonda looks at him in amazement.*)

RHONDA: Come on, Randy! Cancer is bad because it causes suffering and death. (*Now she hopes Randall will accept her new assumption that suffering and death are bad.*)

RANDALL: What's so bad about suffering and death?

RHONDA: Suffering reduces pleasure, while death is a total absence of being. That's awful!

RANDALL: No way. I am a masochist, so I like suffering. And if you don't have any being, you can't feel anything anyway.

RHONDA: O.K., wise guy. Let's assume that instead of absence of being you are dropped head-first into an everlasting lake of boiling oil where you must stay for eternity.

RANDALL: Hey, I said I was a masochist.

As you can see, the conversation becomes ludicrous because Randall refuses to share Rhonda's assumptions. Rhonda's self-evident "truths" (cancer is bad, suffering is bad, an everlasting lake of boiling oil is bad) seem to have no force for Randall. Without assumptions held in common, an argument degenerates into an endless regress of reasons that are based on more reasons that are based on still more reasons, and so forth. Randall's technique here is a bit like Callicles' rebuttals of Socrates—a refusal to accept the starting points of Socrates' argument. Attacking an argument's assumptions is, in fact, a legitimate way of deepening and complicating our understanding of an issue. But taken to an extreme, this technique makes argument impossible.

Perhaps you think this argument about smoking is a cornball case that would never crop up in real situations. In fact, however, a slight variation of it is extremely common. We encounter the problem every time we argue about purely personal opinions: opera is boring, New York City is too big, pizza tastes better than nachos, baseball is more fun than soccer. The problem with these disputes is that they rest on personal preferences rather than on shared assumptions. In other words, there are no common criteria for "boring" or "too big" or "tastes better" that writer and reader can share.

Of course, reasonable arguments about these disputes become possible once common assumptions are established. For example, a nutritionist could argue that pizza is better than nachos because it provides more balanced nutrients per calorie. Such an argument can succeed if the disputants accept the nutritionist's assumption that "more balanced nutrients per calorie" is a criterion for "better." But if one of the disputants responds, "Nah, nachos are better than pizza because nachos taste better," then he makes a different assumption—"My sense of taste is better than your sense of taste." This is a wholly personal standard, an assumption that others are unable to share.

 FOR CLASS DISCUSSION ▬▬▬▬▬▬▬▬▬▬▬▬▬▬▬▬▬▬▬▬

The following questions can all be answered in alternative ways. However, not all of them will lead to reasonable arguments. Try to decide which questions will lead to reasonable arguments and which will lead only to pseudo-arguments:

1. Is Spike Lee a good film director?

2. Are science fiction films better than westerns?

3. Should our city subsidize the development of a convention center?

4. Is this abstract oil painting by Bozo, the ape from the local zoo, a true work of art?

5. Is Danish Modern furniture attractive?

6. Is football a fun sport to play?

7. Does extrasensory perception (ESP) exist?

8. Which would look more attractive in this particular living room, Early American furniture or Danish Modern furniture?

9. Which are better, argumentation essays or short stories?

10. Which is better, Pete's argumentation essay or Janine's?

FRAME OF AN ARGUMENT: A CLAIM SUPPORTED BY REASONS

We have said earlier that an argument originates in an *issue question*, which by definition is any question that provokes disagreement about the best answer. When you write an argument, your task is to take a position on the issue and to support it with reasons and evidence. The *claim* of your essay is the position you want your audience to accept. To put it another way, your claim is your essay's thesis statement, a one-sentence summary answer to your issue question. Your task, then, is to make a claim and support it with reasons.

What Is a Reason?

A *reason* (also called a premise) is a claim used to support another claim. In speaking or writing, a reason is usually linked to the claim with such connecting words as *because, since, for, so, thus, consequently,* and *therefore,* indicating that the claim follows logically from the reason.

Let's take an example. In one of our recent classes a woman naval ROTC student surprised her classmates by remarking that women should not be allowed to serve on submarines. A heated discussion quickly followed, expanding into the more general issue of whether women should be allowed to join military combat units. Here are frameworks the class developed for two alternative positions on that issue.

One View

CLAIM: Women should be barred from joining military combat units.

REASON 1:   Women for the most part don't have the strength or endurance for combat roles.

REASON 2:   Serving in combat isn't necessary for women's career advancement in the military.

REASON 3:   Women in close-knit combat units would hurt unit morale by introducing sexual jealousies.

REASON 4:   Pregnancy or need to care for infants and small children would make women less reliable to a unit.

REASON 5:   Women haven't been socialized into fighters and wouldn't have the "Kill them with a bayonet!" spirit that men can get.

Alternative View

CLAIM: Women should be allowed to join combat units in the military.

REASON 1:   Millions of women are stronger and more physically fit than most men; women selected for combat duty would have the strength and endurance to do the job.

REASON 2:   The image of women as combat soldiers would help society overcome harmful gender stereotyping.

REASON 3:   Serving in combat units would open up many more opportunities for women's career advancement in the military.

REASON 4:   The justice of equal rights for women demands that women be allowed to serve in combat units.

Formulating a list of reasons in this way breaks your argumentative task into a series of subtasks. It gives you a frame for building your argument in parts. In the previous example, the frame for the argument opposing women in combat suggests five different lines of reasoning a writer might pursue. A writer might use all five reasons or select only two or three, depending on which reasons would most persuade the intended audience. Each line of reasoning would be developed in its own separate section of the argument.

For example, one section of an argument opposing women in combat might open with the following sentence: "Women shouldn't be allowed to join combat units because they don't have the strength or endurance for combat roles." In this section, the writer would describe the levels of strength and endurance currently required for combat service and provide evidence that these requirements would have to be lowered if women were to join combat units. In this section the writer might also need to support the unstated assumption that underlies this reason—that a high level of physical strength and endurance is a necessary criterion for combat effectiveness. (How one articulates and supports the underlying assumptions of an argument will be developed in Chapter 6 under our discussion of warrants and backing.)

The writer would proceed the same way for each separate section of the argument. Each section would open with a clear statement of the reason to be developed. The writer would then support each reason with evidence or chains of other reasons. Additionally, if needed for the intended audience, the writer would support any underlying assumptions on which the reason depends.

To summarize our point in this section, the frame of an argument consists of a claim (the thesis statement of the essay), which is supported by one or more reasons, which are in turn supported by evidence or chains of further reasons.

Advantages of Expressing Reasons in *Because* Statements

Chances are that when you were a child *because* contained magical explanatory powers:

DOROTHY: I want to go home now.

TOMMY: Why?

DOROTHY: Because.

TOMMY: Because why?

DOROTHY: Just because.

Somehow *because* seemed decisive. It persuaded people to accept your view of the world; it changed people's minds. Later, as you got older, you discovered that *because* only introduced your arguments and that it was the reasons following *because* that made the difference. Still, *because* introduced you to the powers potentially residing in the adult world of logic.

Of course, there are many other ways to express the logical connection between a reason and a claim. Our language is rich in ways of stating *because* relationships:

- Women shouldn't be allowed to join combat units because they don't have the strength or endurance for combat roles.

- Women don't have the strength or endurance for combat roles. Therefore women should not be allowed to join combat units.

- Women don't have the strength or endurance for combat roles, so they should not be allowed to join combat units.

- One reason that women should not be allowed to join combat units is that they don't have the strength or endurance for combat roles.

- My argument that women should not be allowed to join combat units is based mainly on evidence that women don't have the strength or endurance for combat roles.

Even though logical relationships can be stated in various ways, writing out one or more *because* clauses seems to be the most succinct and manageable way to clarify an argument for oneself. We therefore suggest that sometime in the writing process you create a *working thesis statement* that summarizes your main reasons as *because* clauses attached to your claim.* Just when you compose your own working thesis statement depends largely on your writing process. Some writers like to plan out their whole argument from the start and often compose their working thesis statements with *because* clauses before they write their rough drafts. Others discover their arguments as they write. And sometimes it is a combination of both. For these writers, an extended working thesis statement is something they might write halfway through the composing process as a way of ordering their argument when various branches seem to be growing out of control. Or they might compose a working thesis statement at the very end as a way of checking the unity of the final product.

Whenever you write your extended thesis statement, the act of doing so can be simultaneously frustrating and thought provoking. Composing *because* clauses can be a powerful discovery tool, causing you to think of many different kinds of arguments to support your claim. But it is often difficult to wrestle your ideas into the *because* clause shape, which sometimes seems to be overly tidy for the complex network of ideas you are trying to work with. Nevertheless, trying to summarize your argument as a single claim with reasons should help you see more clearly what you have to do.

 FOR CLASS DISCUSSION

Try the following group exercise to help you see how writing *because* clauses can be a discovery procedure.

Divide into small groups. Each group member should contribute an issue that he or she might like to explore. Discussing one person's issue at a time, help each member develop a claim supported by several reasons. Express each reason as a *because* clause. Then write out the working thesis statement for each person's argument by attaching the *because* clauses to the claim. Finally, try to create *because* clauses in support of an alternative claim for each issue. Recorders should select two or three working thesis statements from the group to present to the class as a whole.

---

*A working thesis statement for an argument opposing women in combat units might look like this: *Women should not be allowed to join combat units because they lack the strength, endurance, and "fighting spirit" needed in combat, because being pregnant or having small children would make them unreliable for combat at a moment's notice, and because women's presence would hurt morale of tight-knit combat units.* (A working thesis statement for an argument supporting women in combat is found on page 93.)

You might not put a bulky thesis statement like this into your essay itself; rather, a working thesis statement is a behind-the-scenes way of summarizing your argument for yourself so that you can see it whole and clear.

APPLICATION OF THIS CHAPTER'S
PRINCIPLES TO YOUR OWN WRITING

In Chapter 2, during our discussion of summary writing, we mentioned that not all arguments are equally easy to summarize. Generally, an argument is easiest to summarize when the writer places her thesis or claim in the essay's introduction and highlights each reason with explicit transitions as the argument progresses. We say that such arguments have a *self-announcing structure,* in that the essay announces its thesis (and sometimes its supporting reasons) and forecasts its shape before the body of the argument begins. Such arguments aim at maximum clarity for readers by focusing attention on the content and structure of the writer's ideas. As we explained in Chapter 3, such hierarchically structured, self-announcing arguments often follow the conventional format of classical argument (see pp. 63–66).

Arguments with self-announcing structures can be distinguished from those with *unfolding structures.* An argument with an unfolding structure often delays its thesis until the end or entwines the argument into a personal narrative, story, or analysis without an explicitly argumentative shape. Often the reader must tease out the writer's thesis and supporting reasons, which remain implied only. Unfolding arguments are often stylistically complex and subtle. As we will explain in Chapters 7 and 8, unfolding structures are often more effective than self-announcing structures for audiences who are hostile to the writer's views or for whom the issues are particularly troubling or complex. In contrast, classical arguments are often best for neutral or undecided audiences weighing alternative views on an issue and seeking an immediately clear and logical exposition of the writer's case.

The strategy for generating ideas set forth in this chapter—thinking of parallel because clauses and combining them into a working thesis statement that nutshells your argument—leads naturally to a classical argument with a self-announcing structure. Each because clause, together with its supporting evidence, becomes a separate building block of your argument. The building blocks, which can vary in length from a single paragraph to a whole series of paragraphs, are linked back to the thesis through appropriate transitions.

In our own classes we ask students early in the course to write arguments with self-announcing structures because such structures force writers to articulate their arguments clearly to themselves and because such structures help students master the art of organizing complex ideas. Later on in the course we encourage students to experiment with structures that unfold their meanings rather than announce them in the introduction.

In writing classical arguments, students often ask how much of the argument to summarize in the introduction. Consider the following options. Within the introduction you could choose to announce only your claim:

Women should be allowed to join combat units.

Or you could also predict a series of parallel reasons:

Women should be allowed to join combat units for several reasons.

Or you could forecast the actual number of reasons:

> Women should be allowed to join combat units for four main reasons.

Or you could forecast the whole argument:

> Women should be allowed to join combat units because they have the stamina, strength, and fighting spirit to do the job; because women as combat soldiers would help society overcome gender stereotyping; because allowing women in combat units would open up many more avenues for career advancement for women; and because opening combat units to women would advance the cause of equal rights.

These, of course, are not your only options. If you choose to delay your thesis until the end (a simple kind of unfolding argument), you might place the issue question in the introduction but not give away your own position:

> Would it best serve the nation to let women join combat units or not?

There are no hardbound rules to help you decide how much of your argument to forecast in the introduction. In Chapter 7 we discuss the different *ethos* projected when the writer places the claim in the introduction versus withholding it until later in the essay. And in Chapter 8 we show how delaying your thesis until the end may be a better strategy for hostile audiences.

It is clear at this point, though, that in deciding how much to forecast in the introduction a writer trades off clarity for surprise. The more you forecast, the clearer your argument is and the easier it is to read quickly. The less you forecast, the more surprising the argument is because the reader doesn't know what is coming. The only general rule is this: Readers sometimes feel insulted by too much forecasting. In writing a self-announcing argument, announce at the beginning only what is needed for clarity. In a short argument, readers usually don't need all the because clauses stated explicitly in the introduction. In longer arguments, however, or in especially complex ones, readers appreciate having the whole argument forecast at the outset.

APPLICATION OF THIS CHAPTER'S PRINCIPLES TO THE READING OF ARGUMENTS

When you read a classical argument, you will have little difficulty discerning the claim and main lines of reasoning of the argument because the writer forecasts the structure and highlights reasons with transitions. When you read an unfolding argument, however, it is often hard to discern its main argumentative core, to identify its claim, and to sort out its reasons and evidence. The more unfolding or implicit the argument, the harder it is to see exactly how the writer makes his or her case. Moreover, complex arguments often contain digressions and subarguments. Thus there may be dozens of small interlinked arguments going on inside a slowly unfolding main argument.

When you feel yourself getting tangled up in a complex argument, one powerful strategy is to apply the principles of this chapter. Try to convert the argument from its complex unfolding structure into a self-announcing, thesis-with-reasons structure. (It might help to imagine the argument's author as a member of your class; pretend he or she has to state his or her argument as a claim with because clauses. What working thesis statement would the writer construct?) Begin by identifying the writer's claim. Then ask yourself, what are the one, two, three, or four main arguments this writer puts forward to support that claim? State those arguments as because clauses attached to the claim. Then compare your because clauses with those of other members of your class. Expect disagreement, since different readers will emphasize different aspects of the argument or summarize them in different ways. However, there should also be considerable overlap.

As a class you can begin to reach consensus on the main lines of reasoning in even the most complex of arguments. Once you have stated these reasons as because clauses attached to the writer's claim, you will find it much easier to analyze the writer's reasoning, underlying assumptions, and use of evidence. And even if you can't agree on the because clauses—or find it difficult to reduce portions of the argument to a clearly stated reason—the exercise will lead you toward better understanding of how the argument works.

CONCLUSION

This chapter has introduced you to the rhetorical triangle with its key concepts of *logos, ethos,* and *pathos.* It has also shown how arguments originate in issue questions, how issue questions differ from information questions, and how arguments differ from pseudo-arguments. The center of the chapter explains that the frame of an argument is a claim supported by reasons. As you generate reasons to support your own arguments, it is often helpful to articulate them as because clauses attached to the claim. Finally, we explained how you can apply the principles of this chapter to your own writing or to your reading of complex arguments.

Of course, stating your reasons in because clauses is only one part of writing an argument. In the next chapter we will see how to support a reason by examining its logical structure, uncovering its unstated assumptions, and planning a strategy of development.

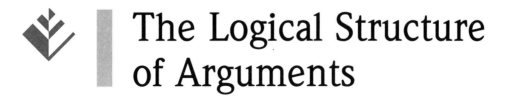

chapter 5

The Logical Structure of Arguments

In Chapter 4 you learned that the core of an argument is a claim supported by reasons and that these reasons can often be stated as because clauses attached to a claim. In the present chapter we examine the logical structure of arguments in more depth.

OVERVIEW TO *LOGOS:* WHAT DO WE MEAN BY THE "LOGICAL STRUCTURE" OF AN ARGUMENT?

As you will recall from our discussion of the rhetorical triangle, *logos* refers to the strength of an argument's support and its internal consistency. *Logos* is the argument's logical structure. But what do we mean by "logical structure"?

First of all, what we *don't* mean by logical structure is the kind of precise certainty you get in a philosophy class in formal logic. Logic classes deal with symbolic assertions that are universal and unchanging, such as "If all ps are qs and if r is a p, then r is a q." This statement is logically certain so long as p, q, and r are pure abstractions. But in the real world, p, q, and r turn into actual things, and the relationships among them suddenly become fuzzy. For example, p might be a class of actions called "Sexual Harassment," while q could be the class of "Actions That Justify Dismissal from a Job." If r is the class "Telling Off-Color Stories," then the logic of our p–q–r statement suggests that telling off-color stories (r) is an instance of sexual harassment (p), which in turn is an action justifying dismissal from one's job (q).

Now, most of us would agree that sexual harassment is a serious offense that might well justify dismissal from a job. In turn, we might agree that telling off-color stories, if the jokes are sufficiently raunchy and are inflicted on an unwilling audience, constitutes sexual harassment. But few of us would want to say categorically that all people who tell off-color stories are harassing their listeners and ought to be fired. Most of us would want to know the particulars of the case before making a final judgment.

In the real world, then, it is difficult to say that ps are always qs or that every instance of a q results in an r. That is why we discourage students from using the word *prove* in claims they write for arguments (as in "This paper will prove that euthanasia is wrong"). Real-world arguments seldom *prove* anything. They can only make a good case for something, a case that is more or less strong, more or less probable. Often the best you can hope for is to strengthen the resolve of those who agree with you or weaken the resistance of those who oppose you. If your audience believes x and you are arguing for y, you cannot expect your audience suddenly, as the result of your argument, to start believing y. If your argument causes an audience to experience a flicker of doubt or an instant of open-mindedness, you've done well. So proofs and dramatic shifts in position are not what real-world arguments are about.

A key difference, then, between formal logic and real-world argument is that real-world arguments are not grounded in abstract, universal statements. Rather, as we shall see, they must be grounded in beliefs, assumptions, or values granted by the audience. A second important difference is that in real-world arguments these beliefs, assumptions, or values are often unstated. So long as writer and audience share the same assumptions, then it's fine to leave them unstated. But if these underlying assumptions aren't shared, the writer has a problem. To illustrate the nature of this problem, consider one of the arguments we introduced in the last chapter.

> Women should be allowed to join combat units because the image of women in combat would help eliminate gender stereotypes.

On the face of it, this is a plausible argument. But the argument is persuasive only if the audience agrees with the writer's assumption that it is a good thing to eliminate gender stereotyping. The writer assumes that gender stereotyping (for example, seeing men as the fighters who are protecting the women and children back home) is harmful and that society would be better off without such fixed gender roles. But what if you believed that some gender roles are biologically based, divinely intended, or otherwise culturally essential and that society should strive to maintain these gender roles rather than dismiss them as "stereotypes"? If such were the case, you might believe as a consequence that our culture should socialize women to be nurturers, not fighters, and that some essential trait of "womanhood" would be at risk if women served in combat. If these were your beliefs, the argument wouldn't work for you because you would reject its underlying assumption. To persuade you with this line of reasoning, the writer would have to show not only how women in combat would help eliminate gender stereotypes but also why these stereotypes are harmful and why society would be better off without them.

The previous core argument ("Women should be allowed to join combat units because the image of women in combat would help eliminate gender stereotypes") is what the Greek philosopher Aristotle would call an enthymeme. An *enthymeme* is an incomplete logical structure that depends, for its completeness, on one or more unstated assumptions (values, beliefs, principles) that serve as the starting point of the argument. The successful arguer, said Aristotle, is the person who knows how to formulate and develop enthymemes so that the argument is rooted in the audience's values and beliefs.

To clarify the concept of "enthymeme," let's go over this same territory again more slowly, examining what we mean by "incomplete logical structure." The sentence "Women should be allowed to join combat units because the image of women in combat would help eliminate gender stereotypes" is an enthymeme. It combines a claim (women should be allowed to join combat units) with a reason expressed as a because clause (because the image of women in combat would help eliminate gender stereotypes). To render this enthymeme logically complete, you must supply an unstated assumption—that gender stereotypes are harmful and should be eliminated. If your audience accepts this assumption, then you have a starting place on which to build an effective argument. If your audience doesn't accept this assumption, then you must supply another argument to support it, and so on until you find common ground with your audience. To sum up:

1. Claims are supported with reasons. You can usually state a reason as a because clause attached to a claim (see Chapter 4).

2. A because clause attached to a claim is an incomplete logical structure called an enthymeme. To create a complete logical structure from an enthymeme, the unstated assumption (or assumptions) must be articulated.

3. To serve as an effective starting point for the argument, this unstated assumption should be a belief, value, or principle that the audience grants.

Let's illustrate this structure by putting the previous example—plus a new one—into schematic form.

INITIAL ENTHYMEME:	Women should be allowed to join combat units because the image of women in combat would help eliminate gender stereotypes.
CLAIM:	Women should be allowed to join combat units.
STATED REASON:	because the image of women in combat would help eliminate gender stereotypes
UNSTATED ASSUMPTION:	Gender stereotypes are harmful and should be eliminated.
INITIAL ENTHYMEME:	Cocaine and heroin should be legalized because legalization would eliminate the black market in drugs.
CLAIM:	Cocaine and heroin should be legalized.

| STATED REASON: | because legalization would eliminate the black market in drugs |
| UNSTATED ASSUMPTION: | An action that eliminates the black market in drugs is good. (Or, to state the assumption more fully, the benefits to society of eliminating the black market in drugs outweigh the negative effects to society of legalizing drugs.) |

 FOR CLASS DISCUSSION

Working individually or in small groups, identify the claim, stated reason, and unstated assumption that completes each of the following enthymemic arguments.

EXAMPLE:

Rabbits make good pets because they are gentle.

CLAIM:	Rabbits make good pets.
STATED REASON:	because they are gentle
UNSTATED ASSUMPTION:	Gentle animals make good pets.

1. We shouldn't elect Joe as committee chair because he is too bossy.

2. Buy this stereo system because it has a powerful amplifier.

3. Drugs should not be legalized because legalization would greatly increase the number of drug addicts.

4. Practicing the piano is good for kids because it teaches discipline.

5. Welfare benefits for unwed mothers should be eliminated because doing so will greatly reduce the nation's illegitimacy rate.

6. Welfare benefits for unwed mothers should not be eliminated because these benefits are needed to prevent unbearable poverty among our nation's most helpless citizens.

7. We should strengthen the Endangered Species Act because doing so will preserve genetic diversity on the planet.

8. The Endangered Species Act is too stringent because it severely damages the economy.

9. The doctor should not perform an abortion in this case because the mother's life is not in danger.

10. Abortion should be legal because a woman has the right to control her own body. (This enthymeme has several unstated assumptions behind it; see if you can recreate all the missing premises.)

ADOPTING A LANGUAGE FOR DESCRIBING ARGUMENTS: THE TOULMIN SYSTEM

Understanding a new field usually requires us to learn a new vocabulary. For example, if you were taking biology for the first time, you'd spend days memorizing dozens and dozens of new terms. Luckily, the field of argument requires us to learn a mere handful of new terms. A particularly useful set of argument terms, one we'll be using throughout the rest of this text, comes from philosopher Stephen Toulmin. In the 1950s, Toulmin rejected the prevailing models of argument based on formal logic in favor of a very audience-based courtroom model.

Toulmin's courtroom model differs from formal logic in that it assumes (1) that all assertions and assumptions are contestable by "opposing counsel," and (2) that all final "verdicts" about the persuasiveness of the opposing arguments will be rendered by a neutral third party, a judge or jury. Keeping in mind the "opposing counsel" forces us to anticipate counterarguments and to question our assumptions; keeping in mind the judge and jury reminds us to answer opposing arguments fully, without rancor, and to present positive reasons for supporting our case as well as negative reasons for disbelieving the opposing case. Above all else, Toulmin's model reminds us not to construct an argument that appeals only to those who already agree with us.

The system we use for analyzing arguments combines Toulmin's system with Aristotle's concept of the enthymeme. The purpose of this system is to provide writers with an economical language for articulating the structure of argument and, in the process, to help them anticipate their audience's needs. More particularly, it helps writers see enthymemes—in the form of a claim with because clauses—as the core of their argument, and the other structural elements from Toulmin as strategies for elaborating and supporting that core.

This system builds on the one you have already been practicing. We simply need to add a few more key terms from Toulmin. The first key term is Toulmin's *warrant*, the name we will now use for the unstated assumption that turns an enthymeme into a complete logical structure. For example:

INITIAL ENTHYMEME:	Women should be allowed to join combat units because the image of women in combat would help eliminate gender stereotypes.
CLAIM:	Women should be allowed to join combat units.
STATED REASON:	because the image of women in combat would help eliminate gender stereotypes
WARRANT:	Gender stereotypes are harmful and should be eliminated.
INITIAL ENTHYMEME:	Cocaine and heroin should be legalized because legalization would eliminate the black market in drugs.

CLAIM:	Cocaine and heroin should be legalized.
STATED REASON:	because legalization would eliminate the black market in drugs
WARRANT:	An action that eliminates the black market in drugs is good.

Toulmin derives his term *warrant* from the concept of "warranty" or "guarantee." The warrant is the value, belief, or principle that the audience has to hold if the soundness of the argument is to be guaranteed or warranted. We sometimes make similar use of this word in ordinary language when we say "That is an unwarranted conclusion," meaning one has leapt from information about a situation to a conclusion about that situation without any sort of general principle to justify or "warrant" that move. Thus if we claim that cocaine and heroin ought to be legalized because legalization would end the black market, we must be able to cite a general principle or belief that links our prediction that legalization would end the black market to our claim that legalization ought to occur. In this case the warrant is the statement, "An action that eliminates the black market for drugs is good." It is this underlying belief that warrants or guarantees the argument. Just as automobile manufacturers must provide warranties for their cars if they want skeptical customers to buy them, we must provide warrants linking our reasons to our claims if we expect skeptical audiences to "buy" our arguments.

But arguments need more than claims, reasons, and warrants. These are simply one-sentence statements—the frame of an argument, not a developed argument. To flesh out our arguments and make them convincing we need what Toulmin calls *grounds* and *backing*. Grounds are the supporting evidence—facts, data, statistics, testimony, or examples—that cause you to make a claim in the first place or that you produce to justify a claim in response to audience skepticism. Toulmin suggests that grounds are "what you have to go on" in an argument. In short, they are collectively all the evidence you use to support a reason. It sometimes helps to think of grounds as the answer to a "How do you know that . . .?" question preceding a reason. (How do you know that letting women into combat units would help eliminate gender stereotypes? How do you know that legalizing drugs will end the black market?) Here is how grounds fit into our emerging argument schema.

CLAIM:	Women should be allowed to join combat units.
STATED REASON:	because the image of women in combat would help eliminate gender stereotypes
GROUNDS:	data and evidence showing that a chief stereotype of women is that they are soft and nurturing whereas men are tough and aggressive. The image of women in combat gear packing a rifle, driving a tank, firing a machine gun from a foxhole, or radioing for artillery support would shock people into seeing women not as "soft and nurturing" but as equal to men.

CLAIM: Cocaine and heroin should be legalized.

STATED REASON: because legalization would eliminate the black market
                    in drugs

GROUNDS: data and evidence showing how legalizing cocaine and
                    heroin would eliminate the black market (statistics, data,
                    and examples describing the size and effect of current
                    black market, followed by arguments showing how
                    selling cocaine and heroin legally in state-controlled
                    stores would lower the price and eliminate the need
                    to buy them from drug dealers)

In many cases, successful arguments require just these three components: a claim,
a reason, and grounds. If the audience already accepts the unstated assumption behind the reason (the warrant), then the warrant can safely remain in the background
unstated and unexamined. But if there is a chance that the audience will question or
doubt the warrant, then the writer needs to back it up by providing an argument in
its support. *Backing* is the argument that supports the warrant. Backing answers the
question, "How do you know that . . .?" or "Why do you believe that . . .?" prefixed
to the warrant. (Why do you believe that gender stereotyping is harmful? Why do
you believe that the benefits of ending the black market outweigh the costs of legalizing cocaine and heroin?) Here is how *backing* is added to our schema.

WARRANT: Gender stereotypes are harmful and should be eliminated.

BACKING: arguments showing how the existing stereotype of soft and
                    nurturing women and tough and aggressive men is harmful to
                    both men and women (examples of how the stereotype keeps
                    men from developing their nurturing sides and women from
                    developing autonomy and power; examples of other benefits
                    that come from eliminating gender stereotypes include more
                    egalitarian society, no limits on what persons can pursue;
                    deeper respect for both sexes)

WARRANT: An action that eliminates the black market in drugs is good.

BACKING: an argument supporting the warrant by showing why elimi-
                    nating the black market in drugs is good (statistics and exam-
                    ples about the ill effects of the black market, data on crime
                    and profiteering, evidence that huge profits make drug deal-
                    ing more attractive than ordinary jobs, the high cost of crime
                    created by the black market, the cost to taxpayers of waging
                    the war against drugs, the high cost of prisons to house incar-
                    cerated drug dealers, etc.)

Finally, Toulmin's system asks us to imagine how a shrewd adversary would
try to refute our argument. Specifically, the adversary might attack our reason and
grounds by showing how letting women become combat soldiers wouldn't do

much to end gender stereotyping or how legalizing drugs would *not* end the black market. Or the adversary might attack our warrant and backing by showing how some gender stereotypes are worth keeping, or how the negative consequences of legalizing drugs might outweigh the benefit of ending the black market.

In the case of the argument supporting women in combat, an adversary might offer one or more of the following rebuttals:

CONDITIONS OF REBUTTAL

Rebutting the reasons and grounds: evidence that letting women join combat units wouldn't overcome gender stereotyping (very few women would want to join combat units; those that did would be considered freaks; most girls would still identify with Barbie doll models, not with female infantry)

Rebutting the warrant and backing: arguments showing it is important to maintain gender role differences because they are biologically based, divinely inspired, or otherwise important culturally; women should be nurturers and mothers, not fighters; essential nature of "womanhood" sullied by putting women in combat

As this example shows, adversaries can question either an argument's reasons and grounds or its warrant and backing or sometimes both. Conditions of rebuttal remind writers to look at their arguments from the perspective of skeptical readers. To help writers imagine how skeptics might see weaknesses in an argument, conditions of rebuttal are often stated as conditionals using the word *unless,* such as, "It is good to overcome gender stereotyping *unless* those stereotypes are biologically based or otherwise essential for society." Conditions of rebuttal name the exceptions to the rule, the circumstances under which your reason or warrant might not hold. Stated in this manner, the conditions of rebuttal for the legalization-of-drugs argument might look like this:

CONDITIONS OF REBUTTAL

Rebutting the reason and grounds: Legalizing cocaine and heroin would eliminate the black market in drugs unless taxes on legal drugs would keep the price high enough that a black market would still exist; unless new kinds of illegal designer drugs would be developed and sold on the black market.

Rebutting the warrant and backing: Ending the black market is good unless the increased numbers of drug users and addicts were unacceptably high; unless harmful changes in social structure due to acceptance of drugs were too severe; unless the health and economic consequences of increased number of drug users were catastrophic; unless social costs to families and communities associated with addiction or erratic behavior during drug-induced "highs" were too great.

Toulmin's final term, used to limit the force of a claim and indicate the degree of its probable truth, is *qualifier.* The qualifier reminds us that real-world arguments almost never prove a claim. We may say things like "very likely," "probably," or "maybe" to indicate the strength of the claim we are willing to draw from our grounds and warrant. Thus if there are exceptions to your warrant or if your grounds are not very strong, you will have to qualify your claim. For example, you might say "Except in rare cases, women should not be allowed in combat units," or "With full awareness of the potential dangers, I suggest we consider the option of legalizing drugs as a way of ending the ill effects of the black market."

Although the system just described might at first seem complicated, it is actually fairly easy to use after you've had some opportunity to practice. The following chart will help you review the terms.

ORIGINAL ENTHYMEME: your claim with *because* clause

CLAIM: The point or position you are trying to get your audience to accept

STATED REASON: your because clause*; your reasons are the subordinate claims you make in support of your main claim

GROUNDS: the evidence (data, facts, testimony, statistics, examples) supporting your stated reason

WARRANT: the originally unstated assumption behind your enthymeme, the statement of belief, value, principle, and so on, that, when accepted by an audience, warrants or underwrites your argument

BACKING: evidence or other argumentation supporting the warrant (if the audience already accepts the warrant, then backing is usually not needed. But if the audience doubts the warrant, then backing is essential)

CONDITIONS OF REBUTTAL: your acknowledgement of the limits of your claim—those conditions under which it does not hold true, in anticipation of an adversary's counterargument against your reason and grounds or against your warrant and backing

QUALIFIER: words or phrases limiting the force of your claim

---

* Most arguments have more than one because clause or reason in support of a claim. Each enthymeme thus develops only one line of reasoning, one piece of your whole argument.

To help you practice using these terms, here are two more examples, displayed this time so that the conditions of rebuttal are set in an opposing column next to the reason/grounds and the warrant/backing.

INITIAL ENTHYMEME: Women should be barred from combat duty because the presence of women would harm unit morale.

CLAIM: Women should be barred from combat duty.

STATED REASON: because the presence of women would harm unit morale

GROUNDS: evidence and examples of how presence of women would lead to romantic or sexual relationships and create sexual competition and jealousy; evidence that male bonding is difficult when women are present; fear that a woman wouldn't be strong enough to carry a wounded buddy off a battlefield, etc.; fear that men couldn't endure watching a woman with her legs blown off in a mine field

WARRANT: Combat units need high morale to function effectively.

BACKING: arguments supporting the warrant by showing that combat soldiers have to have an utmost faith in buddies to do their job; anything that disrupts male bonding will make the unit less likely to stick together in extreme danger or endure being prisoners of war; examples of how unit cohesion is what makes a fighting unit able to withstand battle

CONDITIONS OF REBUTTAL:
Rebutting the reason and grounds: arguments that letting women join combat units would *not* harm unit morale (times are changing rapidly; men are used to working professionally with women; examples of successful mixed-gender sports teams and mountain climbing teams; example of women astronauts working in close quarters with men; arguments that sexual and romantic liaisons would be forbidden and sexual activity punished; after a period of initial discomfort, men and women would overcome modesty about personal hygiene, etc.)

Rebutting the warrant and backing: arguments that unit morale is not as important for combat efficiency as is training and discipline; unit morale not as important as promoting women's rights; men will have to learn to deal with the presence of women and treat them as fellow soldiers; men can learn to act professionally even if their morale is lower

QUALIFIER: In many cases the presence of women would hurt morale.

ORIGINAL ENTHYMEME: The exclusionary rule is a bad law because it allows drug dealers to escape prosecution.*

CLAIM: The exclusionary rule is a bad law.

STATED REASON: because it allows drug dealers to escape prosecution

GROUNDS: numerous cases wherein the exclusionary rule prevented police from presenting evidence in court; examples of nitpicking rules and regulations that allowed drug dealers to go free; testimony from prosecutors and police about how the exclusionary rule hampers their effectiveness

WARRANT: It is beneficial to our country to prosecute drug dealers.

BACKING: arguments showing the extent and danger of the drug problem; arguments showing that prosecuting and imprisoning drug dealers will reduce the drug problem

CONDITIONS OF REBUTTAL:
Rebuttal of reason and grounds: unless the exclusionary rule does not allow many drug dealers to escape prosecution (counterevidence showing numerous times when police and prosecutors followed the exclusionary rule and still obtained convictions; statistical analysis showing that the percentage of cases in which exclusionary rule threw evidence out of court is very low)

Rebuttal of warrant and backing: unless reversing exclusionary rule would have serious costs that outweigh benefits; unless greatly increasing the pursuit and prosecution of drug dealers would have serious costs (arguments showing that the value of protecting individual liberties outweighs the value of prosecuting drug dealers)

QUALIFIER: perhaps, tentatively

---

*The exclusionary rule is a court-mandated set of regulations specifying when evidence can and cannot be introduced into a trial. It excludes all evidence that police obtain through irregular means. In actual practice, it demands that police follow strict procedures. Opponents of the exclusionary rule claim that its "narrow technicalities" handcuff police.

FOR CLASS DISCUSSION

Working individually or in small groups, imagine that you have to write arguments developing the ten enthymemes listed in the For Class Discussion exercise on page 98. Use the Toulmin schema to help you determine what you need to consider when developing each enthymeme. As an example, we have applied the Toulmin schema to the first enthymeme.

ORIGINAL ENTHYMEME: We should not choose Joe as committee chair because he is too bossy.

CLAIM: We should not choose Joe as committee chair.

STATED REASON: because he is too bossy

GROUNDS: various examples of Joe's bossiness; testimony about his bossiness from people who have worked with him

WARRANT: Bossy people make bad committee chairs.

BACKING: arguments showing that other things being equal, bossy people tend to bring out the worst rather than the best in those around them; bossy people tend not to ask advice, make bad decisions; etc.

CONDITIONS OF REBUTTAL: *Rebuttal of reason and grounds:* unless Joe isn't really bossy (counterevidence of Joe's cooperativeness and kindness; testimony that Joe is easy to work with; etc.)

Rebuttal of the warrant and backing: unless bossy people sometimes make good chairpersons (arguments showing that at times a group needs a bossy person who can make decisions and get things done); unless Joe has other traits of good leadership that outweigh his bossiness (evidence that, despite his bossiness, Joe has many other good leadership traits such as high energy, intelligence, charisma, etc.)

QUALIFIER: In most circumstances, bossy people make bad committee chairs.

USING TOULMIN'S SCHEMA TO DETERMINE A STRATEGY OF SUPPORT

Having introduced you to Toulmin's terminology for describing the logical structure of arguments, we can turn directly to a discussion of how to use these concepts for developing your own arguments. As we have seen, the claim, supporting reasons, and warrant form the frame for a line of reasoning. The majority of words in an argument, however, are devoted to grounds and backing—the supporting sections that develop the argument frame. Generally these supporting sections take one of two forms: either (1) *evidence* such as facts, examples, case studies, statistics, testimony from experts, and so forth; or (2) a *chain of reasons*—that is, further conceptual argument. The Toulmin schema can help you determine what kind of support your argument needs. Let's look at each kind of support separately.

Evidence as Support

It's often easier for writers to use evidence rather than chains of reasons for support because using evidence entails moving from generalizations to specific details—a basic organizational strategy that most writers practice regularly. Consider the following hypothetical case. A student, Ramona, wants to write a complaint letter to the head of the Philosophy Department about a philosophy professor, Dr. Choplogic, whom Ramona considers incompetent. Ramona plans to develop two different lines of reasoning: first, that Choplogic's courses are disorganized and, second, that Choplogic is unconcerned about students. Let's look briefly at how she can develop her first main line of reasoning, which is based on the following enthymeme:

Dr. Choplogic is an ineffective teacher because his courses are disorganized.

The grounds for this argument will be all the evidence she can muster showing that Choplogic's courses are disorganized. Figure 5.1 shows Ramona's initial brainstorming notes based on the Toulmin schema. The information Ramona lists under "grounds" is what she sees as the facts of the case—the hard data she will use as evidence to support her reason. Here is how this argument might look when placed into written form:

Claim and reason

One reason that Dr. Choplogic is ineffective is that his courses are poorly organized. I have had him for two courses—Introduction to Philosophy and Ethics—and both were disorganized. He never gave us a syllabus or explained his grading system. At the beginning of the course he wouldn't tell us how many papers he would require, and he never seemed to know how much of the textbook material he planned to cover. For Intro he told us to read the whole text, but he covered only half of it in class. A week before the final I asked him how much of the text would be on the exam and he said he hadn't decided. The Ethics class was even more disorganized. Dr. Choplogic told us to read the text, which provided one set of terms for ethical arguments, and then he told us he didn't like the text and presented us in lecture with a wholly different set of terms. The result was a whole class of confused, angry students.

Grounds (evidence in support of reason)

Claim: Dr. Choplogic is an ineffective teacher.
Stated reason: because his courses are disorganized
Grounds: What evidence is there that his courses are disorganized?
    —no syllabus in either Intro or Ethics
    —never announced how many papers we would have
    —didn't know what would be on tests
    —didn't like the textbook he had chosen; gave us different terms
    —didn't follow any logical sequence in his lectures

FIGURE 5.1   Ramona's initial planning notes

As you can see, Ramona has plenty of evidence to support her contention that Choplogic is disorganized. But how effective is this argument as it stands? Is this all she needs? The Toulmin schema also encourages Ramona to examine the warrant, backing, and conditions of rebuttal for this argument. Figure 5.2 shows how her planning notes continue.

This section of her planning notes helps her see her argument more fully from the audience's perspective. She believes that no one can challenge her reason and grounds—Choplogic is indeed a disorganized teacher. But she recognizes that some people might challenge her warrant ("Disorganized teachers are ineffective"). A supporter of Dr. Choplogic might say that some teachers, even though they are hopelessly disorganized, might nevertheless do an excellent job of stimulating thought and discussion. Moreover, such teachers might possess other valuable traits that outweigh their disorganization. Ramona therefore decides to address these concerns by adding another section to this portion of her argument.

Backing for warrant (shows why disorganization is bad)   Dr. Choplogic's lack of organization makes it difficult for students to take notes, to know what to study, or to relate one part of the course to another. Moreover, students lose confidence in the teacher because he doesn't seem to care enough to prepare for class.

Response to conditions of rebuttal   In Dr. Choplogic's defense, it might be thought that his primary concern is involving students in class discussions or other activities to teach us thinking skills or get us involved in philosophical discussions. But this isn't the case. Students rarely get a chance to speak in class. We just sit there listening to rambling, disorganized lectures.

Claim: Dr. Choplogic is an ineffective teacher.

Stated reason: because his courses are disorganized

Grounds: What evidence is there that his courses are disorganized?
—no syllabus in either Intro or Ethics
—never announced how many papers we would have
—didn't know what would be on tests
—didn't like the textbook he had chosen; gave us different terms
—didn't follow any logical sequence in his lectures

Warrant: Disorganized teachers are ineffective.

Backing:
—organization helps you learn
—gets material organized in a logical way
—helps you know what to study
—helps you take notes and relate one part of course to another
—when teacher is disorganized you think he hasn't prepared for class; makes you lose confidence

Conditions of rebuttal: Would anybody doubt my reasons and grounds?
—No. Every student I have ever talked to agrees that these are the facts about Choplogic's courses. Everyone agrees that he is disorganized. Of course, the department chair might not know this, so I will have to provide evidence.

Would anybody doubt my warrant and backing? Maybe they would.
—Is it possible that in some cases disorganized teachers are good teachers? Have I ever had a disorganized teacher who was good? My freshman sociology teacher was disorganized, but she really made you think. You never knew where the course was going but we had some great discussions. Choplogic isn't like that. He isn't using classtime to get us involved in philosophic thinking or discussions.
—Is it possible that Choplogic has other good traits that outweigh his disorganization? I don't think he does, but I will have to make a case for this.

FIGURE 5.2   Ramona's planning notes continued

As the marginal notations show, this section of her argument backs the warrant that disorganized teachers are ineffective and anticipates some of the conditions for rebuttal that an audience might raise to defend Dr. Choplogic. Throughout her draft, Ramona has supported her argument with effective use of evidence. The Toulmin schema has shown her that she needed evidence primarily to support her stated reason ("Choplogic is disorganized"). But she also needed some evidence to support her warrant ("Disorganization is bad") and to respond to possible conditions of rebuttal ("Perhaps Choplogic is teaching thinking skills").

In general, the evidence you use for support can come either from your own personal experiences and observations or from reading and research. Although many arguments depend on your skill at research, many can be supported wholly or in part from your own personal experiences, so don't neglect the wealth of evidence from your own life when searching for data. Chapter 6 is devoted to a more detailed discussion of evidence in arguments.

Chain of Reasons as Support

So far we have been discussing how to support reasons with evidence. Many reasons, however, cannot be supported this way; rather, they must be supported with a chain of other reasons. Such passages are often more difficult to write. Let's take as an example a student who wants to argue that the state should require the wearing of seatbelts. His claim, along with his main supporting reason, is as follows:

> The state should require the wearing of seatbelts in moving vehicles because seatbelts save lives.

In planning out the argument, the writer determines the unstated warrant, which in this case is that the state should enact any law that would save lives. The writer's argument thus looks like this:

CLAIM:	The state should enact a mandatory seatbelt law.
STATED REASON:	Such a law will save lives.
WARRANT:	Laws that save lives should be enacted by the state.

The writer's next step is to consider the conditions for rebuttal for these premises. He realizes that he will have no trouble supporting the stated reason ("Seatbelts save lives") since he can use evidence in the form of examples, statistics, and testimony. But the warrant of the argument ("Laws that save lives should be enacted by the state") cannot be defended by an appeal to such data. Although this statement operates as a warrant in the original seatbelt argument, it is actually a new claim that must itself be supported by additional reasons. As this example illustrates, a statement serving as a reason in one argument can become a claim in another, setting off a potentially infinite regress of reasons.

Examining the conditions for rebuttal reveals to the writer how vulnerable the warrant is. If the state is supposed to enact any law that saves lives, should it then pass laws requiring you to take your vitamins, get your blood pressure checked, or put safety strips in your bathtub? How could the writer argue that the state has the right to require seatbelts without opening the way for dozens of other do-gooder laws? Unable to use evidence, the writer proceeded to think of chains of reasons that might add up to a convincing case.

The seatbelt law differs from other do-gooder laws:

- Because it mandates behavior only on public property.
- Because it concerns highway safety, and the state is clearly responsible for public highways.
- Because the connection between wearing seatbelts and safety is immediately clear.
- Because it is similar to already established laws requiring the wearing of motorcycle helmets.
- Because the law is easy to follow, is minimally disruptive, and costs relatively little so that the benefits outweigh the disadvantages.

Each of these arguments distinguishes seatbelt legislation from other, less acceptable laws government might enact in the name of citizen safety, and they thus become ways of qualifying the warrant that the state should enact *all* laws that save lives. Together they constitute some reasons for supporting seatbelt legislation and for arguing that such legislation is not an unreasonable infringement of citizens' rights.

Having worked out these differences between seatbelt laws and other do-gooder laws, the writer is ready to draft the argument in essay form. Here is a portion of the writer's essay, picking up his argument after he has shown that seatbelts do indeed save lives:

> But just because seatbelts save lives does not necessarily mean that the state has the right to make us wear them. Certainly we don't want the state to make us put nonslip safety strips in our bathtubs, to require annual blood-pressure checks, or to outlaw cigarettes, alcohol, and fat. But seatbelt regulation governs our behavior on public roadways, not in the privacy of our homes, and the government is obviously responsible for making the highways as safe as possible. After all, we can sue the government for negligence if it disregards safety in highway construction. Forcing motor vehicle passengers to wear seatbelts can thus be seen as part of their general program to make the highways safe. Moreover, the use of seatbelts constitutes a minimal restriction of personal freedom. Seatbelts are already standard equipment in cars, it costs us nothing to wear them, and they are now designed for maximum comfort.
>
> There are also a number of precedents for seatbelt legislation. Indeed, there are already government regulations requiring the installation of seatbelts in cars. To require their installation but not their use is silly. It is to require people to be potentially, but not actually, safe. In addition, a number of states, following the same sort of rationale as the one I've followed above, require motorcyclists to wear helmets. Such helmets are often costly and uncomfortable and, according to some cyclists, hurt the biker's image. But because they protect lives and save millions of dollars in insurance and hospital costs, such objections have been overridden.

As you can tell, this section is considerably more complex than one that simply cites data as evidence in support of a reason. Here the writer must use an interlocking chain of other reasons, showing all the ways that a seatbelt law is different from a safety-strip-in-the-bathtub law. Certainly it's not a definitive argument, but it is considerably more compelling than saying that the state should pass any law that protects lives. Although chains of reasons are harder to construct than bodies of evidence, many arguments will require them.

CONCLUSION

Chapters 4 and 5 have provided an anatomy of argument. They have shown that the core of an argument is a claim with reasons that usually can be summarized in one or more because clauses attached to the claim. Often, it is as important to support the unstated premises in your argument as it is to support the stated ones. In order to plan out an argument strategy, arguers can use the Toulmin schema, which helps writers discover grounds, warrants, and backings for their arguments and to test them through conditions for rebuttal. Finally, we saw how stated reasons and warrants are supported through the use of evidence or chains of other reasons. In the next chapter we will look more closely at the uses of evidence in argumentation.

 FOR CLASS DISCUSSION

1. Working individually or in small groups, consider ways you could use evidence from personal experience to support the stated reason in each of the following partial arguments:
   a. Another reason to oppose a state sales tax is that it is so annoying.
   b. Professor X should be rated down on his (her) teaching because he (she) doesn't design homework effectively to promote real learning.
   c. Professor X is an outstanding teacher because he (she) generously spends so much time outside of class counseling students with personal problems.

2. Now try to create a chain-of-reasons argument to support the warrants in each of the above partial arguments. The warrants for each of the arguments are stated below.
   a. Support this warrant: We should oppose taxes that are annoying.
   b. Support this warrant: The effective design of homework to promote real learning is an important criterion for rating teachers.
   c. Support this warrant: Time spent counseling students with personal problems is an important criterion for rating teachers.

3. Using Toulmin's conditions of rebuttal, work out a strategy for refuting either the stated reasons or the warrants or both in each of the above arguments.

chapter 6

Evidence in Argument

In the previous chapter, we examined two basic ways to support arguments: through reasons supported by evidence and through reasons supported by chains of other reasons. In this chapter we return to a discussion of evidence—how to find, use, and evaluate it. We focus on four categories of evidence: (1) data from personal experience—either from memory or from observation; (2) data from interviews, surveys, and questionnaires; (3) data from reading, especially library research, and (4) numerical or statistical data. We then examine the knotty problem of what to do when the evidence is inconclusive and the experts disagree. Finally, we discuss how to evaluate evidence in order to use it fairly, responsibly, and persuasively.

USING EVIDENCE FROM PERSONAL EXPERIENCE

Your own life can be the source of supporting evidence in many arguments. Personal narratives can illustrate important points or underscore the human significance of your issue. Such stories build bridges to readers, who often find personal experience more engaging and immediate than dry lists of facts or statistics. Moreover, when readers sense a writer's personal connection to an issue, they are more likely to find the writer's position credible.

Using Personal Experience Data
Collected from Memory

Many arguments can be supported extensively, even exclusively, by data recalled from memory. Here, for example, is how a student from a small Montana town used her memories to support the claim "Small rural schools provide a quality education for children."

> Another advantage of small rural schools is the way they create in students a sense of identity with their communities and a sense of community pride. When children see the active support of the community toward the school, they want to return this support with their best efforts. I remember our Fergus Grade School Christmas programs. Sure, every grade school in Montana has a Christmas program, but ours seemed to be small productions. We started work on our play and songs immediately after Thanksgiving. The Fergus Community Women's Club decorated the hall a few days before the program. When the big night arrived, the whole community turned out, even Mr. and Mrs. Schoenberger, an elderly couple. I and the eleven other students were properly nervous as we performed our play, "A Charlie Brown Christmas." As a finale, the whole community sang carols and exchanged gifts. One of the fathers even dressed up as Santa Claus. Everyone involved had a warm feeling down inside when they went home.

The community bonding described in this paragraph—the father playing Santa Claus, the attendance of the elderly couple, the communal singing of Christmas carols—supports the writer's stated reason that small rural schools help students feel an identity with their communities.

Using Personal Experience Data
Collected from Observations

For other arguments you can gather evidence through personal observations. For example, suppose you favored installing a traffic light at a dangerous pedestrian crossing. You might give an account of a near miss you had at the crossing. Better yet, you could spend a couple of afternoons at the intersection counting cars, observing pedestrian behavior, taking note of dangerous situations, timing how long it takes to cross the street, and so forth. These could then become persuasive data for an argument like the one that follows.

> The intersection at 5th and Montgomery is particularly dangerous. Traffic volume on Montgomery is so heavy that pedestrians almost never find a comfortable break in the flow of cars. On April 29, I watched fifty-seven pedestrians cross this intersection. Not once did cars stop in both directions before the pedestrian stepped off the sidewalk onto the street. Typically, the pedestrian had to move into the street, start tentatively to cross, and wait until a car finally stopped. On fifteen occasions, pedestrians had to stop halfway across the street, with cars speeding by in both directions, waiting for cars in the far lanes to stop before they could complete their crossing.

USING EVIDENCE FROM INTERVIEWS, SURVEYS, AND QUESTIONNAIRES

In addition to direct observations, you can gather evidence by conducting interviews, taking surveys, or passing out questionnaires.

Conducting Interviews

Interviewing people is a useful way not only to gather expert testimony and important data, but also to learn about alternative views. To conduct an effective interview, you must first have a clear sense of purpose: Why are you interviewing the person, and what information is he or she uniquely able to provide? In turn, you need to be professional and courteous.

It's crucial that you write out all questions you intend to ask beforehand, making sure that every question is related to the purpose of your interview. (Of course, be ready to move in unexpected directions if the interview opens up new territory.) Find out as much as possible about the interviewee before the interview. Your knowledge of his or her background will help establish your credibility and build a bridge between you and your source. Be punctual and respectful of your interviewee's time.

In most cases, it is best to present yourself as a listener seeking clarity on an issue rather than as an advocate of a particular position. Except in rare cases, it is a mistake to enter into argument with your interviewee, or to indicate through body language or tone of voice an antagonism toward his or her position. During the interview, play the believing role. Save the doubting role for later, when you are looking over your notes. While conducting the interview, plan either to tape it (in which case you must ask the interviewee's permission) or to take good notes. Immediately after the interview, while your memory is fresh, rewrite your notes more fully and completely.

When you use interview data in your own writing, put quotation marks around any direct quotations. Except when unusual circumstances might require anonymity, identify your source by name and indicate his or her title or credentials—whatever will convince the reader that this person's remarks are to be taken seriously. Here is how one student used interview data to support an argument against carpeting dorm rooms.

> Finally, university-provided carpets will be too expensive. According to Robert Bothell, Assistant Director of Housing Services, the cost will be $300 per room for the carpet and installation. The university would also have to purchase more vacuum cleaners for the students to use. Altogether, Bothell estimated the cost of carpets to be close to $100,000 for the whole campus. [Here the student writer uses interview data from Robert Bothell as evidence that university-provided carpets will be too expensive. As Assistant Director of Housing Services, Bothell has the credentials to be an authoritative source on these costs.]

Using Surveys or Questionnaires

Still another form of field research data can come from surveys or questionnaires. Sometimes an informal poll of your classmates can supply evidence persuasive to a reader. One of our students, in an argument supporting public transportation, asked every rider on her bus one morning the following two questions:

Do you enjoy riding the bus more than commuting by car? If so, why?

She was able to use her data in the following paragraph:

Last week I polled forty-eight people riding the bus between Bellevue and Seattle. Eighty percent said they enjoyed riding the bus more than commuting by car, while 20 percent preferred the car. Those who enjoyed the bus cited the following reasons in this order of preference: It saved them the hassle of driving in traffic; it gave them time to relax and unwind; it was cheaper than paying for gas and parking; it saved them time.

More formal research can be done through developing and distributing questionnaires. Developing a good questionnaire is a task of sufficient complexity that some academic disciplines devote whole courses to the topic. In general, problems with questionnaires arise when the questions are confusing or when response categories don't allow the respondent enough flexibility of choices. If you are writing an argument that depends on an elaborate questionnaire, consider checking out a book from your library on questionnaire design. A simple questionnaire, however, can be designed without formal training. Type it neatly so that it looks clean, uncluttered, and easy to complete. At the head of the questionnaire you should explain its purpose. Your tone should be courteous and, if possible, you should offer the reader some motivation to complete the questionnaire.

INEFFECTIVE EXPLANATION FOR QUESTIONNAIRE

The following questionnaire is very important for my research. I need it back by Tuesday, January 19, so please fill it out as soon as you get it. Thanks. [doesn't explain purpose; reasons for questionnaire are stated in terms of writer's needs, not audience's need]

MORE EFFECTIVE EXPLANATION

This questionnaire is aimed at improving the quality of Dickenson Library for students and staff. It should take no more than three or four minutes of your time and gives you an opportunity to say what you presently like and don't like about the library. Of course, your responses will be kept anonymous. To enable a timely report to the library staff, please return the questionnaire by Tuesday, January 19. Thank you very much. [purpose is clear; respondents see how filling out questionnaire may benefit them]

When you pass out questionnaires, you should seek a random distribution so that any person in your target population has an equal chance of being selected. Surveys lose their persuasiveness if the respondents are unrepresentative of the total population you intended to survey. For example, if your library questionnaire went only to dorm residents, then you wouldn't know how commuting students feel about the library.

USING EVIDENCE FROM READING

Although you can base some arguments on evidence from personal experience or from questionnaires and interviews, most arguments require research evidence gleaned from reading: books, magazines, journals, newspapers, government documents, computerized data banks, Internet sources, chat groups, specialized encyclopedias and almanacs, corporate bulletins, and so forth. How to find such data; how to incorporate it into your own writing through summary, paraphrase, and quotation; and how to cite it and document it are treated in detail in Part IV of this text (Chapters 16 and 17).

When you use research data from reading, it often takes one or more of the following forms: facts and examples, summaries of research studies, and testimony.

Facts and Examples

A common way to incorporate evidence from reading is to cite facts and examples. Here is how one student writer argues that plastic food packaging and styrofoam cups aren't necessarily damaging to the environment.

> It's politically correct today to scorn plastic food wrapping and styrofoam cups. But in the long run these containers may actually help the environment. According to Tierney (1996), a typical household in countries that don't use plastic food wrapping produces one-third more garbage from food spoilage than do U.S. households. Those plastic wrappers on foods allow us to buy foods in small quantities and keep them sterile until use. Tierney also claims that plastic packaging requires far less energy to produce than does paper or cardboard and is lighter to transport (27). Similarly, he claims that the energy costs of producing a ceramic coffee mug and of washing it after each use make it less environmentally friendly than throwaway styrofoam cups (44).

Knowing that experts can disagree about what is a "fact," this writer attributes her evidence to Tierney ("Tierney claims . . .") rather than stating Tierney's claims baldly as facts and simply citing him in parentheses. (She will later provide complete bibliographic information about the Tierney source in her "Works Cited" list; see Chapter 17.)

Summaries of Research

An argument can often be supported by summarizing or quoting summary statements from research studies. Here is how a student writer used a summary statement to support his opposition to mandatory helmet laws for motorcycle riders:

> However, a helmet won't protect against head injury when one is traveling at normal traffic speeds. According to a U.S. Department of Transportation study, "There is no evidence that any helmet thus far, regardless of cost or design, is capable of rejecting impact stress above 13 mph" ("Head Injuries" 8).

Testimony

Research data can also take the form of *testimony,* an expert's opinion that you cite to help bolster your case. Testimony, which we might call secondhand evidence, is often blended with other kinds of data. Using testimony is particularly common wherever laypersons cannot be expected to be experts; thus, you might cite an authority on the technical feasibility of cold fusion, the effects of alcohol on fetal tissue development, or the causes of a recent airplane crash. Here is how a student writer used testimony to bolster an argument on global warming.

> We can't afford to wait any longer before taking action against global warming. At a recent Senate hearing of the Subcommittee on Environmental Pollution, Senator Chafee warned: "There is a very real possibility that man—through ignorance or indifference or both—is irreversibly altering the ability of our atmosphere to [support] life" (qtd. in Begley 64). At this same hearing, Robert Watson of the National Aeronautics and Space Administration (which monitors the upper atmosphere) claimed: "Global warming is inevitable—it's only a question of magnitude and time" (qtd. in Begley 66).

Here the writer uses no factual or statistical data that global warming is occurring; rather, she cites the testimony of experts.

USING NUMERICAL DATA AND STATISTICS

Among the most pervasive kinds of evidence in modern arguments are numerical data and statistics. Many of us, however, are understandably mistrustful of numerical data. "There are three kinds of lies," we have all heard: "lies, damned lies, and statistics."

Those who gather, use, and analyze numerical data have their own language for degrees of data manipulation. *Teasing* and *tweaking* data are usually legitimate attempts to portray data in a better light; *massaging* data may involve a bit of subterfuge but is still within acceptable limits. When the line is crossed and manipulation turns into outright, conscious misrepresentation, however, we say the data have been *cooked*—an unsavory fate for data and people alike. If we are to use data responsibly and protect ourselves from others' abuses of them, it's important for us to understand how to analyze them.

In this section, we explain basic forms of graphic representations—tables, line graphs, bar graphs, and pie charts—and then examine ways to use numerical data both responsibly and persuasively.

Representing Numbers in Tables, Graphs, and Charts

One of the simplest means for presenting numerical data to your audience is in a table. Halfway between a picture and a list, a *table* presents numerical data in columns (vertical groupings) and rows (horizontal groupings), thereby allowing us to see relationships relatively quickly.

The following table (Figure 6.1) is intended to help people perceive how much progress a large southwestern university has made toward diversifying its faculty during a given decade. It offers snapshots of the faculty's ethnic composition in 1984 and again in 1994, followed by a summary of the changes that took place in between.

You read tables in two directions: from the top down and from left to right. The title of the table is usually at the top. In this case, the title "Southwest State University: An Historical Review of Minority Students, Faculty, and Staff" tells us the most general content of the table—the change over time of the ethnic makeup of the university community. Directly below, we encounter the subtitle "Full-Time Faculty by Tenure Status: Fall 1984 and Fall 1994." This subtitle tells us which of the three components of the university community identified in the title—SSU faculty—is the subject of the table and the principle means—tenure status and time—used to organize the table's contents.

Continuing down the table, in the first row of categories beneath the labels we find a breakdown of the major ethnic groups ("American Indian," "Asian American," etc.) comprising SSU's faculty. We then move to the top of the far left column, where we find "Tenure Status." There are three different variations of tenure status: "Tenured," "On Track to Be Tenured" ("on track" faculty typically are eligible to become tenured after six years of successful teaching and scholarship at the institution), or "Not on Track"—which includes adjunct faculty who were hired with no expectation of a long-term contractual commitment from the university.

In the far left of the column immediately below "Tenure Status" we find the data broken down into "1984 Total," "1994 Total," and "10-Year % Change." Reading across each row, we see a series of numbers telling us the number of people in each category and the percent of the whole that number represents. In this case,

Southwest State University: A Historical Review of Minority
Students, Faculty, and Staff
Full-Time Faculty by Tenure Status, Fall 1984 and Fall 1994

Tenure Status	Native American		Asian American		African American		Hispanic		White		Total		Minority	
	No.	%	No.	%	No.	%	No.	%	No.	%	No.	%	No.	%
1984 Total	9	0.6	64	4.2	21	1.4	44	2.9	1,371	90.9	1,509	100.0	138	9.1
Tenured	6	0.6	30	3.2	10	1.1	24	2.6	867	92.5	937	100.0	70	7.5
On track	2	0.7	15	5.5	5	1.8	13	4.7	240	87.3	275	100.0	35	12.7
Not on track	1	0.3	19	6.4	6	2.0	7	2.4	264	88.9	297	100.0	33	11.1
1994 Total	15	0.8	137	7.5	37	2.0	102	5.6	1,533	84.0	1,824	100.0	291	16.0
Tenured	6	0.5	54	4.9	15	1.4	49	4.5	973	88.7	1,097	100.0	124	11.3
On track	8	2.5	32	9.9	11	3.4	39	12.1	232	72.0	322	100.0	90	28.0
Not on track	1	0.2	51	12.6	11	2.7	14	3.5	328	81.0	405	100.0	77	19.0
10-Year % Change	6	66.7	73	114.1	16	76.2	58	131.8	162	11.8	315	20.9	153	110.9
Tenured	0	0.0	24	80.0	5	50.0	25	104.2	106	12.2	160	17.1	54	77.1
On track	6	300.0	17	113.3	6	120.0	26	200.0	-8	-3.3	47	17.1	55	157.1
Not on track	0	0.0	32	168.4	5	83.3	7	100.0	64	24.2	108	36.4	44	133.3

Source: SSU Office of Institutional Analysis

FIGURE 6.1   A table showing relationships among numerical data

the whole is the number in the "Total" column on the right. Thus, in 1984 there were six tenured American Indian faculty, representing .6 percent of the 937 tenured faculty in the university.

When you read a table, avoid the temptation simply to plunge into all the numbers. After you've read the title and headings to make basic sense of what the table is telling you, try randomly selecting several numbers in the table and saying aloud what those numbers "mean" to be sure you understand what the table is really about.

Line Graphs

At first glance, line graphs seem significantly simpler to read than tables. Sometimes we literally see the significance of a line graph at a glance. A *line graph* achieves this simplicity by converting numerical data into a series of points on an imaginary grid created by horizontal and vertical axes, and then by connecting those points. The resulting line gives us a picture of the relationship between whatever is represented on the horizontal (X) axis and whatever is represented on the vertical (Y) axis. Although they are extremely economical, graphs can't convey the same richness of information that tables can. They are most useful when your focus is on a single relationship.

To illustrate how graphs work, consider Figure 6.2, which contains a graphic representation of a learning curve for assembly-line workers.

To determine what this graphic is telling you, you must first clarify what's represented on the two axes. In this case, the X axis represents "Units Produced" while the Y axis represents "Average Labor Hours Required." The first point on the X axis indicates that the number of hours a worker requires to produce the first unit is 100. By the time a worker gets to the 20th unit, however, the number of hours required is down to 63. By the 140th unit, production time is down to only 48 hours.

So what does this graph tell us? How would we generally characterize the nature of the relationship between the X axis and the Y axis? Generally, we could say that X and Y are "inversely related": as X gets greater, Y gets smaller. That general description will hold for all line graphs that look like this one, sloping downward from left to right.

In simple English, we might translate this relationship to something like the following: "As you produce more units of anything, you learn how to produce those units more efficiently and thus spend less time producing each one." But note that the line's slope (its angle of ascent or descent) flattens out as it moves to the right, suggesting that over time the *rate* at which efficiency improves slows down. In the language of data analysis, the flattened slope indicates that changes in Y are less and less "sensitive" to changes in X. At some point, presumably, you would see no further increases in efficiency and the learning curve would be perfectly parallel to the X axis, meaning that Y is no longer sensitive to X.

You can apply the "truth" of this graph to your own situation. Any time you begin learning a new subject, you spend a great deal of time acquiring relatively small amounts of knowledge. The less efficient you are at acquiring knowledge

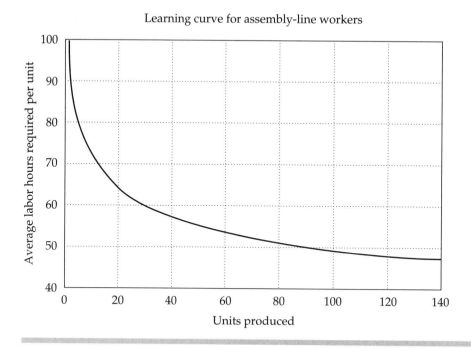

FIGURE 6.2   A graph depicting a dynamic relationship between two variables

initially, the "steeper" the learning curve will be for you. Over time, as you become more familiar with the subject—its terms and basic concepts—you can more quickly build on your base of knowledge and "flatten" the learning curve.

One important advantage of expressing this relationship graphically is that you can see it dynamically, changing at different rates over time. Expressing that same relationship as a numerical average might lead you to distort it. If, for example, you chose to "freeze" the line early in its descent and ask, "How many units on average have you produced?" you would come up with a very low number. Assuming that the purpose of asking the question in the first place is to project the future cost of producing units, an average would never be as helpful as a graph. The graph not only shows the relationship between two variables up to a given point, it can also indicate the probable future direction of that relationship.

Bar Graphs

Bar graphs use bars of varying length and width, extending either horizontally or vertically, to contrast two or more quantities. As with any graphic presentation, you should read from the top down, being especially careful to note the graph's title. Most bar graphs also have *legends,* or explanations of how to read the graph. Bars are typically shaded in various hues, crosshatched, left clear, or filled in with slanting lines, to differentiate among the quantities or items being compared. The legend identifies what quantity or item each bar represents.

The bar graph in Figure 6.3 is from the national newspaper, *USA Today,* well known for its extensive use of graphics as a means of simplifying complex concepts for a broad audience. The title tells us that the purpose of the graph is to illustrate "How Congress could solve the deficit problem in seven years by holding spending to the projected 3% inflation rate" instead of spending at the rate projected by the Congressional Budget Office (CBO). The legend, in turn, shows us which quantity each of the bars in the graph represents: The lightest bar represents revenues, the dark bar represents the CBO's projected spending, and the medium colored bar represents spending at the 3 percent inflation rate.

Again, reading across the horizontal axis, we find the *independent variable,* time—in this case a year-by-year comparison of the three quantities from 1995 to 2002. On the Y axis, we find the *dependent variable,* dollars received and expended. As we move from left to right, the revenue bar and the 3 percent growth bar gradually inch closer together, until by 2002 they are exactly equal, meaning that revenue and spending would be balanced. The black middle bar, the CBO's estimated spending, meanwhile, inches past the other two bars until finally it represents a significant imbalance between revenue and spending.

The power of this visual is that it takes a particularly dodgy set of figures and gives them the certitude of an accomplished fact. National revenue and spending figures are notoriously difficult to project. Both can be markedly affected by a number of economic factors over which we have very limited control. And the further out we make those projections, the more problematic they become. Eight

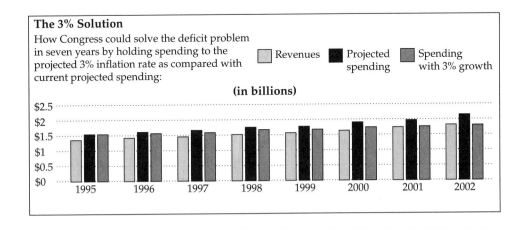

FIGURE 6.3   A bar graph that simplifies a complex concept
Sources: Congressional Budget Office.

years, in the world of macroeconomics, is an extraordinarily long time to project into the future. But cast into a series of bars, each one only slightly different from the previous one, the change seems not only plausible, but almost inevitable. Hey, that 3 percent solution is a great idea!

Pie Charts

Pie charts, as their name suggests, depict different percentages of a total (the pie) in the form of slices. At tax time, pie charts are a favorite way of depicting all the different places that your tax dollars go. If your main point is to demonstrate that a particular portion of a whole is disproportionately large—perhaps you're arguing that too many of our tax dollars are spent on Medicaid or defense—the pie chart can demonstrate that at a glance. (Conversely, of course, it can also demonstrate that some other part of the whole is undersized relative to other shares.) The effectiveness of pie charts diminishes as we add more slices. In most cases, you'll begin to confuse readers if you include more than five or six "slices."

Figure 6.4 shows a pie chart from *USA Today* that, in combination with a line graph, effectively illustrates the size of three parts relative to one another. Note how the editors of *USA Today* chose to use a line graph to plot the growth in collections of child support payments from 1984 to 1993. The impressive upward slope of the line nicely underscores the editors' point that child support collections nearly quadrupled during that time period. They use a line graph to do what line graphs do best—illustrate change over time for a given dependent variable. But when they wanted to depict a static relationship, the editors naturally chose a pie chart to show that a great deal of support is still owed: In 1989, only 51 percent of children granted child support in a divorce settlement received their full amount, while 25 percent received nothing. (In place of a legend, the editors simply identify what each slice of the pie represents within the graph itself.)

Using Graphics for Effect

Any time we present numerical data pictorially, the potential for enhancing the rhetorical presence of our argument, or of manipulating our audience outright, increases markedly. By *presence,* we mean the immediacy and impact of our material. For example, raw numbers and statistics, in large doses, are apt to dull people's minds and perplex them. But numbers turned into pictures are very immediate. Graphs, charts, and tables help an audience see at a glance what long strings of statistics can only hint at.

We can have markedly different effects on our audience according to how we design and construct a graphic. For example, by coloring one variable prominently and enlarging it slightly, a graphic artist can greatly distort the importance of that variable. Although such depictions may carry warnings that they are "not to scale," the visual impact is often more memorable than the warning.

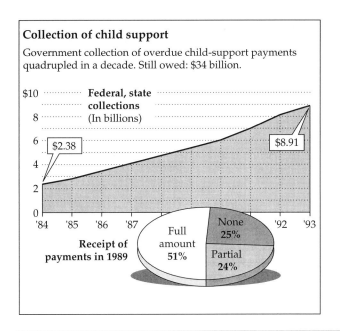

FIGURE 6.4 Pie chart showing relative sizes of three parts

Sources: Office of Child Support Enforcement; Census Bureau. By Cliff Vancura, USA TODAY.

One of the subtlest ways of controlling an audience's perception of a numerical relationship is the way you construct the grids on the X/Y axes (the X axis being horizontal, the Y axis vertical) of a line graph. Consider, for example, the graph in Figure 6.5 depicting the monthly net profits of an ice cream sandwich retailer. If you look at this graph, you'd think that the net profits of "Bite O' Heaven" were themselves shooting heavenward. But if you were considering investing in an ice cream sandwich franchise yourself, you would want to consider how the graph was constructed. Note the quantity assigned to each square on the grid. Although the graph does represent the correct quantities, the designer's choice of increments leads to a wildly inflated depiction of success. If the "Bite O' Heaven" folks had chosen a larger increment for each square on the vertical axis—say, $5,000 instead of $1,000—the company's rise in profitability would look like the graph in Figure 6.6. One can easily distort or overstate a rate of change on a graph by consciously selecting the quantities assigned to each scale unit on the horizontal or vertical axis.

Another way to create a rhetorical effect with a line graph is to vary the scope of time it covers. Note that the two graphs just presented cover net sales from January through August. What do you think the sales figures for this company might typically be from September through December?

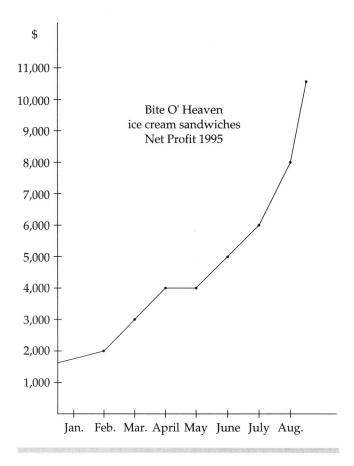

FIGURE 6.5　A line graph that distorts the data

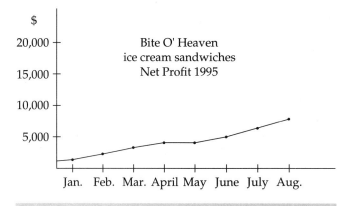

FIGURE 6.6　A line graph that more accurately depicts data

FOR CLASS DISCUSSION

In small groups, create a line graph for the net profits of the Bite O' Heaven company for a whole year based on your best estimates of when people are most apt to buy ice cream sandwiches. Then draw graphs of net profits, quarter by quarter, over a three-year period to represent the following conditions:

1. The Bite O' Heaven company maintains a stable market share with no increase or decrease in the rate of profits over the three years.

2. The Bite O' Heaven company increases its market share, with each year more profitable than the preceding one.

3. The Bite O' Heaven company loses market share with each year leaner than the previous one.

Using Numbers Strategically

As we have suggested, your choice and design of a graphic can markedly affect your audience's perception of your subject. But you can also influence your audience through the kinds of numbers you use: raw numbers versus percentages; or raw numbers versus "adjusted" numbers (for example, wages "adjusted for inflation"); or a statistical presentation versus a narrative one. The choice always depends on the audience you're addressing and the purpose you want to achieve.

One of the most common choices writers have to make is between citing raw numbers or citing percentages or rates. In some cases, for example, a raw number will be more persuasive than a percentage. If you were to say that the cost of attending a state college will increase at a rate 15 percent greater than the Consumer Price Index over the next decade, most audiences would be lost—few would know how to translate that number into terms they could understand. But if you were to say that in the year 2007, the cost of attending a state college for one year will be about $21,000, you would surely grab your audience's attention. So, if you were a financial planner trying to talk a young couple into saving money for their children's college education, you would be more prone to use the raw number rather than the percent increase. But if you were a college administrator trying to play down the increasing costs of college to a hostile legislator, you might well use the percentage increase rather than the raw number.

In turn, how you state raw numbers can markedly increase or decrease their impact on an audience. For example, to say that newspapers consume huge amounts of wood pulp is mildly interesting. To say that publication of the *New York Times* requires 248 million tons of pulp each year is even more impressive. To say that publication of just one Sunday edition of the *New York Times* requires the cutting of 75,000 trees is mind boggling. Again, translate the number into what is most meaningful to your audience and the impact you wish to have on that audience.

Finally, in using numbers you often have a choice of presenting *indexed* or *adjusted* numbers as opposed to simple raw numbers. In the case of economic data, this difference can be particularly important. For example, in the 1996 presidential debates, Republican supporters suggested that President Clinton had signed the "largest tax increase in history" into law. Clinton supporters retorted that if adjustments were made for inflation, the tax increase was in fact smaller than one signed into law by Republican President Bush. Because of the extremely high rates of inflation during the 1980s, any economic data from that decade or prior to it should be adjusted for inflation in making comparisons to present-day dollar values.

 FOR CLASS DISCUSSION

A recent proposal to build a new ballpark in Seattle, Washington yielded a wide range of statistical arguments. All of the following statements are reasonably faithful to the same facts:

- The ballpark would be paid for by raising the sales tax from 8.2 percent to 8.3 percent over a twenty-year period.
- The sales tax increase is one-tenth of 1 percent.
- This increase represents an average of $7.50 per person per year—about the price of a movie ticket.
- This increase represents $750 per five-person family over the twenty-year period of the tax.
- For a family building a new home in the Seattle area, this tax will increase building costs by $200.
- This is a $250 million tax increase for the residents of the Seattle area.

How would you describe the costs of the proposed ballpark if you opposed the proposal? How would you describe the costs if you supported the proposal?

WHAT TO DO WHEN THE EXPERTS DISAGREE

When you research a complex issue, do you seek only to support your own position on an issue? Or do you seek clarification and deepening of understanding? We believe that clarification, which requires an empathic consideration of alternative views, is the worthier goal. We recommend that you use your research time to seek the truth about your issue, not simply to justify your position on that issue. But in making this recommendation, we also acknowledge that clarification is an elusive goal. In trying honestly to hear alternative views on an issue, you may well deepen rather than lessen your confusion. Let's pause to reflect for a bit on how best to deal with this potential confusion.

Suppose you are writing an argument claiming that the United States should take immediate measures to combat global warming. Early in your search for evidence, you come across the following editorial, which appeared in *USA Today* in June 1986.

Imagine a world like this:

Omaha, Neb., sweats through the worst drought in its history. In July 2030, the mercury hits 100 on 20 days. Crops are wiped out; the Midwest is a dust bowl.

New Orleans is under water. The French Quarter has shut down; the Superdome holds a small lake. The governor says property damage will be in the billions.

Washington, D.C., suffers through its hottest summer—87 days above 90 degrees. Water is rationed; brownouts are routine because utilities can't meet demand for electricity. Federal employees, working half-days in unbearable heat, report an alarming rise in skin cancer across the USA.

Abroad, floods have inundated Bangladesh and Indonesia. The seas are four feet above 1986 levels. The United Nations reports millions will die in famines; shocking climate changes have ruined agriculture.

That sounds far-fetched, but if some scientists' worst fears come true, that could be what our children inherit.

Since the beginning of this century, man has been spewing pollutants into the atmosphere at an ever-increasing rate. Carbon dioxide and chlorofluorocarbons—CFC's—are fouling the air, our life support system. Everything that burns releases carbon dioxide. CFC's are used to make refrigerants, Styrofoam, computer chips, and other products.

In the past century, carbon dioxide in the atmosphere has risen 25 percent. The problem is that carbon dioxide holds in heat, just as the roof of a greenhouse does. That's why the Earth's warming is called the greenhouse effect.

CFC's retain heat, too, and break down the atmosphere's protective layer of ozone. If it is damaged, more of the sun's ultraviolet rays will reach Earth, causing skin cancer and damaging sea life.

Combined with the loss of forests that absorb carbon dioxide, the effects of this pollution could be disastrous. By 2030, Earth's temperature could rise 8 degrees, polar ice caps would melt, weather would change, crops would wilt.

There is growing evidence that these pollutants are reaching ominous levels. At the South Pole, the ozone layer has a "hole" in it—it's been depleted by 40 percent. NASA scientist Robert Watson says: "Global warming is inevitable—it's only a question of magnitude and time."

Some say don't panic, probably nothing will happen. The trouble with that is that we know these pollutants are building, and by the time we are sure of the worst effects, it may be too late. Action is needed, now. The USA must:

—Recognize that global warming may worsen and begin planning responses; more research is needed, too.

—Renew the search for safe, clean alternatives to fossil fuels, nuclear fission, and chlorofluorocarbons.

—Report on the extent of the problem to the world and press for international controls on air pollution.

The possible dimensions of this disaster are too big to just "wait and see." If a runaway train heads for a cliff and the engineer does nothing, the passengers are bound to get hurt. Let's check the brakes before it's too late.

When the students in one of our classes first read this editorial, they found it both persuasive and frightening. The opening scenario of potential disasters— New Orleans under water, unbearable heat, water rationing, floods, ruined agriculture, "alarming rise in skin cancer"—scared the dickens out of many readers. The powerful effect of the opening scenario was increased by the editorial's subsequent use of scientific data: carbon dioxide has increased 25 percent, the ozone layer has been depleted by 40 percent, a NASA scientist says that "[g]lobal warming is inevitable . . .," and so forth. Additionally, a plausible cause-and-effect chain explains the approaching disaster: the spewing of pollutants and the cutting down of forests lead to increased CO_2, which traps heat; use of CFC's breaks down the ozone layer, allowing more ultraviolet radiation to reach earth's surface, thereby causing cancer.

Inexperienced students gathering data might be tempted to quote this article. Unwittingly, they might even distort the article slightly by writing something like this:

> According to *USA Today,* our civilization is on a train ride to disaster unless we put on the brakes. If global warming continues on its present course, by the year 2030, New Orleans will be under water, crops will be wiped out by droughts, . . . [and so forth].

But a more careful reading of the *USA Today* piece suggests just how misguided this summary is. First of all, the article is couched in "could's" and "might's." If we read carefully, we see that the opening scenario isn't represented as factual, inevitable, or even likely. Rather, it is represented as the "worst fears" of "some scientists." Near the end of the editorial we learn that "[s]ome say don't panic" but we aren't told whether these "some" are respectable scientists, carefree politicians, crackpots, or what. But the most puzzling aspect of this editorial is the gap between the alarming worst-case scenario at the beginning of the editorial and the tepid recommendations at the end. The final "call for action" calls for no real action at all. Recommendations 1 and 3 call for more research and for "international controls on air pollution"—nicely vague terms that create little reader discomfort. The second recommendation—renew the search for safe alternatives—reveals the writer's comfortable American optimism that scientists will find a way out of the dilemma without causing Americans any real distress. (A curious item in Recommendation 2 is the sandwiching of "nuclear fission" between "fossil fuels" and "chlorofluorocarbons." Nuclear fission is *not* a cause of the greenhouse effect and may be a plausible alternative energy source in our effort to combat global warming. But since nuclear power poses other environmental dangers, the writer tosses it in as one of the enemies.) If the "possible dimensions of this disaster" are as great as the opening scenario leads us to believe, then perhaps wrenching changes in our economy are needed to cut down our dependence on fossil fuels.

But what is the actual truth here? How serious is the greenhouse effect and what should the United States do about it? A search for the truth involves us in the sequence of reading strategies suggested in Chapter 2, "Reading Arguments": (1) reading as a believer; (2) reading as a doubter; (3) seeking out alternative views and asking why the various sides disagree with each other; and (4) evaluating the various positions. When our students applied this strategy to the greenhouse effect, they discovered an unsettling uncertainty among scientists about the facts of the case combined with complex disagreements over values. In your search for clarity, what do you do when the experts disagree?

Coping with Uncertainty

Coping with disagreement among experts is a skill experienced arguers must develop. If there were no disagreements, of course, there would be no need for argument. It is important to realize that experts can look at the same data, can analyze the same arguments, can listen to the same authorities, and still reach different conclusions. Seldom will one expert's argument triumph over another's in a field of dissenting claims. More often, one expert's argument will modify another's and in turn will be modified by yet another. Your own expertise is not a function of your ability to choose the "right" argument, but of your ability to listen to alternative viewpoints, to understand why people disagree, and to synthesize your own argument from those disagreements.

Here briefly is our analysis of some of the disagreements about the greenhouse effect.

Questions of Fact

At the heart of the controversy is the question "How serious is the greenhouse effect?" On the basis of our own research, we discovered that scientists agree on one fact: The amount of carbon dioxide in the earth's atmosphere has increased 7 percent since accurate measurements were first taken during the International Geophysical Year 1957/58. Additionally, scientists seem agreed that the percentage of carbon dioxide has increased steadily since the start of the Industrial Revolution in the 1860s. The statement in the *USA Today* editorial that carbon dioxide has increased by 25 percent is generally accepted by scientists as an accurate estimate of the total increase since 1860.

Where scientists disagree is on the projected effect of this increase. Predictions of global warming are derived from computer models, none of which seems able to encompass all the factors that contribute to global climate, particularly ocean currents and the movements of air masses above the oceans. Because of the enormous complexity of these factors, projections about the future differ considerably from scientist to scientist. *USA Today* took one of the worst-case projections.

Questions of Value

There is also widespread disagreement on what actions the United States or other countries should take in response to the potential warming of the earth. In general, these disputes stem from disagreements about value. In particular, participants in the conversation give different answers to the following questions:

1. In the face of uncertain threat, do we react as if the threat were definite or do we wait and see? If we wait and see, will we be inviting disaster?

2. How much faith can we place in science and technology? Some people, arguing that necessity is the mother of invention, assume that scientists will get us out of this mess. Others believe that technofixes are no longer possible.

3. How much change in our way of life can we tolerate? What, for example, would be the consequences to our economy and to our standard of living if we waged an all-out war on global warming by making drastic reductions, say, in our use of carbon fuels? To what extent are we willing to give up the benefits of industrialization?

4. How much economic disruption can we expect other nations to tolerate? What worldwide economic forces, for example, are making it profitable to cut down and burn tropical rain forests? What would happen to the economies of tropical countries if international controls suddenly prevented further destruction of rain forests? What changes in our own economy would have to take place?

Our whole point here is that the problem of global warming is interwoven into a gigantic web of other problems and issues. One of the benefits you gain from researching a complex technical and value-laden issue such as global warming is learning how to cope with ambiguity.

What advice can we give, therefore, when the experts disagree? Here is the strategy we tend to use. First, we try to ferret out the facts that all sides agree on. These facts give us a starting place on which to build an analysis. In the greenhouse controversy, the fact that all sides agree that the amount of CO_2 in the atmosphere has increased by 25 percent and that this amount increases the percentage of infrared radiation absorbed in the atmosphere suggests that there is scientific cause for concern.

Second, we try to determine if there is a majority position among experts. Sometimes dissenting voices stem from a small but prolific group of persons on the fringe. Our instincts are to trust the majority opinions of experts, even though we realize that revolutions in scientific thought almost always start with minority groups. In the case of the greenhouse effect, our own research suggests that the majority of scientists are cautiously concerned but not predicting doomsday. There seems to be a general consensus that increased greenhouse gases will contribute to global warming but how much and how soon, they won't say.

Third, we try as much as possible to focus, not on the testimony of experts, but on the data the experts use in their testimony. In other words, we try to learn as much as possible about the scientific or technical problem and immerse ourselves in the raw data. Doing so in the case of the greenhouse effect helped us appreciate the problems of creating computer models of global climate and especially of gathering data about oceanic impact on climate.

Finally, we try to determine our own position on the values issues at stake because, inescapably, these values influence the position we ultimately take. For example, the authors of this text tend to be pessimistic about technofixes for most environmental problems. We doubt that scientists will solve the problem of greenhouse gases either through finding alternatives to petrocarbon fuels or by discovering ways to eliminate or counteract greenhouse gases. We also tend not to be risk-takers on environmental matters. Thus we prefer to take vigorous action now to slow the increase of greenhouse gases rather than take a wait-and-see attitude. The conclusion of our own research, then, is that the *USA Today* editorial is irresponsible in two ways: It uses unfair scare tactics in the opening scenario by overstating the fears of most scientists, yet in its conclusion it doesn't call for enough disruption of our present way of life.

What we have attempted to do in the previous section is show you how we try to reach a responsible position in the face of uncertainty. We cannot claim that our position is the right one. We can only claim that it is a reasonable one and a responsible one—responsible to our own understanding of the facts and to our own declaration of values.

WRITING YOUR OWN ARGUMENT: USING EVIDENCE PERSUASIVELY

Once you have arrived at a position on an issue, often after having written a draft that enables you to explore and clarify your own views, you need to select the best evidence possible and to use it persuasively. Whether your evidence comes from research or from personal experience, the following guidelines may be helpful.

When Possible, Select Your Data from Sources Your Reader Trusts

Other things being equal, choose data from sources you think your reader will trust. After immersing yourself in an issue, you will get a sense of who the participants in a conversation are and what their reputations tend to be. One needs to know the political biases of sources and the extent to which a source has a financial or personal investment in the outcome of a controversy. When the greenhouse controversy first struck the national consciousness, two prolific writers on the subject were Carl Sagan and Dixie Lee Ray, both of whom are now deceased. Both writers held Ph.D. degrees in science and both had national reputations for speaking out in the popular press on technical and scientific issues. Carl Sagan, however, was an environmentalist while Dixie Lee Ray tended to support business and industry. To some audiences, neither of these writers were as persuasive as more cautious and less visible scientists who publish primarily in scientific journals. Similarly, citing a conservative magazine such as *Reader's Digest* is apt to be ineffective to liberal audiences, just as citing a Sierra Club publication would be ineffective to conservatives.

Increase Persuasiveness of Factual Data by Ensuring Recency, Representativeness, and Sufficiency

Other things being equal, choose data that are recent, representative, and sufficient. The more your data meet these criteria, the more persuasive they are.

Recency: Although some timeless issues don't depend on recent evidence, most issues, especially those related to science and technology or to current political and economic issues, depend on up-to-date information. Make sure your supporting evidence is the most recent you can find.

Representativeness: Supporting examples are more persuasive when the audience believes they are typical examples instead of extreme cases or rare occurrences. Many arguments against pornography, for example, use violent pornography or child pornography as evidence, even though these are extreme cases quite different from the erotica associated, say, with *Playboy*. These nonrepresentative examples are ineffective if one's purpose is to include such publications as *Playboy* in the category of pornography. Assuring representativeness is an especially important concern of statisticians, who seek random samples to avoid bias toward one point of view. Seeking representative examples helps you guard against selective use of data—starting with a claim and then choosing only those data that support it, instead of letting the claim grow out of a careful consideration of all the data.

Sufficiency: One of the most common reasoning fallacies, called *hasty generalization* (see Appendix 1), occurs when a person leaps to a sweeping generalization based on only one or two instances. The criterion of sufficiency (which means having enough examples to justify your point) helps you guard against hasty generalization. The key here isn't to cite every possible example, but to convince your audience that the examples you have cited don't exhaust your whole supply. In our experience, lack of sufficiency occurs frequently in personal experience arguments. The student praised earlier for her personal experience data in an argument about rural schools suffers from this problem in the following paragraph:

My primary reason for supporting the small, rural grade schools over the larger urban schools is the amount of learning that occurs. I am my own proof. I was the only member of my grade from the third to the eighth grade at Fergus Grade School. I relished the privilege of being able to work on two chapters of math, instead of one, especially if I enjoyed the subject. Upon graduation from the eighth grade, I attended a large high school and discovered that I had a better background than students from larger grade schools. I got straight A's.

The problem here is that the writer's one example—herself—isn't sufficient for supporting the claim that rural schools provide quality learning. To support that claim, she would need either more examples or statistical data about the later achievements of students who attended rural grade schools.

In Citing Evidence, Distinguish Fact from Inference or Opinion

In citing research data, you should be careful to distinguish facts from inferences or opinions. A *fact* is a noncontroversial piece of data that is verifiable through observation or through appeal to communally accepted authorities. Although the distinction between a fact and an inference is a fuzzy one philosophically, at a pragmatic level all of the following can loosely be classified as facts.

The Declaration of Independence was signed in 1776.

An earthquake took place in San Francisco on the opening day of the World Series in 1989.

The amount of carbon dioxide in the atmosphere has increased by 7 percent since 1955.

An *inference,* on the other hand, is an interpretation or explanation of the facts that may be reasonably doubted. This distinction is important because, when reading as a doubter, you often call into question a writer's inferences. If you treat these inferences as facts, you are apt to cite them as facts in your own arguments, thereby opening yourself up to easy rebuttal. For the most part, inferences should be handled as testimony rather than as fact.

WEAK: Flohn informs us that the warming of the atmosphere will lead to damaging droughts by the year 2035. [treats Flohn's inference as a fact about global warming]

BETTER: Flohn interprets the data pessimistically. He believes that the warming of the atmosphere will lead to damaging droughts by the year 2035. [makes it clear that Flohn's view is an inference, not a fact]

To Use Evidence Persuasively, Position It Effectively

Whenever possible, place evidence favorable to your point in rhetorically strong positions in your essay; tuck opposing evidence into rhetorically inconspicuous places. Consider the case of Professor Nutt, who was asked to write a letter of recommendation for Elliot Weasel for a management trainee position at a bank. Professor Nutt remembered Weasel with mixed emotions. On the one hand, Weasel was the most brilliant student Nutt had ever had in class—an excellent mathematical mind, creative imagination, strong writing skills. On the other hand, Weasel was slovenly, rude, irresponsible, and moody. In the first case below, Nutt decides to give Weasel a positive recommendation.

POSITIVE RECOMMENDATION FOR WEASEL

Although Elliot Weasel was somewhat temperamental in my class and occasionally lacked people skills, these problems were the result of brilliance. I am convinced that Weasel is one of the most highly intelligent students I have ever encountered. In fact, in one of my business management classes, he wrote the best term paper I have ever received in five years of teaching management. I gave him an A+ and even learned some new insights from his paper. If he could learn to interact more effectively with others, he would become a superb manager. In sum, I give him a quite high recommendation.

In the next case, Nutt's recommendation is negative.

NEGATIVE RECOMMENDATION FOR WEASEL

Although Elliott Weasel is one of the most intelligent students I have ever encountered, he was somewhat temperamental in my class and occasionally lacked people skills. He would come to class dressed sloppily with unkempt hair and dirty-looking clothes. He also seemed like a loner, was frequently moody, and once refused to participate in a group project. Thus my recommendation of him is mixed. He's highly intelligent and an excellent writer, but I found him rude and hard to like.

Let's analyze the difference between these versions. In the first version, Nutt places the anti-Weasel data in subordinate clauses and phrases and places the pro-Weasel data in main slots, particularly the main clause of the first sentence. The effect is to highlight Weasel's strong points. Because the opening sentence ends with an emphasis on Weasel's brilliance, Nutt brings in additional data to back up the assertion that Weasel is brilliant.

In the second version, Nutt reverses this procedure by putting pro-Weasel data in subordinate positions and highlighting the anti-Weasel data in main clauses. Because the opening sentence ends with an emphasis on Weasel's moodiness and lack of people skills, Nutt brings in additional data to back up these points. Thus through selection of data (deciding which facts to put in and which ones to leave out) and through loading of data into main or subordinate slots in the paragraph, Nutt creates a positive impression in the first version and a negative impression in the second. Although neither version could be regarded as untruthful, neither version tells the "whole truth" either, because the necessity to interpret the data means commitment toward some sort of claim, which necessarily shapes the selection and placement of evidence.

 FOR CLASS DISCUSSION

Suppose that you developed a questionnaire to ascertain students' satisfaction with your college library as a place to study. Suppose further that you got the following responses to one of your questions (numbers in brackets indicate percentage of total respondents who checked each response):

The library provides a quiet place to study.

Strongly agree (10%)

Agree (40%)

Undecided (5%)

Disagree (35%)

Strongly disagree (10%)

Without telling any lies of fact, you can report these data so that they place the current library atmosphere in either favorable or unfavorable light. Working individually or in small groups, use the data provided to complete the following sentences:

There seemed to be considerable satisfaction with the library as a quiet place to study. In response to our questionnaire . . .[complete this sentence by selecting data from the above responses].

Students seem dissatisfied with the noise level of the library. In response to our questionnaire . . .[complete this sentence by selecting data from the above responses].

CONCLUSION

Supporting your reasons with evidence or chains of other reasons is essential if you hope to make your arguments persuasive. As we have seen, evidence includes facts, examples, statistics, testimony, and other forms of data, and it can come from personal experience as well as from reading and research. For many issues, your search for evidence leads you into an ambiguous arena of conflicting views. Adapting to a world where experts disagree requires strategies for sorting out the causes of disagreement and establishing reasonable grounds to justify the claims you finally wish to assert. Learning how to evaluate evidence in your sources and how to use evidence responsibly and persuasively is an important skill that develops gradually. We hope this chapter gives you some helpful groundwork on which to build.

In the next chapters we will consider further strategies for making your arguments as persuasive as possible by turning our attention increasingly toward audience.

 ## WRITING ASSIGNMENTS
FOR CHAPTERS 4–6

The first four writing options that follow are short, skill-building exercises that we call "microthemes." They can be done as overnight out-of-class assignments or as in-class writing or group discussion exercises. These one- or two-paragraph assignments are most successful if approached like games. They are designed to help you learn argumentative "moves" that you can apply later to longer, more formal essays.

The last option is a formal writing assignment that asks you to construct a logical, well-developed argument, putting into practice the principles of structure discussed in Chapters 4–6.

OPTION 1: *A Microtheme that Supports a Reason with Personal Experience Data*
Write a one- or two-paragraph argument in which you support one of the following enthymemes using evidence from personal experience. Most of your microtheme should be devoted to use of personal experience to support the stated reason. However, also include a brief passage supporting the implied warrant for your chosen enthymeme. The opening sentence of your microtheme should be the enthymeme itself, which serves as the thesis statement for your argument.

1. Children should have hobbies because, among other things, hobbies fill up leisure time with enjoyable activity. (Support the stated reason with examples of how hobbies in your life have helped you fill up leisure time with enjoyable activities. Support the warrant by arguing that enjoyable use of leisure time is a good thing for children.)

2. After-school jobs are generally not a good idea for teenagers because they take up too much valuable study time.

3. After-school jobs are beneficial for teenagers because they teach time management.

4. Another reason to oppose a state sales tax is that it is so annoying.

5. *X* (a teacher/professor of your choosing) is an ineffective teacher because, among other things, he (she) doesn't design homework effectively to promote real learning.

6. *X* (a teacher/professor of your choosing) is an outstanding teacher because he (she) generously spends so much time outside of class counseling students with personal problems.

7. Any enthymeme (a claim with a because clause) of your choice that can be supported through personal experience. Clear your enthymeme with your instructor before drafting your microtheme.

OPTION 2: *A Microtheme that Uses Evidence from Research* The purpose of this microtheme is to help you learn how to support reasons with evidence gathered from research. The following presentation of data attempts to simulate the kinds of research evidence one might typically gather on note cards during a research project. (See Chapters 16 and 17 for further advice on incorporating research data into your own writing. For this assignment, assume you are writing for a popular magazine so that you do not need to use academic citations.)

The situation: By means of startling "before and after" photographs of formerly obese people, the commercial diet industry heavily advertises rapid weight loss diets that use liquids and powders or special low-calorie frozen dinners. **Your task:** Drawing on the following data, write a short argument warning people of the hazards of these diets.

Source: Representative Ron Wyden (D–Oregon), chairman of a congressional subcommittee investigating the diet industry:

- Wyden fears that diet programs now include many shoddy companies that use misleading advertisements and provide inadequate medical supervision of their clients.
- "This industry has been built almost overnight on a very shaky foundation."
- "All the evidence says that losing large amounts of weight very fast does more harm than good."
- Wyden believes that the diet industry may need to be federally regulated.

Source: Theodore B. VanItallie, M.D., a founder of the Obesity Research Center at St. Luke's Roosevelt Hospital Center in New York:

- Rapid weight loss systems (such as liquid diets) were originally designed for morbidly obese individuals.
- For people who are only slightly overweight, rapid weight loss can be hazardous.

- When weight loss is too rapid, the body begins using lean muscle mass for fuel instead of excess fat. The result is a serious protein deficiency that can bring on heart irregularities.
- "If more than 25 percent of lost weight is lean body mass, the stage is set not only for early regain of lost weight but for a higher incidence of fatigue, hair loss, skill changes, depression and other undesirable side effects."

Source: Bonnie Blodgett, freelance writer on medical/health issues:

- Rapid weight loss may accelerate formation of gallstones. 179 people are currently suing a major diet company because of gallstone complications while pursuing the company's diet. The company denies responsibility.
- For every five people who start a commercial weight-loss program, only one stays with it long enough to lose a significant amount of weight.
- Up to 90 percent of dieters who lose more than 25 pounds gain it all back within two years.
- Only one in fifty maintains the weight loss for seven years.
- The best way to lose weight is through increased exercise, moderate reduction of calories, and a lifelong change in eating habits.
- Unless one is grossly obese and dieting under a physician's supervision, one should strive to lose no more than 1 or 2 pounds per week.

Source: Philip Kern, M.D., in a study appearing in *The New England Journal of Medicine:*

- Rapid weight loss programs result in the "yo-yo" syndrome—a pattern of compulsive fasting followed by compulsive bingeing.
- This pattern may upset the body's metabolism by producing an enzyme called lipoprotein lipase.
- This protein helps restore fat cells shrunken by dieting.
- It apparently causes formerly fat people to crave fatty foods, thereby promoting regain of lost weight.*

OPTION 3: *A Microtheme that Draws on a Newspaper Story for Data*   Using the following newspaper article, "Deaths Spur New Call for Child-Labor Crackdown," as a source, write a microtheme that could be part of an argument calling for increased enforcement of child-labor laws. Begin your microtheme with the following sentence: "Recent evidence suggests that the child-labor problem is more severe than most people realize." Then select data from the story that focus on the extent and severity of the problem.

---

*Source of these data is Bonnie Blodgett, "The Diet Biz," *Glamour* Jan. 1991, pp. 136ff.

Deaths Spur New Call for
Child-Labor Crackdown

Two children were killed and 4,000 injured on the job in Washington state last year, 1
Department of Labor and Industries officials said yesterday in proposing legislation to protect youngsters in the workplace.

The department investigated 395 of the 4,000 cases and found nearly 44 percent of 2
the employers were violating child-labor laws at the time of a minor's injury.

"Society places a high value on the well-being of children," said Joe Dear, director of 3
the agency. "That should extend to children in the workplace. They're more vulnerable.
They're more susceptible to intimidation by employers, and they're less knowledgeable
about their rights."

It is the third year in a row that the Labor and Industries Department has drafted a bill 4
to strengthen its enforcement capabilities in regulating child-labor laws.

In the past two sessions, the legislation passed the Democrat-controlled House and died 5
in the Republican-dominated Senate.

Attention was focused on child-labor issues in October 1989 when a 14-year-old boy died 6
after being struck by two cars while selling candy door-to-door in the Graham area south of
Tacoma.

The state is seeking an injunction to stop the operation of his employer, Teens for Ac- 7
tion Against Drugs. The state contends the boy was not supervised properly.

The Pierce County prosecutor's office also has filed criminal misdemeanor charges 8
against owners Christopher and Nikita Spice, accusing them of failure to register the company with the state, failure to secure work permits for employees and variances for children under 16, and false advertising.

The other death involved a 12-year-old Oregon boy struck by a car in the Federal Way 9
area. Officials could not provide further information about his case.

In other incidents, a 16-year-old Spanaway boy cut off three fingers while using a table 10
saw, a 15-year-old girl was burned by a motorized iron in Mount Vernon, and a 17-year-old
boy was burned on the face while pouring molten aluminum in a Spokane foundry.

Dear said all were performing duties prohibited by child-labor laws. In its year-long 11
study, the department found injured children in every industry, but particularly in fast-food
and retail businesses.

Another study conducted by the University of Washington, Harborview Medical Cen- 12
ter and the Labor and Industries Department found 17,000 children under 18 were hurt
on the job from 1986 to 1989.

The proposed legislation would allow the department to impose civil penalties on em- 13
ployers who violate the law and to seek felony prosecution for serious violations. That could
mean five years in prison and a fine of $10,000, Dear said.

For less serious violations, the department could issue citations, and employers could 14
avoid penalty by complying with the regulations.

The maximum charge an employer now faces is a misdemeanor, with a fine of up 15
to $1,000.

OPTION 4: *A Microtheme that Uses Statistical Data to Support a Point*   Defend one of the following theses:

Thesis A—"Women (blacks) made only negligible progress toward job equality between 1972 and 1981."

Thesis B—"Women (blacks) made significant progress toward job equality between 1972 and 1981."

Support your thesis with evidence drawn from the following table. You can write your microtheme about the job progress of either women or blacks.

TABLE FOR OPTION 4   Employed persons, by sex, race, and occupation, 1972 and 1981

Occupation	1972			1981		
		Percentage			Percentage	
	Total Employed (1,000)	Female	Black and Other	Total Employed (1,000)	Female	Black and Other
Professional, Technical	11,538	39.3	7.2	16,420	44.6	9.9
Accountants	720	21.7	4.3	1,126	38.5	9.9
Dentists	108	1.9	5.6	130	4.6	6.2
Engineers	1,111	0.8	3.4	1,537	4.4	7.3
Lawyers	322	3.8	1.9	581	14.1	4.6
Librarians	158	81.6	7.0	192	82.8	5.7
Physicians	332	10.1	8.2	454	13.7	14.5
Registered nurses	807	97.6	8.2	1,654	96.8	12.3
College teachers	464	28.0	9.2	585	35.2	9.2
Administrators	8,081	17.6	4.0	11,540	27.5	5.8
Bank officers	430	19.0	2.6	696	37.5	5.5
Office managers	317	41.9	1.0	504	70.6	4.0
Sales managers	574	15.7	1.6	720	26.5	4.6
Clerical Workers	14,329	75.6	8.7	18,564	80.5	11.6
Bank tellers	290	87.5	4.9	569	93.5	7.6
File clerks	274	84.9	18.0	315	83.8	22.9
Secretaries	2,964	99.1	5.2	3,917	99.1	7.2
Skilled Crafts	10,867	3.6	6.9	12,662	6.3	8.5
Carpenters	1,052	0.5	5.9	1,122	1.9	5.8
Construction	2,261	0.6	9.0	2,593	1.9	10.2
Mechanics	1,040	0.5	8.5	1,249	0.6	8.7
Transportation	3,233	4.2	14.8	3,476	8.9	15.5
Bus drivers	253	34.1	17.1	360	47.2	21.1
Truck drivers	1,449	0.6	14.4	1,878	2.7	13.9
Unskilled Labor	4,242	6.0	20.2	4,583	11.5	16.5
Service Workers	9,584	57.0	18.5	12,391	59.2	18.4
Food service	3,286	69.8	13.9	4,682	66.2	14.0
Nurses' aides	1,513	87.0	24.6	1,995	89.2	24.3
Domestic cleaners	715	97.2	64.2	468	95.1	51.5

OPTION 5: *A Formal Argument Using at Least Two Reasons in Support of Your Claim*   Write a multiparagraph essay in which you develop two or more reasons in support of your thesis or claim. Each of your reasons should be summarizable in a because clause attached to your claim. If you have more than two reasons, develop your most important reason last. Give your essay a self-announcing structure in which you highlight your claim at the end of your introduction and begin your body paragraphs with clearly stated reasons. Open your essay with an attention-grabbing lead that attracts your readers' interest; your introduction should also explain the issue being addressed as well as provide whatever background is needed.

Note that this assignment does not ask you to refute opposing views. Nevertheless, it is a good idea to summarize an opposing view briefly to help the reader see the issue more clearly. Because you will not be refuting this view, the best place to summarize it is in your introduction prior to presenting your own claim. (If you place an opposing view in the body of your essay, its prominence obligates you to refute it or concede to it—issues addressed in Chapter 8 of this text. If you briefly summarize an opposing view in the introduction, however, you use it merely to clarify the issue and hence do not need to treat it at length.)

The following essay illustrates this assignment. It was written by a freshman student whose first language is Vietnamese rather than English. Additional essays written to the same assignment (some strong, some weak) are found in the "norming exercise" in Appendix 2 (see pp. 445–450). This exercise is aimed at helping you internalize criteria for a strong performance on this assignment.

Choose Life!

Dao Do (student)

Should euthanasia be legalized? My classmate Paula and her family think it should be. Paula's grandmother was blind from diabetes. For three years she was constantly in and out of the hospital, but then her kidneys shut down and she became a victim of life supports. After three months of suffering, she finally gave up. Paula believes the three-month period was unnecessary, for her grandmother didn't have to go through all of that suffering. If euthanasia were legalized, her family would have put her to sleep the minute her condition worsened. Then, she wouldn't have had to feel pain, and she would have died in peace and with dignity. Despite Paula's strong argument for legalizing euthanasia, I find it is wrong.   1

First, euthanasia is wrong because no one has the right to take the life of another person. Just as our society discourages suicide, it should discourage euthanasia because in both the person is running away from life and its responsibilities. Some people say that euthanasia or suicide will end suffering and pain. But what proofs do they have for such a claim? Death is still mysterious to us; therefore, we do not know whether death will end suffering and pain or not. What seems to be the real claim is that death to those with illnesses will end *our* pain. Such pain involves worrying over them, paying their medical bills,   2 and giving up so much of our time. Their deaths end our pain rather than theirs. And for that reason, euthanasia is a selfish act, for the outcome of euthanasia benefits us, the non-sufferers, more. Once the sufferers pass away, we can go back to our normal lives.

3   My second opposition to euthanasia is its unfavorable consequences. Today, euthanasia is performed on those who we think are suffering from incurable diseases or brain death. But what about tomorrow? People might use euthanasia to send old parents to death just to get rid of them faster, so they can get to the money, the possessions, and the real estate. Just think of all the murder cases on TV where children killed their parents so they can get to the fortune. Legalizing euthanasia will increase the number of these murder cases. The right of euthanasia not only encourages corruption, it encourages discrimination. People who suffer pain would be put into categories according to which should live longer and which shouldn't. Perhaps poor people or people of color will be more apt to be euthanized than rich people, or perhaps people with AIDS will be euthanized sooner so that society won't have to spend money on this very expensive disease.

4   My third objection to euthanasia is that it fails to see the value in suffering. Suffering is a part of life. We only see the value of suffering if we look deeply within our suffering. For example, I never thought my crippled uncle from Vietnam was a blessing to my grandmother until I talked to her. My mother's little brother was born prematurely. As a result of oxygen and nutrition deficiency, he was born crippled. His tiny arms and legs were twisted around his body, preventing him from any normal movements such as walking, picking up things, and lying down. He could only sit. Therefore, his world was very limited, for it consisted of his own room and the garden viewed through his window. Because of his disabilities, my grandmother had to wash him, feed him, and watch him constantly. It was hard but she managed to care for him for forty-three years. He passed away after the death of my grandfather in 1982. Bringing this situation out of Vietnam and into Western society shows the difference between Vietnamese and West's views. In West, my uncle might have been euthanized as a baby. Supporters of euthanasia would have said he wouldn't have any quality of life and that he would have been a great burden. But he was not a burden on my grandmother. She enjoyed taking care of him, and he was always her company after her other children got married and moved away. Neither one of them saw his defect as a form of suffering because it brought them closer together. My uncle was there for us to be thankful to God for not letting us be born with such disabilities. We should appreciate our lives, for they are not so limited.

5   In conclusion, let us be reminded that we do not have the right to take life, but we do have the right to live. We are free to live life to its fullest. Why anticipate death when it ends everything? Why choose a path we know nothing of? There's always room for hope. In hoping, we'll see that forced death is never a solution. Until we can understand the world after, we should choose to live and not to die.

chapter *7*

Moving Your Audience

Audience-Based Reasons, *Ethos,* and *Pathos*

In Chapters 5 and 6 we discussed *logos*—the logical structure of reasons and evidence in an argument. When writers focus on *logos*, they are often trying to clarify their own thinking as much as to persuade. In this chapter and the next, we shift our attention increasingly toward persuasion, in which our goal is to move our audience as much as possible toward our own position on an issue. In this chapter we examine strategies for connecting our argument to our audience's values and beliefs (audience-based reasons), for ensuring that we are credible and trustworthy in their eyes (*ethos*), and for ensuring that our presentation affects their sympathies (*pathos*). In Chapter 8 we explain strategies for varying the tone and structure of an argument to accommodate different kinds of audiences.

While all of these strategies are capable of being misused, of being presented in an "underhanded" or "manipulative" way, our discussion of them presupposes an arguer whose position is based on a reasoned investigation of evidence and a commitment to consistent and articulable values and beliefs. The strategies are in turn designed to help you create arguments that are not only rationally sound, but also effective for a given audience.

STARTING FROM YOUR READERS' BELIEFS: THE POWER OF AUDIENCE-BASED REASONS

Whenever you ask if a given piece of writing is persuasive, the immediate rejoinder should always be, "Persuasive to whom?" What seems a good reason to you may not be a good reason to others. The force of a logical argument, as Aristotle showed in his explanation of enthymemes, depends on the audience's acceptance of underlying assumptions, values, or beliefs (see pp. 96-97). Finding audience-based reasons means discovering enthymemes that are effectively rooted in your audience's values.

Difference Between Writer- and Audience-Based Reasons

To illustrate the difference between writer- and audience-based reasons, consider the following hypothetical case. Suppose you believed that the government should build a dam on the nearby Rapid River—a project bitterly opposed by several environmental groups. Which of the following two arguments might you use to address environmentalists?

1. The government should build a dam on the Rapid River because the only alternative power sources are coal-fired or nuclear plants, both of which pose greater risk to the environment than a hydroelectric dam.
2. The government should build a hydroelectric dam on the Rapid River because this area needs cheap power to attract heavy industry.

Clearly, the warrant of Argument 1 ("Choose the source of power that poses least risk to the environment") is rooted in the values and beliefs of environmentalists, whereas the warrant of Argument 2 ("Growth of industry is good") is likely to make them wince. To environmentalists, new industry means more congestion, more smokestacks, and more pollution. However, Argument 2 may appeal to out-of-work laborers or to the business community, to whom new industry means more jobs and a booming economy.

From the perspective of *logos* alone, Arguments 1 and 2 are both sound. They are internally consistent and proceed from reasonable premises. But they will affect different audiences very differently. Neither argument proves that the government should build the dam; both are open to objection. Passionate environmentalists, for example, might counter Argument 1 by asking why the government needs to build any power plant at all. They could argue that energy conservation would obviate the need for a new power plant. Or they might argue that building a dam hurts the environment in ways unforeseen by dam supporters. Our point, then, isn't that Argument 1 will persuade environmentalists. Rather, our point is that Argument 1 will be more persuasive than Argument 2 because it is rooted in beliefs and values the intended audience shares.

Let's consider a second example by returning to Chapter 1 and student Gordon Adams's petition to waive his math requirement. Gordon's central argument, as you will recall, was that as a lawyer he would have no need for algebra. In Toulmin's terms, Gordon's argument looks like this:

CLAIM:	I should be exempted from the algebra requirement
STATED REASON:	because in my chosen field of law I will have no need for algebra
GROUNDS:	testimony from lawyers and others that lawyers never use algebra
WARRANT:	(largely implicit in Gordon's argument) General education requirements should be based on career utility (that is, if a course isn't needed for a particular student's career, it shouldn't be required).
BACKING:	(not provided) arguments that career utility should be the chief criterion for requiring general education courses

In our discussions of this case with students and faculty, students generally vote to support Gordon's request, whereas faculty generally vote against it. And in fact, the University Standards Committee rejected Gordon's petition, thus delaying his entry into law school.

Why do faculty and students differ on this issue? Mainly they differ because faculty reject Gordon's warrant that general education requirements should serve students' individual career interests. Most faculty believe that general education courses, including math, provide a base of common learning that links us to the past and teaches us modes of understanding useful throughout life.

Gordon's argument thus challenges one of college professors' most cherished beliefs—that the liberal arts are innately valuable. Further, it threatens his immediate audience, the committee, with a possible flood of student requests to waive other general education requirements on the grounds of their irrelevance to a particular career choice.

How might Gordon have created a more persuasive argument? In our view, Gordon might have prevailed had he accepted the faculty's belief in the value of the math requirement and argued that he had fulfilled the "spirit" of that requirement through alternative means. He could have based his argument on an enthymeme like this:

I should be exempted from the algebra requirement because my experience as a contractor and inventor has already provided me with an equivalent mathematical knowledge.

Following this audience-based approach, he would drop all references to algebra's uselessness for lawyers and expand his discussion of the mathematical savvy he acquired on the job. This argument would honor faculty values and reduce their fear of setting a bad precedent. Few students are likely to have Gordon's background, and those who did could apply for a similar exemption without threatening the system. Again, this argument may not have won, but it would have gotten a more sympathetic hearing.

On the other hand, arguments like Gordon's that call fundamental assumptions into doubt may have a long-range effect. Although he probably would have greatly improved his chances of getting a waiver by appealing to his audience's values and beliefs, his challenge of those beliefs might in the long run contribute to the systemic change he desires. By arguing that he's a special case, Gordon would have left the rule itself unchallenged. By challenging the rule itself, he follows a high-risk/high-gain strategy that, even if unsuccessful, may force reexamination of the faculty's basic beliefs. If successful, meanwhile, it could affect thousands of students.

 ## FOR CLASS DISCUSSION

Working in groups, decide which of the two reasons offered in each instance would be more persuasive to the specified audience. Be prepared to explain your reasoning to the class. Write out the implied warrant for each because clause and decide whether the specific audience would likely grant it.

1. Audience: a beleaguered parent
   a. I should be allowed to stay out until 2 A.M. because all my friends do.
   b. I should be allowed to stay out until 2 A.M. because only if I'm free to make my own decisions will I mature.

2. Audience: a prospective employer
   a. I would be a good candidate for a summer job at the Happy Trails Dude Ranch because I have always wanted to spend a summer in the mountains and because I like to ride horses.
   b. I would be a good candidate for a summer job at the Happy Trails Dude Ranch because I am a hard worker, because I have had considerable experience serving others in my volunteer work, and because I know how to make guests feel welcome and relaxed.

3. Audience: people who oppose the present grading system on the grounds that it is too competitive
   a. We should keep the present grading system because it prepares people for the dog-eat-dog pressures of the business world.
   b. We should keep the present grading system because it tells students that certain standards of excellence must be met if individuals are to reach their full potential.

4. Audience: young people aged fifteen to twenty-five
   a. You should become a vegetarian because an all-vegetable diet is better for your heart than a meaty diet.
   b. You should become a vegetarian because that will help eliminate the suffering of animals raised in factory farms.

5. Audience: conservative proponents of "family values"
   a. Same-sex marriages should be legalized because doing so will promote public acceptance of homosexuality.
   b. Same-sex marriages should be legalized because doing so will make it easier for gay people to establish and sustain long-term stable relationships.

Finding Audience-Based Reasons: Asking Questions about Your Audience

As the preceding exercise makes clear, reasons are most persuasive when linked to your audience's values. This principle seems simple enough, yet it is easy to forget. For example, employers frequently complain about job interviewees whose first concern is what the company will do for them, not what they might do for the company. Conversely, job search experts agree that most successful job candidates do extensive background research on a prospective company so that in an interview they can relate their own skills to the company's problems and needs. Successful arguments typically grow out of similar attention to audience needs.

To find out all you can about an audience, we recommend that you explore the following questions:

1. Who is your audience? Your audience might be a single, identifiable person. For example, you might write a letter to a professor arguing for a change in a course grade or to a vice president for research proposing a new research and development project for your company. Or your audience might be a decision-making body such as the University Standards Committee or a philanthropic organization to which you're writing a grant proposal. At other times your audience might be the general readership of a newspaper, church bulletin, magazine, or journal, or you might produce a flier to be handed out on street corners.

2. How much does your audience know or care about your issue? Are they currently part of the conversation on this issue, or do they need considerable background information? If you are writing to specific decision makers (for example, the administration at your college about restructuring the intramural program), are they currently aware of the problem or issue you are addressing and do they care about it? If not, how can you get their attention? Your answers to these questions will especially affect your introduction and conclusion.

3. What is your audience's current attitude toward your issue? Are they supportive of your position on the issue? Neutral or undecided? Skeptical? Strongly opposed? What other points of view besides your own will your audience be weighing? In Chapter 8, we will explain how your answers to these questions can help you decide the structure and tone of your argument.

4. What objections are your audience likely to make to your argument? What weaknesses will they find? What aspects of your position will be most threatening to them and why? How are your basic assumptions, values, or beliefs different from your audience's? Your answers here will help determine the content of your argument and will alert you to extra research you may need to do to bolster your response to audience objections.

5. Finally, what values, beliefs, or assumptions about the world do you and your audience share? Despite differences of view on this issue, where can you find common links with your audience? How might you use these links to build bridges to your audience?

Suppose, for example, that you support universal mandatory testing for the HIV virus. It's important from the start that you understand and acknowledge the interests of those opposed to your position. Who are they and what are their concerns? Gays and others in high-risk categories may fear finding out whether they are infected; certainly they will fear discrimination from being publicly identified as HIV carriers. Moreover, gays may see mandatory AIDS testing as part of an ongoing attempt by homophobes to stigmatize the gay community. Liberals, meanwhile, will question the necessity of invading people's privacy and compromising their civil liberties in the name of public health.

What shared values might you use to build bridges to those opposed to mandatory testing? At a minimum, you share a desire to find a cure for AIDS and a fear of the horrors of an epidemic. Moreover, you also share a respect for the dignity and humanity of those afflicted with AIDS and do not see yourself as part of a backlash against gays.

Given all that, you begin to develop a strategy to reduce your audience's fears and to link your reasons to their values. Your thinking might go something like this:

PROBLEM:	How can I create an argument rooted in shared values?
POSSIBLE SOLUTIONS:	I can try to reduce the audience's fear that mandatory AIDS testing implies a criticism of gays. I must assure that my plan ensures confidentiality. I must make clear that my first priority is stopping the spread of the disease and that this concern is shared by the gay community.
PROBLEM:	How can I reduce fear that mandatory HIV-testing will violate civil liberties?

POSSIBLE SOLUTIONS: I must show that the enemy here is the HIV virus, not victims of the disease. Also, I might cite precedents for how we fight other infectious diseases. For example, many states require marriage license applicants to take a test for sexually transmitted diseases, and many communities have imposed quarantines to halt the spread of epidemics. I could also argue that the right of everyone to be free from this disease outweighs the right to privacy, especially when confidentiality is assured.

The preceding example shows how a writer's focus on audience can shape the actual invention of the argument.

 FOR CLASS DISCUSSION ▬▬▬▬▬▬▬▬▬▬▬▬▬▬▬▬▬▬▬▬▬

Working individually or in small groups, plan an audience-based argumentative strategy for one or more of the following cases. Follow the thinking process used by the writer of the mandatory HIV-testing argument: (1) State several problems that the writer must solve to reach the audience, and (2) develop possible solutions to those problems.

1. An argument for the right of software companies to continue making and selling violent video games: Aim the argument at parents who oppose their children's playing these games.

2. An argument limiting the number of terms that can be served by members of Congress: Aim the argument at supporters of an influential incumbent who would no longer be eligible to hold office.

3. An argument supporting a $1-per-gallon increase in gasoline taxes as an energy conservation measure: Aim your argument at business leaders who oppose the tax for fear it will raise the cost of consumer goods.

4. An argument supporting the legalization of cocaine: Aim your argument at readers of *Reader's Digest*, a conservative magazine that supports the current war on drugs.

ETHOS AND *PATHOS* AS PERSUASIVE APPEALS: AN OVERVIEW

The previous section focused on audience-based reasons as a means of moving an audience. In terms of the rhetorical triangle introduced in Chapter 4, searching for audience-based reasons can be seen primarily as a function of *logos*—finding the best structure of reasons and evidence to sway an audience—although, as we shall see, it also affects the other points of the triangle. In what follows, we turn to the power of *ethos* (the appeal to credibility) and *pathos* (the appeal to an audience's sympathies) as further means of making your arguments more effective.

It's tempting to think of these three kinds of appeals as "ingredients" in an essay, like spices you add to a casserole. Succumbing to this metaphor, you might say to yourself something like this: "Just enough *logos* to give the dish body; but for more piquancy it needs a pinch of *pathos*. And for the back of the palate, a tad more *ethos*."

But this metaphor is misleading because *logos*, *ethos*, and *pathos* are not substances; they are ways of seeing rather than objects of sight. A better metaphor might be that of different lamps and filters used on theater spotlights to vary lighting effects on a stage. Thus, if you switch on a *pathos* lamp (possibly through using more concrete language or vivid examples), the resulting image will engage the audience's sympathy and emotions more deeply. If you overlay an *ethos* filter (perhaps by adopting a different tone toward your audience), the projected image of the writer as a person will be subtly altered. If you switch on a *logos* lamp (by adding, say, more data for evidence), you will draw the reader's attention to the logical appeal of the argument. Depending on how you modulate the lamps and filters, you shape and color your readers' perception of the issue.

Our metaphor is imperfect, of course, but our point is that *logos*, *ethos*, and *pathos* work together to create an impact on the reader. Consider, for example, the different impacts of the following arguments, all having roughly the same logical appeal.

1. People should adopt a vegetarian diet because only through vegetarianism can we prevent the cruelty to animals that results from factory farming.

2. I hope you enjoyed your fried chicken this evening. You know, of course, how much that chicken suffered just so you could have a tender and juicy meal. Commercial growers cram the chickens so tightly together into cages that their beaks are cut off to keep them from pecking each other's eyes out. The only way to end the torture is to adopt a vegetarian diet.

3. People who eat meat are no better than sadists who torture other sentient creatures to enhance their own pleasure. Unless you enjoy sadistic tyranny over others, you have only one choice: Become a vegetarian.

4. People committed to justice might consider the extent to which our love of eating meat requires the agony of animals. A visit to a modern chicken factory—where chickens live their entire lives in tiny darkened coops without room to spread their wings—might raise doubts about our right to inflict such suffering on sentient creatures. Indeed, such a visit might persuade us that vegetarianism is a juster alternative.

Each argument has roughly the same logical core:

CLAIM: People should adopt a vegetarian diet.

STATED REASON: because only vegetarianism will end the suffering of animals subjected to factory farming

GROUNDS: the evidence of suffering in commercial chicken farms, where chickens peck each other's eyes out; evidence that only widespread adoption of vegetarianism will end factory farming

WARRANT: If we have an alternative to making animals suffer, we should adopt it.

But the impact of each argument varies. The difference between Arguments 1 and 2, most of our students report, is the greater emotional power of 2. Whereas Argument 1 refers only to the abstraction "cruelty to animals," Argument 2 paints a vivid picture of chickens with their beaks cut off to prevent their pecking each other blind. Argument 2 makes a stronger appeal to *pathos* (not necessarily a stronger argument), stirring feelings by appealing simultaneously to the heart and to the head.

The difference between Arguments 1 and 3 concerns both *ethos* and *pathos*. Argument 3 appeals to the emotions through highly charged words like "torture," "sadist," and "tyranny." But Argument 3 also draws attention to its writer, and most of our students report not liking that writer very much. His stance is self-righteous and insulting. In contrast, Argument 4's author establishes a more positive *ethos*. He establishes rapport with his audience by assuming they are committed to justice and by qualifying his argument with conditional terms such as *might* and *perhaps*. He also invites sympathy for his problem—an appeal to *pathos*—by offering a specific description of chickens crammed into tiny coops.

Which of these arguments is best? They all have appropriate uses. Arguments 1 and 4 seem aimed at receptive audiences reasonably open to exploration of the issue, whereas Arguments 2 and 3 seem designed to shock complacent audiences or to rally a group of True Believers. Even Argument 3, which is too abusive to be effective in most instances, might work as a rallying speech at a convention of animal liberation activists.

Our point thus far is that *logos, ethos,* and *pathos* are different aspects of the same whole, different lenses for intensifying or softening the light beam you project onto the screen. Every choice you make as a writer affects in some way each of the three appeals. The rest of this chapter examines these choices in more detail.

HOW TO CREATE AN EFFECTIVE *ETHOS:* THE APPEAL TO CREDIBILITY

Classical rhetoricians of ancient Greece and Rome recognized that an argument would be more persuasive if the audience trusted the speaker. Aristotle argued that such trust resides within the speech itself, not in the prior reputation of the speaker. In the speaker's manner and delivery, in his tone, word choice, and arrangement of reasons, in the sympathy with which he treats alternative views, a speaker creates a trustworthy persona. Aristotle called the impact of the speaker's credibility the appeal from *ethos.* How does a writer create credibility? We will suggest three ways.

Be Knowledgeable about Your Issue

The first way to gain credibility is to *be* credible; that is, to argue from a strong base of knowledge, to have at hand the examples, personal experiences, statistics, and other empirical data needed to make a sound case. If you have done your homework (people who "do their homework" are highly respected in business, government, and academe), you will command the attention of most audiences.

Be Fair

Besides being knowledgeable about your issue, you need to demonstrate fairness and courtesy to alternative views. Because true argument can occur only where persons may reasonably disagree with one another, your *ethos* will be strengthened if you demonstrate that you understand and empathize with other points of view. There are times, of course, when you may appropriately scorn an opposing view. But these times are rare, and they mostly occur when you address audiences predisposed to your view. Demonstrating empathy to alternative views is generally the best strategy.

Build a Bridge to Your Audience

A third means of establishing credibility—building a bridge to your audience— has been treated at length in our earlier discussion of audience-based reasons. By grounding your argument in shared values and assumptions, you demonstrate your goodwill and enhance your image as a trustworthy person respectful of your audience's views. We mention audience-based reasons here to show how this aspect of *logos*—finding the reasons that are most rooted in the audience's values— also affects your *ethos* as a person respectful of your readers' views.

HOW TO CREATE *PATHOS:* THE APPEAL TO BELIEFS AND EMOTIONS

At the height of the Vietnam protest movement, a group of demonstrators "napalmed" a puppy by dousing it with gasoline and setting it on fire, thereby outraging people all across the country. Many sent indignant letters to their local newspapers, provoking the following response from the demonstrators: "Why are you outraged by the napalming of a single puppy when you are not outraged by the daily napalming of human babies in Vietnam?"

From the demonstrators' view, napalming the puppy constituted an appeal from *pathos.* Logos-centered arguments, the protesters felt, numbed the mind to human suffering; in napalming the puppy, they intended to reawaken in their audience a capacity for gut-level revulsion that had been dulled by too many statistics, too many abstract moral appeals, and too much superficial TV coverage of the war.

Of course, the napalmed puppy was a real-life event, a street theater protest, not a written argument. But writers often use similar strategies. Anti-abortion proponents use it whenever they graphically describe the dismemberment of a fetus during abortion; euthanasia proponents use it when they describe the prolonged suffering of a terminally ill patient hooked hopelessly to machines. And a student uses it when he argues that a professor ought to raise his grade from a C to a B, lest he lose his scholarship and leave college, shattering the dreams of his dear old grandmother.

Are such appeals legitimate? Our answer is yes, if they intensify our response to an issue rather than divert our attention from it. Because understanding is a matter of feeling as well as perceiving, *pathos* can give access to nonlogical, but not necessarily nonrational, ways of knowing. Used effectively, pathetic appeals reveal the fullest human meaning of an issue, helping us walk in the writer's shoes. That is why arguments are often improved through the use of sensory details that allow us to see the reality of a problem or through stories that make specific cases and instances come alive.

Appeals to *pathos* become illegitimate, we believe, when they confuse an issue rather than clarify it. To the extent that students' grades should be based on performance or effort, the student's image of the dear old grandmother is an illegitimate appeal to *pathos,* for it diverts the reader from rational to irrational criteria. The weeping grandmother may provide a legitimate motive for the student to study harder, but not for the professor to change a grade.

Although it is difficult to classify all the ways that writers can create appeals from *pathos,* we will focus on four strategies: concrete language; specific examples and illustrations; narratives; and connotations of words, metaphors, and analogies.

Use Concrete Language

Concrete language—one of the chief ways that writers achieve voice—can increase the liveliness, interest level, and personality of a writer's prose. When used in argument, concrete language typically heightens *pathos.* For example, consider the differences between the first and second drafts of the following student argument:

First draft: People who prefer driving a car to taking a bus think that taking the bus will increase the stress of the daily commute. Just the opposite is true. Not being able to find a parking spot when in a hurry to work or school can cause a person stress. Taking the bus gives a person time to read or sleep, etc. It could be used as a mental break.

Second draft: Taking the bus can be more relaxing than driving a car. Having someone else behind the wheel gives people time to chat with friends or cram for an exam. They can balance their checkbooks, do homework, doze off, read the daily newspaper, or get lost in a novel rather than foaming at the mouth looking for a parking space.

In this revision, specific details enliven the prose by creating images that trigger positive feelings—who wouldn't want some free time to doze off or to get lost in a novel?

Use Specific Examples and Illustrations

Specific examples and illustrations serve two purposes in an argument: They provide evidence that supports your reasons; simultaneously, they give your argument presence and emotional resonance. Note the flatness of the following draft arguing for the value of multicultural studies in a university core curriculum:

> *Early draft:* Another advantage of a multicultural education is that it will help us see our own culture in a broader perspective. If all we know is our own heritage, we might not be inclined to see anything bad about this heritage because we won't know anything else. But if we study other heritages, we can see the costs and benefits of our own heritage.

Now note the increase in "presence" when the writer adds a specific example.

> *Revised draft:* Another advantage of multicultural education is that it raises questions about traditional Western values. For example, owning private property (such as buying your own home) is part of the American dream and is a basic right guaranteed in our Constitution. However, in studying the beliefs of American Indians, students are confronted with a very different view of private property. When the U.S. Government sought to buy land in the Pacific Northwest from Chief Sealth, he replied:
>
> The president in Washington sends words that he wishes to buy our land. But how can you buy or sell the sky? The land? The idea is strange to us. If we do not own the freshness of the air and the sparkle of the water, how can you buy them?. . . We are part of the earth and it is part of us. . . . This we know: the earth does not belong to man, man belongs to the earth.
>
> Our class was shocked by the contrast between traditional Western views of property and Chief Sealth's views. One of our best class discussions was initiated by this quotation from Chief Sealth. Had we not been exposed to a view from another culture, we would have never been led to question the "rightness" of Western values.

The writer begins his revision by evoking a traditional Western view of private property, which he then questions by shifting to Chief Sealth's vision of land as open, endless, and unobtainable as the sky. Through the use of a specific example, the writer brings to life his previously abstract point about the benefit of multicultural education.

Use Narratives

A particularly powerful way to evoke *pathos* is to tell a story that embodies your thesis implicitly and appeals directly to the reader's feelings and imagination. Brief narratives—whether real or hypothetical—are particularly effective as opening attention grabbers for an argument. To illustrate how an introductory narrative (either a story or a brief scene) can create pathetic appeals, consider the following vignettes from two different arguments about the homeless. The first argument, in support of legislation to help the poor, aims to create sympathy for homeless people. It opens this way:

> It hurts the most when you come home from the theater on a cold January night. As you pull your scarf tighter around your neck and push your gloved hands deeper into the pockets of your wool overcoat, you notice the man huddled over the sewer grate, his feet wrapped in newspapers. He blows on his hands, then tucks them under his armpits and lies down on the sidewalk with his shoulders over the grate, his bed for the night. There are hundreds like him downtown, and their numbers are growing. How can we help?

The second argument, supporting an antiloitering law to keep the homeless out of posh shopping areas, aims to create sympathy not for the homeless but for the shoppers. It opens like this:

> Panhandlers used to sit on corners with tin cups that they rattled politely. Not any more. Today we are besieged by ratty woe mongers who scuttle up behind you, clutching bottles of Mad Dog 20/20 in a sack, breathe their foul fumes down your neck, tap your arm or grab your sleeve, and demand your money. If you ignore them, they try to embarrass or threaten you.

Each of these brief narratives makes a case for a particular point of view toward the homeless. They help us see a problem through the eyes of the person making the argument. Although each makes a powerful appeal to *pathos,* both can face resistance in some quarters. The first narrative may strike some as sentimental; the second may strike others as flippant and callous. The emotional charge set by an introductory narrative can sometimes work against you as well as for you. If you have doubts about an opening narrative, test it out on other readers before using it in your final draft.

  FOR CLASS DISCUSSION

Suppose that you want to write arguments on the following issues. Working individually or in groups, think of an introductory scene or brief story that would create a pathetic appeal favorable to your argument.

1. a. an argument supporting the use of animals for biomedical research
   b. an argument opposing the use of animals for biomedical research
   [Note that the purpose of the first narrative is to create sympathy for the use of animals in medical research; perhaps you could describe the happy homecoming of a child cured by a medical procedure developed through testing on animals. The second narrative, aimed at evoking sympathy for abolishing animal research, might describe a lab rabbit's suffering.]

2. a. an argument for a program to restore a national park to its natural condition
   b. an argument for creating more camping places and overnight sites for recreational vehicles in national parks

3. a. an argument favoring legalization of drugs
   b. an argument opposing legalization of drugs

In addition to their use as opening scenes or as examples and illustrations, narratives can sometimes inform a whole argument. If the argument is conveyed entirely through narrative, then it is an implicit rather than explicit argument (see Chapter 1, pp. 4–6). But explicit arguments can sometimes contain an extensive narrative component. One source of the powerful appeal of Gordon Adams's petition to waive his math requirement (Chapter 1, pp. 19–22) is that the argument embodies aspects of his personal story.

In his appeal to the Standards Committee, Gordon Adams uses numerous standard argument devices (for example, testimony from legal practitioners that knowledge of algebra is not required in the study or practice of law). But he also makes a strong pathetic appeal by narrating the story of how he assembled his case. By foregrounding his encounters with all the people from whom he seeks information, he makes himself an actor in a story that might be called "Gordon's Quest for Truth." Gordon's quest story reveals to us his seriousness simply by the fact that he invested significant time and trouble in preparing his case. Moreover, by quoting and paraphrasing the words of his sources in a series of dramatic vignettes—rather than simply reporting them thirdhand—Gordon gives this testimony a kind of immediacy it might otherwise not have.

The story of Gordon's construction of his argument, meanwhile, is situated inside a larger story that lends weight to the points he makes in the smaller story. The larger story, the story of Gordon's "awakening" to injustice and his fierce commitment to overcoming injustice for his people, links Gordon's desire to waive his algebra requirement to a larger, more significant story about overcoming oppression. And beyond Gordon's story lies an even larger, richer story, the history of Native American peoples in the United States over the past century, which lends an even greater resonance and clarity to his personal story. By telling his story, Gordon makes himself more human and familiar, more understandable and less threatening. This is why whenever we want to break down difference, overcome estrangement, grow closer to people we don't know well, we tell them our stories. In Gordon's case, telling his story allowed him to negotiate some considerable differences between himself and his audience of mostly white, middle-class faculty members. Even though he lost his case, he made a powerful argument that was taken seriously.

Choose Words, Metaphors, and Analogies with Appropriate Connotations

Another way of appealing to *pathos* is to select words, metaphors, or analogies with connotations that match your aim. Thus, a rapidly made decision by a city council might be called "haughty and autocratic" or "bold and decisive," depending on whether you oppose or support the council. Similarly, writers can use favorable or unfavorable metaphors and analogies to evoke different imaginative or emotional responses. Thus, a tax bill might be viewed as a "potentially fatal poison pill" or as "unpleasant but necessary economic medicine."

The writer's control over word selection raises the problem of slant or bias. Some writers choose slanted words that evoke emotional responses favorable to the arguer's aims but that distort the truth. The line between responsible and distortive use of language is not easily drawn. Some contemporary philosophers argue that the notion of bias-free, perfectly transparent language is an impossible ideal; all language is a lens. Thus, when we choose word A rather than word B, when we put this sentence in the passive voice rather than the active, when we select this detail and omit that detail, we create bias.

Let's illustrate. When you see an unshaven man sitting on a city sidewalk with his back up against a doorway, wearing old, slovenly clothes, and drinking from a bottle hidden in a sack, what is the objective, "true" word for this person?

a person on welfare?	a welfare leech?	a beggar?
a panhandler?	a bum?	a hobo?
a wino?	a drunk?	an alcoholic?
a crazy guy?	a homeless person?	a transient?

None of these words can be called "true" or perfectly objective because each creates its own slant. Each word causes us to view the person through that word's lens. If we call the person a beggar, for example, we evoke connotations of helpless poverty and of the biblical call to give alms to the poor. *Beggar,* then, is slightly more favorable than *panhandler,* which conjures up the image of someone pestering you for money. Calling the person "homeless," on the other hand, shifts the focus away from the person's behavior and onto a faulty economic system that fails to provide sufficient housing. The word *wino,* meanwhile, identifies a different cause for the person's condition—alcoholism rather than economics.

Writers face decisions about word choices all the time. If you are supporting the cause of labor unions against big corporations, you might choose to call their top officers "corporate tycoons," "country club elite," or even "fat cat executives." If you supported the corporations, however, you might choose "chief executive officers" or "top-level corporation heads." Or in either case you might choose the most neutral term possible—perhaps "corporation leaders."

Our point is that a purely objective language may be impossible. But the absence of pure objectivity doesn't mean that all language is equally slanted or that truth can never be discerned. Readers can recognize degrees of bias in someone's language and distinguish between a reasonably trustworthy passage and a highly distortive one. By being on the lookout for slanted language—without claiming that any language can be totally objective—we can defend ourselves from distortive appeals to *pathos* while recognizing that responsible use of connotation can give powerful presence to an argument.

THE INTERRELATEDNESS OF *LOGOS*, *ETHOS*, AND *PATHOS*: WHERE SHOULD I REVEAL MY THESIS?

To demonstrate the interrelatedness of *logos, ethos,* and *pathos,* we turn now to a question often asked in our argument classes: "Where should I place my thesis? Should I tell readers up front where I stand on an issue, or should I wait to reveal my own position?" Although this may seem like a small technical matter, thesis placement can profoundly affect your audience's perception of your trustworthiness (*ethos*) as well as their sympathetic engagement with your views (*pathos*).

In Chapter 3, we suggested that the most common form of argument has a classical structure in which you state your thesis in the introduction, support it with reasons and evidence, and then summarize and refute opposing views (see pp. 63–66). Rhetorically, however, it is not always advantageous to tell your readers where you stand at the start of your argument or to separate yourself so definitively from alternative views. Sometimes it's better to keep the issue open, delaying the revelation of your own position until the middle or end of the essay.

As we will explain in more detail in the next chapter, classical argument with its up-front thesis and its clear summary and refutation of alternative views works best when you address a neutral or undecided audience. But it often lacks the subtlety and flexibility necessary when the issue is emotionally charged, when your own views are tentative, or when the audience is hostile. In such cases, it is often more effective to delay your thesis because of the subtle ways that a delayed thesis can increase your appeal to *ethos* and *pathos*.

To illustrate the different effects of classical versus delayed thesis arguments, we have taken a delayed thesis argument by nationally known columnist Ellen Goodman and rewritten it into the classical form. The article appeared shortly after the nation was shocked by a brutal gang rape in New Bedford, Massachusetts, in which a woman was raped on a pool table by patrons of a local bar.* We would like you to read both versions and then answer the class discussion exercises that follow.

---

*The rape occurred in 1985 and was later made into an Academy Award–winning movie, *The Accused,* starring Jody Foster.

Minneapolis Pornography Ordinance

Ellen Goodman

(original version: delayed thesis)

Just a couple of months before the pool-table gang rape in New Bedford, Mass., *Hustler* magazine printed a photo feature that reads like a blueprint for the actual crime. There were just two differences between *Hustler* and real life. In *Hustler,* the woman enjoyed it. In real life, the woman charged rape.

There is no evidence that the four men charged with this crime had actually read the magazine. Nor is there evidence that the spectators who yelled encouragement for two hours had held previous ringside seats at pornographic events. But there is a growing sense that the violent pornography being peddled in this country helps to create an atmosphere in which such events occur.

As recently as last month, a study done by two University of Wisconsin researchers suggested that even "normal" men, prescreened college students, were changed by their exposure to violent pornography. After just ten hours of viewing, reported researcher Edward Donnerstein, "the men were less likely to convict in a rape trial, less likely to see injury to a victim, more likely to see the victim as responsible." Pornography may not cause rape directly, he said, "but it maintains a lot of very callous attitudes. It justifies aggression. It even says you are doing a favor to the victim."

If we can prove that pornography is harmful, then shouldn't the victims have legal rights? This, in any case, is the theory behind a city ordinance that recently passed the Minneapolis City Council. Vetoed by the mayor last week, it is likely to be back before the Council for an overriding vote, likely to appear in other cities, other towns. What is unique about the Minneapolis approach is that for the first time it attacks pornography, not because of nudity or sexual explicitness, but because it degrades and harms women. It opposes pornography on the basis of sex discrimination.

University of Minnesota Law Professor Catherine MacKinnon, who co-authored the ordinance with feminist writer Andrea Dworkin, says that they chose this tactic because they believe that pornography is central to "creating and maintaining the inequality of the sexes. . . . Just being a woman means you are injured by pornography."

They defined pornography carefully as, "the sexually explicit subordination of women, graphically depicted, whether in pictures or in words." To fit their legal definition it must also include one of nine conditions that show this subordination, like presenting women who "experience sexual pleasure in being raped or . . . mutilated. . . ." Under this law, it would be possible for a pool-table rape victim to sue *Hustler.* It would be possible for a woman to sue if she were forced to act in a pornographic movie. Indeed, since the law describes pornography as oppressive to all women, it would be possible for any woman to sue those who traffic in the stuff for violating her civil rights.

In many ways, the Minneapolis ordinance is an appealing attack on an appalling problem. The authors have tried to resolve a long and bubbling conflict among those who have both a deep aversion to pornography and a deep loyalty to the value of free speech. "To date," says Professor MacKinnon, "people have identified the pornographer's freedom with everybody's freedom. But we're saying that the freedom of the pornographer is the subordination of women. It means one has to take a side."

8   But the sides are not quite as clear as Professor MacKinnon describes them. Nor is the ordinance.

9   Even if we accept the argument that pornography is harmful to women—and I do— then we must also recognize that anti-Semitic literature is harmful to Jews and racist literature is harmful to blacks. For that matter, Marxist literature may be harmful to government policy. It isn't just women versus pornographers. If women win the right to sue publishers and producers, then so could Jews, blacks, and a long list of people who may be able to prove they have been harmed by books, movies, speeches or even records. The Manson murders, you may recall, were reportedly inspired by the Beatles.

10   We might prefer a library or book store or lecture hall without Mein Kampf or the Grand Whoever of the Ku Klux Klan. But a growing list of harmful expressions would inevitably strangle freedom of speech.

11   This ordinance was carefully written to avoid problems of banning and prior restraint, but the right of any woman to claim damages from pornography is just too broad. It seems destined to lead to censorship.

12   What the Minneapolis City Council has before it is a very attractive theory. What MacKinnon and Dworkin have written is a very persuasive and useful definition of pornography. But they haven't yet resolved the conflict between the harm of pornography and the value of free speech. In its present form, this is still a shaky piece of law.

Our Rewrite of the Same Essay into the Classical Argument Structure

1   Just a couple of months before the pool-table gang rape in New Bedford, Mass., *Hustler* magazine printed a photo feature that reads like a blueprint for the actual crime. There were just two differences between *Hustler* and real life. In *Hustler,* the woman enjoyed it. In real life, the woman charged rape. Of course, there is no evidence that the four men charged with this crime had actually read the magazine. Nor is there evidence that the spectators who yelled encouragement for two hours had held previous ringside seats at pornographic events. But there is a growing sense that the violent pornography being peddled in this country helps to create an atmosphere in which such events occur. One city is taking a unique approach to attack this problem. An ordinance recently passed by the Minneapolis City Council outlaws pornography not because it contains nudity or sexually explicit acts, but because it degrades and harms women. Unfortunately, despite the proponents' good intentions, the Minneapolis ordinance is a bad law because it has potentially dangerous consequences.

2   Let's begin by looking at the opposing view. The proponents of the Minneapolis City Ordinance argue that pornography should be made illegal because it degrades and humiliates women. To show that it degrades women, they cite a recent study done by two University of Wisconsin researchers that suggests that even "normal" men (prescreened college students) are changed by their exposure to violent pornography. After just ten hours of

viewing, reported researcher Edward Donnerstein, "the men were less likely to convict in a rape trial, less likely to see injury to a victim, more likely to see the victim as responsible." Pornography may not cause rape directly, he said, "but it maintains a lot of very callous attitudes. It justifies aggression. It even says you are doing a favor to the victim."

The core of their argument runs as follows: "If something degrades and humiliates women, then it discriminates against women. Pornography degrades and humiliates women. Therefore, pornography discriminates against women." Since empirical evidence is mounting that pornography indeed degrades and humiliates women, pornography, their argument goes, is a form of sex discrimination. University of Minnesota Law Professor Catherine MacKinnon, who co-authored the ordinance with feminist writer Andrea Dworkin, says that they chose to focus on pornography as a form of discrimination because they believe that pornography is central to "creating and maintaining the inequality of the sexes. . . . Just being a woman means you are injured by pornography." They defined pornography carefully as "the sexually explicit subordination of women, graphically depicted, whether in pictures or in words." To fit their legal definition it must also include one of nine conditions that show this subordination, like presenting women who "experience sexual pleasure in being raped or . . . mutilated. . . ." Under this law it would be possible for a woman to sue if she were forced to act in a pornographic movie. Indeed, since the law describes pornography as oppressive to all women, it would be possible for any woman to sue those who traffic in the stuff for violating her civil rights.   3

In many ways, the Minneapolis ordinance is an appealing solution to an appalling problem. The authors have tried to resolve a long and bubbling conflict among those who have both a deep aversion to pornography and a deep loyalty to the value of free speech. "To date," says Professor MacKinnon, "people have identified the pornographer's freedom with everybody's freedom. But we're saying that the freedom of the pornographer is the subordination of women. It means one has to take a side."   4

One must concede that the argument is attractive. It seems to give liberal thinkers a way of getting around the problem of free speech. But the reasoning behind the ordinance is flawed because its acceptance could lead to the suppression of a wide range of ideas. Even if we accept the argument that pornography is harmful to women—and I do—then we must also recognize that anti-Semitic literature is harmful to Jews and racist literature is harmful to blacks. For that matter, Marxist literature may be harmful to government policy. It isn't just women versus pornographers. If women win the right to sue publishers and producers, then so could Jews, blacks, and a long list of people who may be able to prove they have been harmed by books, movies, speeches, or even records. The Manson murders, you may recall, were reportedly inspired by the Beatles.   5

We might prefer a library or book store or lecture hall without Mein Kampf or the Grand Whoever of the Ku Klux Klan. But a growing list of harmful expressions would inevitably strangle freedom of speech. The ordinance was carefully written to avoid problems of banning and prior restraint, but the right of any woman to claim damages from pornography is just too broad. It seems destined to lead to censorship. What the Minneapolis City Council has before it is a very attractive theory. What MacKinnon and Dworkin have written is a very persuasive and useful definition of pornography. But they haven't yet resolved the conflict between the harm of pornography and the value of free speech. In its present form, this is still a shaky piece of law.   6

FOR CLASS DISCUSSION

The following questions are based on Ellen Goodman's pornography essay, which you have just read. Using whichever version of the essay is most helpful, prepare answers to the questions. Work either as individuals or in small groups.

1. In one or two sentences, summarize the argument supporting the Minneapolis ordinance.

2. In one or two sentences, summarize Goodman's own argument.

3. Which version of the essay, 1 or 2, did you find most useful in answering the preceding two questions?

4. Which version of the essay do you think is most effective? Why?

If you are like our own students, two-thirds of you will prefer Goodman's version. However, many students report that the classical version helped them answer the questions more easily. By placing the thesis statement at the end of the introduction ("... the Minneapolis ordinance is a bad law because it has potentially dangerous consequences") the classical version gives you up front a clear summary of the writer's position. Also, by laying out the syllogistic core of the Minneapolis ordinance, the classical version makes it easier to find and summarize the opposing view.

But even though the argument of the classical version can be grasped more quickly, most readers still prefer Goodman's version? Why is this?

Most people point to the greater sense of complexity and surprise in the delayed-thesis version, a sense that comes largely from the delayed discovery of the writer's position. Whereas the classical version almost immediately labels the ordinance a "bad law," the original version withholds judgment, inviting the reader to examine the law more sympathetically and to identify with the position of those who drafted it. Rather than distancing herself from those who see pornography as a violation of women's rights, Goodman shares with her readers her own struggles to think through these issues, thereby persuading us of her genuine sympathy for the ordinance and for its feminist proponents. In the end, her delayed thesis renders her final rejection of the ordinance not only more surprising but more convincing.

Clearly, then, a writer's decision about when to reveal her thesis is critical. Revealing the thesis early makes the writer seem more hardnosed, more sure of her position, more confident about how to divide the ground into friendly and hostile camps, more in control. Delaying the thesis, in contrast, complicates the issues, increases reader sympathy for more than one view, and heightens interest in the tension among alternative views and in the writer's struggle for clarity.

As this example suggests, the interplay between *pathos* and *ethos* is complex. By delaying her thesis, Goodman projects an image of herself (*ethos*) as sympathetic to feminism and troubled by her own differences with feminist scholars on this issue. This image of herself increases reader sympathy (*pathos*) for her dilemma and offers assurances that her position has been not been lightly chosen.

The Ellen Goodman example reveals the complexity of choices writers make when they draft and revise. It is often conceptually easier to write an argument in the classical form, which works well in many rhetorical situations. Variations on this form, however, can sometimes make your argument more persuasive as well as more stylistically subtle. Further discussion of how and when to vary an argument's structure occurs in Chapter 8.

CONCLUSION

In this chapter, we have explored ways that writers can strengthen the persuasiveness of their arguments by using audience-based reasons and by creating appeals to *ethos* and *pathos.* Arguments are more persuasive if they are rooted in the underlying assumptions, beliefs, and values of the intended audience. Similarly, arguments are more persuasive if readers trust the credibility of the writer and if the argument appeals to readers' hearts and imaginations as well as their intellects. We have also seen how the placement of a writer's thesis—whether stated explicitly in the beginning or delayed until the end of the essay—can have subtle effects on the way both the argument and the writer are received.

chapter 8

Accommodating Your Audience

Treating Differing Views

In the previous chapter we discussed ways of moving an audience. In this chapter we discuss a writer's options for accommodating her audience's views on her issue—whether to omit them, refute them, concede to them, or incorporate them through compromise and conciliation. In particular, we show you how your choices about structure and tone will often differ depending on whether your audience is sympathetic, undecided or neutral, or strongly resistant to your views. The strategies explained in this chapter will increase your flexibility as an arguer and enhance your chance of being persuasive to a wide variety of audiences.

OPENING EXERCISE

As an introduction to these concerns, consider the following case:

SHOULD TEAM WRITING BE REQUIRED IN A FIRST-YEAR COMPOSITION COURSE?

A heated controversy recently occurred in the composition program at University X. As an experiment, instructors for several sections of first-year composition asked their students to write a group proposal argument (written by five-person teams) that offered a solution for a campus problem chosen by each team. Each student's grade for the project was based on the quality of the final team product adjusted upward or downward according to each student's individual contributions to the team effort.

Several teachers in the experiment, enthusiastic about the success of this assignment, proposed to the Composition Committee that a similar team-writing experience be required in all sections of first-year composition. To no one's surprise, this proposal evoked controversy with both students and instructors writing letters to the committee supporting or opposing the proposal.

Based on your initial reaction, what position would you take on this controversy? Would you support or oppose a requirement that first-year composition students write one of their formal essays as a group or team? Why?

Now that you know something of the background of this issue and have made your own initial judgment, please read the following two versions of a professor's letter to the Composition Committee supporting the team-writing proposal. Which of the two versions of the letter do you think is more effective?

VERSION 1

I urge the Composition Committee to approve the proposal that team writing be required in first-year composition courses. As an instructor in the experimental program, I have required a team-writing assignment for the last three semesters with very positive results. Let me highlight briefly my reasons for supporting this proposal.

First, the team-writing assignment promotes true active learning. I was impressed by my students' ability to identify and analyze a problem on campus, imagine alternative solutions, and then propose and justify their chosen solution to the problem. The group discussions revealed a high level of critical thinking and creativity.

The group work also taught students excellent revising skills. Acting alternately as drafters and revisers, the students had to make all the parts of the proposal fit together with unified structure and consistent voice and style. Largely because the process was effective, the final products were excellent. Some of their proposals were so good that I have urged the groups to submit them to appropriate university offices.

Additionally, team writing simulates the kind of writing students will do in professional life. Team writing has long been common in science and engineering and is increasingly common in the business world, where reports and proposals are typically written by teams. By teaching students to function in a group environment, the team-writing experience imparts an essential career skill.

Finally, from a teacher's perspective, the team-writing assignment gives instructors a breathing space in the semester when they can schedule more student conferences and provide more individual help. Relieved from a heavy paper-grading load during the team-writing unit, I worked with students on revisions of earlier assignments and gave other kinds of individualized help.

For these reasons, I strongly urge you to make a team-writing experience a required part of our first-year composition courses. If you would like to discuss these ideas with me personally or would like to see examples of work produced by my student groups, please contact me at xxxx.

Sincerely,
Professor _____ Jones

VERSION 2

Despite real difficulties associated with team-writing assignments, I urge the composition committee to approve the proposal that team writing be required in first-year composition courses. As an instructor in the program, I have required a team-writing assignment for the last three semesters. Although I have had my share of difficulties in requiring team writing, the positive benefits of the assignment outweigh the costs.

Let me begin, though, by acknowledging the problem areas. Teachers and students who dislike team writing point with justification to such problems as dysfunctional groups, unequal sharing of work, group difficulties in scheduling out-of-class meetings, personality conflicts, willingness of weak writers to let the good writers do the work, and the very knotty problem of assigning grades equitably. I know these problems well. Last semester one of my students became so angry at her group that she stormed out of the classroom, telling me in the hall that she would drop the class before she would return to her group. Students are so used to working individually rather than together that the strain on the teacher of trying to help them function as a team can be overwhelming.

Despite these problems, I still enthusiastically support a required team-writing experience for first-year students. Here are my reasons.

First, the team-writing assignment promotes true active learning. I was impressed by my students' ability to identify and analyze a problem on campus, imagine alternative solutions, and then propose and justify their chosen solution to the problem. With only a few exceptions, the group conversations during this project—even among groups that didn't seem to be working well together—showed a high level of critical thinking and creativity.

The group work also taught students excellent revising skills. Acting alternately as drafters and revisers, the students had to make all the parts of the proposal fit together with unified structure and consistent voice and style. Largely because the process was effective, the final products were excellent. Some of their proposals were so good that I have urged the groups to submit them to appropriate university offices.

Additionally, team writing simulates the kind of writing students will do in professional life. Team writing has long been common in science and engineering and is increasingly common in the business world, where reports and proposals are typically written by teams. Even the dysfunctional groups benefit from this aspect of team writing. They learn—perhaps the hard way—that professional working groups, unlike friendship groups, require goal orientation, dutiful work habits, and effective cooperation. By teaching students how to work productively in groups, we are imparting an essential career skill.

Finally, from a teacher's perspective, the team-writing assignment gives instructors a breathing space in the semester when they can schedule more student conferences and provide more individual help. Relieved from a heavy paper-grading load, I worked with students on revisions of earlier assignments and gave other kinds of individualized help that would otherwise be impossible.

For these reasons, I strongly urge you to make a team-writing experience a required part of our first-year composition courses. If you would like to discuss these ideas with me personally or would like to see examples of work produced by my student groups, please contact me at xxxx.

Sincerely,
Professor _____ Jones

 FOR CLASS DISCUSSION

Individual task: Freewrite for several minutes describing the differences between the two versions and explaining your decision about which version is more persuasive. **Small group task:** (1) Share your freewrites with each other. (2) What relationship do you find, if any, between each group member's initial position on the team-writing issue and that person's preference for Version 1 or Version 2 as most persuasive? (3) As a group, reach consensus on which letter the instructor should send to the composition committee. Be prepared to explain your reasoning.

ONE-SIDED VERSUS MULTISIDED ARGUMENTS

The previous exercise introduces you to the differences between one-sided and multisided arguments. Version 1 is a one-sided argument. It presents only a positive view of team writing without attempting to look at an opposing perspective. Version 2, on the other hand, is a multisided argument. It still supports team writing, but at various places summarizes possible objections that other teachers might raise.

Which version is more effective rhetorically? That is, which is apt to be more persuasive to an audience?

According to some researchers, if people already agree with a writer's thesis, they usually find one-sided arguments more persuasive. A multisided argument comes across as wishy-washy and makes the writer seem less decisive. On the other hand, if people initially disagree with a writer's thesis, a multisided argument often seems more persuasive because it shows that the writer has listened to other views and thus seems more open-minded and fair. An especially interesting effect has been documented for neutral audiences. In the short run, one-sided arguments seem more persuasive to neutral audiences; in the long run, however, multisided arguments seem to have more staying power. Neutral audiences who've heard only one side of an issue tend to change their minds when they hear alternative arguments. By anticipating and in some cases refuting opposing views, the multisided argument diminishes the surprise and force of subsequent counterarguments and also exposes their weaknesses.

Now that you've heard from the researchers, go back and examine the results of your own little experiment. Do they bear out the experts' findings? If not, why not?

DETERMINING YOUR AUDIENCE'S
RESISTANCE TO YOUR VIEWS

In the previous chapter we emphasized the power of audience-based reasons. In the rest of this chapter we show you another audience-based strategy for increasing the power of your arguments: how to adapt the structure and tone of your essay to your audience, based on the degree of their resistance to your own views.

One way to imagine your relationship to your audience on any given issue is to place them on a scale of resistance from strong support of your position to strong opposition (see Figure 8.1). At the accord end of this scale are likeminded people who basically agree with your position on the issue. At the resistance end are those who strongly disagree with you, perhaps unconditionally, because their values, beliefs, or assumptions sharply differ from your own. In between the accord and resistance ends of the scale lies a range of opinions. Close to your position will be those leaning in your direction but with less conviction than you. Close to the resistance position will be those basically opposed to your view but willing to listen to your argument and perhaps willing to acknowledge some of its strengths. In the middle are those undecided people who are still sorting out their feelings, seeking additional information, and weighing the strengths and weaknesses of alternative views.

Seldom, however, will you encounter an issue in which the range of disagreement follows a simple line from accord to resistance. Often resistant views fall into different categories so that no single line of argument appeals to all those whose views are different from your own. You have to identify not only your audience's resistance to your ideas but also the causes of that resistance.

Consider, for example, an issue that divided the state of Washington when the Seattle Mariners baseball team demanded a new stadium. A ballot initiative asked citizens to raise taxes to build a new retractable roof stadium for the Mariners. Supporters of the initiative faced a complex array of resisting views (see Figure 8.2). Opponents of the initiative could be placed into four different categories. Some simply had no interest in sports, cared nothing about baseball, and saw no benefit in building a huge sports facility in downtown Seattle. Another group loved baseball, perhaps followed the Mariners passionately, but were philosophically opposed to subsidizing rich players and owners with taxpayer money. They argued that the whole sports industry needed to be restructured so that stadiums were paid for out of sports revenues. Still another group was opposed to tax hikes in general.

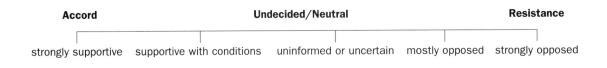

FIGURE 8.1   Scale of resistance

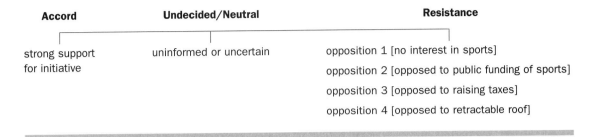

FIGURE 8.2   Scale of resistance, baseball stadium issue

They focused on the principle of reducing the size of government and of using tax revenues only for essential services. Finally, another powerful group supported baseball and supported the notion of public funding of a new stadium, but they opposed the kind of retractable roof stadium specified in the initiative. They wanted an old-fashioned, open-air stadium like Baltimore's Camden Yards or Cleveland's Jacobs Field.

Writers supporting the initiative found it impossible to address all these resisting audiences at once. If a supporter of the initiative wanted to aim an argument at sports haters, he or she could stress the spinoff benefits of a new ballpark (for example, the new ball park would attract tourist revenue, renovate the deteriorating Pioneer Square neighborhood, create jobs, make sports lovers more apt to vote for public subsidies of the arts, and so forth). But these arguments were irrelevant to those who wanted an open-air stadium, who opposed tax hikes categorically, or who objected to public subsidy of millionaires.

Another kind of complexity occurs when a writer is positioned between two kinds of resisting views. Consider the position of student writer Sam, a gay man who wished to argue that gay and lesbian people should actively support legislation to legalize same-sex marriage (see Figure 8.3). Most arguments that support same-sex marriage are aimed at conservative heterosexual audiences who tend to dislike homosexuality and stress traditional family values. But Sam imagined writing for a gay magazine such as the *Harvard Gay and Lesbian Review* or *The Advocate*, and he wished to aim his argument at liberal gay and lesbian activists who opposed traditional marriage on different grounds. These thinkers, critiquing traditional bourgeois marriage for the way it stereotypes gender roles and limits the freedom of partners, argued that heterosexual marriage wasn't a good model for relationships in the gay community. These persons constituted an audience 180 degrees removed from the conservative proponents of family values who oppose same-sex marriage on moral and religious grounds.

In writing his early drafts, Sam was stymied by his attempt to address both audiences at once. It was only after he blocked out the conservative "family values" audience and imagined an audience of what he called "liberationist" gays and lesbians was he able to develop a consistent argument. (You can read Sam's essay on pp. 300–301.)

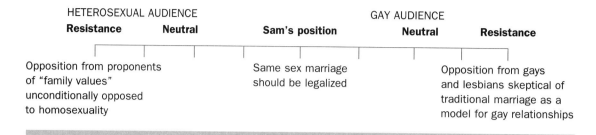

FIGURE 8.3   Scale of resistance for same-sex marriage issue

The Mariners example and the same-sex marriage example illustrate the difficulty of adapting your argument to your audience's position on the scale of resistance. Yet doing so is important because you need a stable vision of your audience before you can determine an effective content, structure, and tone for your argument. As we showed in Chapter 7, an effective content derives from your choosing audience-based reasons that appeal to your audience's values, assumptions, and beliefs. As we show in the rest of this chapter, an effective structure and tone are often a function of where your audience falls on the scale of resistance. The next sections show how you can adjust your arguing strategy depending on whether your audience is supportive, neutral, or hostile.

APPEALING TO A SUPPORTIVE AUDIENCE: ONE-SIDED ARGUMENT

Although arguing to a supportive audience might seem like preaching to the choir, such arguments are common. Usually, the arguer's goal is to convert belief into action—to inspire a party member to contribute to a senator's campaign or a bored office worker to sign up for a change-your-life weekend seminar.

Typically, appeals to a supportive audience are structured as one-sided arguments that either ignore opposing views or reduce them to "enemy" stereotypes. Filled with motivational language, these arguments list the benefits that will ensue from your donations to the cause and the horrors just around the corner if the other side wins. One of the authors of this text recently received a fund-raising letter from an environmental lobbying group declaring, "It's crunch time for the polluters and their pals on Capitol Hill." The "corporate polluters" and "anti-environment politicians," the letter continues, have "stepped up efforts to roll back our environmental protections—relying on large campaign contributions, slick PR firms and well-heeled lobbyists to get the job done before November's election." This letter makes the reader feel part of an in-group of good guys fighting the big business "polluters." Nothing in the letter examines environmental issues from business's perspective or attempts to examine alternative views fairly. Since the intended audience already believes in the cause, nothing in the letter invites readers to consider the issues more complexly. Rather, the goal is to solidify support, increase the fervor of belief, and inspire action. Most appeal arguments make it easy to act, ending with an 800 phone number to call, a tear-out postcard to send in, or a congressperson's address to write to.

APPEALING TO A NEUTRAL OR UNDECIDED AUDIENCE: CLASSICAL ARGUMENT

The in-group appeals that motivate an already supportive audience can repel a neutral or undecided audience. Because undecided audiences are like jurors weighing all sides of an issue, they distrust one-sided arguments that caricature other views. Generally the best strategy for appealing to undecided audiences is the classical argument described in Chapter 3 (pp. 63–66).

What characterizes the classical argument is the writer's willingness to summarize opposing views fairly and to respond to them openly—either by trying to refute them or by conceding to their strengths and then shifting to a different field of values. Let's look at these strategies in more depth.

Summarizing Opposing Views

The first step toward responding to opposing views in a classical argument is to summarize them fairly. Follow the "principle of charity," which obliges you to avoid loaded, biased, or "straw man" summaries that oversimplify or distort opposing arguments, making them easy to knock over. Consider the differences between the following fair and unfair summaries of Professor Jones's hypothetical letter supporting a required team-written paper in freshman English.

UNFAIR SUMMARY

Professor Jones is obviously caught up in recent educational fads as we can see by all her jargon about "active learning," "critical thinking," and "group processes." She supports team writing primarily because it reduces her paper-grading load. She also claims that a single team-writing experience will lead to sudden improvements in thinking skills and to enhanced career success.

Although this summary shows an opposing view, it both distorts and oversimplifies Jones's position. First, it misrepresents Jones's reason for liking the reduced paper-grading feature of team writing. It also exaggerates and hence oversimplifies

Jones's claims about the value of team writing to teach critical thinking and enhance career success. Through distortion and oversimplification, the writer sets up a straw man that is easier to knock down than is Jones's original argument.

FAIR SUMMARY

Professor Jones presents four main reasons for supporting team writing. First, she argues that team writing promotes active learning and teaches critical thinking; second, it helps students learn revising skills, which in turn leads to better written papers; third, she believes that team writing prepares students for the kind of writing environment that prevails in the world of work; fourth, she argues that the time saved in paper grading can be converted profitably to time helping individuals.

This version follows the principle of charity, trying to state Jones's views fairly and accurately.

 FOR CLASS DISCUSSION

Suppose that you believe that ROTC courses ought to receive academic credit and thus you oppose the views of the student writer of "ROTC Courses Should Not Get College Credit" on pp. 448–449. Working individually or in groups, prepare two different summaries of this writer's views as follows:

1. Unfair summary using loaded language or straw man oversimplification or distortion

2. Fair summary following the principle of charity

When you are finished, be prepared to read your summaries aloud to the class as a whole.

Refuting Opposing Views

Once you have summarized opposing views, you can either refute them or concede to their strengths. In refuting an opposing view, you attempt to convince readers that its argument is logically flawed, inadequately supported, or based on erroneous assumptions. In refuting an argument, you can rebut (1) the writer's stated reason and grounds, or (2) the writer's warrant and backing, or (3) both. Put in less specialized language, you can rebut a writer's reasons and evidence or his underlying assumptions. Let's begin with a simple example. Suppose you wanted to refute the argument:

We shouldn't elect Joe as chairperson because he is too bossy.

Displayed in Toulmin terms, this argument looks like this:

CLAIM:	We shouldn't elect Joe as chairperson.
STATED REASON:	because he is too bossy
GROUNDS:	evidence that Joe is bossy
WARRANT:	Bossy people make bad chairpersons.

One way to refute this argument is to rebut the stated reason and grounds.

> I disagree with you that Joe is bossy. In fact, Joe is very non-bossy. He's a good listener who's willing to compromise, and he involves others in decisions. The example you cite for his being bossy wasn't typical. It was a one-time circumstance that doesn't represent his normal behavior. [The writer could then provide examples of Joe's cooperative nature.]

Or you could concede that Joe is bossy but rebut the argument's warrant that bossiness is a bad trait.

> I agree that Joe is bossy, but in this circumstance bossiness is just the trait we need. This committee hasn't gotten anything done for six months and time is running out. We need a decisive person who can come in, get the committee organized, assign tasks, and get the job done.

Let's now illustrate these strategies in a more complex situation. For an example, we'll look at the issue of whether recycling is an effective strategy for saving the environment. A controversial subissue concerning recycling is whether the United States is running out of space for sanitary landfills. Supporters of recycling often argue that there are no places left to dump our garbage. Here is how one environmental writer makes this case:

> Because the United States is running out of landfill space, Americans will simply not be able to put the 180 million tons of solid waste they generate each year into landfills, where 70 percent of it now goes. Since 1979, the United States has exhausted more than two-thirds of its landfills; projections indicate that another one-fifth will close over the next five years. Between 1983 and 1987, for example, New York closed 200 of its 500 landfills; this year Connecticut will exhaust its landfill capacity. If the problem seemed abstract to Americans, it became odiously real in the summer of 1989 as most of the nation watched the notorious garbage barge from Islip, New York wander 6,000 miles, searching for a place to dump its rancid 3,100-ton load.*

---

*Lodge, George C. and Jeffrey F. Rayport. "Knee-deep and Rising: America's Recycling Crisis," *Harvard Business Review* (Sept./Oct. 1991), p. 132.

This passage tries to persuade us that the U.S. is running out of landfill space. Now watch how writer John Tierney attempts to refute this argument in an influential 1996 *New York Times Magazine* article entitled "Recycling Is Garbage."

[Proponents of recycling believe that] our garbage will bury us. The Mobro's[†] saga was presented as a grim harbinger of future landfill scarcity, but it actually represented a short-lived scare caused by new environmental regulations. As old municipal dumps were forced to close in the 1980's, towns had to send their garbage elsewhere and pay higher prices for scarce landfill space. But the higher prices predictably encouraged companies to open huge new landfills, in some regions creating a glut that set off price-cutting wars. Over the past few years, landfills in the South and Middle West have been vying for garbage from the New York area, and it has become cheaper to ship garbage there than to bury it locally.

America has a good deal more landfill space available than it did 10 years ago. . . . A. Clark Wiseman, an economist at Gonzaga University in Spokane, Wash., has calculated that if Americans keep generating garbage at current rates for 1,000 years, and if all their garbage is put in a landfill 100 yards deep, by the year 3000 this national garbage heap will fill a square piece of land 35 miles on each side.

This doesn't seem a huge imposition in a country the size of America. The garbage would occupy only 5 percent of the area needed for the national array of solar panels proposed by environmentalists. The millennial landfill would fit on one-tenth of 1 percent of the range land now available for grazing in the continental United States.*

In this case, Tierney uses counterevidence to rebut the reason and grounds of the original enthymeme: "Recycling is needed because the United States is running out of landfill space." Tierney attacks this argument by disagreeing with the stated reason that the United States is running out of landfill space.

But writers are also apt to question the underlying assumptions (warrants) of an opposing view. For an example, consider another recycling controversy: From an economic perspective, is recycling cost effective? In criticizing recycling, Tierney argues that recycling wastes money; he provides evidence that "every time a sanitation department crew picks up a load of bottles and cans from the curb, New York City loses money." In Toulmin's terms, Tierney's line of reasoning is structured as follows:

TIERNEY'S ENTHYMEME:	Promoting recycling is bad policy because it costs more to recycle material than to bury the same material in a landfill.

[†]The *Mobro* is the name of the notorious garbage barge from Islip, New York, referred to at the end of the previous quotation.

*John Tierney. "Recycling Is Garbage," *New York Times Magazine,* 30 June 1996, p. 28.

CLAIM:	Promoting recycling is bad policy.
STATED REASON:	because it costs more to recycle material than to bury the same material in a landfill
GROUNDS:	evidence of the high cost of recycling [Tierney cites evidence that it costs New York City $200 more per ton to collect and dispose of recyclables than to bury them]
WARRANT:	We should dispose of garbage in the least expensive way.

In rebutting Tierney's argument, proponents of recycling typically accepted Tierney's figures on recycling costs in New York City (that is, they agreed that in New York City recycling was more expensive than burying garbage). But in various ways they attacked his warrant. Typically, proponents of recycling said that even if the costs of recycling were higher than burying wastes in a landfill, recycling still benefited the environment by reducing the amount of virgin materials taken from nature. This argument says, in effect, that saving virgin resources takes precedence over economic costs.

These examples show how a refutation can focus on either the stated reasons and grounds of an argument or upon the warrants and backing.

❧ FOR CLASS DISCUSSION

Imagine how each of the following arguments might be fleshed out with grounds and backing. Then attempt to refute each argument by suggesting ways to rebut the reason and grounds, or the warrant and backing, or both.

1. Writing courses should be pass/fail because the pass/fail system would encourage more creativity.

2. The government should make cigarettes illegal because cigarettes cause cancer and heart disease.

3. Majoring in engineering is better than majoring in music because engineers make more money than musicians.

4. People should not eat meat because doing so causes needless pain and suffering to animals.

5. The endangered species law is too stringent because it seriously hampers the economy.

Strategies for Rebutting Evidence

Whether you are rebutting an argument's reasons and grounds or its warrant and backing, you will frequently need to question a writer's use of evidence. Here are some strategies that you can use:

Deny the Facticity of the Data

Generally a piece of data can be considered a fact when a variety of observers all agree that the datum corresponds with reality. Often, though, what one writer considers a fact another may consider a case of wrong information. If you have reason to doubt a writer's facts, then call them into question.

Cite Counterexamples or Countertestimony

One of the most effective ways to counter an argument based on examples is to cite a counterexample. If someone argues that women are often better managers than men because they are more people conscious, several counterexamples of cold, impersonal women or of kindly, warm-hearted men can cast doubt on the whole argument. The effect of counterexamples is to deny the conclusiveness of the original data. Similarly, citing an authority whose testimony counters other expert testimony is a good way to begin refuting an argument based on testimony.

Cast Doubt on the Representativeness or Sufficiency of Examples

Examples are powerful only if the audience feels them to be representative and sufficient. Many environmentalists complained that John Tierney's attack on recycling was based too largely on data from New York City and that it didn't accurately take into account the more positive experiences of other cities and states. When data from outside New York City were examined, the cost-effectiveness and positive environmental impact of recycling seemed more apparent.

Cast Doubt on the Relevance or Recency of the Examples, Statistics, or Testimony

The best evidence is up to date. In a rapidly changing universe, data that are even a few years out of date are often ineffective. If a writer uses demographic data to argue that your community doesn't need a new nursing home, you could raise questions about the recency of the data, arguing that the percentage of elderly has increased since the time the data were collected. Another problem with data is their occasional lack of relevance. For example, in arguing that an adequate ozone layer is necessary for preventing skin cancers, it is not relevant to cite statistics on the alarming rise of lung cancers.

Call into Question the Credibility of an Authority

One trick of sophistry is to have an authority within one field speak out on issues in a different field. Modern advertising regularly uses this kind of sleight-of-hand whenever movie stars or athletes endorse products about which they have no expertise. The problem of credibility is trickier when an apparent authority has no particular expertise in a specific subfield within the discipline. For example, a psychologist specializing in the appetite mechanisms of monkeys might not be an expert witness on schizophrenic behavior in humans, even though a writer could cite that person as a Ph.D. in psychology. Thus, if you can attack the credibility of the authority, you can sometimes undermine the effectiveness of the testimony. (This procedure is different from the *ad hominem* fallacy discussed in Appendix 1 because it doesn't attack the personal character of the authority but only the authority's expertise on a specific matter.)

Question the Accuracy or Context of Quotations

Evidence based on testimony is frequently distorted by being either misquoted or taken out of context. Often scientists will qualify their findings heavily, but these qualifications will be omitted by the popular media. You can thus attack the use of a quotation by putting it in its original context or by restoring the qualifications accompanying the quotation in its original source.

Question the Way Statistical Data Were Produced or Interpreted

Chapter 6 provides fuller treatment of how to refute statistics. In general you can rebut statistical evidence by calling into account how the data were gathered, treated mathematically, or interpreted. It can make a big difference, for example, whether you cite raw numbers or percentages or whether you choose large or small increments for the axes of graphs.

Example of Student Essay Using Refutation Strategy

The following student essay is an example of a short argument that uses a refutation strategy to appeal to a neutral or undecided audience. Note the way the writer summarizes and then refutes opposing views.

Abstract Versus Representational Art

Have you ever come across a painting by Picasso, Mondrian, Pollock, Miró, or any other modern abstract painter of this century and found yourself engulfed in a brightly colored canvas that your senses cannot interpret? Many people, especially out here in the West, [1] would tend to scoff and denounce abstractionism as senseless trash. For instance, these people are disoriented by Miró's bright, fanciful creatures and two-dimensional canvas. They click their tongues and shake their heads at Mondrian's grid works, declaring the poor guy played too many Scrabble games. They guffaw at Pollock's canvases of splashed paint, and silently shake their heads in sympathy for Picasso, whose gruesome, distorted figures must be a reflection of his mental health. Then, standing in front of a Charlie Russell, the famous Western artist, they'll declare it a work of God. People feel more comfortable with something they can relate to and understand immediately without too much thought. This is the case with the work of Charlie Russell. Being able to recognize the elements in his paintings—such as trees, horses, and cowboys—gives people a safety line to their world of "reality." These people don't realize, however, how much creativity and artistic talent is required to produce abstract art.

2   People who look down on abstract art have several major arguments to support their beliefs. First, they feel that artists turn abstract because they are not capable of the technical drafting skills that appear in Remington, Russell, and Rockwell pieces. Therefore they created an art form that anyone was capable of and that was less time consuming and then paraded it as artistic progress. Secondly, they feel that the purpose of art is to create something of beauty in an orderly, logical composition. Russell's compositions are balanced and rational; everything sits calmly on the canvas, leaving the viewer satisfied that he has seen all there is to see. The modern abstractionists, on the other hand, seem to compose their pieces irrationally. For example, upon seeing Picasso's *Guernica,* a girlfriend of mine was confused as to the center of focus and turned to ask me, "What's the point?" Finally, many people feel that art should portray the ideal and real. The exactness of detail in Charlie Russell's work is an example of this. He has been called a great historian because his pieces depict the lifestyle, dress, and events of the times. His subject matter is derived from his own experiences on the trail, and reproduced to the smallest detail.

3   I agree in part with many of these arguments, and at one time even endorsed them. But now, I believe differently. First I object to the argument that abstract artists are not capable of drafting—representational drawing—and therefore created a new art form that required little technical skill. Many abstract artists, such as Picasso, are excellent draftsmen. As his work matured, Picasso became more abstract in order to increase the expressive quality of his work. *Guernica* was meant as a protest against the bombing of that city by the Germans. To express the terror and suffering of the victims more vividly, he distorted the figures and presented them in a black and white journalistic manner. If he had used representational image and color, much of the emotional content would have been lost and the piece probably would not have caused the demand for justice that it did.

4   Secondly, I disagree that a piece *must* be logical and aesthetically pleasing to be art. More important, I feel, is the message it conveys to its viewers. It should reflect the ideals and issues of its time and be true to itself, not just a flowery, glossy surface. For example, through his work, Mondrian was trying to present a system of simplicity, logic, and rational order. As a result, his pieces did end up looking like a Scrabble board. Miró created powerful, surrealistic images from his dreams and subconscious. Pollock's huge splatter paint canvases surround the viewer with a fantastic linear environment. All of these artists were

trying to evoke a response from society through an expressionistic manner, not just create a pretty picture to be admired and passed by.

Finally, abstract artists and representational artists maintain different ideas about "reality." To the representational artist, reality is what he sees with his eyes. This is the reality he *reproduces* on canvas. To the abstract artist, reality is what he feels about what his eyes see. This is the reality he *interprets* on canvas. This can be illustrated by Mondrian's *Trees* series. You can actually see the progression from the early recognizable, though abstracted, *Trees,* to his final solution, the grid system.   5

A cycle of abstract and representational art began with the first scratching of prehistoric man. From the abstractions of ancient Egypt to representational, classical Rome, returning to abstractionism in early Christian art and so on up to the present day, the cycle has continued. But this day and age may witness its death through the camera. With film, there is no need to produce finely detailed, historical records manually; the camera does this for us faster and more efficiently. Perhaps we will soon be heading for a time where representational art is nonexistent and artists and their work will be redefined. With abstractionism as the victor, maybe another cycle will be touched off. With no need for more Charlie Russells, artists will differ from each other in some other way.   6

 FOR CLASS DISCUSSION ══════════════════════════════════

1. What is the issue being addressed in this essay?

2. What is the writer's claim?

3. Summarize in a single sentence the opposing view that the writer tries to refute. State the claim and then summarize each opposing reason as a because clause attached to that claim.

4. How does the writer attempt to refute each line of reasoning in the opposing argument?

Conceding to Opposing Views

In writing a classical argument, a writer must sometimes concede to an opposing argument rather than refute it. Sometimes you encounter portions of an argument that you simply can't refute. For example, suppose you support the legalization of hard drugs such as cocaine and heroin. Adversaries of legalization cite alarming statistics enumerating the increases in drug users and addicts that will result from legalization. You might dispute the size of their numbers, but you reluctantly agree that legalization will increase drug use and hence addiction. Your strategy in this case is not to refute the opposing argument, but to concede to it by admitting that legalization of hard drugs will promote heroin and cocaine addiction. Having made that concession, your task is then to show that the benefits of drug legalization still outweigh the costs you've just conceded.

As this example shows, the strategy of a concession argument is to switch from the field of values employed by the writer you disagree with to a different field of values more favorable to your position. You don't try to refute the writer's stated reason and grounds (by arguing that legalization will *not* lead to increased drug usage and addiction), nor his warrant (by arguing that increased drug use and addiction is not a problem). Rather, you shift the argument to a new field of values by introducing a new warrant, one that you think your audience can share (that the benefits of legalization—eliminating the black market and ending the crime and violence associated with procurement of drugs—outweigh the costs of increased addiction). To the extent that opponents of legalization share your desire to stop drug-related crime, shifting to this new field of values is a good strategy. Although it may seem that you weaken your own position by conceding to an opposing argument, you may actually strengthen it by increasing your credibility and gaining your audience's goodwill. Moreover, conceding to one part of an opposing argument doesn't mean that you won't refute other parts of that argument.

A good illustration of the concession strategy is Version 2 of the team-writing argument (pp. 168–169). The writer does not try to refute the argument against requiring a team-written paper. She concedes that a team-writing assignment can create a bundle of headaches for teachers, including dysfunctional groups, inequities in grading, and so forth. Rather, her strategy is to shift from the opposing field of values (teacher comfort, ease of grading, reduction of hassles) to a different field of values (active learning, gaining an important career skill, extra time for teachers to schedule conferences). By conceding that team-writing assignments can cause headaches for teachers, the writer achieves a fair-minded *ethos* that may be more persuasive than a combative *ethos.*

APPEALING TO A RESISTANT AUDIENCE: DELAYED THESIS OR ROGERIAN ARGUMENT

Whereas classical argument is effective for neutral or undecided audiences, it is often less effective for audiences strongly opposed to the writer's position. Because resisting audiences often hold values, assumptions, or beliefs widely different from the writer's, they are unswayed by classical argument, which attacks their world view too directly. On many values-laden issues such as abortion, gun control, gay rights, and welfare reform the distance between a writer and a resisting audience can be so great that dialog hardly seems possible.

Because of these wide differences in basic beliefs and values, a writer's goal is seldom to convert resistant readers to the writer's position. The best that the writer can hope for is to reduce somewhat the level of resistance, perhaps by opening up a channel of conversation, increasing the reader's willingness to listen, and preparing the way for future dialog. If you can get a resistant audience to say, "Well, I still don't agree with you at all but I now understand you better and respect your views a bit more," you will have been highly successful.

Delayed Thesis Argument

In some cases, you can reach a resistant audience by using a *delayed thesis* structure. We explained this strategy in Chapter 7, where we showed how professional writer Ellen Goodman, arguing against the Minneapolis city ordinance on pornography, increased her rapport with her audience by delaying her thesis until the end. By not revealing her thesis until after she explored the complexity of the issue and described resisting views sympathetically, she avoided an adversarial us-against-them tone and gained her audience's respect. (See pp. 159–164 for further discussion of delayed thesis arguments.)

Rogerian Argument

An even more powerful strategy for addressing resistant audiences is a conciliatory strategy often called *Rogerian argument,* named after psychologist Carl Rogers, who used this strategy to help people resolve differences.* Rogerian argument emphasizes "empathic listening," which Rogers defined as the ability to see an issue sympathetically from another person's perspective. He trained people to withhold judgment of another person's ideas until after they listened attentively to the other person, understood that person's reasoning, appreciated that person's values, respected that person's humanity—in short, walked in that person's shoes. Before disagreeing with another person, Rogers would tell his clients, you must be able to summarize that person's argument so accurately that he or she will say, "Yes, you understand my position."

What Carl Rogers understood is that traditional methods of argumentation are threatening. When you try to persuade people to change their minds on an issue, Rogers claimed, you are actually demanding a change in their worldview—to get other people, in a sense, to quit being their kind of person and start being your kind of person. Research psychologists have shown that persons are often not swayed by a logical argument if it somehow threatens their own view of the world. Carl Rogers was therefore interested in finding ways to make arguments less threatening. In Rogerian argument the writer typically waits until the end of the essay to present his position, and that position is often a compromise between the writer's original views and those of the resisting audience. Because Rogerian

---

*See Carl Rogers' essay "Communication: Its Blocking and Its Facilitation" in his book *On Becoming a Person* (Boston: Houghton Mifflin, 1961), pp. 329–37. For a fuller discussion of Rogerian argument, see Richard Young, Alton Becker, and Kenneth Pike, *Rhetoric: Discovery and Change* (New York: Harcourt Brace, 1972).

argument stresses the psychological as well as logical dimensions of argument, and because it emphasizes reducing threat and building bridges rather than winning an argument, it is particularly effective when dealing with emotionally laden issues.

Under Rogerian strategy, the writer reduces the sense of threat in her argument by showing that *both writer and resistant audience share many basic values.* Instead of attacking the audience as wrongheaded, the Rogerian writer respects her audience's intelligence and humanity and demonstrates an understanding of the audience's position before presenting her own position. Finally, the Rogerian writer never asks the audience to capitulate entirely to the writer's side—just to shift somewhat toward the writer's views. By acknowledging that he or she has already shifted toward the audience's views, the writer makes it easier for the audience to accept compromise. All of this negotiation ideally leads to a compromise between—or better, a synthesis of—the opposing positions.

The key to successful Rogerian argument, besides the art of listening, is the ability to point out areas of agreement between the writer's and reader's positions. For example, if you support a woman's right to choose abortion and you are arguing with someone completely opposed to abortion, you're unlikely to convert your reader, but you might reduce the level of resistance. You begin this process by summarizing your reader's position sympathetically, stressing your shared values. You might say, for example, that you also value babies; that you also are appalled by people who treat abortion as a form of birth control; that you also worry that the easy acceptance of abortion diminishes the value society places on human life; and that you also agree that accepting abortion lightly can lead to lack of sexual responsibility. Building bridges like these between you and your readers makes it more likely that they will listen to you when you present your own position.

In its emphasis on establishing common ground, Rogerian argument has much in common with recent feminist theories of argument. Many feminists criticize classical argument as rooted in a male value system and tainted by metaphors of war and combat. Thus, classical arguments, with their emphasis on assertion and refutation, are typically praised for being "powerful," "forceful," or "disarming." The writer "defends" his position and "attacks" his "opponent's" position using facts and data as "ammunition" and reasons as "big guns" to "blow away" his opponent's claim. According to some feminists, viewing argument as war can lead to inauthenticity, posturing, and game playing. The traditional pro-con debate—defined in one of our desk dictionaries as "a formal contest of argumentation in which two opposing teams defend and attack a given proposition"—treats argument as verbal jousting, more concerned to determine a winner than to clarify an issue (see Chapter 1, p. 4).

One of our woman students, who excelled as a debater in high school and received straight As in argument classes, recently explained in an essay her growing alienation from male rhetoric. "Although women students are just as likely to excel in 'male' writing . . . we are less likely to feel as if we were saying something authentic and true." Later the student elaborated on her distrust of "persuasion":

FOR CLASS DISCUSSION

1. In this letter, what shared values between writer and audience does the writer stress?

2. Imagine the letter rewritten as a classical argument. How would it be different?

CONCLUSION

This chapter has shown you the difference between one- and multisided arguments and explained why multisided arguments are apt to be more persuasive to neutral or resisting audiences. A multisided argument generally includes a fair summary of differing views, followed by either refutation, concession, or Rogerian synthesis. The strategies you use for treating resistant views depends on the audience you are trying to reach and your purpose. We explained how audiences can be placed on a scale of resistance ranging from strongly supportive to strongly resistant. In addressing supportive audiences, writers typically compose one-sided arguments with strong motivational appeals to action. Neutral or undecided audiences generally respond most favorably to classical arguments that set out strong reasons in support of the writer's position and yet openly address alternative views, which are first summarized and then either rebutted or conceded to. When the audience is strongly resistant, a delayed thesis or Rogerian strategy is most effective at reducing resistance and helping move the audience slightly toward the writer's views.

 ## WRITING ASSIGNMENTS FOR CHAPTERS 7 AND 8

The writing assignments for Chapters 7 and 8 require careful attention to your audience's views. The first two options are short arguments that give you specific practice at addressing alternative views. The last option calls for a longer, classical argument.

OPTION 1: *Summarizing and Refuting Opposing Views* This assignment asks you to practice the summary and refutation section of a standard classical argument. It calls for a self-announcing structure and asks you to adopt an *ethos* of confident self-assurance about the rightness of your own position. Choose an issue where there is a clear opposing view that you disagree with. The purpose of this assignment is to summarize and refute that opposing view. Before drafting this essay, reread pp. 173–181 on "Addressing Neutral or Undecided Audiences."

Write a multiparagraph essay in which you summarize a position different from yours and then show the weaknesses of that position. Your essay should have four main sections. The opening section should introduce your issue, give it presence, and briefly indicate your own position on the issue (without developing that position). Your second section should summarize an alternative view, following the principle of charity. Make clear in your transition to this section that you are summarizing a view different from your own; otherwise your readers will assume it is your view and get confused. Each of the reasons supporting the differing view should be clearly highlighted. The third and longest section of your essay should refute each of the reasons summarized in the previous section. (You may concede to some of the reasons.) Finally, your last section should provide a conclusion.

The student essay on abstract art (pp. 179–181) illustrates this assignment.

OPTION 2: *Rogerian Strategy*   This assignment asks you to practice a Rogerian strategy aimed at reducing the psychological distance between you and a strongly resisting audience. Choose a topic in which you address an audience that has strong psychological or emotional resistance to your position.

Write a multiparagraph essay that refrains from presenting your position until the conclusion. The opening section introduces the issue and provides background. The second section sympathetically summarizes the resistant view. The third section creates a bridge between writer and resistant audience by pointing out major areas of agreement. After examining this common ground, the third section then points out areas of disagreement but stresses that these are minor compared with the major areas of agreement already discussed. Finally, the last section presents the writer's position, which, if possible, should be a compromise or synthesis indicating that the writer has shifted his original position (or at least his sympathies) toward the resistant view and is now asking the opposition to make a similar shift toward the writer's new position. Your goal here, through tone, arrangement, and examination of common values, is to reduce the threat of your argument in the eyes of your audience. Before drafting this essay, reread pages 183–185, where we discuss Rogerian argument.

The student letter to Beth Downey (pp. 185–186) illustrates this strategy.

OPTION 3: *A Classical Argument*   Write a classical argument, as explained on pages 63–66. In essence, this essay combines the two or more reasons assignment on page 143 (Option 5) with the summary and refutation assignment on page 187 (Option 1). A classical argument has a self-announcing structure. Your introduction will present your issue, provide needed background, and announce your thesis. It may also provide a brief forecasting passage to help the reader anticipate the shape of your essay (see p. 143). In the body of your essay, you summarize and refute opposing views as well as present your own reasons and evidence in support of your position. It is your choice whether you summarize and refute opposing views before or after you have made your own case. Generally, try to end your essay with your strongest arguments.

p a r t   t h r e e

Arguments in Depth

Five Categories of Claims

CHAPTER 9   Using the Categories of Claims to Generate Ideas

CHAPTER 10   Definition Arguments: X Is/Is Not a Y

CHAPTER 11   Causal Arguments: X Causes/Does Not Cause Y

CHAPTER 12   Resemblance Arguments: X Is/Is Not Like Y

CHAPTER 13   Evaluation Arguments: X Is/Is Not a Good Y

CHAPTER 14   Proposal Arguments: "We Should/Should Not Do X"

CHAPTER 15   Ethical Arguments

Using the Categories of Claims to Generate Ideas

In Parts I and II, we discussed the arguing process, the basic structure of arguments, and the relation of arguments to audience. In Part III, our goal is to help you understand the different patterns of thought called for by different kinds of argument claims. Once you learn the patterns of organization and thought characteristic of each claim category, you can use those patterns to develop your argument.

In particular, Part III introduces you to five different categories of argument: definitional arguments, cause/consequence arguments, analogy/resemblance arguments, evaluation arguments, and proposal arguments. The first three of these categories concern questions of truth; the last two concern questions of value.

The five-category schema is not primarily a tool for classifying arguments; in fact, you will come across many arguments that resist and some that defy ready classification. Rather, the five-category schema is mainly an invention tool. By understanding how certain categories of claims are typically developed, you can confidently generate reasons and support for your position and evaluate the strengths and weaknesses of alternative views.

The present chapter introduces you to the five-category schema and explains a simple three-step strategy for generating ideas for values arguments. The remaining chapters of Part III treat each of the categories in more detail.

WHAT IS A TRUTH ARGUMENT?

The first three categories in our schema—sometimes called *truth arguments*—involve disputes about the way reality is (or was or will be). Unlike factual claims, which can be confirmed or disconfirmed by using agreed-on empirical measures, truth claims involve interpretation of facts that must be supported by reasons.

Determining the point at which factual claims turn into truth claims, however, is tricky. The French mathematician Poincaré said that a fact is something that is "common to several thinking beings and could be common to all." Water freezes at 32 degrees; Chicago is in Illinois; the state of Illinois did not ratify the Equal Rights Amendment. These are all factual claims insofar as few people would question them in the first place; if they were questioned, we could refer to a common source (e.g., an almanac or science textbook) that would affirm the claim to the skeptic's satisfaction.

But what about an apparently factual claim such as "Joe is literate." Does that mean Joe can read a newspaper? A traffic sign? A fourth-grade reader? A novel? Or does it mean that Joe has read a number of books that we've agreed are essential for all educated members of our culture to have read? Any time an apparent statement of fact requires interpretation (in this case, the meaning of *literate*), any time there is less than universal agreement about the meaning of a given term and no common source has the authority to settle that difference, we are in the realm of truth claims. Here are some examples of the kinds of truth claims we'll be examining:

Bill Clinton is/is not a liberal. (X is a Y—definitional argument)

Gun control laws will/will not reduce the violent crime rate in the United States. (X causes Y—causal argument)

Investing in the stock market is/is not like gambling. (X is like Y—resemblance argument)

WHAT IS A VALUES ARGUMENT?

For many people, arguments over claims of truth are the only legitimate arguments we can have. Values, after all, are personal, whereas truth can be looked at "objectively." But the notion that values are purely personal is a dangerous one. If for no other reason, it's dangerous because every day we encounter values issues that must be resolved. If you think, for example, that you deserve a promotion and your boss disagrees, your own sense of self-worth won't let you ignore the resulting values conflict.

Although it's true that one's values often begin as feelings founded on personal experience, they must be articulated and justified if they are to be influential in the public sphere. Values incapable of being justified are vulnerable to every sort of questioning. They are reduced to mere "opinions" or "tastes" in your own private collection of likes and dislikes. But values can be justified with reasons and evidence; they are transpersonal and shareable. We can articulate criteria for our values that others would agree are significant and coherent and we can apply those criteria to situations, people, and things to create a reasoned argument.

Here are some examples of the kinds of values claims we'll be examining:

Dr. Choplogic is/is not a good teacher. (X is a good/bad Y—evaluation claim)

Congress should/should not pass a bill protecting speech on the Internet. (We should/should not do X—proposal claim)

Dr. Kervorkian is/is not a good person. (special case of evaluation claim—moral argument)

THREE-STEP STRATEGY FOR DEVELOPING VALUES ARGUMENTS

The five-category schema is an especially powerful invention tool for any argument making a good/bad claim (evaluation) or a should claim (proposal) because the supporting reasons for values claims are often truth claims. For example, consider the arguments used in the early 1990s to protest government funding for an exhibition of homoerotic photographs by Robert Mapplethorpe. Those opposed to the exhibit used all three sorts of truth claims to support their central values claim.

> Taxpayer funding for the Mapplethorpe exhibits ought to be withdrawn [*proposal claim*] because the photographs are pornographic [*definitional claim*], because they promote community acceptance of homosexuality [*cause/consequence claim*], and because the photographs are more like political statements than art [*analogy/ resemblance claim*].

Whatever you might think of the argument, the example shows how the because clauses in support of the proposal claim are truth claims of definition, cause/consequence, and analogy/resemblance. The example suggests how the three truth claims can be used as a strategy to help you think of ways to support value arguments. The rest of this chapter explains this three-step strategy in more detail.

The three-step strategy works by focusing your attention on three different approaches to developing a value argument:

1. An *argument from definition,* in which you argue that doing X is right (wrong) according to some value, assumption, principle, or belief that you share with your audience. (This strategy is also called by various other names, such as an "argument from principle" or an "argument from genus or category.")

2. An *argument from consequence,* in which you argue that doing X is right (wrong) because doing X will lead to consequences that you and your audience believe are good (bad).

3. An *argument from resemblance,* in which you argue that doing X is right (wrong) because doing X is like doing Y, which you and your audience agree is right (wrong).

Let's now illustrate the strategy in more detail. In a recent college course, the instructor asked students whether they would report a classmate for plagiarizing a paper. To the instructor's dismay, the majority of students said "No." How might the teacher support her claim that students should report plagiarists?

An Argument from Definition or Principle

One strategy she could use is to argue as follows: "A student should report a classmate for plagiarizing a paper because plagiarism is fraud." We can call this an *argument from principle* because it is based on the assumption that the audience opposes fraud categorically, no matter what form it takes. Such an argument can also be called an argument from definition because it places the term X (plagiarizing a paper) inside the class or category Y (fraud).

Argument from Definition/Principle

To discover reasons using this strategy, you conduct the following kind of search:

We should (should not) do X because X is _____.

Try to fill in the blank with an appropriate adjective or noun (*good, just, ethical, criminal, ugly, violent, peaceful, wrong, inflationary, healing; an act of kindness, terrorism, murder, true art, political suicide,* and so forth). The point is to try to fill in the blank with a noun or adjective that appeals in some way to your audience's values. Your goal is to show that X belongs to the chosen class or category.

In saying that plagiarism is fraud, the teacher assumes that students would report classmates for other kinds of fraud (for example, for counterfeiting a signature on a check, for entering the university's computer system to alter grades, and so forth). In other words, she knows that the term *fraud* has force on the audience because most people will agree that instances of fraud should be reported. Her task is to define *fraud* and show how plagiarism fits that definition. She could show that fraud is an act of deception to obtain a benefit that doesn't rightly belong to a person. She could then argue that plagiarism is such an act in that it uses deception to procure the benefits of a grade that the plagiarizer has not earned. Although the person whose work is plagiarized may not be directly damaged, the reputation and stature of the university is damaged whenever it grants credentials that have been fraudulently earned. The degree earned by a plagiarizer is fraudulent. Although convincing students that plagiarism is fraud won't guarantee that students will report it, putting plagiarism inside the category of seriously bad things does make such whistle blowing more likely.

An Argument from Consequence

Besides arguing from principle, the teacher could argue from consequence: "A student should report a classmate for plagiarizing a paper because the consequences of plagiarism are bad for everyone." An argument of this type shows first that X causes Y and then that Y is bad.

Argument from Consequence

To discover reasons for using this strategy, conduct the following kind of search:

We should (should not) do X because X leads to these consequences:

_____, _____, _____, _____.

Then think of consequences that your audience will agree are good or bad, as your argument requires.

Using this strategy, the teacher now focuses on the ill effects of plagiarism. She might argue that plagiarism raises the grading curve to the disadvantage of honest students or that it can lead to ill-trained people getting into critical professions. How would you like to have your eyes operated on by someone who plagiarized her work in medical school? She might argue that accepting plagiarism leads to acceptance of moral laxity throughout society, thus making tax dodging, bogus repair charges, and petty theft at work more widespread. She might argue that plagiarism hurts the plagiarist by preventing that person from developing skills needed for later success. She could further argue that plagiarism scandals weaken the reputation of the university and dilute the worth of its degrees. Finally, she could argue that reporting plagiarism will reduce its incidence. All the preceding are arguments from consequence.

An Argument from Resemblance

There is a third strategy the teacher might employ. She could say, "You should report someone for plagiarizing an essay just as you should report someone for entering someone else's painting in an art show." Although similar to an argument from definition, this argument from resemblance employs very different sorts of reasoning.

In using this strategy, the teacher encourages her audience to recognize that an essay is a piece of property like a painting. Once her audience accepts an essay as a piece of property, it's easier for that audience to see its unauthorized use as an act of theft. Whenever we deal with new ways of understanding, analogies are a valuable bridge from old to new ways. But beware—argument from analogy can be very persuasive but also vulnerable to the charge of *false analogy*. Chapter 12 treats resemblance arguments in depth.

Argument from Resemblance

To discover supporting reasons using this strategy, conduct the following kind of search:

We should (should not) do X because doing X is like _____.

Then think of analogies or precedents that are similar to doing X but that currently have more force for your audience. Your task is then to transfer your audience's attitude toward X to the precedent or analogy.

These three strategies—trying to support a values claim from the perspectives of principle, consequence, and resemblance—are powerful means of invention. In selecting among these reasons, choose those most likely to appeal to your audience's assumptions, beliefs, and values.

 FOR CLASS DISCUSSION

1. Working individually or in small groups, use the strategies of principle, consequence, and resemblance to create because clauses that support each of the following claims. Try to have at least one because clause from each of the strategies, but generate as many reasons as possible. Don't worry about whether any individual reason exactly fits the strategy. The purpose is to stimulate thinking, not to fill in the slots.

   EXAMPLE:

CLAIM:	Pit bulls make bad pets
PRINCIPLE:	because they are vicious
CONSEQUENCE:	because owning a pit bull leads to conflicts with neighbors
RESEMBLANCE:	because owning a pit bull is like having a shell-shocked roommate—mostly they're lovely companions but they can turn violent if startled

    a.   Marijuana should be legalized.

    b.   Division I college athletes should receive salaries.

    c.   Couples should live together before they marry.

    d.   The United States should end its energy dependence on other nations.

    e–i. Repeat the exercise, taking a different position on each issue. You might try beginning with the claim: "Pit bulls make good pets."

2. Working individually or in groups, use the principle/consequences/resemblance strategy to explore arguments on both sides of the following issues.

    a. Should spanking be made illegal?

    b. Has affirmative action been good or bad for the nation?

    c. Should all eighteen-year-old American citizens be required to perform some sort of public service?

    d. Should high schools pass out free contraceptives?

    e. Should writing students be graded on the basis of effort rather than performance?

c h a p t e r 10

Definition Arguments
X Is/Is Not a Y

CASE 1

In 1989 the city of Seattle passed the Family Leave Ordinance, which allowed city employees to use their sick leave to care for a "domestic partner" who is ill. To be eligible for domestic partnership, a couple, whether heterosexual or homosexual, had to file affidavits declaring that they share the same home with their partner, are each other's sole partners, and are responsible for each other's common welfare. For purposes of sick and bereavement leave, domestic partnership was synonymous with marriage. Supporters of this ordinance argued that, in the words of one local columnist, "[i]f sick and bereavement leave is given to married workers, then those in domestic partnerships equivalent to marriage ought to have the same privilege."* Opponents of the ordinance argued that domestic partnerships are not marriages and shouldn't be treated as such.

CASE 2

In a famous Los Angeles criminal case, black motorist Rodney King was stopped for erratic driving after a high-speed chase. According to the arresting officers, King then became verbally abusive, threatened the officers, and violently resisted arrest. The subsequent events were captured on a seventeen-minute video made by an amateur filmmaker. The video showed numerous officers with nightsticks and "stun guns" beating and stunning King until he was lying on the ground and then continuing the beating for several more minutes. The key point in the trial and subsequent retrial of the officers was whether they had used "reasonable force" in subduing a suspect who was resisting arrest. Clearly the police must

---

*Terry Tang, *Seattle Times*, 1 Nov. 1990, A10.

protect themselves and use sufficient force to put a suspect under their control, but at what point does reasonable force cross the line and become itself criminal violence?

CASE 3

Economist Isabella Sawhill believes that the current distinctions among "poor," "middle income," and "rich" don't help us understand the real problem of poverty in America. She proposes a new term "underclass." According to her definition, the defining characteristic of the underclass is "dysfunctional behavior," which means failure to follow four major norms of middle-class society: (1) Children are supposed to study hard in school; (2) no one is supposed to become a parent until able to afford a child; (3) adults are supposed to hold regular jobs; and (4) everyone is supposed to obey laws. If we use this definition instead of income level, a rich drug dealer may be a member of the underclass while a poor widow might not be. Sawhill believes society can improve the lives of the underclass by changing these dysfunctional characteristics rather than by relieving poverty directly. A new definition thus aims at changing social policy.*

THE SPECIAL NATURE OF A DEFINITIONAL ISSUE

Many arguments require a definition of key terms. If you are arguing, for example, that after-school jobs are harmful to teenagers because they promote materialism, you will have to define *materialism* somewhere in your argument. Writers regularly define words for their readers either by providing synonyms, by citing a dictionary definition, by stipulating a special definition ("Ordinarily word X means such and so, but in this essay I am using word X to mean this"), or by giving an extended definition in which the writer defines the term and then illustrates the definition with several clarifying examples. This chapter shows you ways to provide such definitions for your readers.

However, this chapter does not focus primarily on writing occasional definitions within arguments. Rather, its purpose is to describe how an entire argument can be devoted to a definitional issue. Definitional arguments, according to our usage, occur whenever people disagree about the actual definition of a term or about the "match" or "fit" between an agreed-on definition and a specific object or concept. For example, an argument about whether or not *Penthouse* magazine is pornographic is a definitional argument; as such it will involve two related issues: (1) What do we mean by "pornographic" (the definition issue)? and (2) Does *Penthouse* fit that definition (the match issue)?

---

*Spencer Rich, "Economist: Behavior Draws Lines Between the Classes," *Seattle Times,* 13 Sept. 1989, A4.

Before proceeding with our explanation of definitional arguments, we will present the writing assignment for Chapter 10. This chapter will be more meaningful to you if you read it in the light of a definitional problem that you will need to solve for one of your own essays.

 WRITING ASSIGNMENT FOR CHAPTER 10:
EXTENDED DEFINITION/BORDERLINE
CASE: IS THIS X A Y?

This assignment asks you to solve a definitional problem. In your essay, you must argue whether or not a given X (a borderline case) belongs to concept Y, which you must define.* You will need to write an extended definition of a concept such as "police brutality," "courageous action," "child abuse," "creative act," "cruelty to animals," "free speech," or another, similar concept that is both familiar yet tricky to define precisely. After you have established your definition, you will need to apply it to a borderline case, arguing whether the borderline case fits or does not fit the definition. For example:

1. Is a daring bank robbery an "act of courage"?
2. Is accounting a "creative profession"?
3. Are highly skilled videogame players "true athletes"?
4. Is a case like the following an instance of "cruelty to animals"?

A bunch of starlings build nests in the attic of a family's house, gaining access to the attic through a torn vent screen. Soon the eggs hatch, and every morning at sunrise the family is awakened by the sounds of birds squawking and wings beating against rafters as the starlings fly in and out of the house to feed the hatchlings. After losing considerably early morning sleep, the family repairs the screen. Unable to get in and out, the parent birds are unable to feed their young. The birds die within a day.

One part of your essay should be an extended definition of your Y term (in this case, cruelty to animals), in which you set forth the criteria for your chosen Y, illustrating each criterion with positive and contrastive examples. Once you have established your definition of Y, you will use it to decide whether your chosen X

*The writing assignment for this chapter, as well as the collaborative exercises for exploration and development of ideas, is based on the work of George Hillocks and his research associates at the University of Chicago. See George Hillocks, Jr., Elizabeth A. Kahn, and Larry R. Johannessen, "Teaching Defining Strategies as a Mode of Inquiry: Some Effects on Student Writing," *Research in the Teaching of English,* 17 (October 1983): 275–84. See also Larry R. Johannessen, Elizabeth A. Kahn, and Carolyn Calhoun Walter, *Designing and Sequencing Prewriting Activities,* Urbana, Ill.: NCTE, 1982.

term (the borderline case—in the preceding case, the repairing of the screen, which leads to the death of the starlings) meets or does not meet the criteria. The rest of this chapter explains this arguing strategy in detail.

THE CRITERIA-MATCH STRUCTURE OF DEFINITIONAL ARGUMENTS

Definitional arguments take the form "X is/is not a Y." This claim can be restated in various ways: "X is/is not a case of Y," "X is/is not an instance of Y," "X does/does not belong to the class of Y," and so forth. The Y term can be either a noun phrase ("Writing graffiti on walls is *vandalism*") or an adjective phrase ("Writing graffiti on walls is *politically useless*"—that is, *"belongs to the class of politically useless things"*).

To appreciate the structure of a definitional argument, consider the shape of a typical definitional claim when its reasons are stated as because clauses: X is a Y because it possesses feature A, because it possesses feature B, and because it possesses feature C. Placed in the Toulmin schema, the argument looks like this:

ENTHYMEME:	X is a Y because it possesses features A, B, and C.
CLAIM:	X is a Y.
STATED REASON:	because it possesses features A, B, and C
GROUNDS:	evidence that X possesses features A, B, and C
WARRANT:	Features A, B, and C are sufficient criteria for calling something a Y.
BACKING:	chains of reasons and evidence (or citing of statutes, etc.) that show that true Ys have features A, B, and C
CONDITIONS OF REBUTTAL:	*Attacking the grounds:* unless X doesn't possess features A, B, and C or doesn't possess sufficient quantities of A, B, and C; unless X possesses, in addition to features A, B, and C, a fourth feature Z, which makes it impossible to be a Y
	Attacking the warrant: unless features A, B, and C are not sufficient criteria for calling something a Y
QUALIFIER:	Depends on level of certainty of definition or level of certainty that X meets definition.

As we have shown, definitional arguments of the type "X is a Y" tend to have a two-part structure: (1) How do we define Y? and (2) Does X fit that definition? We use the term *criteria-match* to describe this structure, which occurs regularly not only in definitional arguments but also, as we shall see in Chapter 13, in values arguments of the type "X is a good/bad Y." The "criteria" part of the structure defines the Y term by setting forth the criteria that must be met to be considered a Y (these criteria are the warrants for the argument). The "match" part examines whether or not the X term meets these criteria (evidence that X meets the criteria is the grounds for the argument). Let's consider several more examples:

DEFINITIONAL CLAIM:	Weaving is a craft, not an art.
	Criteria part: What are the criteria for a craft?
	Match part: Does weaving meet these criteria?
DEFINITIONAL CLAIM:	A Honda assembled in Ohio is/is not an American-made car.
	Criteria part: What criteria have to be met before a car can be called "American-made"?
	Match part: Does a Honda assembled in Ohio meet these criteria?

 FOR CLASS DISCUSSION

Consider the following definitional claims. Working as individuals or in small groups, identify the criteria issue and the match issue for each of the following claims. (Any of these examples could be potential topics for an extended definition/ borderline case argument of the kind you are asked to write for this chapter.)

1. Childbirth is/is not a creative act.

2. Writing graffiti on subways is/is not vandalism.

3. The language "spoken" by porpoises is/is not true language.

4. Beauty contests are/are not sexist events.

5. For purposes of state regulation, bungee jumping from a crane is/is not a "carnival amusement ride."

6. Psychology is/is not a true science.

7. Designing advertisements for television is/is not a creative activity.

8. A surrogate mother—one who has had another woman's fertilized egg implanted in her uterus—is/is not the true mother of the child.

9. Cheerleaders are/are not athletes.

10. Poker is/is not a game of luck.

CONCEPTUAL PROBLEMS OF DEFINITION

Before moving on to discuss ways of defining the Y term in a definitional argument, we need to discuss some of the conceptual difficulties of definition. Language, as you quickly discover when you try to analyze it, is a slippery subject. Definitions aren't as easy to make, or as certain, as a handy pocket dictionary might lead you to believe.

Language as a Way of Ordering the World

Language is our primary means of making sense of the world. Through language we convert what psychologist William James called the "buzz and confusion" of the world into a system of classes and relationships that are represented by a network of verbal signs called words. Each naming word in a language depends on our perceiving a set of attributes that any object or concept must have in order to bear that name. Naming words (with the exception of proper names) don't designate particular items but rather attributes of items. Hence, when we want to know what *king* means, we don't need to know every king in history. We simply need to know the characteristics of kings and kingship to understand and use the term. Through naming we are set free from the world of immediate particulars where we can see only this rock or that flower; through naming we are liberated into a shareable world where we possess with other humans the concept "rock" and the concept "flower" along with arbitrary signs—the vocal sounds "rock" and "flower"—that call forth the concepts.

But if naming is the "first act" of language users, it's far from a simple one. Words allow us to share concepts, but they certainly don't assure perfect mutual understanding. Inevitably, as soon as we've named something, someone else will ask "Whaddya mean by that?" Language, for all its wonderful powers, is an arbitrary system that requires agreement among its users before it can work. And it's not always easy to get that agreement. Thus, the second act after naming is defining. And even at the most basic level, defining things can be devilishly complex.

Why Can't We Just Look in the Dictionary?

"What's so hard about defining?" you might ask. Why not just look in a dictionary? To get a sense of the complexity of defining something, consider the word *red*. What does it mean? Although you might agree with us that *red* is difficult to define in words, you could argue that you can escape the problem simply by pointing to something red. Maybe. But consider the following example cited by I. A. Richards and C. K. Ogden in *The Meaning of Meaning*.

An English explorer, investigating an unknown Congolese language, found himself in a hut with five natives standing around a wooden table. The explorer tapped the table and asked "What's this?" Each of the five Congolese gave him a different answer, causing the explorer to congratulate himself for "working among a people who possessed so rich a language that they had five words for one article" (*Meaning*, p. 78).

Only later did he discover that the natives had understood his apparently straightforward gesture in five different ways. One thought he was asking the word for "wood"; another for "table covering"; the third thought he wanted the word for "hardness"; the fourth for "tapping." Only one guessed his actual intention and gave him the Congolese word for "table." Even when we can point to an object in reality, then, there is possibility for confusion. Think how these difficulties multiply as we move on to words standing for things that can't be pointed toward, words like *love* and *freedom* and *cruelty to animals*.

But let's go back to dictionaries and their limitations in resolving definitional disputes. Say you wanted to resolve the debate over whether or not cheerleaders are athletes by turning to your dictionary. An athlete, according to our dictionary, is "one who is trained to compete in exercises, sports, or games requiring physical strength, agility, or skill." So, are cheerleaders athletes? They do train, and the activity itself of leading cheers would appear to require "strength, agility, and skill." But is it a form of "competition"? Do they "compete" against the rival cheerleaders? And is cheerleading "exercise, sport, or game"? Well, you're going to have to keep looking in your dictionary before you can even begin to address these questions. And take it from us, you won't be able to stop once you've defined all the attributes of your first definition.

Dictionaries usually can't resolve real definitional disputes because their function is to tell us the commonly held meanings of words. That is, their purpose is to tell us what words mean in general usage, without getting into the shades and nuances of meaning that are at the heart of most definitional disputes. People arguing over the definition of *athlete* probably already know the approximate dictionary definition of the word. But words aren't facts and an exact meaning common to all is impossible when words are always changing their meaning over time and between contexts. Moreover, dictionary definitions rarely tell us such things as *to what degree* a given condition must be met before it qualifies for class membership. How much do you need to train to qualify as an athlete? *To what extent* must you compete? How strong or agile does an athlete have to be? On all such critical matters, dictionaries are too often silent to settle definitional disputes.

Definitions and the Rule of Justice: At What Point Does X Quit Being a Y?

For some people, all this concern about definition may seem misplaced. How often, after all, have you heard people accuse each other of getting bogged down in "mere semantics"? But how we define a given word can have significant implications for people who must either use the word or have the word used on them. Take, for example, what some philosophers refer to as "the rule of justice." According to this rule, "beings in the same essential category should be treated in the same way." Should an insurance company, for example, treat a woman who needs to miss work following childbirth the same way it treats a woman who needs to miss work following an appendectomy? Should childbirth belong within the category "illness" as far as insurance payments are concerned? Similarly, if a company gives "new baby" leave to a mother, should it also be willing to give "new baby" leave to a father? In other words, is this kind of leave "new mother" leave or is it "new parent" leave? And what if a couple adopts an infant? Should "new mother" or "new parent" leave be available to them also? These questions are all definitional issues involving arguments about what class of beings an individual belongs to and about what actions to take to comply with the "rule of justice," which demands that all members of that class be treated equally.

Let's take a slightly less elevated (and less complex) problem of definitional justice. If your landlord decides to institute a "no pets" rule, then the rule of justice requires that all pets have to go—not just your neighbor's barking dog, but also Mrs. Brown's cat, the kids' hamster downstairs, and your own pet tarantula. In order to keep your friendly spider, though, mightn't you argue that your pet tarantula isn't really a "pet"? Because the rule of justice demands that all pets must be treated equally, the only fair way to save your spider is to get it removed from the class "pets." The rule of justice thus forces the question "How much can any given X vary before it is no longer a Y?"

The rule of justice becomes even harder to apply when we consider Xs that grow, evolve, or otherwise change through time. When Young Person back in Chapter 1 argued that she could set her own curfew because she was mature, she raised the question "What are the attributes or criteria of a 'mature' person?" In this case, a categorical distinction between two separate kinds of things ("mature" versus "not mature") evolves into a distinction of degree ("mature enough"). So perhaps we should not ask whether Young Person is mature, but whether she is "mature enough." At what point does a child become an adult? (When does a fetus become a human person? When does a B essay become an A essay? When does a social drinker become an alcoholic?)

Although we may be able arbitrarily to choose a particular point and declare, through stipulation, that "mature" means eighteen years old or that "human person" includes a fetus at conception, or at three months, or at birth, in the everyday world the distinction between child and adult, between egg and person, between social drinking and alcoholism seems an evolution, not a sudden and definitive step. Nevertheless, our language requires an abrupt shift between classes. In short, applying the rule of justice often requires us to adopt a digital approach to reality—switches are either on or off, either a fetus is a human person or it is not—whereas our sense of life is more analogical—there are numberless gradations between on and off, there are countless shades of gray between black and white.

As we can see in the preceding case, the promise of language to fix the buzz and confusion of the world into an orderly set of categories turns out to be elusive. In most definitional debates, an argument, not a quick trip to the dictionary, is required to settle the matter.

CONDUCTING A
CRITERIA-MATCH ARGUMENT

Having raised some philosophical issues about definition, let's now proceed directly to a discussion of how to conduct a criteria-match argument. When you prepare to develop and write a definitional argument, you need first to determine if the criteria or the match or both are primarily at issue.

In some arguments the criteria part—that is, determining the defining characteristics of Y—is the most difficult. The Minneapolis ordinance against pornography referred to in Chapter 7 is an example of this kind of argument. According to that ordinance, if a magazine or film meets any of nine criteria, it can be considered pornographic. The major difficulty faced by drafters of the ordinance was establishing the nine criteria.

In other arguments the match part will take the majority of your time. If you wanted to argue that your calculus course was badly organized you would probably spend most of your time showing examples of disorganization in the course and little time, if any, defining *disorganized.* In still other arguments—such as the extended definition/borderline case assignment in this chapter—the criteria and match parts might both demand considerable attention. The point is, however, that all definitional arguments have at their core a criteria-match structure even if one part of the structure can be virtually eliminated in specific cases.

DEFINING THE Y TERM
(ESTABLISHING CRITERIA FOR Y)

Unless your Y term is easy to define, you will have to present an extended definition in which you gradually bring your reader step by step toward understanding your criteria. In this section we discuss two methods of definition—Aristotelian and operational.

Aristotelian Definition

In *Aristotelian definitions,* regularly used in dictionaries, one defines a term by placing it within the next larger class or category and then showing the specific attributes that distinguish the term from other terms within the same category. For example, a *pencil* is a "writing implement" (next larger category) that differs from other writing implements in that it makes marks with lead or graphite rather than ink. You could elaborate this definition by saying "usually the lead or graphite is a long, thin column embedded in a slightly thicker column of wood with an eraser on one end and a sharpened point, exposing the graphite, on the other." You could even distinguish a wooden pencil from a mechanical pencil, thereby indicating again that the crucial identifying attribute is the graphite, not the wooden column.

As you can see, an Aristotelian definition of a Y term creates specific criteria that enable you to distinguish it from the next larger class. But whereas our example of a pencil is relatively easy, most criteria arguments are more complex, requiring you not just to state your criteria but to argue for them. For example, when trying to define *true sports car* for the claim "A Dodge Stealth is/is not a true sports car," you might have to defend such criteria as these: "A true sports car is an automobile that has seats for only two people" or "A true sports car is an automobile designed specifically for racing on narrow curving roads." Most of the space in the criteria section of your essay would be spent justifying the criteria you have chosen, usually through examples, contrastive examples, and refutation of opposing criteria.

In constructing Aristotelian definitions it is sometimes helpful to understand and use the concepts of "accidental," necessary," and "sufficient" criteria. An *accidental* criterion is a usual but not essential feature of a concept. For example, "made out of wood" is an accidental feature of a pencil. Most pencils are made out of wood, but something can still be a pencil even if it isn't made out of wood (for example, a mechanical pencil).

Although the distinction between accidental and essential features is relatively clear when discussing things such as pencils, it gets increasingly cloudy as we move into complex definitional debates (for example, what are the accidental, as opposed to essential, characteristics of sexist acts?).

A *necessary* criterion is an attribute that *must* be present for something to be a Y. For example, "is a writing implement" is a necessary criterion for a pencil; "marks with graphite or lead" is also a necessary criterion. However, neither of these criteria by itself is a sufficient criterion for a pencil. Many writing implements aren't pencils (for example, pens); also, many things that mark with lead or graphite aren't pencils (for example, a lead paperweight will make pencil-like marks on paper). To be a pencil, both these criteria together must be present. We say, then, that these two criteria together are *sufficient* criteria for the concept "pencil."

You can appreciate how these concepts can help you carry on a definitional argument with more precision. Felix Ungar might argue that a Stealth is not a true sports car because it has rear seats. (To Felix, having seating for only two people is thus a necessary criterion for a true sports car.) Oscar Madison might argue, however, that having two seats is only an accidental feature of sports cars and that a Stealth is indeed a true sports car because it has a racy appearance and because it handles superbly on curves. (For Oscar, racy appearance and superb handling are together sufficient criteria for a true sports car.)

❧ FOR CLASS DISCUSSION

Working individually or in small groups, try to determine whether each of the following is a necessary criterion, a sufficient criterion, an accidental criterion, or no criterion for defining the indicated concept. Be prepared to explain your reasoning.

CRITERION	CONCEPT TO BE DEFINED
presence of gills	fish
having yellow hair (applied to person)	blond
born inside the United States	American citizen
over sixty-five	senior citizen
knows several programming languages for computers	meets foreign language requirement for graduation
line endings form a rhyming pattern	poem
teaches classes at a college	college professor
eats no meat, ever	vegetarian
kills another human being	murderer
good sex life	happy marriage

Effect of Rhetorical Context on Aristotelian Definitions

It is important to appreciate how the context of a given argument can affect your definition of a term. The question "Is a tarantula kept in the house a pet?" may actually have opposing answers, depending on the rhetorical situation. You may argue that your tarantula is or is not a pet, depending on whether you are trying to exclude it from your landlord's "no pet" rule or include it in your local talk show's "weird pet contest." Within one context you will want to argue that what your landlord really means by *pet* is an animal (next larger class) capable of disturbing neighbors or harming the landlord's property (criteria that distinguish it from other members of the class). Thus you could argue that your tarantula isn't a pet in your landlord's sense because it is incapable of harming property or disturbing the peace (assuming you don't let it loose!). In the other context you would argue that a pet is "any living thing" (note that in this context the "next larger class" is much larger) with which a human being forms a caring attachment and which shares its owner's domicile. In this case you might say, "Tommy Tarantula here is one of my dearest friends and if you don't think Tommy is weird enough, wait 'til I show you Vanessa, my pet Venus's-flytrap."

To apply the same principle to a different field of debate, consider whether or not obscene language in a student newspaper should be protected by the First Amendment. The purpose of school officials' suspending editors responsible for such language is to maintain order and decency in the school. The school officials thus hope to narrow the category of acts that are protected under the free speech amendment in order to meet their purposes. On the other hand, the American Civil Liberties Union (which has long defended student newspaper editors) is intent on avoiding any precedent that will restrict freedom of speech any more than is absolutely necessary. The different definitions of *free speech* that are apt to emerge thus reflect the different purposes of the disputants.

The problem of purpose shows why it is so hard to define a word out of context. Some people try to escape this dilemma by returning to the "original intent" of the authors of precedent-setting documents such as the Constitution. But if we try to determine the original intent of the writers of the Constitution on such matters as "free speech," "cruel and unusual punishment," or the "right to bear arms," we must still ask what their original purposes were in framing the constitutional language. If we can show that those original purposes are no longer relevant to present concerns, we have begun to undermine what would otherwise appear to be a static and universal definition to which we could turn.

Operational Definitions

In some rhetorical situations, particularly those arising in the physical and social sciences, writers need precise definitions that can be measured empirically and are not subject to problems of context and disputed criteria. Consider, for example, an argument involving the concept "aggression." "Do violent television programs increase the incidence of aggression in children?" To do research on this issue a scientist needs a precise, measurable definition of *aggression*. Typically, a scientist might measure aggression by counting "the number of blows or kicks a child gives to an inflatable bozo doll over a fifteen-minute period when other play options are available." The scientist might then define "aggressive behavior" as six or more blows to the bozo doll. Such definitions are useful in that they are precisely measurable, but they are also limited in that they omit criteria that may be unmeasurable but important. Is it adequate, for example, to define a "superior student" as someone with a 3.2 GPA or higher? Or is it adequate to define an "aggressive child" as one who pummels bozo dolls instead of playing with trucks?

CONDUCTING THE MATCH PART OF A DEFINITIONAL ARGUMENT

As we showed at the beginning of this chapter, a typical enthymeme for a definitional argument is as follows: "X is a Y because it possesses attributes A, B, and C." In the criteria part of the argument you show that A, B, and C are the necessary and sufficient criteria for something to be called a Y. Then in the match part of your argument you show that X possesses the attributes A, B, and C. Generally you do so by using either examples or analysis.

Suppose you wanted to argue that your history teacher was an "authoritarian." Since he is in some ways rather lax—for example, he doesn't count off for late papers and he doesn't require class attendance—some of your classmates say he isn't authoritarian at all. (They are in effect saying that harsh treatment for late papers and absences is a necessary condition for calling a teacher "authoritarian.") Consequently you establish the following criteria for "authoritarian": repression of alternative points of view and strict adherence to certain arbitrary procedures. You now need to show that your history teacher meets these criteria. You write the following enthymeme to serve as the core of your argument:

> My history professor is an authoritarian because he represses questions and alternate points of view in his class and because he demands strict adherence to arbitrary procedures for doing the assignments.

To support this argument, you would give various examples of his meeting these two criteria: To show his repression of alternative points of view, you might cite, among other examples, the time he embarrassed a student for disagreeing with him on the rightness of Harry Truman's decision to drop the atomic bomb on Hiroshima. And to show his adherence to arbitrary procedures, you could, among other things, mention how he reduces the grade on an essay if the margins aren't precisely one-and-a-half inches.

In other kinds of arguments, you may have to analyze the features of your X rather than just cite examples. For instance, if you argue that one *necessary* criterion for "police brutality" is "intention"—that is, the police officer must intend the harm—then you will need to analyze your borderline case to see if the police officer intentionally (as opposed to accidentally) harmed the victim. If the harm was accidental, then you could relieve the officer of the charge "police brutality." Thus through the power of example or analysis you show that X possesses the attributes of Y.

 ## WRITING YOUR DEFINITIONAL ARGUMENT

With this background, you are now ready to begin writing your extended definition/borderline case argument. The following should help you in that process.

Starting Point: Finding a Definitional Controversy   The key to this assignment is finding a good controversy about a definition. A fruitful way to begin is through discussion with others. Perhaps your instructor will use the following discussion exercise in class; if not, start a similar conversation with friends.

FOR CLASS DISCUSSION

1. Suppose you wanted to define the concept "courage." Working in groups, try to decide whether each of the following cases is an example of courage:
   a. A neighbor rushes into a burning house to rescue a child from certain death and emerges, coughing and choking, with the child in his arms. Is the neighbor courageous?
   b. A fireman rushes into a burning house to rescue a child from certain death and emerges with the child in his arms. The fireman is wearing protective clothing and a gas mask. When a newspaper reporter calls him courageous, he says, "Hey, this is my job." Is the fireman courageous?
   c. A teenager rushes into a burning house to recover a memento given to him by his girlfriend, the first love of his life. Is the teenager courageous?
   d. A parent rushes into a burning house to save a trapped child. The fire marshal tells the parent to wait because there is no chance the child can be reached from the first floor. The fire marshal wants to try cutting a hole in the roof to reach the child. The parent rushes into the house anyway and is burned to death. Was the parent courageous?
   e. Are mountain climbers and parachutists courageous in scaling rock precipices or jumping out of airplanes during their leisure hours?
   f. Is a robber courageous in performing a daring bank robbery?
   g. Mutt and Jeff are standing on a cliff high above a lake. Mutt dares Jeff to dive into the water. Jeff refuses, saying it is too dangerous. Mutt double dares Jeff, who still refuses. So Mutt dives into the water and, on surfacing, yells up to Jeff, calling him a coward and taunting him to dive. Jeff starts to dive, but then backs off and takes the trail down to the lake, feeling ashamed and silly. Was Mutt courageous? Was Jeff courageous?

2. As you make your decisions on each of these cases, create and refine the criteria you use.

3. Make up your own series of controversial cases, like those above for "courage," for one or more of the following concepts:
   a. cruelty to animals
   b. child abuse
   c. true athlete
   d. sexual harassment
   e. free speech protected by the First Amendment

Once you complete the preceding exercise, choose one of the most controversial cases within a topic area you enjoy and consider using that as the subject of your essay. Or look back through your earlier exploratory writing to see if any of your entries focus on definitional issues. Clear your definitional issue with your instructor.

Exploration Stage I: Developing Criteria for Your Y Term

One effective way to discover criteria is to use a definitional heuristic in which you search for cases that are instances of "Y," "not Y," and "maybe Y." You will find that criteria for Y begin to emerge as your group discusses the characteristics of obvious instances of Y, contrastive instances of not Y, and then borderline instances of maybe Y.

Suppose, for example, you wanted to argue the claim "Accounting is/is not a creative profession." Your first goal is to establish criteria for a creative profession. Using this heuristic, you would begin by thinking of examples of obvious creative behaviors, then of contrastive behaviors that seem similar to the previous behaviors but yet are clearly not creative, and then finally of borderline behaviors that may or may not be creative. Your list might look like this:

Examples of Creative Behaviors

Beethoven composes a symphony.

An architect designs a house.

Edison invents the light bulb.

An engineer designs a machine that will make widgets in a new way.

A poet writes a poem (later revised to "A poet writes a poem that poetry experts say is beautiful"—see following discussion).

Contrastive Examples of Noncreative Behaviors

A conductor transposes Beethoven's symphony into a different key.

A carpenter builds a house from the architect's plan.

I change a lightbulb in my house.

A factory worker uses the new machine to stamp out widgets.

A graduate student writes stupid "love/dove" poems for birthday cards.

Examples of Borderline Cases

A woman gives birth to a child.

An accountant figures out your income tax.

A musician plays Beethoven's symphony with great skill.

A monkey paints an oil painting by smearing paint on canvas: a group of art critics, not knowing a monkey was the artist, call the painting beautiful.

After you have brainstormed for your various cases, develop your criteria by determining what features the "clearly creative" examples have in common and what features the "clearly noncreative" examples lack. Then refine your criteria by deciding on what grounds you might include or eliminate your border-line cases from the category "creative." For example, you might begin with the following criterion:

DEFINITION: FIRST TRY

For an act to be creative, it must result in an end product that is significantly different from other products.

But then, by looking at some of the examples in your creative and noncreative columns, you decide that just producing a different end product isn't enough. A bad poem might be different from other poems, but you don't want to call a bad poet creative. So you refine your criteria.

DEFINITION: SECOND TRY

For an act to be creative, it must result in an end product that is significantly different from other products and is yet useful or beautiful.

This definition would allow you to include all the acts in your creative column but eliminate the acts in the noncreative column.

Your next step is to refine your criteria by deciding whether to include or reject items in your borderline list. You decide to reject the childbirth case by arguing that creativity must be a mental or intellectual activity, not a natural process. You reject the monkey as painter example on similar grounds, arguing that although the end product may be both original and beautiful, it is not creative because it is not a product of the monkey's intellect. Finally, you reject the example of the musician playing Beethoven's symphony. Like the carpenter who builds the house, the musician possesses great skill but doesn't design a new product; rather, he or she follows the instructions of the designer. (A music major in your group reacts bitterly, arguing that musicians "interpret" music and that such behavior is creative. She notes that the music department is housed in a building called the "Creative Arts Complex." Your group, however, can't figure out a way to reword the definition to include performance rather than production. If you call performing musicians creative, the rest of the group argues, then the rule of justice forces you to call carpenters creative also, because both kinds of craftspeople reproduce the creative intentions of others. Once we call performers creative, they argue, the concept of creativity will get so broad that it will no longer be useful.) Your group's final definition, then, looks like this (with the music major dissenting):

DEFINITION: THIRD TRY

For an act to be creative, it must be produced by intellectual design, and it must result in an end product that is significantly different from other products and is yet useful or beautiful.

Having established these criteria, you are ready for your final borderline case, your original issue of whether or not accounting is a creative profession. Based on your criteria, you might decide that accounting is not generally a creative profession because the final products are not significantly new or different. For the most part, accountants do elaborately complex calculations, but they generally follow established procedures in doing so. However, the profession can sometimes offer creative opportunities when an accountant, for example, develops a new kind of computer program or develops new, improved procedures for handling routine business (accounting majors may argue that accounting is creative in other ways).

The definitional heuristic thus produces a systematic procedure for developing criteria for a definitional argument. Moreover, it provides an organizational strategy for writing the criteria part of your argument because one good way to conduct a definitional argument is to take your reader step by step through the process of establishing your criteria. In other words, you would use the examples from your list to show your reader first your rough criteria and then your increasingly refined criteria derived from consideration of your borderline cases.

 FOR CLASS DISCUSSION

1. Working as a group, try the definitional heuristic on the topic "cruelty to animals" (or some other Y chosen by the instructor or your group). Make three lists.
   a. obvious examples of cruelty to animals
   b. contrastive examples—that is, behaviors that are not cruel to animals (Try to vary a few features of each entry under "a" above so that the example switches from cruelty to noncruelty.)
   c. borderline cases (Include the starling example from p. 200.)

2. Once you have created your list of cases, create a one-sentence definition of "cruelty to animals" following the pattern described earlier for creativity. Your definition should include each of the criteria you established.

3. In your journal, make a similar three-column list for the Y term you have chosen for your own definitional essay. Then create a working definition for your Y term by deciding on your criteria.

Exploration Stage II: Exploring Your Match Argument

In doing the earlier class discussion exercises, you have practiced arguing whether borderline cases met your definitions for "courage" or "cruelty to animals." Now try this exercise as a form of exploratory writing. List the criteria for your chosen Y term; then freewrite for five or ten minutes exploring whether your borderline case meets each of the criteria. Before writing the first draft of your argument, you might also explore your ideas further by doing the eight freewriting tasks on pages 73–74 in Chapter 3.

Writing the Discovery Draft—A Possible Organizational Structure for Your Essay

You are now ready to write your discovery draft. At this stage it may be helpful to look at a typical organizational structure for an extended definition/borderline case essay. Such an organization is shown in Figure 10.1. The argument typically begins by introducing the reader to the controversy and by showing that the definition of the Y term or the match between the Y definition and

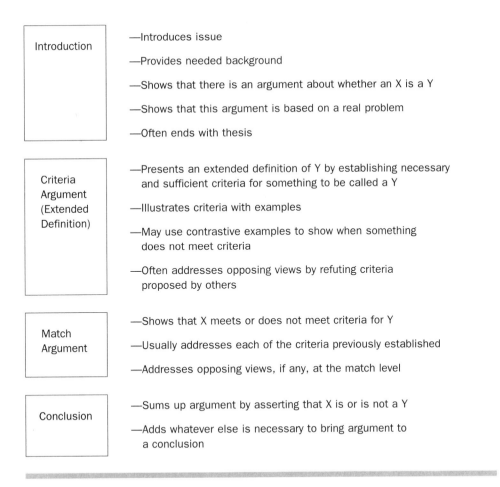

Introduction	—Introduces issue
	—Provides needed background
	—Shows that there is an argument about whether an X is a Y
	—Shows that this argument is based on a real problem
	—Often ends with thesis

Criteria Argument (Extended Definition)	—Presents an extended definition of Y by establishing necessary and sufficient criteria for something to be called a Y
	—Illustrates criteria with examples
	—May use contrastive examples to show when something does not meet criteria
	—Often addresses opposing views by refuting criteria proposed by others

Match Argument	—Shows that X meets or does not meet criteria for Y
	—Usually addresses each of the criteria previously established
	—Addresses opposing views, if any, at the match level

| Conclusion | —Sums up argument by asserting that X is or is not a Y |
| | —Adds whatever else is necessary to bring argument to a conclusion |

FIGURE 10.1 Possible organizational pattern for definition argument

the X term is problematic. The body of the essay usually begins with an extended definition of the Y term, followed by an argument showing that the X term does or does not meet the definition. Sometimes a writer will present all the criteria for the Y term before moving to the match argument. At other times, the writer might choose to proceed one criterion at a time by first describing the criterion, arguing that the X term meets it, and then proceeding to the next criterion.

Revision Stage

Once you have written a discovery draft, you will better appreciate the complexity of your issue and see it more clearly. As you revise your draft, your goal will be to make your argument clear and persuasive for readers. You might find it helpful at this time to summarize your argument as a claim with because clauses and to test it with Toulmin's schema. Here is how student writer Kathy Sullivan used Toulmin to analyze a draft of her essay examining the possible obscenity of photographs displayed in a gay bar in Seattle. The final version of this essay is printed on pages 220–221.

ENTHYMEME:	The photographs displayed in the Oncore bar are not obscene because they do not violate the community standards of the patrons of the bar, because they do not appeal to prurient interest, because children are not apt to be exposed to them, and because they promote an important social value, safe sex, in order to prevent AIDS.
CLAIM:	The photographs are not obscene.
STATED REASONS:	(1) They don't violate community standards; (2) they do not appeal to prurient interests; (3) children are not exposed to them; and (4) they promote an important social purpose of preventing AIDS through safe sex.
GROUNDS:	(1) evidence that most Oncore patrons are homosexual and that these photographs don't offend them (no complaints, etc.); (2) purpose of photographs is not prurient sexuality, they don't depict explicit sexual acts, the only thing complained about by the liquor board is visible body parts; (3) because this is a bar, children aren't allowed; (4) evidence that the purpose of these photographs is to promote safe sex, thus they have a redeeming social value

WARRANT:	Things that don't violate community standards, do not appeal to prurient interests, don't come in view of children, and promote an important purpose are not obscene.
BACKING:	These criteria come from the definition of obscenity in *Black's Law Dictionary,* which in turn is based on recent court cases. This is a very credible source. In addition, arguments showing why the community standard here should be that of the homosexual community rather than the community at large; arguments showing that the social importance of safe sex overrides other considerations.
CONDITIONS OF REBUTTAL:	An opponent might say that the community standards should be those of the Seattle community at large, not those of the gay community. An opponent might say that photographs of male genitalia in a gay bar appeal to prurient interest.
QUALIFIER:	Those photographs would be obscene if displayed anywhere but in a gay bar.

As a result of this analysis, Kathy revised her final draft considerably. By imagining where her arguments were weak ("conditions of rebuttal"), she realized that she needed to include more backing by arguing that the community standards to be applied in this case should be those of the homosexual community rather than the community at large. She also added a section arguing that visible genitalia in the photographs didn't make the photos obscene. By imagining how your argument can be rebutted, you will see ways to strengthen your draft. Consequently, we close out this chapter by looking more carefully at the ways a definitional argument can be rebutted.

CONDITIONS FOR REBUTTAL: TESTING A DEFINITIONAL ARGUMENT

In refuting a definitional argument, you need to appreciate its criteria-match structure. Your refutation can attack either the argument's criteria or its match, or both.

Attacking the Criteria

Might an opponent claim that your criteria are not the right ones?   This is the most common way to attack a definitional argument. Opponents might say that A, B, and C are only accidental criteria for Y, not necessary and sufficient criteria. Or they might say that A, B, and C are necessary but not sufficient and that you don't have a real Y until you have a feature D. For example, you might argue that an action is courageous so long as the doer risks something of value, which you might define as "reputation," "family honor," and so forth. But an opponent might say that an action is truly courageous only if a person risks life and limb. The argument will turn, then, on how much is risked.

Might an opponent find counterexamples—things that possess features A, B, and C but may not be a Y?   If you say that cruelty to animals occurs any time a human being intentionally causes an animal to suffer, an opponent might call this criterion into question by bringing up the case of animal research in medicine. Opponents might argue that causing an animal to suffer intentionally is not cruelty to animals so long as the suffering serves a sufficient human good.

Might an opponent cite extraordinary circumstances that weaken your criteria?   An opponent may also find that the criteria you've developed are perfectly acceptable in ordinary circumstances but are rendered unacceptable by extraordinary circumstances. If you say that starving the starlings (p. 200) is cruelty to animals because the life of the starlings outweighs the inconvenience to the family, an opponent might challenge you by asking, "What if one of the people in the bedroom was ill and needed absolute quiet?" By invoking extraordinary circumstances, an opponent can force us to look at questions of degree—How far are we willing to stretch our criteria?

Might an opponent object to your criteria on the basis of "purpose"?   We have seen how definitional arguments occur in context. If your criteria for "sexual harassment" are based on a male view of the world, with the intention of protecting males from being sued for ogling women, might not your criteria be challenged from a woman's perspective?

Attacking the Match

A match argument usually uses examples to show that X indeed possesses characteristics A, B, and C and thus qualifies as a Y.

Might an opponent claim that your examples are too narrow and unrepresentative?   The most common way to refute a match argument is to show that the examples are too narrow and unrepresentative. In arguing that Dr. Booley, president of State Technical College, is an imaginative leader, you may have cited as examples Booley's creative handling of a labor dispute with the food service and his institution of a new accounting system. But in so doing, have you ignored other, equally important problem areas on campus where Booley has shown no imagination (for example, the clumsy advising system, low faculty morale, outdated curriculum, poor library, etc.)?

Might an opponent claim that your examples are not accurate?   In the previous illustration, an opponent might point out that it was not Dr. Booley's leadership that deserves credit for resolving the labor dispute; rather, it was Vice President Conehead's steady intervention that won the day.

Will your opponent accuse you of using extreme examples? For example, if you are arguing that pornography is degrading to humans, you may well have turned to extreme instances of child pornography. But might your opponent point out that most pornography is different? Your opponent might simply say: "OK, granted explicit sexual material involving children is degrading to humans. But everything else, so long as it involves consenting adults, is OK."

 FOR CLASS DISCUSSION

Read the following two definitional arguments. The first is by a student writer in response to the extended definition/borderline case assignment in this chapter. The second is by professional commentator Charles Krauthammer. In Krauthammer's argument, definitional issues are embedded in a larger proposal issue. Krauthammer proposes to rebuild a national system of asylums in which homeless mentally ill persons could be involuntarily confined. Krauthammer's definitional issues are these: What are the criteria by which a mentally ill person could be involuntarily institutionalized? How can one tell when eccentric behavior means mental illness?

1. Working as a whole class or in small groups, share your responses to the following questions: (a) How persuaded are you by each writer's argument? (b) If you find the arguments persuasive, which parts of them were particularly influential or effective? (c) If you are not persuaded, which parts of the arguments do you find weak or ineffective? (d) How would you attempt to rebut each argument?*

2. Working individually or in groups, create scenarios of cases that would "test" Krauthammer's criteria for permitting involuntary institutionalization of a homeless mentally ill person: (a) a case of a homeless mentally ill person who could be involuntarily confined under both the present criteria (danger to self or others) and Krauthammer's proposed criteria (degradation or helplessness); (b) a case of a homeless mentally ill person who could remain on the streets according to the danger criterion but could be institutionalized involuntarily under Krauthammer's degradation criterion; (c) a case of a homeless mentally ill person who could stay on the streets according to both criteria.

3. If Krauthammer's definition were to become law, how might his criteria be clarified or restricted so that the state couldn't place any eccentric homeless person in an insane asylum?

---

*For a counterargument that attempts to rebut Krauthammer's plan, see the student essay "What Should Be Done about the Mentally Ill Homeless?" on pp. 330–338.

Oncore, Obscenity, and the Liquor Control Board

Kathy Sullivan (student)

1   In early May, Geoff Menasee, a Seattle artist, exhibited a series of photographs with the theme of "safe sex" on the walls of an inner city, predominantly homosexual restaurant and lounge called the Oncore. Before hanging the photographs, Menasee had to consult with the Washington State Liquor Control Board because, under the current state law, art work containing material that may be considered indecent has to be approved by the board before it can be exhibited. Of the almost thirty photographs, six were rejected by the board because they partially exposed "private parts" of the male anatomy. Menasee went ahead and displayed the entire series of photographs, placing bandaids over the "indecent" areas, but the customers continually removed the bandaids.

2   The liquor control board's ruling on this issue has caused controversy in the Seattle community. The *Seattle Times* has provided news coverage, and a "Town Meeting" segment was filmed at the restaurant. The central question is this: Should an establishment that caters to a predominantly homosexual clientele be enjoined from displaying pictures promoting "safe sex" on the grounds that the photographs are obscene?

3   Before I can answer this question, I must first determine whether the art work should truly be classified as obscene. To make that determination, I will use the definition of obscenity in *Black's Law Dictionary:*

> Material is "obscene" if to the average person, applying contemporary community standards, the dominant theme of material taken as a whole appeals to prurient interest, if it is utterly without redeeming social importance, if it goes substantially beyond customary limits of candor in description or representation, if it is characterized by patent offensiveness, and if it is hard core pornography.

An additional criterion is provided by Pember's *Mass Media Laws:* "A work is obscene if it has a tendency to deprave and corrupt those whose minds are open to such immoral influences (children for example) and into whose hands it might happen to fall" (p. 394). The art work in question should not be prohibited from display at predominantly homosexual establishments like the Oncore because it does not meet the above criteria for obscenity.

4   First of all, to the average person applying contemporary community standards, the predominant theme of Menasee's photographs is not an appeal to prurient interests. The first element in this criterion is "average person." According to Rocky Breckner, manager of the Oncore, 90 percent of the clientele at the Oncore is made up of young white homosexual males. This group therefore constitutes the "average person" viewing the exhibit. "Contemporary community standards" would ordinarily be the standards of the Seattle community. However, this art work is aimed at a particular group of people—the homosexual community. Therefore, the "community standards" involved here are those of the gay community rather than the city at large. Since the Oncore is not an art museum or gallery, which attracts a broad spectrum of people, it is appropriate to restrict the scope of "community standards" to that group who voluntarily patronize the Oncore.

Second, the predominant theme of the photographs is not "prurient interest" nor do the photographs go "substantially beyond public limits of candor." There are no explicit sexual acts found in the photographs; instead, their theme is the prevention of AIDS through the practice of safe sex. Homosexual displays of affection could be viewed as "prurient interest" by the larger community, but same-sex relationships are the norm for the group at whom the exhibit is aimed. If the exhibit were displayed at McDonalds or even the Red Robin it might go "substantially beyond customary limits of candor," but it is unlikely that the clientele of the Oncore would find the art work offensive. The manager stated that he received very few complaints about the exhibit and its contents.

Nor is the material pornographic. The liquor control board prohibited the six photographs based on their visible display of body parts such as pubic hair and naked buttocks, not on the basis of sexual acts or homosexual orientation. The board admitted that the photographs depicted no explicit sexual acts. Hence, it can be concluded that they did not consider the suggestion of same-sex affection to be hard-core pornography. Their sole objection was that body parts were visible. But visible genitalia in art work are not necessarily pornographic. Since other art work, such as Michelangelo's sculptures, explicitly depict both male and female genitalia, it is arguable that pubic hair and buttocks are not patently offensive.

It must be conceded that the art work has the potential of being viewed by children, which would violate Pember's criterion. But once again the incidence of minors frequenting this establishment is very small.

But the most important reason for saying these photographs are not obscene is that they serve an important social purpose. One of Black's criteria is that obscene material is "utterly without redeeming social importance." But these photographs have the explicit purpose of promoting safe sex as a defense against AIDS. Recent statistics reported in the *Seattle Times* show that AIDS is now the leading cause of death of men under forty in the Seattle area. Any methods that can promote the message of safe sex in today's society have strong redeeming social significance.

Those who believe that all art containing "indecent" material should be banned or covered from public view would most likely believe that Menasee's work is obscene. They would disagree that the environment and the clientele should be the major determining factor when using criteria to evaluate art. However, in the case of this exhibit I feel that the audience and the environment of the display are factors of overriding importance. Therefore, the exhibit should have been allowed to be displayed because it is not obscene.

How to Save the Homeless Mentally Ill

Charles Krauthammer

Hard cases make bad law. Joyce Brown is a hard case. She was one of the first persons locked up in Bellevue Hospital when New York City decided to begin sweeping the homeless mentally ill off the streets. And she was first to challenge in court her forcible hospitalization. She won, but an appeals court reversed the decision. Now that a court has upheld her right to refuse treatment, the city will release her any day now. The case, like Brown herself, is a muddle and making a muddle of the law. But it dramatically illustrates what is wrong with the current debate about the homeless mentally ill and with the limits of benevolence that our society permits itself to accord them.

2   Everything about Brown allows contradictory explanations. Court documents refer not to Joyce Brown but to Billie Boggs, the name of a local TV personality and one of the several false names Brown adopted. Is she delusional or did she choose new names the better to hide from her sisters who in the past had tried to get her hospitalized? She cut up and publicly urinated on paper money. Is that crazy or, as her lawyers claim, was she symbolically demonstrating disdain for the patronizing solicitude of strangers who gave her money? She shouted obscenities in the street. Is that the result of demented rage or was it her only effective means of warding off the busybodies of the city's Project HELP (Homeless Emergency Liaison Project) who might take her away to a hospital?

3   In sum, was she living on a grate at 2nd and East 65th because she is mentally ill or because she has chosen the life of a professional (her word) street person?

4   "A lucid and rational woman who is down on her luck," Brown's ACLU lawyer calls her. Being down on one's luck can just be that. But it can be a sign of something graver, namely the downward social mobility that is characteristic of schizophrenia and that is caused by the gradual disintegration of the personality that marks its course. The classic picture is: brilliant physics major drops out, becomes cabbie, becomes unemployed, drifts, becomes homeless. Brown was a secretary, lost her job, did drugs, wandered from sister's house to sister's house, then ended up a bag lady.

5   She is a puzzle. The first judge thought the ACLU's psychiatrists correct. The appeals court bought the city's diagnosis. Dr. Francine Cournos, the most recent court-appointed (and thus disinterested) psychiatrist, determined that she did suffer from "a serious mental illness," that she "would benefit from medication," but that, since she refused, forcing it upon her would do more harm than good.

6   My guess is that Dr. Cournos is right. Brown most likely is a chronic schizophrenic. But that is a condition more reliably diagnosed by observing a patient's course than by a snapshot observation. The symptoms can remit for a time. When Brown was cleaned up, dressed up, and given attention, she appeared lucid and rational in court. Left on her own, however, her course had been relentlessly downhill. The proof will come if, as is likely, she ends up back at the hospital.

7   But the lawyer's duel was not just over whether Brown is mentally ill. Mental illness is a necessary, but not a sufficient, condition for involuntary commitment. The other condition is dangerousness: a person must also be a danger to himself or to others before he may be forcibly taken care of.

8   Brown's ACLU lawyers argued for the now traditional standard of dangerousness: imminent danger, meaning harm—suicide or extreme neglect leading to serious injury or death—within hours or days. The city was pushing for a broader standard: eventual danger, meaning that Brown's life was such that she inevitably would come to grief, even if it could not now be foreseen exactly when and how. Maureen McLeod, one of the city's lawyers, protested having "to wait until something happens to her. It is our duty to act before it is too late."

Is it? Generally speaking, the answer is no. We don't permit preventive detention even for criminals who we "know" are going to commit crimes. We have to wait and catch them. If involuntary commitment requires that dangerousness be shown, then it is not enough to say that something awful will happen eventually. By that standard, heavy smoking ought to be a criterion for commitment. 9

The city, trying desperately to stretch the dangerousness criterion to allow the forced hospitalization of Joyce Brown, had to resort to a very strained logic. After all, Brown had spent a year on the grate without any apparent physical harm from illness, malnutrition, or exposure. As the appeals court dissent pointed out, the city's case came down to a claim that Brown would ultimately be assaulted if she continued living and acting as provocatively as she was. But there is hardly a New Yorker who is not subject to assault merely by passing through the streets of New York. It is odd to blame the pathology of the city on her and lock her up to protect her from it. 10

The idea of eventual harm as opposed to imminent harm is slippery and arbitrary. Brown had already been exposed to all the things that the city said would do her in—traffic, disease, strangers, the elements—and had survived quite nicely. The city was reduced to arguing that her luck was going to run out. It had to make this claim because it had to prove dangerousness. But why should a civilized society have to prove that a person's mental incapacity will lead to death before it is permitted to save that person? Should not degradation be reason enough? 11

The standard for the involuntary commitment of the homeless mentally ill is wrong. It should not be dangerousness but helplessness. We have a whole array of laws (e.g., on drug abuse and prostitution) that prohibit certain actions not primarily because they threaten life but because they degrade the person. In order to override the liberty of the severely mentally ill, one should not be forced to claim—as the city disingenuously claimed in the Brown case—that life is at stake, but that a minimal human dignity is at stake. 12

Joyce Brown is a tough case because it is at least possible that she is, in fact, not mentally ill at all, only unlucky, eccentric and willful. Fine. But you cannot make that case for thousands of other homeless people. Helen Phillips, for example, picked up in the same New York City round-up as Brown, lives in Pennsylvania Station and is convinced that plutonium is poisoning the water. For the homeless who are clearly mentally ill, why should it be necessary to convince a judge that, left alone, they will die? The vast majority won't. It should be enough to convince a judge that, left alone, they will suffer. 13

Moreover, the suffering is needless. It can be mitigated by a society that summons the courage to give the homeless mentally ill adequate care, over their objections if need be. In a hospital they will at the very least get adequate clothing and shelter. And for some, medication will relieve the torment of waking dreams. 14

What prevents us from doing this is the misguided and pernicious civil libertarian impulse that holds liberty too sacred to be overridden for anything other than the preservation of life. For the severely mentally ill, however, liberty is not just an empty word but a cruel hoax. Free to do what? To defecate in one's pants? To wander around Grand Central station begging for sustenance? To freeze to death in Central Park? The week that Joyce Brown won her reprieve from forced medication, three homeless men were found frozen 15 dead in New York. What does freedom mean for a paranoid schizophrenic who is ruled by voices commanded by his persecutors and rattling around in his head?

16   What to do? The New York City sweep is only the first temporary step. It yields a bath, a check-up, a diagnosis, and the beginning of treatment. The sicker patients will need long-term custodial care in a psychiatric hospital. Others might respond to treatment and graduate to the less restrictive environment of a local clinic or group home. Many of these people will fall apart and have to be swept up and cycled through the system again.

17   A sensible approach to the problem begins with the conviction that those helpless, homeless, and sick are the responsibility of the state. Society must be willing to assert control even if protection and treatment have to be given involuntarily. These people are owed asylum. Whether the asylums should be large or small, rural or urban is a matter for debate. (In my view a mix of asylum size and location would serve the widest spectrum of patients' needs.) What should by now be beyond debate is that the state must take responsibility for the homeless mentally ill. And that means asserting control over their lives at least during their most severe incapacity.

18   In 1963 President Kennedy helped launch the community mental health revolution that emptied America's state mental hospitals. Kennedy said in his message to Congress, "Reliance on the cold mercy of custodial isolation will be supplanted by the open warmth of community concern." It wasn't. In the turbulence of urban life even the mentally well have trouble finding community, let alone deriving from it any warmth. The mentally ill are even less likely to find it. Everyone is for community mental health care—until it comes to his community. This may be deplorable but it is a fact. And it is cruel to allow the mentally ill to suffer neglect pending rectification of that fact, under the assumption that until the community is ready to welcome the mentally ill, the street is better than the asylum. It is not.

19   In 1955 state psychiatric hospitals had 559,000 patients. Today there are about 130,000, a decline of 75 percent. Now, the incidence of severe mental illness has not changed. (Schizophrenia, for example, afflicts about one percent of the population.) Nor have drugs and modern treatment yielded a cure rate of 75 percent. Many of the 75 percent discharged from the state hospitals have simply been abandoned. They have become an army of grate-dwellers.

20   Helping them will require, first, rebuilding the mental hospital system. These hospitals do not have to be rural, they do not have to be massive, and they do not have to be run-down. The entire American medical care system runs on incentives. Psychiatry, social work, and nursing are not immune to the inducement that good money would offer to work with the severely ill.

21   Second, a new asylum system will require support for a string of less restrictive halfway environments and for the personnel to run them. New York State has just announced a program to supply another element of psychiatric care: a new cadre of case workers to supervise intensively the most severely ill. They would follow the mentally ill through all parts of the system, even back onto the streets, and offer supervision, advice, and some services. But facilitators cannot be enough. If there are no beds in a state mental hospital when the patient is severely delusional or self-destructive, if there are no halfway houses during recovery or remission, then the case worker is left helpless. Anybody who has worked with the mentally ill knows that all the goodwill in the world is

insufficient if the institutions are not there. Intensive case management can guide a patient through a rebuilt asylum system. Without such a system, however, they can only provide the most superficial succor. The basic facts of the homeless mentally ill, destitution and degradation, will remain unchanged.

Rebuilding an asylum system is one problem we can and should throw money at. It will take a lot. The way to do it is to say to Americans: You are pained and offended by homelessness. We propose to get the most wretched, confused, and disruptive of the homeless off the streets and into clean and humane asylums. We need to pay for them. We propose capping the mortgage interest deduction: less of a tax break on your house so that others can be housed. (A cap at $20,000 would yield $1 billion of revenues annually.) A new asylum system begins with concern for the elementary dignity of the homeless mentally ill. But it does not end there. The rest of us need it too. Not just, as the cynics claim, for reasons of cleanliness, so that the comfortable bourgeois does not have his daily routine disturbed by wretchedness. Getting the homeless mentally ill off the streets is an exercise in morality, not aesthetics.

It is not our aesthetic but our moral sensibilities that are most injured by the spectacle of homelessness. The city, with its army of grate-dwellers, is a school for callousness. One's natural instincts to help are suppressed every day. Moreover, they have to be suppressed if one is to function: there are simply too many homeless. Thirty years ago if you saw a person lying helpless on the street, you ran to help him. Now you step over him. You know that he is not an accident victim. He lives there. Trying to get him out of his cardboard house is not a simple act of mercy of which most people are quite capable. It is a major act of social work that only the professional and the saintly can be expected to undertake. To expect saintliness of the ordinary citizen is bad social policy. Further, to expose him hourly to a wretchedness far beyond his power to remedy is to make moral insensitivity a requirement of daily living. Society must not leave the ordinary citizen with no alternative between ignoring the homeless and playing Mother Teresa. A civilized society ought to offer its people some communal act that lies somewhere in between, such as contributing to the public treasury to build an asylum system to care for these people.

Project HELP, the necessary first stage in such a system, is already under attack. First, because it curtails civil liberties. Second, because it sets up a revolving door: off the street, into a hospital for 21 days, then to some lightly supervised home, then back on the streets. In fact, those picked up in Project HELP have been given a high priority for scarce state hospital and other psychiatric beds. (Of the 29 New York patients who have thus far left Bellevue, 21 went to a special 50-bed unit at Creedmoor Psychiatric Center and eight have been discharged to family or adult homes.) It is hard to place the rest in state hospitals or in existing community services because there are few of either: the first as a matter of conscious policy, the second as a matter of political neglect. The way to avert the revolving-door problem is not by leaving the homeless mentally ill on the streets, but by building a long-term psychiatric care system that can accommodate them.

Third, charge the critics, Project HELP deals only with the very tip of the iceberg, so far 70 out of thousands. True. But those 70 are, after all, real suffering people. MForeover, as proper long-term facilities are built, there is no reason why Project HELP cannot become their triage service, assigning the homeless mentally ill to appropriate care.

26   Still, it will not do to have illusions about what can be achieved. After winning the appeal in the Brown case, Mayor Ed Koch declared himself eager "to treat her medically. I want this woman to get well, as quickly as possible." Unfortunately, chronic schizophrenics do not get well quickly. Some never get well. This is not a question of getting them off the street, giving them an injection, and letting them go. It is a question of getting people permanently off the street and into a system of comprehensive long-term care.

27   Rebuilding that system is a question of money. But being prepared to pick people up and send them into it—and keep them in it, if necessary—is a question of political will. It requires relinquishing the illusions of community and the phony promise of liberty that led to the dismantling of the system over the last 30 years. It requires a new consensus that a life of even minimal dignity is preferable to a wretchedness the homeless endure in the name of rights from which, like the world around them, they have long been alienated. Most of the homeless mentally ill picked up so far seem to share, as far as they can, that view. They have not protested the city's efforts. Less than a fifth of those hospitalized thus far have lodged legal challenges against their commitment. Two challenges, including Brown's, have met with some success. Most are grateful for a safe and warm hospital bed. What they seem to fear is being carted off to one of the wretched emergency shelters, where they feel—rightly—more endangered than they do on the street.

28   A new asylum system will not solve the homeless problem. Obviously the mentally ill are not the only category of homeless people in America. There are at least two others. Some of the homeless are not helpless but defiantly indigent. This is Joyce Brown, as she depicts herself: a professional street person, a lucid survivor who has chosen a life of drift. "It was my choice to live on the streets," she says. "It was an experience." Such people used to be called hoboes. Then there are the victims of economic calamity, such as family breakup or job loss. Often these are single mothers with children. Unlike the hoboes, they hate the street and want to get off, but lack the money, skills, and social supports. Some nonetheless try very hard: two homeless mothers who testified recently at a House hearing are actually working and putting kids through school.

29   We can debate for years what to do for these people. Should the hoboes who prefer street life be forced off the street in the name of order? And how best to help the homeless who are simply too poor to buy decent housing in the city? Whatever the answers to these questions, it is both cruel and dishonest to defer addressing the mentally ill homeless—for whom choice is not an issue and for whom poverty is a symptom, not the cause, of their misery—until we have figured out a solution to the rest.

30   When the mentally ill infiltrate the ranks of another deviant group, criminals, we try to segregate them and treat them differently. We do not await a cure for psychopathy or a solution to criminality before applying different standards of treatment for the criminally insane. There is no reason to defer saving the homeless mentally ill until the solution to the rest of homelessness is found. Moreover, whatever solutions are eventually offered the non-mentally ill homeless, they will have little relevance to those who are mentally ill. Housing vouchers, counseling, and job training won't do much for Helen Phillips until we get the plutonium out of the water. And since we may never succeed, she will need more than housing vouchers, counselling, job training. She will need constant care.

The argument over how many of the homeless are mentally ill is endless. The estimates, which range from one-quarter to three-quarters, vary with method, definition, and ideology. But so what if even the lowest estimates are right? Even if treating the mentally ill does not end homelessness, how can that possibly justify not treating the tens, perhaps hundreds of thousands who would benefit from a partial solution? 31

In the end, the Brown case boils down to a problem of category, not a problem of principle. Is she a schizophrenic or a hobo? There is inevitably some blurring of the lines between categories. (Studies of homeless families in New York have shown that many heads of these families exhibit signs of mental illness.) But even the judge who ruled in her favor on the grounds that she was not mentally ill upheld the city's program. 32

In Brown's case, we will not know which category she really belongs to until her illness, if it is there, plays itself out. We will find out soon enough if she is a professional street person or a chronic schizophrenic. But there are others for whom there is no need to wait. The diagnosis is clear, and treatment, or at least care, is available. In their cases, to wait is a dereliction of social duty bordering on criminal neglect. 33

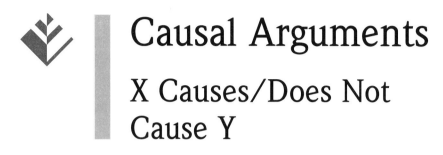

chapter 11

Causal Arguments

X Causes/Does Not Cause Y

CASE 1

Many U.S. citizens wonder why it is so difficult to stop illegal immigration into the United States from Mexico. They want more intensive patroling of the borders, and some have even advocated building a wall along the entire Mexican-American border. A number of economists, however, have shown that manufacturing companies and agribusinesses profit from illegal immigration, which supplies cheap, mobile, nonunion labor. While taking a public stand against illegal immigration—thus winning lots of votes—many legislators and government officials are beholden to under-the-table corporate interests that want illegal immigration to continue. "Illegal immigration," says analyst Wade Gordon, "is only epiphenomenally a law-enforcement issue; it is at root a labor-market event."* To understand the phenomenon of illegal immigration, says Gordon, we must understand the complex causal forces that drive it.

CASE 2

What's the best way to invest your money during periods of high inflation? According to one analyst, gold is the best bet because precious metals erode less in value than paper currencies when inflation is high. According to a second analyst, the best bet is to buy stocks in companies with extensive holdings of natural resources because high inflation rates are typically sparked by overheated economies.

---

*"Masters of the Game: How the U.S. Protects the Traffic in Cheap Mexican Labor," *Harper's,* July 1996, p. 36.

The reasoning here is that an overheated economy creates high demand for raw materials derived from natural resources; because the supply of natural resources remains relatively fixed, increased demand drives up prices, providing disproportionately high profits for investors. According to a third analyst, almost any stock market investment is better than bond funds because bonds do not benefit from all the activity in the economy in the way that stocks do. One's choice here depends on an analysis of cause and effect in a complex economy.

CASE 3

A great national debate in the 1990s centers on how to fight the drug war. Some people want to increase penalties for drug pushers and users. Others want to legalize drugs, saying that legalization will take the profit out of the black market. At the heart of this controversy is a series of causal issues. What causes people to take drugs? What will be the consequences of different courses of action? For example, opponents of legalization say that open access to drugs will cause an increase, not a decrease, in drug usage and that the greatest losers will be minority communities. Proponents of legalization claim that the glamour of drug pushing is itself a cause of drug demand.

CASE 4

During July and August 1986, the death rate for infants rose an unexplained 235 percent in the state of Washington. A medical school professor at the University of Pittsburgh attributed the increase to radioactive fallout from the Chernobyl nuclear meltdown accident in the Ukraine. Using weather reports and empirical evidence gathered in Washington state, he documented the increased radiation received on the northwestern coast of the United States. He used this evidence to bolster his argument that low levels of radiation are more dangerous than the scientific community currently believes. Opponents of the professor's hypothesis urged the public to view his argument with caution. They said that other factors may explain the increase in infant mortality.

THE FREQUENCY OF CAUSAL ARGUMENTS

We encounter causal issues all the time. What are the causes of illegal immigration and of the United States' failure to stem it? Where should people invest their savings in periods of high inflation? Will legalization of drugs cause an increase or decrease in drug addicts? What caused the death rate of infants in Washington to rise by 235 percent in July and August 1986?

Some arguments are devoted entirely to causal issues; just as frequently, causal arguments support should arguments in which the writer argues that we should or should not do X *because X will lead to specified consequences.* Convincing readers how X will lead to these consequences—a causal argument—thus constitutes much of the should argument. (Later we call should arguments by the more general term *proposal arguments,* which we treat at length in Chapter 14.)

Causal arguments are often found in debates about moral or legal guilt. For example, before we can assign guilt in a crime, we have to show that those being charged were not insane or otherwise driven to act by forces beyond their control. A shrewd attorney might point to her client's life of poverty or to a chemical imbalance such as premenstrual stress syndrome. In one real-life example, a California murderer's sentence was mitigated in part because the defense convinced the jury that the defendant's actions resulted from a diet too heavy in refined sugar. This so-called "Twinkie defense" is an extreme case of a causal argument's playing an important role in a judgment about human responsibility.

THE NATURE OF CAUSAL ARGUING

Typically, causal arguments try to show how one event brings about another. On the surface, causal arguments may seem a fairly straightforward matter—more concrete, to be sure, than the larger moral issues in which they are often embedded. But consider for a moment the classic illustration of causality—one billiard ball striking another on a pool table. Surely we are safe in saying that the movement of the second ball was "caused" by a transfer of energy from the first ball at the moment of contact. Well, yes and no. British philosopher David Hume (among others) argued long ago that we don't really perceive "causality"; what we perceive is one ball moving and then another ball moving. We infer the notion of causality, which is a human construct, not a property of billiard balls. Contemporary philosophers and scientists have argued that Newtonian notions of mathematically calculable causality—often associated with billiard ball examples—don't hold even for the inanimate world. Imagine how complex causality becomes when we start talking about humans instead of inanimate objects.

When humans become the focus of a causal argument, the very definition of causality is immediately vexed. When we say, for example, that a given factor X "caused" a person to do Y, we might mean that X "forced her to do Y," thereby negating her free will (for example, the presence of a brain tumor caused my erratic behavior, which caused me to lose my job); on the other hand, we might simply mean that factor X "motivated" her to do Y, in such a way that doing Y is still an expression of freedom (for example, my allergic reaction to polyester caused me to give up my job as a Wal-Mart greeter and become a roadie for Hootie and the Blowfish).

When we argue about causality in human beings, we must guard against confusing these two senses of "cause" or assuming that human behavior can be predicted or controlled in the same way that nonhuman behavior can. A rock dropped from a roof will always fall to the ground at 32 feet per second squared; and a rat zapped for making left turns in a maze will always quit making left turns. But if we raise interest rates, will consumers save more? If so, how much? This is the sort of question we debate endlessly.

Fortunately, most causal arguments can avoid the worst of these scientific and philosophic quagmires. As human beings, we share a number of assumptions about what causes events in the observable world, and we can depend on the goodwill of our audiences to grant us most of these assumptions. Most of us, for example, would be satisfied with the following explanation for why a car went into a skid: "In a panic the driver locked the brakes of his car, causing the car to go into a skid."

panic → slamming brake pedal → locking brakes → skid

We probably do not need to defend this simple causal chain because the audience will grant the causal connections between events A, B, C, and D. The sequence seems reasonable according to our shared assumptions about psychological causality (panic leads to slamming brake pedal) and physical causality (locked brakes lead to skid).

But if you are an attorney defending a client whose skidding car caused considerable damage to an upscale boutique, you might see all sorts of additional causal factors. ("Because the stop sign at that corner was obscured by an untrimmed willow tree, my client innocently entered what he assumed was an open intersection only to find a speeding beer truck bearing down on him. When my client took immediate decelerating corrective action, the improperly maintained, oil-slicked roadway sent his car into its near-fatal skid and into the boutique's bow windows—windows that extrude into the walkway 11 full inches beyond the limit allowed by city code.") Okay, now what's the cause of the crash and who's at fault?

Our point is that establishing causal connections often requires persuasive argument rather than scientific calculation. Consider another hypothetical case, this time at a more complex level: a congressional hearing on increased tobacco use by American teenager males. The star witness for the hearing is Phil "Wink" Blankenship, account executive for a major tobacco company's PR firm. The senators are questioning him on the company's use of a fictional cartoon character, Nick O. Teen, a raffish, boyishly handsome and irreverent huckster for smokeless tobacco.

SENATOR A: Mr. Blankenship, in the six months that you have been using this character Nick O. Teen as a spokesperson for your product, sales for smokeless tobacco among teenage boys went up 28 percent. Do you have any comment on that?

WINK: Well, Senator, since it is illegal for youths under the age of eighteen to buy tobacco of any sort, I can only deplore this surge of lawlessness among American youth. Personally, I attribute this deplorable conduct to the breakdown of the American family.

SENATOR B: So if I understand you correctly, Mr. Blankenship, you attribute none of the increased consumption of smokeless tobacco to the $60 million advertising campaign your company created around the character of a Nick O. Teen?

WINK (*dabbing at his eyes with a hankie*):   Most certainly not, Senator. And I am deeply wounded by the insidious implications of that question. The Nick O. Teen ads are aimed at adults, and part of their message is purely educational since each ad says that "moderation" is important in the use of smokeless tobacco. The fact that a bunch of teenagers decided to start using snuff at the same time we started using Nick O. Teen to encourage moderate tobacco use is a coincidence. You cannot conclude that our ads had any influence on these lawless youths.

SENATOR C: What do you have to say about the mounting evidence that regular use of smokeless tobacco causes mouth and throat cancers?

WINK (*instantly*):   That's never been proven, Senator! And we in the tobacco industry have underwritten millions of dollars of research, conducted by the finest scientists money can buy, into the effects of tobacco on humans and to this date have never found an unambiguous linkage between tobacco and cancer. Moreover, we are proud that we never encourage overconsumption of our products. And as we all know, too much of anything, no matter how refreshing and enjoyable in the moment, can lead to negative consequences.

SENATOR B: But why, if you are concerned not to encourage overconsumption, did you launch a mail-in campaign whereby consumers could get a free Nick O. Teen black leather jacket or twenty rock CDs with proof of purchase seals from your smokeless tobacco products?

WINK: Senator, our assumption there was that older users of our product would save proof-of-purchase seals to buy birthday and Christmas gifts for family members.

SENATORS: Thank you, Mr. Blankenship, for your testimony this morning.

WINK: And thank you, Senators, for the opportunity to meet with you this morning and share my industry's point of view. Let me also remind those of you up for reelection in the coming year that my firm is sponsoring its annual gala fundraiser for incumbents next week and will have a number of industry representatives on hand to answer questions and provide further information.

DESCRIBING THE LOGICAL STRUCTURE OF A CAUSAL ARGUMENT: *BECAUSE* CLAUSES AND THE TOULMIN SCHEMA

Causal arguments can usually be stated using *because* clauses. Typically, a causal because clause pinpoints one or two key elements in the causal chain rather than trying to summarize every link. If we wished to argue that Nick O. Teen ads influenced teenage males to buy smokeless tobacco, one of our lines of reasoning might be nutshelled this way:

ENTHYMEME: The Nick O. Teen ads influenced teenage males to buy smokeless tobacco because the ads created a subconscious link between chewing snuff and being cool like Nick.

Like other kinds of arguments, causal arguments can be analyzed using the Toulmin schema. (It is easiest to apply Toulmin's schema to causal arguments if you think of the grounds as the observable phenomena at any point in the causal chain and the warrants as the shareable assumptions about causality that join links together.) Here is how the preceding argument could be displayed in Toulmin terms.

CLAIM: The Nick O. Teen ads influenced teenage males to buy smokeless tobacco.

STATED REASON: because the ads created a subconscious link between chewing snuff and being cool like Nick

GROUNDS: arguments and evidence showing how the Nick O. Teen character created an image of being cool, tough, and rebellious; arguments and evidence that these are subconscious desires of teenage males

WARRANT: Consumers will buy products that appeal subliminally to their desires.

BACKING: studies of how contemporary advertising works; testimony of psychologists who study advertising; comparisons to other successful ad campaigns

CONDITIONS OF REBUTTAL: *Attacking the grounds:* unless Nick O. Teen doesn't portray a tough, rebellious character at all (Wink might say: "You pointy-headed intellectual types are reading too much into this innocent cartoon character; Nick O. Teen is just a humorous drawing"); unless the ad makes no subliminal appeal ("I don't know what psychological problems you senators have, but this ad isn't making any kind of subconscious appeal to anything")

Attacking the warrant: unless ad campaigns work entirely on name recognition and not on psychological appeals; unless this campaign isn't similar to other campaigns

QUALIFIER: This is a likely explanation for how the ads work.

 FOR CLASS DISCUSSION

1. Working individually or in small groups, create a causal chain to show how the first-mentioned item could help lead to the last one.

   a. invention of the automobile   redesign of cities

   b. invention of the automobile   changes in sexual mores

   c. Elvis Presley arrives   rise of the drug culture in the 1960s

   d. invention of the telephone   loss of a sense of community in neighborhoods

   e. development of the "pill"   rise in the divorce rate

   f. development of way to prevent rejections in transplant operations   liberalization of euthanasia laws

2. For each of your causal chains, compose a claim with an attached because clause summarizing one or two key links in the causal chain. For example, "The invention of the automobile helped cause the redesign of cities because automobiles made it possible for people to live farther away from their places of work."

Of course, the previous argument linking Nick O. Teen ads to rising teen tobacco use doesn't prove causality. At best, it offers a plausible explanation of how the ads might induce a teenage male to try smokeless tobacco. If you wanted to build a stronger case that the tobacco company's ad campaign *caused* the increase in smokeless tobacco use, you would have to produce a more extended argument, perhaps something like this:

ENTHYMEMES: We are reasonably certain that the $60 million Nick O. Teen campaign caused the increase in smokeless tobacco use among male teenagers because the rise in smokeless tobacco use began within several weeks of the start of the ad campaign, because the ads were designed specifically to appeal to the subconscious desires of teenage males, and because the ads were targeted directly at teenage males by appearing in magazines and other venues where the primary audience is male teenagers.

A Toulmin analysis of this argument looks like this:

CLAIM:	We are reasonably certain that the $60 million Nick O. Teen campaign caused the increase in smokeless tobacco use among male teenagers.
STATED REASONS:	(a) because the rise in smokeless tobacco use began within several weeks of the start of the ad campaign; (b) because the ads were designed specifically to appeal to the subconscious desires of teenage males; and (c) because the ads were targeted directly at teenage males by appearing in magazines and other venues where the primary audience is male teenagers
GROUNDS:	(a) evidence that teen use of smokeless tobacco has increased significantly and that the increase began shortly after the start of the ad campaign; (b) evidence that the ads appeal to the subconscious desires of teenage males; (c) evidence that the campaign focused on print media associated with teen readership, bought billboard space near thoroughfares frequented by teens and offered product inducements particularly attractive to teenage consumers; research evidence showing that new teen users of smokeless tobacco are familiar with Nick O. Teen
WARRANTS:	(a) If one event follows another event, the first event may have caused the second event providing that other plausible causal links can be established to overrule coincidence; (b) consumers will buy products that appeal subliminally to their subconscious desires; (c) expensive ad campaigns aimed at target audiences are usually successful
BACKING:	(a) arguments showing that a plausible causal explanation linking the ads to the rise in

smokeless tobacco use can be established (thus the temporal connection between the ads and increased usage is not coincidental); (b) arguments showing how skillful ads work psychologically; (c) evidence of other expensive ad campaigns that have been successful

CONDITIONS OF REBUTTAL: *Attacking the grounds:*   (a) unless the temporal link is simply coincidence; unless other causal explanations are plausible: for example, much of the increased use of smokeless tobacco might be attributed to increasing intolerance of smoking in public places, forcing nicotine users to find less visible alternatives for satisfying their craving; perhaps the recent campaigns against the use of smokeless tobacco by major sports teams gave teens a new outlet for rebelling against adult norms; perhaps, as Wink maintains, the breakdown of the family causes kids to become lawless; (b) unless people are reading too much into the ads and they don't really appeal to subconscious desires or have a subliminal effect; (c) unless the ads were not targeted at teenage males

Attacking the warrants: (a) unless argument A is a clear example of a *post hoc* fallacy (see p. 329); (b) unless psychological advertising doesn't really work; (c) unless targeting specific audiences doesn't really work

QUALIFIER: We are *reasonably certain.*

 ## WRITING ASSIGNMENT FOR CHAPTER 11: AN ARGUMENT INVOLVING SURPRISING OR DISPUTED CAUSES

By looking back through your previous explorations or by developing new ideas through the exploration tasks at the end of this chapter, choose an issue question about the causes (or consequences) of a trend, event, or other phenomenon. Write a three- to five-page argument that persuades an audience to accept your explanation of the causes (or consequences) of your chosen phenomenon. Within your essay you should examine alternative hypotheses or opposing views and explain your reasons for rejecting them.

You can imagine your issue either as a puzzle or as a disagreement. If a puzzle, your task will be informational as well as persuasive because your role will be that of an analyst explaining causes or consequences of an event to an audience that doesn't have an answer already in mind. If you see your issue as a disagreement, your task will be more directly persuasive since your goal will be to change your audience's views so as to align more closely with your own.

The rest of this chapter will help you write your essay by giving you more background about causal arguments and by providing suggestions for each stage of the writing process.

THREE METHODS FOR ARGUING THAT ONE EVENT CAUSES ANOTHER

One of the first things you need to do when preparing a causal argument is to note just what sort of causal relationship you're dealing with. Are you concerned with the causes of a specific event or phenomenon such as the increase in homelessness in the 1980s, the collapse of the Soviet Union, the sudden increase in the number of homeruns in the 1996 baseball season, or the breakdown in communication between you and your father? Or are you planning to write about the cause of some recurring phenomenon such as cancer, laughter, math anxiety among females, or teen suicide?

With recurring phenomena, you have the luxury of being able to study multiple cases over long periods of time and establishing correlations between suspected causal factors and effects. In some cases you can even intervene in the process and test for yourself whether diminishing a suspected causal factor results in a lessening of the effect or whether increasing the causal factor results in a corresponding increase in the effect. Additionally, you can spend a good deal of time exploring just how the mechanics of causation might work.

But with a one-time occurrence your focus is on the details of the event and specific causal chains that may have contributed to the event. Sometimes evidence has disappeared or changed its nature. You often end up in the position more of a detective than of a scientific researcher and your conclusion will have to be more tentative as a result.

Having briefly stated these words of caution, let's turn now to the various ways you can argue that one event causes another.

First Method: Explain the Causal Mechanism Directly

The most convincing kind of causal argument identifies every link in the causal chain, showing how X causes A, which causes B, which in turn causes C, which finally causes Y. In some cases, all you have to do is fill in the missing links;

in other cases—when your assumptions about causality may seem questionable to your audience—you have to argue for the causal connection with more vigor.

A careful spelling out of each step in the causal chain is the technique used by astronomer Carl Sagan in "The Warming of the World" (pp. 253–257), in which he explains the greenhouse effect and predicts its consequences. His causal chain looks like this:

Starting Point A	Starting Point B
Cutting down of forests leads to fewer plants on Earth's land surface.	Burning of fossil fuels produces carbon dioxide.
Fewer plants lead to more carbon dioxide in the atmosphere.	(*Warrant:* because carbon dioxide is a product of combustion)
(*Warrant:* because plants convert carbon dioxide to oxygen)	Production of carbon dioxide leads to more carbon dioxide in the atmosphere.

LINK 2

More carbon dioxide in atmosphere reduces amount of infrared light radiated into space. (*Warrant:* because carbon dioxide absorbs infrared radiation; Sagan backs this warrant with further explanation)

LINK 3

Earth heats up. (*Warrant:* because Earth stays cool by reflecting heat back into space through infrared radiation)

LINK 4

Land will become parched; seas will rise. (*Warrant:* because heat causes changes in precipitation patterns causing land to parch; also because heat causes glacial ice to melt)

LINK 5

Massive global danger (*Warrant:* because parched farmland and rising seas will cause social and economic upheaval)

Sagan concludes his essay with a proposal based on this causal argument. Placed into a claim with a because clause, Sagan's should argument looks like this:

Nations should initiate worldwide efforts to find alternative energy sources because the continued burning of fossil fuels will lead to global catastrophe.

Thus, in Sagan's essay, a lengthy causal argument in the beginning supports a final should argument.

This causal chain method is also used by student writer Mary Lou Torpey in predicting the consequences of mandatory drug testing (pp. 257–258). Figure 11.1 shows Torpey's planning diagram for her argument "What Drugs I Take Is None of Your Business—The Consequences of Mandatory Drug Testing." Her diagram shows the links of the chain beginning with a mandatory drug-testing program and culminating in prejudice against employees with certain treatable disorders such as narcolepsy.

Second Method: Use Various Inductive Methods to Establish a High Probability of a Causal Link

Informal Induction

Although few of us are scientists, all of us practice the scientific method informally through *induction.* Induction is a form of reasoning by which we make generalizations based on a limited number of specific cases. For example, if on several occasions you got a headache after drinking red wine but not after drinking white wine, you would be apt to conclude inductively that red wine causes you to get headaches. However, because there are almost always exceptions to rules arrived at inductively and because we can't be certain that the future will always be like the past, inductive reasoning gives only probable truths, not certain ones.

When your brain thinks inductively, it sorts through data looking for patterns of similarity and difference. Toddlers are thinking inductively when they learn the connection between flipping a wall switch and watching the ceiling light come on. Like scientists, they are holding all variables constant except the position of the switch. But the inductive process does not explain the causal mechanism itself. Thus, through induction you know that red wine gives you a headache, but you don't know how the wine actually works on your nervous system—the causal chain itself.

Largely because of its power, the process of induction often can lead you to wrong conclusions. You should be aware of two common fallacies of inductive reasoning that can tempt you into erroneous assumptions about causality. (Both fallacies are treated more fully in Appendix 1.)

The *post hoc, ergo propter hoc* fallacy ("after this, therefore because of this") mistakes precedence for cause. Just because event A regularly precedes event B doesn't mean that event A causes event B. The same reasoning that tells us that flipping a switch causes the light to go on can make us believe that the Chernobyl nuclear disaster caused the rise in infant death rates in the state of Washington (see Case 4). The nuclear disaster clearly preceded the rise in death rates. But did it clearly *cause* it? Our point is that precedence alone is no proof of causality and that we are guilty of this fallacy whenever we are swayed to believe that X causes Y primarily because X precedes Y. We can guard against this fallacy by seeking plausible link-by-link connections showing how X causes Y.

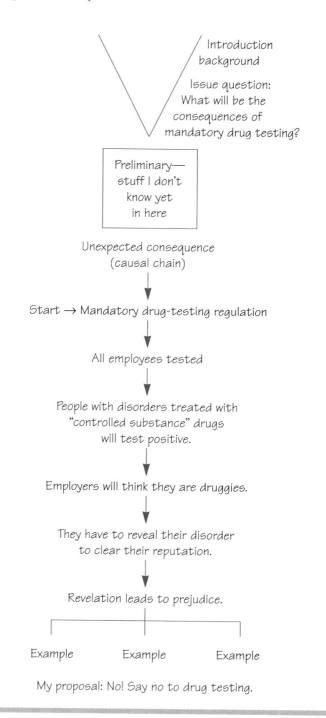

FIGURE 11.1   Initial planning diagram for Mary Lou Torpey's essay (pp. 257–258)

The *hasty generalization* fallacy occurs when you make a generalization based on too few cases or too little consideration of alternative explanations: You flip the switch, but the light bulb doesn't go on. You conclude—too hastily—that the power has gone off. (Perhaps the light bulb has burned out or the switch is broken.) How many trials does it take before you can make a justified generalization rather than a hasty generalization? It is difficult to say, for sure. Both the post hoc fallacy and the hasty generalization fallacy remind us that induction requires a leap from individual cases to a general principle and that it is always possible to leap too soon.

Scientific Experimentation

One way to avoid inductive fallacies is to examine our causal hypotheses as carefully as possible. When we deal with a recurring phenomenon such as cancer, we can create scientific experiments that give us inductive evidence of causality with a fairly high degree of certainty. If, for example, we were concerned that a particular food source such as spinach might contain cancer-causing chemicals, we could test our hypothesis experimentally. We could take two groups of rats and control their environment carefully so that the only difference between them (in theory, anyway) was that one group ate large quantities of spinach and the other group ate none. Spinach eating, then, is the one variable between the two groups that we are testing. After a specified period of time, we would check to see what percentage of rats in each group developed cancer. If twice as many spinach-eating rats contracted cancer, we could probably conclude that our hypothesis had held up.

Correlation

Still another method of induction is correlation, which expresses a statistical relationship between X and Y. A correlation between X and Y means that when X occurs, Y is likely to occur also, and vice versa. To put it another way, correlation establishes a possibility that an observed link between an X and a Y is a causal one rather than a mere coincidence. The existence of a correlation, however, does not tell us whether X causes Y, whether Y causes X, or whether both are caused by some third phenomenon. For example, there is a fairly strong correlation between nearsightedness and intelligence. (That is, in a given sample of nearsighted people and people with normal eyesight, a higher percentage of the nearsighted people will be highly intelligent. Similarly, in a sample of high-intelligence people and people with normal intelligence, a higher percentage of the high-intelligence group will be nearsighted.) But the direction of causality isn't clear. It could be that high intelligence causes people to read more, thus ruining their eyes (high intelligence causes nearsightedness). Or it could be that nearsightedness causes people to read more, thus raising their intelligence (nearsightedness causes high intelligence). Or it could be that some unknown phenomenon inside the brain causes both nearsightedness and high intelligence.

In recent years, correlation studies have been made stunningly sophisticated through the power of computerized analyses. For example, we could attempt to do the spinach-cancer study without resorting to a scientific experiment. If we identified a given group that ate lots of spinach (for example, vegetarians) and another group that ate little if any spinach (Inuits) and then checked to see if their rates of cancer correlated to their rates of spinach consumption, we would have the beginnings of a correlation study. But it would have no scientific validity until we factored out all the other variables between vegetarians and Inuits that might skew the findings—variables such as lifestyle, climate, genetic inheritance, differences in diet other than spinach, and so forth. Factoring out such variables is one of the complex feats that modern statistical analyses attempt to accomplish. But the fact remains that the most sophisticated correlation studies still cannot tell us the direction of causality or even for certain that there is causality.

By way of illustrating the uses of correlation arguments, consider Victor Fuchs's article "Why Married Mothers Work" (pp. 259–262). The graph on page 260 shows that the number of married mothers in the workforce has been steadily rising since 1948. Fuchs rejects several common explanations for this phenomenon (growth of feminism, government affirmative action, economic need) on the grounds that the timing is wrong. He proposes another hypothesis: Increased wages and increased job openings in the service sector are for him the best causal candidates because their slow, steady rate of increase correlates with the increase in working married mothers. Moreover, he provides a hypothesis for why women are attracted to service sector jobs (they require less physical strength, offer flexible hours including part-time work, and are located near residential areas).

Note that Fuchs is careful to have two kinds of reasons for his argument. The first is the statistical data that show that the increase of married mothers in the workplace correlates with the increase of wages and the increase of available jobs in the service sector. The second is a hypothesis explaining why increased wages and increased service sector jobs attract married mothers. Whenever you make a causal argument supported by statistical correlations, you should be aware—as is Fuchs—that you must be able to offer some reason for thinking that there is a particular "direction" to the relationship.

Conclusion about Inductive Methods

Induction, then, can tell us within varying degrees of certainty whether or not X causes Y. It does not, however, explain the causal mechanism itself. Typically, the because clause structure of an inductive argument would take one of the following three shapes: (1) "Although we cannot explain the causal mechanism directly, we believe that X and Y are very probably causally linked because we have repeatedly observed their conjunction"; (2) ". . . because we have demonstrated the linkage through controlled scientific experiments"; or (3) ". . . because we have shown that they are statistically correlated and have provided a plausible hypothesis concerning the causal direction."

FOR CLASS DISCUSSION

Working individually or in small groups, develop plausible causal chains that might explain the correlations between the following pairs of phenomena:

a. A person registers low stress level on electrochemical stress meter.   Does daily meditation.

b. Person regularly consumes frozen dinners.   Is likely to vote for improved rapid transit.

c. High achiever   Is first-born child.

d. Member of the National Rifle Association   Favors tough treatment of criminals.

Third Method: Argue by Analogy or Precedent

Another common method of causal arguing is through analogy or precedent. (See also Chapter 12, which deals in more depth with the strengths and weaknesses of this kind of arguing.) When you argue through resemblance, you try to find a case that is similar to the one you are arguing about but is better known and less controversial to the reader. If the reader agrees with your view of causality in the similar case, you then try to transfer this understanding to the case at issue. Causal arguments by analogy and precedent are logically weaker than arguments based on causal chains or on induction and will typically be used in cases where empirical evidence is weak. Here are some examples of this method in causal arguing:

1. If you wanted to argue that overcrowding in high-density apartment houses causes dangerous stress in humans, you could compare humans to mice, which develop symptoms of high stress when they are crowded together in cages. (This argument depends on the warrant that humans and mice will respond similarly to the condition of crowding.)

2. If you want to argue that doing regular thinking skills exercises will result in improved thinking ability, you could compare the mind to a muscle and the thinking skills exercises to daily weight training. (Because the audience will probably accept the causal chain of weight training leading to improved physical strength, you hope to transfer that acceptance to the field of mental activity. This argument depends on the warrant that the mind is like a muscle.)

3. If you wanted to argue that forced piano lessons won't make a child a musician, you could argue that parents can't mold a child like clay; rather, children are like plants—you can't mold them into something that is not in their nature any more than a gardener can mold a tulip into a rose. (This argument depends on the warrant that children are more like plants than like clay.)

All of these arguments have a persuasive power. However, any two things that are alike in some ways (analogous) are different in others (disanalogous), and these differences are apt to be ignored in arguments from analogy. You should realize, then, that the warrant that says X is like Y is almost always vulnerable. Psychologists, for example, have pretty much demonstrated that the mind is not like a muscle, and we can all think of ways that children are not like plants. *All* resemblance arguments, therefore, are in some sense "false analogies." But some analogies are so misleading that logicians have labeled them as fallacious—the fallacy of *false analogy*. The false analogy fallacy covers those truly blatant cases where the differences between X and Y are too great for the analogy to hold. An example might be the following: "Putting red marks all over students' papers causes great emotional distress just as putting knife marks over their palms would cause great physical distress." It is impossible to draw a precise line, however, between an analogy that has true clarifying and persuasive power and one that is fallacious.

GLOSSARY OF TERMS ENCOUNTERED IN CAUSAL ARGUMENTS

Because causal arguments are often easier to conduct if writer and reader share a few specialized terms, we offer the following glossary for your convenience.

Fallacy of Oversimplified Cause: One of the greatest temptations when establishing causal relationships is to fall into the habit of looking for *the* cause of something. Most phenomena, especially the ones we argue about, will have multiple causes. For example, few presidents have won elections on the basis of one characteristic or event. Usually elections result from a combination of abilities, stances on key issues, personal characteristics, mistakes on the part of the competition, events in the world, and so forth. Similarly, scientists know that a number of different causes must work together to create a disease such as cancer. But though we know all this, we still long to make the world less complex by attributing a single cause to puzzling effects.

Immediate/Remote Causes: Every causal chain links backward indefinitely into the past. An immediate cause is the closest in time to the event being examined. If a normally passive man goes on a killing rampage, the immediate cause may be a brain tumor or a recent argument with his wife that was the "last straw" in a long chain of events. A number of earlier events may have led up to the present—failure to get medical attention for headaches or failure to get counseling when a marriage began to disintegrate. Such causes going further back into the past are considered remote causes. It's sometimes difficult to determine the relative significance of remote causes insofar as immediate causes are so obviously linked to the event whereas remote causes often have to be dug out or inferred. It's difficult to know, for example, just how seriously to take serial murderer Ted Bundy's defense that he was "traumatized" at age twelve by the discovery that he was illegitimate. How big a role are we willing to grant a causal factor so remote in time and so apparently minor in relation to the murder of thirty-five young women?

Precipitating/Contributing Causes: These terms are similar to *immediate* and *remote* causes but don't designate a temporal linking going into the past. Rather, they refer to a main cause emerging out of a background of subsidiary causes. The contributing causes are a set of conditions that give rise to the precipitating cause, which triggers the effect. If, for example, a husband and wife decide to separate, the precipitating cause may be a stormy fight over money, which itself is a symptom of their inability to communicate with each other any longer. All the factors that contribute to that inability to communicate— preoccupation with their respective careers, anxieties about money, in-law problems—may be considered contributing causes. Note that the contributing causes and precipitating cause all coexist simultaneously in time—none is temporally more remote than another. But the marriage might have continued had the contributing causes not finally resulted in frequent angry fighting, which doomed the marriage.

Constraints: Sometimes an effect occurs, not because X happened, but because another factor—a constraint—was removed. At other times a possible effect will not occur because a given constraint prevents it from happening. A constraint is a kind of negative cause that limits choices and possibilities. As soon as the constraint is removed, a given effect may occur. For example, in the marriage we have been discussing, the presence of children in the home might have been a constraint against divorce; as soon as the children graduate from high school and leave home, the marriage may well dissolve.

Necessary/Sufficient Causes: We speak of necessary causes as those that must be present when a given effect takes place. If a necessary cause is absent, the effect cannot take place. Thus the presence of a spark is a necessary cause for the operation of a gasoline engine. A sufficient cause, on the other hand, is one that guarantees a given effect. An electric spark is thus a *necessary cause* for the operation of a gasoline engine but not a *sufficient cause* since other causes must also be present to make the engine work (fuel, etc.). Few causes are ever both necessary and sufficient to bring about a given effect.

❧ FOR CLASS DISCUSSION

The terms in the preceding glossary can be used as an effective heuristic for thinking of possible causes of an event. For the following events, try to think of as many causes as possible by making idea maps with branches labeled *immediate cause, remote cause, precipitating cause, contributing cause,* and *constraint* (see Figure 11.2).

1. Working individually, make a map identifying causes for one of the following:
   a. your decision to attend your present college

b. an important event in your life or your family (a divorce, a major move, etc.)

c. a personal opinion you hold that is not widely shared

2. Working as a group, make a map identifying causes for one of the following:

a. why women's fashion and beauty magazines are the most frequently purchased magazines in college bookstores

b. why the majority of teenagers don't listen to classical music

c. why the number of babies born out of wedlock has increased dramatically in the last thirty years

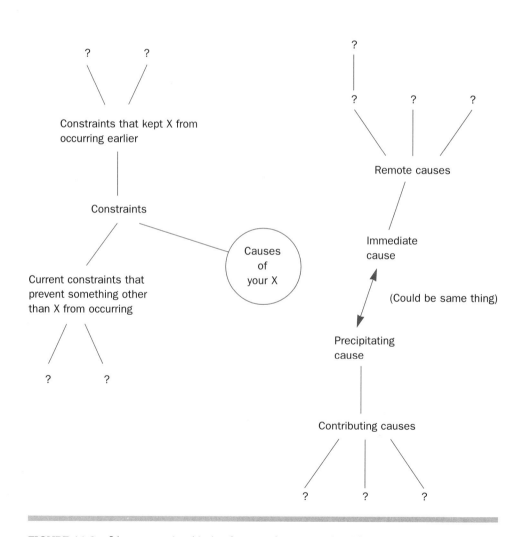

FIGURE 11.2   Idea map using kinds of causes for generating ideas

WRITING YOUR CAUSAL ARGUMENT

The stages of the writing process that we discussed in Chapter 3 can be fruitfully applied to a causal argument. What follows are some suggestions that may help you find a good causal issue and produce an effective argument.

The Starting Point: Finding a Causal Issue

You already may have discovered some good causal issues and recorded them in your journal. If not, here are some exploration tasks that might help you get started.

Make a List of People's Unusual Likes and Dislikes

One way to become engaged with a causal issue is to make a list of unusual things that anger people, scare them, or inspire their hatred. Alternatively, you can list unusual things that people like, value, or desire. You could then write a causal argument explaining why one of these phenomena produces this emotional response. Try to choose likes or dislikes that are fairly common but are puzzling to explain. Typical titles might be: "Why Are People Afraid of Bats?" "Why Do Certain Students Dislike Writing?" or "Why Do So Many People Like Professional Wrestling?"

Make Lists of Trends and Other Puzzling Phenomena

Besides lists of unusual likes and dislikes, try adding your own Xs to the following list.

1. trends

    popularity of expensive basketball shoes for street wear

    growth of alternative schools

    increase in nationwide sales of premium coffees

2. one-time events

    the defeat of Bob Dole in the 1996 elections

    rash of mysterious illnesses of Gulf War veterans two years after returning to the United States

    the sudden appearance of deformed frogs in Minnesota lakes

3. repeatable events

    Why are children attracted to violent video games?

    What are the effects of telecommuting on the workplace?

    What are the causes of reading difficulties?

4. other puzzling phenomena

> Why are lotteries popular?
>
> Why do people watch professional wrestling?
>
> Why is so much hatred of women reflected in gangsta rap?

Make Some Idea Maps to Explore
Causes or Consequences

Another way to find a causal issue is to try out some arguments. Make idea maps in which you brainstorm possible causes for several of the following phenomena: failure of many sexually active teenagers to use birth control; growth of the home computer industry; decline of interest in home videogames; popularity of rock groups with bisexual identities; increase of popularity of "home birthing" methods; graffiti on subways; the dominance of blacks in college and professional basketball; popularity of Eddie Murphy movies; growth in the pornography industry. Then add at least three phenomena of your own to the list.

Another fruitful area for idea-maps is to explore possible consequences of real or hypothetical events. What might be the consequences, for example, of some of the following: a cure for cancer; total prevention of illegal immigration; the legalization of same-sex marriage; a heavy tax on families having more than two children; replacement of federal income tax with a federal sales tax; a four-day workweek; several topics of your own choice.

Exploration Stage

Once you have decided on a causal issue, we recommend that you explore it by going through the eight guided tasks for exploring an argument (on pp. 73–74). You can also make an idea map on your causal issue like the ones in the For Class Discussion exercise in the preceding glossary of causal terms.

Writing the Discovery Draft: Typical Ways
of Organizing a Causal Argument

Your goal at the discovery draft stage is to get your developing argument onto paper. At this stage it is useful to know some of the standard ways that a causal argument can be organized. Later, you may decide on a quite different organizational pattern, but these standard ways will help you get started.

Plan 1

When your purpose is to describe and explain all the links in a causal chain:

- Introduce phenomenon to be explained and show why it is problematical.
- Present your thesis in summary form.
- Describe and explain each link in the causal chain.

Carl Sagan's essay on the greenhouse effect (pp. 253–257) follows this format.

Plan 2

When your purpose is to explore the relative contribution of all causes to a phenomenon or to explore all possible consequences of a phenomenon:

- Introduce the phenomenon to be explained and suggest how or why it is controversial.
- Devote one section to each possible cause/consequence and decide whether it is necessary, sufficient, contributory, remote, and so forth. (Arrange sections so that those causes most familiar to the audience come first and the most surprising ones come last.)

Victor Fuchs's argument "Why Married Mothers Work" (pp. 259–262) follows this format.

Plan 3

When your purpose is to argue for a cause or consequence that is surprising or unexpected to your audience:

- Introduce a phenomenon to be explained and show why it is controversial.
- One by one, examine and reject the causes or consequences your audience would normally assume or expect.
- Introduce your unexpected or surprising cause or consequence and argue for it.

Plans 2 and 3 are similar in that they examine numerous possible causes or consequences. Plan 2, however, tries to establish the relative importance of each cause or consequence, whereas Plan 3 aims at rejecting the causes or consequences normally assumed by the audience and argues for an unexpected surprising cause or consequence. Plan 3 is the strategy used by Mary Lou Torpey (pp. 257–258) in arguing for an unexpected consequence of drug testing and by Walter S. Minot in proposing an overlooked cause of decline in American education (pp. 262–263).

Plan 4

When your purpose is to change your audience's mind about a cause or consequence:

- Introduce issue and show why it is controversial.
- Summarize your opponent's causal argument and then refute it.
- Present your own causal argument.

Plan 4 is a standard structure for all kinds of arguments. This is the structure you would use if you were the attorney for the person whose car skidded into the boutique (p. 231). The opposing attorney would blame your client's reckless driving. You would lay blame on a poorly signed intersection, a speeding beer truck, and violation of building codes.

Revision: Seeing Your Argument Afresh

Once you have written a discovery draft, you will have a clearer idea of what you are trying to do in your essay. Through further drafting and discussions with others, your next goal is to clarify your argument for yourself and then finally to make it clear and persuasive for your readers.

If you haven't already done so, now is the time to summarize your argument as a claim with because clauses and to analyze your argument either using the Toulmin schema or making a diagram of your causal chain similar to the one we made for Carl Sagan's essay on the greenhouse effect or that Mary Lou Torpey made for herself (Figure 11.1). To strengthen your argument from the perspective of a skeptical audience, pay particular attention to Toulmin's "conditions for rebuttal." Try to see the weaknesses of your argument from an opposing perspective and use that knowledge to bolster your support. The following section shows you some ways to role play an opposing view in order to discover weaknesses in your own argument.

CONDITIONS FOR REBUTTAL: CRITIQUING CAUSAL ARGUMENTS

Because of the strenuous conditions that must be met before causality can be proven, causal arguments are vulnerable at many points. The following strategies will generally be helpful.

If You Described Each Link in a Causal Chain, Would Skeptics Point Out Weaknesses in Any of the Links?

As the diagram of Carl Sagan's article suggests, describing a causal chain can be complex business. A skeptic can raise doubts about an entire argument simply by undercutting one of the links. Your best defense is to make a diagram of the linkages and role play a skeptic trying to refute each link in turn. Whenever you find possible arguments against your position, see how you can strengthen your own argument at that point.

If Your Argument Is Based on a Scientific Experiment, Could Skeptics Question the Validity of the Experiment?

The scientific method attempts to demonstrate causality experimentally. If the experiment isn't well designed, however, the demonstration is less likely to be acceptable to skeptical audiences. Here are ways to critique a scientific argument:

Question the findings.   Skeptics may have reason to believe that the data collected were not accurate or representative. They might provide alternative data or simply point out flaws in the way the data were collected.

Question the interpretation of the data.   Many research studies are divided into a "findings" and a "discussion" section. In the discussion section the researcher analyzes and interprets the data. A skeptic might provide an alternative interpretation of the data or otherwise argue that the data don't support what the original writer claims.

Question the design of the experiment.   A detailed explanation of research design is beyond the scope of this text, but we can give a brief example of how a typical experiment did go wrong. Graduate students recently completed an experiment to test the effect of word processors on students' writing in junior high school. They reported that students who used the word processors for revising all their essays did significantly better on a final essay than a control group of students who didn't use word processors.

It turned out, however, that there were at least two major design flaws in the experiment. First, the researchers allowed students to volunteer for the experimental group. Perhaps these students were already better writers than the control group from the start. (Can you think of a causal explanation of why the better students might volunteer to use the computers?) Second, when the teachers graded essays from both the computer group and the control group, the essays were not retyped uniformly. Thus the computer group's essays were typed with "computer perfection," whereas the control group's essays were handwritten or typed on ordinary typewriters. Perhaps the readers were affected by the pleasing appearance of the computer-typed essays. More significantly, perhaps the graders were biased in favor of the computer project and unconsciously scored the computer-typed papers higher.

This example illustrates just a few of the ways a scientific study can be flawed. Our point is that skeptics might not automatically accept your citation of a scientific study as a proof of causality. By considering opposing views in advance, you may be able to strengthen your argument.

If You Have Used Correlation Data, Could Skeptics Argue that the Correlation Is Much Weaker than You Claim or that You Haven't Sufficiently Demonstrated Causality?

As we discussed earlier, correlation data tell us only that two or more phenomena are likely to occur together. They don't tell us that one caused the other. Thus, correlation arguments are usually accompanied by hypotheses about causal connections between the phenomena. Correlation arguments can often be refuted as follows:

- Find problems in the statistical methods used to determine the correlation.
- Weaken the correlation by pointing out exceptions.
- Provide an alternative hypothesis about causality.

If You Have Used an Analogy Argument, Could Skeptics Point Out Disanalogies?

Although among the most persuasive of argumentative strategies, analogy arguments are also among the easiest to refute. The standard procedure is to counter your argument that X is like Y by pointing out all the ways that X is *not* like Y. Once again, by role playing an opposing view you may be able to strengthen your own analogy argument.

Could a Skeptic Cast Doubt on Your Argument by Reordering Your Priority of Causes?

Up to this point we've focused on refuting the claim that X causes Y. However, another approach is to concede that X helps cause Y but that X is only one of several contributing causes and not the most significant one at that.

 FOR CLASS DISCUSSION

In "Students Who Push Burgers" (pp. 262–263), the author, Walter Minot, blames part-time jobs as a primary cause of the decline of educational performance by American students, a decline that leads in turn (so claims Minot) to a decline in our economy. You, however, want to defend the practice of American teenagers holding part-time jobs. Using procedures outlined in this chapter, how might you attempt to weaken Minot's argument and create greater audience adherence to your own?

1. Do a ten-minute freewrite in which you explore ways to undercut Minot's argument and support your own.

2. In groups, discuss your individual responses.

3. Elect one member of your group to give a brief speech before the class, arguing that Minot's essay either fails to see important benefits in part-time work or diverts attention from other, more important causes of the decline of American education.

The Warming of the World

Carl Sagan

When humans first evolved—in the savannahs of East Africa a few million years ago—our numbers were few and our powers feeble. We knew almost nothing about controlling our environment—even clothing had yet to be invented. We were creatures of the climate, utterly dependent upon it.

A few degrees hotter or colder on average, and our ancestors were in trouble. The toll taken much later by the ice ages, in which average land temperatures dropped some 8° C (centigrade, or Celsius), must have been horrific. And yet, it is exactly such climatic change that pushed our ancestors to develop tools and technology, science and civilization. Certainly, skills in hunting, skinning, tanning, building shelters and refurbishing caves must owe much to the terrors of the deep ice age.

Today, we live in a balmy epoch, 10,000 years after the last major glaciation. In this climatic spring, our species has flourished; we now cover the entire planet and are altering the very appearance of our world. Lately—within the last century or so—humans have acquired, in more ways than one, the ability to make major changes in that climate upon which we are so dependent. The Nuclear Winter findings are one dramatic indication that we can change the climate—in this case, in the spasm of nuclear war. But I wish here to describe a different kind of climatic danger, this one slower, more subtle and arising from intentions that are wholly benign.

It is warm down here on Earth because the Sun shines. If the Sun were somehow turned off, the Earth would rapidly cool. The oceans would freeze, and eventually the atmosphere itself would condense out and our planet would be covered everywhere by snowbanks of solid oxygen and nitrogen 10 meters (about 30 feet) high. Only the tiny trickle of heat from the Earth's interior and the faint starlight would save our world from a temperature of absolute zero.

We know how bright the Sun is; we know how far from it we are; and we know what fraction of the sunlight reaching the Earth is reflected back to space (about 30 percent). So we can calculate—with a simple mathematical equation—what the average temperature of the Earth should be. But when we do the calculation, we find that the Earth's temperature should be about 20° C below the freezing point of water, in stark contradiction to our everyday experience. What have we done wrong?

6   As in many such cases in science, what we've done wrong is to forget something—in this case, the atmosphere. Every object in the universe radiates some kind of light to space; the colder the object, the longer the wavelength of radiation it emits. The Earth—much colder than the Sun—radiates to space mainly in the infrared part of the spectrum, not the visible. Were the Sun turned off, the Earth would soon be indetectable in ordinary visible light, though it would be brilliantly illuminated in infrared light.

7   When sunlight strikes the Earth, part is reflected back into the sky; much of the rest is absorbed by the ground and heats it—the darker the ground, the greater the heating. The ground radiates back upward in the infrared. Thus, for an airless Earth, the temperature would be set solely by a balance between the incoming sunlight absorbed by the surface and the infrared radiation that the surface emits back to space.

8   When you put air on a planet, the situation changes. The Earth's atmosphere is, generally, still transparent to visible light. That's why we can see each other when we talk, glimpse distant mountains and view the stars.

9   But in the infrared, all that is different. While the oxygen and nitrogen in the air are transparent in both the infrared and the visible, minor constituents such as water vapor (H_2O) and carbon dioxide (CO_2) tend to be much more opaque in the infrared. It would be useless for us to have eyes that could see at a wavelength, say, of 15 microns in the infrared, because the air is murky black there.

10   Accordingly, if you add air to a world, you heat it: The surface now has difficulty when it tries to radiate back to space in the infrared. The atmosphere tends to absorb the infrared radiation, keeping heat near the surface and providing an infrared blanket for the world. There is very little CO_2 in the Earth's atmosphere—only 0.03 percent. But that small amount is enough to make the Earth's atmosphere opaque in important regions of the infrared spectrum. CO_2 and H_2O are the reason the global temperature is not well below freezing. We owe our comfort—indeed, our very existence—to the fact that these gases are present and are much more transparent in the visible than in the infrared. Our lives depend on a delicate balance of invisible gases. Too much blanket, or too little, and we're in trouble.

11   This property of many gases to absorb strongly in the infrared but not in the visible, and thereby to heat their surroundings, is called the "greenhouse effect." A florist's greenhouse keeps its planty inhabitants warm. The phrase "greenhouse effect" is widely used and has an instructive ring to it, reminding us that we live in a planetary-scale greenhouse and recalling the admonition about living in glass houses and throwing stones. But, in fact, florists' greenhouses do not keep warm by the greenhouse effect; they work mainly by inhibiting the movement of air inside, another matter altogether.

12   We need look only as far as the nearest planet to see an example of an atmospheric greenhouse effect gone wild. Venus has in its atmosphere an enormous quantity of carbon dioxide (roughly as much as is buried as carbonates in all the rocks of the Earth's crust). There is an atmosphere of CO_2 on Venus 90 times thicker than the atmosphere on the Earth and containing some 200,000 times more CO_2 than in our air. With water vapor and other minor atmospheric constituents, this is enough to make a greenhouse effect that keeps the surface of Venus around 470° C (900° F)—enough to melt tin or lead.

13   When humans burn wood or "fossil fuels" (coal, oil, natural gas, etc.), they put carbon dioxide into the air. One carbon atom (C) combines with a molecule of oxygen (O_2) to pro-

duce CO_2. The development of agriculture, the conversion of dense forest to comparatively sparsely vegetated farms, has moved carbon atoms from plants on the ground to carbon dioxide in the air. About half of this new CO_2 is removed by plants or by the layering down of carbonates in the oceans. On human time-scales, these changes are irreversible: Once the CO_2 is in the atmosphere, human technology is helpless to remove it. So the overall amount of CO_2 in the air has been growing—at least since the industrial revolution. If no other factors operate, and if enough CO_2 is put into the atmosphere, eventually the average surface temperature will increase perceptibly.

There are other greenhouse gases that are increasingly abundant in the Earth's atmosphere—halocarbons, such as the freon used in refrigerator cooling systems; or nitrous oxide (N_2O), produced by automobile exhausts and nitrogenous fertilizers; or methane (CH_4), produced partly in the intestines of cows and other ruminants.   14

But let's for the moment concentrate on carbon dioxide: How long, at the present rates of burning wood and fossil fuels, before the global climate becomes significantly warmer? And what would the consequences be?   15

It is relatively simple to calculate the immediate warming from a given increase in the CO_2 abundance, and all competent calculations seem to be in good agreement. More difficult to estimate are (1) the rate at which carbon dioxide will continue to be put into the atmosphere (it depends on population growth rates, economic styles, alternative energy sources and the like) and (2) feedbacks—ways in which a slight warming might produce other, more drastic, effects.   16

The recent increase in atmospheric CO_2 is well documented. Over the last century, this CO_2 buildup should have resulted in a few tenths of a degree of global warming, and there is some evidence that such a warming has occurred.   17

The National Academy of Sciences estimates that the present atmospheric abundance of CO_2 is likely to double by the year 2065, although experts at the academy predict a one-in-20 chance that it will double before 2035—when an infant born today becomes 50 years old. Such a doubling would warm the air near the surface of the Earth by 2° C or 3° C— maybe by as much as 4° C. These are average temperature values; there would naturally be considerable local variation. High latitudes would be warmed much more, although a baked Alaska will be some time coming.   18

There would be precipitation changes. The annual discharge of rivers would be altered. Some scientists believe that central North America—including much of the area that is now the breadbasket of the world—would be parched in summer if the global temperature increases by a few degrees. There would be some mitigating effects; for example, where plant growth is not otherwise limited, more CO_2 should aid photosynthesis and make more luxuriant growth (of weeds as well as crops). If the present CO_2 injection into the atmosphere continued over a few centuries, the warming would be greater than from all other causes over the last 100,000 years.   19

As the climate warms, glacial ice melts. Over the last 100 years, the level of the world's oceans has risen by 15 centimeters (6 inches). A global warming of 3° C or 4° C over the next century is likely to bring a further rise in the average sea level of about 70 centimeters (28 inches). An increase of this magnitude could produce major damage to ports all over the world and induce fundamental change in the patterns of land development. A   20

serious speculation is that greenhouse temperature increases of 3° C or 4° C could, in addition, trigger the disintegration of the West Antarctic Ice Sheet, with huge quantities of polar ice falling into the ocean. This would raise sea level by some 6 meters (20 feet) over a period of centuries, with the eventual inundation of all coastal cities on the planet.

21   There are many other possibilities that are poorly understood, including the release of other greenhouse gases (for example, methane from peat bogs) accelerated by the warming climate. The circulation of the oceans might be an important aspect of the problem. The scientific community is attempting to make an environmental-impact statement for the entire planet on the consequences of continued burning of fossil fuels. Despite the uncertainties, a kind of consensus is in: Over the next century or more, with projected rates of burning coal, oil and gas, there is trouble ahead.

22   The problem is difficult for at least three different reasons:

(1) We do not yet fully understand how severe the greenhouse consequences will be.

(2) Although the effects are not yet strikingly noticeable in everyday life, to deal with the problem, the present generation might have to make sacrifices for the next.

(3) The problem cannot be solved except on an international scale: The atmosphere is ignorant of national boundaries. South African carbon dioxide warms Taiwan, and Soviet coal-burning practices effect productivity in America. The largest coal resources in the world are found in the Soviet Union, the United States and China, in that order. What incentives are there for a nation such as China, with vast coal reserves and a commitment to rapid economic development, to hold back on the burning of fossil fuels because the result might, decades later, be a parched American sunbelt or still more ghastly starvation in sub-Saharan Africa? Would countries that might benefit from a warmer climate be as vigorous in restraining the burning of fossil fuels as nations likely to suffer greatly?

23   Fortunately, we have a little time. A great deal can be done in decades. Some argue that government subsidies lower the price of fossil fuels, inviting waste; more efficient usage, besides its economic advantage, could greatly ameliorate the CO_2 greenhouse problem. Parts of the solution might involve alternative energy sources, where appropriate: solar power, for example, or safer nuclear fission reactors, which, whatever their other dangers, produce no greenhouse gases of importance. Conceivably, the long-awaited advent of commercial nuclear fusion power might happen before the middle of the next century.

24   However, any technological solution to the looming greenhouse problem must be worldwide. It would not be sufficient for the United States or the Soviet Union, say, to develop safe and commercially feasible fusion power plants: That technology would have to be diffused worldwide, on terms of cost and reliability that would be more attractive to developing nations than a reliance on fossil fuel reserves or imports. A serious, very high-level look at patterns of U.S. and world energy development in light of the greenhouse problem seems overdue.

25   During the last few million years, human technology, spurred in part by climatic change, has made our species a force to be reckoned with on a planetary scale. We now find, to our astonishment, that we pose a danger to ourselves. The present world order is, unfortunately, not designed to deal with global-scale dangers. Nations tend to be concerned about themselves, not about the planet; they tend to have short-term rather than long-term

objectives. In problems such as the increasing greenhouse effect, one nation or region might benefit while another suffers. In other global environmental issues, such as nuclear war, all nations lose. The problems are connected: Constructive international efforts to understand and resolve one will benefit the others.

Further study and better public understanding are needed, of course. But what is essential is a global consciousness—a view that transcends our exclusive identification with the generational and political groupings into which, by accident, we have been born. The solution to these problems requires a perspective that embraces the planet and the future. We are all in this greenhouse together.

26

What Drugs I Take Is None of Your Business— The Consequences of Drug Testing

Mary Lou Torpey (student)

So you have a job interview with a new company tomorrow? Well my advice is to go home, get some rest, and drink plenty of fluids, because chances are you'll have to leave more than just a good impression with your prospective employer. You may have to leave a full specimen bottle to check you out for drug use, too. Imagine having to stand in a line in your business suit with your application in one hand and a steaming cup of urine in the other, waiting to turn each of them in, wondering which one is really more important in the job selection process. Some companies and every branch of the Armed Forces require a witness present during the test so the person being tested doesn't try to switch specimens with someone who is drug or alcohol free. As one can imagine, having to be witnessed during a drug test could give a whole new meaning to the term "stage fright." The embarrassing situation of being drug tested is a real possibility, since mandatory drug testing is becoming more and more prevalent in today's workplaces.

1

Despite the embarrassment, many employers, including western Washington's largest, Boeing, believe the consequences of mandatory drug testing would be beneficial. By trying to ensure safe work environments by cutting down on drug abusers who could create potential hazards for other employees, such companies believe that quality in workmanship will improve. They also believe that their employees will operate at peak performance levels to keep productivity up. However, there is a consequence of mandatory drug testing that is not being considered by the employers who have instituted it, a consequence that will be devastating for hundreds of thousands of people.

2

Perhaps the most potentially damaging result of mandatory drug testing lies with people who have legitimate uses for controlled substance drugs—people like me. I have narcolepsy, a serious lifelong disorder that causes crippling sleepiness without the help of controlled substance drugs, similar to the way a mobility impaired person would be crippled without crutches, a walker, or a wheelchair. In other words, I, as a narcoleptic, must

3

have a controlled substance drug to maintain any sort of normal lifestyle at all. Without amphetamines, I could not drive a car, go to college, read, or even hold a decent conversation without falling asleep.

4   The damaging consequence of mandatory drug testing here is that if I, or other with a myriad of other chronic disorders requiring the use of controlled substance drugs, such as epilepsy, depression due to chemical imbalance, or a number of other seizure disorders, were seeking employment where a drug test is administered, we would be forced to divulge information about the illness. It should be every person's choice whether or not they will inform their employer, especially if their medications manage their illness adequately.

5   Having to inform a prospective employer about an illness would open the way for prejudice. In all honesty, why would an employer hire a "sick" person when there are so many "normal" ones on the job market? This prejudice is ironic since people like me with narcolepsy or other "silent disabilities" try so hard to compensate that they make exemplary employees. The way I think of it is like that commercial for "Scrubbing Bubbles." That's the commercial where the little bubbles go down the bathtub drain after making it sparkling clean, shouting "we work hard so you don't have to." When it comes to my job, I work hard so my employer doesn't have to think about making special exceptions for me.

6   In the case of a random test for employees already with a company, those individuals would be forced to explain why a controlled substance is coming up on their test results. When this happens to an employee who has not previously told his employer about an illness or medication he must take, that employee runs the strong chance of being terminated or prejudiced against in the promotion process. After all, what would make an employer believe an employee's explanation about a necessary drug if the employer already showed so little trust as to administer a test at all?

7   In addition, the emphasis in drug testing for the abuse of drugs such as Ritalin® and Dexedrine® is making them increasingly difficult to purchase in pharmacies. Quotas are now being put on their production, and some states are working on banning them or making them more and more difficult to get. For example, many times I have taken a prescription to be filled into a pharmacy only to find that they had run out of their allotment and would not have any for a few days. A few days is like a lifetime for most narcoleptics without medication, some of whom can be virtually housebound without it. Imagine, in the hysteria over these drugs caused by being targeted in mandatory drug testing, what would happen if a few days turned into weeks or maybe even a month?

8   There is no denying the need for programs to address drug and alcohol abuse. The beneficial causes the employers are seeking are reasonable in themselves, but just won't happen through mandatory drug testing. Instead, why can't employers take a positive approach to dealing with substance abuse within the workplace? Employers could set up counseling programs and encourage people with problems to step forward and get help. Employers who show trust and respect for their employees will get trust and respect in return. A positive, caring approach would be better for everyone, considering the far-reaching negative consequences of mandatory drug testing. After all, one should never forget that disorders requiring the use of controlled substance drugs have no prejudice. They can strike anyone at anytime. Believe me, I know.

Why Married Mothers Work

Victor Fuchs

Among single women ages 25–44 four out of five work for pay, and this proportion has   1
not changed since 1950. Divorced and separated women have also traditionally worked,
and their participation rates (about 75 percent) have grown only slightly. The truly astonishing changes have taken place in the behavior of married women with children, as shown
in Figure 1. . . .

Why has the participation of married mothers grown so *rapidly* and so *steadily*? Popu-   2
lar discussions frequently attribute this growth to changes in attitudes that were stimulated
by the feminist movement, but the time pattern portrayed in Figure 1 does not lend much
support to this view. Betty Friedan's *The Feminine Mystique,* which is often credited with
sparking the modern feminist movement, was published in 1963, long after the surge of
married mothers into the labor force was under way. Moreover, there is no evidence of any
sudden acceleration in response to this movement. Similarly, widespread public expressions
of feminism *followed* rather than preceded the rise in the age of marriage and the fall in
the birth rate. Divorce is the one variable whose change coincided with the burgeoning
feminist movement, rising rapidly between 1965 and 1975. Thus, the feminist writings and
discussion, valid as they may be in their own terms, will probably not be viewed by future
historians as a basic cause of social change but primarily as a rationale and a rhetoric for
changes that were already occurring for other reasons.

Government affirmative action programs are regarded by many as fostering female em-   3
ployment, but the timing again suggests that too much has been claimed for this explanation. These programs, which did not gain force until well into the 1960s, cannot explain
the rapid rise in participation of married mothers in the 1950s—a rise that was even more
rapid for older women with grown children. The timing of changes in the occupational distribution of employed married women is also contrary to what one would expect if the feminist movement or government affirmative action had a great deal of effect. The proportion
who were in professional and technical occupations rose rapidly between 1948 and 1965,
from 7.7 percent to 14.7 percent, but thereafter the rate of increase was more modest, only
to 17.7 percent by 1979.

One of the most popular explanations for the two-earner family is that the wife's earn-   4
ings are "needed to help make ends meet." This answer is the one most frequently given
by women to survey researchers, and it receives some support from analytical studies that
attempt to explain why, at any particular time, some wives work and some don't. There is
a strong consensus among economists that, other things held constant, the higher the husbands income, the less likely it is that the wife will work for pay.

This explanation, however, does not contribute much to an understanding of changes   5
over time. "Need," in an absolute sense, can hardly be the reason for the rapid rise in labor
force participation of married mothers in the 1950s, when the real hourly earnings of their
husbands were increasing at an unprecedented pace. Nathan Keyfitz (1980) observed that
when women are asked why they work outside the home, they tend to reply that they need

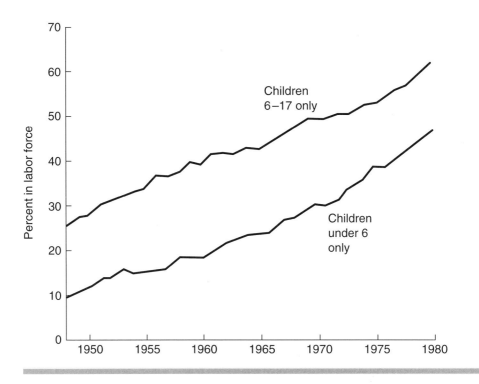

FIGURE 1   Labor force participation rates of married women with husband present, by presence and age of own children, 1948–1980

(*Sources:* Employment and Training Administration, *Employment and Training Report of the President, 1980,* table B-4; idem, *Employment and Training Report of the President, 1981,* table B-7.)

the money. "But," he writes, "the answer cannot be correct, since in earlier decades their husbands were earning less, presumably families needed money, and yet wives were content to stay home. Needing money is a universal, a constant, and a first rule of method is that one cannot explain a variable . . . with a constant."

6   One frequently mentioned but inadequately evaluated explanation for the surge of women into paid employment is the spread of time-saving household innovations such as clothes washers and dryers, frozen foods, and dishwashers. There is little doubt that it is easier to combine paid employment with home responsibilities now than it was fifty years ago, but it is not clear whether these time-saving innovations were the cause of the rise in female labor force participation or whether they were largely a *response* to meet a demand created by working women. Confusion about this point is most evident in comments that suggest that the rapid growth of supermarkets and fast-food outlets is a cause of women going to work. Similar time-saving organizations were tried at least sixty years ago, but with less success because the value of time was much lower then. The absence of supermarkets and fast-food eating places in low-income countries today also shows that their rapid growth

in the United States is primarily a *result* of the rising value of time and the growth of women in the work force, not the reverse.

Within the economics profession the explanation that commands the widest consensus is that *higher wages* have attracted more married mothers into the labor force. This explanation is more firmly grounded in economic theory than many of the others and is reasonably consistent with observed behavior, both over time and among families at a given point in time. Ever since the pioneering work of Jacob Mincer (1962), numerous cross-section analyses—studies that examine differences among individual families or groups of families—uniformly report that the probability of a wife's working is *positively* related to her potential wage rate, holding constant spouse's education. This is the opposite of the previously noted *negative* effect of the husband's wage rate on the wife's labor force participation. . . .

In addition to higher wages, the rapid expansion of jobs in the service sector has contributed to the rise in female labor force participation (Fuchs 1968). The service industries (retail trade, financial service, education, health, personal services, public administration) have traditionally offered much greater employment opportunities for women than have mining, manufacturing, construction, and other branches of the industrial sector. For instance, 73 percent of nonfarm female employment was in the service sector in 1960, whereas the comparable figure for males was only 44 percent.

There are many reasons for this large differential. First, most occupations in the service sector do not place a premium on physical strength. Second, hours of work are frequently more flexible in service industries and there are many more opportunities for part-time work. Other things held constant, mothers of small children are more likely to be working in those metropolitan areas where there is a large variation in the weekly hours of men (King 1978). This variation is a good indicator of the existence of part-time employment opportunities, and women are much more likely than men to seek part-time employment. Third, service sector jobs are more likely to be located in or near residential areas, thus making them more attractive to women who bear large responsibilities for child care and homemaking.

The propensity of women to seek service sector employment is particularly relevant because it is this sector that has provided nearly all of the additional job opportunities in the U.S. economy since the end of World War II. Between 1947 and 1980 U.S. employment expanded by 39 million; the service sector provided 33 million of these additional jobs. To be sure, some of the growth of service employment is the *result* of the increase in female labor force participation rather than the cause (Fuchs 1981a). Families with working mothers are more likely to eat out, to send their children to nursery school, and to purchase a wide range of personal and professional services. This feedback effect, however, accounts for only a part of the growth of service employment. The major explanation is that rapid increases in output per worker in agriculture and industry cut the demand for labor in those sectors and shifted employment to services. A secondary reason is that consumer demand shifted slightly toward services in response to the growth of real income.

I conclude that the growth of real wages and the expansion of the service sector have been the most important reasons for the growth of female labor force participation. This participation, in turn, has had important effects on marriage, fertility, and divorce, but there is also some feedback from fertility and divorce to labor force participation. Better control of fertility makes a career in the labor market more promising to women, not only because of a reduction in the *number* of children but also because women now have better control over the *timing* of births. The increase in the *probability* of divorce contributes to the rise in female labor force participation because women recognize that complete commitment to home and husband can leave them in a perilous economic position if the marriage should dissolve. Alimony and child support payments are often inadequate, and are not paid at all in a large proportion of cases. An old song says that "diamonds are a girl's best friend," but today the ability to earn a good wage is likely to prove a more reliable asset.

Students Who Push Burgers

Walter S. Minot

1   A college freshman squirms anxiously on a chair in my office, his eyes avoiding mine, those of his English professor, as he explains that he hasn't finished his paper, which was due two days ago. "I just haven't had the time," he says.

2   "Are you carrying a heavy course load?"

3   "Fifteen hours," he says—a normal load.

4   "Are you working a lot?"

5   "No, sir, not much. About 30 hours a week."

6   "That's a lot. Do you have to work that much?"

7   "Yeah, I have to pay for my car."

8   "Do you really need a car?"

9   "Yeah, I need it to get to work."

10   This student isn't unusual. Indeed, he probably typifies today's college and high school students. Yet in all the lengthy analyses of what's wrong with American education, I have not heard employment by students being blamed.

11   I have heard drugs blamed and television—that universal scapegoat. I have heard elaborate theories about the decline of the family, of religion, and of authority, as well as other sociological theories. But nobody blames student employment. The world seems to have accepted the part-time job as a normal feature of adolescence. A parochial school in my town even had a day to honor students who held regular jobs, and parents often endorse this employment by claiming that it teaches kids the value of the dollar.

12   But such employment is a major cause of educational decline. To argue my case, I will rely on memories of my own high school days and contrast them with what I see today. Though I do have some statistical evidence, my argument depends on what anyone over 40 can test through memory and direct observation.

13   When I was in high school in the 1950s, students seldom held jobs. Some of us baby-sat, shoveled snow, mowed lawns, and delivered papers, and some of us got jobs in department stores around Christmas. But most of us had no regular source of income other than the generosity of our parents.

The only kids who worked regularly were poor. They worked to help their families. If   14
I remember correctly, only about five people in my class of 170 held jobs. That was in a
working-class town in New England. As for the rest of us, our parents believed that going
to school and helping around the house were our work.

In contrast, in 1986 my daughter was one of the few students among juniors and se-   15
niors who didn't work. According to Bureau of Labor statistics, more than 40 percent of
high school students were working in 1980, but sociologist Ellen Greenberger and Lau-
rence Steinberg in "When Teenagers Work" came up with estimates of more than 70 percent working in 1986, though I suspect that the figure may be even higher now.

My daughter, however, did not work; her parents wouldn't let her. Interestingly, some   16
of the students in her class implied that she had an unfair advantage over them in the classroom. They were probably right, for while she was home studying they were pushing burgers, waiting on tables, or selling dresses 20 hours a week. Working students have little time
for homework.

I attended a public high school, while she attended a Roman Catholic preparatory   17
school whose students were mainly middle class. By the standards of my day, her classmates
did not "have to" work. Yet many of them were working 20 to 30 hours a week. Why?

They worked so that they could spend $60 to $100 a week on designer jeans, rock   18
concerts, stereo and video systems, and, of course, cars. They were living lives of luxury,
buying items on which their parents refused to throw hard-earned money away. Though
the parent would not buy such tripe for their kids, the parents somehow convinced themselves that the kids were learning the value of money. Yet, according to Ms. Greenberger
and Mr. Steinberg, only about a quarter of those students saved money for college or other
long-term goals.

How students spend their money is their business, not mine. But as a teacher, I have   19
witnessed the effects of employment. I know that students who work all evening aren't
ready for studying when they get home from work. Moreover, because they work so hard
and have ready cash, they feel that they deserve to have fun—instead of spending all their
free time studying.

Thus, by the time they get to college, most students look upon studies as a spare-time   20
activity. A survey at Pennsylvania State University showed that most freshmen believed they
could maintain a B average by studying about 20 hours a week. (I can remember when college guidebooks advised two to three hours of studying for every hour in class—30 to 45
hours a week.)

Clearly individual students will pay the price for lack of adequate time studying, but   21
the problem goes beyond the individual. It extends to schools and colleges that are finding
it difficult to demand quantity or quality of work from students.

Perhaps the reason American education has declined so markedly is because America has   22
raised a generation of part-time students. And perhaps our economy will continue to decline
as full-time students from Japan and Europe continue to out-perform our part-time students.

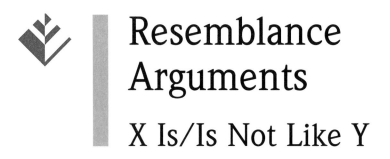

chapter 12

Resemblance Arguments

X Is/Is Not Like Y

CASE 1

In May 1987, a controversy arose between Israeli and West German historians over the reinterpretation of the Holocaust, the Nazi attempt to destroy the Jews. According to one West German historian, the Nazi annihilation of the Jews was comparable to Stalin's massacre of the Russian peasants and Pol Pot's murder of his opponents in Cambodia. The effect of this comparison, in the eyes of many Israeli historians, was to diminish the horror of the Holocaust by denying its uniqueness. Israeli historian Shaul Friedlander responded that while the scale and criminality of the murders might be compared, "there is no other example to my knowledge of a government deciding that an entire race of millions of people spread all over a continent is to be brought together by all means at the disposal of the state and eliminated."*

CASE 2

To further her argument against the notion that motherhood is a predestined role for women, a psychiatrist used the following analogy: "Women don't need to be mothers any more than they need spaghetti. But if you're in a world where everyone is eating spaghetti, thinking they need it and want it, you will think so too."†

---

*From Karen Winkler, "German Scholars Sharply Divided over Place of Holocaust in History," *Chronicle of Higher Education,* 27 May 1987, pp. 4–5.

†From Betty Rollin, "Motherhood: Who Needs It?"

264

CASE 3

Lawyer Charles Rembar attacked the American Civil Liberties Union (ACLU) for its opposition to the mandatory reporting of AIDS cases. Rembar claimed that the ACLU position didn't take into account the seriousness of the AIDS problem. According to Rembar, the ACLU "clings to once useful concepts that are inappropriate to current problems. Like the French military, which prepared for World War II by building the Maginot Line, which was nicely adapted to the trench warfare of World War I, the ACLU sometimes hauls up legal arguments effective in old libertarian battles but irrelevant to those at hand. . . ."*

CASE 4

When the voting age was reduced from twenty-one to eighteen, many people argued for the lower voting age by saying, "If you are old enough to fight for your country in a war, you are old enough to vote." But author Richard Weaver claimed that this analogy was true "only if you believe that fighting and voting are the same kind of thing which I, for one, do not. Fighting requires strength, muscular coordination and, in a modern army, instant and automatic response to orders. Voting requires knowledge of men, history, reasoning power; it is essentially a deliberative activity. Army mules and police dogs are used to fight; nobody is interested in giving them the right to vote. This argument rests on a false analogy."†

THE DIFFERENCE BETWEEN RESEMBLANCE ARGUMENTS AND DEFINITION ARGUMENTS

In some cases it may seem that a resemblance argument (X is like Y) is not very different from a definitional argument (X is Y). For example, if you were to say that the Sandinista government of Nicaragua was "like" the Somoza regime that it replaced, you might really be making a definitional argument, claiming that both regimes belong to the same class—say, the class "totalitarian governments" or the class "benevolent dictatorships." Their similarities would be restricted to the traits of whatever class they are being put into. In effect, the "like" statement is a definitional claim in which both X and Y are said to belong to class Z.

But if you were to draw an analogy between the Reagan presidency or the Clinton presidency and a third thing different in kind from recent American politics—say, to a TV sitcom or a sporting event—or if you were to argue that some other

---

*From the *New York Times,* May 15, 1987.

†From Richard M. Weaver, "A Responsible Rhetoric," *The Intercollegiate Review,* Winter 1976–1977, pp. 86–87.

situation remote in time—say, American Revolutionary politics or nineteenth-century Balkan politics—should serve as a precedent for Nicaragua, the argument moves over into the realm of resemblance. In either case, there are no preexisting definitional criteria to which the event can be matched. There certainly isn't a "Dictionary of Similar Things" we can use to certify the rightness of our comparison. We have to discover and develop the grounds on which the two terms of our comparison are similar.

When we're developing analogies as opposed to establishing definitions, we must be conscious at all times that the two things being compared are essentially different, not members of the same class. In the end we may well be left with several important points of comparison that don't lead to a neat category or concept that somehow "sums" up all the points of comparison and ties them all together. Analogies, in short, reveal different sides of events or things without forcing us to put the things being compared into the same category.

And although the two (or more) things being compared in a relationship of precedence are going to be closer in identity than the terms of an analogy, a precedent doesn't define a term as strictly as does a definition. In a precedent, we are claiming a relationship of resemblance between two actual events. We're saying that this case and that case have sufficient similarities to warrant our drawing similar conclusions from them; we are not saying that the two cases share an identity. The points of comparison between the two may be numerous, but it would be impossible to establish essential conditions that if met would ensure "class membership."

Obviously, an argument of resemblance has to be considerably more tentative than an argument of definition. Suppose, for example, that you wanted to write an argument favoring a balanced federal budget. In one section of your argument you might develop the following claim of resemblance: "Just as a family will go bankrupt if it continually spends more than it makes, so the federal government will go bankrupt if its expenses exceed its revenues." This claim depends on the resemblance between the fiscal problems of the federal government and the fiscal problems of a private family. For many audiences, this comparison might be persuasive: It uses an area of experience familiar to almost everyone (the problem of balancing the family budget) to help make sense of a more complex area of experience (the problem of balancing the federal budget). At its root is the warrant that what works for the family will work for the Fed.

Such an argument can be powerful, but dangerous, if it ignores important differences ("disanalogies") between the terms of comparison. One can think, for instance, of many differences between the economics of a family and that of the federal government. For example, unlike a private family, the federal government prints its own money and does most of its borrowing from its own members. Perhaps these differences negate the claim that family debt and federal debt are similar in their effects. It is thus essential that an argument based on resemblance acknowledge important disanalogies.

One way of illustrating the necessarily tentative nature of a resemblance claim is to look at it via Toulmin's schema. If we take the preceding example for our illustration, we might get something like this:

ENTHYMEME:	If the Fed doesn't balance its budget, it will go bankrupt because families that don't balance their budgets go bankrupt.
CLAIM:	If the Fed doesn't balance its debt, it will go bankrupt.
STATED REASON:	because families that don't balance their budgets go bankrupt
GROUNDS:	evidence showing that indeed families overspending their budget do go bankrupt
WARRANT:	The economic laws that apply to families apply also to governments.
BACKING:	evidence that when governments and families behave in economically similar ways, they suffer similar consequences
CONDITIONS OF REBUTTAL:	all cases in which governments and families behaved in similar ways and did not suffer similar consequences; all the ways that families and governments differ
QUALIFIER:	The claim is supported by the analogy only to the extent that family and government economics resemble each other.

As you look at this schema, you can see just how troublesome it would be to support your warrant that economic laws apply equally to families and governments. As noted earlier, resemblance arguments require you to compare two or more actual cases as opposed to simply applying a concept to an actual case. Whereas the definition of a concept is limited by certain conventions of usage, the comparison between family and government economics is wide open. You have, in sum, undertaken an extraordinary burden of proof since, under the conditions of rebuttal, the possible exceptions to your warrant are in danger of multiplying like exemptions in a tax reform bill (so to speak).

❦ WRITING ASSIGNMENTS FOR CHAPTER 12

OPTION 1: *An Analogy Microtheme*   Because few arguments are devoted entirely to a resemblance claim and because many arguments from resemblance are used in service of other claims, this assignment asks you simply to write a piece of an argument. Imagine that you are writing a longer argument for or against an X of your choice. As part of your argument you want to influence your reader's emotional or intellectual understanding of X, in either a positive or a negative direction, by comparing it to a more familiar Y. Write the portion of your argument that develops the extended analogy. A good model for this assignment is the argument on pages 269–270. The writer opposes a proficiency exam in writing by comparing it to a proficiency exam in physical fitness. The For Class Discussion exercise on pages 270–271 will give you ideas for topics.

OPTION 2: *A Precedence Microtheme*   Imagine that you are writing a proposal argument of the kind "We should/should not do X" and that one of your reasons will develop a precedence argument as follows: "We should/should not do X because doing X will lead to the same good/bad consequences that we experienced when we did Y." Write the portion of your argument that develops this precedence claim.

OPTION 3: *An Analysis of a Resemblance Argument*   Write an analysis of Susan Brownmiller's argument that pornography hurts women (pp. 278–280), which uses an analogy between pornography and Nazi anti-Semitic propaganda, or of some other resemblance argument provided by your instructor.

FIRST TYPE OF RESEMBLANCE ARGUMENT: ARGUMENTS BY ANALOGY

In this section we deal with the first class of resemblance arguments, argument by *analogy*. Although it's rare to find an entire argument that rests on an analogy, analogies are used extensively in the service of all the other claim types. The ubiquity of analogies in argument is undoubtedly a function of their power to make new relationships clear to reader and writer alike.

The use of analogies can constitute the most imaginative form of argumentation. Consider the case of an outraged prep school student upset about the quality of the high teas at Whitebread-on-Perrier Prep, where he matriculates. Suppose he were to compare his lot to that of a political prisoner in a Russian prison. His resemblance claim would undoubtedly get some attention, particularly from parents paying huge sums of money for their offspring to attend the place.

But getting attention is not enough. In fact, if your argument is particularly weak, getting attention may not be at all desirable. The question now facing our enraged student, the question that faces any author of a resemblance claim, is "How far can I go with this thing?" Analogies can be short and suggestive, used as tools for getting an audience's attention and sympathy, or they can be developed at length and used as tools for guiding their understanding.

Using Undeveloped Analogies

If you put yourself in the shoes of our hypothetical Whitebread-on-Perrier inmate, what would you choose to do? Develop the analogy or let it lie? Our advice would be to get past it as quickly as possible before the disanalogies come back to haunt you. The analogy may serve briefly to suggest certain aspects of the case that you want emphasized—lack of voice in the institution, poor quality of food—but if one goes much past those points of comparison, your suffering is going to pale in comparison to that of the political prisoner. Here, as in many analogies, the differences between the two situations aren't just qualitative but quantitative. And quantitative differences, if extreme, can be fatal to an analogy. In this regard, keep in mind Karl Marx's maxim that "differences in degree, if large enough, become differences in kind."

Using undeveloped analogies to convey feelings and points of view is common in many arguments. The effect is to bring to your argument about topic X (say, the importance of discipline to freedom) the full weight, emotion, and understanding your audience already has about Y (the importance of staying on the tracks to the progress of a train). Thus, one writer, arguing against the complexities of recent tax legislation, showed his disgust by drawing an analogy between tax laws and rotting plants or festering wounds.

> It does not take a deep or broadly informed analysis to sense the reek of economic decay and social fester that such irresponsible legislation cultivates.*

Later this writer went on to compare recent tax legislation to an infection by a new virus. Through his use of the analogy, the writer hoped to transfer to the new tax law the audience's already existing revulsion to disease-producing virus.

Using Extended Analogies

Instead of using undeveloped analogies, you may choose to extend your comparison, using your readers' greater understanding of Y to illuminate X. And if your audience is already favorably or unfavorably disposed to Y, then the analogy helps create similar feelings for X. As an example of a claim based on an extended analogy, consider the following excerpt from a professor's argument opposing a proposal to require a writing-proficiency exam for graduation. In the following portion of his argument, the professor compares development of writing skills to the development of physical fitness.

> A writing proficiency exam gives the wrong symbolic messages about writing. It suggests that writing is simply a skill, rather than an active way of thinking and learning. It suggests that once a student demonstrates proficiency then he or she doesn't need to do any more writing.
>
> Imagine two universities concerned with the physical fitness of their students. One university requires a junior-level physical fitness exam in which students must run a mile in less than 10 minutes, a fitness level it considers minimally competent. Students at this university see the physical fitness exam as a one-time hurdle. As

---

*From C. Thomas Higgins, *Seattle Times*, 21 Sept. 1986.

many as 70 percent of them can pass the exam with no practice; another 10–20 percent need a few months' training; and a few hopeless couch potatoes must go through exhaustive remediation. After passing the exam, any student can settle back into a routine of TV and potato chips having been certified as "physically fit."

The second university, however, believing in true physical fitness for its students, is not interested in minimal competency. Consequently, it creates programs in which its students exercise 30 minutes every day for the entire four years of the undergraduate curriculum. There is little doubt which university will have the most physically fit students. At the second university, fitness becomes a way of life with everyone developing his or her full potential.

If you choose to write an extended analogy such as this, you will focus on the points of comparison that serve your purposes. The writer's purpose in the preceding case is to support the achievement of mastery rather than minimalist standards as the goal of the university's writing program. Whatever other disanalogous elements are involved (for example, writing requires the use of intellect, which may or may not be strengthened by repetition), the comparison reveals vividly that a commitment to mastery involves more than a minimalist test. The analogy serves primarily to underscore this one crucial point. In reviewing the different groups of students as they "prepare" for the fitness exam, the author makes clear just how irrelevant such an exam is to the whole question of mastery. Typically, then, in developing your analogy you are not developing all possible points of comparison so much as you are bringing out those similarities consistent with the point you are trying to make.

 ## FOR CLASS DISCUSSION

The following is a two-part exercise to help you clarify for yourself how analogies function in the context of arguments. Part 1 is to be done outside class; part 2 is to be done in class. This exercise is an excellent "Starting Point" task for the Option 1 writing assignment for this chapter.

PART 1   Think of an analogy that accurately expresses your feeling toward each of the following topics. Then write your analogy in the following one-sentence format:

X is like Y: A, B, C . . . (where X is the main topic being discussed; Y is the analogy; and A, B, and C are the points of comparison).

EXAMPLES:

Cramming for an exam to get better grades is like pumping iron for 10 hours straight to prepare for a weightlifting contest: exhausting and counterproductive.

A right-to-lifer bombing an abortion clinic is like a vegetarian bombing a cattle barn: futile and contradictory.

a. Spanking a child to teach obedience is like . . .

b. Building low-cost housing for poor people is like . . .

c. The use of steroids by college athletes is like . . .

d. Mandatory AIDS testing for all U.S. residents is like . . .

e. A legislative proposal to eliminate all federally subsidized student loans is like . . .

f. The effect of American fast food on our health is like . . .

g. The personal gain realized by people who have committed questionable or even illegal acts and then made money by selling book and movie rights is like . . .

In each case, begin by asking yourself how you feel about the subject. If you have negative feelings about a topic, then begin by calling up negative pictures that express those feelings (or if you have positive feelings, call up positive comparisons). As they emerge, test each one to see if it will work as an analogy. An effective analogy will convey both the feeling you have toward your topic and your understanding of the topic. For instance, the writer in the "cramming for an exam" example obviously believes that pumping iron for 10 hours before a weightlifting match is stupid. This feeling of stupidity is then transferred to the original topic—cramming for an exam. But the analogy also clarifies understanding. The writer imagines the mind as a muscle (which gets exhausted after too much exercise and which is better developed through some exercise every day rather than a lot all at once) rather than as a large container (into which lots of stuff can be "crammed").

PART 2   Now, bring your analogies to class and compare them to those of your classmates. Select the best analogies for each of the topics and be ready to say why you think they are good. If you choose, you can then use your analogy as the basis for an extended analogy for this chapter's writing assignment.

SECOND TYPE OF RESEMBLANCE ARGUMENT: ARGUMENTS BY PRECEDENT

Precedent arguments are like analogy arguments in that they make comparisons between an X and a Y. In precedent arguments, however, the Y term is always a past event, usually an event where some sort of decision was reached, often a moral, legal, or political decision. An argument by precedent tries to show that a similar decision should or should not be reached for the present issue X because the situation of X is or is not like the situation of Y.

A good example of a precedent argument is the following excerpt from a speech by President Lyndon Johnson in the early years of the Vietnam War:

> Nor would surrender in Vietnam bring peace because we learned from Hitler at Munich that success only feeds the appetite of aggression. The battle would be renewed in one country and then another country, bringing with it perhaps even larger and crueler conflict, as we have learned from the lessons of history.*

Here the audience knows what happened at Munich: France and Britain tried to appease Hitler by yielding to his demand for a large part of Czechoslovakia, but Hitler's armies continued their aggression anyway, using Czechoslovakia as a staging area to invade Poland. By arguing that surrender in Vietnam would lead to the same consequences, Johnson brings to his argument about Vietnam the whole weight of his audience's unhappy knowledge of World War II. Administration white papers developed Johnson's precedent argument by pointing toward the similarity of Hitler's promises with those of the Viet Cong: You give us this and we will ask for no more. But Hitler didn't keep his promise. Why should the Viet Cong?

As with analogies, we often turn to precedents in the early stages of planning an argument. Whereas analogies stimulate our thinking about alternative ways of describing a situation or solving a problem, precedents offer us advice from the past. Let's say, for example, that you are arguing for the mandatory use of seatbelts in cars. Here we might turn to the precedent of mandatory motorcycle helmet law in our own state or a mandatory seatbelt law in a neighboring state. We would want to review the whole story of how the seatbelt laws were enacted, how opposition arguments were met, what consequences followed their passage, and so forth, to help us plan our own argument. Once we have explored possible arguments using the precedents as guides, we can also cite those precedents in our arguments, using them as evidence as well as structural models.

In a relatively straightforward legal example such as the seatbelt law example, a precedent argument is particularly persuasive. We can see this more clearly if we apply the Toulmin schema to the argument.

ENTHYMEME:	The state should enact a seatbelt law because seatbelt laws have had good consequences in other states.
CLAIM:	The state should enact a seatbelt law.
STATED REASON:	because seatbelt laws have had good consequences in other states
GROUNDS:	evidence that seatbelt laws in other states have had good consequences (saved lives, relatively high compliance, few enforcement problems)

*From *Public Papers of the Presidents of the United States,* Vol. 2: *Lyndon B. Johnson,* 1965, p. 794.

WARRANT:	Seatbelt laws will be at least as effective in this state as they have been in the other states that have enacted them.
BACKING:	evidence that there are no significant differences between this state and other states that might diminish the effectiveness of seatbelt laws in this state
CONDITIONS OF REBUTTAL:	acknowledged differences between states that might well impair the effectiveness of a seatbelt law in this state
QUALIFIERS:	statements to the effect than even if the seatbelt law is less effective here than it has been in other states it will still improve conditions.

As you can see, the key to a precedent argument is showing that the similarities between W and Y outweigh the dissimilarities. In the seatbelt example, it is difficult to imagine how states would differ so that seatbelt laws would be successful in one state but not in another. But if one state is more urban than another (perhaps city drivers are less apt to wear seatbelts because they have to make so many short trips), or if one state regularly elects a Democratic government and the other elects a Republican government (Republicans are generally less tolerant of governmental regulations than Democrats), or if one state has much higher gasoline taxes than another (perhaps people who can afford to drive cars when gasoline is high priced have a different attitude toward seatbelts than poorer people), then there might be predictable differences in the way citizens would react to a seatbelt law.

FOR CLASS DISCUSSION

1. Consider the following claims of precedent and evaluate just how effective you think each precedent might be in establishing the claim:
   a. Don't vote for Governor Frick for president because governors have not proven to be effective presidents.
   b. Gays should be allowed to serve openly in the U.S. military because they are allowed to serve openly in most other Western countries.
   c. The United States should avoid military involvement in the former Yugoslavia because it will end up in another mess like Vietnam.

2. Recently, voters in the state of Montana considered an initiative to abolish property taxes. Supporters of the initiative responded to predictions that it would have disastrous consequences for public service in the state by saying, "Similar dire predictions were made in Massachusetts and California when they passed initiatives to lower property taxes and none of these predictions came to pass, so you can ignore these nay-sayers."

You have been hired by a lobbying group who opposes the initiative. Your task is to do the background research that your group needs in order to refute the above precedent argument. Working in small groups, make a list of research questions you would want to ask.

WRITING YOUR RESEMBLANCE ARGUMENT

The class discussion exercises in this chapter should help you find a starting point for your analogy or precedent and explore its usefulness. The optional microtheme assignments for this chapter will not require as extensive a process as that required for a full-scale argument. After you have written a rough draft of your microtheme, however, we recommend that you examine your argument using Toulmin's schema. Once again, test your argument by looking carefully at the conditions for rebuttal.

CONDITIONS FOR REBUTTAL: TESTING A RESEMBLANCE ARGUMENT

Once you've written a draft of your resemblance argument, you need to test that argument by attempting to refute it. What follows are some typical questions audiences will raise about arguments of resemblance.

Will My Audience Say I Am Trying to Prove Too Much with My Analogy or Precedent?

The most common mistake people make with resemblance arguments is to ask them to prove more than they're capable of proving. Too often, an analogy is treated as if it were a syllogism or algebraic ratio wherein necessary truths are deduced (*a* is to *b* as *c* is to *d*) rather than as a useful, but basically playful, figure that suggests uncertain but significant insight. The best way to guard against this charge is to qualify your argument and to find other means of persuasion to supplement an analogy or precedent argument.

For a good example of an analogy that tries to do too much, consider former President Reagan's attempt to prevent the United States from imposing economic sanctions on South Africa. Reagan wanted to argue that harming South Africa's economy would do as much damage to blacks as to whites. In making this argument, he compared South Africa to a zebra and concluded that one couldn't hurt the white portions of the zebra without also hurting the black.

Now, the zebra analogy might work quite well to point up the interrelatedness of whites and blacks in South Africa. But it has no force whatsoever in supporting Reagan's assertion that economic sanctions would hurt blacks as well as whites.

To refute this analogy, one need only point out the disanalogies between the zebra stripes and racial groups. (There are, for example, no differences in income, education, and employment between black and white stripes on a zebra.)

Will My Audience Point Out Disanalogies in My Resemblance Argument?

Although it is easy to show that a country is not like a zebra, finding disanalogies is sometimes quite tricky. Often displaying the argument in Toulmin terms will help. Here is the Toulmin schema for former President Johnson's "Munich analogy" for supporting the war in Vietnam:

ENTHYMEME:	The United States should not withdraw its troops from Vietnam because doing so will have the same disastrous consequences as did giving in to Hitler prior to World War II.
CLAIM:	The United States should not withdraw its troops from Vietnam.
STATED REASON:	because doing so will have the same disastrous consequences as did giving in to Hitler before World War II
GROUNDS:	evidence that withdrawal of military support backfired in Europe in 1939
WARRANT:	The situation in Europe in 1939 closely parallels the situation in Southeast Asia in 1965.
BACKING:	evidence of similarities (for example, in political philosophy, goals, and military strength of the enemy; the nature of the conflict between the disputants; and the American commitment to its allies) between the two situations
CONDITIONS OF REBUTTAL:	acknowledged differences between the two situations that might make the outcome of the present situation different from the outcome of the first situation

Laid out like this, some of the problems with the analogy are quickly evident. One has to make a considerable leap to go from undeniably true, historically verifiable grounds to a highly problematic claim. This means that the warrant will have to be particularly strong to license the movement. And although there are undeniable similarities between the two events (as there will be between any two sufficiently complex events), the differences are overwhelming. Thus, during the Vietnam era, critic Howard Zinn attacked the warrant of Johnson's analogy by claiming three crucial differences between Europe in 1938 and Vietnam in 1967.

First, Zinn argued, the Czechs were being attacked from without by an external aggressor (Germany), whereas Vietnam was being attacked from within by rebels as part of a civil war; second, Czechoslovakia was a prosperous, effective democracy, whereas the official Vietnam government was corrupt and unpopular; finally, Hitler wanted Czechoslovakia as a base for attacking Poland, whereas the Viet Cong and North Vietnamese aimed at reunification of their country as an end in itself.*

The Munich example shows again how arguments of resemblance depend on emphasizing the similarities between X and Y and playing down the dissimilarities. One could try to refute the counterargument made by Zinn by arguing first that the Saigon government was more stable than Zinn thinks and second that the Viet Cong and North Vietnamese were driven by goals larger than reunification of Vietnam, namely, communist domination of Asia. Such an argument would once again highlight the similarities between Vietnam and prewar Europe.

Will My Audience Propose a Counteranalogy?

A final way of testing a resemblance claim is to propose an alternative analogy or precedent that counters the original claim. Suppose you wanted to argue for the teaching of creationism along with evolution in the schools and your opponent said, "Teaching creationism along with evolution is like teaching the stork theory of where babies come from along with the biological theory." After showing the disanalogies between creationism and the stork theory of reproduction, you could counter with your own analogy: "No, teaching creationism along with evolution is like bilingual education, where you respect the cultural heritage of all peoples." To the extent that your audience values pluralism and the preservation of different beliefs, your analogy may well provide them with a new perspective on the topic, a perspective that allows them to entertain an otherwise alien notion.

❧ FOR CLASS DISCUSSION

Examine the following resemblance claims and then attempt to refute them by pointing out disanalogies between the phenomena being compared.

1. In the following example, the author is arguing that it is not unconstitutional to require drug testing of federal employees. Within the argument the author draws an analogy between testing for drugs and checking for weapons or bombs at an airport. Using the techniques suggested in this chapter, test the soundness of the argument.

---

*Based on the summary of Zinn's argument in J. Michael Sproule, *Argument: Language and Its Influence* (New York: McGraw-Hill, 1980), pp. 149–50.

The Constitution does not prohibit all searches and seizures. It makes the people secure in their persons only from "unreasonable" searches and seizures, and there is nothing unreasonable in Reagan's executive order.

. . . Those who challenge this sensible program [drug testing by urinalysis] ought to get straight on this business of "rights." Like any other employer, the government has a right—within certain well-understood limits—to fix the terms and conditions of employment. The individual's right, if he finds these conditions intolerable, is to seek employment elsewhere. A parallel situation may be observed at every airport in the land. Individuals may have a right to fly, but they have no right to fly without having their persons and baggage inspected for weapons. By the same token, the federal worker who refuses to provide a urine specimen under the president's order can clean out his desk and apply to General Motors or General Electric or Kodak—only to discover that private industry is equally interested in a drug-free work place.*

2. In the following passage, former NAACP administrator Jack Greenberg defends affirmative action on the basis of analogy to other cases in the free market in which certain groups are given preferences not related to merit.

The moral legitimacy of affirmative action and quotas favoring racial minorities must be assessed in a social and historical context, in the light of the many conflicting values that our society holds. . . . [There are many examples of instances in which criteria other than merit result in the selection of persons] other than those best qualified.

A tenured professor will hold his position in spite of competition from younger, better, more vigorous scholars. Tenure is thought, however, to serve the important societal interest in academic freedom by enabling teachers to take controversial positions without fear and by shielding them against petty politics.

Seniority rights advance individual security, worker satisfaction and job loyalty by promoting older workers although younger persons may be objectively more qualified, while, paradoxically, compulsory retirement favors younger persons over older, experienced, and perhaps more competent workers. . . .

[Similarly, preference is given to veterans or union members even though non-veterans or non-union members might be more highly qualified. Both examples serve larger national interests.]

Even the most prestigious schools consider more than marks as criteria for admission—to obtain a geographically and otherwise diverse student body and thereby enhance the educational experience of all. . . .†

---

*From "A Conservative View" by James J. Kilpatrick. © Universal Press Syndicate. Reprinted with permission. All rights reserved.

†"Affirmative Action, Quotas, and Merit." *New York Times*, 7 Feb. 1976.

Analyze Greenberg's argument. Is he right that affirmative action to hire more minorities can be justified by comparison to other instances when criteria other than merit affect hiring decisions: tenure, seniority, union membership, veteran status, geographic diversity?

3. Analyze the strengths and weaknesses of various kinds of resemblance arguments in the following excerpt from Susan Brownmiller's *Against Our Will: Men, Women and Rape.*

From *Against Our Will: Men, Women and Rape*

Susan Brownmiller

1   Pornography has been so thickly glossed over with the patina of chic these days in the name of verbal freedom and sophistication that important distinctions between freedom of political expression (a democratic necessity), honest sex education for children (a societal good) and ugly smut (the deliberate devaluation of the role of women through obscene, distorted depictions) have been hopelessly confused. Part of the problem is that those who traditionally have been the most vigorous opponents of porn are often those same people who shudder at the explicit mention of any sexual subject. Under their watchful, vigilante eyes, frank and free dissemination of educational materials relating to abortion, contraception, the act of birth, the female biology in general is also dangerous, subversive and dirty. (I am not unmindful that frank and free discussion of rape, "the unspeakable crime," might well give these righteous vigilantes further cause to shudder.) Because the battle lines were falsely drawn a long time ago, before there was a vocal women's movement, the antipornography forces appear to be, for the most part, religious, Southern, conservative and right-wing, while the pro-porn forces are identified as Eastern, atheistic and liberal.

2   But a woman's perspective demands a totally new alignment, or at least a fresh appraisal. The majority report of the President's Commission on Obscenity and Pornography (1970), a report that argued strongly for the removal of all legal restrictions on pornography, soft and hard, made plain that 90 percent of all pornographic material is geared to the male heterosexual market (the other 10 percent is geared to the male homosexual taste), that buyers of porn are "predominantly white, middle-class, middle-aged married males" and that the graphic depictions, the meat and potatoes of porn, are of the naked female body and of the multiplicity of acts done to that body.

3   Discussing the content of stag films, "a familiar and firmly established part of the American scene," the commission report dutifully, if foggily, explained, "Because pornography historically has been thought to be primarily a masculine interest, the emphasis in stag films seems to represent the preferences of the middle-class American male. Thus male homosexuality and bestiality are relatively rare, while lesbianism is rather common."

The commissioners in this instance had merely verified what purveyors of porn have   4
always known: hard-core pornography is not a celebration of sexual freedom; it is a cynical
exploitation of female sexual activity through the device of making all such activity, and consequently all females, "dirty." Heterosexual male consumers of pornography are frankly
turned on by watching lesbians in action (although never in the final scenes, but always as
a curtain raiser); they are turned off with a sudden swiftness of a water faucet by watching
naked men act upon each other. One study quoted in the commission report came to the
unastounding conclusion that "seeing a stag film in the presence of male peers bolsters masculine esteem." Indeed. The men in groups who watch the films, it is important to note,
are *not* naked.

When male response to pornography is compared to female response, a pronounced   5
difference in attitude emerges. According to the commission, "Males report being more
highly aroused by depictions of nude females, and show more interest in depictions of nude
females than [do] females." Quoting the figures of Alfred Kinsey, the commission noted that
a majority of males (77 percent) were "aroused" by visual depictions of explicit sex while
a majority of females (68 percent) were not aroused. Further, "females more often than
males reported 'disgust' and 'offense.' "

From whence comes this female disgust and offense? Are females sexually backward   6
or more conservative by nature? The gut distaste that a majority of women feel when we
look at pornography, a distaste that, incredibly, it is no longer fashionable to admit, comes,
I think, from the gut knowledge that we and our bodies are being stripped, exposed and
contorted for the purpose of ridicule to bolster that "masculine esteem" which gets its kick
and sense of power from viewing females as anonymous, panting playthings, adult toys, de-
humanized objects to be used, abused, broken and discarded.

This, of course, is also the philosophy of rape. It is no accident (for what else could be   7
its purpose?) that females in the pornographic genre are depicted in two cleanly delineated
roles: as virgins who are caught and "banged" or as nymphomaniacs who are never sated.
The most popular and prevalent pornographic fantasy combines the two: an innocent, un-
tutored female is raped and "subjected to unnatural practices" that turn her into a raving,
slobbering nymphomaniac, a dependent sexual slave who can never get enough of the big,
male cock.

There can be no "equality" in porn, no female equivalent, no turning of the tables in   8
the name of bawdy fun. Pornography, like rape, is a male invention, designed to dehu-
manize women, to reduce the female to an object of sexual access, not to free sensuality
from moralistic or parental inhibition. The staple of porn will always be the naked female
body, breasts and genitals exposed, because as man devised it, her naked body is the female's "shame," her private parts the private property of man, while his are the ancient,
holy, universal, patriarchal instrument of his power, his rule by force over *her.*

Pornography is the undiluted essence of anti-female propaganda. Yet the very same lib-   9
erals who were so quick to understand the method and purpose behind the mighty propaganda machine of Hitler's Third Reich, the consciously spewed-out anti-Semitic caricatures
and obscenities that gave an ideological base to the Holocaust and the Final Solution, the
very same liberals who, enlightened by blacks, searched their own conscience and came to
understand that their tolerance of "nigger" jokes and portrayals of shuffling, rolling-eyed

servants in movies perpetuated the degrading myths of black inferiority and gave an ideological base to the continuation of black oppression—these very same liberals now fervidly maintain that the hatred and contempt for women that find expression in four-letter words used as expletives and in what are quaintly called "adult" or "erotic" books and movies are a valid extension of freedom of speech that must be preserved as a Constitutional right.

10   To defend the right of a lone, crazed American Nazi to grind out propaganda calling for the extermination of all Jews, as the ACLU has done in the name of free speech, is, after all, a self-righteous and not particularly courageous stand, for American Jewry is not currently threatened by storm troopers, concentration camps and imminent extermination, but I wonder if the ACLU's position might change if, come tomorrow morning, the bookstores and movie theaters lining Forty-second Street in New York City were devoted not to the humiliation of women by rape and torture, as they currently are, but to a systematized commercially successful propaganda machine depicting the sadistic pleasures of gassing Jews or lynching blacks?

11   Is this analogy extreme? Not if you are a woman who is conscious of the ever-present threat of rape and the proliferation of a cultural ideology that makes it sound like "liberated" fun. The majority report of the President's Commission on Obscenity and Pornography tried to pooh-pooh the opinion of law enforcement agencies around the country that claimed their own concrete experience with offenders who were caught with the stuff led them to conclude that pornographic material is a causative factor in crimes of sexual violence. The commission maintained that it was not possible at this time to scientifically prove or disprove such a connection.

12   But does one need scientific methodology in order to conclude that the antifemale propaganda that permeates our nation's cultural output promotes a climate in which acts of sexual hostility directed against women are not only tolerated but ideologically encouraged? A similar debate has raged for many years over whether or not the extensive glorification of violence (the gangster as hero; the loving treatment accorded bloody shoot-'em-ups in movies, books and on TV) has a causal effect, a direct relationship to the rising rate of crime, particularly among youth. Interestingly enough, in this area—nonsexual and not specifically related to abuses against women—public opinion seems to be swinging to the position that explicit violence in the entertainment media does have a deleterious effect; it makes violence commonplace, numbingly routine and no longer morally shocking.

13   More to the point, those who call for a curtailment of scenes of violence in movies and on television in the name of sensitivity, good taste and what's best for our children are not accused of being pro-censorship or against freedom of speech. Similarly, minority group organizations, black, Hispanic, Japanese, Italian, Jewish, or American Indian, that campaign against ethnic slurs and demeaning portrayals in movies, on television shows and in commercials are perceived as waging a just political fight, for if a minority group claims to be offended by a specific portrayal, be it Little Black Sambo or the Frito Bandito, and relates it to a history of ridicule and oppression, few liberals would dare to trot out a Constitutional argument in theoretical opposition, not if they wish to maintain their liberal credentials. Yet when it comes to the treatment of women, the liberal consciousness remains fiercely obdurate, refusing to be budged, for the sin of appearing square or prissy in the age of the so-called sexual revolution has become the worst offense of all.

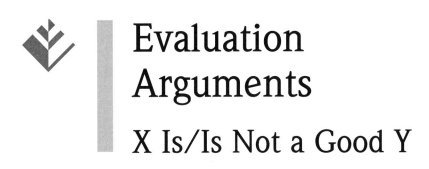

chapter 13

Evaluation Arguments

X Is/Is Not a Good Y

CASE 1

A young engineer has advanced to the level of a design group leader. She is now being considered for promotion to a management position. Her present supervisor is asked to write a report evaluating her as a prospective manager. He is asked to pay particular attention to the criteria of "creativity," "leadership," "interpersonal skill," "communication skills," and "technical competence."

CASE 2

A medical research group is asked to prepare guidelines for physicians on the best way to manage insulin-dependent diabetes. Some physicians want strict control of blood sugar levels. These physicians expect patients to take readings of their blood sugars every four hours and to take as many as three or four insulin injections per day. Other physicians allow blood sugars to fluctuate through a wider range of readings. They ask patients to monitor their blood sugars less often and to take only one or two injections per day. Which of these management programs is better? The research group has been asked to deal specifically with the following criteria: risk of long-range complications from diabetes; psychological well-being; and quality of life.

CASE 3

When former tennis star Margaret Court argued that Martina Navratilova's admitted homosexuality kept her from being a proper role model for young tennis players, sports writer Steve Kelley disagreed: "Navratilova is, in fact, an excellent role model. . . . She is self-made. She didn't learn the game playing with the privileged classes. She is honest and well-spoken in interviews. She doesn't kiss off questions with stock cliches. . . . Navratilova is a voracious reader, fluent in four languages. She belongs to the Sierra Club, reads several newspapers a day. She is a political junkie who has the courage of her convictions." Additionally, Kelly admires her courage and integrity in openly acknowledging her relationship with her longtime lover Judy Nelson, an admission that "has cost Navratilova millions in endorsements."*

CASE 4

A large southwestern city is evaluating its transportation systems. Faced with rapid growth, urban sprawl, budget shortfalls for highway construction and maintenance, and an EPA order to improve rapidly deteriorating air quality (largely caused by automobile exhaust), city planners must make some hard decisions. On one hand, the cost of highway construction and maintenance is mushrooming, but taxpayers have gotten so accustomed to taxes for highways that they view highway travel as "free." On the other hand, the suggested alternative forms of transportation, chief among them light rail transit, cost riders considerably less per mile than automotive transport, involve significant reduction in pollution (if drivers can be lured from their cars to the trains), and require fewer public dollars to maintain than highways. But light rail requires huge initial investments, new taxes for financing, and visible fares to be paid for each usage. Moreover, public response to recently built light rail systems in Los Angeles, Miami, and Portland has been mixed. So which way do the planners go? How do they evaluate the desirability of alternative transportation systems?

In our roles as citizens and professionals we are continually expected to make difficult evaluations, to defend them, and even to persuade others to accept them. Often we will defend our judgments orally—in committees making hiring and promotion decisions, in management groups deciding which of several marketing plans to adopt, or at parent advisory meetings evaluating the success of school policies. Sometimes, too, we will be expected to put our arguments in writing.

Practice in thinking systematically about the process of evaluation, then, is valuable experience. In this chapter we focus on *evaluation* arguments of the type "X is/is not a good Y" (or "X is a good/bad Y") and the strategy needed for conducting such arguments.† In Chapter 15, we will return to evaluation arguments to examine in more detail some special problems raised by ethical issues.

---

*Steve Kelley, *Seattle Times,* 26 Aug. 1990, C3.

†In addition to the contrasting words *good/bad,* there are a number of other evaluative terms that involve the same kind of thinking: *effective/ineffective, successful/unsuccessful, workable/unworkable,* and so forth. Throughout this chapter, terms such as these can be substituted for *good/bad.*

WRITING ASSIGNMENT FOR CHAPTER 13:
EVALUATE A "CONTROVERSIAL" X

Write an argument in which you evaluate something controversial. Possible examples include the following:

- Is a sales tax a good method of taxation? Which method of income tax is preferable, a flat rate or a progressive rate?

- Do Top Forty stations play the best music? Is the classic rock music from the late sixties better than the rock music being produced today? Why is one musician (group) better than another?

- Is *Platoon* a great war movie? What is the best horror movie of all time? What is the best Steven Spielberg movie? Does the movie *Taxi Driver* deserve the praise it has received from critics? How good was the Mel Gibson *Hamlet* versus the Kenneth Branagh *Hamlet*?

- Is [a controversial teacher at your school] a good teacher? How good is the Canadian health care system? Is Rosie O'Donnell a good talk show host? Was Pete Rose as great a baseball player as is popularly believed? How effective is homeopathic medicine in treating disease?

- Is *USA Today* a good newspaper? Do network news shows do a good job at giving the news? Are America's prisons effective? How serious a problem is the budget deficit? Have the *Miranda* warnings improved or harmed police enforcement?

The X you choose should be controversial or at least problematic. While you are safe in arguing that a Mercedes Benz is a good car or that smoking is bad for your health, your claim is unlikely to surprise anyone. By "controversial" or "problematic," then, we mean that people are apt to disagree with your evaluation of X or that you are somehow opposing the common view of X. By choosing a controversial or problematic X, you will be able to focus on a clear issue. Somewhere in your essay you should summarize alternative views and either refute them or concede to them (see Chapter 8).

Note that this assignment asks you to do something different from a typical movie review, restaurant review, or product review in a consumer magazine. Many reviews are simply informational or analytic, where the writer's purpose is to describe the object or event being reviewed and explain its strengths and weaknesses. In contrast, your purpose here is persuasive. You must change someone's mind about the evaluation of X.

The rest of this chapter explains the thinking processes that underlie evaluation arguments and gives you some advice on how to compose an evaluation essay.

CRITERIA-MATCH STRUCTURE OF EVALUATION ARGUMENTS

An "X is/is not a good Y" argument follows the same criteria-match structure that we examined in definitional arguments (Chapter 10). A typical claim for such an argument has the following form:

X is/is not a good Y because it meets/fails to meet criteria A, B, and C.

The main structural difference between an evaluation argument and a definition argument involves the Y term. In a definition argument, one argues whether a particular Y term is the correct class in which to place X. (Is a tarantula a *pet*?) In an evaluation argument, we know the Y term—that is, what class to put X into (Dr. Choplogic is a *teacher*)—but we don't know whether X is a good or bad instance of that class. (Is Dr. Choplogic a *good* teacher?) As in definition arguments, warrants specify the criteria to be used for the evaluation, whereas the stated reasons and grounds assert that X meets these criteria.

Let's look at some examples that, for the sake of illustration, assert just one criterion for "good" or "bad." (Most arguments will, of course, develop several criteria.) For the first example, we examine only the claim, stated reason, and warrant:

ENTHYMEME:	Computer-aided instruction (CAI) is an effective teaching method because it encourages self-paced learning.
CLAIM:	Computer-aided instruction is an effective teaching method.
STATED REASON:	Computer-aided instruction encourages self-paced learning.
WARRANT (CRITERION):	If a teaching method encourages self-paced learning, then it is effective.

To develop this argument, the writer would have to defend both the criterion (warrant) and the match (stated reason). Somewhere in the essay the writer would have to argue that an effective teaching method is one that allows students to work at their own pace; he would also have to argue that CAI instruction actually meets this criterion. (Of course, if self-paced instruction is the only criterion for effectiveness that the writer is proposing, he will have to justify the great weight he is giving to that criterion, which most readers would not believe is a necessary criterion for effectiveness, much less a sufficient one.)

Let's take a second example, and this time display the complete argument according to the Toulmin schema:

ENTHYMEME:	Pete Rose is not a Hall of Fame quality ballplayer because he was strong primarily in batting average and career hits but weak in most other categories.
CLAIM:	Pete Rose does not belong in the Hall of Fame.
STATED REASON:	He wasn't a complete player (he was strong primarily in batting average and career hits but weak in most other categories).
GROUNDS:	A thorough analysis of Pete Rose's career statistics reveals that in many aspects of fielding, hitting, baserunning, and run production his record is below average.
WARRANT:	Well-rounded performance is a necessary criterion for inclusion in the Hall of Fame.
BACKING:	evidence that shows that all present members of the Hall of Fame were well-rounded players; testimony from experts arguing that Hall of Fame players should be well rounded
CONDITIONS OF REBUTTAL:	unless Pete Rose's career records in several areas (e.g., games played, at bats, total career hits, batting average) are so overwhelming that Hall of Fame electors choose to ignore his lack of power, his poor baserunning, his mediocre defense; unless intangibles like competitive zeal are given precedence over the player's record
QUALIFIER:	Given the surprising nature of this claim— most people who oppose Pete Rose's election to the Hall of Fame do so on the basis of his gambling problems and his income tax evasion, not on the basis of his baseball record— one should acknowledge in the qualifier that one faces an uphill battle. Hence, "Pete Rose *may not* belong in the Hall of Fame" is probably as emphatic a claim as one can expect to get away with.

In this case, establishing a match between X and the criteria is fairly easy, but gaining support for the appropriateness of the criteria will be trickier. Baseball experts probably will agree that Pete Rose was not a well-rounded ball player. But many will reject "well-roundedness" as a necessary criterion for election to the Hall of Fame. Similarly, baseball experts will agree that Pete Rose has damaged his reputation through ethical and legal mistakes. But many will reject ethical purity as a criterion for election.

GENERAL STRATEGY FOR EVALUATION ARGUMENTS

The general strategy for evaluation arguments is to establish criteria and then to argue that X meets or does not meet the criteria. In writing your argument, you have to decide whether your audience is apt to accept your criteria or not. If you want to argue, for example, that pit bulls do not make good pets because they are potentially vicious, you can assume that most readers will share your assumption that viciousness is bad. Likewise, if you want to praise the new tax bill because it cuts out tax cheating, you can probably assume readers agree that tax cheating is bad.

Often, however, selecting and defending your criteria are the most difficult parts of a criteria-match argument. For example, people who own pit bulls because they *want* a vicious dog for protection may not agree that viciousness is bad. In this case, you would need to argue that another kind of dog, such as a German shepherd or a doberman, would make a better choice than a pit bull or that the bad consequences of a vicious dog outweigh the benefits. Several kinds of difficulties in establishing criteria are worth discussing in more detail.

The Problem of Standards: What's Normal or What's Ideal?

To get a sense of this problem, consider again Young Person's archetypal argument with The Parents about her curfew (see Chapter 1). She originally argued that staying out until 2:00 A.M. is fair "because all the other kids' parents let their kids stay out late," to which The Parents might respond: "Well, *ideally*, all the other parents should not let their kids stay out that late." Young Person based her criterion for fairness on what is *normal;* her standards arose from common practices of a social group. The Parents, however, argued from what is *ideal*, basing their criteria on some external standard that transcends social groups.

We experience this dilemma in various forms throughout our lives. It is the conflict between absolutes and cultural relativism, between written law and customary practice. There is hardly an area of human experience that escapes the dilemma: Is it fair to get a ticket for going 70 mph on a 65 mph freeway when most of the drivers go 70 mph or higher? Is it better for high schools to pass out free contraceptives to students because the students are having sex anyway (what's *normal*), or is it better not to pass them out in order to support abstinence (what's *ideal*)? When you select criteria for an evaluation argument, you may well have to choose one side or the other of this dilemma, arguing for what is ideal or for what is normal. Neither position should be seen as necessarily better than the other; normal practice may be corrupt just as surely as ideal behavior may be impossible.

The Problem of Mitigating Circumstances

When confronting the dilemma raised by the "normal" versus the "ideal," we sometimes have to take into account circumstances as well as behavior. In particular, we have the notion of *mitigating* circumstances, or circumstances that are extraordinary or unusual enough to cause us to change our standard measure of judgment. Ordinarily it is wrong to be late for work or to miss an exam. But what if your car had a flat tire?

When you argue for mitigating circumstances as a reason for modifying judgment in a particular case, you are arguing against the conditions of both normal behavior and ideal behavior as the proper criterion for judgment. Thus, when you make such an argument, you will likely assume an especially heavy burden of proof. People assume the rightness of usual standards of judgment unless there are compelling arguments for abnormal circumstances.

The Problem of Choosing Between Two Goods or Two Bads

Not all arguments of value, of course, clearly deal with bad and good, but with choosing between two bads or two goods. Often we are caught between a rock and a hard place. Should we cut pay or cut people? Put our parents in a nursing home or let them stay at home where they have become a danger to themselves? In such cases one has to weigh conflicting criteria, knowing that the choices are too much alike—either both bad or both good.

The Problem of Seductive Empirical Measures

The need to make distinctions among relative goods or relative bads has led many persons to seek quantifiable criteria that can be weighed mathematically. Thus we use grade point averages to select scholarship winners, MCAT scores to decide who gets into medical school, and student evaluation scores to decide which professor gets the University Teaching Award.

In some cases, such empirical measures can be quite acceptable. But they can be dangerous if they don't adequately measure the value of the people or things they purportedly evaluate. (Some people would argue that they *never* adequately measure anything significant.) To illustrate the problem further, consider the problems of relying on grade point average as a criterion for employment. Many employers rely heavily on grades when hiring college graduates. But according to every major study of the relationship between grades and work achievement, grades are about as reliable as palm reading when it comes to predicting life success. Why do employers continue to rely so heavily on grades? Clearly because it is so easy to classify job applicants according to a single empirical measure that appears to rank order everyone along the same scale.

The problem with empirical measures, then, is that they seduce us into believing that complex judgments can be made mathematically, thus rescuing us from the messiness of alternative points of view and conflicting criteria. Empirical measures seem extremely persuasive next to written arguments that try to qualify and hedge and raise questions. We suggest, however, that a fair evaluation of any X might require such hedging.

The Problem of Cost

A final problem that can crop up in evaluations is cost. In comparing an X to others of its kind, we may find that on all the criteria we can develop, X comes out on top. X is the best of all possible Ys. But if X costs too much, we have to rethink our evaluation.*

If we're looking to hire a new department head at Median State University, and the greatest scholar in the field, a magnificent teacher, a regular dynamo of diplomacy, says she'll come—for a hundred Gs a year—we'll probably have to withdraw our offer. Whether the costs are expressed in dollars or personal discomfort or moral repugnance or some other terms, our final evaluation of X must take cost into account, however elusive that cost might be.

HOW TO DETERMINE CRITERIA FOR YOUR ARGUMENT

Now that we have explored some of the difficulties you may encounter in establishing and defending criteria for your evaluation of X, let's turn to the practical problem of trying to determine criteria themselves. How do you go about finding the criteria you'll need for distinguishing a good teacher from a poor teacher, a good movie from a bad movie, a successful manager from an unsuccessful manager, a healthy diet from an unhealthy diet, and so forth?

Step 1: Determine the Category in Which the Object Being Evaluated Belongs

In determining the quality or value of any given X, you must first figure out what your standard of comparison is. If, for example, you asked one of your professors to write you a letter of recommendation for a summer job, what class of

---

*We can avoid this problem somewhat by placing items into different classes on the basis of cost. For example, a Mercedes may come out far ahead of a Hyundai, but the more relevant evaluative question to ask is, "How does a Mercedes compare to a Cadillac?"

things should the professor put you into? Is he or she supposed to evaluate you as a student? a leader? a worker? a storyteller? a party animal? or what? This is an important question because the criteria for excellence in one class (student) may be very different from criteria for excellence in another class (party animal).

To write a useful letter, your professor should consider you first as a member of the general class "summer job holder" and base her evaluation of you on criteria relevant to that class. To write a truly effective letter, however, your professor needs to consider your qualifications in the context of the smallest applicable class of candidates: not "summer job holder," but "law office intern" or "highway department flagperson" or "golf course groundsperson." Clearly, each of these subclasses has very different criteria for excellence that your professor needs to address.

We thus recommend placing X into the smallest relevant class because of the apples-and-oranges law. That is, to avoid giving a mistaken rating to a perfectly good apple, you need to make sure you are judging an apple under the class "apple" and not under the next larger class "fruit" or a neighboring class "orange." And to be even more precise, you may wish to evaluate your apple in the class "eating apple" as opposed to "pie apple" because the latter class is supposed to be tarter and the former class juicier and sweeter.

Obviously, there are limits to this law. For example, the smallest possible class of apples would contain only one member—the one being evaluated. At that point, your apple is both the best and the worst member of its class. And hence, evaluation of it is meaningless. Also, we sometimes can't avoid apples-and-oranges comparisons because they are thrust upon us by circumstances, tradition, or some other factor. Thus, the Academy Award judges selecting "Best Movie" aren't allowed to distinguish between Great Big Box Office Hits and "serious little films that make socially significant points."

Step 2: Determine the Purpose or Function of This Class

Once you have located X in its appropriate class, you should next determine what the purpose or function of this class is. Let's suppose that the summer job you are applying for is tour guide at the city zoo. The function of a tour guide is to make people feel welcome, to give them interesting information about the zoo, to make their visit pleasant, and so forth. Consequently, you wouldn't want your professor's evaluation to praise your term paper on Napoleon Bonaparte or your successful synthesis of some compound in your chemistry lab. Rather, the professor should highlight your dependability, your neat appearance, your good speaking skills, and your ability to work with groups. On the other hand, if you were applying for graduate school, then your term paper on Bonaparte or your chem lab wizardry would be relevant. In other words, the professor has to evaluate you according to the class "tour guide," not "graduate student," and the criteria for each class derive from the purpose or function of the class.

Let's take another example. Suppose that you are the chair of a committee charged with evaluating the job performance of Lillian Jones, director of the admissions office at Clambake College. Ms. Jones has been a controversial manager because several members of her staff have filed complaints about her management style. In making your evaluation, your first step is to place Ms. Jones into an appropriate class, in this case, the general class "manager," and then the more specific class "manager of an admissions office at a small, private college." You then need to identify the purpose or function of these classes. You might say that the function of the general class "managers" is to "oversee actual operations of an organization so that the organization meets its goals as harmoniously and efficiently as possible," whereas the function of the specific class "manager of an admissions office at a small, private college" is "the successful recruitment of the best students possible."

Step 3: Determine Criteria Based on the Purposes or Function of the Class to Which X Belongs

Once you've worked out the purposes of the class, you are ready to work out the criteria by which you judge all members of the class. Criteria for judgment will be based on those features of Y that help it achieve the purposes of its class. For example, once you determine the purpose and function of the position filled by Lillian Jones, you can develop a list of criteria for managerial success:

1. Criteria related to "efficient operation"
   - articulates priorities and goals for the organization
   - is aggressive in achieving goals
   - motivates fellow employees
   - is well organized, efficient, and punctual
   - is articulate and communicates well
2. Criteria related to "harmonious operation"
   - creates job satisfaction for subordinates
   - is well groomed, sets good example of professionalism
   - is honest, diplomatic in dealing with subordinates
   - is flexible in responding to problems and special concerns of staff members
3. Criteria related to meeting specific goals of a college admissions office
   - creates a comprehensive recruiting program
   - demonstrates that recruiting program works

Step 4: Give Relative Weightings to the Criteria

Even though you have established criteria, you must still decide which of the criteria are most important. In the case of Lillian Jones, is it more important that she bring in lots of students to Clambake College or that she create a harmonious, happy office? These sorts of questions are at the heart of many evaluative controversies. Thus, a justification for your weighting of criteria may well be an important part of your argument.

DETERMINING WHETHER X MEETS THE CRITERIA

Once you've established your criteria, you've got to figure out how well X meets them. You proceed by gathering evidence and examples. The success of the recruiting program at Clambake College can probably be measured empirically, so you gather statistics about applications to the college, SAT scores of applicants, number of acceptances, academic profiles of entering freshmen, and so forth. You might then compare those statistics to those compiled by Ms. Jones's predecessor or to her competitors at other, comparable institutions.

You can also look at what the recruiting program actually does—the number of recruiters, the number of high school visitations, quality of admissions brochures, and other publications. You can also look at Ms. Jones in action, searching for specific incidents or examples that illustrate her management style. For example, you can't measure a trait such as diplomacy empirically, but you can find specific instances where the presence or absence of this trait was demonstrated. You could turn to examples where Ms. Jones may or may not have prevented a potentially divisive situation from occurring or where she offered or failed to offer encouragement at psychologically the right moment to keep someone from getting demoralized. As with criteria-match arguments in definition, one must provide examples of how the X in question meets each of the criteria that have been set up.

Your final evaluation of Ms. Jones, then, might include an overview of her strengths and weaknesses along the various criteria you have established. You might say that Ms. Jones has done an excellent job with recruitment (an assertion you can support with data on student enrollments over the last five years) but was relatively poor at keeping the office staff happy (as evidenced by employee complaints, high turnover, and your own observations of her rather abrasive management style). Nevertheless, your final recommendation might be to retain Ms. Jones for another three-year contract because you believe that an excellent recruiting record is the most important criterion for her position at Clambake. You might justify this heavy weighting of recruiting on the grounds that the institution's survival depends on its ability to attract adequate numbers of good students.

As a way of testing your argument in preparation for your committee's meeting, you lay out your argument according to Toulmin's schema:

ENTHYMEME:	Despite some weaknesses, Ms. Jones has been a good manager of the admissions office at Clambake College because her office's recruitment record is excellent.
CLAIM:	Ms. Jones has been a good manager of the admissions office at Clambake College.
STATED REASON:	Her office's recruitment record is excellent.
GROUNDS:	statistical data demonstrating the excellence of the recruitment program
WARRANT:	Successful recruitment is the most important criterion for rating job performance of the director of admissions.
BACKING:	Evidence that low recruitment leads to financial problems and even closing of a college; maintaining enrollment through recruitment is the lifeblood of the college. Although her opponents have complained that Ms. Jones has serious problems maintaining harmony among her staff, a happy staff serves no purpose if we don't have enough students to keep the college open.
CONDITIONS OF REBUTTAL:	unless the recruitment record isn't as good as I have said (Note: I'll need to be sure of my standards when I say her record is excellent. Am I arguing about "what's normal" by comparing Clambake's record with other colleges? Or am I arguing about what is ideal? Will one of Jones's critics bring in an argument saying she isn't doing a particularly good job of recruiting? Might they argue that plenty of people in the office could do the same good job of recruitment—after all, Clambake sells itself—without stirring up any of the personnel problems that Ms. Jones has caused?)
	Unless the recruitment record isn't the most important criterion. Ms. Jones is obviously weak in maintaining good relationships with staff. How might an opponent argue that staff problems in Ms. Jones's office are severe

enough that we ought to search for a new director? I will have to counter that argument
some way.

QUALIFIER: I will need to qualify my general rating of
excellent by acknowledging Ms. Jones's weaknesses in some areas. But I want to be definite
in saying that recruitment is the most important criterion and that she definitely meets
this criterion.

 FOR CLASS DISCUSSION

The following small-group exercise can be accomplished in one or two class
hours. It gives you a good model of the process you will need to go through in
order to write your own evaluation essay. Working in small groups, suppose that
you are going to evaluate a controversial member of one of the following classes:

    a. a teacher
    b. a political figure
    c. an athlete
    d. a school newspaper
    e. a school policy
    f. a recent Supreme Court decision
    g. a rock singer or group or MTV video
    h. a dorm or living group
    i. a restaurant or college hangout
    j. an X of your choice

1. Choose a controversial member within one of these classes as the specific person, thing, or event you are going to evaluate (Professor Choplogic, the Wild
   Dog Bar, Madonna, and so forth).

2. Narrow down the general class by determining the smallest relevant class to
   which your X belongs (from "athlete" to "basketball guard"; from "college
   hangout" to "college hangout for people who want to hold late-night bull
   sessions").

3. Make a list of the purposes or functions of that class and then list the criteria
   that a good member of that class would have to have in order to accomplish
   the purposes.

4. If necessary, rank order your criteria.

5. Evaluate your X by matching X to each of the criteria.

WRITING YOUR
EVALUATION ARGUMENT

Starting Point: Finding and Exploring an Evaluation Issue   If you have not already listed some evaluation issues, try creating idea maps with spokes chosen from among the following categories: *people* (athletes, political leaders, musicians, clergypeople, entertainers, businesspeople); *science and technology* (weapons systems, word-processing programs, spread sheets, automotive advancements, treatments for diseases); *media* (a newspaper, a magazine or journal, a TV program, a radio station, an advertisement); *government and world affairs* (an economic policy, a Supreme Court decision, a law or legal practice, a government custom or practice, a foreign policy); *the arts* (a movie, a book, a building, a painting, a piece of music); *your college or university* (a course, a teacher, a textbook, a curriculum, an administrative policy, the financial aid system); *world of work* (a job, a company operation, a dress policy, a merit pay system, a hiring policy, a supervisor); or any other categories of your choice.

Then brainstorm possibilities for controversial Xs that might fit into the categories on your map. As long as you can imagine disagreement about how to evaluate X, you have a potentially good topic for this assignment.

Once you have found an issue and have taken a tentative position on it, explore your ideas by freewriting your responses to the eight guided tasks in Chapter 3, pages 73–74.

Writing a Discovery Draft: Some Suggestions for Organizing Your Evaluation Argument   As you write your discovery draft, you might find useful the following typical structure for an evaluation argument. Of course, many evaluation arguments don't follow this shape, but many do, and you can always alter the shape later if its structure seems too formulaic to you.

- Introduce your issue and show why evaluating X is problematic or controversial.
- Summarize opposing views.
- Refute or concede to opposing views.
- Present your own claim.
    State Criterion 1 and defend it if necessary.
        Show that X meets criterion.
    State Criterion 2 and defend it if necessary.
        Show that X meets criterion.
    Continue with additional criteria and match arguments.
- Sum up your evaluation

Revision   At this stage you should be able to summarize your argument as a claim with because clauses. To test the structure of your argument, you may find it useful to analyze it with the Toulmin schema. This method will help you see to what extent you need to defend each of your criteria. As the example on evaluating Lillian Jones shows (pp. 292–293), the main testing of the argument can occur when you consider the conditions of rebuttal. In the final section of this chapter, we turn to some of the questions you might ask yourself when testing your argument.

CONDITIONS FOR REBUTTAL: TESTING YOUR EVALUATION ARGUMENT

After you've gone through a process like the one sketched out here, you should have a thoughtful rough draft ready for more careful scrutiny. Once again, put yourself in the role of the critic.

Will My Audience Accept My Criteria?

Many evaluative arguments are weak because the writers have simply assumed that readers will accept their criteria. Whenever your audience's acceptance of your criteria is in doubt, you will need to make your warrants clear and provide backing in their support.

Are My Criteria Based on the "Smallest Applicable Class" for X?

For example, the James Bond movie *Golden Eye* will certainly be a failure if you evaluate it in the general class "movies," in which it would have to compete with *Citizen Kane* and other great classics. But if you evaluated it as an "escapist movie" or a "James Bond movie" it would have a greater chance for success and hence of yielding an arguable evaluation. All of this isn't to say that you couldn't evaluate "escapist movies" as a class of, say, "popular films" and find the whole class deficient. Evaluations of this type are, however, more difficult to argue because of the numbers of items you must take into account.

Will Readers Accept My General Weighting of Criteria?

Another vulnerable spot in an evaluation argument is the relative weight of the criteria. How much anyone weights a given criterion is usually a function of his or her own interests relative to the X in question. You should always ask whether some particular group affected by the quality of X might not have good reasons for weighting the criteria differently.

Will Readers Question My Standard of Reference?

In questioning the criteria for judging X, we can also focus on the standard of reference used—what's normal versus what's ideal. If you have argued that X is bad because it doesn't live up to what's ideal, you can expect some readers to defend X on the basis of what's normal. Similarly, if you argue that X is good because it is better than its competitors, you can expect some readers to point out how short it falls from what is ideal.

Will Readers Criticize My Use of Empirical Measures?

The tendency to mistake empirical measures for criteria is a common one that any critic of an argument should be aware of. As we have discussed earlier, what's most measurable isn't always significant when it comes to assessing the essential traits needed to fulfill whatever function X is supposed to fulfill. A 95-mph fastball is certainly an impressive empirical measure of a pitcher's ability—but if the pitcher doesn't get batters out, that measure is a misleading gauge of performance.

Will Readers Accept My Criteria but Reject My Match Argument?

The other major way of testing an evaluation argument is to anticipate how readers might object to your stated reasons and grounds. Will readers challenge you by finding sampling errors in your data or otherwise find that you used evidence selectively? For example, if you think your opponents will emphasize Lillian Jones's abrasive management style much more heavily than you did, you may be able to undercut their arguments by finding counterexamples that show Ms. Jones acting diplomatically. Be prepared to counter objections to your grounds.

 FOR CLASS DISCUSSION

Read the following examples of evaluation arguments. Then, working as individuals or in a group, answer the following questions:

1. What criteria are used to evaluate the X in question?

2. Does the writer create an argument for the appropriateness of these criteria? If so, how effective is it?

3. How effective is the argument that X matches each of the established criteria?

4. How would you go about refuting each of the arguments?

How to Reform the Federal Tax System: Just the Basics, Please

Murray Weidenbaum

After more than a year of public debate, it is fair to say that there is no universal agreement on the details of how to reform the federal tax system. Do we replace the entire income-tax system with a new national sales tax? Or do we streamline the income tax by shifting to a flat tax? Do we adopt a savers-friendly reform of the income tax (known as the USA Tax)?

It will take more discussion, analysis, and congressional deliberation before a specific tax reform emerges that has broad enough support to be enacted. Yet some progress has been made in developing a consensus on the direction of change.

There is a widespread belief that the current tax system is unfair and too complicated. It also is viewed as hurting the individual family and individual business, especially the smaller enterprise. And, when we step back from the mass of specific provisions and exceptions, we see that the present Internal Revenue Code depresses the American economy. That means it reduces jobs and living standards at home and erodes our competitiveness in the global marketplace. These issues transcend traditional political partisanship, which may make it unlikely that real progress can occur in the midst of a presidential election campaign.

Given the variety of personal interests, it is especially difficult to develop any new approach to fundamental tax policy that can garner majority support. The following is an attempt to concentrate on basic themes rather than on specific approaches. These six characteristics of the desired revenue system are based on extended discussions with groups ranging from technical experts to ordinary taxpayers.

The new tax system should:

1. Be fair to the average taxpayer—and should be seen that way. People in the same economic circumstances should be taxed the same, regardless of where they live or whom they know.

2. Be understandable to the average citizen. Eliminating special privileges will help simplify the tax system and achieve greater fairness. Most of the complications in Form 1040 result from the requirements of statutes passed by Congress, rather than from the shortcomings of the form designers in the Internal Revenue Service.

3. Have lower tax rates than today's. How flat the tax structure can get will depend on the success in eliminating those costly loopholes and in energizing the economy. That also means it would be helpful to defer the array of tax cuts being suggested by various candidates until next year, when they can be included in a more carefully drafted comprehensive tax-reform bill.

4. Help the average family achieve financial independence. That means it should do more to encourage saving and investment. We will also have a stronger economy if more of our fellow citizens have a direct financial stake in the operation of the private-enterprise system.

5. Make it easier to start a new business and for that business to grow and compete. This is the key to job creation, and it requires a tax system that looks at business enterprise not as a burden to society but as a positive benefit. As former President Reagan was fond of reminding us, business collects taxes—people pay taxes.

6. Foster a stronger economy on a sustainable basis. It will take a more rapid rate of economic growth to produce a higher living standard today and a brighter outlook for the future.

6   A final thought: Just as there may be more than one path to salvation, there is more than one approach to tax reform that can achieve these six objectives. It will take the ability of competing interest groups to work together and to adopt a middle-of-the-road position.

Clinton Can Show Courage by Vetoing Bad Welfare Bill

Terry Tang

1   Conservative pundit George Will is no friend of people living off the public dole. And yet he, and others honest enough to say so, are appalled at what passes for welfare reform in Congress. Last fall, shrinking back from the sight of the welfare-reform juggernaut, Will wrote: "Conservatives say, well, nothing could be worse than the current system. They are underestimating their ingenuity."

2   The latest welfare plan proves again that Congress is perfectly capable of making an already flawed system disastrous for 9 million children surviving on welfare.

3   Forget trying to puzzle out what the proposal will do to needy kids in your neighborhood or in your school. Neither the White House nor supporters of the legislation (which changed hour by hour in the Senate this week) will release any numbers on the plan's impact on poverty rates. The only incontrovertible fact is, just about every claim made for this welfare package is a lie.

4   First of all, $23 billion of the package's $60 billion expected savings over six years would be achieved not by getting more people to work, but by denying legal immigrants food stamps, Medicaid and other welfare benefits (illegal immigrants are ineligible for such aid). Legal immigrants, who pay taxes like everyone else, make up only 5 percent of the welfare population, but they and their children will bear 35 percent of the cuts. So much for fairness in a nation of immigrants.

5   Second, $28 billion of the savings in the Senate bill ($31 billion in the House version) come straight out of food programs that keep the poorest Americans fed, including millions of the working poor who don't receive any welfare. In Washington, some 477,000 people depend on food stamps, more than half of them are children. It's a measure of the radicalization of the debate that the cut is now $4.5 billion deeper than the cut in last year's Senate bill. President Clinton vetoed that version because it would push one million children into poverty; this bill would be worse.

Third, nothing in the package will help put more welfare mothers to work. It will, how- 6
ever, force the least able of them—the illiterate, the mentally impaired, those without any
job experience—off welfare after five years regardless of their job prospects. The legislation
would allow states to exempt 20 percent of the welfare population from the time limit, but
that doesn't solve the problem.

The most employable people will get jobs (provided the economy is sound and jobs 7
exist), and only those facing multiple problems will be left in the system. That is precisely
what happens now. Women who have skills cycle out of welfare relatively quickly (about
70 percent of families leave welfare within two years), but those who are in the system for
more than five years typically have huge hurdles to overcome. The legislation would deny
kids public aid even if their mothers are incapable of supporting them.

The aim is to put 50 percent of all welfare recipients into work by 2002. But there's 8
no new money to educate or train these people. About 60 percent of the welfare mothers
in Washington state, for example, never finished high school. A good 30 percent of them
will need a lot more help than a resumé service to land even a low-skill job.

The Congressional Budget Office estimates that shepherding more people into jobs 9
would cost $13 billion more than is now spent on welfare-to-work services. And that's as-
suming there is no improvement in the services offered. Even the CBO says the work requirements are so underfunded that most states will ignore the 50 percent work rule.

In other words, welfare recipients could very well receive no help or training (even if 10
they are willing to work) and still be shoved off welfare after five years. As for the women
who do land jobs, they may not be able to keep them. The CBO estimates that child-care
money would be short $2.3 billion over six years given the increased work rates among
welfare-receiving mothers.

Finally, here's the biggest lie of all. The repeal of the welfare entitlement—touted as 11
the cornerstone of reform—has absolutely nothing to do with increasing self-sufficiency.

Congress can and should make welfare mothers work, ferret out fraud, tighten child-
support enforcement, and increase child-care subsidies so that women earning minimum
wage can afford to go to work. It can do all these things without destroying the slim guarantee of federal aid for destitute children.

By all means, give states maximum freedom to experiment with new approaches; 44 12
of them are beginning to do just that. But the anti-entitlement push in Congress isn't about
regulatory freedom. It's about reducing federal spending, regardless of where those discarded children end up.

Clinton faces the toughest political test of the season when the bill comes out of the 13
House-Senate conference committee. He can sign a lie and claim he's a reformer or tell the
truth and veto the bill. Given his record for truthfulness, how he'll go is anybody's guess.

This week in a campaign speech in Denver, he said to booming applause: "What do
you want from all these poor folks that are on welfare? What do you want from them? They
all have kids. . . . You want them to have kids that turn out to be the mayor of Denver, right?
Isn't that what you want?"

It was a nice rhetorical flourish. The legislation Clinton faces wouldn't even ensure that 14
poor children in Denver survive their childhood.

Would Legalization of Gay Marriage Be Good for the Gay Community?

Sam Isaacson (student)

1   For those of us who have been out for a while, nothing seems shocking about a gay pride parade. Yet at this year's parade, I was struck by the contrast between two groups—the float for the Toys in Babeland store (with swooning drag queens and leather clad, whip-wielding, topless dykes) and the Northwest chapters of Integrity and Dignity (Episcopal and Catholic organizations for lesbians and gays), whose marchers looked as conservative as the congregation of any American church.

2   These stark differences in dress are representative of larger philosophical differences in the gay community. At stake is whether or not we gays and lesbians should act "normal." Labeled as deviants by many in straight society, we're faced with various opposing methods of response. One option is to insist that we are normal and work to integrate gays into the cultural mainstream. Another response is to form an alternative gay culture with its own customs and values; this culture would honor deviancy in response to a society which seeks to label some as "normal" and some as "abnormal." For the purposes of this paper I will refer to those who favor the first response as "integrationists" and those who favor the second response as "liberationists". Politically, this ideological clash is most evident in the issue of whether legalization of same-sex marriage would be good for the gay community. Nearly all integrationists would say yes, but many liberationists would say no. My belief is that while we must take the objections of the liberationists seriously, legalization of same-sex marriage would benefit both gays and society in general.

3   Let us first look at what is so threatening about gay marriage to many liberationists. Many liberationists fear that legalizing gay marriage will reinforce current social pressures that say monogamous marriage is the normal and right way to live. In straight society, those who choose not to marry are often viewed as self-indulgent, likely promiscuous, and shallow—and it is no coincidence these are some of the same stereotypes gays struggle against. If gays begin to marry, married life will be all the more the norm and subject those outside of marriage to even greater marginalization. As homosexuals, liberationists argue, we should be particularly sensitive to the tyranny of the majority. Our sympathies should lie with the deviants—the transsexual, the fetishist, the drag queen, and the leather-dyke. By choosing marriage, gays take the easy route into "normal" society; we not only abandon the sexual minorities of our community, we strengthen society's narrow notions of what is "normal" and thereby further confine both straights and gays.

4   Additionally, liberationists worry that by winning the right to marry gays and lesbians will lose the distinctive and positive characteristics of gay culture. Many gay writers have commented on how as a marginalized group gays have been forced to create different forms of relationships that often allow for a greater and often more fulfilling range of life experiences. Writer Edmund White, for instance, has observed that there is a greater fluidity in the relationships of gays than straights. Gays, he says, are more likely than straights to stay friends with old lovers, are more likely to form close friendships outside the romantic relationship, and are generally less likely to become compartmentalized into isolated couples. It has also been noted that gay relationships are often characterized by more equality and

better communication than are straight relationships. Liberationists make the reasonable assumption that if gays win the right to marry they will be subject to the same social pressure to marry that straights are subject to. As more gays are pressured into traditional life patterns, liberationists fear the gay sensibility will be swallowed up by the established attitudes of the broader culture. All of society would be the poorer if this were to happen.

I must admit that I concur with many of the arguments of the liberationists that I have outlined above. I do think if given the right, gays would feel social pressure to marry; I agree that gays should be especially sensitive to the most marginalized elements of society; and I also agree that the unique perspectives on human relationships that the gay community offers should not be sacrificed. However, despite these beliefs, I feel that legalizing gay marriage would bring valuable benefits to gays and society as a whole.   5

First of all, I think it is important to put the attacks the liberationists make on marriage into perspective. The liberationist critique of marriage claims that marriage in itself is a harmful institution (for straights as well as gays) because it needlessly limits and normalizes personal freedom. But it seems clear to me that marriage in some form is necessary for the well-being of society. Children need a stable environment in which to be raised. Studies have shown that children whose parents divorce often suffer long-term effects from the trauma. Studies have also shown that people tend to be happier in stable long-term relationships. We need to have someone to look over us when we're old, when we become depressed, when we fall ill. All people, gay or straight, parents or nonparents, benefit from the stabilizing force of marriage.   6

Second, we in the gay community should not be too quick to overlook the real benefits that legalizing gay marriage will bring. We are currently denied numerous legal rights of marriage that the straight community enjoys: tax benefits, insurance benefits, inheritance rights, and the right to have a voice in medical treatment or funeral arrangements for a dying partner.   7

Further, just as important as the legal impacts of being denied the right to marriage is the socially symbolic weight this denial carries. We are sent the message that while gay sex in the privacy of one's home will be tolerated, gay love will not be respected. We are told that it is not important to society whether we form long-term relationships or not. We are told that we are not worthy of forming families of our own. By gaining the same recognitions by the state of our relationships and all the legal and social weight that recognition carries, the new message will be that gay love is just as meaningful as straight love.   8

Finally, let me address what I think is at the heart of the liberationist argument against marriage—the fear of losing social diversity and our unique gay voice. The liberationists are wary of society's normalizing forces. They fear that if gays win the right to marry gay relationships will simply become imitations of straight relationships—the richness gained through the gay experience will be lost. I feel, however, this argument unintentionally plays into the hands of conservatives. Conservatives argue that marriage is, by definition, the union between man and woman. As a consequence, to the broad culture gay marriage can only be a mockery of marriage. As gays and lesbians we need to argue that conservatives are imposing arbitrary standards on what is normal and not normal in society. To fight the conservative agenda, we must suggest instead that marriage is, in essence, a contract of love and commitment between two people. The liberationists, I think, unwittingly feed into conservative identification and classification by pigeonholing gays as outsiders. Reacting against social norms is simply another way of being held hostage by them.   9

10   We need to understand that the gay experience and voice will not be lost by gaining the right to marry. Gays will always be the minority by simple biological fact and this will always color the identity of any gay person. But we can only make our voice heard if we are seen as full-fledged members of society. Otherwise we will remain an isolated and marginalized group. And only when we have the right to marry will we have any say in the nature and significance of marriage as an institution. This is not being apologetic to the straight culture, but is a demand that we not be excluded from the central institutions of Western culture. We can help merge the fluidity of gay relationships with the traditionally more compartmentalized married relationship. Further, liberationists should realize that the decision *not* to marry makes a statement only if one has the ability to choose marriage. What would be most radical, most transforming, is two women or two men joined together in the eyes of society.

Beauty Pageant Fallacies

Debra Goodwin (student)

1   "You will be beautiful up there on the stage, Jessica," said the beauty pageant director. "You've spent your whole life preparing for this contest. The judges will examine you and all they will see is a perfect ten. You look gorgeous." There are many in our society who believe beauty pageants are a harmless way to celebrate the beauty of women in our culture. These same individuals boast that the beauty pageants provide many opportunities for the winners of such contests. In some contests women are even awarded scholastic scholarships for their beauty. Advocates of beauty pageants claim that winners of these contests win because of their talent not because of their looks. Despite these claims, I believe that beauty pageants damage our society. First, beauty pageants hurt a woman's self-esteem. Second, beauty contests present women as objects and are thus a kind of pornography. Finally, beauty pageants perpetuate and condone the exploitation of women in our society.

2   Beauty pageants are harmful because they severely damage a woman's self-esteem by creating an impossible standard of beauty that leads to serious medical and mental problems. My sister Pam pursued her ambition to be a beauty queen. She explained, "I read everything I could find on pageants back to the 1950s to determine if there was a standard of beauty and whether I could seem to fit it. And I could—with the help of heavy makeup to cover my acne scars, enough hair spray to defy gravity for hours, tape for my boobs, and spray adhesive to hold down my swimsuit." Pam felt that being transformed into a beauty queen made absolutely clear how "artificial, dangerous, and self-denying the beauty standard really is." After winning in the local pageants Pam explained, "I was whisked away for a session with two pageant advisors who dissected my body: 'Okay, you really need to work on your legs; we definitely have to find you a better bra.' No matter how I looked, I was inadequate." Pam's obsession with winning in the beauty pageant circle landed her in the hospital diagnosed as anorexic with a severely low self-esteem. After months of counseling, Pam realized that her identity as a woman was replaced by ideas of what others thought she should act and look like.

Unfortunately, Pam's problem is not an isolated case. She said, "There were women   3
who were always making themselves vomit so that they would not gain any weight. Also,
there were women in tears during many of our rehearsals because they didn't look exactly
like the pageant organizers wanted." According to Ruby Koppes, a retired beauty pageant
organizer whom I interviewed, "Diseases such as anorexia and bulimia are very common
problems in the beauty pageant ring. Many girls would have to drop out of the contest because they would become ill from erratic dieting methods." The problems that manifest
themselves within the beauty pageant circle indicate the extent to which women have been
socialized to pursue the elusive ideal of beauty at any cost.

Another reason why beauty pageants are harmful is that they are a subtle form of   4
pornography which portrays women as objects. Although beauty pageants are not usually
thought of as pornographic, they have been a major platform for the reduction of women
from full human beings into objects. These competitions are such a way of life that we rarely
stop to challenge the concept of a woman walking down a platform in a bathing suit, parading in front of a group of male judges who look over her legs, her breasts, and her waist,
who compare her bodily measurements with those of other contestants, and who make a
choice of the "best" female based primarily on these exterior qualities, just as judges at dog
or livestock shows do. Beauty contests create a fantasy world where women are meant to
be ogled and men are polite voyeurs. Looking at women as objects helps men to "keep
women in their place." When women are totally equated with their physical beauty, they
won't be taken seriously in any other respect.

Closely related to the pornographic nature of beauty pageants is the harmful way that they   5
exploit women. There are two major areas of exploitation that I would like to address. First,
beauty pageants exploit women by stereotyping their sexuality. For a woman to be successful
and to win approval, women must have the unbeatable Madonna-Whore combination—they
must be sexy but wholesome. Women who pursue the pageant's approval with more than ordinary determination may get caught by our society's limits on how far women can "properly"
go in presenting themselves. The case of Vanessa Williams, chosen Miss America for 1984, is
a good example. When a photographer for whom she had posed nude sold her pictures to a
magazine for men, she was publicly disgraced and forced to give up her title. Vanessa Williams
went "too far." To exhibit one's body scantily clothed and to be seductive conforms to our society's standards for womanhood, but over-titillating men with nude photos does not.

Finally, beauty pageants exploit women by perpetuating our society's focus on *young*   6
women. Women are continually reminded that our society does not have any roles for older
women. Older women in our society are seen as the antithesis of the beauty pageant queen.
The White House Conference on Older Women held in 1981 concluded that "popular images that portray older women as inactive, unhealthy, asexual, unattractive, and ineffectual
are prevalent." On television, older women continue to be shown fending off old age with
Geritol or aspirin, baking cookies for the grandchildren, or retreating into the world of soap
operas. Although the population of older women is expanding and diverse, and older
women continue to grow and lead interesting lives, negative stereotypes persist. These prevailing stereotypes will continue as long as beauty pageant contestants are the standard of
what our society believes women are and should be.

c h a p t e r 14

Proposal Arguments

"We Should/ Should Not Do X"

CASE 1

A medical school professor wishes to further her research into the effect of alcohol consumption on fetal development in pregnant women. Focusing on the development of fetal blood vessels, she decides to do a study using laboratory rats. She and her research partner, a professor of anatomy, develop a research design to study how the ingestion of alcohol by pregnant rats affects blood vessel development in fetal eye tissue. She and the anatomist devote three months to the planning and writing of a grant proposal to be submitted to the National Science Foundation.

CASE 2

A student dissatisfied with the noise level in a study lounge in a campus dormitory proposes that a soundproofed wall and door be installed between the study lounge and an adjoining TV/relaxation lounge. In preparing the proposal, which she submits to the university housing office, the student interviews dormitory residents about their study habits and researches the cost of the proposed wall by taking measurements and visiting a local hardware store.

CASE 3

A forestry professor weighs the economic advantages of maintaining a healthy lumber industry versus the environmental advantages of protecting the spotted owl and the grandeur of old growth forests. As a partial solution to the problem of competing needs, he proposes the development of a new industry specializing in thinning and pruning forest lands—making usable products with lumber presently considered scrap and at the same time increasing the quality of forests.*

CASE 4

Barry Commoner, director of the Center for the Biology of Natural Systems at Queens College, poses the following dilemma: "To what extent should the choice of production technologies be governed—as it is now—by private, generally short-term, profit-maximizing response to market forces, and to what extent by long-term social concerns like environmental quality?" In examining the problem of atmospheric pollutants, he opts for governmental control based on long-term social concerns. Specifically, he proposes that the government shift from trying to "clean up" pollutants to issuing an outright ban on pollutant-causing technologies.†

THE NATURE OF PROPOSAL ARGUMENTS

Although *proposal* or "should" arguments are the last type we examine, they are among the most common arguments that you will encounter or be called on to write. Their essence is that they call for action. In reading a proposal, the audience is enjoined to make a decision and then to act upon it—to *do* something. Proposal arguments are sometimes called "should" or "ought" arguments because these helping verbs express the obligation to act: "We *should* do X" or "We *ought* to do X."

For instructional purposes, we will distinguish between two kinds of proposal arguments, even though they are closely related and involve the same basic arguing strategies. The first kind we will call *practical proposals*, which propose an action to solve some kind of local or immediate problem. A student's proposal to change the billing procedures for scholarship students would be an example of a practical proposal, as would an engineering firm's proposal for the design of a new bridge being planned by a city government. The second kind we will call *policy proposals*, in which the writer offers a broad plan of action to solve major social, economic, or political problems affecting the common good. An argument that the United States should adopt a national health insurance plan or that the terms for senators and representatives should be limited to twelve years would be examples of policy proposals.

Seattle Times, 27 Aug. 1990, A9.

†"Free Markets Can't Control Pollution," *New York Times*, 15 April 1990.

The primary difference is the narrowness versus breadth of the concern. Practical proposals are narrow, local, and concrete; they focus on the nuts and bolts of getting something done in the here and now. They are often concerned with the exact size of a piece of steel, the precise duties of a new person to be hired, or a close estimate of the cost of paint or computers to be purchased. Policy proposals, on the other hand, are concerned with the broad outline and shape of a course of action, often on a regional, national, or even international issue. What government should do about overcrowding of prisons would be a problem addressed by policy proposals. How to improve the security alarm system for the county jail would be addressed by a practical proposal.

Learning to write both kinds of proposals is valuable. Researching and writing a policy proposal is an excellent way to practice the responsibilities of citizenship. By researching a complex issue, by attempting to weigh the positive and negative consequences of any policy decision, and then by committing yourself to a course of action, you will be doing the kind of thinking necessary for the survival of a democratic society. On the other hand, writing practical proposals may well be among your most important duties on the job. Writing persuasive practical proposals is the lifeblood of engineering companies and construction firms because through such proposals a company wins bids and creates work. In many companies, employees can initiate improvements in company operations through practical proposals, and it is through grant proposals that innovative people gain funding for research or carry on the work of volunteer and nonprofit organizations throughout our society.

THE GENERAL STRUCTURE AND STRATEGY OF PROPOSAL ARGUMENTS

Proposal arguments, whether practical proposals or policy proposals, generally have a three-part structure: (1) description of a problem, (2) proposed solution, and (3) justification for the proposed solution. Luckily, proposal arguments don't require different sorts of argumentative strategies from the ones you have already been using. In the justification section of your proposal argument, you develop because clauses of the kinds you have practiced all along throughout this text.

SPECIAL REQUIREMENTS OF PROPOSAL ARGUMENTS

Although proposal arguments combine elements from other kinds of claims, they differ from other arguments in that they call for action. Calls to action don't entail any strategies that we haven't already considered, but they do entail a unique set of emphases. Let's look briefly at some of the special requirements of proposal arguments.

Adding "Presence" to Your Argument

It's one thing for a person to assent to a value judgment, but it's another thing to act on that judgment. The personal cost of acting may be high for many people in your audience. That means that you have to engage not only your audience's intellect, but their emotions as well. Thus proposal arguments often require more attention to *pathos* than do other kinds of arguments (see pp. 154–155).

In most cases, convincing people to act means that an argument must have "presence" as well as intellectual force. An argument is said to have presence when the reader senses the immediacy of the writer's words. Not only does the reader recognize the truth and consistency of the argument, but he experiences its very life. An argument with presence is one in which the reader can share the writer's point of view—the writer's emotions, the force of the writer's personal engagement with the issue—as well as assent to the writer's conclusions.

How does one achieve presence in an argument? There are a number of ways. For one, you can appeal directly to the reader's emotions through the effective use of details, brief scenes, and compelling examples that show the reader the seriousness of the problem you are addressing or the consequences of not acting on your proposal. Consider the following example of presence from a policy argument favoring euthanasia:

> There are hundreds of thousands of persons today living in continuing, sustained, baffled misery, pain, and anguish; thousands literally imprisoned in nursing homes and hospitals; thousands isolated, alone, family gone, just prolonging miserable day after miserable day.
>
> Mist clouds my eyes as I remember the last days of my own father, begging the doctors to let him go home and die peacefully in the room he so loved, overlooking the trees and gardens that he had created over the years.
>
> "No," they said, "you must stay here where we can watch you." Maybe brutal is not a strong enough word to describe the situation. And so my father was refused his sacred right to die with integrity, quality and with some dignity left intact in the life of a proud and good man.*

In addition to scenes such as this, writers can use figurative language such as metaphor and analogy to make the problem being addressed more vivid or real to the audience, or they can shift from abstract language to descriptions, dialogues, statistics, and illustrative narratives. Here is how one student used personal experience in the problem section of her proposal calling for redesign of the mathematics department's introductory calculus curriculum.

> My own experience in the Calculus 134 and 135 sequence last year showed me that it was not the learning of calculus that was difficult for me. I was able to catch on to the new concepts. The problem for me was in the fast pace. Just as I

---

*From William Edelen, *The Idaho Statesman.*

was assimilating new concepts and feeling the need to reinforce them, the class was on to a new topic before I had full mastery of the old concept. . . . Part of the reason for the fast pace is that calculus is a feeder course for computer science and engineering. If prospective engineering students can't learn the calculus rapidly, they drop out of the program. The high dropout rate benefits the Engineering School because they use the math course to weed out an overabundance of engineering applicants. Thus the pace of the calculus course is geared to the needs of the engineering curriculum, not to the needs of someone like me who wants to be a high school mathematics teacher and who believes that my own difficulties with math—combined with my love for it—might make me an excellent math teacher.

Here the writer creates presence through an effective *ethos:* She is not a complainer or whiner but a serious student genuinely interested in learning calculus. She has given presence to the problem by calling attention to it in a new way.

Overcoming the Natural Conservatism of People

Another difficulty faced by a proposal maker is the innate conservatism of all human beings, whatever their political persuasion. One philosopher refers to this conservatism as the law of inertia, the tendency of all things in the universe, including human beings, to remain at rest if possible. The popular adage "If it ain't broke, don't fix it" is one expression of this tendency. Hence, proposers of change face an extraordinary burden of proof. Specifically, they have to prove that something needs fixing, that it can be fixed, and that the cost of fixing it will be outweighed by the benefits of fixing it.

The difficulty of proving that something needs fixing is compounded by the fact that frequently the status quo appears to be working. So sometimes when writing a proposal, you can't argue that what we have is bad, but only that what we could have is better. Often, then, a proposal argument will be based not on present evils but on the evils of lost potential. And getting an audience to accept lost potential may be difficult indeed, given the inherently abstract nature of potentiality.

The Difficulty of Predicting Future Consequences

Further, most proposal makers will be forced to predict consequences of a given act. As we've seen in our earlier discussions of causality, it is difficult enough to argue backward from event Y in order to establish that X caused Y. Think how much harder it is to establish that X will, in the future, cause certain things to occur. We all know enough of history to realize that few major decisions have led neatly to their anticipated results. This knowledge indeed accounts for much of our conservatism. All the things that can go wrong in a causal argument can go wrong in a proposal argument as well; the major difference is that in a proposal argument we typically have less evidence for our conjectures.

The Problem of Evaluating Consequences

A final difficulty faced by all proposal arguments concerns the difficulty of evaluating the consequences of the proposal. In government and industry, managers often turn to a tool known as *cost-benefit analysis* to calculate the potential consequences of a given proposal. As much as possible, a cost-benefit analysis tries to reduce all consequences to a single scale for purposes of comparison. Most often, the scale will be money. Although this scale may work well in some circumstances, it can lead to grotesquely inappropriate conclusions in other situations.

Just how does one balance the money saved by cutting Medicare benefits against the suffering of the people denied benefits? How does one translate the beauty of a wilderness area into a dollar amount? On this score, cost-benefit analyses often run into a problem discussed in the previous chapter: the seductiveness of empirical measures. Because something can't be readily measured doesn't mean it can be safely ignored. And finally, what will be a cost for one group will often be a benefit for others. For example, if social security benefits are cut, those on social security will suffer, but current workers who pay for it with taxes will take home a larger paycheck.

These, then, are some of the general difficulties facing someone who sets out to argue in favor of a proposal. Although not insurmountable, they are at least daunting. Given those difficulties, let's now set forth the writing assignment for this chapter and then turn to the question of how one might put together a proposal argument.

 ## WRITING ASSIGNMENT FOR CHAPTER 14: OPTIONS FOR PROPOSAL ARGUMENTS

OPTION 1: *A Practical Proposal Addressing a Local Problem*   Write a practical proposal offering a solution to a local problem. Your proposal should have three main sections: (1) description of the problem, (2) proposed solution, and (3) justification. You may include additional sections or subsections as needed. Longer proposals often include an *abstract* at the beginning of the proposal to provide a summary overview of the whole argument. (Sometimes called the *executive summary,* this abstract may be the only portion of the proposal read by high-level managers.) Sometimes proposals are accompanied by a *letter of transmittal*—a one-page business letter that introduces the proposal to its intended audience and provides some needed background about the writer.

Your proposal can be either an *action proposal,* in which you specify exactly the action that needs to be taken to solve the problem, or a *planning proposal,* in which you know what the problem is but don't yet know how to solve it. A planning proposal usually calls for the formation of a committee or task force to address the problem, so that your "solution" doesn't specify an actual solution but rather specifies the mission of the committee you want to establish. To make a planning proposal as effective as possible, you are wise to suggest several ideas for possible solutions—that is, several alternative courses of action that you want the committee to examine in more detail and refine. An example of a practical proposal with a planning focus is included at the end of this chapter ("A Proposal to Save Bernie's Blintzes Restaurant" by student writer Jeff Cain).

Document design is important in practical proposals, which are aimed at busy people who have to make many decisions under time constraints. Because the writer of a practical proposal usually produces the finished document (practical proposals are seldom submitted to newspapers or magazines for publication), he or she must pay particular attention to the attractive design of the document. An effective design helps establish the writer's *ethos* as a quality-oriented professional and helps make the reading of the proposal as easy as possible. Document design includes effective use of headings and subheadings, attractive typeface and layout, flawless editing, and other features enhancing the visual appearance of the document.*

OPTION 2: *A Policy Proposal as a Guest Editorial*   Write a two- to three-page policy proposal suitable for publication as a feature editorial in a college or city newspaper or in some publication associated with a particular group or activity such as a church newsletter or employee bulletin. By *feature editorial* we mean a well-developed argument as opposed to a short *opinion editorial* (also known as an *op-ed* piece) that simply sets forth an editorial view without development and support. The voice and style of your argument should be aimed at general readers of your chosen publication. Your editorial should have the following features:

1. The identification of a problem (Persuade your audience that this is a genuine problem that needs solving; give it presence.)
2. A proposal for action that will help alleviate the problem
3. A justification of your solution (the reasons that your audience should accept your proposal and act on it)

OPTION 3: *A Researched Argument Proposing Public Policy*   Write an eight- to twelve-page proposal argument as a formal research paper, using research data for support. (See Chapters 16 and 17 for advice on writing a researched argument.) Your argument should include all the features of the shorter argument in Option 2 and also a summary and refutation of opposing views (in the form of alternative proposals and/or differing cost-benefit analyses of your proposal). An example of a researched policy proposal is student writer Stephen Bean's "What Should Be Done about the Mentally Ill Homeless?" on pages 330–338.

---

*It is usually a mistake, however, to use all the bells and whistles available on recent hardware and software for desktop publishing. Different styles and sizes of fonts, fancy title pages, and extraneous visuals such as pointing fingers, daggers, stars, and so forth, make you look like a computer doodler rather than a serious writer. Tasteful, conservative use of boldface and underlining is usually the best approach. Even if you have available only a typewriter, you can create several levels of attractive headings by using different combinations of indentation, underlining, and capital letters.

DEVELOPING A PROPOSAL ARGUMENT

Writers of proposal arguments must focus in turn on three main phases or stages of the argument: showing that a problem exists, explaining the proposed solution, and offering a justification.

Convincing Your Readers That a Problem Exists

There is one argumentative strategy generic to all proposal arguments: awakening in the reader a sense of a problem. Typically, the development of a problem occurs in one of two places in a proposal argument—either in the introduction prior to the presentation of the arguer's proposal claim or in the body of the paper as the first main reason justifying the proposal claim. In the second instance the writer's first because clause has the following structure: "We should do X *because a problem exists (and X will solve it)."*

At this stage of your argument, it's important to give your problem presence. You must get people to see how the problem affects people, perhaps through examples of suffering or other loss or through persuasive statistics and so forth. Your goal is to awaken your readers to the existence of a problem, a problem they may well not have recognized before.

Besides giving presence to the problem, a writer must also gain the readers' intellectual assent to the depth, range, and potential seriousness of the problem. Suppose, for illustration, that you wanted to propose a special tax to increase funding for higher education in your state. In trying to convince taxpayers in your state that a problem exists, what obstacles might you face? First of all, many taxpayers never went to college and feel that they get along just fine without it. They tend to worry more about the quality of roads, social services, elementary and secondary schools, police and fire protection, and so forth. They are not too convinced that they need to worry about professors' salaries or better equipped research labs. Thus, it's not enough to talk about the importance of education in general or to cite figures showing how paltry your state's funding of higher education is.

To convince your audience of the need for your proposal, you'll have to describe the consequences of low funding levels in terms they can relate to. You'll have to show them that potential benefits to the state are lost because of inadequate funding. Perhaps you can show the cost in terms of inadequately skilled graduates, disgruntled teachers, high turnover, brain drain to other states, inadequate educational services to farmers and businesspeople, lost productivity, and so forth. Or perhaps you can show your audience examples of benefits realized from better college funding in other states. Such examples give life to the abstract notion of lost potential.

All of this is not to say that you can't or shouldn't argue that higher education is inherently good. But until your reader can see low funding levels as "problematic" rather than "simply the way things are," your proposal stands little chance of being enacted.

Showing the Specifics of Your Proposal

Having decided that there is a problem to be solved, you should lay out your thesis, which is a proposal for solving the problem. Your goal now is to stress the feasibility of your solution, including costs. The art of proposal making is the art of the possible. To be sure, not all proposals require elaborate descriptions of the implementation process. If you are proposing, for example, that a local PTA chapter should buy new tumbling mats for the junior high gym classes, the procedures for buying the mats will probably be irrelevant. But in many arguments the specifics of your proposal—the actual step-by-step methods of implementing it—may be instrumental in winning your audience's support.

You will also need to show how your proposal will solve the problem either partially or wholly. Sometimes you may first need to convince your reader that the problem is solvable, not something intractably rooted in "the way things are," such as earthquakes or jealousy. In other words, expect that some members of your audience will be skeptical about the ability of any proposal to solve the problem you are addressing. You may well need, therefore, to "listen" to this point of view in your refutation section and to argue that your problem is at least partially solvable.

In order to persuade your audience that your proposal can work, you can follow any one of several approaches. A typical approach is to lay out a causal argument showing how one consequence will lead to another until your solution is effected. Another approach is to turn to resemblance arguments, either analogy or precedent. You try to show how similar proposals have been successful elsewhere. Or, if similar things have failed in the past, you try to show how the present situation is different.

The Justification: Convincing Your Reader That Your Proposal Should Be Enacted

This phase of a proposal argument will need extensive development in some arguments and minimal development in others, again depending on your particular problem and the rhetorical context of your proposal. If your audience already acknowledges the seriousness of the problem you are addressing and has simply been waiting for the right solution to come along, then your argument will be successful so long as you can convince your audience that your solution will work and that it won't cost too much. Such arguments depend on the clarity of your proposal and the feasibility of its being implemented.

But what if the costs are high? Or what if your audience doesn't think that the problem you are addressing is particularly serious? In such cases you have to develop your main reasons for believing that X should be done. A good strategy is to use the three-step process described in Chapter 9 when you examined arguments from principle, from consequence, and from resemblance. Here are some examples of how the three-step strategy can be used for proposal arguments.

PROPOSAL CLAIM:	Our university should abolish fraternities and sororities.
PRINCIPLE:	because they are elitist (or "a thing of the past" or "racist" or "sexist" or whatever)
CONSEQUENCE:	because eliminating the Greek system will improve our school's academics (or "fill our dormitories," "allow us to experiment with new living arrangements," "replace rush with a better freshman orientation," and so forth)
RESEMBLANCE:	because other universities that have eliminated the Greek system have reported good results
PROPOSAL CLAIM:	We should eliminate mandatory busing of children to achieve racial equality.
PRINCIPLE:	because it is unjust (or "ineffective," "a misuse of judicial authority," "a violation of individual rights," and so forth)
CONSEQUENCE:	because it puts too many psychological burdens on kids (or "costs too much," "destroys neighborhood schools," "makes it difficult to have parental involvement in the schools," "splits up siblings," "causes kids to spend too much time on buses," and so forth)
RESEMBLANCE:	because busing schoolchildren to solve a social problem such as racism makes about as much sense as sending alcoholics' kids through a detox center to cure their parents
PROPOSAL CLAIM:	Our church should start an active ministry to AIDS patients.
PRINCIPLE:	because doing so would be an act of love (or "justice" or "an example of Christian courage," and so forth)
CONSEQUENCE:	because doing so will help increase community understanding of the disease and also reduce fear
RESEMBLANCE:	because Jesus ministered to the lepers and in our society AIDS victims have become the outcasts that lepers were in Jesus' society

Each of these arguments attempts to appeal to the value system of the audience. Each tries to show how the proposed action is within the class of things that the audience already values, will lead to consequences desired by the audience, or is similar to something the audience already values (or will alleviate something the audience disvalues).

Touching the Right Pressure Points

Having defined and weighed the problem, having worked out a feasible solution, and having motivated your audience to act on your proposal, you may well wish to take your argument a step further. You may thus have to determine who has the power to act on your proposal and apply arguments directly to that person's or agency's immediate interests. More than any other form of argument, a proposal argument needs finally to be addressed to those with the power to act on the proposal. You need to know to whom or to what your power source is beholden or responsive and what values your power source holds that can be appealed to. You're looking, in short, for pressure points.

While attempting to get a university to improve wheelchair access to the student union building, one student with multiple sclerosis discovered that the university had recently paid $100,000 to put oak trim in a new faculty office building. She knew officials were a bit embarrassed by that figure, and it became an effective pressure point for her essay. "The university can afford to pay $100,000 for oak trim for faculty, but can't spend one quarter of that amount helping its disabled students get full access to the student union building." This hard-to-justify discrepancy put considerable pressure on the administration to find money for more wheelchair ramps. The moral here is that it makes good sense to tie one's proposal as much as possible to the interests of those in power.

USING THE "STOCK ISSUES" STRATEGY TO DEVELOP A PROPOSAL ARGUMENT

An effective way to generate ideas for a proposal argument is to ask yourself a series of questions based on the "stock issues" strategy. Suppose, for example, you wanted to develop the following argument: "In order to solve the problem of students who won't take risks with their writing, the faculty at Weasel College should adopt a pass/fail method of grading in all writing courses." The stock issues strategy invites the writer to consider "stock" ways (that is, common, usual, frequently repeated ways) that such arguments can be conducted.

Stock issue 1: *Is there really a problem here that needs to be solved?* Is it really true that a large number of student writers won't take risks in their writing? Is this problem more serious than other writing problems such as undeveloped ideas, lack of organization, poor sentence structure, and so forth? This stock issue invites the writer to convince her audience that a true problem exists. Conversely, an opponent to the proposal might argue that a true problem does not exist.

Stock issue 2: *Will the proposed solution really solve this problem?* Is it true that a pass/fail grading system will cause students to take more risks with their writing? Will more interesting, surprising, and creative essays result from pass/fail grading? Or will students simply put less effort into their writing?

This stock issue prompts a supporter to demonstrate that the proposal will solve the problem; in contrast, it prompts the opponent to show that the proposal won't work.

Stock issue 3: *Can the problem be solved more simply without disturbing the status quo?* An opponent of the proposal might agree that a problem exists and that the proposed solution might solve it. However, the opponent might say, "Are there not less radical ways to solve this problem? If we want more creative and risk-taking student essays, can't we just change our grading criteria so that we reward risky papers and penalize conventional ones?" This stock issue prompts supporters to show that *only* the proposed solution will solve the problem and that no minor tinkering with the status quo will be adequate. Conversely, opponents will argue that the problem can be solved without acting on the proposal.

Stock issue 4: *Is the proposed solution really practical? Does it stand a chance of actually being enacted?* Here an opponent to the proposal might agree that the proposal would work but that it involves pie-in-the-sky idealism. Nobody will vote to change the existing system so radically; therefore, it is a waste of our time to debate it. Following this prompt, supporters would have to argue that pass/fail grading is workable and that enough faculty are disposed to it that the proposal is worth debating. Opponents might argue that the faculty at Weasel College are so traditional that pass/fail has utterly no chance of being accepted, despite its merits.

Stock issue 5: *What will be the unforeseen positive and negative consequences of the proposal?* Suppose we do adopt a pass/fail system. What positive or negative consequences might occur that are different from what we at first predicted? Using this prompt, an opponent might argue that pass/fail grading will reduce the effort put forth by students and that the long-range effect will be writing of even lower quality than we have now. Supporters would try to find positive consequences—perhaps a new love of writing for its own sake rather than the sake of a grade.

USING THE TOULMIN SCHEMA TO DEVELOP A PROPOSAL ARGUMENT

The Toulmin schema is also a helpful way to think through a proposal argument. Consider the following proposal argument laid out according to Toulmin's schema and later modified as a result of the Toulmin analysis:

INITIAL ENTHYMEME:	All college students should be required to take an ethics course because most students are not effective ethical thinkers and because an ethics course would help solve this problem.

CLAIM:	All college students should be required to take an ethics course.
STATED REASONS:	(a) Students are not effective thinkers about ethical issues; (b) An ethics course will help solve this problem.
GROUNDS:	(a) evidence that college students lack the ability to think effectively about ethical issues; (b) evidence that ethics courses help students think more effectively about ethical issues (e.g., pre- and post-course tests asking students to think coherently about ethical issues; follow-up studies of students who take ethics courses and a control group of students who don't take ethics to see if there are significant differences in ethical behavior)
WARRANT FOR BOTH A AND B:	The ability to think effectively about ethical issues is such an important skill that a proposal to develop that skill should be enacted.
BACKING:	evidence of the benefits of ethical thinking and the costs of ineffective ethical thinking
CONDITIONS OF REBUTTAL:	examples of people who've studied ethics and have been incapable of effective ethical thinking, of effective ethical thinkers who've never had a course in college ethics (perhaps it is the home or the church that teaches ethical thinking, not a college course), or of societies in which effective ethical thinking has not led to the promised benefits
QUALIFIERS:	a statement to the effect that college ethics courses will make it "more likely" that students can think effectively about ethical issues and that more effective ethical thinking will "probably" be beneficial to society

The stated reasons in support of the claim are evaluation and causal claims. The first stated reason—college students are not effective ethical thinkers—is an evaluative claim that requires the writer to create criteria for effective ethical thinking and to show that today's students don't meet the criteria. The second claim—that a course in ethics will help solve this problem—is a causal one and forces the writer to provide evidence that the course will work. The conditions for rebuttal highlight potential weaknesses in the stated reasons and grounds because they point out so many possible exceptions—people who think ethically without taking an ethics course, people who take an ethics course and still don't think ethically, and so forth. The possibility that one really learns ethics in the home or church seems particularly troubling to the argument.

The main warrant for this proposal—that effective ethical thinking is good and that methods for developing it should therefore be enacted—also presents problems. Although your audience might grant that effective ethical thinking is a good thing, plenty of opponents will not grant that an ethics course should be required. Requiring students to take ethics courses means forcing them to forgo other courses, many of which can lay claim to being inherently good as well. Moreover, students uninterested in ethics and professors who don't teach ethics can't be expected to accept the proposal readily because they are the ones who will bear most of the "costs" of implementing it. So the writer has a considerable burden of proof in getting his readers to accept the warrant.

Seeing the argument displayed this way, the writer decided that more support was needed in two places: First, the writer had to find more evidence that ethics courses really work. Second, the writer had to provide a more convincing argument that the benefits of an ethics course were significant enough to justify a required course for all students. The writer decided to do more research into contemporary problems caused by poor ethical thinking in order to bolster his argument that such a course would bring long-range benefits to society. To strengthen his case further, he decided to argue also that ethics courses would in general make for more thoughtful and questioning students. Finally, he turned to a resemblance argument by citing precedents at many liberal arts colleges around the nation where required courses in ethics have been enacted.

 FOR CLASS DISCUSSION

The following collaborative task takes approximately two class days to complete. The exercise takes you through the process of creating a proposal argument.

1. In small groups, identify and list several major problems facing students in your college or university.

2. Decide among yourselves which are the most important of these problems and rank them in order of importance.

3. Take your group's number one problem and explore answers to the following questions. Group recorders should be prepared to present your group's answers to the class as a whole:
   a. Why is the problem a problem?
   b. For whom is the problem a problem?
   c. How will these people suffer if the problem is not solved? (Give specific examples.)
   d. Who has the power to solve the problem?
   e. Why hasn't the problem been solved up to this point?
   f. How can the problem be solved? (That is, create a proposal.)

g. What are the probable benefits of acting on your proposal?

h. What costs are associated with your proposal?

i. Who will bear those costs?

j. Why should this proposal be enacted?

k. Why is it better than alternative proposals?

4. As a group, draft an outline for a proposal argument in which you:

a. Describe the problem and its significance.

b. Propose your solution to the problem.

c. Justify your proposal by showing how the benefits of adopting that pro-posal outweigh the costs.

5. Recorders for each group should write their group's outline on the board and be prepared to explain it to the class.

WRITING THE PROPOSAL ARGUMENT

Starting Points: Finding a Proposal Issue   Since "should" or "ought" issues are among the most common sources of arguments, you may already have good ideas for proposal issues. To think of topics for practical proposals, try making an idea map of local problems you would like to see solved. For initial spokes, try trigger words such as the following: problems at my university (dorms, parking, registra-tion system, grading system, campus appearance, clubs, curriculum, intramural program, football team); problems in my city or town (dangerous intersections, ugly areas, inadequate lighting, a poorly designed store, a shopping center that needs a specific improvement); problems at my place of work (office design, flow of customer traffic, merchandise display, company policies, customer relations); or problems related to my hobbies, recreational time, life as a consumer, life as a homeowner, and so forth. If you can offer a solution to the problem you identify, consider an action proposal. If you can't solve the problem but believe it is worth serious attention, consider a planning proposal.

To find a topic for policy proposals, stay in touch with the news, which will keep you aware of current debates on regional and national issues. Skimming re-cent issues of *Time* or *Newsweek*, thumbing through a recent *Wall Street Journal,* or looking at the table of contents in public policy magazines such as *The Atlantic, The New Republic, National Review,* and others will also give you excellent leads.

You can also try freewriting in response to trigger questions such as these:

- I would really like to solve the problem of . . .

- I believe that X should . . . [substitute for X words such as *my teachers, the president, the school administration, Congress, my boss,* and so forth]

Exploration Stage   Once you have decided on a proposal issue, we recommend you explore it by trying one or more of the following activities:

Explore ideas by using the "stock issues" strategy. Much of what we say about proposal arguments in this chapter has been influenced by the stock issues questions: (1) Is there really a problem here that has to be solved? (2) Will the proposed solution really solve this problem? (3) Can the problem be solved in a simpler way without disturbing the status quo? (4) Is the proposed solution practical enough that it really stands a chance of being acted upon? (5) What will be the positive and negative consequences of the proposal?

Explore your problem by freewriting answers to the eleven questions (3a–k) in the preceding For Class Discussion exercise. These questions cover the same territory as the stock issues strategy, but the arrangement and number of questions might stimulate additional thought.

Explore ideas for the justification section of your proposal by using the three-step strategy introduced in Chapter 9. Briefly, this strategy invites you to justify your proposal to do X by arguing (1) that doing X is the right thing to do in principle, (2) that doing X will lead to various good consequences, and (3) that doing X (or something similar) has been done with good results elsewhere or that doing X is like doing Y, which we agree is good. This strategy is particularly powerful for proposal arguments because it focuses on finding audience-based reasons.

Explore ideas for your argument by completing the eight exploratory tasks in Chapter 3 (pp. 73–74).

Writing the Discovery Draft: Some Ways to Organize a Proposal Argument   When you write your discovery draft, you may find it helpful to have at hand some plans for typical ways of organizing a proposal argument. What follows are two common methods of organization. Option 1 is the plan most typical for practical proposals. Either Option 1 or Option 2 is an effective plan for a policy proposal.

OPTION 1

- Presentation of a problem that needs solving:
     description of problem (give problem presence)
     background, including previous attempts to solve problem
     argument that the problem is solvable (optional)
- Presentation of writer's proposal:
     succinct statement of the proposed solution serves as thesis statement
     explain specifics of proposed solution
- Summary and rebuttal of opposing views (in practical proposals, this section is often a summary and rejection of alternative ways of solving the problem)

- Justification persuading reader that proposal should be enacted:
    - Reason 1 presented and developed
    - Reason 2 presented and developed
    - and so forth
- Conclusion that exhorts audience to act (Give presence to final sentences.)

OPTION 2

- Presentation of issue, including background
- Presentation of writer's proposal
- Justification
    - Reason 1:   Show that proposal addresses a serious problem.
    - Reason 2:   Show that proposal will solve problem.
    - Reason 3:   Give additional reasons for enacting proposal.
- Summary and refutation of opposing views
- Conclusion that exhorts audience to act

Revision Stage   Once you have written a discovery draft and have begun to clarify your argument for yourself, you are ready to begin making your argument clear and persuasive for your readers. Once again, exploring your argument using the Toulmin schema should prove useful. Pay particular attention to the ways a skeptical audience might rebut your argument.

CONDITIONS FOR REBUTTAL: TESTING YOUR PROPOSAL ARGUMENT

As we've suggested throughout the foregoing discussion, proposal arguments are vulnerable on many grounds—the innate conservatism of most people, the difficulty of clearly anticipating all the consequences of the proposal, and so forth. What questions, then, can one put specifically to proposal arguments to help us anticipate these vulnerabilities?

Will My Audience Deny That My Problem Is Really a Problem?

The first question to ask of your proposal is "What's so wrong with the status quo that change is necessary?" The second question is "Who loses if the status quo is changed?" Be certain not to overlook this second question. Most proposal makers can demonstrate that some sort of problem exists, but often it is a problem only for certain groups of people. Solving the problem will thus prove a benefit to some people but a cost to others. If your audience examines the problem from the perspective of the potential losers rather than the winners, they can often raise doubts about your proposal.

For example, one state recently held an initiative on a proposed "bottle bill" that would fight litter by permitting the sale of soda and beer only in returnable bottles. Sales outlets would be required to charge a substantial deposit on the bottles in order to encourage people to return them. Proponents of the proposal emphasized citizens as "winners" sharing in the new cleanliness of a landscape no longer littered with cans. To refute this argument, opponents showed consumers as "losers" burdened with the high cost of deposits and the hassle of collecting and returning bottles to grocery stores.

Will My Audience Doubt the Effectiveness of My Solution?

Assuming that you've satisfied yourself that a significant problem exists for a significant number of people, a number of questions remain to be asked about the quality of the proposed solution to solve the problem. First, "Does the problem exist for the reasons cited, or might there be alternative explanations?" Here we return to the familiar ground of causal arguments. A proposal supposedly strikes at the cause of a problem. But perhaps striking at that "cause" won't solve the problem. Perhaps you've mistaken a symptom for a cause, or confused two commonly associated but essentially unlinked phenomena for a cause-effect relationship. For example, will paying teachers higher salaries improve the quality of teaching or merely attract greedier rather than brighter people? Maybe more good teachers would be attracted and retained if they were given some other benefit (fewer students? smaller classes? more sabbaticals? more autonomy? more prestige?).

Another way to test your solution is to list all the uncertainties involved. This might be referred to as the "The Devil you know is better than the Devil you don't know" strategy. Remind yourself of all the unanticipated consequences of past changes. Who, for example, would have thought back in the days when aerosol shaving cans were being developed that they might lead to diminished ozone layers, which might lead to more ultraviolet rays getting through the atmosphere from the sun, which would lead to higher incidences of skin cancer? The history of technology is full of such cautionary tales that can be invoked to remind you of the uncertain course that progress can sometimes take.

Will My Audience Think My Proposal Costs Too Much?

The most commonly asked question of any proposal is simply, "Do the benefits of enacting the proposal outweigh the costs?" As we saw above, you can't foresee all the consequences of any proposal. It's easy, before the fact, to exaggerate both the costs and the benefits of a proposal. So, in asking how much your proposal will cost, we urge you to make an honest estimate. Will your audience discover costs you hadn't anticipated—extra financial costs or unexpected psychological or environmental or aesthetic costs? As much as you can, anticipate these objections.

Will My Audience Suggest Counterproposals?

Related to all that's been said so far is the counterproposal. Can you imagine an appealing alternative to both the status quo and the proposal that you're making? The more clearly your proposal shows that a significant problem exists, the more important it is that you be able to identify possible counterproposals. Any potential critic of a proposal to remedy an acknowledged problem will either have to make such a counterproposal or have to argue that the problem is simply in the nature of things. So, given the likelihood that you'll be faced with a counterproposal, it only makes sense to anticipate it and to work out a refutation of it before you have it thrown at you. And who knows, you may end up liking the counterproposal better and changing your mind about what to propose!

 FOR CLASS DISCUSSION

The following proposal arguments—both by student writers—illustrate the range of proposal writing. The first argument is a practical proposal, the second a policy proposal. Both arguments are reproduced in typewriter format to illustrate conventional typescript form for formal papers. The first argument, as a practical proposal, uses heading and subheadings. When sent to the intended audience, it is accompanied by a single-spaced letter of transmittal following the conventional format of a business letter. The second argument is a formal research paper using the documentation format of the Modern Language Association (MLA). A full explanation of this format occurs in Chapter 17.* Working in groups, identify the argumentation strategies used by each writer. Specifically, be able to answer the following questions:

1. Does the writer demonstrate that a problem exists? What strategies does the writer use to demonstrate the problem?

2. Does the writer persuade you that the proposed solution will solve the problem? What strategies does the writer use to try to persuade you that the solution will work?

3. Does the writer attempt to listen to opposing views? How successful is the writer in refuting those views? What strategies does the writer use?

4. Does the writer argue effectively that the solution should be enacted? Does the writer use arguments from principle? from consequence? from resemblance?

5. How would you try to refute each writer's argument?

---

*Stephen Bean's essay attempts to refute a proposal argument by Charles Krauthammer, "How to Save the Homeless Mentally Ill," which is reprinted in Chapter 10 (pages 221–227). Bean's method of refutation is to propose a counterproposal. Both Bean's and Krauthammer's arguments are examples of proposals.

August 30, 1996

Jeffrey Cain
515 West Olympic Pl.
Seattle, Washington
98119

Martin _____
Owner, Bernie's Blintzes Restaurant
1201 10th Avenue
Seattle, Washington 98185

Dear Mr. _____:

Enclosed is a proposal that addresses Bernie's Blintzes present economic trouble. It provides an inexpensive alternative to the $60,000 "makeover" plan proposed by the recently hired restaurant consultant. Having been an employee of Bernie's Blintzes for over three years, and having previously been an employee of a catering business, I hope that my observations will be of some interest and help to you.

In brief, my proposal suggests that investing $60,000 into a complete restaurant upgrade not only exposes you to unnecessary economic risk, but also fails to build on Bernie's Blintzes' strengths and sixteen-year legacy. Instead, I propose that through the production and distribution of Bernie's Blintzes' chocolate chip cookies to area espresso stands and coffee shops, Bernie's Blintzes restaurant can reestablish itself as a viable money making business. Unlike the consultant's proposal, this plan recommends that Bernie's Blintzes build on what it has done well for sixteen years, preserving an important part of Seattle's Jewish culture—something I know that is important to you.

As a member of the Bernie's Blintzes staff, I share your interest in keeping the restaurant economically viable. I hope my thoughts are of some benefit. Thank you for your consideration.

Sincerely,

Jeffrey Cain

A PROPOSAL TO SAVE
BERNIE'S BLINTZES RESTAURANT

Submitted to the Owner, Mr. Martin _____

Jeffrey Cain

Summary

This proposal argues that investing $60,000 into a complete restaurant upgrade not only exposes the owners of Bernie's Blintzes restaurant to unnecessary economic risk, it also fails to build on Bernie's Blintzes' strengths and sixteen-year legacy. Instead, I propose that through the production and distribution of Bernie's Blintzes' chocolate chip cookies to area espresso stands and coffee shops, Bernie's Blintzes restaurant can reestablish itself as a viable money making business.

1

Problem

Bernie's Blintzes restaurant is currently in financial crisis and must either close its doors or substantially increase its sales and profits.

2

Background on Bernie's Blintzes Restaurant

For over sixteen years Bernie's Blintzes restaurant has been serving traditional kosher-style food in a family dining atmosphere in Seattle's Queen Anne district. Known for its excellent matzoh ball soup, blintzes, potato latkes, pastrami sandwiches, and giant chocolate chip cookies, Bernie's Blintzes remains one of Seattle's only family-operated ethnic Jewish restaurants. In addition to providing sit-down and take-out dining, Bernie's Blintzes also offers an extensive catering service that has steadily grown since its inception five years ago.

3

During the past two years, however, a slow but constant decrease in restaurant patronage has led to a decline in Bernie's Blintzes' sales and profits. In an effort to reestablish their restaurant as a money-making business, the owners of Bernie's Blintzes have employed the professional services of a restaurant consultant. After three months of observation and study, the consultant identified three areas that have led to Bernie's Blintzes' decline in patronage: (1) increased competition with the addition of seven new restaurants in the neighborhood over the past three years; (2) menu items that are out of fashion with health-conscious consumers; (3) a lack of marketing and name familiarity—although Bernie's Blintzes is well known around the neighborhood, few in the greater Seattle area would recognize its name. As a remedy, the consultant has recommended a $60,000 restaurant upgrade, including a complete interior remodel, new menu, and an advertising and marketing plan that would include changing Bernie's Blintzes name and logo. In short, the consultant envisions an entirely new restaurant: rebuilding Bernie's Blintzes from the ground up.

4

Problems with the Consultant's Proposal

5   A continued loss of patronage would certainly force the owners of Bernie's Blintzes to discontinue their sixteen-year-old labor; yet the prospect of investing $60,000 into a completely "new" restaurant brings economic risk and great uncertainty. A $60,000 investment would require the owners to assume a second home mortgage, and there are certainly no guarantees that their investment would pay off. The owners are rightfully apprehensive. But putting economic considerations aside for the moment, the consultant's "ground-up" proposal also brings great uncertainty because it fails to build on Bernie's Blintzes' strengths in three significant ways.

6   <u>First, increased competition is not necessarily a bad thing</u>. Paragon consultants are correct in observing that new restaurants have brought more competition to Bernie's Blintzes' neighborhood, but these same new restaurants have also brought more potential customers. Bernie's Blintzes' sixteen-year tenure in the neighborhood is a strength that could lure some of the neighborhood's new visitors. A well-established restaurant is a welcome respite from today's ever-changing fast-food culture.

7   <u>Second, a dated menu can be advantageous</u>. While it may be true that consumers have become more health conscious, it is also the case that consumers have become more aware of ethnic cuisine—consider the popularity of Thai food. Bernie's Blintzes' traditional kosher-style menu is a rarity in Seattle and may be a welcome alternative to other more familiar ethnic foods, like Chinese or Mexican.

8   <u>Finally, new isn't always better</u>. The consultant rightfully recognizes that Bernie's Blintzes has poor name familiarity throughout the city; however, it does have strong name familiarity within its neighborhood. Changing Bernie's Blintzes' name, as the consultant's proposal calls for, would take away whatever name familiarity that already exists, obscuring what for some is a local landmark.

9   A proposal that builds on Bernie's Blintzes' existing strengths could be less risky and certainly less expensive than the consultant's plan.

Proposal

10   This proposal is offered as a cost-effective, low-risk alternative to the consultant's plan that would utilize Bernie's Blintzes' existing facilities, build on its time-tested strengths, and maintain its traditional ethnic cuisine and character. The nucleus of this proposal involves the production and distribution of Bernie's Blintzes' chocolate

chip cookies to area espresso carts and coffee shops. This plan capitalizes on the popularity of Bernie's Blintzes' cookies and the booming espresso cart and coffee shop industry in Seattle.

Bernie's Blintzes' chocolate chip cookies are well known to customers as "the best coffee cookies in the world." This is because unlike other cookies, Bernie's Blintzes' cookies are a little harder than most, making them excellent for dipping into a hot cup of coffee. It is not unusual for customers to special-order a dozen cookies to have with their coffee at home, and at catering events the cookies quickly disappear when coffee is served.   11

Bernie's Blintzes' chocolate chip cookies are a perfect match for the booming coffee industry in the greater Seattle area. Espresso stands and coffee shops decorate nearly every public place in Seattle, from schools and gas stations to shopping malls and street corners. In addition to selling coffee products, these coffee vendors also sell pastries and sweets. Some carts sell in excess of 200 cookies a week. With very few companies currently distributing quality pastries to espresso carts, the potential for the owners of Bernie's Blintzes to tap into this new and growing market is excellent.   12

Because Bernie's Blintzes already has the means for cookie production, this plan could begin almost immediately. Presently, the restaurant experiences slow hours during the evening and in between lunches when restaurant employees, particularly kitchen staff, have little to do. During this slow time, employees could assist in the production of the chocolate chip cookies, particularly kitchen personnel. Orders for the cookies would be taken via phone or fax by employees who are already being paid. If cookie production exceeded the amount of time that employees who were already on the clock were available, then extended working hours could be offered to existing employees without having to hire new help, at least initially. Delivery would be made the following morning, within twenty-four hours. (The cookies would be delivered, until it became necessary to hire a new employee, by the owner—reducing costs and ensuring positive customer relations.)   13

At least initially, then, the labor cost involved in producing the cookies would be minimal. Therefore, the cookies could continue to sell at their present retail price of $.75, maintaining a $.45 net profit on each cookie. With this scenario, it may be possible to lower the wholesale price of the cookie to $.50. However, it is recommended that Bernie's Blintzes increase the retail price of its cookies to   14

$1.00 instead, with a wholesale price of $.75. A random sampling of area espresso carts reveals that most carts market their cookies for $1.00 to $1.50, some as high as $1.75. In raising the retail cost of the cookie to $1.00 and the wholesale cost to $.75, Bernie's Blintzes would be announcing its cookie as a "high-end" cookie that is competitively priced. Cookies at a wholesale price of $1.00 would realize a $.70 net profit.

15   Distribution to ten coffee carts that each sold 100 cookies a week would yield $700.00, weekly. Given the hundreds of coffee carts in the greater Seattle area, it is likely that Bernie's Blintzes' distribution would far exceed ten coffee carts. Thus, there is a genuine opportunity to make a substantial amount of money from a product that Bernie's Blintzes is already producing. Yet the benefits from such a simple endeavor would far exceed the monetary profit from each cookie.

Justification

16   In several important ways, the production and distribution of Bernie's Blintzes' chocolate chip cookies would help restore Bernie's Blintzes to financial prosperity.

17   First, this proposal builds on existing strengths. Bernie's Blintzes' chocolate chip cookies have already been market tested—sixteen years of experience shows that Bernie's Blintzes' cookies sell. Moreover, establishing a cookie distribution system would open the door for Bernie's Blintzes to distribute more of its other time tested items, like its famous matzoh ball soup. Also, distribution need not be limited to Seattle; in time, Bernie's Blintzes' cookies could be distributed throughout the region.

18   Second, initial costs and risks are very low. Because producing chocolate chip cookies takes advantage of existing facilities and labor, the cookies could be distributed and marketed at a very competitive rate, allowing Bernie's Blintzes to establish itself in a citywide market at a nominal cost—producing and distributing cookies would not require a second mortgage.

19   Third, cookie distribution would increase name familiarity. Each cookie would carry a label on one side that would include the Bernie's Blintzes logo, phone number and address. Coffee drinkers across town will want to visit Bernie's Blintzes restaurant after they come to appreciate these fine cookies. Curious new visitors to the neighborhood will match the restaurant sign to the label on the cookie they purchased at the espresso cart near their home. Another label on the other side of the cookie could promote Bernie's Blintzes' catering and specialty menu items.

<u>Finally, Bernie's Blintzes could continue to do what it does best: serve</u>   20
<u>traditional kosher-style food</u>. Unlike the consultant's proposal, this plan allows
Bernie's Blintzes to build on what it has done well for sixteen years, preserving an
important part of Seattle's Jewish culture.

Skeptics may criticize a plan such as this because it is simplistic in appearance.   21
After all, it does seem somewhat "starry-eyed" to think that chocolate chip cookies
could be the source of economic prosperity. Yet one might consider the millions of
dollars made today by Famous Amos Cookies, a company that began on nothing
more than a dream and a kitchen in a garage. Sometimes the most effective plans
are the simplest ones.

Conclusion

By building on existing strengths and doing what Bernie's Blintzes has been doing   22
well for sixteen years, the owners of Bernie's Blintzes restaurant can reestablish it
as a profitable business. Producing and distributing chocolate chip cookies
addresses Bernie's Blintzes' shortcomings while building on its strengths, and in
contrast to the Paragon plan, this proposal can be executed immediately with a
nominal investment.

Stephen Bean
Professor Arness
English 110
June 1, 1993

What Should Be Done about the Mentally Ill Homeless?

1   Winter paints Seattle's streets gray with misting rain that drops lightly but
steadily into pools. Walking to work through one of Seattle's oldest districts, Pioneer
Square, I see an incongruous mixture of people: both successful business-types
and a large population of homeless. Some walk to offices or lunches grasping cups
of fresh ground coffee; others slowly push wobbling carts containing their earthly
possessions wrapped carefully in black plastic. These scenes of homelessness have
become common throughout America's urban centers—so common, perhaps, that
despite our feelings of guilt and pity, we accept the presence of the homeless as
permanent. The empty-stomach feeling of confronting a ragged panhandler has
become an often accepted fact of living in the city. What can we do besides giving
a few cents spare change?

2   Recently, a growing number of commentators have been focusing on the
mentally ill homeless. In response to the violent murder of an elderly person by
a homeless mentally ill man, New York City recently increased its efforts to locate
and hospitalize dangerous homeless mentally ill individuals. New York's plan will
include aggressive outreach—actively going out into the streets and shelters to
locate mentally ill individuals and then involuntarily hospitalizing those deemed
dangerous either to others or themselves (Dugger, "Danger" B1). Although the
New York Civil Liberties Union has objected to this action on the grounds that
involuntary hospitalization may violate the rights of the mentally ill, many applaud
the city's action as a first step in dealing with a problem which the nation has
grossly ignored. One highly influential commentator, Charles Krauthammer, has
recently called for widescale involuntary reinstitutionalization of the mentally ill
homeless—a seemingly persuasive proposal until one begins to do research on the
mentally ill homeless. Adopting Krauthammer's proposal would be a dangerous and
wrong-headed policy for America. Rather, research shows that community-based
care in which psychiatrists and social workers provide coordinated services in the

Bean 2

community itself is a more effective solution to the problems of the mentally ill homeless than widescale institutionalization.

In his article "How to Save the Homeless Mentally Ill," Charles Krauthammer argues that the federal government should assist the states in rebuilding a national system of asylums. He proposes that the criteria for involuntary institutionalization be broadened: The state should be permitted to institutionalize mentally ill persons involuntarily not only if they are deemed dangerous to others or themselves (the current criterion for institutionalization) but also if they are "degraded" or made helpless by their illness. He points to the large number of patients released from state institutions in the 60s and 70s who, finding no support in communities, ended up on the streets. Arguing that the mentally ill need the stability and supervision that only an institution can provide, Krauthammer proposes substantial increases in federal taxes to fund rebuilding of asylums. He argues that the mentally ill need unique solutions because of their unique problems; their homelessness, he claims, stems from mental illness not poverty. Finally, Krauthammer rebuts the argument that involuntary hospitalization violates civil liberties. He argues that "liberty" has no meaning to someone suffering from severe psychosis. To let someone suffer the pains of mental illness and the pains of the street when they could be treated and recover is a cruel right indeed. He points to the project HELP program where less than a fifth of those involuntarily hospitalized protested their commitment; most are glad, he claims, for a warm bed, nutritious food, and a safe environment.

Krauthammer's argument, while persuasive on first reading, is based on four seriously flawed assumptions. His first assumption is the widely accepted notion that deinstitutionalization of state mental hospitals in the 1960s and 70s is a primary cause of the current homelessness problem in America. Krauthammer talks about the hundreds of thousands released from the hospitals who have become "an army of grate-dwellers" (24). However, recent research has shown that the relationship of deinstitutionalization to homelessness is vastly overstated. Ethnologist Kim Hopper argues that while deinstitutionalization has partly contributed to increased numbers of mentally ill homeless its influence is far smaller than popularly believed. She argues that the data many used to support this claim were methodologically flawed and that researchers who found symptoms of mental illness in homeless people didn't try to ascertain whether these symptoms were the cause or effect of living on the street. Finally, she points out that a lag time of five years existed between the major release of state hospital patients and the rise of mentally ill individuals in shelters. This time lag suggests that other social and economic factors might have come into play to account for the rise of homelessness (Hopper 156–57). Carl Cohen and Kenneth Thompson also point to this time lag as evidence to reject deinstitutionalization as the major cause of mentally ill homelessness (817). Jonathan Kozol argues that patients released from state hospitals in the late sixties and early seventies didn't go directly to the streets but went to single-room occupancy housing, such as cheap hotels or boarding houses. Many of these ex-patients became homeless, he argues, when almost half of single-room occupancy housing was replaced by more expensive housing between 1970 and 1980 (Kozol 18). The effects of this housing shortage might account for the lag time that Hopper and Cohen and Thompson cite.

5   Krauthammer's focus on mental illness as a cause of much of the homelessness problem leads to another of the implicit assumptions in his argument: that the mentally ill comprise a large percentage of the homeless population. Krauthammer avoids mentioning specific numbers until the end of his article when he writes:

> The argument over how many of the homeless are mentally ill is endless.
> The estimates, which range from one-quarter to three-quarters, vary with
> method, definition, and ideology. But so what if even the lowest estimates
> are right? Even if treating the mentally ill does not end homelessness,
> how can that possibly justify not treating the tens, perhaps hundreds
> of thousands who would benefit from a partial solution? (25)

This paragraph is rhetorically shrewd. It downplays the numbers issue and takes the moral high road. But by citing estimates between one-quarter and three-quarters, Krauthammer effectively suggests that a neutral estimate might place the number around fifty percent—a high estimate reinforced by his leap from "tens" to "perhaps hundreds of thousands" in the last sentence.

6   Close examination of the research, however, reveals that the percentage of mentally ill people on the streets may be even lower than Krauthammer's lowest figure of 25%. In an extensive study conducted by David Snow and colleagues, a team member lived among the homeless for 12 months to collect data on mental illness. Additionally, the researchers tracked the institutional histories of a random

sample of homeless. The study found that only 10% of the street sample and 16% of the tracking sample showed mental illness. The researchers pointed to a number of reasons why some previous estimates and studies may have inflated the numbers of mentally ill homeless. They suggest that the visibility of the mentally ill homeless (their odd behaviors make them stand out) combined with the widespread belief that deinstitutionalization poured vast numbers of mentally ill onto the streets caused researchers to bias their data. Thus researchers would often interpret behavior such as socially inappropriate actions, depression, and sleeping disorders as indications of mental illness, when in fact these actions may simply be the natural response to living in the harsh environment of the street. Additionally, the Snow study points to the medicalization of homelessness. This phenomenon means that when doctors and psychiatrists treat the homeless they focus on their medical and psychological problems while ignoring their social and economic ones. Because studies of the mentally ill homeless have been dominated by doctors and psychologists, these studies tend to inflate the numbers of mentally ill on the streets (Snow et al. 419–21).

Another persuasive study showing low percentages of mentally ill homeless—   7
although not as low as Snow's estimates—comes from Deborah Dennis and colleagues who surveyed the past decade of research on mentally ill homeless. The combined findings of all these research studies suggest that the mentally ill comprise between 28% and 37% of the homeless population (Dennis et al. 1130). Thus we see that while the mentally ill make up a significant proportion of the homeless population they do not approach a majority as Krauthammer and others would have us believe.

Krauthammer's third assumption is that the causes of homelessness among   8
the mentally ill are largely psychological rather than socioeconomic. By this thinking, the solutions to their problems involve the treatment of their illnesses rather than the alleviation of poverty. Krauthammer writes, "Moreover, whatever solutions are eventually offered the non-mentally ill homeless, they will have little relevance to those who are mentally ill" (25). Closer examination, however, shows that other factors play a greater role in causing homelessness among the mentally ill than mental illness. Jonathan Kozol argues that housing and the economy played the largest role in causing homelessness among the mentally ill. He points to two million jobs lost every year since 1980, an increase in poverty, a massive shortage

in low income housing, and a drop from 500,000 subsidized private housing units to 25,000 during the Reagan era (Kozol 17–18). Cohen and Thompson also place primary emphasis on poverty and housing shortages:

> Data suggest that most homeless mentally ill persons lost their rooms in single-room-occupancy hotels or low-priced apartments not because of psychoticism but because they 1) were evicted because of renewal projects and fires, 2) were victimized by unscrupulous landlords or by other residents, or 3) could no longer afford the rent. (818)

Douglas Mossman and Michael Perlin cite numerous studies which show that mental illness itself is not the primary factor causing homelessness among the mentally ill; additionally, they point out that the severity of mental illness itself is closely linked to poverty. They argue that lack of private health care increases poor health and the frequency of severe mental illness. They conclude, "Homelessness is, if nothing else, a condition of poverty, and poor individuals in general are at increased risk for episodes of psychiatric illness" (Mossman and Perlin 952). Krauthammer's article conveniently ignores the role of poverty, suggesting that much of the homeless problem could be solved by moving the mentally ill back into institutions. But the evidence suggests that symptoms of mental illness are often the <u>results</u> of being homeless and that any efforts to treat the psychological problems of the mentally ill must also address the socioeconomic problems.

9   Krauthammer's belief that the causes of mentally ill homelessness are psychological rather than social and economic leads to a fourth assumption that the mentally ill homeless are a distinct subgroup who need different treatment from the other homeless groups. Krauthammer thus divides the homeless into three primary groups: (1) the mentally ill; (2) those who choose to live on the street; and (3) "the victims of economic calamity, such as family breakup or job loss" (25). By believing that the mentally ill homeless are not also victims of "economic calamity," Krauthammer greatly oversimplifies their problems. As Cohen and Thompson show, it is difficult to separate the mentally ill homeless and the non-mentally ill homeless. "On closer examination, 'not mentally ill' homeless people have many mental health problems; similarly, the 'mentally ill' homeless have numerous nonpsychiatric problems that arise from the sociopolitical elements affecting all homeless people" (Cohen and Thompson 817). Because the

two groups are so similar, it is counterproductive to insist on entirely different solutions for both groups.

Krauthammer's proposal thus fails on a number of points. It won't solve nearly as much of the homelessness problem as he leads us to believe. It would commit valuable taxpayer dollars to building asylums rather than attacking the underlying causes of homelessness in general. And perhaps most importantly, its emphasis on involuntary confinement in asylums is not the best long-range method to treat the mentally ill homeless. Instead of moving the mentally ill homeless away from society into asylums, we would meet their needs far more effectively through monitored community-based care. Instead of building expensive institutions we should focus on finding alternative low cost housing for the mentally ill homeless and meet their needs through teams of psychiatrists and social workers who could oversee a number of patients' treatments, monitoring such things as taking medications and receiving appropriate counseling. Involuntary hospitalization may still be needed for the most severely deranged, but the majority of mentally ill homeless people can be better treated in their communities.

From a purely financial perspective, perhaps the most compelling reason to prefer community-based care is that it offers a more efficient use of taxpayer dollars. In a letter to the <u>New York Times</u> on behalf of the Project for Psychiatric Outreach to the Homeless, Drs. Katherine Falk and Gail Albert give us the following statistics:

> It costs $105,000 to keep someone in a state hospital for a year. But it costs only $15,000 to $35,000 (depending on the intensity of services) to operate supported residences in the community with the necessary onsite psychiatrists, case workers, case managers, drug counselors, and other rehabilitation services. (A30)

It can be argued, in fact, that the cost of maintaining state hospitals for the mentally ill actually prevents large numbers of mentally ill from receiving treatment. When large numbers of mentally ill persons were released from state hospitals during the deinstitutionalization movement of the 60s and 70s, the original plan was to convert resources to community-based care. Even though the number of patients in state institutions has dramatically decreased over the past two decades, institutions have continued to maintain large shares of state funding. According to David Rothman of Columbia University, "Historically, the dollars have remained locked in the institutions and did not go into community mental health" (qtd. in

Dugger, "Debate" B2). In fact, cutting New York's state hospital budget would provide enough money for over 20,000 units in supported community residences (Falk and Albert A30). Furthermore, Linda Chafetz points out that having the money to pay for such resources as clothes, bathing facilities, meals, and housing is the most urgent concern among caregivers in treating the mentally ill homeless. According to Chafetz, "The immediate and urgent nature of the resource dilemma can make other issues appear almost frivolous by comparison" (451). With such an obvious shortage of resources, pouring what money we have into the high-cost institutional system would be a grave disservice to the majority of the mentally ill homeless population and to the homeless population as a whole.

12   A second reason to adopt community-based care over widescale institutionalization is that the vast majority of the homeless mentally ill do not need the tight control of the hospital system. Cohen and Thompson cite a number of studies which show "that only 5%–7% of single adult homeless persons are in need of acute inpatient care" (820). Involuntarily hospitalizing a large number of homeless who don't demand institutionalized care is not only a waste of resources but also an unnecessary assault on individual freedom for many.

13   Finally, the community-based care system is preferable to institutionalization because it most often gives the best treatment to its patients. Although Krauthammer claims that less than a fifth of involuntarily hospitalized patients have legally challenged their confinement (25), numerous studies indicate there is widespread resistance to institutional care by the homeless mentally ill. Mossman and Perlin cite multiple sources indicating that many mentally ill have legitimate reasons to fear state hospitals. Moreover, they provide evidence that many would rather suffer the streets and their mental illness than suffer the conditions of state hospitals and the side effects of medications. The horrible track record of conditions of state hospitals supports the logic of this thinking. On the other hand, Mossman and Perlin point out many homeless mentally ill will accept treatment from the type of alternative settings community-based care offers (953). Further, Cohen and Thompson tell us that most mentally ill homeless don't see themselves as mentally ill; treatment has often left them feeling humiliated and disempowered (819). Obviously, these feelings of powerlessness would be exacerbated by forced institutionalization. Because the patient plays a large role in the success of his or

her treatment, these attitudes make a huge difference. In fact, Mossman and Perlin cite numerous sources that point to the success non-institutional approaches have had in integrating even the chronically mentally ill homeless into the community. For quality of care alone, Mossman and Perlin claim, community-based solutions are the best approach (953).

Given the advantages of community-based care, what is the appeal of Krauthammer's proposal? Involuntary institutionalization appeals to our common impulse to lock our problems out of sight. As crime increases, we want to build more prisons; when we see ragged men and women mumbling in the street, we want to shut them up in institutions. But the simple solutions are not often the most effective ones. Institutionalization is tempting, but alternative methods have shown themselves to be more effective. Community-based care works better because it's based on a better understanding of the problem. Community-based care, by allowing the psychiatrist and social worker to work together, attacks both the mental and social dimensions of the problem: the client not only receives psychological counseling and medication, but also help on how to find affordable housing, how to manage money and shop effectively, and how to live in a community. Without roots in a community, a patient released from a mental asylum will quickly return to the streets. To pour scarce resources into the expensive project of rebuilding asylums—helping the few while ignoring the many—would be a terrible misuse of taxpayer dollars.

Krauthammer's argument appeals in another way also. By viewing the homeless as mentally ill, we see them as inherently different from ourselves. We needn't see any connection to those mumbling bag ladies and those ragged men lying on the grates. When we regard them as mentally ill, we see ourselves as largely unresponsible for the conditions that led them to the streets. Those professional men and women carrying their espresso Starbuck's coffees to their upscale offices in Seattle's Pioneer Square don't have to be reminded that this historic district used to contain a number of single-occupancy boarding houses. The professionals work where the homeless used to live. The rich and the poor are thus interconnected, reminding us that homelessness is primarily a social and economic problem, not a mental health problem. And even the most deranged of the mentally ill homeless are messengers of a nationwide scourge of poverty.

Works Cited   Bean 9

Chafetz, Linda. "Withdrawal from the Homeless Mentally Ill." <u>Community Mental Health Journal</u> 26 (1990): 449–61.

Cohen, Carl I., and Kenneth S. Thompson. "Homeless Mentally Ill or Mentally Ill Homeless?" <u>American Journal of Psychiatry</u> 149 (1992): 816–23.

Dennis, Deborah L. et al. "A Decade of Research and Services for Homeless Mentally Ill Persons: Where Do We Stand?" <u>American Psychologist</u> 46 (1991): 1129–38.

Dugger, Celia W. "A Danger to Themselves and Others." <u>New York Times</u> 24 Jan. 1993: B1+.

———. "A Debate Unstilled: New Plan for Homeless Mentally Ill Does Not Address Larger Questions." <u>New York Times</u> 22 Jan. 1993: B2.

Falk, Katherine, and Gail Albert. Letter. <u>New York Times</u> 11 Feb. 1993: A30.

Hopper, Kim. "More than Passing Strangers: Homelessness and Mental Illness in New York City." <u>American Ethnologist</u> 15 (1988): 155–57.

Kozol, Jonathan. "Are the Homeless Crazy?" <u>Harper's Magazine</u> Sept. 1988: 17–19.

Krauthammer, Charles. "How to Save the Homeless Mentally Ill." <u>New Republic</u> 8 Feb. 1988: 22–25.

Mossman, Douglas, and Michael L. Perlin. "Psychiatry and the Homeless Mentally Ill: A Reply to Dr. Lamb." <u>American Journal of Psychiatry</u> 149 (1992): 951–56.

Snow, David A. et al. "The Myth of Pervasive Mental Illness among the Homeless." <u>Social Problems</u> 33 (1986): 407–23.

chapter **15**

Ethical
Arguments

The line between ethical arguments ("Is X morally good?") and other kinds of values disputes is often pretty thin. Many apparently straightforward practical values issues can turn out to have an ethical dimension. For example, in deciding what kind of car to buy, most people would base their judgments on criteria such as cost, reliability, safety, comfort, stylishness, and so forth. But some people might feel morally obligated to buy the most fuel-efficient car, or not to buy a car from a manufacturer whose investment or labor policies they found morally repugnant. Depending on how large a role ethical considerations played in the evaluation, we might choose to call this an *ethical argument* as opposed to a simpler kind of values argument. In any case, we here devote a separate chapter to ethical arguments because we believe they represent special difficulties to the student of argumentation. Let's take a look now at some of those special difficulties.

SPECIAL DIFFICULTIES OF
ETHICAL ARGUMENTS

One crucial difficulty with ethical arguments concerns the role of "purpose" in defining criteria for judgment. In Chapter 13, we assumed that every class of beings has a purpose, that the purpose should be defined as narrowly as possible, and that the criteria for judgment derive directly from that purpose. For example, the purpose of a computer repairperson is to analyze the problem with my computer, to fix it, and to do so in a timely and cost-efficient manner. Once I formulate this purpose, it is easy for me to define criteria for a good computer repairperson.

In ethics, however, the place of purpose is much fuzzier. Just what is the purpose of human beings? Before I can begin to determine what ethical duties I have to myself and to others, I'm going to have to address this question; and because the chance of reaching agreement on that question remains remote, many ethical arguments are probably unresolvable. In ethical discussions we don't ask what a "manager" or a "judge" or a "point guard" is supposed to do in situations relevant to the respective classes; we're asking what John Doe is supposed to be or what Jane Doe is supposed to do with her life. Who they are or what their social function is makes no difference to our ethical assessment of their actions or traits of character. A morally bad person may be a good judge and a morally good person may be a bad manager.

As the discussion so far has suggested, disagreements about ethical issues often stem from different systems of belief. We might call this problem the problem of warrants. This is, people disagree because they do not share common assumptions on which to ground their arguments.

If, for example, you say that good manners are necessary for keeping us from reverting to a state of raw nature, your implied warrant is that raw nature is bad. But if you say that good manners are a political tool by which a ruling class tries to suppress the natural vitality of the working class, then your warrant is that liberation of the working classes from the corrupt habits of the ruling class is good. It would be difficult, therefore, for people representing these opposing belief systems to carry on a reasonable discussion of etiquette—their whole assumptions about value, about the role of the natural self, and about political progress are different. This is why ethical arguments are often so acrimonious—they frequently lack shared warrants to serve as starting places for argument.

It is precisely because of the problem of warrants, however, that you should try to confront issues of ethics with rational deliberation. The arguments you produce may not persuade others to your view, but they should lay out more clearly the grounds and warrants of your own beliefs. Such arguments serve the purpose of clarification. By drafting essays on ethical issues, you begin to see more clearly what you believe and why you believe it. Although the arguments demanded by ethical issues require rigorous thought, they force us to articulate our most deeply held beliefs and our richest feelings.

AN OVERVIEW OF MAJOR ETHICAL SYSTEMS

When faced with an ethical issue, such as the issue of whether terrorism can be justified, we must move from arguments of good or bad to arguments of right or wrong. The terms *right* and *wrong* are clearly different from the terms *good* and *bad* when the latter terms mean simply "effective" (meets purposes of class, as in "This is a good stereo system") or "ineffective" (fails to meet purposes of class, as in "This is a bad cookbook"). But *right* and *wrong* often also differ from what seems to be a moral use of the terms *good* and *bad*. We might say, for example, that warm sunshine is good in that it brings pleasure and that cancer is bad in that it brings pain and death, but that is not quite the same thing as saying that sunshine is "right" and cancer is "wrong." It is the problem of "right" and "wrong" that ethical arguments confront.

Thus it is not enough to say that terrorism is "bad"; obviously everyone, including most terrorists, would agree that terrorism is "bad" in that it causes suffering and anguish. If we want to condemn terrorism on ethical grounds, we have to say that it's also "wrong" as well as "bad." In saying that something's wrong, we're saying that all people ought to refrain from doing it. We're also saying that acts that are morally "wrong" are in some way blameworthy and deserve censure, a conclusion that doesn't necessarily follow a negative nonethical judgment, which might lead simply to our not buying something or not hiring someone. From a nonethical standpoint, you may even say that someone like Abu Nidal is a "good" terrorist in that he fully realizes the purposes of the class "terrorist": He causes great damage with a minimum of resources, brings a good deal of attention to his cause, and doesn't (as of this writing) get caught. The ethical question here, however, is not whether or not Nidal is a good member of the class, but whether it is wrong for such a class to exist.

In asking the question "Ought the class 'terrorist' exist?" or, to put it more colloquially, "Are there ever cases where terrorism is justified?" we need to seek some consistent approach or principle. In the phrase used by some philosophers, ethical judgments are typically "universalizable" statements. That is, when we oppose a terrorist act, our ethical argument (assuming it's a coherent one) should be capable of being generalized into an ethical principle that will hold for all similar cases. Ethical disputes usually involve clashes between such principles. For example, a pro-terrorist might say, "My ends justify my means," whereas an antiterrorist might say, "The sanctity of human life is not to be violated for any reason." The differences in principles such as these account for different schools of ethical thought.

There are many different schools of ethical thought—too many to present in this chapter. But to help you think your way through ethical issues, we'll look at some of the most prevalent methods of resolving ethical questions. The first of these methods, "naive egoism," is really less a method than a retreat from method. It doesn't represent a coherent ethical view, but it is a position that many people lapse into on given issues. It represents, in short, the most seductive alternative to rigorous ethical thought.

Naive Egoism

Back in Chapter 1, we touched on the morality of the Sophists and suggested that their underlying maxim was something like "might makes right." That is, in ethical terms, they were essentially egoists who used other people with impunity to realize their own ends. The appeal of this position, however repugnant it may sound when laid out like this, is enormous. It is a rationalization for self-promotion and pleasure seeking. We are all prone to sink into it occasionally. In recent years, people have gotten rich by rationalizing this position into an "enlightened egoism" and by arguing, in numerous best-selling books with words like *Number One* or *Self* in the titles, that if we all follow the bidding of our egos, we'll be happy.

On closer examination, this philosophy proves to be incoherent, incapable of consistent application. Not many philosophers take it seriously, however persistently it returns with new sets of disciples. It should be noted, however, that philosophers don't reject naive egoism simply because they believe "selfishness is bad." Rather, philosophers tend to assess ethical systems according to such factors as their scope (how often will principles derived from a system provide a guide for our moral action?) and their precision (how clearly can we analyze a given situation using the tools of the system?) rather than their intuition about whether the system is right or wrong.

Although naive egoism has great scope (you can always ask "What's in it for me?"), it is far from precise, as we'll try to show. Take the case of young Ollie Unger, who has decided that he wants to quit living irrationally and to join some official school of ethical thought. The most appealing school at the moment—recommended to him by a philosophy major over at the Phi Upsilon Nu house—is the "I'm Number One!" school of scruples. He heads downtown to their opulent headquarters and meets with the school's guru, one Dr. Pheelgood.

"What's involved in becoming a member of your school?" Ollie inquires.

"Ahhh, my apple-cheeked chum, that's the beauty of it. It's so simple. You just give me all your worldly possessions and do whatever I tell you to do."

Ollie's puzzled. He had in mind something a bit more, well, gratifying. He was hoping for something closer to the *Playboy* philosophy of eat, drink and make merry—all justified through rational thought.

"You seem disappointed," Pheelgood observes. "What's the matter?"

"Well, gee, it just doesn't sound like I'm going to be number one here. I thought that was the idea. To look out for numero uno."

"Of course not, silly boy. This is after all the 'I'm Number One School of Scruples.' And I, *moi,* am the I who's Number One. There can be only one Number One, of course, and since I founded the school, I'm it."

"But I thought the idea of your school was for everyone to have the maximum amount of enjoyment in life."

Peevishness clouds Pheelgood's face. "Look here, Unger, if I arrange things for you to have a good time, my day has to dim. The demand that I curb my own pleasure for the sake of your own, well that's simply subversive, undermines the very foundation of this philosophy. Next you'll be asking me to open soup kitchens and retread the downtrodden. If I'm to look out for Number One, then you've got to act entirely differently from me. I take, you give. Capiche? If you want to be Number One, then you go somewhere else. After paying me to teach you how to do it, of course."

With that, we'll stop the dialogue. As should be obvious by now, it's very diffi-cult to systematize egoism. You have two sets of demands in constant conflict—the demands of your own personal ego and those of everyone else's. It's impossible, hence, to universalize a statement that all members of the school could hold equally without contradicting all other members of the school. Thus, for example, if I write a book saying that it's okay to rip people off to satisfy their own desires, I am au-thorizing others to steal my book and prevent me from realizing my own desires for profit. In the end, the philosophy is not only contradictory, but also not very ef-ficient at delivering the desired end product—personal gratification.

That's not to say, of course, that people can't or don't act on the principle of me-firstism. It's just to say that it's impossible to systematize it without returning us to what philosopher Thomas Hobbes called the condition of nature, wherein life is "nasty, brutish, and short." The immediate practical problem of any survival-of-the-fittest school of morals is that it benefits a few (the fittest of the fit) at the ex-pense of the many. Some egoists try to get around this problem by conceding that we must limit our self-gratification either by entering into contracts or institutional arrangements with others or by sacrificing short-term interests for long-term ones. We might, for example, give to the poor now in order to avoid a revolution of the masses later. But once they've let the camel's nose of concern for others into the tent, it's tough to hang onto egoistic philosophy. Having considered naive egoism, let's turn to a pair of more workable alternatives.

In shifting to the two most common forms of ethical thought, we shift point of view from "I" to "us." Both groups, those who make ethical judgments ac-cording to the consequences of any act and those who make ethical judgments according to the conformity of any act with a principle, are guided by their con-cern for the whole of humanity rather than simply the self.

Consequences as the Grounds of Ethics

Perhaps the best-known example of evaluating acts according to their ethical consequences is John Stuart Mill's Utilitarianism. The goal of Utilitarianism, ac-cording to Mill, is "the greatest good for the greatest number." It is a very down-to-earth philosophy that grew out of nineteenth-century British philosophers' concern to demystify ethics and to make it work in the practical world.

As Mill makes clear, a focus on ethical consequences allows you readily to as-sess a wide range of acts. You can apply the principle of utility—which says that an action is morally right if it produces a greater net value (benefits minus costs) than any available alternative action—to virtually any situation and it will help you reach a decision. Obviously, however, it's not always easy to make the calcu-lations called for by the principle, since, like any prediction of the future, an esti-mate of consequences is conjectural. In particular, it's often very hard to assess the long-term consequences of any action. Too often, Utilitarianism seduces us into a short-term analysis of a moral problem simply because long-term consequences are very difficult to predict.

Principles as the Grounds of Ethics

Any ethical system based on principles will ultimately rest on one or two moral tenets that we are duty-bound to uphold, no matter what the consequences. Sometimes the moral tenets come from religious faith—for example, the Ten Commandments. At other times, however, the principles are derived from philosophical reasoning, as in the case of German philosopher Immanuel Kant. Kant held that no one should ever use another person as a means to his own ends and that everyone should always act as if his acts were the basis of universal law. In other words, Kant held that we were duty-bound to respect other people's sanctity and to act in the same way that we would want all other people to act. The great advantage of such a system is its clarity and precision. We are never overwhelmed by a multiplicity of contradictory and difficult-to-quantify consequences; we simply make sure we are not violating a principle of our ethical system and proceed accordingly.

The Two Systems Compared

In the eyes of many people, a major advantage of a system such as Utilitarianism is that it impels us to seek out the best solution, whereas systems based on principle merely enjoin us not to violate a principle by our action. In turn, applying an ethical principle will not always help us resolve necessarily relativistic moral dilemmas. For instance, what if none of our available choices violates our moral principles? How do we choose among a host of permissible acts? Or what about situations where none of the alternatives is permitted by our principles? How might we choose the least bad alternative?

To further our comparison of the two systems, let's ask what a Mill or a Kant might say about the previously mentioned issue of terrorism. Here the Kantian position is clear: To kill another person to realize your own ends is palpably evil and forbidden.

But a follower of Mill will face a less clear choice. A Utilitarian could not automatically rule out terrorism or any other means so long as it led ultimately to the greatest good for the greatest number. If a nation is being slowly starved by those around it, if its people are dying, its institutions crumbling and its future disappearing, who's to say that the aggrieved nation is not justified in taking a few hundred lives to improve the lot of hundreds of thousands? The Utilitarian's first concern is to determine if terrorism will most effectively bring about that end. So long as the desired end represents the best possible net value and the means are effective at bringing about the end, the Utilitarian can, in theory anyway, justify almost any action.

Given the shared cultural background and values of most of us, not to mention our own vulnerability to terrorism, the Kantian argument is probably very appealing here. Indeed, Kantian ethical arguments have overwhelming appeal for us when the principle being invoked is already widely held within our culture, and when the violation of that principle will have clear and immediate negative consequences for us. But in a culture that doesn't share that principle and for whom the consequences of violation are positive rather than negative, the argument will undoubtedly appear weaker, a piece of fuzzy-headed idealism.

 FOR CLASS DISCUSSION

Working as individuals or in small groups:

1. Try to formulate a Utilitarian argument to persuade terrorist leaders in a country such as Libya to stop terrorist action.

2. Try to formulate an ethical principle or rule that would permit terrorism.

Some Compromise Positions Between Consequences and Principles

In the end, most of us would not be entirely happy with an ethic that forced us to ignore either principles or consequences. We all have certain principles that we simply can't violate no matter what the consequences. Thus, for example, some of us would not have dropped the bomb on Hiroshima even if it did mean saving many lives ultimately. And certainly, too, most of us will compromise our principles in certain situations if we think the consequences justify it. For instance, how many of us would not deceive, harm, or even torture a kidnapper to save the life of a stolen child? Indeed, over the years, compromise positions have developed on both sides to accommodate precisely these concerns.

Some "consequentialists" have acknowledged the usefulness of general rules for creating more human happiness over the long run. To go back to our terrorism example, a consequentialist might oppose terrorist action on the grounds that "Thou shalt not kill another person in the name of greater material happiness for the group." This acknowledgment of an inviolable principle will still be based on a concern for consequences—for instance, a fear that terrorist acts may lead to World War III—but having such a principle allows the consequentialist to get away from a case-by-case analysis of acts and to keep more clearly before himself the long-range consequences of acts.

Among later-day ethics of principle, meanwhile, the distinction between absolute obligation and what philosophers call *prima facie* obligation has been developed to take account of the force of circumstances. An absolute obligation would be an obligation to follow a principle at all times, no matter what. A *prima facie* obligation, on the other hand, is an obligation to do something "other things being equal," that is, in a normal situation. Hence, to use a classic moral example, you would not, other things being equal, cannibalize an acquaintance. But if there are three of you in a lifeboat, one is dying and the other two will surely die if they don't get food, your *prima facie* obligation not to eat another might be waived. (However, the Royal Commission, which heard the original case, took a more Kantian position and condemned the action of the seamen who cannibalized their mate.)

These, then, in greatly condensed form, are the major alternative ways of thinking about ethical arguments. Let's now briefly summarize the ways you can use your knowledge of ethical thought to develop your arguments and refute those of others.

DEVELOPING AN ETHICAL ARGUMENT

To help you see how familiarity with these systems of ethical thought can help you develop an ethical argument, let's take an example case. How, for example, might we go about developing an argument in favor of abolishing the death penalty?

Our first task is to examine the issue from the two points of view just discussed. How might a Utilitarian or a Kantian argue that the death penalty should be abolished? The argument on principle, as is usually the case, would appear to be the simpler of the two. Taking another life is difficult to justify under most ethical principles. For Kant, the sanctity of human life is a central tenet of ethics. Under Judeo-Christian ethics, meanwhile, one is told that "Vengeance is Mine, saith the Lord" and "Thou shalt not kill."

But, unfortunately for our hopes of simplicity, Kant argued in favor of capital punishment:

> There is no sameness of kind between death and remaining alive even under the most miserable conditions, and consequently there is no equality between the crime and the retribution unless the criminal is judicially condemned and put to death.*

Kant is here invoking an important principle of justice—that punishments should be proportionate to the crime. Kant appears to be saying that this principle must take precedence over his notion of the supreme worth of the individual. Some philosophers think he was being inconsistent in taking this position. Certainly, in establishing your own position, you could support a case against capital punishment based on Kant's principles, even if Kant himself did not reach the same conclusion. But you'd have to establish for your reader why you are at odds with Kant in this case. Kant's apparent inconsistency here illustrates how powerfully our intuitive judgments can affect our ethical judgment.

Likewise, with the Judeo-Christian position, passages can be found in the Bible that would support capital punishment, notably, the Old Testament injunction to take "an eye for an eye and a tooth for a tooth." The latter principle is sim-

---

*From Immanuel Kant, *The Metaphysical Elements of Justice.*

ply a more poetic version of "Let the punishment fit the crime." Retribution should be of the same kind as the crime. And the commandment "Thou shalt not kill" is often interpreted as "Thou shalt not commit murder," an interpretation that not only permits just wars or killing in self-defense but is also consistent with other places in the Bible that suggest that people have not only the right but the obligation to punish wrongdoers and not leave their fate to God.

So, there appears to be no clearcut argument in support of abolishing capital punishment on the basis of principle. What about an argument based on consequences? How might abolishing capital punishment result in a net good that is at least as great as allowing it?

A number of possibilities suggest themselves. First, in abolishing capital punishment, we rid ourselves of the possibility that someone may be wrongly executed. To buttress this argument, we might want to search for evidence of how many people have been wrongly convicted of or executed for a capital crime. In making arguments based on consequence we must, whenever possible, offer empirical evidence that the consequences we assert exist—and exist to the degree we've suggested.

There are also other possible consequences that a Utilitarian might mention in defending the abolition of capital punishment. These include leaving open the possibility that the person being punished will be reformed, keeping those charged with executing the murderer free from guilt, putting an end to the costly legal and political process of appealing the conviction, and so forth.

But in addition to calculating benefits, you will need also to calculate the costs of abolishing the death penalty and to show that the net result favors abolition. Failure to mention such costs is a serious weakness in many arguments of consequence. Moreover, in the issue at hand, the consequences that favor capital punishment— deterrence of further capital crimes, cost of imprisoning murderers, and so forth— are well known to most members of your audience.

In our discussion of capital punishment, then, we employed two alternative ways of thinking about ethical issues. In pursuing an argument from principle, we looked for an appropriate rule that permitted or at least did not prohibit our position. In pursuing an argument from consequence, we moved from what's permissible to what brings about the most desirable consequences. Most ethical issues, argued thoroughly, should be approached from both perspectives, so long as irreconcilable differences don't present themselves.

Should you choose to adopt one of these perspectives to the exclusion of the other, you will find yourself facing many of the problems mentioned above. This is not to say that you can't ever go to the wall for a principle or focus solely on consequences to the exclusion of principles; it's simply that you will be hard pressed to convince those of your audience who happen to be of the other persuasion and demand different sorts of proof. For the purpose of developing arguments, we encourage you to consider both the relevant principles and the possible consequences when you evaluate ethical actions.

TESTING ETHICAL ARGUMENTS

Perhaps the first question you should ask in setting out to analyze your draft of an ethical argument is, "To what extent is the argument based on consequences or on ethical principles?" If it's based exclusively on one of these two forms of ethical thought, then it's vulnerable to the sorts of criticism discussed above. A strictly principled argument that takes no account of the consequences of its position is vulnerable to a simple cost analysis. What are the costs in the case of adhering to this principle? There will undoubtedly be some, or else there would be no real argument. If the argument is based strictly on consequentialist grounds, we should ask if the position violates any rules or principles, particularly such commandments as the Golden Rule—"Do unto others as you would have others do unto you"—which most members of our audience adhere to. By failing to mention these alternative ways of thinking about ethical issues, we undercut not only our argument but our credibility as well.

Let's now consider a more developed examination of the two positions, starting with some of the more subtle weaknesses in a position based on principle. In practice people will sometimes take rigidly "principled" positions because they live in fear of "slippery slopes"; that is, they fear setting precedents that might lead to ever more dire consequences. Consider, for example, the slippery slope leading from birth control to euthanasia if you have an absolutist commitment to the sanctity of human life. Once we allow birth control in the form of condoms or pills, the principled absolutist would say, then we will be forced to accept birth control "abortions" in the first hours after conception (IUDs, "morning after" pills), then abortions in the first trimester, then in the second or even the third trimester. And once we have violated the sanctity of human life by allowing abortions, it is only a short step to euthanasia and finally to killing off all undesirables.

One way to refute a slippery-slope argument of this sort is to try to dig a foothold into the side of the hill to show that you don't necessarily have to slide all the way to the bottom. You would thus have to argue that allowing birth control does not mean allowing abortions (by arguing for differences between a fetus after conception and sperm and egg before conception), or that allowing abortions does not mean allowing euthanasia (by arguing for differences between a fetus and a person already living in the world).

Consequentialist arguments have different kinds of difficulties. As discussed before, the crucial difficulty facing anyone making a consequentialist argument is to calculate the consequences in a clear and reliable way. Have you considered all significant consequences? If you project your scenario of consequences further into the future (remember, consequentialist arguments are frequently stronger over the short term than over the long term, where many unforeseen consequences can occur), can you identify possibilities that work against the argument?

As also noted, consequentialist arguments carry a heavy burden of empirical proof. What evidence can you offer that the predicted consequences will in fact come to pass? Do you offer any evidence that alternative consequences won't occur? And just how do you prove that the consequences of any given action are a net good or evil?

In addition to the problems unique to each of the two positions, ethical arguments are vulnerable to the more general sorts of criticism, including consistency, recency, and relevance of evidence. Obviously, however, consequentialist arguments will be more vulnerable to weaknesses in evidence, whereas arguments based on principle are more open to questions about consistency of application.

 ## FOR CLASS DISCUSSION

1. Prior to beginning this exercise, read the following short story by Ursula Le Guin. Then, working individually or in small groups, prepare answers to the following questions:
   a. How would someone such as Mill evaluate the actions of those who walk away?
   b. How would someone such as Kant evaluate the same action?
   c. If you are working in groups, try to reach a group consensus on how the action should be evaluated. Recorders for the group should explain how your group's evaluation differs from a Utilitarian or a Kantian approach.

2. Read "The Case for Torture" (pages 387–389) by philosopher Michael Levin. Levin creates an argument that torture not only can be justified but is positively mandated under certain circumstances. Analyze Levin's argument in terms of our distinction between arguments from principle and arguments from consequence.

3. In "The Case for Torture," Levin mentions the possibility of some "murkier" cases in which it is difficult to draw a line demarcating the legitimate use of torture. Try to come up with several examples of these "murkier" cases and explain what makes them murky.

The Ones Who Walk Away from Omelas
(Variations on a Theme by William James)

Ursula Le Guin

With a clamor of bells that set the swallows soaring, the Festival of Summer came to   1
the city Omelas, bright-towered by the sea. The rigging of the boats in harbor sparkled with flags. In the streets between houses with red roofs and painted walls, between old moss-grown gardens and under avenues of trees, past great parks and public buildings, processions moved. Some were decorous: old people in long stiff robes of mauve and grey, grave

master workmen, quiet, merry women carrying their babies, and chatting as they walked. In other streets the music beat faster, a shimmering of gong and tambourine, and the people went dancing, the procession was a dance. Children dodged in and out, their high calls rising like the swallows' crossing flights over the music and the singing. All the processions wound towards the north side of the city, where on the great water-meadow called the Green Fields boys and girls, naked in the bright air, with mud-stained feet and ankles and long, lithe arms, exercised their restive horses before the race. The horses wore no gear at all but a halter without bit. Their manes were braided with streamers of silver, gold, and green. They flared their nostrils and pranced and boasted to one another; they were vastly excited, the horse being the only animal who has adopted our ceremonies as his own. Far off to the north and west the mountains stood up half encircling Omelas on her bay. The air of morning was so clear that the snow still crowning the Eighteen Peaks burned with white-gold fire across the miles of sunlit air, under the dark blue of the sky. There was just enough wind to make the banners that marked the racecourse snap and flutter now and then. In the silence of the broad green meadows one could hear the music winding through the city streets, farther and nearer and ever approaching, a cheerful faint sweetness of the air that from time to time trembled and gathered together and broke out into the great joyous clanging of the bells.

2   Joyous! How is one to tell about joy? How describe the citizens of Omelas?

3   They were not simple folk, you see, though they were happy. But we do not say the words of cheer much any more. All smiles have become archaic. Given a description such as this one tends to make certain assumptions. Given a description such as this one tends to look next for the King, mounted on a splendid stallion and surrounded by his noble knights, or perhaps in a golden litter borne by great-muscled slaves. But there was no king. They did not use swords, or keep slaves. They were not barbarians. I do not know the rules and laws of their society, but I suspect that they were singularly few. As they did without monarchy and slavery, so they also get on without the stock exchange, the advertisement, the secret police, and the bomb. Yet I repeat that these were not simple folk, not dulcet shepherds, noble savages, bland utopians. They were not less complex than us. The trouble is that we have a bad habit, encouraged by pedants and sophisticates, of considering happiness as something rather stupid. Only pain is intellectual, only evil interesting. This is the treason of the artist: a refusal to admit the banality of evil and the terrible boredom of pain. If you can't lick 'em join 'em. If it hurts, repeat it. But to praise despair is to condemn delight, to embrace violence is to lose hold of everything else. We have almost lost hold; we can no longer describe a happy man, nor make any celebration of joy. How can I tell you about the people of Omelas? They were not naive and happy children—though their children were, in fact, happy. They were mature, intelligent, passionate adults whose lives were not wretched. O miracle! but I wish I could describe it better. I wish I could convince you. Omelas sounds in my words like a city in a fairy tale, long ago and far away, once upon a time. Perhaps it would be best if you imagined it as your own fancy bids, assuming it will rise to the occasion, for certainly I cannot suit you all. For instance, how about technology? I think that there would be no cars or helicopters in and above the streets; this follows from the fact that the people of Omelas are happy people. Happiness is based on a just discrimination

of what is necessary, what is neither necessary nor destructive, and what is destructive. In the middle category, however—that of the unnecessary but undestructive, that of comfort, luxury, exuberance, etc.—they could perfectly well have central heating, subway trains, washing machines, and all kinds of marvelous devices not yet invented here, floating light-sources, fuelless power, a cure for the common cold. Or they could have none of that: it doesn't matter. As you like it. I incline to think that people from towns up and down the coast have been coming in to Omelas during the last days before the Festival on very fast little trains and double-decked trams, and that the train station of Omelas is actually the handsomest building in town, though plainer than the magnificent Farmers' Market. But even granted trains, I fear that Omelas so far strikes some of you as goody-goody. Smiles, bells, parades, horses, bleh. If so, please add an orgy. If an orgy would help, don't hesitate. Let us not, however, have temples from which issue beautiful nude priests and priestesses already half in ecstasy and ready to copulate with any man or woman, lover or stranger, who desires union with the deep godhead of the blood, although that was my first idea. But really it would be better not to have any temples in Omelas—at least, not manned temples. Religion yes, clergy no. Surely the beautiful nudes can just wander about, offering themselves like divine souffles to the hunger of the needy and the rapture of the flesh. Let them join the processions. Let tambourines be struck above the copulations, and the glory of desire be proclaimed upon the gongs, and (a not unimportant point) let the offspring of these delightful rituals be beloved and looked after by all. One thing I know there is none of in Omelas is guilt. But what else should there be? I thought at first there were no drugs, but that is puritanical. For those who like it, the faint insistent sweetness of *drooz* may perfume the ways of the city, *drooz* which first brings a great lightness and brilliance to the mind and limbs, and then after some hours a dreamy languor, and wonderful visions at last of the very arcana and inmost secrets of the Universe, as well as exciting the pleasure of sex beyond all belief; and it is not habit-forming. For more modest tastes I think there ought to be beer. What else, what else belongs in the joyous city? The sense of victory, surely, the celebration of courage. But as we did without clergy, let us do without soldiers. The joy built upon successful slaughter is not the right kind of joy; it will not do; it is fearful and it is trivial. A boundless and generous contentment, a magnanimous triumph felt not against some outer enemy but in communion with the finest and fairest in the souls of all men everywhere and the splendor of the world's summer: this is what swells the hearts of the people of Omelas, and the victory they celebrate is that of life. I really don't think many of them need to take *drooz.*

Most of the processions have reached the Green Fields by now. A marvelous smell of cooking goes forth from the red and blue tents of the provisioners. The faces of small children are amiably sticky; in the benign grey beard of a man a couple of crumbs of rich pastry are entangled. The youths and girls have mounted their horses and are beginning to group around the starting line of the course. An old woman, small, fat and laughing, is passing out flowers from a basket, and tall young men wear her flowers in their shining hair. A child of nine or ten sits at the edge of the crowd alone, playing on a wooden flute. People pause to listen, and they smile, but they do not speak to him, for he never ceases playing and never sees them, his dark eyes wholly rapt in the sweet, thin magic of the tune.

He finishes, and slowly lowers his hands holding the wooden flute.

6   As if that little private silence were the signal, all at once a trumpet sounds from the pavilion near the starting line: imperious, melancholy, piercing. The horses rear on their slender legs, and some of them neigh in answer. Soberfaced, the young riders stroke the horses' necks and soothe them, whispering, "Quiet, quiet, there my beauty, my hope. . . ." They begin to form in rank along the starting line. The crowds along the racecourse are like a field of grass and flowers in the wind. The Festival of Summer has begun.

7   Do you believe? Do you accept the festival, the city, the joy? No? Then let me describe one more thing.

8   In a basement under one of the beautiful public buildings of Omelas, or perhaps in the cellar of one of its spacious private homes, there is a room. It has one locked door, and no window. A little light seeps in dustily between cracks in the boards, secondhand from a cob-webbed window somewhere across the cellar. In one corner of the little room a couple of mops, with stiff, clotted, foul-smelling heads, stand near a rusty bucket. The floor is dirt, a little damp to the touch, as cellar dirt usually is. The room is about three paces long and two wide: a mere broom closet or disused tool room. In the room a child is sitting. It could be a boy or a girl. It looks about six, but actually is nearly ten. It is feeble-minded. Perhaps it was born defective, or perhaps it has become imbecile through fear, malnutrition, and neglect. It picks its nose and occasionally fumbles vaguely with its toes or genitals, as it sits hunched in the corner farthest from the bucket and the two mops. It is afraid of the mops. It finds them horrible. It shuts its eyes, but it knows the mops are still standing there; and the door is locked; and nobody will come. The door is always locked; and nobody ever comes, except that sometimes—the child has no understanding of time or interval—sometimes the door rattles terribly and opens, and a person, or several people, are there. One of them may come in and kick the child to make it stand up. The others never come close, but peer in at it with frightened, disgusted eyes. The food bowl and the water jug are hastily filled, the door is locked, the eyes disappear. The people at the door never say anything, but the child, who has not always lived in the tool room, and can remember sunlight and its mother's voice, sometimes speaks. "I will be good," it says. "Please let me out. I will be good!" They never answer. The child used to scream for help at night, and cry a good deal, but now it only makes a kind of whining, "eh-haa, eh-haa," and it speaks less and less often. It is so thin there are no calves to its legs; its belly protrudes; it lives on a half-bowl of corn meal and grease a day. It is naked. Its buttocks and thighs a mass of festered sores, as it sits in its own excrement continually.

9   They all know it is there, all the people of Omelas. Some of them have come to see it, others are content merely to know it is there. They all know that it has to be there. Some of them understand why, and some do not, but they all understand that their happiness, the beauty of their city, the tenderness of their friendships, the health of their children, the wisdom of their scholars, the skill of their makers, even the abundance of their harvest and the kindly weathers of their skies, depends wholly on this child's abominable misery.

10   This is usually explained to children when they are between eight and twelve, when-ever they seem capable of understanding; and most of those who come to see the child are young people, though often enough an adult comes, or comes back, to see the child. No matter how well the matter has been explained to them, these young spectators are always

shocked and sickened at the sight. They feel disgust, which they had thought themselves superior to. They feel anger, outrage, impotence, despite all the explanations. They would like to do something for the child. But there is nothing they can do. If the child were brought up into the sunlight out of that vile place, it if were cleaned and fed and comforted, that would be a good thing, indeed; but if it were done, in that day and hour all the prosperity and beauty and delight of Omelas would wither and be destroyed. Those are the terms. To exchange all the goodness and grace of every life in Omelas for that single, small improvement: to throw away the happiness of thousands for the chance of the happiness of one: that would be to let guilt within the walls indeed.

The terms are strict and absolute; there may not even be a kind word spoken to the child.   11

Often the young people go home in tears, or in a tearless rage, when they have seen   12
the child and faced this terrible paradox. They may brood over it for weeks or years. But as time goes on they begin to realize that even if the child could be released, it would not get much good of its freedom: a little vague pleasure of warmth and food, no doubt, but little more. It is too degraded and imbecile to know any real joy. It has been afraid too long even to be free of fear. Its habits are too uncouth for it to respond to humane treatment. Indeed, after so long it would probably be wretched without walls about it to protect it, and darkness for its eyes, and its own excrement to sit in. Their tears at the bitter injustice dry when they begin to perceive the terrible justice of reality, and to accept it. Yet it is their tears and anger, the trying of their generosity and the acceptance of their helplessness, which are perhaps the true source of the splendor of their lives. Theirs is no vapid, irresponsible happiness. They know that they, like the child, are not free. They know compassion. It is the existence of the child, and their knowledge of its existence, that makes possible the nobility of their architecture, and poignancy of their music, the profundity of their science. It is because of the child that they are so gentle with children. They know that if the wretched one were not there snivelling in the dark, the other one, the flute-player, could make no joyful music as the young riders line up in their beauty for the race in the sunlight of the first morning of summer.

Now do you believe in them? Are they not more credible? But there is one more thing   13
to tell, and this is quite incredible.

At times one of the adolescent girls or boys who go to see the child does not go home   14
to weep or rage, does not, in fact, go home at all. Sometimes also a man or woman much older falls silent for a day or two, and then leaves home. These people go out into the street, and walk down the street alone. They keep walking, and walk straight out of the city of Omelas, through the beautiful gates. They keep walking across the farmlands of Omelas. Each one goes alone, youth or girl, man or woman. Night falls; the traveler must pass down village streets, between the houses with yellow-lit windows, and on out into the darkness of the fields. Each alone, they go west or north, towards the mountains. They go on. They leave Omelas, they walk ahead into the darkness, and they do not come back. The place they go towards is a place even less imaginable to most of us than the city of happiness. I cannot describe it at all. It is possible that it does not exist. But they seem to know where they are going, the ones who walk away from Omelas.

p a r t   f o u r

Writing from Sources

The Argument as Formal Research Paper

CHAPTER 16   Finding and Selecting Sources: The Library
              and the Internet

CHAPTER 17   Using and Documenting Sources

chapter 16

Finding and Selecting Sources

The Library and the Internet

Although the "research paper" is a common writing assignment in college, students are often baffled by their professor's expectations when they are given a research paper assignment. The problem is that students often think of research writing as presenting information rather than as creating an argument. One of our business school colleagues calls these sorts of research papers "data dumps." "You ask students to write a research paper on the American banking system," he will tell you, "and they fill you up a truckload of information on banking and unload it on your desk. 'There's your fresh load of info, Prof; you make sense out of it.' "

But a research paper shouldn't be a data dump. Like any other essay, it should use its data to support a thesis. Consider the following excerpt from an article in *Family Circle,* a typical supermarket magazine for the home consumer:

> Despite the enormous expansion of the female labor force in recent years (the number of working women has doubled since 1960), there has been little improvement in women's economic position. In 1939 American women earned 63 cents to a man's dollar. Today, they earn 64 cents to a man's dollar. In 1984 the median income of women who worked full time, year-round was $14,479, while similarly employed men earned $23,218. A woman with four years of college still earns less than a male high school dropout.*

---

*From Sylvia Ann Hewlett, "How Our Laws Hurt Working Mothers and Their Families," *Family Circle,* 21 Oct. 1986, p. 54.

This essay has many features of a good research paper. Note that it has a clear thesis (". . . there has been little improvement in women's economic position"). Note also that the author's supporting data come from research, that is, from external sources rather than personal experience—data she has found by reading books, journals, newspapers, statistical tables, and so forth.

However, there is one major difference between this essay and a formal academic research paper. In this essay, we can't check her data. Because the essay has no citations and no list of works cited, we can't tell where she got her information; we have no way of verifying her figures, of deciding about the reliability of her sources. The purpose of citations and a bibliography in an academic research paper is to enable readers to follow the trail of the author's research. Perhaps the writer has misquoted somebody, has taken information out of context or from a biased source, has fallen victim to some of the statistical traps we discuss in Chapter 6, and so forth. If a research essay is properly "documented" (accurate use of citations placed in correct form), it is possible to locate all the sources and verify the author's data. The proper formats for citations and bibliography entries are simply conventions within an academic discipline to facilitate the reader's retrieval of the original sources. These conventions, like other jargon shared by people with special interests, permit rapid communication among those familiar with the discipline.

Thus, you will find that writing an argument as a formal research paper draws on the same argumentation skills you have been using all along. What distinguishes a formal research argument from less formal arguments is more extensive use of research data to support the writer's argument and special care in documenting sources properly. In this chapter and the next, we look at the special skills you will need to find and use sources effectively.

FORMULATING A RESEARCH QUESTION

The best way to avoid writing a data dump essay is to begin with a good research question—the formulation of a problem or issue that your essay will address. The research question, usually in the form of an issue question, will give you a guiding purpose in doing your library research. If you begin only with a general topic—say, the American banking system—all you can do is look at books and articles on banks, dozens and dozens of them perhaps. But to what purpose? What are you looking for?

If, on the other hand, you come to the library with a clearly formulated issue question, then you know what you are looking for in your research. For example, you might formulate specific issue questions on the American banking system such as these: "Will the elimination of tax deductions for consumer loans substantially reduce demand for car loans from banks?" Or "Will the elimination of tax deductions for consumer loans benefit banks?" The sooner you can settle on a research question, the easier it will be for you to find the source materials you need in a time-saving, efficient manner. The exploration methods we suggested in Chapter 3 can help you find a research topic that interests you.

A good way to begin an exploration is to freewrite for ten minutes or so, reflecting on recent readings that have stimulated your interest, on recent events that have sparked arguments, or on personal experiences that might open up onto public issues. If you have no idea for a topic, try starting with the trigger question "What possible topics am I interested in?" If you already have an idea for a topic area, explore why you are interested in it. Search for the personal connections or the particular angles that most intrigue you. Here is how Lynnea, a student writer, began exploring a topic related to police work. She chose this topic because she had a friend who was a patrol officer.

LYNNEA'S FIRST FREEWRITE

Why am I attracted to this issue? What personal connections do I have?

My friend is a police officer and has been telling me about some of the experiences he has had while walking "the beat" downtown. The people he has to deal with are mostly street people: bums, gang members, drug dealers, etc. He tells me how he just harasses them to get them to move on and to leave the area, or he looks for a reason to give them a ticket so that eventually they will accumulate a few unpaid tickets, and they will have to go to jail. My friend told me about an experience where an alcoholic tramp started kicking his feet against the patrol car after he and his partner had walked about a block away to begin their night shift. The bum started yelling at them to come back and kept hitting and throwing himself against the car. "OK, what are you doing that for?" they asked. The bum stammered that he wanted to go to "detox." They told the tramp that they would not take him to detox, and so he kept on banging the car. What can be done about these people? Not only the alcoholics and bums, but what about the gang members, prostitutes, drug dealers, etc.? The police forces out on the streets at night seem to be doing little more than just ruffling a few feathers, but what else can they do under the circumstances?

On finishing this freewrite, Lynnea was certain she wanted to write her research argument on something related to police work. The topic interested her, and having a patrol officer as a friend gave her an opportunity for interview data. She decided she was most interested in gangs and called her friend to get some more insights. Several days later, she met her friend at a local restaurant during his lunch break. After that meeting, she again did a freewrite.

LYNNEA'S SECOND FREEWRITE

Today I went with my friend for a cup of coffee to discuss some possible topics for my paper. He took me to a coffee shop where several of the officers in the area meet for lunch. I had wanted to ask Bob specific questions about gangs in the area, but when we joined the rest of the officers, I didn't have the chance. However, something they brought into the discussion *did* interest me. They were talking about a woman who had recently graduated from the academy and was now trying to pass the student officer's phase. This woman, I was informed, was 4'9" and weighed about 90 pounds. Apparently, at the academy she couldn't perform many of the physical exercises that her fellow trainees could. Where most of the men could pull a trigger between 80 and 90 times during the allotted time, she could pull the trigger of her police issue .38 revolver only once. And she was so tiny that they had to make a booster seat for the patrol car. One of the instructors said that her being in the academy was a joke. Well, it does seem that way to me. I can imagine this woman trying to handle a situation. How could she handcuff someone who resisted arrest? It seems dangerous that someone who is so weak should be allowed to be on patrol duty. I wouldn't want her as my back-up.

Lynnea now knew she had a topic that interested her. She wanted to research women patrol officers, especially the success rate of small women. She formulated her initial research question this way: "Can a small, physically weak woman, such as this 4'9" police candidate, make a good patrol officer?" Her initial thesis was that small, physically weak women could not make good patrol officers, but she wanted to keep an open mind, using argument as a means of clarification. As this chapter progresses, we will return occasionally to Lynnea's research project. (Her final argument essay is reproduced in full at the end of Chapter 17.)

EXPLORING ON THE INTERNET

Besides freewriting and sharing ideas with friends, today's researchers have the vast resources of the Internet and the World Wide Web as sources of ideas and help. Throughout a project, many researchers get invaluable assistance from listserv discussions, Usenet newsgroups, or real-time chat groups.

Listserv Discussions

Among the most productive ways to use e-mail is to join a listserv interest group. A *listserv* compiles any number of e-mail accounts into a mailing list and forwards copies of messages to all people on the list. There are thousands of well-established listservs about a wide variety of topics. You need to know the address of a list in order to join. Specific information about joining various listservs and an index of active lists can be found by entering the Uniform Resource Locator (URL) address "http://tile.net/lists/" once you are on the World Wide Web in a browser.* Once you have subscribed to a listserv, you receive all messages sent to the list and any message you send to the list address will be forwarded to the other members.

A message sent to a listserv interest group is sure to find a responsive audience because all members on the list have chosen to take part in an ongoing dis-

---

*Each file on the World Wide Web has a unique address, or URL, which allows writers to link to information on the Web and lets users move to specific sites. *http* stands for hypertext transfer protocol. There are a number of different systems, or protocols, on the Internet that facilitate the sharing of information. E-mail, for example, is often transferred using the simple mail transfer protocol. Since all the servers and clients that e-mail users work with understand this particular protocol, messages can be exchanged. The http protocol is more advanced and subsumes many earlier Internet protocols.

cussion on the list's specific topic. Often lists archive and periodically post important messages or frequently asked questions (FAQs) for you to study. Most lists are for serious students of the list's topic, so to avoid offending any list members, learn the conventions for posting a message before you jump in.

Although you might find all kinds of interactions on a listserv, many users expect thoughtful, well-organized statements. If you are posting a message that introduces a new thread of discussion, you should clearly state your position (or question) and summarize those of others. Here is a sample posting to a listserv on the environment.

```
To: environL@brahms.usdg.org
From: alanw@armadillo.edu (Alan Whigum)
Subject: Acid Rain and Action

I've been doing research on acid rain and am
troubled by some of the things I've found. For
instance, I've learned that washing coal gases
with limestone before they are released could
reduce sulfur emissions. I know that the
government has the power to mandate such devices,
but the real problem seems to be lack of public
pressure on the government. Why don't people push
for better legislation to help end acid rain? I
suppose it's an economic issue.
```

In turn, you can expect cogent, thoughtful responses from the list members. Here's a possible reply to the preceding message.

```
To: environL@brahms.usdg.org
From: bboston@armadillo.edu
Subject: Re Acid Rain and Action

I think you are right in pointing out that it is
ultimately public pressure that will need to be
applied to reduce acid rain. I've heard the
argument that it is cost that prevents steps from
being taken; people will pay more for goods and
services if these measures are taken, so they
resist. However, judging from the people I've
talked to about the subject, I would say that a
bigger problem may be knowledge. Most of them
said they would be willing to pay a little bit
more for their electricity if it meant a safer
environment. People aren't aware that action needs
to be taken now, because the problem seems remote.
```

When you join a listserv, you are granted instant access to a discourse community that is committed and knowledgeable about its topic. You can join one of the discussions already taking place on the list or post a request to get information and clarification about your own interests.

Listservs can take your ideas through a productive dialectic process as your message is seconded, refuted, complicated, and reclarified by the various list members. They also afford valuable opportunities to practice your summarizing skills as you respond to messages or provide additional information in a second posting. For example, suppose you take issue with a long message that placed the blame for homelessness on Reagan administration policies during the 1980s. Rather than reproducing that entire message, you might provide a brief summary of the main point. The summary would not only give the readers enough background information to appreciate fully your response, it would also help you determine the main points of the original message and pinpoint the issues on which you disagree.

Usenet Newsgroups

Among the most useful sections of the Internet for writers are the bulletin-boardlike forums of Usenet newsgroups. Newsgroups are electronic forums that allow you to post or respond to messages about virtually any topic imaginable. Newsgroups can be powerful tools for exploring problems and considering alternative viewpoints. The news server at your school determines the organization and number of groups available to you. Some schools carry groups that provide articles from professional news services, such as AP, Reuters, and UPI. Others provide topic-centered discussion groups. Your campus system may also offer class newsgroups for exchanging messages and drafts with others at your school. Check with your instructor or computer center to find out how to access the groups available to you.

Newsgroups feature messages that remain posted for a relatively long time, depending on the amount of traffic in the group. This practice allows for the development of various threads of discussion in response to the postings. An example, shown in Figure 16.1, shows both the nested postings to a newsgroup and an excerpt from one of the postings. Matt Giwer's posting mentions revisionists who want to reduce the estimates of the number of Holocaust victims. A response from William C. Anderson asks for a source. Giwer then claims that the information is common knowledge. The posting by John Morris again challenges Giwer for a source. Finally, Giwer responds to the challenges by citing the source for his information. Although this thread was continued after these postings and Giwer was further challenged, you can see that the postings constitute a kind of dialectic that interrogates the initial assumption.

Although you may be tempted to join such a thread immediately, you should familiarize yourself with some of the style conventions and the audience for that newsgroup before jumping in. Take time to read and listen in (lurk) to the group's postings. Debate on Usenet can become fairly heated, and a message that ignores previous postings can elicit angry responses ("flames"). In addition, a message that doesn't consider the newsgroup's audience or its favored style will likely

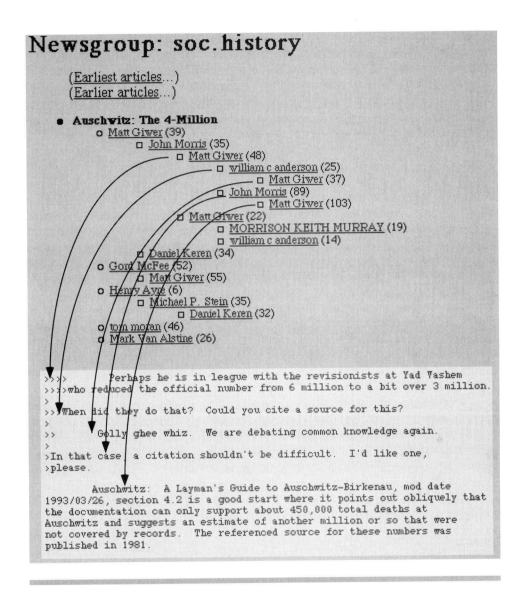

FIGURE 16.1   A sample newsgroup thread

be challenged. For example, if you want to post something in the "alt.fan.rush-limbaugh" group, you should be cautious about composing a message that openly contradicts Rush Limbaugh's brand of politics. If you send a message to the news-group "soc.history," you might be able to tread less carefully—this list is more po-litically diverse—but members of this group might take offense if asked an obvious factual question.

Regardless of their makeup, most groups resent being asked questions that have already been answered. Some groups provide an archive of frequently asked questions (FAQs). If your interest is in something practical that is likely to be covered in the FAQ files, refer to them before posting a query. You should use the expertise of the group to find information that you might not be able to uncover otherwise.

When you are ready to post a message, use some of the strategies outlined for composing a message to a listserv: try to summarize and synthesize your own position as well as those of others; highlight what you see as the most problematic or murky aspects of the topic. Carefully constructed messages are more likely to receive useful responses.

When you do receive feedback, evaluate it with special care. The unfiltered nature of all Internet media makes critical reading an essential skill. Because anyone with an Internet connection can take part in a discussion or post a message or article, you need to evaluate this information differently than you would articles from national newsmagazines, which are professionally written, edited for clarity, and checked for accuracy.

Although most postings are thoughtful, you will also find carelessly written messages that misconstrue an argument, personal rants that offer few, if any, stated reasons for their claims, and propaganda and offensive speech of many kinds in certain newsgroups. It is your responsibility, and unique opportunity, to read newsgroup messages critically, looking for their various biases and making decisions about their relative authority.

Of course, printed sources are marked by their own biases. Deadlines and space constraints may limit the depth and accuracy of printed coverage, and first-hand insights may be screened by authors and editors. If you were studying attitudes toward the Middle East peace process, a newsgroup exchange between a conservative Jew in Israel and a Palestinian student in the United States might provide better insight than a news article for your work. As you read through newsgroup messages, take time to evaluate the users' personal investments in the issue. Compare their comments to those in traditional sources, check for accuracy, and look for differing perspectives. Work these perspectives into your own thinking and writing about the topic. Treat information and points of view gathered from the Internet as primary rather than as secondary material; many of the people who contribute such material care passionately about an issue. It is up to you to place this material in context and edit it for your own audience.

Real-Time Discussion or Chat

Real-time discussions, or *chat*, are synchronous exchanges that take place on a network—meaning that messages are transferred instantly back and forth among members taking part in the discussion. We focus on real-time interactions that take place on the Internet, but you can apply many of the strategies outlined here to local chat programs in your writing class. One of the most popular forms of real-time interaction takes place in the various channels of *Internet Relay Chat* (IRC). As with newsgroup and listserv communications, in chat you compose messages on your own computer and send them through the chat program to other users on the network. Some schools allow you to connect directly to a computer-center server and issue a command that will activate an IRC program. You may also have an IRC program on your workstation or PC that will make the connection for you. Once you are connected, you will want to issue a "list" command to see which topics are being discussed. You can then use the "join" command to log on to a particular channel. Since the specifics for connecting and issuing the various commands vary, you will need to check with your instructor or an experienced user for information about using IRCs at your school.

Like other Internet forums, chat groups are organized around common interests; but IRC sessions are more spontaneous and informal than is communication through newsgroups or listservs, because they consist of exchanges from people who are logged on at the same time. Moreover, in most cases, anyone can drop in on a chat, so the composition and focus of the group shifts from moment to moment. In these conversations, typographical and spelling errors are mostly overlooked, and abbreviations are an acceptable part of real-time style. The pace can be extremely fast, so users generally focus on getting their thoughts out rather than on producing highly polished messages.

IRC conversations and many other real-time exchanges also allow users to act as characters and to include scripted actions in the conversations. Imagine three users discussing flag burning.

```
William: I'm studying the constitutionality of flag-
burning amendments. Does anybody have any opinions?

Pat Buchanan: I think that if you are an American,
you should respect the country enough not to deface
her symbols.

*Thomas Jefferson takes out a match and sets fire
to the corner of an old thirteen star flag. It's
probably more important to respect the underlying
principles of our country than its symbols.
```

The asterisk denotes that the user Thomas Jefferson has issued an "action" command. By putting his name at the beginning of the message, other users see whatever follows as an action performed by that character. Users can construct a third-person narrative by mixing speech with the actions of their characters. You may use this feature in role-playing exercises or to explore some open-ended thinking about your topic.

When you join an IRC channel, you will be asked to choose a nickname. As you ponder your choice, think about some of the issues of *ethos* that we discussed in Chapter 7. How do you want others to perceive you? What kind of personality do you want to adopt? As you work in IRCs, you will refine your ability to weave various personae into your writing.

Perhaps even more than newsgroup or listserv discussions, chat sessions tend to heat up easily. Many real-time forums on the Internet allow users to take on pseudonyms, and some people use the opportunity to become irresponsible in what they say and write.

IRCs give rise to several ethical issues. In these uncensored forums, you will undoubtedly encounter discussions and materials that aren't appropriate for your assignments and class work. You may be challenged to assess your own feelings about censorship, pornography, hate speech, and free speech. And you will need to consider the impact of your persona and words on others as you take on a character or act out an idea.

Perhaps the most useful function of chat sessions is that they promote brainstorming and freewriting. When you are writing in a real-time environment, treat the activity as an exploratory one. Expect the message that you send to be challenged, seconded, or modified by the other writers in the session. Keep an open mind about the various messages that fly back and forth and be sure to respond to points that you find particularly useful or problematic. If you are using a local classroom chat program, you will be talking to people you know, so the conversation will be more predictable. When it's over, you might ask your instructor for a transcript of a chat session; reading it later will help solidify the free thinking that goes into a real-time discussion.

LOCATING SOURCES IN THE LIBRARY OR ONLINE

To be a good researcher, you need to know how to unlock the resources of your college's or university's library. Today, many researchers are also using the vast resources of the Internet and the World Wide Web to find materials.

When they enter a library, most students think of "books"; they tend to focus on the bookshelves and thereby neglect the wealth of other resources a library contains, particularly articles in magazines and journals, statistical reports from government agencies, articles and editorials in newspapers (often on microfilm or microfiche), congressional records, and so forth. Books, of course, are important, but they tend to be less current than periodical sources. The key is to become skilled at using all of a library's resources.

Today, many libraries have converted their card catalog systems to online computer-based systems, making card catalogs obsolete. However, some libraries still have traditional card catalogs, so we will explain first the traditional system of card catalogs and print indexes, and then we will turn to electronic catalogs and databases.

Using the Card Catalog

The library's card catalog is your first source of information about the library's holdings. Indexed by subject, title, and author, cards in the card catalog identify most of the library's holdings: books, magazines and journals (but not the titles of articles in them), newspapers, theses and dissertations, major government documents (but not minor ones), and most multimedia items including records, cassettes, and filmstrips.

Each book in the library has at least three cards—a title card, an author card, and a subject card. Figure 16.2 shows a subject card for one of the books Lynnea used in her research. Filed under the subject heading "POLICEWOMEN," this card shows the book's title (*Women Police; A Study of the Development and Status of the Women Police Movement*), its author (Chloe Owings), and other information. This book would have two additional cards—one filed under "Owings" in the author file and one under "*Women Police; A Study of . . .*" under the title file. The call number at the left (a Dewey Decimal System number—see later) indicates where the book can be found in the stacks.

To help you find cards in the files, you should know something about the rules of alphabetizing:

- Subjects and titles are alphabetized word by word (*On Becoming a Person* comes before *On Matrimony*) and then letter by letter (*Neutral Zone* comes before *Neutrons in Electromicroscopy*).

- In alphabetizing, follow the rule "nothing comes before something." In other words, a blank space comes before the letter *a*. *Sea Through a Sailor's Eyes* comes before *Seatbelts and Other Controversies* (the blank space after "Sea" comes before the *t* in "Seatbelts").

- Abbreviations are arranged as though spelled out (for example, "St. Augustine" is filed in the *S* section under "Saint Augustine").

- Titles containing numbers are filed as though the numbers were spelled out (*2000 Leagues under the Sea* is filed under *Two Thousand Leagues . . .*).

- Articles (*a, an,* and *the*) and their foreign language equivalents are disregarded for purposes of alphabetizing (*A Midsummer Night's Dream* is filed under the *M*s).

- Names beginning with "Mc" or "Mac" are filed under "Mac" ("McKinnon" comes before "MacRae").

To find the book in the stacks, you will need to know the two major systems for shelving books—the Dewey Decimal System, which uses a series of numbers and decimals, and the Library of Congress System, which uses letters followed by numbers. The Library of Congress System is used by most college and university libraries, although they may have an older book collection still classified in the Dewey Decimal System.

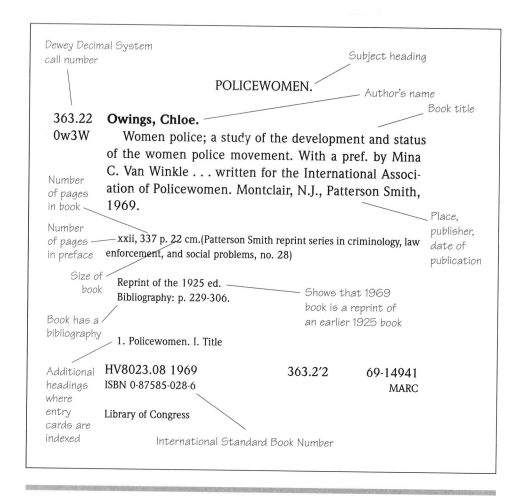

FIGURE 16.2   Book entry in card catalog

Dewey Decimal System

000	General Works
100	Philosophy and Related Disciplines
200	Religion
300	Social Sciences
400	Language
500	Pure Science
600	Technology and Applied Science
700	The Arts
800	Literature and Rhetoric
900	General Geography and History

Library of Congress System

A   General Works, Polygraphy

B   Philosophy, Psychology, and Religion

C   Auxiliary Sciences of History

D   General and Old World History (except America)

E–F   American History

G   Geography, Anthropology, Manners and Customs, Folklore, Recreation

H   Social Science, Statistics, Economics, Sociology

J   Political Science

K   Law

L   Education

M   Music

N   Fine Arts

P   Language and Literature

Q   Science

R   Medicine

S   Agriculture, Plant and Animal Industry, Fish Culture, Fisheries, Hunting, Game Protection

T   Technology

U   Military Science

V   Naval Science

Z   Bibliography and Library Science

Each of these headings is further subdivided according to an elaborate system of subclassifications. For example, in the Library of Congress System the book by William C. Grimm called *Familiar Trees of America* is filed under QK481 (Q = Science; K = Botany; 481 = North American trees). Knowing something of the system's logic helps you browse.

Using Periodical and Newspaper Indexes

Often the best sources of information come from periodicals (magazines and scholarly journals) and from newspapers. The library's card catalog doesn't help you find titles of articles appearing in these periodical sources. Unless your library uses online indexes (see pp. 372–377), you will need to use bookbound print indexes. Most libraries locate their indexes in a central area in the reference section of the library, so it is usually a simple matter to find out where they are housed.

What follows is a list of what we consider the most important and useful indexes. We begin with "current affairs" indexes, useful for finding information on current controversies and issues related to public affairs. Then we turn to a variety of more specialized indexes.

Current Affairs

1. *Readers' Guide to Periodical Literature.* The best-known index to periodical literature. Includes popular, general interest topics such as current events, famous people, movie reviews, and hobbies. Focuses primarily on "general audience" magazines such as *Time, Newsweek, Popular Mechanics, National Geographic, Scientific American,* and so forth.

2. *Social Sciences Index.* Covers all subjects and disciplines within the social sciences, including anthropology, area studies, psychology, political science, and sociology. (Before 1974 this was called *Social Sciences and Humanities Index.*) Although this index lists some articles from popular magazines, it concentrates on articles published in scholarly journals carried in academic libraries. Articles listed in this index will often be more technical and academic, aimed at professional scholars rather than the general audience.

3. *Biography Index.* Quarterly and annual index to biographical material in current books and periodicals. Here is where you should turn if you want to find out biographical information about a person.

4. *Business Periodical Index.* This index covers articles on all business-related topics such as advertising, public relations, marketing, management, and topics relating to economics.

5. *General Science Index.* A subject index to articles in general science periodicals. Covers areas such as biology, botany, chemistry, environment and conservation, medicine and health, physics, zoology.

6. *New York Times Index.* Subject index to the *New York Times,* giving exact references to date, page, and column and including brief synopses of articles.

7. *Wall Street Journal Index.* Monthly and annual index to the *Wall Street Journal.* Organized in two parts: (1) corporate news indexed by name of company, and (2) general news indexed by subject.

8. *Public Affairs Information Service (P.A.I.S.) Bulletin.* Lists articles, pamphlets, and books dealing with economic and social conditions, public administration, politics, and international relations. This index is especially useful for topics related to current public policy, domestic or international.

Specialized Indexes: Education

1. *Education Index.* Indexes by author and subject about 300+ periodicals, proceedings, and yearbooks covering all phases of education. Especially good coverage of topics related to children and child development.

2. *Current Index to Journals in Education.* Detailed author and subject index for articles from more than seven hundred education and education-related journals.

Specialized Indexes: History and Literature

1. *America: History and Life.* Includes abstracts of scholarly articles on the history of the United States and Canada.

2. *Annual Bibliography of English Language and Literature.* Subject index of scholarly articles in English language and literature. Literature section is arranged chronologically and includes articles on the major writers of each century.

3. *Historical Abstracts.* Includes abstracts of scholarly articles on world history (excluding United States and Canada) from 1775 to 1945.

4. *Humanities Index.* Subject index to various topics in the humanities, including archaeology, classics, folklore, history, language and literature, politics, performing arts, philosophy, and religion. (Before 1974 this was called *Social Sciences and Humanities Index.*)

5. *MLA (Modern Language Association) International Bibliography of Books and Articles in Modern Language and Literature.* Comprehensive index of scholarly articles on the languages and literature of various countries. Arranged by national literatures with subdivisions by literary periods.

Specialized Indexes: Nursing and Medical Sciences

1. *Cumulative Index to Nursing and Allied Health Literature.* Major index for topics related to nursing and public health.

2. *Index Medicus.* Monthly index, by subject, of periodical literature on medicine and medical-related topics. Covers publication in all principal languages.

Specialized Indexes: Philosophy and Religion

1. *Philosopher's Index.* Author and subject index to scholarly articles in books and periodicals. Subject section includes abstracts of articles.

2. *Religion Index One: Periodicals.* Subject and author index to scholarly articles on topics in religion. Protestant in viewpoint, but also indexes a number of Catholic and Jewish periodicals.

Specialized Indexes: Psychology and Sociology

1. *Psychological Abstracts.* Subject and author index covering books, journals, technical reports, and scientific documents. Each item includes an abstract.

2. *Social Sciences Index.* See under Current Affairs on page 370.

3. *Applied Science and Technology Index.* Subject index to periodical articles in fields of aeronautics and space sciences, automation, earth sciences, engineering, physics, telecommunications, transportation, and related topics.

4. *Biological and Agricultural Index.* Subject index to English-language periodicals in the agricultural and biological sciences.

5. *General Science Index.* See Current Affairs.

Once you locate these indexes in the library, you will quickly get the hang of using them. Most of the indexes listed above are used in approximately the same way. In general, each volume in an index lists articles that appeared in journals and magazines for a one-year period. The year is stated on the outside cover of the index volume and sometimes at the top of each page. To use the index, you have to be flexible in selecting subject headings. Lynnea, for example, found most of her articles indexed under "policewomen," but one index used the heading "women" and the subheading "and police." It is often difficult to know what headings an index will use, but because most indexes cross-reference listings under a variety of headings, with patience and perseverance you can usually track down what you want.

Because indexes are generally bound by year, you need to look in a different volume for each year you wish to search. Thus, if you wanted to find all the articles written on women in police forces between 1980 and 1990, you would need to look under the subject heading "policewomen" in ten separate volumes. Each entry uses a series of abbreviations (you may have to look in the explanatory codes at the front of the index to decipher some of them) that give you all the information you need to locate the article. Figures 16.3 and 16.4 show entries on policewomen from the *Readers' Guide* and the *Social Sciences Index.*

When you find entries that seem relevant to your topic, jot down the title of the article; the name of the magazine or journal; and the volume, year, and page numbers (remember that the year often doesn't appear in the entry; the year is on the cover of the volume).

Once you have a preliminary list of articles, you will need to find out how your library shelves its periodical collection so that you can retrieve the journals or magazines you need. (Small libraries can afford only small collections of journals, so you may have to cross some of your titles off your list or depend on interlibrary loan.)

Using Online Catalogs and Electronic Databases

Now that library indexing systems are becoming increasingly computerized, the old-fashioned, one-volume-at-a-time, hands-on searching method described earlier is becoming obsolete. However, methods of using online computer searches vary so much from institution to institution that it is impossible to describe a single, generalized method of conducting a computer search.

To use an online catalog—or most other electronic research technology—effectively, you need to be adept at keyword searching. Be persistent and flexible. For example, if you are trying to find information on the economic influence of the

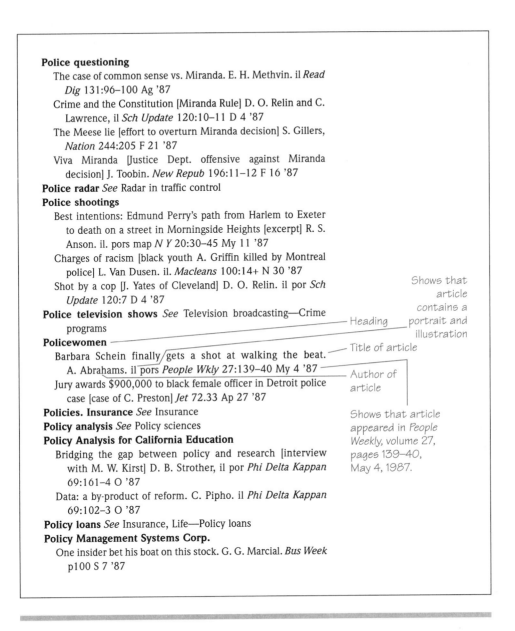

Police questioning

The case of common sense vs. Miranda. E. H. Methvin. il *Read Dig* 131:96–100 Ag '87

Crime and the Constitution [Miranda Rule] D. O. Relin and C. Lawrence, il *Sch Update* 120:10–11 D 4 '87

The Meese lie [effort to overturn Miranda decision] S. Gillers, *Nation* 244:205 F 21 '87

Viva Miranda [Justice Dept. offensive against Miranda decision] J. Toobin. *New Repub* 196:11–12 F 16 '87

Police radar *See* Radar in traffic control

Police shootings

Best intentions: Edmund Perry's path from Harlem to Exeter to death on a street in Morningside Heights [excerpt] R. S. Anson. il. pors map *N Y* 20:30–45 My 11 '87

Charges of racism [black youth A. Griffin killed by Montreal police] L. Van Dusen. il. *Macleans* 100:14+ N 30 '87

Shot by a cop [J. Yates of Cleveland] D. O. Relin. il por *Sch Update* 120:7 D 4 '87

Police television shows *See* Television broadcasting—Crime programs

Policewomen

Barbara Schein finally gets a shot at walking the beat. A. Abrahams. il pors *People Wkly* 27:139–40 My 4 '87

Jury awards $900,000 to black female officer in Detroit police case [case of C. Preston] *Jet* 72.33 Ap 27 '87

Policies. Insurance *See* Insurance

Policy analysis *See* Policy sciences

Policy Analysis for California Education

Bridging the gap between policy and research [interview with M. W. Kirst] D. B. Strother, il por *Phi Delta Kappan* 69:161–4 O '87

Data: a by-product of reform. C. Pipho. il *Phi Delta Kappan* 69:102–3 O '87

Policy loans *See* Insurance, Life—Policy loans

Policy Management Systems Corp.

One insider bet his boat on this stock. G. G. Marcial. *Bus Week* p100 S 7 '87

Shows that article contains a portrait and illustration

Heading

Title of article

Author of article

Shows that article appeared in *People Weekly*, volume 27, pages 139–40, May 4, 1987.

FIGURE 16.3   Entry from *Readers' Guide,* 1987

timber industry in South America, you might enter the keywords "timber and economics." If these keywords produce numerous entries on the spotted owl controversy in the Pacific Northwest, you might alter your keywords to "timber and economics not owl" and free your screen of owl references. Most online catalogs

Poles in France
Immigration and emigration
History
Comparative immigrant history: Polish workers in the Ruhr area
   and the north of France. C. Klessmann. *J Soc Hist* 20:335–53
   Wint '86
Police
See also
Communication in police work
Conflict of interests (Police)
Criminal investigation
Decision making in police work
Detectives
Off-duty police
Police patrol
Sardino, Thomas J.
Secret service
Tamm, Quinn, 1910–1986
Administration
See Police administration
Alcoholism
Alcoholism and the police officer: impact on police administra-
   tors. H. W. Stege. *Police Chief* 53:82–4 Mr '86
Amount of education, experience, etc.
Education and training requirements in law enforcement: a na-
   tional comparison. A. D. Sapp. *Police Chief* 53:48+ N '86
Learning the skills of policing. D. H. Bayley and E. Bittner. *Law
   Contemp Probl* 47:35–59 Aut '84

Subject heading ——————————————— **Attitudes**
Attitudes of police toward violence. S. L. Brodsky and G. D.
   Williamson. *Psychol Rep* 57:1179–80 D '85 pt2
Title —————————————— A comparison of male and female peace officers' stereotypic
   perceptions of women and women peace officers. L. K. Lord.
Author —————————————— bibl *J Police Sci Adm* 14:83–97 Je '86
Contains bibliography —————— Police solidarity and tolerance for police misbehavior. D.
   Lester and W. T. Brink. *Psychol Rep* 57:326 Ag '85
Article appears in —————— **Budget**
Journal of Police *See* Police—Finance
Science Administration, **Diseases and hygiene**
June 1986, volume 14, Cardiovascular intervention among police officers: a two-year re-
pages 83–97 port. R. A. Mostardi and others. il *Police Chief* 53:32–4 Je '86
Disease risk and mortality among police officers: new evidence
   and contributing factors. J. M. Violanti and others. bibl *J Po-
   lice Sci Adm* 14:17–23 Mr '86
Management of training-related injury. P. A. Callicutt. il *FBI Law
   Enforc Bull* 55:16–24 My '86
NYC's physical performance testing program. D. B. Jordan and S.
   Schwartz. *Police Chief* 53:29–30 Je '86

FIGURE 16.4 Entry from *Social Sciences Index,* 1986

allow you to refine keyword searches in a similar way, but you should check the options available before you begin working with an unfamiliar system.

Many libraries also provide computerized indexes that tap into international databases of articles and information or that are built around specific subject areas, and most of these indexes offer the option of keyword searching. The Lexis Nexis catalog, which provides information about, and access to, news and legal publications, is particularly useful for writers. Many schools charge a fee to use these resources, but the breadth of information they offer makes the fee worthwhile. Other subject-area indexes useful to writers include the Modern Language Association's bibliographic listings, the ERIC abstracts of articles on education, the General Science Index, and the Academic Periodical index. Check with the reference desk in your library to learn how to make the best use of the indexes available. Many of these indexes are moving to the Internet via the World Wide Web.

Many libraries also have simple, easy-access computer terminals for searching specific databases on CD-ROM. One typical system, called INFOTRAC, provides rapid access to a multiyear database of popular journals and magazines. However, the number of entries in the data bank is much smaller than the number in the *Readers' Guide to Periodical Literature* or the *Social Sciences Index* so that INFOTRAC is a good starting place but not an adequate source for an extensive search of periodicals. INFOTRAC is easy to use because of its simple menu options and clear prompts. In general, you type in the subject heading you wish to search and then select from a menu of subheadings. When you have identified the heading and subheading of your choice, you can ask the computer to list its entries in that category. You can either read the entries from the screen or ask for a hard copy printout.

Using the World Wide Web and Gopher

In addition to the many conversational resources that we described earlier in this chapter, the Internet offers an unsurpassed collection of government documents, online articles, and other useful files. In the past, researchers had to use several different programs to find these files and to wade through the information; today, technologies such as Gopher and the World Wide Web offer far more efficient options for searching the Internet.

Gopher is designed to tunnel through archives of information. Many institutions have cataloged Gopher resources under large geographic or subject headings. With Gopher, you can tap into these categories and browse through items logically. Most Gopher programs are set to open at a site that lists these useful categories. As Figure 16.5 shows, a Gopher listing typically includes a "search" option. Within this category, you should be able to find a powerful search engine called Veronica. Veronica uses keywords to find information on the net, so you can refine your searches as you would a search using an online catalog. The help files within Veronica provide more information about performing keyword searches.

If you have access to the World Wide Web, we recommend that you do most of your searching there. The Web has a number of powerful search engines. In a similar manner to Gopherhosts, these search engines have collected and categorized

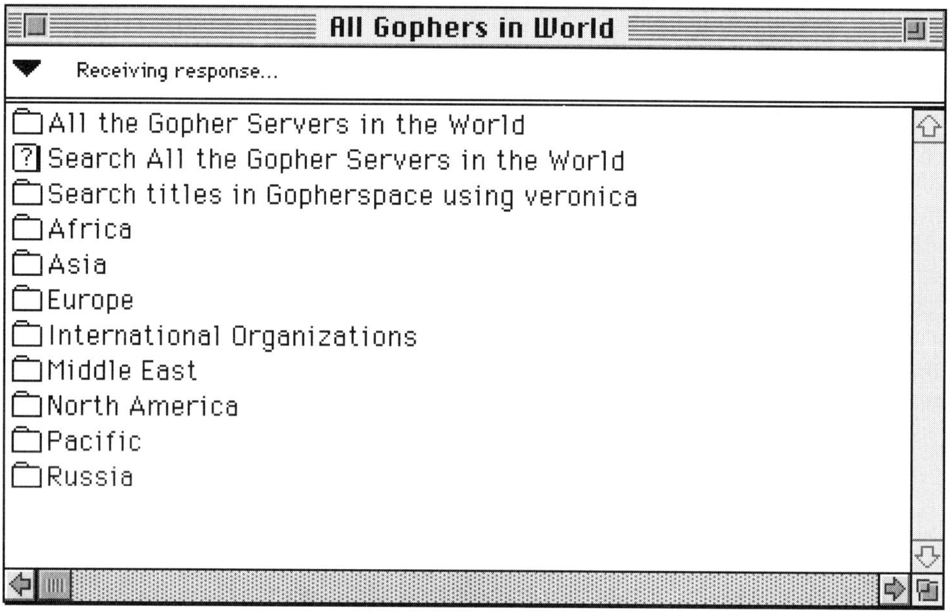

FIGURE 16.5   A gopher site listing geographical resource categories

a large number of Internet files and will perform keyword searches. Most of these search engines will find not only text files, but also graphical, audio, and video files. Some look through the titles of files, whereas others scan the entire text of documents. Different search engines can scan different resources, so it is important that you try a variety of searches when you look for information. Although the Web is evolving rapidly, some of the best search engines are fairly stable. For starters, you might try the following:

Yahoo (http://www.yahoo.com)

Lycos (http://www.lycos.com)

Webcrawler (http://www.webcrawler.com)

These search engines will also let you browse through large subject categories, or trees. Subject trees often incorporate resources from both Gopher and Web sites, but browsing on the Web is the easiest way to navigate through them. The most important thing to keep in mind as you move through these trees (or do any browsing on the Web) is that it is easy to lose track of where various resources are located. Most Internet software allows you to compile lists of locations that you've visited. These lists—usually referred to as *Bookmarks* or *Hotlists*—allow you to return quickly to previously visited sites. We recommend that you save on a diskette or drive any items that you think are particularly valuable. Web and Gopher sites can disappear over time; the only way to ensure that an item will be available for you to use later is to save a copy.

Browsing the Web is an excellent way to help focus your thinking about an issue or topic. For example, suppose that you were searching for information about mining and its impact on Third World countries. As you browsed through some subject trees related to the environment, you might discover an item listing a protest over human rights abuses at Third World mining sites. If you followed the thread of information in the protest listing, you might find out that American students were upset because they felt that an international mining corporation was using their university as part of a public relations effort. This information might prompt you to reconsider your topic; you might decide to broaden your focus to include ways in which mining firms try to shape perceptions at home of their activities abroad.

As you search the Internet for resources, you will be exposed to new information and perspectives. You will want to remain flexible in the early stages of your research effort so that you can reap the benefits of the wealth of information available online. You will also want to play both the explorer and the investigator as you move through the research process. Your initial searches on the Web can help you scout for resources. Some of the links that you follow will be dead ends; others will lead to new discoveries and useful collections of subject-related resources.

Once you've arrived at a topic and gathered some resources, you'll need to investigate them with care. Just as anyone with a connection can post thoughts to a newsgroup or chat forum, anyone can put up a Web page that furthers his or her own agenda. Flashy graphics and other design elements on Web pages can sometimes overwhelm the information that is being presented or lend an air of authority to an otherwise suspect argument or position. Judge these sites critically, with an eye on both the presentation and the reliability of the information.

Using Other Library Sources

Besides being a storehouse for books and periodicals, your library has a wealth of material in the reference section that may be useful to you in finding background information, statistics, and other kinds of evidence. Here are some sources that we have found particularly useful in our own research.

1. *Encyclopedias.* For getting quick background information on a topic, you will often find that a good encyclopedia is your best bet. Besides the well-known general-purpose encyclopedias such as the *Encyclopedia Britannica,* there are excellent specialized encyclopedias devoted to in-depth coverage of specific fields. Among the ones you might find most useful are these:

The International Encyclopedia of the Social Sciences

Dictionary of American History

Encyclopedia of World Art

McGraw-Hill Encyclopedia of Science and Technology

2. *Facts on File.* These interesting volumes give you a year-by-year summary of important news stories. If you wish to assemble a chronological summary of a news event such as Hillary Clinton's task force on national health coverage, ethnic wars in the Balkan countries, or the end of apartheid in South Africa, *Facts on File* gives you a summary of the events along with information about exact dates so that you can find the full stories in newspapers. A special feature is a series of excellent maps in the back of each volume, allowing you to find all geographical place names that occur in the year's news stories. The front cover of each volume explains how to use the series.

3. *Statistical Abstracts of the United States.* Don't even consider picking up one of these volumes if you don't have some spare time. You will get hooked on the fascinating graphs, charts, and tables compiled by the Bureau of Statistics. For statistical data about birth rates and abortions, marriages and divorces, trends in health care, trends in employment and unemployment, nutritional habits, and a host of other topics, these yearly volumes are a primary source of quantitative information about life in the United States.

4. *Congressional Abstracts.* For people working on current or historical events related to politics or any controversy related to the public sector, this index can guide you to all debates about the topic in the Senate or the House of Representatives.

5. *Book Review Digest.* For writers of argument, this series can be a godsend because it provides not only a brief summary of a book but also excerpts from a variety of reviews of the book, allowing the writer to size up quickly the conversation surrounding the book's ideas. To use *Book Review Digest,* you need to know the publishing date of the book for which you want to find reviews. Generally, reviews first appear in the same year the book was published and for several years thereafter. If you want to read reviews, for example, of a book appearing in 1992, you would probably find them in the 1992, 1993, and (if the book were very popular or provocative) 1994 volumes of *Book Review Digest.*

 FOR CLASS DISCUSSION

Working in groups, visit your college's library and learn to use the indexes and other sources listed in the preceding pages. Choose an issue of interest to the members of your group (preferably one about current public affairs so that you can find sources from the *New York Times Index* and *Congressional Abstracts*); then locate titles of two or three articles addressing your issue from as many of the indexes and sources as possible. Group members can divide up the work, each person taking several indexes as a special project and then teaching the others how to use them. Your goal is to feel confident that you can use these indexes to unlock most of the resources contained in your library.

USING YOUR SOURCES: SITTING DOWN TO READ

Once you have developed a working bibliography of books and articles and have gathered a collection of materials, how do you go about reading and note-taking? There is no easy answer here. At times you need to read articles carefully, fully, and empathically—reading as a believer and as a doubter, as discussed in Chapter 2, trying to understand various points of view on your issue, seeing where the disagreements are located, and so forth. Your goal at this time is to clarify your own understanding of the issue in order to join responsibly the on-going conversation.

At other times you need to read quickly, skimming an article in search of a needed piece of information, an alternative view, or a timely quotation. All these considerations and others—how to get your ideas focused, how to take notes, how to incorporate source material into your own writing, and how to cite and document your sources—are the subjects of the next chapter.

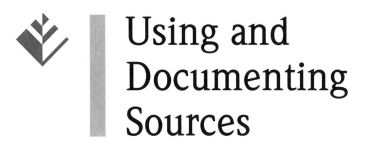

chapter **17**

Using and Documenting Sources

The previous chapter helped you pose a good research question and begin unlocking some of the resources of your library. This chapter helps you see what to do with your sources once you have found them—how to use them to clarify your own thinking and how to incorporate them into your writing through effective use of quotations, paraphrases, and summaries along with appropriate conventional formats for citations and documentation.

CLARIFYING YOUR OWN THINKING: THE CASE OF LYNNEA

In the previous chapter, we followed Lynnea's progress as she posed her research question on the effectiveness of policewomen and began her search for sources. Once Lynnea located several articles on policewomen, she found a quiet spot in the library and began to read. She was guided by two related questions: What physical requirements must someone meet in order to be an effective patrol officer? How successful have policewomen been when assigned to patrol duty? After reading some recent articles, Lynnea noticed that writers often referred to significant earlier studies, particularly a 1984 study called *Policewomen on Patrol, Final Report* by P. B. Bloch and D. Anderson. Lynnea tracked down this study as well as several others referred to in the first articles she read.

Both Lynnea's experience and her research strategy are typical. As a researcher becomes familiar with the ongoing conversation on an issue, she will notice that recent writers frequently refer to the same earlier studies or to the same earlier voices in the conversation. In scientific writing, this background reading is so important that the introductions to scientific studies usually include a "review of the literature" section, wherein writers summarize important research done to date on the question under investigation and identify areas of consensus and disagreement.

Therefore, during the first hours of her research project, Lynnea conducted her own "review of the literature" concerning women on patrol. During an early visit to her university's writing center, she reported that she had found three kinds of studies:

1. Studies attempting to identify the attitude of the police establishment (overwhelmingly male) toward women entering the police profession and the attitude of the general public toward women patrol officers. Although the findings weren't entirely consistent, Lynnea reported that male police officers generally distrusted women on patrol and felt that women didn't have the required physical strength or stamina to be patrol officers. The public, however, was more accepting of women patrol officers.

2. Studies attempting to evaluate the success of women on patrol by examining a variety of data such as arrests made, use of force, firing of weapons, interviews with persons involved in incidents, evaluation reports by superiors, and so forth. Lynnea reported that these studies were generally supportive of women police officers and showed that women cops were as successful as men cops.

3. Studies examining the legal and political battles fought by women to gain access to successful careers in police work. Lynnea reported being amazed at how much prejudice against women was evident in the police establishment.

At a writing center conference Lynnea confessed that, as a result of her readings, she was beginning to change her mind: She was now convinced that women could be effective patrol officers. But she wasn't convinced that *all* women could be effective officers any more than *all* men could be. She still felt that minimum size and strength requirements should be necessary. The problem was, she reported, that she couldn't find any information related to size and strength issues. Moreover, the research on women police officers did not mention anything about the size or strength of the women being studied. Were these successful patrol officers "big, husky" women, Lynnea asked, or "petite" women? She left the writing center in pursuit of more data.

Lynnea's dilemma is again typical. As we discussed in Chapter 6, the search for clarification often leads to uncertainty. As you immerse yourself in the conversation surrounding an issue, you find that the experts often disagree and that no easy answers emerge. Your goal under these circumstances is to find the best reasons available and to support them with the best evidence you can muster. But the kind of uncertainty Lynnea felt is both healthy and humbling. If your own research leads to similar feelings, we invite you to reread those sections of Chapter 6 where, in our discussion of the greenhouse effect, we suggest our own strategy for coping with ambiguity.

We'll leave Lynnea at this point to take up the technical side of writing research arguments. Besides using research to clarify your own thinking, you also need to have strategies for note taking and for incorporating the results of your reading into your own writing through proper citations and documentation.

DEVELOPING A GOOD SYSTEM OF NOTE TAKING

There is no one right way to take notes. For short research papers, many students keep all their notes in a spiral notebook; others use a system of 3 × 5 cards (for bibliographic information) and 5 × 8 cards (for actual notes). Increasingly, researchers use database software on their personal computers. Whatever system you use, the key is to take notes that are complete enough so that you don't have to keep going back to the library to reread your sources. Some students get around this problem by photocopying all articles they might use in their essays, but this is an expensive habit that may in the long run be less efficient than careful note taking in the first place.

It is much easier to take good notes for a research project if you have your issue question clearly formulated. When you know your issue question, you can anticipate how information from books and articles is apt to get incorporated into your essay. Sometimes you will need to write an accurate summary of a whole article as part of your research notes; at other times you may want to jot down only some facts or figures from an article; at still other times you may want to copy a passage word for word as a potential quotation. There is no way to know what kind of notes you will need to take on each book or article unless you can predict what kind of thesis you will be supporting. We therefore continue our comments on the art of note taking as we discuss ways information can be used in a research essay.

INCORPORATING SOURCES INTO YOUR ARGUMENT: SOME GENERAL PRINCIPLES

To illustrate different ways that you can use a source, we will use the following brief article from the magazine *Science '86*.

Reading, Writing, and (Ugh!) You Know What

1   ANN ARBOR, Mich.—Not only are American high school students worse at mathematics than their Japanese and Chinese peers, they start falling behind in kindergarten.

2   That's one conclusion of a five-year study done by psychologist Harold Stevenson and graduate student Shin-ying Lee, both of the University of Michigan, and psychologist James Stigler of the University of Chicago. The study also shows for the first time that parents must share the blame.

More than 2,000 children in kindergarten and the first and fifth grades were tested   3
and interviewed in Minneapolis, in Sendai, Japan, and in Taipei, China. The researchers
composed the test for each grade from math problems found in textbooks in all three cities.

All the children in each grade performed equally well on reading and general intelli-   4
gence tests, but math scores differed from the start. While average scores for U.S. and Chinese kindergarten students were the same, Japanese kindergartners scored about 10
percent higher. First graders in the U.S. were surpassed by their peers in both China and
Japan by an average of 10 percent. Then the gap widened. The top U.S. fifth-grade class
scored below the lowest Japanese class and the second lowest Chinese class. Of the 100
highest scoring fifth graders, one was American.

A crucial difference is time: Chinese and Japanese students spend more hours in math   5
class and attend school some 240 days a year, Americans about 180. But another difference, the researchers found, is parental influence. Chinese and Japanese parents give their
children more help with math homework than U.S. parents, who tended to believe that
"ability" was the premier reason for academic success, according to the researchers' interviews. Chinese and Japanese parents, in contrast, most often said "effort" was most important. And more than 90 percent of U.S. parents believed the schools did an "excellent"
job teaching math and other subjects; most Japanese and Chinese parents said the schools
did a "fair" job.

"American parents are very involved in teaching reading," says Stigler. "But they seem   6
to think that teaching math is the school's job. It's as if it gets them off the hook."

Citing Information

Sometimes the complete argument of an article may not be relevant to your
essay. Often you will use only a piece of information from the article. For example, let's suppose you are writing an argument claiming that American society,
as a whole, values individual creativity more than does Japanese society. You
plan to contrast an open classroom in an American grade school with a more regimented Japanese classroom. At the end of the passage, you might write something like this:

> Not only is education in Japan more regimented than it is in the United States, it con-
> tinues through a much longer school year. A typical Japanese grade school student
> attends classes 240 days a year compared with 180 days a year in the United States.
> (*Science '86* 7). Although such a system might produce more academic achievement,
> it provides little time for children to be children, to play and daydream—essential
> ingredients for nurturing creativity.

Here the total argument of the *Science '86* article isn't relevant to the writer's
essay. He has borrowed only the small detail about the length of the school year
(which, of course, the writer documents by means of a citation in parentheses). In
his original notecards, the writer would not have had to summarize the whole *Science '86* article. By knowing his research question, he would have known that only
this piece of information was relevant.

Summarizing an Argument: Different Contexts Demand Different Summaries

On other occasions, however, you may need to summarize the entire argument of an essay, or at least a major portion of the argument. How you summarize it depends once again on the context of your own essay because your summary must focus on your own thesis. To illustrate how context influences a summary, we will examine passages by two different writers, Cheryl and Jeff, each of whom uses the *Science '86* article, but in the context of different arguments. Cheryl is writing on the issue of heredity versus environment in the determination of scholastic achievement. She is making the causal claim that environment plays a key role in scholastic high achievement. Jeff, on the other hand, is writing on American mathematics education. He is making the evaluation claim that American mathematics education is in a dangerous shambles. Both writers include a summary of the *Science '86* article,* but their summaries are written in different ways in order to emphasize different aspects of the article.

PASSAGE FROM CHERYL'S ESSAY ON HEREDITY VERSUS ENVIRONMENT

Another argument showing the importance of environment on scholastic achievement comes from a research study done by psychologists at the University of Chicago and the University of Michigan (*Science '86*). These researchers compared the mathematics achievement of 2000 kindergartners, first graders, and fifth graders from the United States, Japan, and China. At the beginning of the study the researchers determined that the comparison groups were equal in terms of reading ability and general intelligence. But the American students were far behind in mathematics achievement. At the first grade level, the researchers reported, American students were 10 percent behind Japanese and Chinese students and considerably further behind by the end of the fifth grade. In fact, only one American student scored in the top 100 of all students.

What is significant about this study is that heredity seems to play no factor in accounting for the differences between American students and their Japanese and Chinese counterparts since the comparison groups were shown to be of equal intelligence at the beginning of the study. The researchers attribute the differences between the groups to the time they spent on math (Japanese students go to class 240 days per year while Americans are in class only 180 days per year) and to parental influence. According to the study, American parents believe that native "ability" is the key factor in math achievement and don't seem to push their children as much. Japanese and Chinese parents, however, believe that "effort" is the key factor and spend considerably more time than American parents helping their

---

*The citations follow the MLA format described later in this chapter.

children with their math homework (8). Thus, it is the particular environment created by Chinese and Japanese societies, not inherited intelligence, that accounts
for the greater math achievement of children in those cultures.

PASSAGE FROM JEFF'S ESSAY ON THE FAILURE OF
MATHEMATICS EDUCATION IN THE UNITED STATES

Further evidence of the disgraceful nature of mathematics education in the United
States is the dismal performance of American grade school students in mathematics achievement tests as compared to children from other cultures. One study,
reported in the magazine *Science '86*, revealed that American kindergarten students
scored 10 percent lower on mathematics knowledge than did kindergartners from
Japan. This statistic suggests that American parents don't teach arithmetical skills
in the home to preschoolers the way Japanese parents do.

But the most frightening part of the study showed what happens by the fifth
grade. The best American class in the study scored below the worst Chinese or
Japanese class, and of the top 100 students only one was an American (8). The
differences between the American students and their Chinese and Japanese
counterparts cannot be attributed to intelligence because the article reports that
comparison groups were matched for intelligence at the beginning of the study.
The difference can be accounted for only by the quality of education and the effort
of students. The researchers who did this study attributed the difference first of all
to time. According to the study, Chinese and Japanese students spend 240 days per
year in school while Americans spend only 180. The second reason for the difference is parental influence, since Japanese and Chinese parents spend much more
time than American parents helping their children with mathematics. The study
suggests that if we are to do anything about mathematics education in the United
States we need a revolution not only in the schools but in the home.

 FOR CLASS DISCUSSION

Although both the preceding passages summarize the *Science '86* article, they
use the article to support somewhat different claims. Working as individuals or in
groups, prepare short answers to the following questions. Be ready to elaborate on
your answers in class if called on to defend them.

1. What makes each passage different from a data dump?

2. In what ways are the summaries different? (Compare the summaries to each
   other and to the original article.)

3. How does the difference between the summaries reflect a different purpose in
   each passage?

Article Summaries as a Note-Taking Tool

Both Cheryl's passage and Jeff's summarize the *Science '86* article accurately. To be able to write summaries such as these when you compose your rough drafts, you need to have the articles at hand (by photocopying them from the library) or you need to have written summaries of the articles in your notecards. We strongly recommend the second practice—writing summaries of articles in your notecards when their arguments seem relevant to your research project. Taking notes this way is time consuming in the short run but time efficient in the long run. The act of summarizing forces you to read the article carefully and to perceive its whole argument. It also steers you away from the bad habit of noting facts or information from an article without perceiving how the information supports a meaning. Because summary writing is a way of reading as a believer (see Chapter 2), it helps you listen to the various voices in the conversation about your issue.

Paraphrasing Portions of an Argument

Whereas a summary places a whole argument in a nutshell by leaving out supporting details but keeping the main argument, a paraphrase is about the same length as the original but places the ideas of the original in the writer's own words. Paraphrase often includes pieces of quotation worked neatly into the writer's passage. When you are summarizing a short article, such as the *Science '86* article used in the previous section, parts of your summary can blend into paraphrase. The distinction isn't important. What is important is that you avoid plagiarism by making sure you are restating the original argument in your own words. Generally you should avoid paraphrasing a lengthy passage because then you will simply be turning someone else's argument into your own words. A good research argument weaves together supporting material from a variety of sources; it doesn't paraphrase someone else's argument.

Quoting

Inexperienced writers tend to quote too much material and at too great a length. To see a skillful use of quotations, look again at the *Science '86* article we have been using as an illustration. That article is actually a summary of a much longer and more technical research study written by the researchers Stevenson, Shin-ying Lee, and Stigler. Note that the summary includes only two kinds of quotation: quotation of the single words *ability, effort, excellent,* and *fair;* and a brief quotation from Stigler to conclude the article.

The first kind of quotation—quoting individual words or short phrases—is a matter of accuracy. The writer summarizing the original research study wanted to indicate the exact terms the researchers used at key points in their argument. The second kind of quotation—quoting a brief passage from an article—has a different purpose. Sometimes writers want to give readers a sense of the flavor of their original source, particularly if the source speaks in a lively, interesting style. At other times a writer wishes to quote a source exactly on an especially important point, both to highlight the point and to increase readers' confidence that the writer has elsewhere been summarizing or paraphrasing accurately. The ending quotation in the *Science '86* article serves both purposes.

As a general rule, avoid too much quotation, especially long quotations. Remember that a research essay, like any other essay, should present *your* argument in *your* voice. When you use summary and to a lesser extent paraphrase, you are in command because you are fitting the arguments of your sources to your own purposes. When you quote, on the other hand, you are lifting material from a different context with a different purpose and plunking it into an alien home, inevitably mixing voices and styles. Too much quotation is the hallmark of a data dump essay; the writer strings together other people's words instead of creating his own argument.

INCORPORATING SOURCES INTO YOUR ARGUMENT: TECHNICAL ADVICE ON SUMMARIZING, PARAPHRASING, AND QUOTING

As a research writer, you need to be able to move back and forth gracefully between conducting your own argument and using material from your research in the form of summary, paraphrase, or quotation. For purposes of illustration, we ask you to read the following essay entitled "The Case for Torture" by Michael Levin. We will assume you want to use Levin's ideas in an argument that you are writing. You will need to be familiar with Levin's essay in order to understand our explanations of summary, paraphrase, and quotation.

The Case for Torture

Michael Levin

It is generally assumed that torture is impermissible, a throwback to a more brutal age. 1 Enlightened societies reject it outright, and regimes suspected of using it risk the wrath of the United States.

I believe this attitude is unwise. There are situations in which torture is not merely 2 permissible but morally mandatory. Moreover, these situations are moving from the realm of imagination to fact.

Death: Suppose a terrorist has hidden an atomic bomb on Manhattan Island which 3 will detonate at noon on July 4 unless . . . (here follow the usual demands for money and release of his friends from jail). Suppose, further, that he is caught at 10 A.M. of the fateful day, but—preferring death to failure—won't disclose where the bomb is. What do we do? If we follow due process—wait for his lawyer, arraign him—millions of people will die. If the only way to save those lives is to subject the terrorist to the most excruciating possible pain, what grounds can there be for not doing so? I suggest there are none. In any case, I ask you to face the question with an open mind.

4   Torturing the terrorist is unconstitutional? Probably. But millions of lives surely outweigh constitutionality. Torture is barbaric? Mass murder is far more barbaric. Indeed, letting millions of innocents die in deference to one who flaunts his guilt is moral cowardice, an unwillingness to dirty one's hands. If *you* caught the terrorist, could you sleep nights knowing that millions died because you couldn't bring yourself to apply the electrodes?

5   Once you concede that torture is justified in extreme cases, you have admitted that the decision to use torture is a matter of balancing innocent lives against the means needed to save them. You must now face more realistic cases involving more modest numbers. Someone plants a bomb on a jumbo jet. He alone can disarm it, and his demands cannot be met (or if they can, we refuse to set a precedent by yielding to his threats). Surely we can, we must, do anything to the extortionist to save the passengers. How can we tell 300, or 100, or 10 people who never asked to be put in danger, "I'm sorry, you'll have to die in agony, we just couldn't bring ourselves to . . ."

6   Here are the results of an informal poll about a third, hypothetical, case. Suppose a terrorist group kidnapped a newborn baby from a hospital. I asked four mothers if they would approve of torturing kidnappers if that were necessary to get their own newborns back. All said yes, the most "liberal" adding that she would like to administer it herself.

7   I am not advocating torture as punishment. Punishment is addressed to deeds irrevocably past. Rather, I am advocating torture as an acceptable measure for preventing future evils. So understood, it is far less objectionable than many extant punishments. Opponents of the death penalty, for example, are forever insisting that executing a murderer will not bring back his victim (as if the purpose of capital punishment were supposed to be resurrection, not deterrence or retribution). But torture, in the cases described, is intended not to bring anyone back but to keep innocents from being dispatched. The most powerful argument against using torture as a punishment or to secure confessions is that such practices disregard the rights of the individual. Well, if the individual is all that important—and he is—it is correspondingly important to protect the rights of individuals threatened by terrorists. If life is so valuable that it must never be taken, the lives of the innocents must be saved even at the price of hurting the one who endangers them.

8   Better precedents for torture are assassination and pre-emptive attack. No Allied leader would have flinched at assassinating Hitler, had that been possible. (The Allies did assassinate Heydrich.) Americans would be angered to learn that Roosevelt could have had Hitler killed in 1943—thereby shortening the war and saving millions of lives—but refused on moral grounds. Similarly, if nation A learns that nation B is about to launch an unprovoked attack, A has a right to save itself by destroying B's military capability first. In the same way, if the police can by torture save those who would otherwise die at the hands of kidnappers or terrorists, they must.

Idealism: There is an important difference between terrorists and their victims that   9
should mute talk of the terrorists' "rights." The terrorist's victims are at risk unintentionally, not having asked to be endangered. But the terrorist knowingly initiated his actions.
Unlike his victims, he volunteered for the risks of his deed. By threatening to kill for profit
or idealism, he renounces civilized standards, and he can have no complaint if civilization
tries to thwart him by whatever means necessary.

Just as torture is justified only to save lives (not extort confessions or recantations), it   10
is justifiably administered only to those *known* to hold innocent lives in their hands. Ah,
but how can the authorities ever be sure they have the right malefactor? Isn't there a danger of error and abuse? Won't We turn into Them?

Questions like these are disingenuous in a world in which terrorists proclaim them-   11
selves and perform for television. The name of their game is public recognition. After all,
you can't very well intimidate a government into releasing your freedom fighters unless you
announce that it is your group that has seized its embassy. "Clear guilt" is difficult to define, but when 40 million people see a group of masked gunmen seize an airplane on the
evening news, there is not much question about who the perpetrators are. There will be
hard cases where the situation is murkier. Nonetheless, a line demarcating the legitimate
use of torture can be drawn. Torture only the obviously guilty, and only for the sake of saving innocents, and the line between Us and Them will remain clear.

There is little danger that the Western democracies will lose their way if they choose   12
to inflict pain as one way of preserving order. Paralysis in the face of evil is the greater danger. Some day soon a terrorist will threaten tens of thousands of lives, and torture will be
the only way to save them. We had better start thinking about this.

For incorporating Levin's ideas into your own writing, you have a number
of options.

Summary

When you wish to include a writer's complete argument (or a large sustained
portion of it) in your own essay, you will need to summarize it. For a detailed explanation of how to summarize, see Chapter 2. Summaries can be quite long or very
short. The following condensation of Levin's essay illustrates a short summary.

> Levin believes that torture can be justifiable if its purpose is to save innocent lives
> and if it is certain that the person being tortured has the power to save those lives.
> Torture is not justifiable as punishment. Levin likens the justified use of torture to
> the justified use of assassination or preemptive strikes in order to preclude or
> shorten a war.

This short passage summarizes the main points of the Levin argument in a few
sentences. As a summary, it condenses the whole down to a small nutshell. For an
example of a somewhat longer summary, see Chapter 2, pages 35–37.

Paraphrase

Unlike summary, which is a condensation of an essay, a paraphrase is a "translation" of an essay into the writer's own words. It is approximately the same length as the original, but converts the original into the writer's own voice. Be careful when you paraphrase to avoid both the original writer's words and the original writer's grammatical structure and syntax. If you follow the original sentence structure while replacing occasional words with synonyms, you are cheating: That practice is plagiarism, not paraphrase. Here is a paraphrase of paragraph 4 in Levin's essay:

> Levin asks whether it is unconstitutional to torture a terrorist. He believes that it probably is, but he argues that saving the lives of millions of innocent people is a greater good than obeying the Constitution. Although torture is brutal, so is letting innocent people die. In fact, Levin believes that we are moral cowards if we don't torture a guilty individual in order to save millions of lives.

This paraphrase of paragraph 4 is approximately the same length as the original paragraph. The purpose of a paraphrase is not to condense the original, but to turn the original into one's own language. Even though you are not borrowing any language, you will still need to cite the source to indicate that you are borrowing ideas.

Block Quotation

Occasionally, you will wish to quote an author's words directly. You must be meticulous in copying down the words *exactly* so that you make no changes. You must also be fair to your source by not quoting out of context. When the quoted material takes up more than three lines in your original source, use the following block quotation method:

> In his argument supporting torture under certain circumstances, Levin is careful to insist that he doesn't see torture as punishment but solely as a way of preventing loss of innocent lives:
>
>> I am not advocating torture as punishment. Punishment is addressed to deeds irrevocably past. Rather, I am advocating torture as an acceptable measure for preventing future evils. So understood, it is far less objectionable than many extant punishments.

Here the writer wants to quote Levin's words as found in paragraph 7. Because the passage to be quoted is longer than three lines, the writer uses the block quotation method. Note that the quotation is introduced with a colon and that no quotation marks are used. The block format with indentations takes the place of quotation marks.

Inserted Quotation

If the passage you wish to quote is less than three lines, you can insert it directly into your own sentences by using quotation marks instead of the block method:

> In his argument favoring torture, Levin is careful to distinguish between torture and punishment. "I am not advocating torture as punishment," Levin asserts. "Punishment is addressed to deeds irrevocably past. Rather, I am advocating torture as an acceptable measure for preventing future evils."

Here the writer breaks the same quotation into parts so that no part is longer than three lines. Thus the writer uses quotation marks rather than the block quotation method.

If the inserted quotation is a complete sentence in your own essay, then it should begin with a capital letter. The quotation is usually separated from preceding explanatory matter by a colon or comma. However, if the quotation is not a complete sentence in your own essay, then you insert it using quotation marks only and begin the quotation with a small letter.

QUOTATION AS INDEPENDENT SENTENCE

According to Levin, "Punishment is addressed to deeds irrevocably past."

QUOTATION AS CLAUSE OR PHRASE THAT IS NOT AN INDEPENDENT SENTENCE

Levin claims that punishment is concerned with "deeds irrevocably past," while torture is aimed at "preventing future evils."

In the first example, the quotation begins with a capital *P* because the quotation comprises an independent sentence. Note that it is separated from the preceding phrase by a comma. In the second example the quotations do not comprise independent sentences. They are inserted directly into the writer's sentence, using quotation marks only.

Shortening or Modifying Quotations

Sometimes you wish to quote the exact words from a source, but in order to make the quotation fit gracefully into your own sentence you need to alter it in some way, either by shortening it, by changing it slightly, or by adding explanatory material to it. There are several ways of doing so: through judicious selection of phrases to be quoted or through use of ellipses and brackets.

SHORTEN A PASSAGE BY SELECTING ONLY KEY PHRASES FOR QUOTING

In his argument favoring torture, Levin is careful to distinguish between torture and punishment. "I am not advocating torture as punishment," Levin asserts, but only "as an acceptable measure for preventing future evils."

Here the writer quotes only selected pieces of the longer passage and weaves them into her own sentences.

USE ELLIPSIS TO OMIT MATERIAL FROM A QUOTATION

Levin continues by distinguishing torture from capital punishment:

> Opponents of the death penalty . . . are forever insisting that executing a murderer will not bring back his victim. . . . But torture . . . is intended not to bring anyone back but to keep innocents from being dispatched.

In this block quotation from paragraph 7, the writer uses ellipses in three places. Made with three spaced periods, an ellipsis indicates that words have been omitted. Note that the second ellipsis in this passage seems to contain four periods. The first period ends the sentence; the last three periods are the ellipsis.

USE BRACKETS TO MAKE SLIGHT CHANGES IN A
QUOTATION OR TO ADD EXPLANATORY MATERIAL

According to Levin, "By threatening to kill for profit or idealism, he [the torturer] renounces civilized standards."

The writer puts "the torturer" in brackets to indicate the antecedent of the quoted pronoun "he." This passage is from paragraph 9.

According to Levin, "[T]orture [is] an acceptable measure for preventing future evils."

This passage, from paragraph 7, changes the original slightly: a small *t* has been raised to a capital *T*, and the word *as* has been changed to *is*. These changes are indicated by brackets. You don't usually have to indicate when you change a small letter to a capital or vice versa. But it is important to do so here because the writer is actually changing the grammar of the original by converting a phrase into a sentence.

Using Quotations Within Quotations

Sometimes you may wish to quote a passage that already has quotation marks within it. If you use the block quotation method, keep the quotation marks exactly as they are in the original. If you use the inserted quotation method, then use single quotation marks (') instead of double marks (") to indicate the quotation within the quotation.

Levin is quick to dismiss the notion that a terrorist has rights:

> There is an important difference between terrorists and their victims that should mute talk of the terrorists' "rights." The terrorist's victims are at risk

unintentionally, not having asked to be endangered. But the terrorist know-ingly initiated his actions.

Because the writer uses the block quotation method, the original quotation marks around *rights* remain. See the original passage in paragraph 9.

> Levin claims that "an important difference between terrorists and their victims . . . should mute talk of the terrorists' 'rights.' "

Here the writer uses the inserted quotation method. Therefore the original double quotation marks (") around *rights* have been changed to single quotation marks ('), which on a typewriter are made with an apostrophe.

An Extended Illustration: Martha's Argument

To help you get a feel for how a writer integrates brief quotations into para-phrases or summaries, consider the following passage written by Martha, a stu-dent who was disturbed by a class discussion of Levin's essay. Several classmates argued that Levin's justification of torture could also be used to justify terrorism. Martha did not believe that Levin's argument could be applied to terrorism. Here is the passage from Martha's argument that summarizes Levin. (Page references in Martha's passage refer to the original *Newsweek* source that she used—part of the MLA citation system to be described shortly.)

> Now it may seem that if terrorism is always wrong then torture should always be wrong also since torture, even more so than terrorism, is a barbaric practice from a pre-civilized age. But philosopher Michael Levin shows a flaw in this reasoning. Torture is justifiable, says Levin, but only in some cases. First of all, he says that torture should be applied only to those "*known* to hold innocent lives in their hands" and only if the person being tortured is clearly guilty and clearly can pre-vent a horrible act from occurring (13). Levin uses the example of using torture on a captured terrorist to find the location of an atomic bomb set to go off on Man-hattan Island. The principle here is that you are saving the lives of millions of in-nocent bystanders by applying systematic pain to one person who "renounc[ed] civilized standards" (13) when becoming a terrorist. For Levin, saving the lives of innocent bystanders is a higher moral imperative than refusing to torture the per-son who can prevent the deaths. In fact, Levin claims, refusal to torture the ter-rorist is "moral cowardice, an unwillingness to dirty one's hands" (13). "If life is . . . valuable," Levin argues, then "the lives of the innocents must be saved even at the price of hurting the one who endangers them" (13).
>
> We can now return to the problem I posed earlier. If Levin is able to justify tor-ture under some conditions, why can't we also justify terrorism under some con-ditions? The answer is that . . . [Martha's argument continues].

FOR CLASS DISCUSSION

Working as individuals or as small groups, prepare brief answers for the following questions:

1. How is Martha's passage different from a data dump?

2. Without being able to read her whole essay, can you determine Martha's purpose for summarizing Levin within her own argument on terrorism? If so, what is her purpose?

3. Why did the writer use brackets [ ] within one quotation and ellipses (. . .) within another?

4. What effects did Martha achieve by using only short quotations instead of longer block quotations from Levin's argument?

Signaling Directions:
The Use of Attributive Tags

In all of our examples of citing, summarizing, paraphrasing, and quoting, the writers have used attributive tags to signal to readers which ideas are the writer's own and which ideas are being taken from another source. Attributive tags are phrases such as the following: "according to the researchers . . . ," "Levin claims that . . . ," "the author continues . . . ," and so forth. Such phrases signal to the reader that the material immediately following is from the cited source. Parenthetical citations are used only to give readers follow-up information on where the source can be found, not to indicate that the writer is using a source. The source being cited should always be mentioned in the text. Note how confusing a passage becomes if these attributive tags are omitted.

CONFUSING ATTRIBUTION

Now it may seem that if terrorism is always wrong then torture should always be wrong also since torture, even more so than terrorism, is a barbaric practice from a pre-civilized age. But there is a flaw in this reasoning. Torture should be applied only to those *"known* to hold innocent lives in their hands (Levin 13)" and only if the person being tortured is clearly guilty and clearly can prevent a terrorist act from occurring. A good example is using torture on a captured terrorist to find the location of an atomic bomb set to go off on Manhattan Island.

Although this writer cites Levin as the source of the quotation, it is not clear just when the borrowing from Levin begins or ends. For instance, is the example of the captured terrorist on Manhattan Island the writer's own or does it come from Levin? As the following revision shows, the use of attributive tags within the text makes it clear exactly where the writer's ideas leave off and a borrowed source begins or ends.

CLEAR ATTRIBUTION

Now it may seem that if terrorism is always wrong then torture should always be wrong also since torture, even more so than terrorism, is a barbaric practice from a pre-civilized age. But **philosopher Michael Levin shows** a flaw in this reasoning. Torture is justifiable, **says Levin,** but only in some cases. First of all, **he says that** torture should be applied only to those *"known* to hold innocent lives in their hands" and only if the person being tortured is clearly guilty and clearly can prevent a horrible act from occurring (13). **Levin uses** the example of using torture on a captured terrorist to find the location of an atomic bomb set to go off on Manhattan Island.

AVOIDING PLAGIARISM

Plagiarism, a form of academic cheating, is always a serious academic offense. You can plagiarize in one of two ways: (1) by borrowing another person's ideas without indicating the borrowing with attributive tags in the text and a proper citation, or (2) by borrowing another person's language without putting the borrowed language in quotation marks or block indentations. The first kind of plagiarism is usually outright cheating; the writer usually knows he is stealing material and tries to disguise it.

The second kind of plagiarism, however, often begins in a hazy never-never land between paraphrasing and copying. We refer to it in our classes as "lazy cheating" and still consider it a serious offense, like stealing from your neighbor's vegetable garden because you are too lazy to do your own planting, weeding, and harvesting. Anyone who appreciates how hard it is to write and revise even a short passage will appreciate why it is wrong to take someone else's language readymade. Thus, in our classes, we would fail a paper that included the following passage. (Let's call the writer Lucy.)

> Another argument showing the importance of environment on scholastic achievement comes from a research study done by psychologists at the University of Chicago and the University of Michigan (*Science '86* 7, 8). The study shows that parents must share the blame for the poor math performance of American students. In this study more than 2,000 children in kindergarten and the fifth grade were tested and interviewed in Minneapolis, in Sendai, Japan, and in Taipei, China. The researchers made up a test based on math problems found in textbooks used in all three cities. All the children in each grade performed equally well on reading and general intelligence tests, but their math scores differed from the start. The kindergartners from Japan scored about 10 percent higher than American kindergartners. The gap widened by the fifth grade. The top U.S. fifth-grade class scored below the lowest Japanese class and the second lowest Chinese class. Of the 100 highest scoring fifth graders, one was American (*Science '86* 8).

FOR CLASS DISCUSSION

Do you think it was fair to flunk Lucy's essay? She claimed she wasn't cheating since she gave two different parenthetical citations accurately citing the *Science '86* article as her source. Before answering this question, compare the above passage with the original article on pages 382–383; also compare the above passage with the opening paragraph from Cheryl's summary (pages 384–385) of the *Science '86* article. What justification could a professor use for giving an A to Cheryl's essay while flunking Lucy's essay?

Note Taking to Avoid Plagiarism

When you take notes on books or articles, be extremely careful to put all borrowed language in quotation marks. If you write summaries of arguments, as we strongly recommend you do, take time at the note-taking stage to put the summaries in your own words. If you wish to paraphrase an important passage, make sure you either copy the original into your notes word for word and indicate that you have done so (so that you can paraphrase it later) or paraphrase it entirely in your language when you take the notes. Inadvertent plagiarism can occur if you copy something in your notes word for word and then later assume that what you copied was actually a paraphrase.

DOCUMENTING YOUR SOURCES

To many students, the dreariest aspect of research writing is documenting their sources—that is, getting citations in the proper places and in the correct forms. As we noted at the beginning of the previous chapter, however, documentation of sources is a service to readers who may want to follow up on your research. Documentation in the proper form allows them to find your sources quickly.

There are two questions that you must answer to ensure proper documentation: "When do I cite a source?" and "What format do I use?"

When to Cite Sources

As a general rule, cite everything you borrow. Some students take this rule to unnecessary extremes, arguing that everything they "know" comes from somewhere. They end up citing lectures, conversations with a friend, notes from an old high school class, and so forth. Use common sense. If you successfully avoid writing a data dump essay, then your research will be used to support a thesis, which will reflect your own individual thinking and synthesis of material. You will know when you are using evidence from your own personal experience as source material and when you are using evidence you got from doing library research. Document all the material you got from the library or from another external source.

What Format to Use

Formats for citations and bibliographies vary somewhat from discipline to discipline. At the present time, footnotes have almost entirely disappeared from academic writing as a means of citing sources. Rather, citations for quotations or paraphrased material are now usually made in the text itself by putting brief identifying symbols inside parentheses.

OVERVIEW OF THE MLA AND APA SYSTEMS OF DOCUMENTATION

The two main systems used today for academic essays aimed at general college audiences are the MLA (Modern Language Association) system, generally favored in the humanities, and the APA (American Psychological Association) system, generally favored in the social sciences. Other general systems are sometimes encountered—for example, the *University of Chicago Manual of Style*—and many specialized disciplines such as biology or chemistry have their own style manuals. But familiarity with the MLA and APA systems should serve you well throughout college. The sample research argument written by Stephen Bean (pp. 330–338) follows the MLA style. The sample research argument written by Lynnea Clark (pp. 414–420) follows the APA style.

Neither the MLA nor the APA system uses footnotes to document sources. In both systems a source is cited by means of a brief parenthetical reference following the quotation or the passage in which the source is used. Complete bibliographic information on each source is then included in an alphabetical list at the end of the text. Let us now turn to a more complete discussion of these two features.

Feature 1: Place a Complete Bibliographic List at the End of the Text

In both the MLA and the APA styles, a list of all the sources you have cited is included at the end of the research paper. In the MLA system, this bibliographic list is called "Works Cited." In the APA system this list is called "References." In both systems, entries are listed alphabetically by author (if no author is given for a particular source, then that source is alphabetized by title).

Let's look at how the two style systems would have you cite the Levin article on torture. The article appears in the June 7, 1982, issue of *Newsweek* on page 13. In the MLA style the complete bibliographic reference would be placed at the end of the paper under "Works Cited," where it would appear as follows:

MLA: Levin, Michael. "The Case for Torture." <u>Newsweek</u> 7 June 1982: 13.

In the APA system, the complete bibliographic reference would be placed at the end of the paper under "References," where it would appear as follows:

APA: Levin, M. (1982, June 7). The case for torture. <u>Newsweek,</u> p. 13.

When you refer to this article in the text—using either system—you place a brief citation in parentheses.

Feature 2: Cite Sources in the Text by Putting Brief References in Parentheses

Both the MLA and the APA systems cite sources through brief parenthetical references in the text. However, the two systems differ somewhat in the way these citations are structured.

In-text Citation: MLA System

In the MLA system, you place the author's name and the page number of the cited source in parentheses. (If the author's name is mentioned in a preceding attributive tag, then only the page number needs to be placed in parentheses.)

Torture, claims one philosopher, should only be applied to those "<u>known</u> to hold innocent lives in their hands" and only if the person being tortured is clearly guilty and clearly can prevent a terrorist act from occurring (Levin 13).

or

Torture, claims Michael Levin, should only be applied to those "<u>known</u> to hold innocent lives in their hands" and only if the person being tortured is clearly guilty and clearly can prevent a terrorist act from occurring (13).

If readers wish to follow up on the source, they will look up the Levin article in the "Works Cited" at the end. If more than one work by Levin has been used as sources in the essay, then you would include in the in-text citation an abbreviated title of the article following Levin's name.

(Levin, "Torture" 13)

Once Levin has been cited the first time and it is clear that you are still quoting from Levin, then you need put in parentheses only the page number and eliminate the author's name.

In-text Citation: APA System

In the APA system, you place the author's name and the date of the cited source in parentheses. If you are quoting a particular passage or citing a particular table, include the page number where the information is found. Use a comma to separate each element of the citation and use the abbreviation *p.* or *pp.* before the page number. (If the author's name is mentioned in a preceding attributive tag, then only the date needs to be placed in parentheses.)

> Torture, claims one philosopher, should only be applied to those "<u>known</u> to hold innocent lives in their hands" and only if the person being tortured is clearly guilty and clearly can prevent a terrorist act from occurring (Levin, 1982, p. 13).

> or

> Torture, claims Michael Levin, should only be applied to those "<u>known</u> to hold innocent lives in their hands" and only if the person being tortured is clearly guilty and clearly can prevent a terrorist act from occurring (1982, p. 13).

If readers wish to follow up on the source, they will look for the 1982 Levin article in the "References" at the end. If Levin had published more than one article in 1982, the articles would be distinguished by small letters placed alphabetically after the date:

> (Levin, 1982a)

> or

> (Levin, 1982b)

In the APA style, if an article or book has more than one author, the word *and* is used to join them in the text but the ampersand (&) is used to join them in the parenthetical reference:

> Smith and Peterson (1983) found that . . .

> More recent data (Smith & Peterson, 1983) have shown . . .

Citing a Quotation or Other Data from a Secondary Source

Occasionally, you may wish to use a quotation or other kinds of data from a secondary source. For example, suppose you are writing an argument that the United States should reconsider its trade policies with China. You read an article entitled "China's Gilded Age" by Xiao-huang Yin appearing in the April 1994 issue of *The Atlantic*. This article contains the following passage appearing on page 42:

> Dual ownership has in essence turned this state enterprise into a private business. Asked if such a practice is an example of China's "socialist market economy," a professor of economics at Nanjing University, where I taught in the early 1980's, replied, "Nobody knows what the concept means. It is only rhetoric, and it can mean anything but socialism."

When citing material from a secondary source, it is always best, when possible, to locate the original source and cite your data directly. But in the above case, no other source is likely available. Here is how you would cite it in both the MLA and APA systems.

MLA: According to an economics professor at Nanjing University, the term "socialist market economy," has become confused under capitalistic influence. "Nobody knows what the concept means. It is only rhetoric, and it can mean anything but socialism." (qtd. in Yin 42).

APA: According to an economics professor at Nanjing University, the term "socialist market economy," has become confused under capitalistic influence. "Nobody knows what the concept means. It is only rhetoric, and it can mean anything but socialism" (cited in Yin, 1994, p. 42).

In both systems you would place the Yin article in the end-of-text bibliographic list. What follows is a description of the format for the end-of-text bibliographic entries under "Works Cited" in the MLA system and under "References" in the APA System.

Form for Entries in "Works Cited" (MLA) and "References" (APA)

The remaining pages in this section show examples of MLA and APA formats for different kinds of sources, including electronic sources. Following these examples is a typical page from a "Works Cited" or "References" list that features formats for the most commonly encountered kinds of sources.

General Format for Books

MLA: Author. Title. Edition. City of Publication: Publisher, year of publication.

APA: Author. (Year of Publication). Title. City of Publication: Publisher.

One Author

MLA: Coles, Robert. The Spiritual Life of Children. Boston: Houghton, 1990.

APA: Coles, R. (1990). The spiritual life of children. Boston: Houghton Mifflin.

In the MLA style, author entries include first names and middle initials. In the APA style only the initials of the first and middle names are given, unless full names are needed to distinguish persons with the same initials. In the APA style only the first word and proper names in a title are capitalized. Note also that the year of publication follows immediately after the author's name. In the MLA system, names of publishers have standard abbreviations, listed on pages 218–20 in the MLA Handbook for Writers of Research Papers. In the APA system, names of publishers are not usually abbreviated, except for the elimination of unnecessary words such as *Inc., Co.,* and *Publishers.* Note also that in the MLA style, punctuation following the underlined title is not underlined, but in the APA style, punctuation following the underlined title *is* underlined.

Two Listings for One Author

MLA: Doig, Ivan. <u>Dancing at the Rascal Fair</u>. New York: Atheneum, 1987.

- - -. <u>English Creek</u>. New York: Atheneum, 1984.

In the MLA style, when two or more works by one author are cited, the works are listed in alphabetical order by title. For the second and all additional entries, type three hyphens and a period in place of the author's name. Then skip two spaces and type the title.

APA: Doig, I. (1984). <u>English creek.</u> New York: Atheneum.

Doig, I. (1987). <u>Dancing at the rascal fair.</u> New York: Atheneum.

Selfe, C. L. (1984a). The predrafting processes of four high- and four low-apprehensive writers. <u>Research in the Teaching of English,</u> <u>18,</u> 45–64.

Selfe, C. L. (1984b). <u>Reading as writing and revising strategy.</u> ERIC Document Reproduction Service No. ED 244-295.

In APA style, when an author has more than one entry in "References," the author's name is repeated and the entries are listed chronologically (oldest to newest) rather than alphabetically. When two entries by the same author have the same date, they are then listed in alphabetical order. Lower-case letters are added after the year of publication to distinguish them from each other when cited by date in the text.

Two or More Authors

MLA: Ciochon, Russell, John Olsen, and Jamie James. <u>The Search for the</u> <u>Giant Ape in Human Prehistory</u>. New York: Bantam, 1990.

APA: Ciochon, R., Olsen, J., & James, J. (1990). <u>The search for the giant</u> <u>ape in human prehistory.</u> New York: Bantam Books.

Note that the APA style uses the ampersand (&) to join the names of multiple authors.

Using *et al.* for Works with Several Authors

MLA: Maimon, Elaine P. et al. <u>Writing in the Arts and Sciences</u>. Cambridge, MA: Winthrop, 1981.

In the MLA system, if there are four or more authors, you have the option of using *et al.* (meaning "and others") after the name of the first author listed on the title page.

APA: Maimon, E. P., Belcher, G. L., Hearn, G. W., Nodine, B. F., & O'Connor,
F. W. (1981). <u>Writing in the arts and sciences.</u> Cambridge, MA:
Winthrop.

APA style allows the use of *et al.* only when there are six or more authors for one work.

Anthology with an Editor

MLA: Rabkin, Norman, ed. <u>Approaches to Shakespeare</u>. New York:
McGraw-Hill, 1964.

APA: Rabkin, N. (Ed.). (1964). <u>Approaches to Shakespeare.</u> New York:
McGraw-Hill.

Essay in an Anthology or Other Collection

MLA: Stein, Robert B., Lon Polk, and Barbara Bovee Polk. "Urban
Communes." <u>Old Family/New Family</u>. Ed. Nona Glazer-Malbin.
New York: Nostrand, 1975. 171–88.

APA: Stein, R. B., Polk, L., & Polk, B. B. (1975). Urban communes. In N.
Glazer-Malbin (Ed.), <u>Old family/new family</u> (pp. 171–188). New
York: Van Nostrand.

Book in a Later Edition

MLA: Valette, Rebecca M. <u>Modern Language Testing</u>. 2nd ed. New York:
Harcourt, 1977.

Williams, Oscar, Ed. <u>A Little Treasury of Modern Poetry</u>. Rev. ed.
New York: Scribner's, 1952.

APA: Valette, R. M. (1977). <u>Modern language testing</u> (2nd ed.). New York:
Harcourt, Brace, Jovanovich.

Williams, O. (Ed.). (1952). <u>A little treasury of modern poetry</u> (Rev. ed.).
New York: Scribner's.

Multivolume Work

Cite the whole work when you have used more than one volume of the work.

MLA: Churchill, Winston S. <u>A History of the English-Speaking Peoples</u>.
4 vols. New York: Dodd, 1956–58.

APA: Churchill, W. S. (1956–1958). <u>History of the English-speaking peoples</u>
(Vols. 1–4). New York: Dodd, Mead.

Include the volume number when you have used only one volume of a multivolume work.

MLA: Churchill, Winston S. <u>The Great Democracies</u>. New York: Dodd,
        1957. Vol. 4 of <u>A History of the English-Speaking Peoples</u>.
        4 vols. 1956–58.

APA: Churchill, W. S. (1957). <u>A history of the English-speaking peoples:</u>
        <u>Vol. 4. The great democracies.</u> New York: Dodd, Mead.

Reference Work with Frequent Editions

MLA: Pei, Mario. "Language." <u>World Book Encyclopedia</u>. 1976 ed.

In citing familiar reference works under the MLA system, you don't need to include all the normal publication information.

APA: Pei, M. (1976). Language. In <u>World book encyclopedia</u> (Vol. 12,
        pp. 62–67). Chicago: Field Enterprises.

APA does not give a specific example for use of a reference book. The APA manual directs the writer to follow an example similar to the source and to include more information rather than less.

Less Familiar Reference Work Without Frequent Editions

MLA: Ling, Trevor O. "Buddhism in Burma." <u>Dictionary of Comparative</u>
        <u>Religion</u>. Ed. S. G. F. Brandon. New York: Scribner's, 1970.

APA: Ling, T. O. (1970). Buddhism in Burma. In S. G. F. Brandon (Ed.),
        <u>Dictionary of comparative religion.</u> New York: Scribner's.

Edition in Which Original Author's Work Is Prepared by an Editor

MLA: Brontë, Emily. <u>Wuthering Heights</u>. 1847. Ed. V. S. Pritchett. Boston:
        Houghton, 1956.

APA: Brontë, E. (1956). <u>Wuthering Heights</u> (V. S. Pritchett, Ed.).
        Boston: Houghton, Mifflin. (Original work published 1847)

Translation

MLA: Camus, Albert. <u>The Plague</u>. Trans. Stuart Gilbert. New York: Modern
        Library, 1948.

APA: Camus, A. (1948). <u>The plague</u> (S. Gilbert, Trans.). New York: Modern
        Library. (Original work published 1947)

In APA style, the date of the translation is placed after the author's name; the date of original publication of the work is placed in parentheses at the end of the reference. In text, this book would be cited as follows:

(Camus, 1947/1948)

Corporate Author (a Commission, Committee, or Other Group)

MLA: American Medical Association. <u>The American Medical Association's Handbook of First Aid and Emergency Care</u>. New York: Random, 1980.

APA: American Medical Association. (1980). <u>The American Medical Association's handbook of first aid and emergency care.</u> New York: Random House.

Anonymous Work

MLA: <u>The New Yorker Cartoon Album: 1975–1985</u>. New York: Penguin, 1987.

APA: <u>The New Yorker cartoon album: 1975–1985.</u> (1987). New York: Penguin Books.

Republished Work (For Example, a Newer Paperback Published After the Original Hardbound)

MLA: Sagan, Carl. <u>The Dragons of Eden: Speculations on the Evolution of Human Intelligence</u>. 1977. New York: Ballantine, 1978.

APA: Sagan, C. (1978). <u>The dragons of Eden: Speculations on the evolution of human intelligence.</u> New York: Ballantine. (Original work published 1977)

General Format for Articles

MLA: Author. "Article Title." <u>Magazine or Journal Title</u> volume number (Date): inclusive pages.

APA: Author. (Date). Article title. <u>Magazine or Journal Title, volume number,</u> inclusive pages.

Scholarly Journal with Continuous Annual Pagination

MLA: Barton, Ellen L. "Evidentials, Argumentation, and Epistemological Stance." <u>College English</u> 55 (1993): 745–69.

APA: Barton, E. L. (1993). Evidentials, argumentation, and epistemological stance. <u>College English, 55,</u> 745–769.

Scholarly Journal with Each Issue Paged Separately

MLA: Pollay, Richard W., Jung S. Lee, and David Carter-Whitney. "Separate, but Not Equal: Racial Segmentation in Cigarette Advertising." <u>Journal of Advertising</u> 21.1 (1992): 45–57.

APA: Pollay, R. W., Lee, J. S., & Carter-Whitney, D. (1992). Racial segmentation in cigarette advertising. <u>Journal of Advertising, 21</u>(1), 45–57.

Note that in both systems when each issue is paged separately, both the volume (in this case, 21) and the issue number (in this case, 1) are given.

Magazine Article

MLA: Fallows, James. "Vietnam: Low-Class Conclusions." <u>Atlantic</u> Apr. 1993: 38–44.

APA: Fallows, J. (1993, April). Vietnam: Low-class conclusions. <u>Atlantic,</u> 38–44.

Note that this form is for a magazine published each month. The next entry shows the form for a magazine published each week.

Anonymous Article

MLA: "The Rebellious Archbishop." <u>Newsweek</u> 11 July 1988: 38.

APA: The rebellious archbishop. (1988, July 11). <u>Newsweek,</u> 38.

Review

MLA: Bliven, Naomi. "Long, Hot Summer." Rev. of <u>We Are Not Afraid: The Story of Goodman, Schwerner, and Cheney and the Civil Rights Campaign of Mississippi,</u> by Seth Cagin and Philip Dray. <u>New Yorker</u> 11 July 1988: 81+.

This is a review of a book. The "81+" indicates that the articles begins on page 81 but continues later in the magazine, perhaps on pages 83, 87, and 89. For both movie and book reviews, if the reviewer's name is not given, begin with the title of the reviewed work, preceded by "Rev. of" in the MLA system or "[Review of *title*]" in the APA system. Begin with the title of the review if the review is titled but not signed.

APA: Bliven, N. (1988, July 11). Long, hot summer [Review of the book <u>We are not afraid: The story of Goodman, Schwerner, and Cheney and the civil rights campaign of Mississippi</u>]. <u>The New Yorker,</u> 81–86.

Newspaper Article

MLA: Healy, Tim. "The Politics of Real Estate." <u>Seattle Times</u> 14 June 1988: 1E.

APA: Healy, T. (1988, June 14). The politics of real estate. <u>The Seattle Times,</u> p. 1E.

Note that the section is indicated if each section is paged separately.

Newspaper Editorial

MLA: Smith, Charles Z. "Supreme Court Door Opens for a Minority." Editorial. <u>Seattle Times</u> 14 July 1988: 18A.

APA: Smith, C. Z. (1988, July 14). Supreme Court door opens for a minority [Editorial]. <u>The Seattle Times,</u> p. 18A.

Letter to the Editor of a Magazine or Newspaper

MLA: Fleming, Deb. Letter. <u>Ms.</u> July 1988: 14.

APA: Fleming, D. (1988, July). [Letter to the editor]. <u>Ms.,</u> 14.

Include a title if one is given to the letter in the publication.

Information Service such as ERIC (Educational Resources Information Center) or NTIS (National Technical Information Service)

MLA: Eddy, P. A. <u>The Effects of Foreign Language Study in High School on Verbal Ability as Measured by the Scholastic Aptitude Test-Verbal</u>. Washington: Center for Applied Linguistics, 1981. ERIC ED 196 312.

APA: Eddy, P. A. (1981). <u>The effects of foreign language study in high school on verbal ability as measured by the Scholastic Aptitude Test-Verbal.</u> Washington, DC: Center for Applied Linguistics. (ERIC Document Reproduction Service No. ED 196 312)

Formats for Electronic Sources

You should list source information if you incorporate material from any of the electronic sources described in Chapter 16, including interactions on the Internet. The following categories cover electronic materials that the MLA and APA have specified as of this writing

Books, Pamphlets, or Texts in Online Databases or CD-ROMs that Are Also Available in Print

MLA: Melville, Herman. <u>Moby-Dick, or The White Whale</u>. Ed. Howard Vincent. New York: Viking, 1957. Online. U of Virginia Lib. Internet. 10 Mar. 1995. Available FTP: etext.virginia.edu.

Note that the last two lines list the medium, archive name, computer network, date of access, and supplementary electronic access information.

APA: NCTE. (1987). <u>On writing centers</u> [CD-ROM], Urbana, IL: ERIC Clearinghouse for Resolutions on the Teaching of Composition, II. SilverPlatter.

Include the medium in brackets next to the title, the location, and then the name of the publisher, producer, or distributor.

The entry in "Works Cited" or "References" should document the electronic source, not the printed one. Even if the material is available in printed form, the electronic version may be substantially different.

Journals or Periodicals in Online Databases or CD-ROMs that Are Also Available in Print

MLA: Kettel, Raymond P. "An Interview with Jerry Spinelli: Thoughts on Teaching Writing in the Classroom." <u>English Journal</u> 83 (1994): 61–64. Urbana: ERIC Clearinghouse on Elementary and Early Childhood Educ., 1966–1995/Feb. <u>ERIC</u>. CD-ROM. SilverPlatter. 21 Mar. 1995.

List the medium, vendor name, and issue date. You should list supplementary electronic access information if it is available.

APA: Kettel, R. P. (1994). An interview with Jerry Spinelli: Thoughts on teaching writing in the classroom. English Journal, 83, (1994): 61–64. Urbana, IL: ERIC Clearinghouse on Elementary and Early Childhood Educ. 1966–1995/Feb. ERIC ipps.lsa.uminn.edu

Note that the last item in this format is a retrieval location.

Books, Journals, or Periodicals in Online Databases or CD-ROMs that Are Not Available in Print

MLA: Knuuttila, Simo. "Remarks on Induction in Aristotle's Dialectic and Rhetoric." Revue Internationale de Philosophie 47 (1993): 78–88. CD-ROM. Bowling Green: Bowling Green State University, 1980.

Include the medium, vendor name, and date of issue. You should also list supplementary electronic access information if it is available.

The APA style follows the specifications for online journals available in print.

Computer Disks that Are Not Available in Print

MLA: Microsoft Word. Vers. 6.0. Diskette. Everett: Microsoft, 1994.

APA: Microsoft word 6.0 [Computer software]. (1994). Everett, CA: Microsoft.

Include the medium, city of issue, vendor name, and date of issue.

The APA style follows the specifications for online books available in print.

Information Service Data Bank

MLA: Department of Labor. "U.S. Population by Ethnic Origin: Urban and Urbanized Areas." 1990 U.S. Census of Population and Housing. Online. Human Resource Information Network. 10 Apr. 1995.

Include the medium, network name, and date of issue. You should also include supplementary access information if it is available.

APA: Shimabukuru, J., (Ed.). (1995, February). Internet in ten years-Essays [62 paragraphs]. Electronic Journal on Virtual Culture, 3.(1). Available FTP: 138.122.118.1

Note that this format lists retrieval information, including the server and retrieval path.

Electronic Newsletter or Conference

MLA: Meynell, H. A., ed. "Grace, Politics and Desire: Essays on
            Augustine." <u>Bryn Mawr Medieval Review</u> 93, 8.2 (1990): 7 pp.
            Online. Internet. 10 Mar. 1995.

Include the medium, network name, and date of access. You should also include supplementary access information if it is available.

The APA style follows the specifications for material from an information service data bank.

E-Mail, Listservs, and Other Nonretrievable Sources

MLA: Rushdie, Salman. "My Concern About the Fatwa." E-mail to the
            author. 1 May 1995.

Note that this format specifies that the document is an e-mail letter, to whom it was addressed, and the date of transmission.

In APA style, this material is not listed in "References." You should, however, acknowledge it in in-text citations.

The novelist has repeated this idea recently (Salman Rushdie, E-mail to the author, May 1, 1995).

Bulletin Board or Newsgroup Posting

MLA: MacDonald, James C. "Suggestions for Promoting Collaborative
            Writing in College Composition." 10 Nov. 1994. Online posting.
            NCTE Forum/current topics/bulletin posting. America Online.
            12 Mar. 1995.

Include the date of transmission or posting, the medium, network name, location information, an address or path for electronic access, and date of access.

In APA style, this material is acknowledged in in-text citations only. See the specifications for e-mail, listservs, and other nonretrievable sources.

Miscellaneous Materials

Films, Filmstrips, Slide Programs, and Videotapes

MLA: <u>Chagall</u>. Dir. Kim Evans. Ed. Melvyn Bragg. Videocassette. London
            Weekend Television, 1985.

APA: Evans, K. (Director), & Bragg, M. (Editor). (1985). <u>Chagall</u>
            [Videocassette]. London: London Weekend Television.

Television and Radio Programs

MLA: <u>Korea: The Forgotten War</u>. Narr. Robert Stack. KCPQ, Seattle. 27 June 1988.

APA: Stack, R. (Narrator). (1988, June 27). <u>The forgotten war</u>. Seattle: KCPQ.

Interview

MLA: Deltete, Robert. Personal interview. 27 Feb. 1994.

APA: Deltete, R. (1994, February 27). [Personal interview].

The APA publication manual says to omit nonrecoverable material—such as personal correspondence, personal interviews, lectures, and so forth—from "References" at the end. However, in college research papers, professors usually like to have such information included.

Lecture, Address, or Speech

MLA: North, Oliver. Speech. Washington Policy Council. Seattle. 20 July 1988.

APA: North, O. (1988, July 20). Speech presented to Washington Policy Council, Seattle, WA.

In the MLA system, if the title of the speech is known, give the title in quotation marks in place of "Speech." The *Publication Manual of the American Psychological Association* has no provisions for citing lectures, addresses, or speeches because these are nonrecoverable items. However, the manual gives authors leeway to design citations for instances not covered explicitly in the manual. This format is suitable for college research papers.

For more complicated entries, consult the *MLA Handbook for Writers of Research Papers,* fourth edition, or the *Publication Manual of the American Psychological Association,* fourth edition. Both books should be available in your library or bookstore.

CONCLUSION

If you see research writing as a variation on the thesis-governed writing you do for all your argument essays, you shouldn't have any particular difficulty writing an argument as a research paper. Keep in mind the issue question, thesis, and purpose of your own essay as a guide to taking notes and incorporating sources into your own work. Avoid data dumping by using borrowed material as a way of supporting your own argument instead of as an end in itself. Take particular care to indicate the beginning and end of borrowed material by putting attributive tags in your text and indicate any borrowed language with quotation marks or block indentations. Simply add the conventions of documentation appropriate to your topic and field, and you will have produced a satisfying research paper.

 ## FOR CLASS DISCUSSION

1. Read Stephen's essay, pages 330–338, which is an example of a fully documented argument using the MLA style. Go to your library and locate several of the sources he has cited in his essay. Read one or two of the articles he cites and then prepare a brief report on whether he uses those sources accurately and fairly.*

2. Read Lynnea's essay (following this section), which is an example of a fully documented argument using the APA style. Give this essay the same scrutiny requested for Stephen's essay. Go to your library and locate several of the sources she has cited in her essay. Then prepare a brief report on whether or not she uses those sources accurately and fairly.

3. Pages 412–13, arranged as facing pages for easy comparison, show a "Works Cited" list (MLA) and a "References" list (APA). These lists give you a "quick check" summary of the formats for the most commonly used sources. Review the formats for MLA and APA bibliographic lists, noting similarities and differences. Then respond to the questions below.

 ## DISCUSSION QUESTIONS

Now that you have reviewed the formats of the most commonly used kinds of sources, consider the differences between the MLA and the APA systems. The MLA system is used most frequently in the humanities, while the APA system is used in the social sciences. Why do you suppose the MLA system gives complete first names of authors as well as middle initials, while the APA system uses only initials for the first and middle names? Why does the APA system emphasize date of publication by putting dates prominently near the front of an entry just after the author's name? On the basis of the MLA and APA formats, could you make some observations about differences in values between the humanities and the social sciences?

---

*The Charles Krauthammer essay cited by Stephen is reprinted on pages 330–338 of this text.

Works Cited: MLA Style Sheet for the Most Commonly Used Sources

Ross 27

Works Cited

Adler, Freda. <u>Sisters in Crime</u>. New York: McGraw,
    1975.

Andersen, Margaret L. <u>Thinking About Women:</u>
    <u>Sociological Perspectives on Sex and Gender</u>.
    3rd ed. New York: Macmillan, 1993.

Bart, Pauline, and Patricia O'Brien. <u>Stopping Rape:</u>
    <u>Successful Survival Strategies</u>. New York:
    Pergamon, 1985.

Durkin, Kevin. "Social Cognition and Social Context
    in the Construction of Sex Differences." <u>Sex</u>
    <u>Differences in Human Performances</u>. Ed. Mary
    Anne Baker. New York: Wiley, 1987. 45–60.

Fairburn, Christopher G., et al. "Predictors of 12-month
    Outcome in Bulimia Nervosa and the Influence
    of Attitudes to Shape and Weight." <u>Journal of</u>
    <u>Consulting and Clinical Psychology</u> 61 (1993):
    696–98.

Kantrowitz, Barbara. "Sexism in the Schoolhouse."
    <u>Newsweek</u> 24 Feb. 1992: 62.

Langewiesche, William. "The World in Its Extreme."
    <u>Atlantic</u> Nov. 1991: 105–40.

Taylor, Chuck. "After Cobain's Death: Here Come the
    Media Ready to Buy Stories." <u>Seattle Times</u>
    10 Apr. 1994: A1+.

Author's last name and page number in upper right corner.

Book entry, one author. Use standard abbreviations for common publishers.

Book entry in a revised edition.

Book with two or three authors. With four or more authors use "et al", as in Jones, Peter, et al.

Article in anthology; author heads the entry; editor cited after the title. Inclusive page numbers come two spaces after the period following year.

Article in scholarly journal paginated consecutively throughout year. This article has three or more authors.

Weekly or biweekly popular magazine; abbreviate all months except May, June, and July.

Monthly, bimonthly, or quarterly magazine.

Newspaper article with identified author; if no author, begin with title.

References: APA Style Sheet for the Most Commonly Used Sources

Women, Health, and Crime

27

References

Adler, F. (1975). <u>Sisters in crime.</u> New York: McGraw-Hill.

Andersen, M. L. (1993). <u>Thinking about women: Sociological perspectives on sex and gender</u> (3rd ed.). New York: Macmillan.

Bart, P., & O'Brien, P. (1985). <u>Stopping rape: Successful survival strategies.</u> New York: Pergamon Press.

Durkin, K. (1987). Social cognition and social context in the construction of sex differences. In M. A. Baker (Ed.), <u>Sex differences in human performances</u> (pp. 45–60). New York: Wiley & Sons.

Fairburn, C. G., Pevaler, R. C., Jones, R., & Hope, R. A. (1993). Predictors of 12-month outcome in bulimia nervosa and the influence of attitudes to shape and weight. <u>Journal of Consulting and Clinical Psychology, 61,</u> 696–98.

Kantrowitz, B. (1992, February 24). Sexism in the schoolhouse. <u>Newsweek,</u> p. 62.

Langewiesche, W. (1991, November). The world in its extreme. <u>Atlantic,</u> pp. 105–40.

Taylor, C. (1993, April 10). After Cobain's death: Here come the media ready to buy stories. <u>Seattle Times,</u> pp. A1+.

Running head with page number doublespaced below.

Book entry, one author. Don't abbreviate publisher but omit unnecessary words.

Book entry in a revised edition.

Book with multiple authors; uses ampersand instead of "and" before last name. Authors' names listed last name first.

Article in anthology; no quotes around article. Name of editor comes before book title.

Article in scholarly journal paginated consecutively throughout year. APA lists all authors rather than using "et al." (except when there are six or more authors).

Weekly or biweekly popular magazine; abbreviate all months except May, June, and July.

Monthly, bimonthly, or quarterly magazine.

Newspaper article with identified author; if no author, begin with title.

Women Police Officers:

Should Size and Strength Be Criteria for Patrol Duty?

Lynnea Clark

English 301

15 November

_____

This research paper follows the APA style for format and documentation.

Women Police Officers:

Should Size and Strength Be Criteria for Patrol Duty?

A marked patrol car turns the corner at 71st and Franklin Avenue and 1
cautiously proceeds into the parking lot of an old shopping center. About a dozen
gang members, dressed in their gang colors, stand alert, looking down the alley
that runs behind the store. As the car moves toward the gathering, they suddenly
scatter in all directions. Within seconds, several shots are fired from the alley.
Switching on the overhead emergency lights, the officer bolts from the car when
he sees two figures running past him. "Freeze! Police!" the officer yells. The men
dart off in opposite directions. Chasing one, the policeman catches up to him, and,
observing no gun, tackles him. After a violent struggle, the officer manages to
handcuff the man, just as the backup unit comes screeching up.

This policeman is my friend. The next day I am with him as he sits at a 2
cafe with three of his fellow officers, discussing the incident. One of the officers
comments, "Well, at least you were stronger than he was. Can you imagine if
Connie Jones was on patrol duty last night?" "What a joke," scoffs another officer.
"How tall is she anyway?" "About 4'10" and 90 pounds," says the third officer.
"She could fit in my backpack." Connie Jones (not her real name) has just completed
police academy training and has been assigned to patrol duty in _____ . Because
she is so small, she has to have a booster seat in her patrol car and has been given
a special gun, since she can barely manage to pull the trigger of a standard police-
issue .38 revolver. Although she passed the physical requirements at the academy,
which involved speed and endurance running, situps, and monkey bar tests, most
of the officers in her department doubt her ability to perform competently as a patrol
officer. But nevertheless she is on patrol because men and women receive equal
assignments in most of today's police forces. But is this a good policy? Can a person
who is significantly small and weak make an effective patrol officer?

Because the "small and weak" people in question are almost always women, 3
the issue becomes a woman's issue. Considerable research has been done on
women in the police force, and much of it suggests that women, who are on the
average smaller and weaker than men, can perform competently in law enforcement,
regardless of their size or strength. More specifically, most research concludes that

female police workers in general perform just as well as their fellow officers in patrolling situations. A major study by Bloch and Anderson (1984), commissioned by the Urban Institute, revealed that in the handling of violent situations, women performed well. In fact, women and men received equally satisfactory evaluation ratings on their overall performances.

4   In another more recent study (Grennan, 1987) examining the relationship between outcomes of police-citizen confrontations and the gender of the involved officers, female officers were determined to be just as productive as male officers in the handling of violent situations. In his article on female criminal justice employment, Potts (1982) reviews numerous studies on evaluation ratings of policewomen and acknowledges that "the predominant weight of evidence is that women are equally capable of performing police work as are men" (p. 11). Additionally, female officers score higher on necessary traits for leadership (p. 10), and it has been often found that women are better at dealing with rape and abuse victims. Again, a study performed by Grennan (1987), concentrating on male and female police officers' confrontations with citizens, revealed that the inborn or socialized nurturing ability possessed by female police workers makes them "just as productive as male officers in the handling of a violent confrontation" (p. 84).

5   This view has been strengthened further by the recent achievement of Katherine P. Heller, who was honored by receiving the nation's top award in law enforcement for 1990 (Proctor, 1990). Heller, a United States park policewoman, risked her life by stepping in the open to shoot dead an assailant while he levelled his gun to shoot at her fellow police officer. Five feet three inches and 107 pounds, Heller is not only the first woman to be awarded with Police Officer of the Year, but she is also the smallest recipient ever. Maybe Heller's decisiveness will help lay to rest doubts about many women's abilities as police workers.

6   However, despite the evidence provided by the above cited research, I am not convinced. Although these studies show that women make effective police officers, I believe the studies must be viewed with skepticism. My concern is public safety. In light of that concern, the evidence suggests that police departments should set stringent size and strength requirements for patrol officers, even if these criteria exclude many women.

7   First of all, the research studies documenting the success of women as patrol officers are marred by two major flaws: the amount of evidence gathered is scanty

and the way that the data have been gathered doesn't allow us to study factors of size and strength. Because of minimal female participation in patrol work prior to the past decade, limited amounts of research and reports exist on the issue. And of the research performed, many studies have not been based on representative samples. Garrison, Grant, and McCormick (1988) found that

> [l]iterature on women in patrol or nontraditional police roles tends to be idiosyncratic. . . . Many of the observations written about a relatively small number of women performing successfully in a wider range of police tasks support the assumption that they are exceptions rather than the norm. (p. 32)

Similarly, Bloch and Anderson (1984) note that in the course of their study

> it was not possible to observe enough incidents to be sure that men and women are equally capable in all such situations. It is clear from the incidents which were described that women performed well in the few violent situations which did arise. (p. 61)

Another problem with the available research is that little differentiation has been made within the large group of women being considered; all women officers seem to be grouped and evaluated based on only two criteria: that they are on the police force and that they are female. But like men, women come in all shapes and sizes. To say that women as a class make effective or ineffective police workers is to make too general a claim. The example of women officers such as Katherine Heller proves that some women make excellent patrol cops. But, presumably, some women probably would not make good patrol cops just as some men would not. The available data do not allow us to determine whether size and strength are factors. Because no size differentiation has been made within the groups of women officers under observation in the research studies, it is impossible to conclude whether or not smaller, weaker women performed patrol duties as well as larger, stronger women did. In fact, for Bloch and Anderson's study (which indicates that, from a performance viewpoint, it is appropriate to hire women for patrol assignments on the same basis as men) both men and women had to meet a minimum height requirement of 5'7". Therefore, the performance of smaller, weaker women in handling violent situations remained unevaluated. Thus the data show that many women are great cops; the data do <u>not</u> show that many small women with minimal strength make great cops.

8

9   The case of Katherine Heller might seem to demonstrate that smaller women can perform patrol duties successfully. Heller acknowledged in an interview in <u>Parade</u> magazine that ninety percent of her adversaries will be bigger than herself (Proctor, 1990, p. 5). But she is no fluttering fluffball; rather, she has earned the reputation for being an extremely aggressive cop and has compensated for her size by her bearing. But how many women (or men) of Heller's size or smaller could maintain such "officer presence"? How can we be certain that Heller is in fact representative of small women rather than being an exception?

10   This question leads to my second reason for supporting stringent size and strength requirements: Many police officers, both male and female, have real doubts about the abilities of small and physically weak patrol workers, most of whom are women. In a study done by Vega and Silverman (1982), almost 75% of male police officers felt that women were not strong enough to handle the demands of patrol duties, and 42% felt women lacked the needed assertiveness to enforce the law vigorously (p. 32). Unfortunately, however, because of frequent media reports of discrimination and sexism among police personnel and because of pressure from the Equal Employment Opportunity Commission (EEOC) on police agencies and other employers (Vega & Silverman, 1982; Lord, 1986), these reservations and attitudes have not been seriously taken into account. The valid concerns and opinions of police workers who feel that some women officers are not strong enough to deal effectively with violent situations have been asphyxiated by the smoldering accusations of civil rights activists and feminists, who see only layers of chauvinism, conservatism, cynicism, and authoritarianism permeating our law enforcement agencies. These activists view the problem as being only a "women" issue rather than a "size" issue. But the fact remains that both male and female officers think that many patrol workers are incapable of handling violent situations because of small stature and lack of physical strength. Another policewoman belonging to the same department as Connie Jones explained, "She [Jones] doesn't have the authoritarian stance needed to compensate for her size. She's not imposing and is too soft spoken. Once she responded to a call and was literally picked up and thrown out the door" (anonymous personal communication, October 6, 1990).

11   Finally, patrol duties, unlike other areas of police work, constitute one of the few jobs in our society that may legitimately require above average strength. Because

Women Police

6

the job involves great personal risk and danger, the concern for public safety
overrides the concern for equal rights in this instance. Patrolling is a high visibility
position in police departments as opposed to jobs such as radio dispatching,
academy training, or clerical duties. Patrol workers directly face the challenges
presented by the public, and violence is always a threat for officers on patrol (Vega
& Silverman, 1982; Grennan, 1987). Due to the nature of patrol work, officers many
times must cope with violent situations by using physical force, such as that needed
for subduing individuals who resist arrest. However, pressure from liberal groups
has prevented special consideration being given to these factors of patrol duty. As
long as student officers pass the standard academy Physical Ability Test (in addition
to the other academy requirements), then they are eligible for patrol assignments; in
fact, everyone out of the academy <u>must</u> go on patrol. But the minimum physical
requirements are not challenging. According to Lord (1986), police agencies
"struggle to find a nondiscriminatory, empirically valid entry level physical agility
test which does not discriminate against women by overemphasizing upper body
strength" (Lord, 1986, p. 91). In short, the liberal agenda leading to women on patrol
has forced the lowering of strength requirements.

Without establishing minimum size and strength requirements for patrol   12
workers, police departments are not discharging their duties with maximum
competency or effectiveness. Police training programs stress that police officers
should be able to maintain an authoritarian presence in the face of challenges
and possess the ability to diffuse a situation just by making an appearance.
But some individuals who are able to pass basic training programs still lack
the size needed to maintain an imposing physical stance. And as many citizens
obviously do not respect the uniform, police workers must possess the strength
to efficiently handle violent encounters. Even if size and strength requirements
have a disproportionate impact on women, these physical standards are lawful,
so long as they relate to the demands of the job and "constitute valid predictors
of an employee's performance on the job" (Steel & Lovrich, 1987, p. 53). Patrol
duties demand highly capable and effective workers, and in order to professionalize
law-enforcement practices and to maintain the degree of order necessary for a
free society, police agencies must maintain a high level of competency in their
street-patrol forces.

References

Bloch, P., & Anderson, D. (1974). Police women on patrol: Final report. Washington, D.C.: Police Foundation.

Garrison, C., Grant, N., & McCormick, K. (1988). Utilization of police women. The Police Chief, 55(9), 32–73.

Golden, K. (1981). Women as patrol officers: A study of attitudes. Police Studies, 4(3), 29–33.

Grennan, S. (1987). Findings on the role of officer gender in violent encounters with citizens. Journal of Police Science and Administration, 15(1), 78–84.

Igbinovia, P. (1987). African women in contemporary law enforcement. Police Studies, 10(1), 31–34.

Lord, L. (1986). A comparison of male and female peace officers' stereotypic perceptions of women and women peace officers. Journal of Police Science and Administration, 14(2), 83–91.

Potts, L. (1981). Equal employment opportunity and female criminal justice employment. Police Studies, 4(3), 9–19.

Proctor, P. (1990, September 30). "I didn't have time to taste the fear." Parade Magazine, pp. 4–5.

Steel, B., & Lovrich, N., Jr. (1987). Equality and efficiency tradeoffs in affirmative action—real or imagined? The case of women in policing. The Social Science Journal, 24(1), 53–67.

Vega, M., & Silverman, I. (1982). Female police officers as viewed by their male counterparts. Police Studies, 5(1), 31–39.

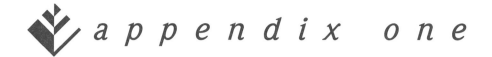 *a p p e n d i x   o n e*

Logical Fallacies

In this appendix, we look at ways of testing the legitimacy of an argument. Sometimes, there are fatal logical flaws hiding in the heart of a perfectly respectable looking argument, and if we miss them, we may find ourselves vainly defending the indefensible. Take, for example, the following cases. Do they seem persuasive to you?

Creationism must be a science because hundreds of scientists believe in it.

I am opposed to a multicultural curriculum because it will lead to ethnic separatism similar to what is happening in Eastern Europe.

Smoking must cause cancer because a higher percentage of smokers get cancer than do nonsmokers.

Smoking doesn't cause cancer because my grandfather smoked two packs per day for fifty years and died in his sleep at age ninety.

An abnormal percentage of veterans who were marched to ground zero during atomic tests in Nevada died of leukemia and lung cancer. Surely their deaths were caused by the inhalation of radioactive isotopes.

THE PROBLEM OF CONCLUSIVENESS
IN AN ARGUMENT

Although it may distress us to think so, none of the above arguments is conclusive. But that doesn't mean they're false, either. So what are they? Well, they are, to various degrees, "persuasive" or "unpersuasive." The problem is that some people will mistake arguments such as those above for "conclusive" or airtight arguments. A person may rest an entire argument on them and then fall right through the holes that observant logicians open in them. Although few people will mistake an airtight case for a fallacious one, lots of people mistake logically unsound arguments for airtight cases. So let's see how to avoid falling into specious reasoning.

Some arguments are flawed because they fail to observe certain formal logical rules. In constructing syllogisms, for example, there are certain formal laws that must be followed if we are to have a valid syllogism. The following argument is beyond doubt invalid and inconclusive:

No Greeks are bald.

No Lithuanians are Greek.

Therefore, all Lithuanians are bald.

But to say the argument is invalid isn't to say that its conclusion is necessarily untrue. Perhaps all Lithuanians really are bald. The point is, if the conclusion were true, it would be by coincidence, not design, because the above argument is invalid. All invalid arguments are inconclusive. And, by the same token, a perfectly valid syllogism may be untrue. Just because the premises follow the formal laws of logic doesn't mean that what they say is true. For a syllogistic argument to be absolutely conclusive, its form must be valid and its premises must be true. A perfectly conclusive argument would therefore yield a noncontroversial truth—a statement that no one would dispute.

This is a long way around to reach one point: The reason we argue about issues is that none of the arguments on any side of an issue is absolutely conclusive; there is always room to doubt the argument, to develop a counterargument. We can only create more or less persuasive arguments, never conclusive ones.

We have examined some of these problems already. In Chapter 11 on causal arguments we discussed the problem of correlation versus causation. We know, for example, that smoking and cancer are correlated but that further arguments are needed in order to increase the conclusiveness of the claim that smoking *causes* cancer.

In this appendix we explore the problem of conclusiveness in various kinds of arguments. In particular, we use the *informal fallacies* of logic to explain how inconclusive arguments can fool us into thinking they are conclusive.

AN OVERVIEW OF INFORMAL FALLACIES

The study of informal fallacies remains the murkiest of all logical endeavors. It's murky in the sense that informal fallacies are as unsystematic as formal fallacies are rigid and systematized. Whereas formal fallacies of logic have the force of laws, informal fallacies have little more than explanatory power. Informal fallacies are quirky; they identify classes of less conclusive arguments that recur with some frequency, but they do not contain formal flaws that make their conclusions illegitimate no matter what the terms may say. Informal fallacies require us to look at the meaning of the terms to determine how much we should trust or distrust the conclusion. The most common mistake one can make with informal fallacies is to assume that they have the force of laws like formal fallacies. They don't. In evaluating arguments with informal fallacies, we usually find that arguments are "more or less" fallacious, and determining the degree of fallaciousness is a matter of judgment.

Knowledge of informal fallacies is most useful when we run across arguments that we "know" are wrong, but we can't quite say why. They just don't "sound right." They look reasonable enough, but they remain unacceptable to us. Informal fallacies are a sort of compendium of symptoms for arguments flawed in this way. We must be careful, however, to make sure that the particular case before us "fits" the descriptors for the fallacy that seems to explain its problem. It's much easier, for example, to find informal fallacies in a hostile argument than in a friendly one simply because we are more likely to expand the limits of the fallacy to make the disputed case fit.

Not everyone agrees about what to include under the heading of informal fallacies. In selecting the following set of fallacies, we left out far more candidates than we included. Since Aristotle first developed his list of thirteen *elenchi* (refutations) down to the present day, literally dozens of different systems of informal fallacy have been put forward. Although there is a good deal of overlap among these lists, the terms are invariably different and the definition of fallacy itself shifts from age to age. In selecting the following set of fallacies, we left out a number of other candidates. We chose the following because they seemed to us to be the most commonly encountered.

In arranging the fallacies we have, for convenience, put them into three categories derived from classical rhetoric: *pathos, ethos,* and *logos.* Fallacies of *pathos* rest on a flawed relationship between what is argued and the audience for the argument. Fallacies of *ethos* rest on a flawed relationship between the argument and the character of those involved in the argument. Fallacies of *logos* rest on flaws in the relationship among statements of an argument.

Fallacies of *Pathos*

Argument to the People (Appeal to Stirring Symbols)

This is perhaps the most generic possible example of a *pathos* fallacy. Argument to the people appeals to the fundamental beliefs, biases, and prejudices of the audience in order to sway opinion through a feeling of solidarity among those of the group. For example, when a politician says, "My fellow Americans, I stand here, draped in this flag from head to foot, to indicate my fundamental dedication to the values and principles of these sovereign United States," he's redirecting to his own person our allegiance to nationalistic values by linking himself with the prime symbol of those values, the flag. The linkage is not rational, it's associative. It's also extremely powerful—which is why arguments to the people crop up so frequently.

Appeal to Ignorance (Presenting Evidence the Audience Can't Examine)

Those who commit this fallacy present assumptions, assertions, or evidence that the audience is incapable of judging or examining. If, for example, a critic were to praise the novel *Clarissa* for its dullness on the grounds that this dullness was the intentional effect of the author, we would be unable to respond because we have no idea what was in the author's mind when he created the work.

Appeal to Irrational Premises (Appealing to Reasons That May Have No Basis in Logic)

This mode of short-circuiting reason may take one of three forms:

1. Appeal to common practice. (It's all right to do X because everyone else does it.)

2. Appeal to traditional wisdom. (It's all right because we've always done it this way.)

3. Appeal to popularity—the bandwagon appeal. (It's all right because lots of people like it.)

In all three cases, we've moved from saying something is popular, common, or persistent to saying it is right, good, or necessary. You have a better chance of rocketing across the Grand Canyon on a motorcycle than you have of going from "is" to "ought" on a because clause. Some examples of this fallacy would include (1) "Of course I borrowed money from the company slush fund. Everyone on this floor has done the same in the last eighteen months"; (2) "We've got to require everyone to read *Hamlet* because we've always required everyone to read it"; and (3) "You should buy a Ford Escort because it's the best-selling car in the world."

Provincialism (Appealing to the Belief That the Known Is Always Better than the Unknown)

Here is an example from the 1960s: "You can't sell small cars in America. In American culture, automobiles symbolize prestige and personal freedom. Those cramped little Japanese tin boxes will never win the hearts of American consumers." Although we may inevitably feel more comfortable with familiar things, ideas, and beliefs, we are not necessarily better off for sticking with them.

Red Herring (Shifting the Audience's Attention from a Crucial Issue to an Irrelevant One)

A good example of a red herring showed up in a statement by former Secretary of State James Baker that was reported in the November 10, 1990 *New York Times.* In response to a question about the appropriateness of using American soldiers to defend wealthy, insulated (and by implication, corrupt) Kuwaiti royalty,

Baker told an anecdote about an isolated encounter he had with four Kuwaitis who had suffered; he then made a lengthy statement on America's interests in the Gulf. Although no one would argue that America is unaffected by events in the Middle East, the question of why others with even greater interests at stake had not contributed more troops and resources went unanswered.

Fallacies of *Ethos*

Appeal to False Authority (Appealing to the Authority of a Popular Person Rather than a Knowledgeable One)

Appeals to false authority involve relying on testimony given by a person incompetent in the field from which the claims under question emerge. Most commercial advertisements are based on this fallacy. Cultural heroes are paid generously to associate themselves with a product without demonstrating any real expertise in evaluating that product. In at least one case, consumers who fell victim to such a fallacy made a legal case out of it. People bilked out of their life savings by a Michigan mortgage company sued the actors who represented the company on TV. Are people fooled by such appeals to false authority entitled to recover assets lost as a result?

The court answered no. The judge ruled that people gullible enough to believe that George Hamilton's capped-tooth smile and mahogany tan qualify him as a real estate consultant deserve what they get. Their advice to consumers? "Buyers beware," because even though sellers can't legally lie, they can legally use fallacious arguments—all the more reason to know your fallacies.

Keep in mind, however, that occasionally the distinction between a false authority fallacy and an appeal to legitimate authority can blur. Suppose that Arnold Palmer were to praise a particular company's golf club. Because he is an expert on golf, it is possible that Palmer actually speaks from authority and that the golf club he praises is superior. But it might also be that he is being paid to advertise the golf club and is endorsing a brand that is no better than its competitors'. The only way we could make even a partial determination of Palmer's motives would be if he presented an *ad rem* ("to the thing") argument showing us scientifically why the golf club in question is superior. In short, appeals to authority are legitimate when the authority knows the field and when her motive is to inform others rather than profit herself.

Appeal to the Person / Ad Hominem (Attacking the Character of the Arguer Rather than the Argument Itself)

Literally, *ad hominem* means "to the man or person." Any argument that focuses on the character of the person making the argument rather than the quality of the reasoning qualifies as an *ad hominem* argument. Ideally, arguments are supposed to be *ad rem,* or "to the thing," that is, addressed to the specifics of the case itself. Thus an *ad rem* critique of a politician would focus on her voting record, the consistency and cogency of her public statements, her responsiveness to constituents, and so forth. An *ad hominem* argument would shift attention from her record to irrelevant features of her personality or personal life. Perhaps an *ad hominem* argument would suggest that she had a less than stellar undergraduate academic record.

But not all *ad hominem* arguments are *ad hominem* fallacies. It's not always fallacious to address your argument to the arguer. There are indeed times when the credibility of the person making an opposing argument is at issue. Lawyers, for example, when questioning expert witnesses who give damaging testimony, will often make an issue of their credibility, and rightfully so. And certainly it's not that clear, for instance, that an all-male research team of social scientists would observe and interpret data in the same way as a mixed-gender research group. An *ad hominem* attack on an opponent's argument in not fallacious so long as (1) personal authority is what gives the opposing argument much of its weight, and (2) the critique of the person's credibility is fairly presented.

An interesting example of an *ad hominem* argument occurred in the 1980s in context of the Star Wars debate. Many important physicists around the country signed a statement in which they declared their opposition to Star Wars research. Another group of physicists supportive of that research condemned them on the grounds that none of the protesting physicists stood to get any Star Wars research funds anyway.

This attack shifted attention away from the reasons given by the protesting physicists for their convictions and put it instead on the physicists' motives. To some extent, of course, credibility is an issue here, because many of the key issues raised in the debate required some degree of expertise to resolve. Hence, the charges meet the first test for nonfallacious reasoning directed to the arguer.

But we must also ask ourselves if the charges being made are fair. If you'll recall from earlier discussions of fairness, we said that fairness requires similar treatment of similar classes of things. Applying this rule to this situation, we can simply reverse the charge being levied against the anti–Star Wars group and say of its supporters: "Because you stand to gain a good deal of research money from this project, we can't take your support of the Star Wars initiatives seriously." The Star Wars supporters would thus become victims of their own logic. *Ad hominem* attacks are often of this nature: The charges are perfectly reversible. (E.g., "Of course you support abortion; all your friends are feminists." "Of course you oppose abortion; you've been a Catholic all your life.") *Ad hominem* debates resemble nothing so much as mental quick-draw contests. Whoever shoots first wins because the first accuser puts the burden of proof on the opposition.

It's important to see here that an *ad hominem* argument, even if not fallacious, can never be definitive. Like analogies, they are simply suggestive; they raise doubts and focus our attention. Catholic writers can produce reasonable arguments against abortion, and feminists can produce reasonable ones for it. *Ad hominem* attacks don't allow us to discount arguments; but they do alert us to possible biases, possible ways the reasoned arguments themselves are vulnerable.

Several subcategories of the *ad hominem* argument that are almost never persuasive include:

1. Name calling (referring to a disputant by unsavory names)
2. Appeal to prejudice (applying ethnic, racial, gender, or religious slurs to an opponent)
3. Guilt by association (linking the opposition to extremely unpopular groups or causes)

Name calling is found far more often in transcripts of oral encounters than in books or essays. In the heat of the moment, speakers are more likely to lapse into verbal abuse than are writers who have time to contemplate their words. The Congressional Record is a rich source for name calling. Here, for example, one finds a duly elected representative referring to another duly elected representative as "a pimp for the Eastern establishment environmentalists." One of the biggest problems with such a charge is that it's unlikely to beget much in the way of reasoned response. It's far easier to respond in kind than it is to persuade people rationally that one is not a jackass of *that* particular sort.

When name calling is "elevated" to include slighting reference to the opponent's religion, gender, race, or ethnic background, we have encountered an appeal to prejudice. When it involves lumping an opponent with unsavory, terminally dumb, or extremely unpopular causes and characters, it constitutes guilt by association.

Strawperson (Greatly Oversimplifying an Opponent's Argument to Make It Easier to Refute or Ridicule)

Although typically less inflammatory than the preceding sorts of *ethos* fallacies, the strawperson fallacy changes the character of the opposition in order to suit the arguer's own needs. In committing a strawperson fallacy, you basically make up the argument you *wish* your opponents had made and attribute it to them because it's so much easier to refute than the argument they actually made. Some political debates consist almost entirely of strawperson exchanges such as: "You may think that levying confiscatory taxes on homeless people's cardboard dwellings is the surest way out of recession, but I don't." Or: "While my opponent would like to empty our prisons of serial killers and coddle kidnappers, I hold to the sacred principles of compensatory justice."

Fallacies of *Logos*

Logos fallacies comprise flaws in the relationships among the statements of an argument. Thus, to borrow momentarily from the language of the Toulmin schema discussed earlier, you can think of *logos* fallacies as breakdowns between arguments' warrants and their claims, between their warrants and their backing, or between their claims and their reasons and grounds.

Begging the Question (Supporting a Claim with a Reason that Is Really a Restatement of the Claim in Different Words)

Question begging is probably the most obvious example of a *logos* fallacy in that it involves stating a claim as though it warranted itself. For example, the statement "Abortion is murder because it involves the intentional killing of an unborn human being" is tantamount to saying "Abortion is murder because it's murder." The warrant "If something is the intentional killing of a human life, it is murder" simply repeats the claim; murder is *by definition* the intentional killing of another human being. Logically, the statement is akin to a statement like "That fellow is fat because he's considerably overweight." The crucial issue in the abortion debate is whether or not a fetus is a human being in the legal sense; this crucial issue is avoided in the argument, which begins by assuming that the fetus is a legal human being. Hence the argument goes in an endless circle from claim to warrant and back again.

Or consider the following argument: "How can you say Minnie Minoso belongs in the Hall of Fame? He's been eligible for over a decade and the Selection Committee turned him down every year. If he belonged in the Hall of Fame, the Committee would already have chosen him." Because the point at issue is whether or not the Hall of Fame Selection Committee *should* elect Minnie Minoso (and they should), the use of their vote as proof of the contention that they should not elect him is wholly circular and begs the question.

In distinguishing valid reasoning from fallacious examples of question begging, some philosophers say that the question has been begged when the premises of an argument are at least as uncertain as the claim. In such cases, we are not making any movement from some known general principle toward some new particular conclusion; we are simply asserting an uncertain premise in order to give the appearance of certainty to a shaky claim.

To illustrate the preceding observation, consider the controversy that arose in the late 1980s over whether or not to impose economic sanctions against South Africa in order to pressure the South Africans into changing their racial policies. One argument against economic sanctions went like this: "We should not approve economic sanctions against South Africa (claim) because economic sanctions will hurt blacks as much as whites" (premise or stated reason). The claim ("We should not impose economic sanctions") is only as certain as the premise from which it was derived ("because blacks will suffer as much as whites"), but many people argued that that premise was extremely uncertain. They thought that whites would suffer the most under sanctions and that blacks would ultimately benefit. The question would no longer be begged if the person included a documented defense of the premise. But without such a defense, the arguer's claim is grounded on a shaky premise that sounds more certain than it is.

Complex Question (Confronting the Opponent with
a Question that Will Put Her in a Bad Light
No Matter How She Responds)

A complex question is one that requires, in legal terms, a self-incriminating response. For example, the question "When did you stop abusing alcohol?" requires the admission of alcohol abuse. Hence the claim that a person has abused alcohol is silently turned into an assumption.

False Dilemma/Either–Or (Oversimplifying a
Complex Issue So That Only Two Choices
Appear Possible)

A good extended analysis of this fallacy is found in sociologist Kai Erickson's analysis of President Truman's decision to drop the A-bomb on Hiroshima. His analysis suggests that the Truman administration prematurely reduced numerous options to just two: Either drop the bomb on a major city or sustain unacceptable losses in a land invasion of Japan. Erickson, however, shows there were other alternatives. Typically, we encounter false dilemma arguments when people are trying to justify a questionable action by creating a false sense of necessity, forcing us to choose between two options, one of which is clearly unacceptable. Hence, when someone orders us to do it "My way or hit the highway," or to "Love it or leave it," it's probably in response to some criticism we made about the "way" we're supposed to do it or the "it" we're supposed to love.

But of course not all dilemmas are false. People who reject all binary oppositions (that is, thinking in terms of pairs of opposites) are themselves guilty of a false dilemma. There are times when we might determine through a rational process of elimination that only two possible choices exist. Deciding whether a dilemma is truly a dilemma or only an evasion of complexity often requires a difficult judgment. Although we should initially suspect any attempt to convert a complex problem into an either/or choice, we may legitimately arrive at such a choice through thoughtful deliberation.

Equivocation (Using to Your Advantage
at Least Two Different Definitions of
the Same Term in the Same Argument)

For example, if we're told that people can't "flourish" unless they are culturally literate, we must know which of the several possible senses of *flourish* are being used before we can test the persuasiveness of the claim. If by *flourishing* the author means acquiring great wealth, we'll look at a different set of grounds than if *flourishing* is synonymous with moral probity, recognition in a profession, or simple contentment. To the extent that we're not told what it means to flourish, the relationship between the claim and the grounds and between the claim and the warrant remains ambiguous and unassailable.

*Confusing Correlation for Cause/*Post Hoc, Ergo
Propter Hoc *(After This, Therefore Because of This)*
(Assuming that Event X Causes Event Y
Because Event X Preceded Event Y)

Here are two examples in which this fallacy may be at work:

Cramming for a test really helps. Last week I crammed for a psychology test and I got an A on it.

I am allergic to the sound of a lawn mower because every time I mow the lawn I start to sneeze.

We've already discussed this fallacy in Chapter 11, particularly in our discussion of the difference between correlation and causation. This fallacy occurs when a sequential relationship is mistaken for a causal relationship. To be sure, when two events occur frequently in conjunction with each other in a particular sequence, we've got a good case for a causal relationship. But until we can show how one causes the other, we cannot be certain that a causal relationship is occurring. The conjunction may simply be a matter of chance, or it may be attributable to some as-yet-unrecognized other factor. For example, your A on the psych test may be caused by something other than your cramming. Maybe the exam was easier, or perhaps you were luckier or more mentally alert.

Just when an erroneous causal argument becomes an example of the *post hoc* fallacy, however, is not cut and dried. Many reasonable arguments of causality later turn out to have been mistaken. We are guilty of the *post hoc* fallacy only when our claim of causality seems naively arrived at, without reflection or consideration of alternative hypotheses. Thus in our lawn mower argument, it is probably not the sound that creates the speaker's sneezing, but all the pollen stirred up by the spinning blades.

We arrived at this more likely argument by applying a tool known as Occam's Razor—the principle that "what can be explained on fewer principles is explained needlessly by more," or "between two hypotheses, both of which will account for a given fact, prefer the simpler." If we posit that sound is the cause of our sneezing, all sorts of intermediate causes are going to have to be fetched from afar to make the explanation persuasive. But the blades stirring up the pollen will cause the sneezing more directly. So, until science connects lawn mower noises to human eardrums to sneezing, the simpler explanation is preferred.

Slippery Slope

The slippery slope fallacy is based on the fear that once we take a first step in a direction we don't like we will have to keep going.

We don't dare send weapons to Eastern Europe. If we do so, we will next send in military advisers, then a special forces battalion, and then large numbers of troops. Finally, we will be in all-out war.

Look, Blotnik, no one feels worse about your need for open-heart surgery than I do. But I still can't let you turn this paper in late. If I were to let you do it, then I'd have to let everyone turn in papers late.

We run into slippery slope arguments all the time, especially when person A opposes person B's proposal. Those opposed to a particular proposal will often foresee an inevitable and catastrophic chain of events that would follow from taking a first, apparently harmless step. In other words, once we put a foot on that slippery slope, we're doomed to slide right out of sight. Often, such arguments are fallacious insofar as what is seen as an inevitable effect is in fact dependent on some intervening cause or chain of causes to bring it about. Will smoking cigarettes lead inevitably to heroin addiction? Overwhelming statistical evidence would suggest that it doesn't. A slippery slope argument would, however, lovingly trace a teenager's inevitable descent from a clandestine puff on the schoolground through the smoking of various controlled substances to a degenerate end in some Needle Park somewhere. The power of the slippery slope argument lies as much as anything in its compelling narrative structure. It pulls us along irresistibly from one plausible event to the next, making us forget that it's a long jump from plausibility to necessity.

One other common place to find slippery slope arguments is in confrontations between individuals and bureaucracies or other systems of rules and laws. Whenever individuals ask to have some sort of exception made for them, they risk the slippery slope reply. "Sorry, Mr. Jones, if we rush your order, then we will have to rush everyone else's order also."

The problem, of course, is that not every slippery slope argument is an instance of the slippery slope fallacy. We all know that some slopes are slippery and that we sometimes have to draw the line, saying "to here, but no farther." And it is true also that making exceptions to rules is dangerous; the exceptions soon get established as regular procedures. The slippery slope becomes a fallacy, however, when we forget that some slopes don't *have* to be slippery unless we let them be slippery. Often we do better to imagine a staircase with stopping places all along the way. The assumption that we have no control over our descent once we take the first step makes us unnecessarily rigid.

Hasty Generalization (Making a Broad Generalization on the Basis of Too Little Evidence)

Typically, a hasty generalization occurs when someone reaches a conclusion on the basis of insufficient evidence. But what constitutes "sufficient" evidence? No generalization arrived at through empirical evidence would meet a logician's strict standard of certainty. And generally acceptable standards of proof in any given field are difficult to determine.

The Food and Drug Administration (FDA), for example, generally proceeds very cautiously before certifying a drug as "safe." However, whenever doubts arise about the safety of an FDA-approved drug, critics accuse the FDA of having made a hasty generalization. At the same time, patients eager to have access to a new drug and manufacturers eager to sell a new product may lobby the FDA to "quit dragging its feet" and get the drug to market. Hence, the point at which a hasty generalization about drug safety passes over into the realm of a prudent generalization is nearly always uncertain and contested.

A couple of variants of hasty generalization that deserve mention are

1. Pars pro toto/*Mistaking the part for the whole (assuming that what is true for a part will be true for the whole).*   *Pars pro toto* arguments often appear in the critiques of the status quo. If, say, someone wanted to get rid of the National Endowment for the Arts, they might focus on several controversial grants they've made over the past few years and use them as justification for wiping out all NEA programs.

2. *Suppressed evidence (withholding contradictory or unsupportive evidence so that only favorable evidence is presented to an audience).*   The flip side of *pars pro toto* is suppressed evidence. If the administrator of the NEA were to go before Congress seeking more money and conveniently forgot about those controversial grants, he would be suppressing damaging but relevant evidence.

Faulty Analogy (Claiming that Because X Resembles Y in One Regard, X Will Resemble Y in All Regards)

Faulty analogies occur whenever a relationship of resemblance is turned into a relationship of identity. For example, the psychologist Carl Rogers uses a questionable analogy in his argument that political leaders should make use of discoveries about human communication derived from research in the social sciences. "During the war when a test-tube solution was found to the problem of synthetic rubber, millions of dollars and an army of talent was turned loose on the problem of using that finding. . . . But in the social science realm, if a way is found of facilitating communication and mutual understanding in small groups, there is no guarantee that the finding will be utilized."

Although Rogers is undoubtedly right that we need to listen more carefully to social scientists, his analogy between the movement from scientific discovery to product development and the movement from insights into small group functioning to political change is strained. The laws of cause and effect at work in a test tube are much more reliable and generalizable than the laws of cause and effect observed in small human groups. Whereas lab results can be readily replicated in different times and places, small group dynamics are altered by a whole host of factors, including the cultural background, gender, age of participants, and so forth. The warrant that licenses you to move from grounds to claim in the realm of science runs up against a statute of limitation when it tries to include the realm of social science.

Non Sequitur (Making a Claim that Doesn't Follow Logically from the Premises, or Supporting a Claim with Irrelevant Premises)

The *non sequitur* fallacy (literally, "it does not follow") is a miscellaneous category that includes any claim that doesn't follow logically from its premises or that is supported with irrelevant premises. In effect, any fallacy is a kind of *non sequitur* because what makes all fallacies fallacious is the absence of a logical connection between claim and premises. But in practice the term *non sequitur* tends to be restricted to problems like the following:

A completely illogical leap: "Clambake University has one of the best faculties in the United States because a Nobel Prize winner used to teach there." (How does the fact that a Nobel Prize winner used to teach at Clambake University make its present faculty one of the best in the United States?)

A clear gap in the chain of reasoning: "People who wear nose rings are disgusting. There ought to be a law against wearing nose rings in public." (This is a *non sequitur* unless the arguer is willing to state and defend the missing premise: "There ought to be a law against anything that I find disgusting.")

Use of irrelevant reasons to support a claim: "I should not receive a C in this course because I have received Bs or As in all my other courses (here is my transcript for evidence) and because I worked exceptionally hard in this course (here is my log of hours worked)." (Even though the arguer has solid evidence to support each premise, the premises themselves are irrelevant to the claim. Course grades should be based on actual performance in the class, not on performance in other classes or on amount of effort devoted to the material.)

  FOR CLASS DISCUSSION

Working individually or in small groups, determine the potential persuasiveness of each argument. If the arguments are nonpersuasive because of one or more of the fallacies discussed in this appendix, identify the fallacies and explain how they render the argument nonpersuasive.

1. a. All wars are not wrong. The people who say so are cowards.
   b. Either we legalize marijuana or we watch a steady increase in the number of our citizens who break the law.
   c. The Bible is true because it is the inspired word of God.
   d. Mandatory registration of handguns will eventually lead to the confiscation of hunting rifles.
   e. All these tornadoes started happening right after they tested the A-bombs. The A-bomb testing has changed our weather.
   f. Most other progressive nations have adopted a program of government-provided health care. Therefore, it is time the United States abandoned its outdated practice of private medicine.
   g. The number of Hollywood movie stars who support liberal policies convinces me that liberalism is the best policy. After all, they are rich and will not benefit from better social services.

h. Society has an obligation to provide housing for the homeless because people without adequate shelter have a right to the resources of the community.

i. I have observed the way the two renters in our neighborhood take care of their rental houses and have compared that to the way homeowners take care of their houses. I have concluded that people who own their own homes take better care of them than those who rent. [This argument goes on to provide detailed evidence about the housecaring practices of the two renters and of the homeowners in the neighborhood.]

j. Since the universe couldn't have been created out of nothing, it must have been created by a divine being.

2. Consider the following statements. Note places where you think the logic is flawed. If you were asked by writers or speakers to respond to their statements, what advice would you give to those who wrote or said them to rescue them from charges of fallaciousness? What would each of these speakers/writers have to show, in addition to what's given, to render the statement cogent and persuasive?

a. "America has had the luxury throughout its history of not having its national existence directly threatened by a foreign enemy. Yet we have gone to war. Why?

   "The United States of America is not a piece of dirt stretching mainly from the Atlantic to the Pacific. More than anything else, America is a set of principles, and the historical fact is that those principles have not only served us well, but have also become a magnet for the rest of the world, a large chunk of which decided to change course last year.

   "Those principles are not mere aesthetic ideas. Those principles are in fact the distillation of 10,000 years of human social evolution. We have settled on them not because they are pretty; we settled on them because they are the only things that work. If you have trouble believing that, ask a Pole." (novelist Tom Clancy)

b. "What particularly irritated Mr. Young [Republican Congressman from Alaska] was the fact that the measure [to prohibit logging in Alaska's Tongass National Forest] was initiated by . . . Robert Mrazek, a Democrat from Long Island. 'Bob Mrazek never saw a tree in his entire life until he went to Alaska' said Mr. Young. . . ." (*New York Times*, 11/10/90)

c. "When Senator Tim Wirth . . . was in Brazil earlier this year on behalf of an effort to save the tropical rain forest of the Amazon basin, the first thing Brazilian President Jose Sarney asked him was, 'What about the Tongass?'" (*New York Times*, 11/10/90)

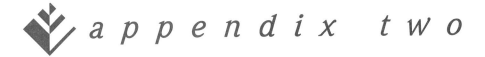

appendix two

The Writing Community
Working in Groups

In Chapter 1 we stressed that today truth is typically seen as a product of discussion and persuasion by members of a given community. Instead of seeing "truth" as grounded in some absolute and timeless realm such as Plato's forms or the unchanging laws of logic, many modern thinkers assert that truth is the product of a consensus among a group of knowledgeable peers. Our own belief in the special importance of argumentation in contemporary life follows from our assumption that truth arises out of discussion and debate rather than dogma or pure reason.

In this appendix, we extend that assumption to the classroom itself. We introduce you to a mode of learning often called collaborative learning. It involves a combination of learning from an instructor, learning independently, and learning from peers. Mostly it involves a certain spirit—the same sort of inquiring attitude that's required of a good arguer.

FROM CONFLICT TO CONSENSUS: HOW TO GET THE MOST OUT OF THE WRITING COMMUNITY

Behind the notion of the writing community lies the notion that thinking and writing are social acts. At first, this notion may contradict certain widely accepted stereotypes of writers and thinkers as solitary souls who retreat to cork-lined studies where they conjure great thoughts and works. But although we agree that every writer at some point in the process requires solitude, we would point out that most writers and thinkers also require periods of talk and social interchange before they retreat to solitude. Poets, novelists, scientists, philosophers, and technological innovators tend to belong to communities of peers with whom they share their ideas, theories, and work. In this section, we try to provide you with some practical advice on how to get the most out of these sorts of communities in developing your writing skills.

Avoiding Bad Habits of Group Behavior

Over the years, most of us have developed certain bad habits that get in the way of efficient group work. Although we use groups all the time to study and accomplish demanding tasks, we tend to do so spontaneously and unreflectively without asking why some groups work and others don't. Many of us, for example, have worked on committees that just didn't get the job done and wasted our time, or else got the job done because one or two tyrannical people dominated the group. Just a couple of bad committee experiences can give us a healthy skepticism about the utility of groups in general. "A committee," according to some people, "is a sort of centipede. It has too many legs, no brain, and moves very slowly."

At their worst, this is indeed how groups function. In particular, they have a tendency to fail in two opposite directions, failures that can be avoided only by conscious effort. Groups can lapse into "clonethink" and produce a safe, superficial consensus whereby everyone agrees with the first opinion expressed in order to avoid conflict or to get on to something more interesting. At the other extreme is a phenomenon we'll call "egothink." In egothink, all members of the group go their own way and produce a collection of minority views that have nothing to do with each other and would be impossible to act on. Clonethinkers view their task as conformity to a norm; egothinkers see their task as safeguarding the autonomy of individual group members. Both fail to take other people and other ideas seriously.

Successful groups avoid both extremes and achieve unity out of diversity. This means that any successful community of learners must be willing to endure creative conflict. Creative conflict results from an initial agreement to disagree respectfully with each other and to focus that disagreement on ideas, not people. For this reason, we say that the relationship among the members of a learning community is not so much interpersonal or impersonal as transpersonal or "beyond the personal." Each member is personally committed to the development of ideas and does whatever is necessary to achieve that development.

The Value of Group Work for Writers

Because we are basically social animals, we find it natural, pleasurable even, to deal with problems in groups. Proof of this fact can be found on any given morning in any given student union in the country. Around the room you will find many students working in groups. Math, engineering, and business majors will be solving problems together, comparing solutions and their ways of arriving at solutions. Others will be comparing their class notes and testing their understanding of concepts and terms by explaining them to each other and comparing their explanations. To be sure, their discussions will occasionally drift off the topic to encompass pressing social issues such as what they're going to do next weekend, or why they like or dislike the class they're working on, but much of the work of college students seems to get done in convivial conversation over morning coffee or late-night popcorn. Why not ease into the rigors of writing in a similar fashion?

A second major advantage of working on writing in a group is that it provides a real and immediate audience for people's work. Too often, when students write in a school setting they get caught up in the writing-for-teacher racket, which may distort their notion of audience. Argumentative writing is best aimed either at opponents or at a neutral "jury" who will be weighing both sides of a controversy. A group of peers gives you a better sense of a real-world audience "out there" than does a single teacher.

There's danger, of course, in having several audiences consider your writing. Your peer audience may well respond differently to your writing than your instructor. You may feel misled if you are praised for something by a peer and then criticized for the same thing by your instructor. These things can and will happen, no matter how much time you spend developing universally accepted criteria for writing. Grades are not facts but judgments, and all judgments involve uncertainty. Students who are still learning the criteria for making judgments will sometimes apply those criteria differently than an instructor who has been working with them for years. But you should know too that two or more instructors might give you conflicting advice also, just as two or more doctors might give you different advice on what to do about the torn ligaments in your knee. In our view, the risks of misunderstanding are more than made up for by gains in understanding of the writing process, an understanding that comes from working in writing communities where everyone functions both as a writer and a writing critic.

A third advantage to working in writing communities is closely related to the second advantage. The act of sharing your writing with other people helps you get beyond the bounds of egocentrism that limit all writers. By egocentrism, we don't mean pride or stuck-upness; we mean the failure to consider the needs of your readers. Unless you share your writing with another person, your audience is always a "mythical group," a fiction or a theory that exists only in your head. You must always try to anticipate the problems others will have in reading your work, but until others actually read it and share their reactions to it with you, you can never be fully sure you have understood your audience's point of view. Until another reads your writing critically, you can't be sure you aren't talking to yourself.

FORMING WRITING COMMUNITIES: SKILLS AND ROLES

Given that there are advantages to working in groups, just how do we go about forming writing communities in the classroom? We first have to decide how big to make the groups. From our experience, the best groups consist of either five to seven people or simply two people. Groups of three to four tend to polarize and become divisive, and larger groups tend to be unmanageable. Because working in five- to seven-person groups is quite different from working in pairs, we discuss each of these different-sized groups in turn.

Working in Groups of Five to Seven People

The trick to successful group work is to consider the maximum number of viewpoints and concerns without losing focus. Because these two basic goals frequently conflict, you need some mechanisms for monitoring your progress. In particular, it's important that each group member is assigned to perform those tasks necessary to effective group functioning. (Some teachers assign roles to individual students, shifting the roles from day to day; other teachers let the groups themselves determine the roles of individuals.) That is, the group must recognize that it has two objectives at all times: the stated objectives of a given task and the objective of making the group work well. It is very easy to get so involved with the given task that you overlook the second objective, generally known as "group maintenance."

The first role is group leader. We hesitate to call persons who fill this role "leaders" because we tend sometimes to think of leaders as know-it-alls who take charge and order people about. In classroom group work, however, being a group leader is a role you play, not a fixed part of your identity. The leader, above all else, keeps the groups focused on agreed-on ends and protects the right of every group member to be heard. It's an important function, and group members should share the responsibility from task to task. Here is a list of things for the leader to do during a group discussion:

1. Ensure that everyone understands and agrees on the objectives of any given task and on what sort of final product is expected of the group (for example, a list of criteria, a brief written statement, oral response to a question, and so forth).

2. Ask that the group set an agenda for completing the task and have some sense of how much time they will spend at each stage. (Your instructor should always make clear what time limits you have to operate within and when he or she expects your task to be completed. If a time limit isn't specified, you should request a reasonable estimate.)

3. Look for signs of getting off the track and ask individual group members to clarify how their statements relate to agreed-on objectives.

4. Actively solicit everyone's contributions and take care that all viewpoints are listened to and that the group does not rush to incomplete judgment.

5. Try to determine when the task has been adequately accomplished.

In performing each of these functions, the leader must be concerned to turn criticisms and observations into questions. Instead of saying to one silent and bored-looking member of the group, "Hey, Gormley, you haven't said diddley squat here so far; say something relevant or take a hike," the leader might ask, "Irwin, do you agree with what Beth just said about this paper being disorganized?" Remember, every action in nature is met with an equal and opposite reaction—commands tend to be met with resistance, questions with answers.

A second crucial role for well-functioning groups is that of recorder. The recorder's function is to provide the group with a record of their deliberations so they can measure their progress. It is particularly important that the recorder write down the agenda and the solution to the problem in precise form. Because the recorder must summarize the deliberations fairly precisely, he must ask for clarifications. In doing this, he ensures that group members don't fall into the "ya know?" syndrome (a subset of clonethink) in which people assent to statements that are in fact cloudy to them. (Ya know?) At the completion of the task, the recorder should also ask if there are any significant remaining disagreements or unanswered questions. Finally, the recorder is responsible for reporting the group's solutions to the class as a whole.*

If these two roles are conscientiously filled, the group should be able to identify and solve problems that temporarily keep it from functioning effectively. Maybe you are thinking that this sounds dumb. Whenever you've been in a group everyone has known if there were problems or not without leaders or recorders. Too often, however, a troubled group may sense that there is a problem without being perfectly clear about the nature of the problem or the solution. Let's say you are in a group with Elwood Lunt, Jr., who is very opinionated and dominates the discussions. (For a sample of Elwood's cognitive style, see his essay in Task 1 at the end of this Appendix.) Group members may represent their problem privately to themselves with a statement such as "Lunt's such a jerk nobody can work with him. He talks constantly and none of the rest of us can get a word in." The group may devote all of its energies to punishing Lunt with ridicule or silence rather than trying to solve the problem. Although this may make you feel better for a short time, Lunt is unlikely to get any better and the group is unlikely to get much done.

If Lunt is indeed bogging the group down by airing his opinions at great length, it is the leader's job to limit his dominance without excluding him. Because group members all realize that it is the group leader's role to handle such problems, the leader has a sort of license that allows her or him to deal directly with Lunt. Moreover, the leader also has the explicit responsibility to do so, so that each member is not forced to sit, silently seething and waiting for someone to do something.

The leader might control Lunt in one of several ways: (1) by keeping to the agenda ("Thanks, Elwood, hate to interrupt, but we're a bit behind schedule and we haven't heard from everyone on this point yet. Jack, shall we move on to you?"); (2) by simply asking Lunt to demonstrate how his remarks are relevant to the topic at hand. ("That's real interesting, Elwood, that you got to see Kurt Cobain in his last performance, but can you tell us how you see that relating to Melissa's point about ending welfare?"); or (3) by introducing more formal procedures such as asking group members to raise their hands and be called on by the chair. These

---

*There is a debate among experts who study small group communications whether or not the roles of leader and recorder can be collapsed into one job. Your group may need to experiment until it discovers the structure that works best for bringing out the most productive discussions.

procedures might not satisfy your blood lust, your secret desire to stuff Lunt into a dumpster; however, they are more likely to let the group get its work done and perhaps, just maybe, to help Lunt become a better listener and participant.

The rest of the group, though they have no formally defined roles, have an equally important obligation to participate fully. To ensure full participation, group members can do several things. They can make sure that they know all the other group members by their first names and speak to them in a friendly manner. They can practice listening procedures wherein they try not to dissent or disagree without first charitably summarizing the view with which they are taking issue. Most importantly, they can bring to the group as much information and as many alternative points of view as they can muster. The primary intellectual strength of group work is the ability to generate a more complex view of a subject. But this more complex view cannot emerge unless all individuals contribute their perspectives.

One collaborative task for writers that requires no elaborate procedures or any role playing is reading your essays aloud within the group. A good rule for this procedure is that no one responds to any one essay until all have been read. This is often an effective last step before handing in any essay. It's a chance to share the fruits of your labor with others and to hear finished essays that you may have seen in the draft stages. Hearing everyone else's final draft can also help you get a clearer perspective on how your own work is progressing. Listening to the essays read can both reassure you that your work is on a par with other people's and challenge you to write up to the level of the best student writing in your group.

Many of you may find this process a bit frightening at first. But the cause of your fright is precisely the source of the activity's value. In reading your work aloud, you are taking responsibility for that work in a special way. Writing specialist Kenneth Bruffee, whose work on collaborative learning introduced us to many of the ideas in this chapter, likens the reading of papers aloud to reciting a vow, of saying "I do" in a marriage ceremony. You are taking public responsibility for your words, and there's no turning back. The word has become deed. If you aren't at least a little nervous about reading an essay aloud, you probably haven't invested much in your words. Knowing that you will take public responsibility for your words is an incentive to make that investment—a more real and immediate incentive than a grade.

Working in Pairs

Working in pairs is another effective form of community learning. In our classes we use pairs at both the early-draft and the late-draft stages of writing. At the early-draft stage, it serves the very practical purpose of clarifying a student's ideas and sense of direction at the beginning of a new writing project. The interaction best takes place in the form of pair interviews. When you first sit down to interview each other, each of you should have done a fair amount of exploratory writing and thinking about what you want to say in your essay and how you're going to say it. Here is a checklist of questions you can use to guide your interview:

1. "What is your issue?" Your goal here is to help the writer focus an issue by formulating a question that clearly has alternative answers.

2. "What is your position on the issue and what are alternative positions?" After you have helped your interviewee formulate the issue question, help her clarify this issue by stating her own position and show how that position differs from opposing ones. Your interviewee might say, for example, that "many of my friends are opposed to building more nuclear power plants, but I think we need to build more of them."

3. "Can you walk me through your argument step by step?" Once you know your interviewee's issue question and intended position, you can best help her by having her walk you through her argument talking out loud. You can ask prompting questions such as "What are you going to say first?" "What next?" and so on. At this stage your interviewee will probably still be struggling to discover the best way to support the point. You can best help by brainstorming along with her, both of you taking notes on your ideas. Often at this stage you can begin making a schematic plan for the essay and formulating supporting reasons as because clauses. Along the way give your interviewee any information or ideas you have on the issue. It is particularly helpful at this stage if you can provide counterarguments and opposing views.

The interview strategy is useful before writers begin their rough drafts. After the first drafts have been written, there are a number of different ways of using pairs to evaluate drafts. One practice that we've found helpful is simply to have writers write a one-paragraph summary of their own drafts and of their partner's. In comparing summaries, writers can often discover which, if any, of their essential ideas are simply not getting across. If a major idea is not in the reader's summary, writer and reader need to decide if it's due to a careless reading or to problems within the draft. The nice thing about this method is that the criticism is given indirectly and hence isn't as threatening to either party. At other times, your instructor might also devise a checklist of features for you to consider, based on the criteria you have established for the assignment.

FOR CLASS DISCUSSION

1. As a group, consider the following quotation and then respond to the questions that follow: "In most college classrooms there is a reluctance to assume leadership. The norm for college students is to defer to someone else, to refuse to accept the position even if it is offered. There is actually a competition in humility and the most humble person usually ends up as the leader."*
   a. Do you think this statement is true?

---

*Gerald Philips, Douglas Pederson, and Julia Wood. *Group Discussion: A Practical Guide to Participant Leadership* (Boston: Houghton Mifflin, 1979).

b. On what evidence do you base your judgment of its truthfulness?

c. As a group, prepare an opening sentence for a paragraph that would report your group's reaction to this quotation.

2. Read the following statements about group interaction and decide as a group whether these statements are true or false.

a. Women are less self-assertive and less competitive in groups than are men.

b. There is a slight tendency for physically superior individuals to become leaders in a group.

c. Leaders are usually more intelligent than nonleaders.

d. Females conform to majority opinion more than males in reaching group decisions.

e. An unconventional group member inhibits group functioning.

f. An anxious group member inhibits group functioning.

g. Group members with more power are usually better liked than low-power group members.

h. Groups usually produce more and better solutions to problems than do individuals working alone.

With the assistance of the group, the recorder should write a four- to five-sentence description of the process your group used to reach agreement on the true-false statements. Was there discussion? Disagreement? Did you vote? Did every person give an opinion on each question? Were there any difficulties?

A SEVERAL-DAYS' GROUP PROJECT: DEFINING "GOOD ARGUMENTATIVE WRITING"

The problem we want you to address in this sequence of tasks is how to define and identify "good argumentative writing." This is a particularly crucial problem for developing writers insofar as you can't begin to measure your growth as a writer until you have some notion of what you're aiming for. To be sure, it's no easy task defining good argumentative writing. In order for even experienced teachers to reach agreement on this subject, some preliminary discussions and no small amount of compromise are necessary. By the end of this task you will most certainly not have reached a universally acceptable description of good argumentative writing. (Such a description doesn't exist.) But you will have begun a dialogue with each other and your instructor on the subject. Moreover, you will have developed a vocabulary for sharing your views on writing with each other.

For this exercise, we give you a sequence of four tasks, some homework and others in-class group tasks. Please do the tasks in sequence.

Task 1 (Homework):
Preparing for the Group Discussion

Freewrite for five minutes on the question: "What is good argumentation writing?" After finishing your freewrite, read fictional student Lunt's argument that follows and, based on the principles that Lunt seems to break, develop a tentative list of criteria for good argumentative writing.

Explanation   Before you come together with a group of people to advance your understanding and knowledge collectively, you first need to explore your own thoughts on the matter. Too often, groups collapse not because the members lack goodwill, but because they lack preparation. To discharge your responsibility as a good group member, you must therefore begin by doing your homework. By using a freewriting exercise, you focus your thinking on the topic, explore what you already know or feel about it, and begin framing questions and problems.

To help you establish a standard for good argumentative writing, we've produced a model of bad arguing by a fictional student, one Elwood P. Lunt, Jr. If you can figure out what's bad about Lunt's argument, then you can formulate the principles of good argument that he violates. Of course, no student of our acquaintance has ever written anything as bad as Lunt's essay. That's the virtue of this contrived piece. It's an easy target. In going over it critically, you may well find that Lunt violates principles of good writing you hadn't thought of in your freewrite. (We tried to ensure that he violated as many as possible.) Thus, you should be sure to go back and modify your ideas from your freewrite accordingly.

A couple of important points to keep in mind here as you prepare to critique another person's work: (1) Remember the principle of charity. Try to look past the muddied prose to a point or intention that might be lurking in the background. Your critique should speak as much as possible to Lunt's failure to realize this intent. (2) Direct your critique to the prose, not the writer. Don't settle for "He just doesn't make sense" or "He's a dimwit." Ask yourself why he doesn't make sense and point to particular places where he doesn't make sense. In sum, give Lunt the same sort of reading you would like to get: compassionate and specific.

Good Writing and Computers for Today's Modern American Youth of America

(A partial fulfillment of writing an argument in the course in which I am attending)

In todays modern fast paced world computers make living a piece of cake. You can do a lot with computers which in former times took a lot of time and doing a lot of work. Learning to fly airplanes, for example. But there are no such things as a free lunch. People who think computers will do all the work for you need to go to the Iron Curtain and take a look around, that's the place for people who think they can be replaced by computers. The precious computer which people think is the dawn of a new civilization but which is in all reality a pig in a poke makes you into a number but can't even add right! So don't buy computers for two reasons.

2   The first reason you shouldn't buy a computer is writing. So what makes people think that they won't have to write just because they have a computer on his desk. "Garbage in and garbage out one philosopher said." Do you want to sound like garbage? I don't. That's why modern American fast paced youth must conquer this affair with computers and writing by ourselves is the answer to our dreams and not just by using a computer for that aforementioned writing. A computer won't make you think better and that's the problem because people think a computer will do your thinking for you. No way, Jose.

3   Another thing is grammar. My Dad Elwood P. Lunt Sr. hit the nail on the head; when he said bad grammar can make you sound like a jerk. Right on Dad. He would be so upset to think of all the jerks out there who wasted their money on a computer so that the computer could write for them. But do computers know grammar? So get on the bandwagon and write good and get rich with computers. Which can make you write right. You think any computer could catch the errors I just made? Oh, sure you do. Jerk. And according to our handbook on writing writing takes intelligence which computers don't have. Now I'm not against computers. I am just saying that computers have there place.

4   In conclusion there are two reasons why you shouldn't buy a computer. But if you want to buy one that is all right as long as you understand that it isn't as smart as you think.

Task 2 (In-Class Group Work): Developing a Master List of Criteria

As a group, reach a consensus on at least six or seven major problems with Lunt's argumentative essay. Then use that list to prepare a parallel list of criteria for a good written argument. Please have your list ready in thirty minutes.

Explanation   Your goal for this task is to reach consensus about what's wrong with Lunt's argument. As opposed to a "majority decision," in which more people agree than disagree, a "consensus" entails a solution that is generally acceptable to all members of the group. In deciding what is the matter with Lunt's essay, you should be able to reach consensus also on the criteria for a good argument. After each group has completed its list, recorders should report each group's consensus to the class as a whole. Your instructor will facilitate a discussion leading to the class's "master list" of criteria.

Task 3 (Homework): Applying Criteria to Student Essays

At home, consider the following five samples of student writing. (This time they're real examples.) Rank the essays "1" through "5," with 1 being the best and 5 the worst. Once you've done this, develop a brief rationale for your ranking.

This rationale should force you to decide which criteria you rank highest and which lowest. For example, does "quality of reasons" rank higher than "organization and development"? Does "colorful, descriptive style" rank high or low in your ranking system?

Explanation   The following essays were all written in response to Option 5, page 145, in Writing Assignments for Chapters 4–6. Before judging the arguments, read over that assignment so you know what students were asked to do. Judge the essays on the basis of the criteria established in class.

Bloody Ice

It is March in Alaska. The ocean-side environment is full of life and death. Man and animal share this domain but not in peace. The surrounding iceflows, instead of being cold and white, are steaming from the remains of gutted carcasses and stained red. The men are hunters and the animals are barely six weeks old. A slaughter has just taken place. Thousands of baby Harp seals lie dead on the ice and thousands more of adult mothers lay groaning over the death of their babies. Every year a total limit of 180,000 seals set by the U.S. Seal Protection Act is filled in a terrifying bloodbath. But Alaska with its limit of 30,000 is not alone. Canadians who hunt seals off the coast of Northern Newfoundland and Quebec are allowed 150,000 seals. The Norwegians are allowed 20,000 and native Eskimos of Canada and Greenland are allowed 10,000 seals per year. Although this act appears heartless and cruel, the men who hunt have done this for 200 years as a tradition for survival. They make many good arguments supporting their traditions. They feel the seals are in no immediate danger of extinction. Also seal furs can be used to line boots and gloves or merely traded for money and turned into robes or fur coats. Sometimes the meat is even used for food in the off hunting months when money is scarce. But are these valid justifications for the unmerciful killings? No, the present limit on Harp seal killings should be better regulated because the continued hunting of the seals will lead to eventual extinction and because the method of slaughter is so cruel and inhumane.   1

The Harp seal killing should be better regulated first because eventual extinction is inevitable. According to *Oceans* magazine, before the limit of 180,000 seals was established in 1950, the number of seals had dwindled from 3,300,000 to 1,250,000. Without these limitations hundreds of thousands were killed within weeks of birth. Now, even with this allotment, the seals are being killed off at an almost greater rate than they can remultiply. Adult female seals give birth once every year but due to pollution, disease, predation, whelping success and malnutrition they are already slowly dying on their own without being hunted. Eighty percent of the seals slaughtered are pups and the remaining twenty percent are adult seals and even sometimes mothers who try attacking the hunters after seeing their babies killed. The hunters, according to the Seal Protection Act, have this right.   2

3   Second, I feel the killing should be better regulated because of the inhumane method used. In order to protect the fur value of the seals, guns are not used. Instead, the sealers use metal clubs to bludgeon the seal to death. Almost immediately after being delivered a direct blow, the seals are gutted open and skinned. Although at this stage of life the seal's skull is very fragile, sometimes the seals are not killed by the blows but merely stunned; thus hundreds are skinned alive. Still others are caught in nets and drowned, which according to *America* magazine, the Canadian government continues to deny. But the worst of the methods used is when a hunter gets tired of swinging his club and uses the heel of his boot to kick the seal's skull in. Better regulation is the only way to solve this problem because other attempts seem futile. For example, volunteers who have traveled to hunting sites trying to dye the seals to ruin their fur value have been caught and fined heavily.

4   The plight of the Harp seals has been long and controversial. With the Canadian hunters feeling they have the right to kill the seals because it has been their industry for over two centuries, and on the other hand with humane organizations fearing extinction and strongly opposing the method of slaughter, a compromise must be met among both sides. As I see it, the solution to the problem is simple. Since the Canadians do occasionally use the whole seal and have been sealing for so long they could be allowed to continue but at a more heavily regulated rate. Instead of filling the limit of 180,000 every year and letting the numbers of seals decrease, Canadians could learn to ranch the seals as Montanans do cattle or sheep. The United States has also offered to help them begin farming their land for a new livelihood. The land is adequate for crops and would provide work all year round instead of only once a month every year. As a result of farming, the number of seals killed would be drastically cut down because Canadians would not be so dependent on the seal industry as before. This would in turn lead back to the ranching aspect of sealing and allow the numbers to grow back and keeping the tradition alive for future generations and one more of nature's creatures to enjoy.

RSS Should Not Provide Dorm Room Carpets

1   Tricia, a University student, came home exhausted from her work-study job. She took a blueberry pie from the refrigerator to satisfy her hunger and a tall glass of milk to quench her thirst. While trying to get comfortable on her bed, she tipped her snack over onto the floor. She cleaned the mess, but the blueberry and milk stains on her brand new carpet could not be removed. She didn't realize that maintaining a clean carpet would be difficult and costly. Tricia bought her own carpet. Some students living in dorm rooms want carpeted rooms provided for them at the expense of the University. They insist that since they pay to live on campus, the rooms should reflect a comfortable home atmosphere. However, Resident Student Services (RSS) should not be required to furnish the carpet because other students do not want carpets. Furthermore, carpeting all the rooms totals into a very expensive project. And lastly, RSS should not have to provide the carpet because many students show lack of respect and responsibility for school property.

2   Although RSS considers the carpeting of all rooms a strong possibility, students like Tricia oppose the idea. They feel the students should buy their own carpets. Others claim the

permanent carpeting would make dorm life more comfortable. The carpet will act as insulation and as a sound proofing system. These are valid arguments, but they should not be the basis for changing the entire residence hall structure. Those students with "cold feet" can purchase house footwear, which cost less than carpet. Unfortunately carpeting doesn't muffle all the noise; therefore, some students will be disturbed. Reasonable quietness should be a matter of respect for other students' privacy and comfort. Those opposed to the idea reason out the fact that students constantly change rooms or move out. The next person may not want carpet. Also, if RSS carpets the rooms, the students will lose the privilege they have of painting their rooms any color. Paint stains cannot be removed. Some students can't afford to replace the carpet. Still another factor, carpet color may not please everyone. RSS would provide a neutral color like brown or gray. With tile floors, the students can choose and purchase their own carpets to match their taste.

Finally, another reason not to have carpet exists in the fact that the project can be expensive due to material costs, installation cost, and the maintenance cost caused mainly by the irresponsibility of many students. According to Rick Jones, Asst. Director of Housing Services, the cost will be $300 per room for the carpet and installation. RSS would also have to purchase more vacuum cleaners for the students use. RSS will incur more expense in order to maintain the vacuums. Also, he claims that many accidents resulting from shaving cream fights, food fights, beverage parties, and smoking may damage the carpet permanently. With floor tiles, accidents such as food spills can be cleaned up easier than carpet. The student's behavior plays an important role in deciding against carpeting. Many students don't follow the rules of maintaining their rooms. They drill holes into the walls, break mirrors, beds, and closet doors, and leave their food trays all over the floor. How could they be trusted to take care of school carpet when they violate the current rules? Many students feel they have the "right" to do as they please. This irresponsible and disrespectful behavior reflects their future attitude about carpet care.

In conclusion, the university may be able to afford to supply the carpets in each room, but maintaining them would be difficult. If the students want carpets, they should pay and care for the carpets themselves. Hopefully, they will be more cautious and value it more. They should take the initiative to fundraise or find other financial means of providing this "luxury." They should not rely on the school to provide unnecessary room fixtures such as carpets. Also, they must remember that if RSS provides the carpet and they don't pay for the damages, they and future students will endure the consequences. What will happen???? Room rates will skyrocket!!!!!

Sterling Hall Dorm Food

The quality of Sterling Hall dorm food does not meet the standard needed to justify the high prices University students pay. As I watched a tall, medium-built University student pick up his Mexican burrito from the counter it didn't surprise me to see him turn up his nose. Johnny, our typical University student, waited five minutes before he managed to make it through the line. After he received his bill of $4.50 he turned his back to the cash register and walked away displeased with his meal.

2   As our neatly groomed University student placed his ValiDine eating card back into his Giorgio wallet, he thought back to the balance left on his account. Johnny had $24 left on his account and six more weeks left of school. He had been eating the cheapest meals he could and still receive a balanced meal, but the money just seemed to disappear. No student, not even a thrifty boy like Johnny, could possibly afford to live healthfully according to the University meal plan system.

3   Johnny then sat down at a dirty table to find his burrito only half way cooked. Thinking back to the long-haired cook who served him the burrito, he bit into the burrito and noticed a long hair dangling from his lips. He realized the cook's lack of preparation when preparing his burrito.

4   Since the food costs so much, yet the quality of the food remains low, University students do not get the quality they deserve. From the information stated I can conclude that using the ValiDine service system University students would be jeopardizing their health and wasting their hard-earned money. University students deserve something more than what they have now.

ROTC Courses Should Not Get College Credit

1   One of the most lucrative scholarships a student can receive is a four-year R.O.T.C. scholarship that pays tuition and books along with a living allowance. It was such a scholarship that allowed me to attend an expensive liberal arts college and to pursue the kind of well rounded education that matters to me. Of course, I am obligated to spend four years on active duty—an obligation that I accept and look forward to. What I am disappointed in, however, is the necessity to enroll in Military Science classes. Strong ROTC advocates argue that Military Science classes are essential because they produce good citizens, teach leadership skills, and provide practical experience for young cadets. Maybe so. But we could get the same benefits without having to take these courses for credit. Colleges should make ROTC training an extracurricular activity, not a series of academic courses taken for academic credit.

2   First of all, ROTC courses, unlike other college courses, do not stress inquiry and true questioning. The ROTC program has as its objective the preparation of future officers committed to the ideals and structure of the military. The structure of the military is based upon obediently following the orders of military superiors. Whereas all my other teachers stress critical thinking and doing independent analysis, my ROTC instructors avoid political or social questions saying it is the job of civilian leaders to debate policies and the job of the military to carry them out. We don't even debate what role the military should play in our country. My uncle, who was an ROTC cadet during the Vietnam war, remembers that not only did ROTC classes never discuss the ethics of the war but that cadets were not allowed to protest the war outside of their ROTC courses. This same obedience is demanded in my own ROTC courses, where we are not able to question administration policies and examine openly the complexity of the situation in Iraq and Kuwait.

3   A second reason that Army ROTC courses do not deserve academic credit is that the classes are not academically strenuous, thus giving cadets a higher G.P.A. and an unfair advantage over their peers. Much of what a cadet does for academic credit involves non-

academic activities such as physical training for an hour three days a week so that at least some of a cadet's grade is based on physical activity, not mental activity. In conducting an informal survey of 10 upper-classmen, I found out that none of them has ever gotten anything lower than an A in a Military Science class and they do not know of anyone who got anything lower than an A. One third-year cadet stated that "the classes are basic. A monkey coming out of the zoo could get college credit for a Military Science class." He went on to say that most of the information given in his current class is a brush-up to 8th grade U.S. history. In contrast, a typical liberal arts college class requires much thought, questioning, and analysis. The ROTC Military Science class is taught on the basis of "regurgitated knowledge," meaning that once you are given a piece of information you are required to know it and reproduce it at any time without thought or question. A good example is in my class Basic Officership. Our first assignment is to memorize and recite in front of the class the Preamble to the Constitution of the United States. The purpose of doing so doesn't seem to be to understand or analyze the constitution because we never talk about that. In fact, I don't know what the purpose is. I just do it because I am told to. Because the "A" is so easy to get in my ROTC class, I spend all my time studying for my other classes. I am a step ahead of my peers in the competition for a high GPA, even though I am not getting as good an education.

Finally, having to take ROTC classes means that I can't take other liberal arts courses 4 which would be more valuable. One of the main purposes for ROTC is to give potential officers a liberal education. Many cadets have the credentials to get into an armed forces academy, but they chose ROTC programs because they could combine military training with a well-rounded curriculum. Unfortunately, by taking Military Science classes each quarter, cadets find that their electives are all but eaten up by the time they are seniors. If ROTC classes were valuable in themselves, I wouldn't complain. But they aren't, and they keep me from taking upper division electives in philosophy, literature, and the humanities.

All of these reasons lead me to believe that Army ROTC cadets are getting short- 5 changed when they enroll for Military Science classes. Because cadets receive a lucrative scholarship, they should have to take the required military science courses. But these courses should be treated as extra-curricular activities, like a work-study job or like athletics. Just as a student on a full-ride athletic scholarship does not receive academic credit for football practices and games, so should a student on a full-ride R.O.T.C. scholarship have to participate in the military education program without getting academic credit. By treating R.O.T.C. courses as a type of extra-curricular activity like athletics, students can take more elective credits that will expand their minds, better enabling them to have the knowledge to make moral decisions and to enjoy their world more fully.

Legalization of Prostitution

Prostitution . . . it is the world's oldest profession. It is by definition the act of offering 1 or soliciting sex for payment. It is, to some, evil. Yet the fact is it exists.

Arguments are not necessary to prove the existence of prostitution. Rather, the argu- 2 ment arises when trying to prove something must be done to reduce the problems of this profession. The problems which exist are in the area of crime, of health, and of environment.

Crime rates are soaring, diseases are spreading wildly, and the environment on the streets is rapidly decaying. Still, it has been generally conceded that these problems cannot be suppressed. However, they can be reduced. Prostitution should be legalized because it would reduce the wave of epidemics, decrease high crime rates, provide good revenue by treating it like other businesses, and get girls off the streets where sexual crimes often occur.

3   Of course, there are those who would oppose the legalization of prostitution stating that it is one of the main causes for the spread of venereal diseases. Many argue that it is inter-related with drug-trafficking and other organized crimes. And probably the most controversial is the moral aspect of the subject; it is morally wrong, and legalizing it would be enforcing, or even justifying, such an existence.

4   These points propose good arguments, but I shall counter each point and explain the benefits and advantages of legalizing prostitution. In the case of prostitution being the main cause for the spread of epidemics, I disagree. By legalizing it, houses would be set up which would solve the problem of girls working on the streets and being victims of sexual crimes. It would also provide regular health checks, as is successfully done in Nevada, Germany, and other parts of the U.S. and Europe, which will therefore cut down on diseases spreading unknowingly.

5   As for the increase of organized crime if prostitution is legalized, I disagree again. Firstly, by treating it like businesses, then that would make good state revenue. Secondly, like all businesses have regulations, so shall these houses. That would put closer and better control in policing the profession, which is presently a problem. Obviously, if the business of prostitution is more closely supervised, that would decrease the crime rates.

6   Now, I come to one of the most arguable aspects of legalizing prostitution: the moral issue. Is it morally wrong to legalize prostitution? That is up to the individual. To determine whether anything is "right or wrong" in our society is nearly impossible to do since there are various opinions. If a person were to say that prostitution is the root of all evil, that will not make it go away. It exists. Society must begin to realize that fear or denial will not make the "ugliness" disappear. It still exists.

7   Prostitution can no longer go ignored because of our societal attitudes. Legalizing it is beneficial to our society, and I feel in time people may begin to form an accepting attitude. It would be the beginning of a more open-minded view of what is reality. Prostitution . . . it is the world's oldest profession. It exists. It is a reality.

Task 4 (In-Class Group Work):
Reaching Consensus on Ranking of Essays

Working again in small groups, reach consensus on your ranking of the five essays. Groups should report both their rankings and their justification for the rankings based on the criteria established in Task 2 or as currently modified by your group.

Explanation   You are now to reach consensus on how you rank the papers and why you rank them the way you do. Feel free to change the criteria you established earlier if they seem to need modification. Be careful in your discussions to distinguish between evaluation of the writer's written product and your own personal position on the writer's issue. In other words, there is a crucial difference between saying "I don't like Pete's essay because I disagree with his ideas" and "I don't like Pete's essay because he didn't provide adequate support for his ideas." As each group reports back the results of their deliberations to the class as a whole, the instructor will highlight discrepancies among the groups' decisions and collate the criteria as they emerge. If the instructor disagrees with the class consensus or wants to add items to the criteria, he or she might choose to make these things known now. By the end of this stage, everyone should have a list of criteria for good argumentative writing established by the class.

A CLASSROOM DEBATE

In this exercise, you have an opportunity to engage in a variant of a formal debate. Although debates of this nature don't always lead to truth for its own sake, they are excellent forums for the development of analytical and organizational skills. The format for the debate is as follows.

First Hour   Groups will identify and reach consensus on "the most serious impediment to learning at this institution." Participants should have come to class prepared with their own individual lists of at least three problems. Once the class has reached consensus on the single most serious impediment to learning on your campus, your instructor will write it out as a formal statement. This statement constitutes the preliminary topic, which will eventually result in a proposition for your debate.

The instructor will then divide the class into an equal number of Affirmative and Negative teams (three to five members per team). Homework for all the Affirmative team members is to identify proposals for solving the problem identified by the class. Negative team members, meanwhile, will concentrate on reasons that the problem is not particularly serious and/or that the problem is "in the nature of things" and simply not soluble by any sort of proposal.

Second Hour   At the beginning of the period, the instructor will pair up each Affirmative team with a Negative team. The teams will be opponents during the actual debate, and there will be as many debates as there are paired teams. Each Affirmative team will now work on choosing the best proposal for solving the problem, while the Negative team pools its resources and builds its case against the seriousness and solubility of the problem. At the end of the period, each Affirmative team will share its proposal with its corresponding Negative team. The actual topic for each of the debates is now set: "Resolved: Our campus should institute Z (the Affirmative team's proposal) in order to solve problem X (the class's original problem statement)."

Homework for the next class is for each team to conduct research (interviewing students, gathering personal examples, polling students, finding data or expert testimony from the library, and so forth) to support its case. Each Affirmative team's research will be aimed at showing that the problem is serious and that the solution is workable. Each Negative team will try to show that the proposal won't work or that the problem isn't worth solving.

Third Hour   At this point each Affirmative team and each Negative team will select two speakers to represent their sides. During this hour each team will pool its ideas and resources to help the speakers make the best possible cases. Each team should prepare an outline for a speech supporting its side of the debate. Team members should then anticipate the arguments of the opposition and prepare a rebuttal.

Fourth (and Fifth) Hour(s)   The actual debates. (There will be as many debates as there are paired Affirmative and Negative teams.) Each team will present two speakers. Each speaker is limited to five minutes. The order of speaking is as follows:

FIRST AFFIRMATIVE:	Presents best case for the proposal
FIRST NEGATIVE:	Presents best case against the proposal
SECOND NEGATIVE:	Rebuts argument of First Affirmative
SECOND AFFIRMATIVE:	Rebuts argument of First Negative

Those team members who do not speak will be designated observers. Their task is to take notes on the debate, paying special attention to the quality of support for each argument and to those parts of the argument that are not rebutted by the opposition. By the next class period (fifth or sixth), they will have prepared a brief, informal analysis titled "Why Our Side Won the Debate."

Fifth or Sixth Hour   The observers will report to the class on their perceptions of the debates by using their prepared analysis as the basis of the discussion. The instructor will attempt to synthesize the main points of the debates and the most telling arguments for either side. At this point, your instructor may ask each of you to write an argument on the debate topic, allowing you to argue for or against any of the proposals presented.

part five

An Anthology of Arguments

OVERVIEW OF THE ANTHOLOGY

Up to this point, we've concentrated mostly on how to write arguments. In Part V of this text we present a number of finished arguments for you to study. These aren't intended to be "model" arguments in the sense that simply by imitating them you can be guaranteed a great argument. By now, it should be clear that writing is more complex than that. What typically makes these arguments worthy of our attention is the writers' commitment to and knowledge of their subjects and their ability to find a form appropriate to what they have to say. Often, the hardest aspects of an essay to imitate are the keys to the essay's success. But this doesn't mean we can't learn something about how to write better arguments from reading a variety of good arguments. And, provided that we don't treat the essays with too much reverence, provided that we're willing to play with them as well as imitate them, we can certainly adapt specific features of various essays to our own ends.

Here we would underscore the need to make the essays work for you. Every argument has a specific occasion, a set of circumstances that gave rise to the writer's choice of voice, structure, and evidence. In order to "translate" another writer's argument to your own occasion, you'll need to make adjustments. An essay you like very much may deal with its topic in an irreverent and funny way; but when you turn to your own topic, you may find humor inappropriate and distracting. Data that are extremely persuasive in one writer's argument may be almost wholly unpersuasive or even irrelevant in the context of your own argument. But by the same token, you may well find that the same author's adroit use of narrative illustrations will serve your essay well. Our advice is to use the following essays as models only in the sense that they are analogues of, not patterns for, arguments you might want to write. The essays represent a range of choices that other writers have made and in that sense are intended to expand your own sense of available options.

One good method for dealing with the essays in this section is to approach them in the manner of the *bricoleur* mentioned by French anthropologist Claude Levi-Strauss. A *bricoleur* is a sort of jack-of-all-trades who keeps a large supply of diverse materials on hand in order to "make do" with them: "A particular cube of oak could be a wedge to make up for the inadequate length of a plank of pine or it could be a pedestal—which would allow the grain and polish of the old wood to show to advantage. In one case it will serve as an extension, in the other as material." If you examine the essays with the *bricoleur*'s irreverent eye for new possibilities and adapt them for your own use, you do them more honor than if you passively "appreciate" them or mechanically ape them.

To help you see these essays in the proper spirit, we've attempted to place some of them in the context of the ongoing conversation that they come from. Instead of standing as the last word on some problematical subject, they are presented as positions on an issue. However eloquent and persuasive they may be, each should be recognized as one voice in a conversation. Indeed, we may well decide that one of the essays is right and another wrong. But even then, the essay of choice will almost always be understood differently by virtue of the fact that we've considered another point of view. After reading divergent points of view on a given subject, the reader is left with the responsibility to synthesize what's given and to create yet another point of view. This process of synthesis and dissent is the very lifeblood of argument.

The anthology addresses eleven important social issues. In each issue, writers express a wide range of views with many overlapping areas of agreement and disagreement. The collected arguments include essays for general audiences as well as academic essays with academic format and documentation.

As you read through the arguments in Part V, you might want to keep in mind the question of where each of them fits into a larger context of issues—those recurrent questions and dilemmas that we struggle with in different guises all the time. No matter what the specific issue is, certain recurring patterns of concern keep cropping up such as the conflict between principles and consequences in ethical arguments, or between spiritual and material values, individual rights and public duties, duties to self and duties to others, short-range consequences and long-range consequences, and commitment to tradition and commitment to progress. For example, whether you are considering a proposal for mandatory drug testing or for a new zoning regulation to prevent homeowners from building too high a fence, you are dealing with the conflict between "rights of the individual" and "rights of the society." One advantage of an anthology of arguments is that in reading through them you can see for yourself how frequently these large issues recur in different guises.

GUIDE QUESTIONS FOR THE ANALYSIS AND EVALUATION OF ARGUMENTS

As you read various arguments from this anthology, we hope that you will internalize habits of analysis and evaluation that we believe are essential for arguers. These habits derive from the principles of argument analysis covered throughout this text so that what follows is simply a summary and review of concepts you have already studied.

Questions for Analyzing and Evaluating a Conversation

Whenever you read two or more arguments addressing the same issue, we recommend that you follow the principles of reading described in Chapter 2.

1. *What does each argument say?* (Reading as a believer, be able to summarize each argument, stating its main claim and supporting reasons in a single sentence, if possible.)

2. *How can each argument be doubted?* (Reading as a doubter, search for weaknesses in the argument and for important questions that you would like to raise if you could talk to the author.)

3. *Why do the disputants disagree?* (Do they disagree at the level of truth or facts? At the level of values, assumptions, and beliefs?)

4. *Which arguments appear to be stronger?* (Which arguments seem most persuasive to you? Before you could take a stand on the issue yourself, what further questions would you need to have answered? Which of your own assumptions, values, and beliefs would you have to examine further and clarify?)

Questions for Analyzing and Evaluating an Individual Argument

The previous questions ask you to examine arguments in the context of the conversations to which they belong. This next set of questions asks you to look closely at a single argument, examining in detail its structure, its argumentative strategies, and its rhetorical force.

1. *How effective is the writer at creating logical appeals?*
   - What is the claim?
   - What reasons support the claim?
   - What are the ground and warrants for each of the reasons?

- How effective is the argument, particularly its use of evidence (grounds) and its support of its basic assumptions (warrants)?
- Does the argument exhibit any of the *logos* fallacies explained in Appendix 1?

2. *How effective is the writer at creating ethical appeals?*
   - What *ethos* does the writer project? What is the writer's stance toward the audience?
   - Is the writer's *ethos* effective?
   - Does the writer commit any of the *ethos* fallacies explained in Appendix 1?

3. *How effective is the writer at creating pathetic appeals?*
   - How effective is the writer at using audience-based reasons?
   - How effective is the writer's use of concrete language, word choice, powerful examples, and analogies for enhancing the pathetic appeal of the argument?

4. *How could the writer's argument be refuted?*
   - Can the writer's grounds be called into question?
   - Can the writer's warrants be called into question?

IMMIGRATION POLICY

The Case for Greatly Increased Immigration

Julian L. Simon

By increasing somewhat the flow of immigrants—from about 600,000 to about 750,000 admissions per year—the immigration legislation passed by Congress late in 1990 will improve the standard of living of native-born Americans. The bill represents a sea change in public attitude toward immigration; it demonstrates that substantially increasing immigration is politically possible now. That's all good news, and we should celebrate it.

The bad news is that the legislation does not *greatly* increase immigration. The new rate is still quite low by historical standards. A much larger increase in numbers—even to, say, only half the rate relative to population size that the United States accepted around the turn of the century—would surely increase our standard of living even more.

The political problem for advocates of immigration is to avoid the letdown to be expected after the passage of this first major legal immigration bill in a quarter-century. And since the new law seems to contemplate additional legislation (by providing for a commission to collect information on immigration), it is important to educate the public about how immigration benefits the nation as well as the immigrants.

Increased immigration presents the United States with an opportunity to realize many national goals with a single stroke. It is a safe and sure path—open to no other nation—to achieve all of these benefits: 1) a sharply increased rate of technological advance, spurred by the addition of top scientific talent from all over the world; 2) satisfaction of business's demand for the labor that the baby-bust generation makes scarce; 3) reduction of the burden that retirees impose upon the ever-shrinking cohort of citizens of labor-force age, who must support the Social Security System; 4) rising tax revenues—resulting from the increase in the proportion of workers to retirees—that will provide the only painless way of shrinking and perhaps even eliminating the federal deficit; 5) improvement in our competitive position vis-á-vis Japan, Europe, and the rest of the world; 6) a boost to or image abroad, stemming from immigrants' connections with their relatives back home, and from the remittances that they send back to them; and 7) not least, the opportunity given to additional people to enjoy the blessings of life in the United States.

All the U.S. need do to achieve the benefits is further to relax its barriers against skilled immigrants. Talented and energetic people want to come here. Yet we do not greatly avail ourselves of this golden opportunity, barring the door to many of the most economically productive workers in the world.

If immigration is such an across-the-border winner, why aren't we welcoming skilled and hardworking foreigners with open arms? These are some of the reasons: 1) The public is ignorant of the facts to be presented here; it therefore charges immigrants with increasing unemployment, abusing welfare programs, and lowering the quality of our work force.

2) Various groups fear that immigrants would harm their particular interests; the groups are less concerned with the welfare of the country as a whole. 3) Well-organized lobbies oppose immigration, which receives little organized support. 4) Nativism, which may or may not be the same as racism in any particular case, continues to exert an appeal.

THE DIMENSIONS OF PRESENT-DAY IMMIGRATION

7   The most important issue is the total number of immigrants allowed into the United States. It is important to keep our eyes fixed on this issue, because it tends to get obscured in emotional discussions of the desirability of reuniting families, the plight of refugees, the geographic origin and racial composition of our immigrant population, the needs of particular industries, the illegality of some immigration, and so on.

8   The Federation for American Immigration Reform (FAIR)—whose rhetoric I shall use as illustration—says that "[i]mmigration to the United States is at record levels." This claim is simply false: Figure I shows the absolute numbers of legal immigrants over the decades. The recent inflow clearly is far below the inflow around the turn of the century—even though it includes the huge number of immigrants who took advantage of the 1986 amnesty; they are classified as having entered in 1989, although most of them actually arrived before 1980. Even the inclusion of illegal immigrants does not alter the fact that there is less immigration now than in the past.

9   Economically speaking, more relevant than these absolute numbers is the volume of immigration as a proportion of the native population, as shown in Figure II. Between 1901 and 1910 immigrants arrived at the yearly rate of 10.4 per thousand U.S. population, whereas between 1981 and 1987 the rate was only 2.5 percent of the population. So the recent flow is less than a fourth as heavy as it was in that earlier period. Australia and Canada admit three times that many immigrants as a proportion of their populations.

10   Another way to think about the matter: in 1910, 14.6 percent of the population was born abroad, but in 1980 less than 6 percent of us were. Not only is the present stock of immigrants much smaller proportionally than it was earlier, but it is a small proportion considered by itself. We tend to think of ourselves as a "nation of immigrants," but less than one out of fifteen people now in the U.S. was born abroad, including those who arrived many years ago. Who would guess that the U.S. has a smaller share of foreign-born residents than many countries that we tend to think have closed homogeneous populations—including Great Britain, Switzerland, France, and Germany? We are a nation not of immigrants, but rather of the descendants of immigrants.

11   Furthermore, the absorption of immigrants is much easier now than it was in earlier times. One has only to read the history of the Pilgrims in Plymouth Colony to realize the enormity of the immediate burden that each new load of immigrants represented. But it is the essence of an advanced society that it can more easily handle material problems than can technically primitive societies. With every year it becomes easier for us to make the material adjustments that an increase in population requires. That is, immigrant assimilation becomes ever less of an economic problem—all the more reason that the proportion of immigrants now seems relatively small, compared with what it was in the past.

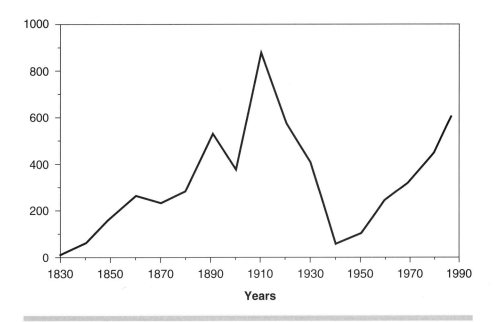

FIGURE I: Annual number of U.S. immigrants (in 1,000s)

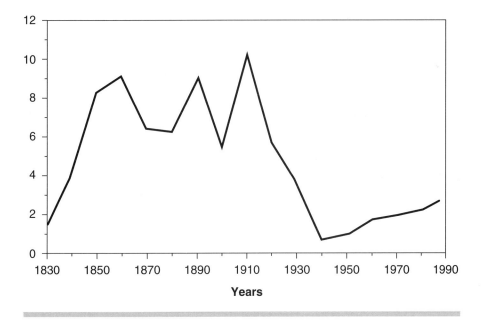

FIGURE II: Immigrants to the U.S. per 1,000 inhabitants

12   Unfortunately, despite recent changes favoring skilled immigrants, our present admissions policy remains largely nepotistic. Most visas are granted to foreigners who have family connections here. Even with the 1990 legislation, the U.S. will admit only about 110,000 people—perhaps 20 percent of all immigrants—on the basis of their job skills. Compare our policy with Australia's, which admits almost 50 percent of its immigrants according to "economic" criteria, and only 30 percent as relatives of citizens. Many of those whom we admit via family preferences also are skilled, of course, but it would be beneficial to us as well as fair to deserving foreigners to admit more people on the basis of merit alone. Indeed, George Borjas of the University of California at Santa Barbara has presented evidence that the economic "quality" of immigrants with given levels of education has declined in recent decades—though the magnitude of the decline remains controversial; the likeliest explanation for the decline is an increase in the proportion of immigrants who are admitted as relatives rather than on their merits alone. On the other hand, Harriet Duleep of the U.S. Civil Rights Commission has recently shown that despite the different admissions policies of the U.S. and Canada (which uses a point system), immigration affects the economies of the two countries similarly—probably because families carefully evaluate the economic potential of relatives before deciding to bring them in.

13   For years, phony inflated estimates of the stocks and flows of illegal immigrants were bandied about by opponents of immigration in order to muddy the waters. Since the 1986 Simpson-Mazzoli law's amnesty we know that the numbers are actually quite modest, much lower than even the "mainstream" estimates cited in the press. So that scare no longer serves as an effective red herring for opponents of immigration.

MALTHUSIAN AND OTHER OBJECTIONS

14   Now let us consider the costs and benefits of immigration—even though economic issues may not be the real heart of the matter, often serving only as a smoke screen to conceal the true motives for opposition. Only thus can one explain why the benefits of immigration do not produce more open policies. Because opponents of immigration wield economic arguments to justify their positions, however, we must consider their assertions.

15   Malthusian objections to immigration begin with "capital dilution." The supposed "law of diminishing returns"—which every economics text explains should not be thought of as a law—causes output per worker to fall. The "law" is so marvelously simple, direct, and commonsensical that it easily seduces thought—especially among academics, for whom such abstractions are bread and butter. Its simplicity also makes the Malthusian notion excellent fare for the family newspaper. In contrast, the arguments that demonstrate the inapplicability of Malthusian capital dilution in the context of immigration are relatively complex and indirect. As a consequence, simple—though incorrect—Malthusianism easily attracts adherents.

16   ⌐ Nowadays, however, the most important capital is human capital—education and skills, which people own themselves and carry with them—rather than capitalist-supplied physical capital. The bugaboo of production capital has been laid to rest by the experience of the years since World War II, which taught economics that, aside from the shortest-run considerations, physical capital does not pose a major constraint to economic growth. It is

human capital that is far more important in a country's development. And immigrants supply their own human capital.

The main real cost that immigration imposes on natives is the extra capital needed for additional schools and hospitals. But this cost turns out to be small relative to benefits, in considerable part because we finance such construction with bond issues, so that we operate largely on a pay-as-you-go basis. Immigrants therefore pay much of their share.   17

The supposed cost that most captures the public's imagination, of course, is welfare payments. According to popular belief, no sooner do immigrants arrive than they become public charges, draining welfare money from American taxpayers, and paying no taxes.   18

Solid evidence gives the lie to this charge. In an analysis of Census Bureau data I found that, aside from Social Security and Medicare, about as much money is spent on welfare services and schooling for immigrant families as for citizens. When programs for the elderly are included, immigrant families receive far *less* in public services than natives. During the first five years in the U.S., the average immigrant family receives $1,400 in welfare and schooling (in 1975 dollars), compared with the $2,300 received by the average native family. The receipts gradually become equal over several decades. Athur Akhbari of St. Mary's College in Canada has shown that recent Canadian data produce almost identical results. And Duleep's finding that the economic results of Canadian and U.S. immigration are quite similar, despite the different admissions systems, adds weight to the conclusion that U.S. immigrants pay much more in taxes than they receive in benefits.   19

Of course there must be some systematic abuses of the welfare system by immigrants. But our legislative system is capable of devising adequate remedies. Even now there are provisions in the Immigration and Naturalization Act that deny visas to aliens who are "likely to become public charges" and provide for the deportation of immigrants who have within five years after entry become public charges "from causes not affirmatively shown to have arisen after entry."   20

As to illegal immigrants and welfare, FAIR typically says that "[t]axpayers are hurt by having to pay more for social services." Ironically, several surveys—for example, one by Sidney Weintraub and Gilberto Cardenas of the University of Texas—show that illegals are even heavier net contributors to the public coffers than legal immigrants; many illegals are in the U.S. only temporarily and are therefore without families, and they are often afraid to apply for services for fear of being apprehended. Illegals do, however, pay taxes.   21

Some cities and states with disproportionately high immigration do incur significant costs and complications when immigrants first arrive. They deserve sympathy and perhaps federal assistance, though officials should note that immigrants' federal taxes will later effectively pay for such temporary assistance.   22

THE NON-THREAT OF DISPLACED NATIVE WORKERS

The most dramatic argument against immigration—the bogeyman in the mind of organized labor, which has been its most powerful political opponent since the nineteenth century—has been that foreigners take jobs held by natives and thereby increase native unemployment. The logic is simple: if the number of jobs is fixed, and immigrants occupy some jobs, there must be fewer available jobs for natives.   23

24   In the shortest run, the demand for any particular sort of worker is indeed inflexible. Therefore, additional immigrants in a given occupation must to some degree lower wages and/or increase unemployment in that occupation. For example, the large recent influx of foreign physicians increases the competition that U.S. physicians face, lowering their earnings. But because immigrants come with a variety of skills, workers in most occupations feel little impact. And in the longer run, workers in most occupations are not injured at all.

25   A good-sized body of competent recent research shows that immigration does not exacerbate unemployment, even among directly competing groups; in California, for instance, immigrants have not increased unemployment among blacks and women. And the research, done by several independent scholars from a variety of angles, uses several kinds of data. For example, Stephen Moore and I systematically studied immigration's effects upon overall unemployment, by looking at the changes in unemployment in various U.S. cities that have experienced different levels of unemployment. We found that if there is displacement, it is too little to be observable.

26   The explanation is that immigrants not only take jobs, but also create them. Their purchases increase the demand for labor, leading to new hires roughly equal in number to the immigrant workers. Immigrants also create jobs directly by opening new businesses. A Canadian government survey of immigrants, which should also describe U.S. experience, found that almost 5 percent—ninety-one of the 1,746 males and 291 single females in its panel sample—had started businesses within their first three years in Canada. Not only did they employ themselves, but they also employed others, creating a total of 606 jobs. Thus the total of 2,037 immigrants personally created roughly 30 percent as many jobs as they collectively held. Furthermore, these numbers surely rose rapidly after the three-year study period; after one year seventy-one self-employed immigrants had created 264 jobs, compared with the ninety-one immigrant entrepreneurs and 606 jobs observed after three years.

27   We can interpret this result as follows: even if one native Canadian was pushed out of a preexisting job by every five immigrants—an improbably high number—this effect would be more than made up for by the new jobs, occupied by natives, created by the immigrants' businesses.

28   The businesses that immigrants start are at first small, of course. But surprisingly, small businesses are the most important source of new jobs. And immigrant entrepreneurs tend to succeed in a dynamic economy, because they are innovative and mobile.

29   Furthermore, potential immigrants are well aware of labor-market conditions in the U.S., and they tend not to come if there is little demand for their skills. Natives tend not to be harmed even in the few industries—like the restaurant and hotel businesses—in which immigrants concentrate, because natives do not want jobs in these industries. Evidence for this comes from experiments conducted by the Immigration and Naturalization Service and San Diego County. In one case, 2,154 illegal aliens were removed from jobs, but the California State Human Resources Agency had almost no success in filling the jobs with U.S. citizens.

30   Wages are admittedly pushed downward somewhat in industries and localities in which immigrants are concentrated. Barton Smith and Robert Newman of the University of Houston found that adjusted wages are 8 percent lower in the Texas border cities in which the proportion of Mexicans is relatively high. Much of the apparent difference is accounted

for by a lower cost of living in the border cities, however. And because immigrants tend to be heterogeneous in their skills, their presence does not disproportionately affect any particular industry; and of course salaries rise in the occupations that few immigrants enter. (Indeed, if immigrants were spread evenly throughout all occupations, wages would not fall in any occupation.) At the same time, immigrants, who consume a wide variety of goods and services, increase the demand for labor across the range of occupations.

TAX PAYMENTS

If immigrants paid relatively little in taxes they might still burden natives, despite using fewer welfare services. But data on family earnings, which allow us to estimate tax payments, show that this is not at all the case.   31

Immigrants pay more than their share of taxes. Within three to five years, immigrant-family earnings reach and pass those of the average American family. The tax and welfare data together indicate that, on balance, an immigrant family enriches natives by contributing an average of $1,300 or more per year (in 1975 dollars) to the public coffers during its stay in the U.S. Evaluating the future stream of these contributions as one would a dam or harbor, the present value of an immigrant family—discounted at the risk-free interest rate of 3 percent—adds up to almost two years' earnings for a native family head. This means that the economic activities of an average immigrant family reduce the taxes of a native head of household enough to advance his or her possible date of retirement by two years.   32

Curiously, contemporary welfare-state policies render immigration more beneficial to natives than it was in earlier times when welfare was mainly voluntary. There are two main reasons why today's immigrants make net contributions to the public coffers. First, far from being tired, huddled masses, immigrants tend to come when they are young, strong, and vibrant, at the start of their work lives. For example, perhaps 46 percent of immigrants are in the prime labor-force ages of twenty to thirty-nine, compared with perhaps 26 percent of natives. And only 4 percent of immigrants are aged sixty or over, compared with about 15 percent of natives. Second, many immigrants are well educated and have well-paying skills that produce hefty tax contributions.   33

Because immigrants arrive in the early prime of their work lives, they ward off a major looming threat to U.S. economic well-being. This threat is the graying of the population, which means that each working native has an increasing burden of retired dependents to support. In 1900, there were five and one-half people aged twenty-five to fifty-four for each person aged sixty and above, whereas the Census Bureau projects that in the year 2000 the ratio will shrink to two and one-half to one—resulting in a burden that will be more than twice as heavy on workers.   34

Being predominantly youthful adults, immigrants mitigate this looming problem of more retired natives being supported by fewer workers. Indeed, immigration is the only practical way to alleviate the burden of increasing dependency that native workers would otherwise feel.   35

In the public sphere this means that immigrants immediately lessen the Social Security burden upon native workers. (The same holds for the defense burden, of course.) And   36 if there is a single factor currently complicating the government's economic policies, it is the size of Social Security payments and other assistance to the aged. Immigration—and the resulting increase in tax payments by immigrants—provides the only way to reduce the federal budget deficit without making painful cuts in valued services.

BOOSTING PRODUCTIVITY

37   Most important in the long run is the boost that immigrants give to productivity. Though hard to pin down statistically, the beneficial impact of immigration upon productivity is likely to dwarf all other effects after these additional workers and consumers have been in the country a few years. Some of the productivity increase comes from immigrants working in industries and laboratories that are at the forefront of world technology. We benefit along with others from the contribution to world productivity in, say, genetic engineering that immigrants could not make in their home countries. More immigrants mean more workers, who will think up productivity-enhancing ideas. As Soichiro Honda (of motorcycle and auto fame) said: "Where 100 people think, there are 100 powers; if 1,000 people think, there are 1,000 powers."

38   It is well to remember that the development of the atomic bomb hinged on the participation of such immigrants as Enrico Fermi, John von Neumann, and Stan Ulam, among many others. Contemporary newspaper stories continue this historical saga, noting the disproportionate numbers of Vietnamese and other Asian immigrant youths who achieve distinction in competitions such as the Westinghouse Science Talent Search. Ben Wattenberg and Karl Zinsmeister of the American Enterprise Institute write that among the forty 1988 finalists, "twenty-two were foreign-born or children of foreign-born parents: from Taiwan, China, Korea, India, Guyana, Poland, Trinidad, Canada, Peru, Iran, Vietnam and Honduras." They also note that one-fourth of recent valedictorians and salutatorians in San Diego have been Vietnamese, and that thirteen of the seventeen public high school valedictorians in Boston in 1989 were foreign born. Sometimes it seems as if such names as Wang Computers and Steve Chen dominate our most vigorous industry.

THE BOTTOM LINE

39   An economist always owes the reader a cost-benefit assessment for policy analysis. So I combined the most important elements pertaining to legal immigrants with a simple macroeconomic model, making reasonable assumptions where necessary. The net effect is slightly negative for the early years, but four or five years later the net effect turns positive and large. And when we tote up future costs and benefits, the rate of "investment" return from immigrants to the citizen public is about 20 percent per annum—a good return for any portfolio.

40   Does all this seem to be a far-out minority view? In 1990 the American Immigration Institute surveyed prominent economists—all the ex-presidents of the American Economic Association, and then-members of the Council of Economic Advisers—about immigration. Economists ought to understand the economic effects of immigration better than others, so their views are of special interest. More than four-fifths of the respondents said that immi-

gration has a very favorable impact on economic growth; none said that its impact is unfavorable. Almost three-fourths said that illegals have a positive economic impact. And almost all agree that recent immigrants have had the same kind of impact as immigrants in the past.

THE REAL REASONS FOR OPPOSITION

I began by citing various reasons for our failure to take in more immigrants, despite the clear-cut benefits of doing so. The first is ignorance of the benefits described above. Second is the opposition by special interests, such as organized labor (which wants to restrict competition for jobs) and ethnic groups (whose members often fear that immigration will cause their proportion of the population to decrease). The third reason is well-organized opposition to immigration and a total lack of organized support for it.   41

FAIR, for example, has a large budget—it amassed $2,000,000 in revenues in 1989— and a large staff. It supports letter-writing campaigns to newspapers and legislators, gets its representatives onto television and radio, and is in the rolodex of every journalist who writes on the subject. Several other organizations play a similar role. On the other side, until recently no organization advocated more immigration generally. Now at least there is the fledgling American Immigration Institute; and the de Tocqueville Institute did excellent work on immigration in 1989 and 1990, before taking on other issues.   42

The fourth check to immigration is nativism or racism, a motive that often lies beneath the surface of the opposition's arguments.   43

Rita Simon of American University, who has studied the history of public opinion toward immigrants, has found that the arguments against immigration have remained eerily identical. In the first half of the nineteenth century, Irish immigrants in New York and Boston were seen as the unassimilable possessors of all bad qualities. One newspaper wrote: "America has become the sewer into which the pollutions of European jails are emptied." Another asked: "Have we not a right to protect ourselves against the ravenous dregs of anarchy and crime, the tainted swarms of pauperism and vice Europe shakes on our shores from her diseased robes?"   44

The 1884 platform of the Democratic party stated its opposition to the "importation of foreign labor or the admission of servile races unfitted by habit, training, religion or kindred for absorption into the great body of our people or for the citizenship which our laws confer."   45

Francis Walker, Commissioner General of the Immigration Service, wrote in 1896:   46

> The question today is . . . protecting the American rate of wages, the American standard of living, and the quality of American citizenship from degradation through the tumultuous access of vast throngs of ignorant and brutalized peasantry from the countries of Eastern and Southern Europe.

In the 1920s the *Saturday Evening Post* also directed fear and hatred at the "new immigrations" from Southern and Eastern Europe: "More than a third of them cannot read and write; generally speaking they have been very difficult to assimilate. . . . They have been hot beds of dissent, unrest, sedition and anarchy."   47

48   Although statements like these are no longer acceptable in public, many people still privately sympathize with such views. One can see the traces in nativist codewords that accuse immigrants of "disturbing national homogeneity" and "changing our national culture."

IMPROVING OUR POLICIES

49   In addition to admitting more immigrants into the United States, we should also consider instituting other desirable changes in policy. Specifically, we must go further to increase the benefits that accrue to the United States from the inflow of highly educated people with high productive potential—especially people with technical skills. To its credit, the 1990 legislation will increase the flow of talented people by increasing the proportion of immigrants who are admitted because of their economic characteristics rather than their familial ties to U.S. citizens. This was worth doing to reduce nepotistic "family connections" admissions, and to treat meritorious applicants without such connections more fairly.

50   The new system does not greatly increase the flow of highly skilled people, however. An additional 100,000 or so immigrants will be admitted under the new provisions for economic selection; only 40,000 will be skilled people, the other 60,000 being their dependents. The overall increase in numbers admitted will yield perhaps another 30,000 highly skilled people. This is still only a small—though a most valuable—increment to our economy.

51   The 1990 legislation also contains a beneficial provision allowing entry to people who will invest a million dollars and create employment for ten Americans. Although this provision will not be as profitable for natives as an outright sale of the opportunity to immigrate, as permitted by some other countries, it does move in the right direction. But the new law does not go far enough; it permits entry to a maximum of only 10,000 persons per year under this provision—a piddling number by any standard.

52   Another policy that the U.S. might employ is simply to give permanent-resident visas to foreigners studying in the U.S. Many foreign students already find ways to remain under the present rules—about half of them students of engineering and science. And even more foreign graduates would remain if they could, which would push up our rate of progress even more.

53   Furthermore, if young foreigners knew that they could remain in the United States after completing their education here, more would choose to study here. This would provide multiple benefits to the United States. Given assurance that they could remain, these students could pay more realistic tuition rates than are now charged, which would benefit U.S. universities. And these increased rates would enable universities to expand their programs to serve both foreign and native students better. Best of all would be the increased number of highly competent scientific and managerial workers who would be part of the American work force.

54   In addition, a larger number of students requires a larger number of professors. And a larger number of openings for professors, especially in such fields as engineering and science, would attract more of the world's best scientists from abroad. This would enhance the process that has brought so many foreigners who subsequently won Nobel prizes to the U.S.—to the advantage as well as the honor of this country.

POLITICAL ADVANTAGES

Political power and economic well-being are intimately related; a nation's international   55
standing is heavily influenced by its economic situation. And today the future of any country—
especially of a major country that is in the vanguard with respect to production and living standards—depends entirely on its progress in knowledge, skill, and productivity. This is more true
now than in the past, because technology changes more rapidly than in earlier times. Even a
single invention can speedily alter a country's economic or military future—consider, for example, the atom bomb or the computer—as no invention could in the past, even the invention of the gun. That's why immigration safely, cheaply, and surely provides the U.S. with
perhaps the greatest opportunity that a country has ever had to surpass its political rivals.

And the best way for the U.S. to boost its rate of technological advance, and to raise its   56
standard of living, is simply to take in more immigrants. To that end, I would suggest that
the number of visas be increased by half a million per year for three years. If no major problems arise with that total (and there is no reason to expect a problem, since even another
one or two million immigrants a year would still give us an admissions rate lower than we
successfully coped with in earlier times, when assimilation was more difficult), then we
should boost the number by another half-million, and so on, until unexpected problems arise.

Immigration policy presents the U.S. with an opportunity like the one that faced the   57
Brooklyn Dodgers in 1947, before blacks played baseball on any major-league team. Signing Jackie Robinson and then Roy Campanella, at the price of antagonizing some players
and club owners, put the Dodgers way ahead of the pack. In the case of immigration, unlike baseball, no other "team" can duplicate our feat, because immigrants mainly want to
come here. All we need is the vision, guts, and ambition of Dodger general manager Branch
Rickey. (A bit of his religious zeal mixed in would do no harm.)

Can we see our national interest clearly enough to reject unfounded beliefs that some   58
groups will lose jobs to immigrants, and to surmount the racism that remains in our society?
Or will we pay a heavy price in slower growth and lessened efficiency for maintaining our
prejudices and pandering to the supposed interests of groups—organized labor, environmentalists, and others—whose misguided wishes will not benefit even them in the long run?

Huddled Excesses

Michael Lind

> Sooner or later America must face reality. It is going to be painful. . . . [W]hat America
> is fighting is a piece of poetry. . . . The poetry is thrilling. It is on the Statue of Liberty: "Give
> me your tired, your poor, your huddled masses yearning to breathe free. . . ." The trouble
> is that huddled masses need jobs.

Patrick Buchanan? No, Richard Strout, the eminent liberal journalist who wrote this   1
column for several decades. Since Strout wrote those words in 1980, more than 10 million

people have immigrated to the United States legally. The number of new immigrants, and their higher-than-average birthrate, recently forced the Census Bureau to revise its 1989 estimate of U.S. population in 2080 upward, by an additional *100 million*—to 400 million.

2   But it is not numbers alone that should convert liberal immigration defenders. As Strout observed, the "huddled masses need jobs." According to a 1995 Bureau of Labor Statistics study, competition with immigrants has accounted for roughly half the recent decline in wages among unskilled American workers. According to University of Michigan demographer William Frey, competition for jobs with poorly paid Latin American and Asian immigrants is driving low-income whites and blacks out of high-immigration states like California and high-immigration cities like New York. No wonder Steve Forbes and Dick Armey favor high levels of immigration, and *The Wall Street Journal* has proposed a five-word amendment to the U.S. Constitution—"There shall be open borders." It's great for business.

3   But not so great for poor Americans. And they're not the only ones under threat. U.S. companies can legally hire 140,000 *skilled* foreign workers each year. Business lobbyists have claimed that the U.S. computer industry needs a never-ending supply of East Asian and Indian scientists because there are not enough Americans able to do the work. Really? Why can't American industry train native and naturalized citizens for high-tech jobs? Some companies do the reverse. In 1994, the American International Group Insurance Company fired more than 250 American computer programmers and replaced them with Indian workers brought in under the H-1B visa program (which allows firms to pay only the foreign prevailing wage plus a living allowance). To add insult to injury, the laid-off workers, on pain of losing their severance pay, were forced to train their foreign replacements for sixty days.

4   The greatest gains in income by the American middle and working classes, both white and black, took place during the era of immigration restriction, from the 1920s to the 1960s. Not coincidentally, this was also the heyday of union membership, which is inevitably hampered when mass immigration produces a workforce divided by ethnicity. And, of course, it was the golden age of public support for universal entitlements and anti-poverty efforts. Coincidence? Not likely. The most generous and egalitarian countries in modern times have been culturally homogeneous nation-states admitting few or no poor immigrants, like those of northern Europe and Japan (where corporate paternalism substitutes for social democracy). The equation of social justice and national solidarity seems much less compelling in the modern U.S., where immigrants overall are much more likely than native-born Americans to receive welfare benefits. (In Chinese-speaking Asia, one widely distributed book tells potential immigrants how to obtain SSI and other benefits of the American welfare state.)

5   There is, then, a liberal case for immigration restriction that has nothing to do with the absurd and offensive claims of some conservatives that growing numbers of nonwhites threaten our civilization (Patrick Buchanan) or our gene pool (Charles Murray). What's more, the obsession with illegal immigration on the part of politicians like Pete Wilson evades the main issue. Each year, 300,000 to 400,000 illegal immigrants arrive in the U.S. to stay, a fraction of the roughly 1 million legal immigrants who take up permanent residence each year. We can and should crack down on illegal immigration—with a stronger border patrol, fences and a computerized national employment verification system—but legal immigration represents the greater threat to American wages and unions.

Reducing legal immigration is a perfectly legitimate liberal cause—if "liberal" means   6
protecting the interests of ordinary wage-earning Americans. Unfortunately, for thirty years
the Democratic Party has not acted like a liberal or social-democratic party. It has acted as
a coalition of ethnic patronage machines (each seeking to enlarge the numbers of its group
eligible for affirmative action) and affluent white social liberals (whose lifestyles in many
cases depend on a supporting cast of low-wage Latin American maids and nannies). Unlike
free-market conservatives, who can at least invoke a principled libertarian viewpoint, pro-
immigration liberals have no theory, merely the "piece of poetry" of which Strout wrote—
and the N-word (nativist). But now that majorities of black Americans and even a slight
majority of Hispanics, according to a Roper poll commissioned by Negative Population
Growth Institute, support reducing immigration to less than 300,000 a year, it will no
longer do to accuse all supporters of immigration reform of racism and xenophobia.

As Strout concluded in a critique of immigration policy back in 1981, "people must   7
face facts, whether they like them or not." A brave minority of liberal Democrats, including Wisconsin Congressman David Obey, have done so, signing on as cosponsors of the immigration reform bills introduced by Alan Simpson in the Senate and Lamar Smith in the
House. Though the bills wisely cut back on extended-family reunification—a Ponzi scheme
that has resulted in escalating immigrant numbers—they would reduce legal immigration
by only a third, to about 700,000 a year.

That's still much too high. The numerical cap envisioned by the original Kennedy-   8
Johnson reform in 1965—290,000 a year—would do more to bring U.S. population growth
in line with other developed countries and to raise U.S. wages, particularly at the bottom
of the income scale. Yet there would still be room for plenty of humanitarian refugees,
spouses and children of Mexican-American citizens, Taiwanese grad students and English
journalists. Though the U.S. would no longer take half the world's legal immigrants, we
would still have the world's most generous immigration policy.

TRB was right. Genuine liberals should unite with populist conservatives to reform an   9
immigration policy that benefits few Americans other than exploitative employers. It is easy
to talk in poetry. But it is necessary to govern in prose.

Timeout: The United States Needs a Moratorium on Immigration

Dan Stein

People often talk reverently about our nation's "immigration tradition." So let's begin   1
by citing a few facts to set the record straight:

Between 1820 and 1965 an average of 297,000 new immigrants settled in the United   2
States each year. In 1991, the United States admitted more than 1.8 million legal immigrants, up from about 1.5 million in 1990. In addition, it is estimated that between 250,000
and 500,000 illegal immigrants settle here permanently each year.

3   Thus, the magnitude of immigration we are witnessing today is anything but traditional. Moreover, immigration is no longer doing what public policies are supposed to do—
namely, serve the interests of the United States and the American people.

4   In states such as Florida, California, Texas, and New York, state and local budgets are
being stretched to the breaking point to pay for the costs of resettling unprecedented numbers of new immigrants. Schools can no longer educate, public hospitals can no longer care
for the indigent, and jobs and affordable housing are at a premium.

WE NEED A RESPITE

5   After 20 years of untraditional high levels of immigration, the United States needs a
respite. Throughout our history we have had periods of relatively high levels of immigration followed by extended periods when immigration was quite low.

6   These periods of low immigration had allowed American society to absorb and assimilate the immigrants and their children and grandchildren. Most notably, the great wave of
immigration at the beginning of the 20th century was followed by a more than 40-year period when immigration was extremely low.

7   Free from the constant cultural and linguistic reinforcement of new arrivals from their
countries of origin, the ethnic ghettos eventually dissipated and the second and third generations became part of the American mainstream. Free from the massive influx of immigrant labor, many African Americans began to migrate north and west, helping to establish
a black middle class.

8   An immigration moratorium, which would exempt spouses and minor children of U.S.
citizens and legitimate refugees, would afford the country an opportunity to absorb this latest wave of immigration and begin to deal with the stress it has placed on many states and
urban areas.

9   It would also allow the nation an opportunity to develop legal-immigration policies that
are suited to the realities of modern times and to get the problem of illegal immigration
under control.

10   The primary reason that legal immigration numbers have grown so rapidly in recent
years is that some 85 percent to 90 percent of the visas go to family members of other recent immigrants. The right to bring a relative to this country is not limited to U.S. citizens,
and the relatives who are eligible go well beyond immediate family members.

11   Thus, not only have we developed never-ending chains of family-based immigration,
but each time we admit a new immigrant, we also actually increase the demand for still further immigration.

12   Keeping the nuclear family together is an important objective. Immigrants, when they
come, ought to be allowed to bring a spouse and unmarried minor children. But beyond
that, there should be no special consideration given for extended families. The United
States cannot be responsible for reuniting extended families that immigrants themselves
separate when they immigrate.

13   Instead, we need to set a firm ceiling on immigration—at the traditional annual levels
of about 300,000 annually. And we must choose our immigrants based on their potential

to make a positive contribution to this country. Other immigrant-receiving nations, like Canada and Australia, have already adopted a merit-based system for selecting newcomers to those countries.

SHUT DOWN OLD SYSTEM

An immigration moratorium would allow us to shut down the old system, which the vast majority of Americans (of all races and ethnic groups) believe is failing to serve the national interest. At the same time it would give us an opportunity to figure out how to deal with the backlog of 3.4 million people who have already applied for family-based visas.   14

An additional benefit of a moratorium is that it would free up manpower and resources to deal with the large and ever-growing problem of illegal immigration. It is estimated that between 2 million and 3 million people enter the United States illegally each year (though only a fraction of that number settle permanently). Uncontrolled illegal immigration has become not only a very costly problem in places like Florida, California and the other states where illegal immigrants settle, but it has become a threat to our national security.   15

Several of the principal suspects in the World Trade Center bombing and the shooting outside CIA headquarters last winter were illegal aliens. It must be stressed that only a very tiny fraction of illegal aliens are terrorists, but it takes only a handful to perpetrate a lot of murder and mayhem. The same lax rules that permit millions of people to enter the United States without inspection each year made it appallingly easy for terrorists to get here and then live here with little fear of being detected.   16

Controlling our borders is not an impossible task. Though we share a 2,000-mile border with Mexico, nearly all illegal immigration takes place along only about 200 miles of border in California and Texas. Mountainous terrain and unmerciful desert have taken care of the rest.   17

The entire Border Patrol has about 3,700 agents, roughly the size of the Capitol Hill police force that protects members of Congress. Twice in the past seven years, Congress has promised to increase the Border Patrol manpower to 6,600, and both times it failed to provide the funds. Under a moratorium, additional resources could be redirected to regain control of the border.   18

WORK VERIFICATION SYSTEM

The most important step in controlling illegal immigration would be to enact a secure work-verification system in this country. Employer sanctions, the law that prohibits the employment of illegal aliens, is being seriously undermined by rampant document fraud. Bogus Social Security cards can be purchased for as little as $25, and 48 out of the 50 states issue drivers' licenses without even checking whether applicants are legal residents of the United States.   19

In an age when credit cards and ATM cards are routinely verified electronically millions of times a day, there is no reason why the Social Security card—which everyone who works in this country must already have anyway—can't be similarly protected. A verifiable Social Security card would ensure that only those people who are in the country legally could find employment and gain access to public benefits. Moreover, it would make the government, not individual employers, responsible for determining who is here legally.   20

21   Most important, a temporary break from extremely high levels of immigration would permit the nation to begin absorbing and assimilating the millions of newcomers who have settled here in recent years. Unless we declare a moratorium on most immigration and get a handle on illegal immigration, we will be faced with a further influx of new immigrants during the 1990s equivalent to the entire population of Florida.

22   It is time to restore our immigration tradition by restoring immigration to its traditional levels. To achieve that, we need to take a timeout.

FOR CLASS DISCUSSION

1. Analyze and evaluate the disagreement over immigration by applying the first set of guide questions from page 455. How do you account for the disagreement between those who support and those who oppose increased immigration?

2. Choose one of the arguments for closer analysis, applying the second set of guide questions on page 455–456.

Optional Writing Assignment   In commenting on the experience of immigrants earlier in U.S. history, Stein notes that "[f]ree from the constant cultural and linguistic reinforcement of new arrivals from their countries of origin, the ethnic ghettos eventually dissipated and the second and third generations became part of the American mainstream." To what extent do you think that immigrants should strive to maintain their own language and ethnicity as opposed to adopting American ways and blending into mainstream culture?

MERCY KILLING AND THE RIGHT TO DIE

Active and Passive Euthanasia
James Rachels

1   The distinction between active and passive euthanasia is thought to be crucial for medical ethics. The idea is that it is permissible, at least in some cases, to withhold treatment and allow a patient to die, but it is never permissible to take any direct action designed to kill the patient. This doctrine seems to be accepted by most doctors, and it is endorsed in a statement adopted by the House of Delegates of the American Medical Association on December 4, 1973:

The intentional termination of the life of one human being by another—mercy killing—is contrary to that for which the medical profession stands and is contrary to the policy of the American Medical Association.

The cessation of the employment of extraordinary means to prolong the life of the body when there is irrefutable evidence that biological death is imminent is the decision of the patient and/or his immediate family. The advice and judgment of the physician should be freely available to the patient and/or his immediate family.

However, a strong case can be made against this doctrine. In what follows I will set out some of the relevant arguments, and urge doctors to reconsider their views on this matter.

To begin with a familiar type of situation, a patient who is dying of incurable cancer of the throat is in terrible pain, which can no longer be satisfactorily alleviated. He is certain to die within a few days, even if present treatment is continued, but he does not want to go on living for those days since the pain is unbearable. So he asks the doctor for an end to it, and his family joins in the request.

Suppose the doctor agrees to withhold treatment, as the conventional doctrine says he may. The justification for his doing so is that the patient is in terrible agony, and since he is going to die anyway, it would be wrong to prolong his suffering needlessly. But now notice this. If one simply withholds treatment, it may take the patient longer to die, and so he may suffer more than he would if more direct action were taken and a lethal injection given. This fact provides strong reason for thinking that, once the initial decision not to prolong his agony has been made, active euthanasia is actually preferable to passive euthanasia, rather than the reverse. To say otherwise is to endorse the option that leads to more suffering rather than less, and is contrary to the humanitarian impulse that prompts the decision not to prolong his life in the first place.

Part of my point is that the process of being "allowed to die" can be relatively slow and painful, whereas being given a lethal injection is relatively quick and painless. Let me give a different sort of example. In the United States about one in 600 babies is born with Down's syndrome. Most of these babies are otherwise healthy—that is, with only the usual pediatric care, they will proceed to an otherwise normal infancy. Some, however, are born with congenital defects such as intestinal obstructions that require operations if they are to live. Sometimes, the parents and the doctor will decide not to operate, and let the infant die. Anthony Shaw describes what happens then:

> . . . When surgery is denied [the doctor] must try to keep the infant from suffering while natural forces sap the baby's life away. As a surgeon whose natural inclination is to use the scalpel to fight off death, standing by and watching a salvageable baby die is the most emotionally exhausting experience I know. It is easy at a conference, in a theoretical discussion, to decide that such infants should be allowed to die. It is altogether different to stand by in the nursery and watch as dehydration and infection wither a tiny being over hours and days. This is a terrible ordeal for me and the hospital staff—much more so than for the parents who never set foot in the nursery.

I can understand why some people are opposed to euthanasia, and insist that such infants must be allowed to live. I think I can also understand why other people favor destroying these babies quickly and painlessly. But, why should anyone favor letting "dehydration and infection wither a tiny being over hours and days?" The doctrine that says that a baby may be allowed to dehydrate and wither, but may not be given an injection that would end its life without suffering, seems so patently cruel as to require no further refutation. The strong language is not intended to offend, but only to put the point in the clearest possible way.

5   My second argument is that the conventional doctrine leads to decisions concerning life and death made on irrelevant grounds.

6   Consider again the case of the infants with Down's syndrome who need operations for congenital defects unrelated to the syndrome to live. Sometimes, there is no operation, and the baby dies, but when there is no such defect, the baby lives on. Now, an operation such as that to remove an intestinal obstruction is not prohibitively difficult. The reason why such operations are not performed in these cases is, clearly, that the child has Down's syndrome and the parents and doctor judge that because of that fact it is better for the child to die.

7   But notice that this situation is absurd, no matter what view one takes of the lives and potentials of such babies. If the life of such an infant is worth preserving, what does it matter if it needs a simple operation? Or, if one thinks it better that such a baby should not live on, what difference does it make that it happens to have an unobstructed intestinal tract? In either case, the matter of life and death is being decided on irrelevant grounds. It is the Down's syndrome, and not the intestines, that is the issue. The matter should be decided, if at all, on that basis, and not be allowed to depend on the essentially irrelevant question of whether the intestinal tract is blocked.

8   What makes this situation possible, of course, is the idea that when there is an intestinal blockage, one can "let the baby die," but when there is no such defect there is nothing that can be done, for one must not "kill" it. The fact that this idea leads to such results as deciding life or death on irrelevant grounds is another good reason why the doctrine should be rejected.

9   One reason why so many people think that there is an important moral difference between active and passive euthanasia is that they think killing someone is morally worse than letting someone die. But is it? Is killing, in itself, worse than letting die? To investigate this issue, two cases may be considered that are exactly alike except that one involves killing whereas the other involves letting someone die. Then, it can be asked whether this difference makes any difference to the moral assessments. It is important that the cases be exactly alike, except for this one difference, since otherwise one cannot be confident that it is this difference and not some other that accounts for any variation in the assessments of the two cases. So, let us consider this pair of cases:

10   In the first, Smith stands to gain a large inheritance if anything should happen to his six-year-old cousin. One evening while the child is taking his bath, Smith sneaks into the bathroom and drowns the child, and then arranges things so that it will look like an accident.

11   In the second, Jones also stands to gain if anything should happen to his six-year-old cousin. Like Smith, Jones sneaks in planning to drown the child in his bath. However, just as he enters the bathroom Jones sees the child slip and hit his head, and fall face down in the water. Jones is delighted; he stands by, ready to push the child's head back under if it is necessary, but it is not necessary. With only a little thrashing about, the child drowns all by himself, "accidentally," as Jones watches and does nothing.

12   Now Smith killed the child, whereas Jones "merely" let the child die. That is the only difference between them. Did either man behave better, from a moral point of view? If the

difference between killing and letting die were in itself a morally important matter, one should say that Jones's behavior was less reprehensible than Smith's. But does one really want to say that? I think not. In the first place, both men acted from the same motive, personal gain, and both had exactly the same end in view when they acted. It may be inferred from Smith's conduct that he is a bad man, although that judgment may be withdrawn or modified if certain further facts are learned about him—for example, that he is mentally deranged. But would not the very same thing be inferred about Jones from his conduct? And would not the same further considerations also be relevant to any modification of this judgment? Moreover, suppose Jones pleaded, in his own defense, "After all, I didn't do anything except just stand there and watch the child drown. I didn't kill him; I only let him die." Again, if letting die were in itself less bad than killing, this defense should have at least some weight. But it does not. Such a "defense" can only be regarded as a grotesque perversion of moral reasoning. Morally speaking, it is no defense at all.

Now, it may be pointed out, quite properly, that the cases of euthanasia with which   13
doctors are concerned are not like this at all. They do not involve personal gain or the destruction of normal healthy children. Doctors are concerned only with cases in which the patient's life is of no further use to him, or in which the patient's life has become or will soon become a terrible burden. However, the point is the same in these cases: the bare difference between killing and letting die does not, in itself, make a moral difference. If a doctor lets a patient die, for humane reasons, he is in the same moral position as if he had given the patient a lethal injection for humane reasons. If his decision was wrong—if, for example, the patient's illness was in fact curable—the decision would be equally regrettable no matter which method was used to carry it out. And if the doctor's decision was the right one, the method used is not in itself important.

The AMA policy statement isolates the crucial issue very well; the crucial issue is "the   14
intentional termination of the life of one human being by another." But after identifying this issue, and forbidding "mercy killing," the statement goes on to deny that the cessation of treatment is the intentional termination of a life. This is where the mistake comes in, for what is the cessation of treatment, in these circumstances, if it is not "the intentional termination of the life of one human being by another?" Of course it is exactly that, and if it were not, there would be no point to it.

Many people will find this judgment hard to accept. One reason, I think, is that it is   15
very easy to conflate the question of whether killing is, in itself, worse than letting die, with the very different question of whether most actual cases of killing are more reprehensible than most actual cases of letting die. Most actual cases of killing are clearly terrible (think, for example, of all the murders reported in the newspapers), and one hears of such cases every day. On the other hand, one hardly ever hears of a case of letting die, except for the actions of doctors who are motivated by humanitarian reasons. So one learns to think of killing in a much worse light than of letting die. But this does not mean that there is something about killing that makes it in itself worse than letting die, for it is not the bare difference between killing and letting die that makes the difference in these cases. Rather, the other factors—the murderer's motive of personal gain, for example, contrasted with the doctor's humanitarian motivation—account for different reactions to the different cases.

16   I have argued that killing is not in itself any worse than is letting die; if my contention is right, it follows that active euthanasia is not any worse than passive euthanasia. What arguments can be given on the other side? The most common, I believe, is the following:

Rebuttal

17   "The important difference between active and passive euthanasia is that, in passive euthanasia, the doctor does not do anything to bring about the patient's death. The doctor does nothing, and the patient dies of whatever ills already afflict him. In active euthanasia, however, the doctor does something to bring about the patient's death: he kills him. The doctor who gives the patient with cancer a lethal injection has himself caused his patient's death; whereas if he merely ceases treatment, the cancer is the cause of the death."

18   A number of points need to be made here. The first is that it is not exactly correct to say that in passive euthanasia the doctor does nothing, for he does do one thing that is very important: he lets the patient die. "Letting someone die" is certainly different, in some respects, from other types of action—mainly in that it is a kind of action that one may perform by way of not performing certain other actions. For example, one may let a patient die by way of not giving medication, just as one may insult someone by way of not shaking his hand. But for any purpose of moral assessment, it is a type of action nonetheless. The decision to let a patient die is subject to moral appraisal in the same way that a decision to kill him would be subject to moral appraisal: it may be assessed as wise or unwise, compassionate or sadistic, right or wrong. If a doctor deliberately let a patient die who was suffering from a routinely curable illness, the doctor would certainly be to blame for what he had done, just as he would be to blame if he had needlessly killed the patient. Charges against him would then be appropriate. If so, it would be no defense at all for him to insist that he didn't "do anything." He would have done something very serious indeed, for he let his patient die.

19   Fixing the cause of death may be very important from a legal point of view, for it may determine whether criminal charges are brought against the doctor. But I do not think that this notion can be used to show a moral difference between active and passive euthanasia. The reason why it is considered bad to be the cause of someone's death is that death is regarded as a great evil—and so it is. However, if it has been decided that euthanasia—even passive euthanasia—is desirable in a given case, it has also been decided that in this instance death is no greater an evil than the patient's continued existence. And if this is true, the usual reason for not wanting to be the cause of someone's death simply does not apply.

20   Finally, doctors may think that all of this is only of academic interest—the sort of thing that philosophers may worry about but that has no practical bearing on their own work. After all, doctors must be concerned about the legal consequences of what they do, and active euthanasia is clearly forbidden by the law. But even so, doctors should also be concerned with the fact that the law is forcing upon them a moral doctrine that may well be indefensible, and has a considerable effect on their practices. Of course, most doctors are not now in the position of being coerced in this matter, for they do not regard themselves as merely going along with what the law requires. Rather, in statements such as the AMA policy statement that I have quoted, they are endorsing this doctrine as a central point of medical ethics. In that statement, active euthanasia is condemned not merely as illegal but as "contrary to that for which the medical profession stands," whereas passive euthanasia is approved. However, the preceding considerations suggest that there is really no moral difference between the

two, considered in themselves (there may be important moral differences in some cases in their *consequences,* but, as I pointed out, these differences may make active euthanasia, and not passive euthanasia, the morally preferable option). So, whereas doctors may have to discriminate between active and passive euthanasia to satisfy the law, they should not do any more than that. In particular, they should not give the distinction any added authority and weight by writing it into official statements of medical ethics.

Saying What We Mean

David B. McCurdy

1   A subtle shift in habits of thought and language has infiltrated discussions of euthanasia and related issues. The prevalent understanding of euthanasia as an action or an omission of treatment motivated by mercy has been joined to—and sometimes replaced by—a conception of euthanasia as an economically motivated denial of medical treatment.

2   Not surprisingly, this shift occurs at a time when economic considerations are playing an increasing role in public policy discussions of the morality and legality of euthanasia. Economic arguments have long been employed both to support and to oppose public sanction of euthanasia. What has changed is that, in some instances, economic considerations have become part of the definition of euthanasia.

3   A clear example of this shift occurs in a *New York Times* op-ed piece addressing the congressional debate over Medicare reform. Burke J. Balch, a representative of the National Right to Life Committee, worries that private managed-care plans will lead to the rationing of life-sustaining medical treatments. In opposing such rationing, he claims that "denial of life-saving medical treatment against the patient's will amounts to involuntary euthanasia."

4   His fears should be taken seriously. The argument that supports his view, however, relies on an unacknowledged replacement of the generally accepted meaning of euthanasia with an understanding of euthanasia as the product of a cost-benefit assessment.

5   Those who debated the morality of euthanasia in the 1970s and 1980s generally agreed that euthanasia was characterized by a merciful desire to relieve another's suffering or end mere existence in a hopeless condition. A deliberate action or an omission of treatment that led to a person's death was termed euthanasia only if its intent was beneficent—if it sought the patient's good—and was motivated by compassion. This understanding is still widely shared, even among opponents of euthanasia.

6   In the National Right to Life Committee's grim depiction of managed Medicare, however, the real force behind "euthanasia" is the overriding drive to save money. Beneficence is barely in view, and compassion is nowhere to be seen.

7   If this definitional shift appeared only in one special-interest group's polemic, it might merit little attention, but similar deviations have also appeared in the writings of philosophers and bioethicists—those who might be expected to act as guardians of moral discourse.

8   Some of these authors seem unaware of the shift they make. Philosopher Larry Churchill observes that opponents of a proposal to ration medical treatment on the basis of age are wrong to characterize the proposal as "advocating passive euthanasia for the elderly on utilitarian grounds." Yet Churchill overlooks the most crucial point. Such opponents of age-rationing not only allege that "passive euthanasia" has a utilitarian justification; they also redefine "passive euthanasia" as an economically based denial of treatment. They then feel free to charge that "euthanasia" is the intent of the proposed rationing of care. By failing to note the redefinition, Churchill is drawn into the new use and appears to concede its legitimacy.

9   Other writers are more deliberate about shifting the definition. Bioethicist Margaret Pabst Battin observes that society is "coming to use the term euthanasia not just for pain-sparing deaths but for resource-conserving deaths as well." She comments that euthanasia's Greek root meaning "good death," a death that is good for the patient, is thereby compromised, and she decries the change: "Our very language invites us to overlook distinctions that we ought to make." Yet after noting society's "rapid change" in usage, Battin adopts the economically based definition herself. She argues that justice requires "the practice of euthanasia" as resource-saving denial of treatment "in certain kinds of scarcity situations."

10   Right-to-life activists alter their usage for different purposes. The National Right to Life Committee hopes to capitalize on the stigma that "euthanasia" is presumed to carry by applying the term to a wide range of cases. Some activists insinuate a parallel between the "euthanasia" that includes limits on health care funding and the "euthanasia" that eliminated "life unworthy of life" in Nazi Germany.

11   Such strategies may backfire. Those who apply the euthanasia label too freely may generate political support for the very practices they oppose. Most Americans still associate euthanasia with compassion and a genuine desire to relieve suffering. In the Kevorkian era these positive associations give euthanasia an aura of moral legitimacy. They are too strong to be dispelled by opponents' attempts to redefine the word or play on fears of Nazi-style genocide. Even physicians and nurses, whose professional codes prohibit participation in euthanasia, often find it hard to reject euthanasia because they associate its aim with values and virtues at the heart of their own practice.

12   Since euthanasia has become a morally permissible option for increasing numbers of Americans, activists would be wise to recognize that the motives of most supporters are quite different from the crude utilitarianism that is fueling the policies deplored by the National Right to Life Committee.

13   Those who would deny life-sustaining treatments in order to conserve resources should not be allowed, let alone encouraged, to call the consequences of their proposal "euthanasia." Proponents should be pressed to adopt a more truthful label—such as Battin's "age rationing by denial of treatment."

14   The importance of such a dialogue extends beyond its relevance to public policy and the common good. Many people experience the anguish reflected in debates on euthanasia and assisted suicide. They use the public discussion of these questions to examine their own stance toward euthanasia or assisted suicide as a possible option for themselves or a loved one. Moreover, the controversy about euthanasia reaches to the very heart of the church's identity. Euthanasia discussions inevitably provoke questions about the meaning

and purpose of life and death before God, the nature of our obligations to care for one another and the ethics of a faithful response to suffering.

The church should carefully monitor its internal dialogue lest a resource-conserving understanding of euthanasia infiltrate its own language and obscure the real moral challenge of euthanasia: the attractiveness of its compassionate motivation and beneficent intent.

15

Proponents of euthanasia and assisted suicide deserve a sympathetic if critical hearing both in the church and in the public arena. We should reject a definition of euthanasia that ignores the differences between those motivated by compassion and beneficence and those who would deny life-sustaining treatment for reasons of financial and societal expediency. Any equation of the two positions slanders sincere proponents of euthanasia, and undercuts the possibility of fruitful dialogue about euthanasia and public policy.

16

Rising to the Occasion of Our Death

William F. May

For many parents, a Volkswagen van is associated with putting children to sleep on a camping trip. Jack Kevorkian, a Detroit pathologist, has now linked the van with the veterinarian's meaning of "putting to sleep." Kevorkian conducted a dinner interview with Janet Elaine Adkins, a 54-year-old Alzheimer's patient, and her husband and then agreed to help her commit suicide in his VW van. Kevorkian pressed beyond the more generally accepted practice of passive euthanasia (allowing a patient to die by withholding or withdrawing treatment) to active euthanasia (killing for mercy).

1

Kevorkian, moreover, did not comply with the strict regulations that govern active euthanasia in, for example, the Netherlands. Holland requires that death be imminent (Adkins had beaten her son in tennis just a few days earlier); it demands a more professional review of the medical evidence and the patient's resolution than a dinner interview with a physician (who is a stranger and who does not treat patients) permits; and it calls for the final, endorsing signatures of two doctors.

2

So Kevorkian-bashing is easy. But the question remains: Should we develop a judicious, regulated social policy permitting voluntary euthanasia for the terminally ill? Some moralists argue that the distinction between allowing to die and killing for mercy is petty quibbling over technique. Since the patient in any event dies—whether by acts of omission or commission—the route to death doesn't really matter. The way modern procedures have made dying at the hands of the experts and their machines such a prolonged and painful business has further fueled the euthanasia movement, which asserts not simply the right to die but the right to be killed.

3

But other moralists believe that there is an important moral distinction between allowing to die and mercy killing. The euthanasia movement, these critics contend, wants to engineer death rather than face dying. Euthanasia would bypass dying to make one dead as quickly as possible. It aims to relieve suffering by knocking out the interval between life and death. It solves the problem of suffering by eliminating the sufferer.

4

5   The impulse behind the euthanasia movement is understandable in an age when dying has become such an inhumanly endless business. But the movement may fail to appreciate our human capacity to rise to the occasion of our death. The best death is not always the sudden death. Those forewarned of death and given time to prepare for it have time to engage in acts of reconciliation. Also, advanced grieving by those about to be bereaved may ease some of their pain. Psychiatrists have observed that those who lose a loved one accidentally have a more difficult time recovering from the loss than those who have suffered through an extended period of illness before the death. Those who have lost a close relative by accident are more likely to experience what Geoffrey Gorer has called limitless grief. The community, moreover, may need its aged and dependent, its sick and its dying, and the virtues which they sometimes evince—the virtues of humility, courage, and patience—just as much as the community needs the virtues of justice and love manifest in the agents of care.

6   On the whole, our social policy should allow terminal patients to die but it should not regularize killing for mercy. Such a policy would recognize and respect that moment in illness when it no longer makes sense to bend every effort to cure or to prolong life and when one must allow patients to do their own dying. This policy seems most consonant with the obligations of the community to care and of the patient to finish his or her course.

7   Advocates of active euthanasia appeal to the principle of patient autonomy—as the use of the phrase "voluntary euthanasia" indicates. But emphasis on the patient's right to determine his or her destiny often harbors an extremely naive view of the uncoerced nature of the decision. Patients who plead to be put to death hardly make unforced decisions if the terms and conditions under which they receive care already nudge them in the direction of the exit. If the elderly have stumbled around in their apartments, alone and frightened for years, or if they have spent years warehoused in geriatrics barracks, then the decision to be killed for mercy hardly reflects an uncoerced decision. The alternative may be so wretched as to push patients toward this escape. It is a huge irony and, in some cases, hypocrisy to talk suddenly about a compassionate killing when the aging and dying may have been starved for compassion for many years. To put it bluntly, a country has not earned the moral right to kill for mercy unless it has already sustained and supported life mercifully. Otherwise we kill for compassion only to reduce the demands on our compassion. This statement does not charge a given doctor or family member with impure motives. I am concerned here not with the individual case but with the cumulative impact of a social policy.

8   I can, to be sure, imagine rare circumstances in which I hope I would have the courage to kill for mercy—when the patient is utterly beyond human care, terminal, and in excruciating pain. A neurosurgeon once showed a group of physicians and an ethicist the picture of a Vietnam casualty who had lost all four limbs in a landmine explosion. The catastrophe had reduced the soldier to a trunk with his face transfixed in horror. On the battlefield I would hope that I would have the courage to kill the sufferer with mercy.

9   But hard cases do not always make good laws or wise social policies. Regularized mercy killings would too quickly relieve the community of its obligation to provide good care. Further, we should not always expect the law to provide us with full protection and coverage for what, in rare circumstances, we may morally need to do. Sometimes the moral life calls us out into a no-man's-land where we cannot expect total security and protection under the law. But no one said that the moral life is easy.

FOR CLASS DISCUSSION

1. Analyze and evaluate the discussion on the right to die by applying the first set of guide questions from page 455. How do you account for the disagreement among the authors?

2. Choose one of the arguments for closer analysis, applying the second set of guide questions on page 455–456. Also consider student writer Dao Do's essay on pages 143–144.

Optional Writing Assignment   As a member of the state medical board, you have been asked by a local civic organization to give your thoughts on the recent controversy over "Dr. Death," the Detroit physician who designed and made available a "suicide machine" to ensure that those who are suffering from incurable diseases and who wish to kill themselves have a speedy and painless death. (For more background on the Jack Kevorkian case, see the opening of William May's essay, p. 479).

Do people have the right to avail themselves of such machines? Do doctors have a right (or even an obligation) to help patients die? What's the state's role in deciding this issue? These are some of the questions the group would like you to consider in a brief (no more than four pages) speech at their weekly Wednesday luncheon. Drawing on your reading of the preceding essays, personal experience, and any other research you may have done, write your speech.

THE RESPONSIBILITY OF THE RICH FOR THE POOR

Lifeboat Ethics: The Case Against Aid that Harms

Garrett Hardin

Environmentalists use the metaphor of the earth as a "spaceship" in trying to persuade   1
countries, industries and people to stop wasting and polluting our natural resources. Since we all share life on this planet, they argue, no single person or institution has the right to destroy, waste or use more than a fair share of its resources.

But does everyone on earth have an equal right to an equal share of its resources? The   2
spaceship metaphor can be dangerous when used by misguided idealists to justify suicidal

policies for sharing our resources through uncontrolled immigration and foreign aid. In their enthusiastic but unrealistic generosity, they confuse the ethics of a spaceship with those of a lifeboat.

3   A true spaceship would have to be under the control of a captain, since no ship could possibly survive if its course were determined by committee. Spaceship Earth certainly has no captain; the United Nations is merely a toothless tiger, with little power to enforce any policy upon its bickering members.

4   If we divide the world crudely into rich nations and poor nations, two thirds of them are desperately poor, and only one third comparatively rich, with the United States the wealthiest of all. Metaphorically each nation can be seen as a lifeboat full of comparatively rich people. In the ocean outside each lifeboat swim the poor of the world, who would like to get in, or at least to share some of the wealth. What should the lifeboat passengers do?

5   First, we must recognize the limited capacity of any lifeboat. For example, a nation's land has a limited capacity to support a population and as the current energy crisis has shown us, in some ways we have already exceeded the carrying capacity of our land.

ADRIFT IN A MORAL SEA

6   So here we sit, say fifty people in our lifeboat. To be generous, let us assume it has room for ten more, making a total capacity of sixty. Suppose the fifty of us in the lifeboat see 100 others swimming in the water outside, begging for admission to our boat or for handouts. We have several options: We may be tempted to try to live by the Christian ideal of being "our brother's keeper," or by the Marxist ideal of "to each according to his needs." Since the needs of all in the water are the same, and since they can all be seen as "our brothers," we could take them all into our boat, making a total of 150 in a boat designed for sixty. The boat swamps, everyone drowns. Complete justice, complete catastrophe.

7   Since the boat has an unused excess capacity of ten more passengers, we could admit just ten more to it. But which ten do we let in? How do we choose? Do we pick the best ten, the neediest ten, "first come, first served"? And what do we say to the ninety we exclude? If we do let an extra ten into our lifeboat, we will have lost our "safety factor," an engineering principle of critical importance. For example, if we don't leave room for excess capacity as a safety factor in our country's agriculture, a new plant disease or a bad change in the weather could have disastrous consequences.

8   Suppose we decide to preserve our small safety factor and admit no more to the lifeboat. Our survival is then possible, although we shall have to be constantly on guard against boarding parties.

9   While this last solution clearly offers the only means of our survival, it is morally abhorrent to many people. Some say they feel guilty about their good luck. My reply is simple: "Get out and yield your place to others." This may solve the problem of the guilt-ridden person's conscience, but it does not change the ethics of the lifeboat. The needy person to whom the guilt-ridden person yields his place will not himself feel guilty about his good luck. If he did, he would not climb aboard. The net result of conscience-stricken people giving up their unjustly held seats is the elimination of that sort of conscience from the lifeboat.

This is the basic metaphor within which we must work out our solutions. Let us now   10
enrich the image, step by step, with substantive additions from the real world, a world that
must solve real and pressing problems of overpopulation and hunger.

The harsh ethics of the lifeboat become even harsher when we consider the repro-   11
ductive differences between the rich nations and the poor nations. The people inside the
lifeboats are doubling in numbers every eighty-seven years; those swimming around outside are doubling, on the average, every thirty-five years, more than twice as fast as the
rich. And since the world's resources are dwindling, the difference in prosperity between
the rich and the poor can only increase.

As of 1973, the U.S. had a population of 210 million people, who were increasing by   12
0.8 percent per year. Outside our lifeboat, let us imagine another 210 million people (say
the combined populations of Colombia, Ecuador, Venezuela, Morocco, Pakistan, Thailand
and the Philippines), who are increasing at a rate of 3.3 percent per year. Put differently,
the doubling time for this aggregate population is twenty-one years, compared to eighty-
seven years for the U.S.

MULTIPLYING THE RICH AND THE POOR

Now suppose the U.S. agreed to pool its resources with those seven countries, with   13
everyone receiving an equal share. Initially the ratio of Americans to non-Americans in this
model would be one-to-one. But consider what the ratio would be after eighty-seven years,
by which time the Americans would have doubled to a population of 420 million. By then,
doubling every twenty-one years, the other group would have swollen to 3.54 billion. Each
American would have to share the available resource with more than eight people.

But, one could argue, this discussion assumes that current population trends will con-   14
tinue, and they may not. Quite so. Most likely the rate of population increase will decline
much faster in the U.S. than it will in the other countries, and there does not seem to be
much we can do about it. In sharing with "each according to his needs," we must recognize that needs are determined by population size, which is determined by the rate of reproduction, which at present is regarded as a sovereign right of every nation, poor or not.
This being so, the philanthropic load created by the sharing ethic of the spaceship can only
increase.

THE TRAGEDY OF THE COMMONS

The fundamental error of spaceship ethics, and the sharing it requires, is that it leads   15
to what I call "the tragedy of the commons." Under a system of private property, the men
who own property recognize their responsibility to care for it, for if they don't they will
eventually suffer. A farmer, for instance, will allow no more cattle in a pasture than its carrying capacity justifies. If he overloads it, erosion sets in, weeds take over, and he loses the
use of the pasture.

If a pasture becomes a commons open to all, the right of each to use it may not be   16
matched by a corresponding responsibility to protect it. Asking everyone to use it with discretion will hardly do, for the considerate herdsman who refrains from overloading the

commons suffers more than a selfish one who says his needs are greater. If everyone would restrain himself, all would be well; but it takes only one less than everyone to ruin a system of voluntary restraint. In a crowded world of less than perfect human beings, mutual ruin is inevitable if there are no controls. This is the tragedy of the commons.

17   One of the major tasks of education today should be the creation of such an acute awareness of the dangers of the commons that people will recognize its many varieties. For example, the air and water have become polluted because they are treated as commons. Further growth in the population or per-capita conversion of natural resources into pollutants will only make the problem worse. The same holds true for the fish of the oceans. Fishing fleets have nearly disappeared in many parts of the world, technological improvements in the art of fishing are hastening the day of complete ruin. Only the replacement of the system of the commons with a responsible system of control will save the land, air, water and oceanic fisheries.

THE WORLD FOOD BANK

18   In recent years there has been a push to create a new commons called a World Food Bank, an international depository of food reserves to which nations would contribute according to their abilities and from which they would draw according to their needs. This humanitarian proposal has received support from many liberal international groups, and from such prominent citizens as Margaret Mead, U.N. Secretary General Kurt Waldheim, and Senators Edward Kennedy and George McGovern.

19   A world food bank appeals powerfully to our humanitarian impulses. But before we rush ahead with such a plan, let us recognize where the greatest political push comes from, lest we be disillusioned later. Our experience with the "Food for Peace program," or Public Law 480, gives us the answer. This program moved billions of dollars' worth of U.S. surplus grain to food-short, population-long countries during the past two decades. But when P.L. 480 first became law, a headline in the business magazine *Forbes* revealed the real power behind it: "Feeding the World's Hungry Millions: How It Will Mean Billions for U.S. Business."

20   And indeed it did. In the years 1960 to 1970, U.S. taxpayers spent a total of $7.9 billion on the Food for Peace program. Between 1948 and 1970, they also paid an additional $50 billion for other economic-aid programs, some of which went for food and food-producing machinery and technology. Though all U.S. taxpayers were forced to contribute to the cost of P.L. 480, certain special interest groups gained handsomely under the program. Farmers did not have to contribute the grain; the Government, or rather the taxpayers, bought it from them at full market prices. The increased demand raised prices of farm products generally. The manufacturers of farm machinery, fertilizers and pesticides benefited by the farmers' extra efforts to grow more food. Grain elevators profited from storing the surplus until it could be shipped. Railroads made money hauling it to ports, and shipping lines profited from carrying it overseas. The implementation of P.L. 480 required the creation of a vast Government bureaucracy, which then acquired its own vested interest in continuing the program regardless of its merits.

EXTRACTING DOLLARS

Those who proposed and defended the Food for Peace program in public rarely mentioned its importance to any of these special interests. The public emphasis was always on its humanitarian effects. The combination of silent selfish interests and highly vocal humanitarian apologists made a powerful and successful lobby for extracting money from taxpayers. We can expect the same lobby to push now for the creation of a World Food Bank.   21

However great the potential benefit to selfish interests, it should not be a decisive argument against a truly humanitarian program. We must ask if such a program would actually do more good than harm, not only momentarily but also in the long run. Those who propose the food bank usually refer to a current "emergency" or "crisis" in terms of world food supply. But what is an emergency? Although they may be infrequent and sudden, everyone knows that emergencies will occur from time to time. A well-run family, company, organization or country prepares for the likelihood of accidents and emergencies. It expects them, it budgets for them, it saves for them.   22

LEARNING THE HARD WAY

What happens if some organizations or countries budget for accidents and others do not? If each country is solely responsible for its own well-being, poorly managed ones will suffer. But they can learn from experience. They may mend their ways, and learn to budget for infrequent but certain emergencies. For example, the weather varies from year to year, and periodic crop failures are certain. A wise and competent government saves out of the production of the good years in anticipation of bad years to come. Joseph taught this policy to Pharaoh in Egypt more than 2,000 years ago. Yet the great majority of the governments in the world today do not follow such a policy. They lack either the wisdom or the competence, or both. Should those nations that do manage to put something aside be forced to come to the rescue each time an emergency occurs among the poor nations?   23

"But it isn't their fault!" some kindhearted liberals argue. "How can we blame the poor people who are caught in an emergency? Why must they suffer for the sins of their governments?" The concept of blame is simply not relevant here. The real question is, what are the operational consequences of establishing a world food bank? If it is open to every country every time a need develops, slovenly rulers will not be motivated to take Joseph's advice. Someone will always come to their aid. Some countries will deposit food in the world food bank, and others will withdraw it. There will be almost no overlap. As a result of such solutions to food shortage emergencies, the poor countries will not learn to mend their ways, and will suffer progressively greater emergencies as their populations grow.   24

POPULATION CONTROL THE CRUDE WAY

On the average, poor countries undergo a 2.5 percent increase in population each year; rich countries, about 0.8 percent. Only rich countries have anything in the way of food reserves set aside, and even they do not have as much as they should. Poor countries have   25 none. If poor countries received no food from the outside, the rate of their population growth would be periodically checked by crop failures and famines. But if they can always draw on a world food bank in time of need, their populations can continue to grow unchecked, and so will their "need" for aid. In the short run, a world food bank may diminish that need, but in the long run it actually increases the need without limit.

26   Without some system of worldwide food sharing, the proportion of people in the rich and poor nations might eventually stabilize. The overpopulated poor countries would decrease in numbers, while the rich countries that had room for more people would increase. But with a well-meaning system of sharing, such as a world food bank, the growth differential between the rich and the poor countries will not only persist, it will increase. Because of the higher rate of population growth in the poor countries of the world, 88 percent of today's children are born poor, and only 12 percent rich. Year by year the ratio becomes worse, as the fast-reproducing poor outnumber the slow-reproducing rich.

27   A world food bank is thus a commons in disguise. People will have more motivation to draw from it than to add to any common store. The less provident and less able will multiply at the expense of the abler and more provident, bringing eventual ruin upon all who share in the commons. Besides, any system of "sharing" that amounts to foreign aid from the rich nations to the poor nations will carry the taint of charity, which will contribute little to the world peace so devoutly desired by those who support the idea of a world food bank.

28   As past U.S. foreign-aid programs have amply and depressingly demonstrated, international charity frequently inspires mistrust and antagonism rather than gratitude on the part of the recipient nation.

CHINESE FISH AND MIRACLE RICE

29   The modern approach to foreign aid stresses the export of technology and advice, rather than money and food. As an ancient Chinese proverb goes: "Give a man a fish and he will eat for a day; teach him how to fish and he will eat for the rest of his days." Acting on this advice, the Rockefeller and Ford Foundations have financed a number of programs for improving agriculture in the hungry nations. Known as the "Green Revolution," these programs have led to the development of "miracle rice" and "miracle wheat," new strains that offer bigger harvests and greater resistance to crop damage. Norman Borlaug, the Nobel Prize winning agronomist who, supported by the Rockefeller Foundation, developed "miracle wheat," is one of the most prominent advocates of a world food bank.

30   Whether or not the Green Revolution can increase food production as much as its champions claim is a debatable but possibly irrelevant point. Those who support this well-intended humanitarian effort should first consider some of the fundamentals of human ecology. Ironically, one man who did was the late Alan Gregg, a vice president of the Rockefeller Foundation. Two decades ago he expressed strong doubts about the wisdom of such attempts to increase food production. He likened the growth and spread of humanity over the surface of the earth to the spread of cancer in the human body, remarking that "cancerous growths demand food; but, as far as I know, they have never been cured by getting it."

OVERLOADING THE ENVIRONMENT

Every human born constitutes a draft on all aspects of the environment: food, air, water, forests, beaches, wildlife, scenery and solitude. Food can, perhaps, be significantly increased to meet a growing demand. But what about clean beaches, unspoiled forests, and solitude? If we satisfy a growing population's need for food, we necessarily decrease its per-capita supply of the other resources needed by men. 31

India, for example, now has a population of 600 million, which increases by 15 million each year. This population already puts a huge load on a relatively impoverished environment. The country's forests are now only a small fraction of what they were three centuries ago, and floods and erosion continually destroy the insufficient farmland that remains. Every one of the 15 million new lives added to India's population puts an additional burden on the environment, and increases the economic and social costs of crowding. However humanitarian our intent, every Indian life saved through medical or nutritional assistance from abroad diminishes the quality of life for those who remain, and for subsequent generations. If rich countries make it possible, through foreign aid, for 600 million Indians to swell to 1.2 billion in a mere twenty-eight years, as their current growth rate threatens, will future generations of Indians thank us for hastening the destruction of their environment? Will our good intentions be sufficient excuse for the consequences of our actions? 32

My final example of a commons in action is one for which the public has the least desire for rational discussion—immigration. Anyone who publicly questions the wisdom of current U.S. immigration policy is promptly charged with bigotry, prejudice, ethnocentrism, chauvinism, isolationism or selfishness. Rather than encounter such accusations, one would rather talk about other matters, leaving immigration policy to wallow in the crosscurrents of special interests that take no account of the good of the whole, or the interest of posterity. 33

Perhaps we still feel guilty about things we said in the past. Two generations ago the popular press frequently referred to Dagos, Wops, Polacks, Chinks and Krauts, in articles about how America was being "overrun" by foreigners of supposedly inferior genetic stock. But because the implied inferiority of foreigners was used then as justification for keeping them out, people now assume that restrictive policies could only be based on such misguided notions. There are no other grounds. 34

A NATION OF IMMIGRANTS

Just consider the numbers involved. Our Government acknowledges a net inflow of 400,000 immigrants a year. While we have no hard data on the extent of illegal entries, educated guesses put the figure at about 600,000 a year. Since the natural increase (excess of births over deaths) of the resident population now runs about 1.7 million per year, the yearly gain from immigration amounts to at least 19 percent of the total annual increase, and may be as much as 37 percent if we include the estimate for illegal immigrants. Considering the growing use of birth-control devices, the potential effect of educational campaigns by such organizations as Planned Parenthood Federation of America and Zero Population 35

Growth, and the influence of inflation and the housing shortage, the fertility rate of American women may decline so much that immigration could account for all the yearly increase in population. Should we not at least ask if that is what we want?

36   For the sake of those who worry about whether the "quality" of the average immigrant compares favorably with the quality of the average resident, let us assume that immigrants and native-born citizens are of exactly equal quality, however one defines that term. We will focus here only on quantity; and since our conclusions will depend on nothing else, all charges of bigotry and chauvinism become irrelevant.

IMMIGRATION VS. FOOD SUPPLY

37   World food banks *move food to the people,* hastening the exhaustion of the environment of the poor countries. Unrestricted immigration, on the other hand, *moves people to the food,* thus speeding up the destruction of the environment of the rich countries. We can easily understand why poor people should want to make this latter transfer, but why should rich hosts encourage it?

38   As in the case of foreign-aid programs, immigration receives support from selfish interests and humanitarian impulses. The primary selfish interest in unimpeded immigration is the desire of employers for cheap labor, particularly in industries and trades that offer degrading work. In the past, one wave of foreigners after another was brought into the U.S. to work at wretched jobs for wretched wages. In recent years, the Cubans, Puerto Ricans and Mexicans have had this dubious honor. The interests of the employers of cheap labor mesh well with the guilty silence of the country's liberal intelligentsia. White Anglo-Saxon Protestants are particularly reluctant to call for a closing of the doors to immigration for fear of being called bigots.

39   But not all countries have such reluctant leadership. Most educated Hawaiians, for example, are keenly aware of the limits of their environment, particularly in terms of population growth. There is only so much room on the islands, and the islanders know it. To Hawaiians, immigrants from the other forty-nine states present as great a threat as those from other nations. At a recent meeting of Hawaiian government officials in Honolulu, I had the ironic delight of hearing a speaker, who like most of his audience was of Japanese ancestry, ask how the country might practically and constitutionally close its doors to further immigration. One member of the audience countered: "How can we shut the doors now? We have many friends and relatives in Japan that we'd like to bring here some day so that they can enjoy Hawaii too." The Japanese-American speaker smiled sympathetically and answered: "Yes, but we have children now, and someday we'll have grandchildren too. We can bring more people here from Japan only by giving away some of the land that we hope to pass on to our grandchildren some day. What right do we have to do that?"

40   At this point, I can hear U.S. liberals asking, "How can you justify slamming the door once you're inside? You say that immigrants should be kept out. But aren't we all immigrants, or the descendants of immigrants? If we insist on staying, must we not admit all others?" Our craving for intellectual order leads us to seek and prefer symmetrical rules and morals: a single rule for me and everybody else; the same rule yesterday, today, and tomorrow. Justice, we feel, should not change with time and place.

We Americans of non-Indian ancestry can look upon ourselves as the descendants of   41
thieves who are guilty morally, if not legally, of stealing this land from its Indian owners.
Should we then give back the land to the now living American descendants of those Indians? However morally or logically sound this proposal may be, I, for one, am unwilling to
live by it and I know no one else who is. Besides, the logical consequence would be absurd.
Suppose that, intoxicated with a sense of pure justice, we should decide to turn our land
over to the Indians. Since all our wealth has also been derived from the land, wouldn't we
be morally obliged to give that back to the Indians too?

PURE JUSTICE VS. REALITY

Clearly, the concept of pure justice produces an infinite regression to absurdity. Cen-   42
turies ago, wise men invented statutes of limitations to justify the rejection of such pure
justice, in the interest of preventing continual disorder. The law zealously defends property
rights, but only relatively recent property rights. Drawing a line after an arbitrary time has
elapsed may be unjust, but the alternatives are worse.

We are all descendants of thieves, and the world's resources are inequitably distrib-   43
uted. But we must begin the journey to tomorrow from the point where we are today. We
cannot remake the past. We cannot safely divide the wealth equitably among all peoples so
long as people reproduce at different rates. To do so would guarantee that our grandchildren, and everyone else's grandchildren, would have only a ruined world to inhabit.

To be generous with one's own possessions is quite different from being generous with   44
those of posterity. We should call this point to the attention of those who, from a com-
mendable love of justice and equality, would institute a system of the commons, either in
the form of a world food bank, or of unrestricted immigration. We must convince them if
we wish to save at least some parts of the world from environmental ruin.

Without a true world government to control reproduction and the use of available re-   45
sources, the sharing ethic of the spaceship is impossible. For the foreseeable future, our survival demands that we govern our actions by the ethics of a lifeboat, harsh though they may
be. Posterity will be satisfied with nothing less.

Rich and Poor

Peter Singer

Consider these facts: by the most cautious estimates, 400 million people lack the   1
calories, protein, vitamins and minerals needed for a normally healthy life. Millions are
constantly hungry; others suffer from deficiency diseases and from infections they would
be able to resist on a better diet. Children are worst affected. According to one estimate,
15 million children under five die every year from the combined effects of malnutrition
and infection. In some areas, half the children born can be expected to die before their
fifth birthday.

2   Nor is lack of food the only hardship of the poor. To give a broader picture, Robert Mc-Namara, President of the World Bank, has suggested the term "absolute poverty." The poverty we are familiar with in industrialized nations is relative poverty—meaning that some citizens are poor, relative to the wealth enjoyed by their neighbors. People living in relative poverty in Australia might be quite comfortably off by comparison with old-age pensioners in Britain, and British old-age pensioners are not poor in comparison with the poverty that exists in Mali or Ethiopia. Absolute poverty, on the other hand, is poverty by any standard. In McNamara's words:

> Poverty at the absolute level . . . is life at the very margin of existence.
>
> The absolute poor are severely deprived human beings struggling to survive in a set of squalid and degraded circumstances almost beyond the power of our sophisticated imaginations and privileged circumstances to conceive.
>
> Compared to those fortunate enough to live in developed countries, individuals in the poorest nations have:
> An infant mortality rate eight times higher
> A life expectancy one-third lower
> An adult literacy rate 60% less
> A nutritional level, for one out of every two in the population, below acceptable standards; and for millions of infants, less protein than is sufficient to permit optimum development of the brain.

3   Absolute poverty is, as McNamara has said, responsible for the loss of countless lives, especially among infants and young children. When absolute poverty does not cause death it still causes misery of a kind not often seen in the affluent nations. Malnutrition in young children stunts both physical and mental development. It has been estimated that the health, growth and learning capacity of nearly half the young children in developing countries are affected by malnutrition. Millions of people on poor diets suffer from deficiency diseases, like goitre, or blindness caused by a lack of vitamin A. The food value of what the poor eat is further reduced by parasites such as hookworm and ringworm, which are endemic in conditions of poor sanitation and health education.

4   Death and disease apart, absolute poverty remains a miserable condition of life, with inadequate food, shelter, clothing, sanitation, health services and education. According to World Bank estimates which define absolute poverty in terms of income levels insufficient to provide adequate nutrition, something like 800 million people—almost 40% of the people of developing countries—live in absolute poverty. Absolute poverty is probably the principal cause of human misery today. . . .

5   The problem is not that the world cannot produce enough to feed and shelter its people. People in the poor countries consume, on average, 400 lbs of grain a year, while North Americans average more than 2000 lbs. The difference is caused by the fact that in the rich countries we feed most of our grain to animals, converting it into meat, milk and eggs. Because this is an inefficient process, wasting up to 95% of the food value of the animal feed, people in rich countries are responsible for the consumption of far more food than those in poor countries who eat few animal products. If we stopped feeding animals on grains, soybeans and fishmeal the amount of food saved would—if distributed to those who need it—be more than enough to end hunger throughout the world.

These facts about animal food do not mean that we can easily solve the world food   6
problem by cutting down on animal products, but they show that the problem is essentially
one of distribution rather than production. The world does produce enough food. Moreover
the poorer nations themselves could produce far more if they made more use of improved
agricultural techniques.

So why are people hungry? Poor people cannot afford to buy grain grown by American   7
farmers. Poor farmers cannot afford to buy improved seeds, or fertilizers, or the machinery
needed for drilling wells and pumping water. Only by transferring some of the wealth of
the developed nations to the poor of the undeveloped nations can the situation be changed.

That this wealth exists is clear. Against the picture of absolute poverty that McNamara   8
has painted, one might pose a picture of "absolute affluence." Those who are absolutely affluent are not necessarily affluent by comparison with their neighbors, but they are affluent by any reasonable definition of human needs. This means that they have more income
than they need to provide themselves adequately with all the basic necessities of life. After
buying food, shelter, clothing, necessary health services and education, the absolutely affluent are still able to spend money on luxuries. The absolutely affluent choose their food
for the pleasures of the palate, not to stop hunger; they buy new clothes to look fashionable, not to keep warm; they move house to be in a better neighbourhood or have a play
room for the children, not to keep out the rain; and after all this there is still money to
spend on books and records, colour television, and overseas holidays.

At this stage I am making no ethical judgments about absolute affluence, merely point-   9
ing out that it exists. Its defining characteristic is a significant amount of income above the
level necessary to provide for the basic human needs of oneself and one's dependents. By
this standard Western Europe, North America, Japan, Australia, New Zealand and the oil-
rich Middle Eastern states are all absolutely affluent, and so are many, if not all, of their citizens. The USSR and Eastern Europe might also be included on this list. To quote McNamara
once more:

> The average citizen of a developed country enjoys wealth beyond the wildest dreams
> of the one billion people in countries with per capita incomes under $200. . . .

These, therefore, are the countries—and individuals—who have wealth which they could,
without threatening their own basic welfare, transfer to the absolutely poor.

At present, very little is being transferred. Members of the Organization of Petroleum   10
Exporting Countries lead the way, giving an average of 2.1% of their Gross National Product. Apart from them, only Sweden, The Netherlands and Norway have reached the modest UN target of 0.7% of GNP. Britain gives 0.38% of its GNP in official development
assistance and a small amount in unofficial aid from voluntary organizations. The total
comes to less than £1 per month per person, and compares with 5.5% of GNP spent on alcohol, and 3% on tobacco. Other, even wealthier nations, give still less: Germany gives
0.27%, the United States 0.22% and Japan 0.21%.

The Obligation to Assist   The path from the library at my university to the Human-   11
ities lecture theatre passes a shallow ornamental pond. Suppose that on my way to give a
lecture I notice that a small child has fallen in and is in danger of drowning. Would anyone
deny that I ought to wade in and pull the child out? This will mean getting my clothes

muddy, and either cancelling my lecture or delaying it until I can find something dry to change into; but compared with the avoidable death of a child this is insignificant.

12   A plausible principle that would support the judgment that I ought to pull the child out is this: if it is in our power to prevent something very bad happening, without thereby sacrificing anything of comparable moral significance, we ought to do it. This principle seems uncontroversial. It will obviously win the assent of consequentialists; but non-consequentialists should accept it too, because the injunction to prevent what is bad applies only when nothing comparably significant is at stake. Thus the principle cannot lead to the kinds of actions of which non-consequentialists strongly disapprove—serious violations of individual rights, injustice, broken promises, and so on. If a non-consequentialist regards any of these as comparable in moral significance to the bad thing that is to be prevented, he will automatically regard the principle as not applying in those cases in which the bad thing can only be prevented by violating rights, doing injustice, breaking promises, or whatever else is at stake. Most non-consequentialists hold that we ought to prevent what is bad and promote what is good. Their dispute with consequentialists lies in their insistence that this is not the sole ultimate ethical principle: that it is *an* ethical principle is not denied by any plausible ethical theory.

13   Nevertheless the uncontroversial appearance of the principle that we ought to prevent what is bad when we can do so without sacrificing anything of comparable moral significance is deceptive. If it were taken seriously and acted upon, our lives and our world would be fundamentally changed. For the principle applies, not just to rare situations in which one can save a child from a pond, but to the everyday situation in which we can assist those living in absolute poverty. In saying this I assume that absolute poverty, with its hunger and malnutrition, lack of shelter, illiteracy, disease, high infant mortality and low life expectancy, is a bad thing. And I assume that it is within the power of the affluent to reduce absolute poverty, without sacrificing anything of comparable moral significance. If these two assumptions and the principle we have been discussing are correct, we have an obligation to help those in absolute poverty which is no less strong than our obligation to rescue a drowning child from a pond. Not to help would be wrong, whether or not it is intrinsically equivalent to killing. Helping is not, as conventionally thought, a charitable act which it is praiseworthy to do, but not wrong to omit; it is something that everyone ought to do.

14   This is the argument for an obligation to assist. Set out more formally, it would look like this:

FIRST PREMISE: If we can prevent something bad without sacrificing anything of comparable significance, we ought to do it.

SECOND PREMISE: Absolute poverty is bad.

THIRD PREMISE: There is some absolute poverty we can prevent without sacrificing anything of comparable moral significance.

CONCLUSION: We ought to prevent some absolute poverty.

15   The first premise is the substantive moral premise on which the argument rests, and I have tried to show that it can be accepted by people who hold a variety of ethical positions.

The second premise is unlikely to be challenged. Absolute poverty is, as McNamara put   16
it, "beneath any reasonable definition of human decency" and it would be hard to find a
plausible ethical view which did not regard it as a bad thing.

The third premise is more controversial, even though it is cautiously framed. It claims   17
only that some absolute poverty can be prevented without the sacrifice of anything of comparable moral significance. It thus avoids the objection that any aid I can give is just "drops
in the ocean" for the point is not whether my personal contribution will make any noticeable impression on world poverty as a whole (of course it won't) but whether it will
prevent some poverty. This is all the argument needs to sustain its conclusion, since the
second premise says that any absolute poverty is bad, and not merely the total amount of
absolute poverty. If without sacrificing anything of comparable moral significance we can
provide just one family with the means to raise itself out of absolute poverty, the third
premise is vindicated.

I have left the notion of moral significance unexamined in order to show that the ar-   18
gument does not depend on any specific values or ethical principles. I think the third
premise is true for most people living in industrialized nations, on any defensible view of
what is morally significant. Our affluence means that we have income we can dispose of
without giving up the basic necessities of life, and we can use this income to reduce absolute poverty. Just how much we will think ourselves obliged to give up will depend on
what we consider to be of comparable moral significance to the poverty we could prevent:
colour television, stylish clothes, expensive dinners, a sophisticated stereo system, overseas
holidays, a (second?) car, a larger house, private schools for our children. . . . For a utilitarian, none of these is likely to be of comparable significance to the reduction of absolute
poverty; and those who are not utilitarians surely must, if they subscribe to the principle
of universalizability, accept that at least *some* of these things are of far less moral significance than the absolute poverty that could be prevented by the money they cost. So the
third premise seems to be true on any plausible ethical view—although the precise amount
of absolute poverty that can be prevented before anything of moral significance is sacrificed
will vary according to the ethical view one accepts.

Taking Care of Our Own   Anyone who has worked to increase overseas aid will have   19
come across the argument that we should look after those near us, our families and then
the poor in our own country, before we think about poverty in distant places.

No doubt we do instinctively prefer to help those who are close to us. Few could stand   20
by and watch a child drown; many can ignore a famine in Africa. But the question is not
what we usually do, but what we ought to do, and it is difficult to see any sound moral justification for the view that distance, or community membership, makes a crucial difference
to our obligations.

Consider, for instance, racial affinities. Should whites help poor whites before helping   21
poor blacks? Most of us would reject such a suggestion out of hand: people's need for food
has nothing to do with their race, and if blacks need food more than whites, it would be a
violation of the principle of equal consideration to give preference to whites.

The same point applies to citizenship or nationhood. Every affluent nation has some   22
relatively poor citizens, but absolute poverty is limited largely to the poor nations. Those

living on the streets of Calcutta, or in a drought stricken region of the Sahel, are experiencing poverty unknown in the West. Under these circumstances it would be wrong to decide that only those fortunate enough to be citizens of our own community will share our abundance. . . .

23   The element of truth in the view that we should first take care of our own, lies in the advantage of a recognized system of responsibilities. When families and local communities look after their own poorer members, ties of affection and personal relationships achieve ends that would otherwise require a large, impersonal bureaucracy. Hence it would be absurd to propose that from now on we all regard ourselves as equally responsible for the welfare of everyone in the world; but the argument for an obligation to assist does not propose that. It applies only when some are in absolute poverty, and others can help without sacrificing anything of comparable moral significance. To allow one's own kin to sink into absolute poverty would be to sacrifice something of comparable significance; and before that point had been reached, the breakdown of the system of family and community responsibility would be a factor to weigh the balance in favour of a small degree of preference for family and community. This small degree of preference is, however, decisively outweighed by existing discrepancies in wealth and property.

24   **Property Rights**   Do people have a right to private property, a right which contradicts the view that they are under an obligation to give some of their wealth away to those in absolute poverty? According to some theories of rights (for instance, Robert Nozick's)[1] provided one has acquired one's property without the use of unjust means like force and fraud, one may be entitled to enormous wealth while others starve. This individualistic conception of rights is in contrast to other views, like the early Christian doctrine to be found in the works of Thomas Aquinas, which holds that since property exists for the satisfaction of human needs, "whatever a man has in superabundance is owed, of natural right, to the poor for their sustenance." A socialist would also, of course, see wealth as belonging to the community rather than the individual, while utilitarians, whether socialist or not, would be prepared to override property rights to prevent great evils. . . .

25   However, I do not think we should accept such an individualistic theory. It leaves too much to chance to be an acceptable ethical view. For instance, those whose forefathers happened to inhabit some sandy wastes around the Persian Gulf are now fabulously wealthy, because oil lay under those sands; while those whose forefathers settled on better land south of the Sahara live in absolute poverty, because of drought and bad harvests. Can this distribution be acceptable from an impartial point of view? If we imagine ourselves about to begin life as a citizen of either Kuwait or Chad—but we do not know which—would we accept the principle that citizens of Kuwait are under no obligation to assist people living in Chad?

26   **Population and the Ethics of Triage**   Perhaps the most serious objection to the argument that we have an obligation to assist is that since the major cause of absolute poverty

---

[1]Robert Nozick, *Anarchy, State and Utopia* (New York, Basic Books, 1974).

is overpopulation, helping those now in poverty will only ensure that yet more people are born to live in poverty in the future.

In its most extreme form, this objection is taken to show that we should adopt a policy of "triage." The term comes from medical policies adopted in wartime. With too few doctors to cope with all the casualties, the wounded were divided into three categories: those who would probably survive without medical assistance, those who might survive if they received assistance, but otherwise probably would not, and those who even with medical assistance probably would not survive. Only those in the middle category were given medical assistance. The idea, of course, was to use limited medical resources as effectively as possible. For those in the first category, medical treatment was not strictly necessary; for those in the third category, it was likely to be useless. It has been suggested that we should apply the same policies to countries, according to their prospects of becoming self-sustaining. We would not aid countries which even without our help will soon be able to feed their populations. We would not aid countries which, even with our help, will not be able to limit their population to a level they can feed. We would aid those countries where our help might make the difference between success and failure in bringing food and population into balance.

27

Advocates of this theory are understandably reluctant to give a complete list of the countries they would place into the "hopeless" category; but Bangladesh is often cited as an example. Adopting the policy of triage would, then, mean cutting off assistance to Bangladesh and allowing famine, disease and natural disasters to reduce the population of that country (now around 80 million) to the level at which it can provide adequately for all.

28

In support of this view Garrett Hardin has offered a metaphor: we in the rich nations are like the occupants of a crowded lifeboat adrift in a sea full of drowning people. If we try to save the drowning by bringing them aboard our boat will be overloaded and we shall all drown. Since it is better that some survive than none, we should leave the others to drown. In the world today, according to Hardin, "lifeboat ethics" apply. The rich should leave the poor to starve, for otherwise the poor will drag the rich down with them. . . .

29

The consequences of triage on this scale are so horrible that we are inclined to reject it without further argument. How could we sit by our television sets, watching millions starve while we do nothing? Would not that (far more than the proposals for legalizing euthanasia) be the end of all notions of human equality and respect for human life? Don't people have a right to our assistance, irrespective of the consequences?

30

Anyone whose initial reaction to triage was not one of repugnance would be an unpleasant sort of person. Yet initial reactions based on strong feelings are not always reliable guides. Advocates of triage are rightly concerned with the long-term consequences of our actions. They say that helping the poor and starving now merely ensures more poor and starving in the future. When our capacity to help is finally unable to cope—as one day it must be—the suffering will be greater than it would be if we stopped helping now. If this is correct, there is nothing we can do to prevent absolute starvation and poverty, in the long run, and so we have no obligation to assist. Nor does it seem reasonable to hold that under these circumstances people have a right to our assistance. If we do accept such a right, irrespective of the consequences, we are saying that, in Hardin's metaphor, we would continue to haul the drowning into our lifeboat until the boat sank and we all drowned.

31

32   If triage is to be rejected it must be tackled on its own ground, within the framework of consequentialist ethics. Here it is vulnerable. Any consequentialist ethics must take probability of outcome into account. A course of action that will certainly produce some benefit is to be preferred to an alternative course that may lead to a slightly larger benefit, but is equally likely to result in no benefit at all. Only if the greater magnitude of the uncertain benefit outweighs its uncertainty should we choose it. Better one certain unit of benefit than a 10% chance of 5 units; but better a 50% chance of 3 units than a single certain unit. The same principle applies when we are trying to avoid evils.

33   The policy of triage involves a certain, very great evil: population control by famine and disease. Tens of millions would die slowly. Hundreds of millions would continue to live in absolute poverty, at the very margin of existence. Against this prospect, advocates of the policy place a possible evil which is greater still: the same process of famine and disease, taking place in, say, fifty years time, when the world's population may be three times its present level, and the number who will die from famine, or struggle on in absolute poverty, will be that much greater. The question is: how probable is this forecast that continued assistance now will lead to greater disasters in the future?

34   Forecasts of population growth are notoriously fallible, and theories about the factors which affect it remain speculative. One theory, at least as plausible as any other, is that countries pass through a "demographic transition" as their standard of living rises. When people are very poor and have no access to modern medicine their fertility is high, but population is kept in check by high death rates. The introduction of sanitation, modern medical techniques and other improvements reduces the death rate, but initially has little effect on the birth rate. Then population grows rapidly. Most poor countries are now in this phase. If standards of living continue to rise, however, couples begin to realize that to have the same number of children surviving to maturity as in the past, they do not need to give birth to as many children as their parents did. The need for children to provide economic support in old age diminishes. Improved education and the emancipation and employment of women also reduce the birthrate, and so population growth begins to level off. Most rich nations have reached this stage, and their populations are growing only very slowly.

35   If this theory is right, there is an alternative to the disasters accepted as inevitable by supporters of triage. We can assist poor countries to raise the living standards of the poorest members of their population. We can encourage the governments of these countries to enact land reform measures, improve education, and liberate women from a purely child-bearing role. We can also help other countries to make contraception and sterilization widely available. There is a fair chance that these measures will hasten the onset of the demographic transition and bring population growth down to a manageable level. Success cannot be guaranteed; but the evidence that improved economic security and education reduce population growth is strong enough to make triage ethically unacceptable. We cannot allow millions to die from starvation and disease when there is a reasonable probability that population can be brought under control without such horrors.

FOR CLASS DISCUSSION

1. Analyze and evaluate the controversy over the obligation of the rich to help the poor by applying the first set of guide questions from page 455. How do you account for the disagreement between Hardin and Singer?

2. Choose one of the arguments for closer analysis, applying the second set of guide questions on page 455–456.

Optional Writing Assignment   At last, you've won the lottery. You'll be receiving $250,000 per year for the next twenty years. Ever since you got the news, your phone's been ringing off the hook. Your older brother, Fast Eddie, has called urging you to buy a big house and a fast car and to consider putting a couple of big ones on the Blue Jays for the American League pennant. Your younger sister, Sensible Sarah, has outlined a comprehensive investment strategy for you that will put you into CDs, zero coupon bonds, and a few blue chippers. Then Aunt Teresa calls. "What are your plans for charitable giving?" she wants to know.

"I'm looking into that," you lie. "I have a plan," you lie further.

"Good," she responds. "Send it to me next week in my birthday card."

Your time is running out. What will you tell Aunt Teresa? Just what are your obligations? Some? None? All? Drawing on ideas from the preceding essays, personal experience, and any other research you may have done, write a letter to her justifying your decision.

CIVIL DISOBEDIENCE

"Letter from Birmingham Jail" in Response to "Public Statement by Eight Alabama Clergymen"
Martin Luther King, Jr.

We the undersigned clergymen are among those who, in January, issued "An Appeal for Law and Order and Common Sense," in dealing with racial problems in Alabama. We expressed understanding that honest convictions in racial matters could properly be pursued in the courts, but urged that decisions of those courts should in the meantime be peacefully obeyed.

Since that time there had been some evidence of increased forbearance and a willingness to face facts. Responsible citizens have undertaken to work on various problems which cause racial friction and unrest. In Birmingham, recent public events have given indication that we all have opportunity for a new constructive and realistic approach to racial problems.

However, we are now confronted by a series of demonstrations by some of our Negro citizens, directed and led in part by outsiders. We recognize the natural impatience of people who feel that their hopes are slow in being realized. But we are convinced that these demonstrations are unwise and untimely.

We agree rather with certain local Negro leadership which has called for honest and open negotiation of racial issues in our area. And we believe this kind of facing of issues can best be accomplished by citizens of our own metropolitan area, white and Negro, meeting with their knowledge and experience of the local situation. All of us need to face that responsibility and find proper channels for its accomplishment.

Just as we formerly pointed out that "hatred and violence have no sanction in our religious and political traditions," we also point out that such actions as incite to hatred and violence, however technically peaceful those actions may be, have not contributed to the resolution of our local problems. We do not believe that these days of new hope are days when extreme measures are justified in Birmingham.

We commend the community as a whole, and the local news media and law enforcement officials in particular, on the calm manner in which these demonstrations have been handled. We urge the public to continue to show restraint should the demonstrations continue, and the law enforcement officials to remain calm and continue to protect our city from violence.

We further strongly urge our own Negro community to withdraw support from these demonstrations, and to unite locally in working peacefully for a better Birmingham. When rights are consistently denied, a cause should be pressed in the courts and in negotiations among local leaders, and not in the streets. We appeal to both our white and Negro citizenry to observe the principles of law and order and common sense.

Signed by:

C. C. J. Carpenter, D.D., LL.D., *Bishop of Alabama*
Joseph A. Durick, D.D., *Auxiliary Bishop, Diocese of Mobile, Birmingham*
Rabbi Milton L. Grafman, *Temple Emanu-El, Birmingham, Alabama*
Bishop Paul Hardin, *Bishop of the Alabama-West Florida Conference of the Methodist Church*
Bishop Nolan B. Harmon, *Bishop of the North Alabama Conference of the Methodist Church*
George M. Murray, D.D., LL.D., *Bishop Coadjutor, Episcopal Diocese of Alabama*
Edward V. Ramage, *Moderator, Synod of the Alabama Presbyterian Church in the United States*
Earl Stallings, *Pastor, First Baptist Church, Birmingham, Alabama*

Following is the letter Martin Luther King, Jr., wrote in response to the clergymen's public statement.

April 16, 1963

My Dear Fellow Clergymen:

While confined here in the Birmingham city jail, I came across your recent statement calling my present activities "unwise and untimely." Seldom do I pause to answer criticism of my work and ideas. If I sought to answer all the criticisms that cross my desk, my secretaries would have little time for anything other than such correspondence in the course of the day, and I would have no time for constructive work. But since I feel that you are men of genuine good will and that your criticisms are sincerely set forth, I want to try to answer your statement in what I hope will be patient and reasonable terms. 1

I think I should indicate why I am here in Birmingham, since you have been influenced by the view which argues against "outsiders coming in." I have the honor of serving as president of the Southern Christian Leadership Conference, an organization operating in every southern state, with headquarters in Atlanta, Georgia. We have some eighty-five affiliated organizations across the South, and one of them is the Alabama Christian Movement for Human Rights. Frequently we share staff, educational and financial resources with our affiliates. Several months ago the affiliate here in Birmingham asked us to be on call to engage in a non-violent direct-action program if such were deemed necessary. We readily consented, and when the hour came we lived up to our promise. So I, along with several members of my staff, am here because I was invited here. I am here because I have organizational ties here. 2

But more basically, I am in Birmingham because injustice is here. Just as the prophets of the eighth century B.C. left their villages and carried their "thus saith the Lord" far beyond the boundaries of their home towns, and just as the Apostle Paul left his village of Tarsus and carried the gospel of Jesus Christ to the far corners of the Greco-Roman world, so am I compelled to carry the gospel of freedom beyond my own home town. Like Paul, I must constantly respond to the Macedonian call for aid. 3

Moreover, I am cognizant of the interrelatedness of all communities and states. I cannot sit idly by in Atlanta and not be concerned about what happens in Birmingham. Injustice anywhere is a threat to justice everywhere. We are caught in an inescapable network of mutuality, tied in a single garment of destiny. Whatever affects one directly, affects all indirectly. Never again can we afford to live with the narrow, provincial "outside agitator" idea. Anyone who lives inside the United States can never be considered an outsider anywhere within its bounds. 4

You deplore the demonstrations taking place in Birmingham. But your statement, I am sorry to say, fails to express a similar concern for the conditions that brought about the demonstrations. I am sure that none of you would want to rest content with the superficial kind of social analysis that deals merely with effects and does not grapple with underlying causes. It is unfortunate that demonstrations are taking place in Birmingham, but it is even more unfortunate that the city's white power structure left the Negro community with no alternative. 5

In any nonviolent campaign there are four basic steps: collection of the facts to determine whether injustices exist; negotiation; self-purification; and direct action. We have gone through all these steps in Birmingham. There can be no gainsaying the fact that racial injustice engulfs this community. Birmingham is probably the most thoroughly segregated city in the United States. Its ugly record of brutality is widely known. Negroes 6 have experienced grossly unjust treatment in the courts. There have been more unsolved bombings of Negro homes and churches in Birmingham than in any other city in the nation. These are the hard, brutal facts of the case. On the basis of these conditions, Negro leaders sought to negotiate with the city fathers. But the latter consistently refused to engage in good-faith negotiation.

7   Then, last September, came the opportunity to talk with leaders of Birmingham's economic community. In the course of the negotiations, certain promises were made by the merchants—for example, to remove the stores' humiliating racial signs. On the basis of these promises, the Reverend Fred Shuttlesworth and the leaders of the Alabama Christian Movement for Human Rights agreed to a moratorium on all demonstrations. As the weeks and months went by, we realized that we were the victims of a broken promise. A few signs, briefly removed, returned; the others remained.

8   As in so many past experiences, our hopes had been blasted, and the shadow of deep disappointment settled upon us. We had no alternative except to prepare for direct action, whereby we would present our very bodies as a means of laying our case before the conscience of the local and the national community. Mindful of the difficulties involved, we decided to undertake a process of self-purification. We began a series of workshops on nonviolence, and we repeatedly asked ourselves: "Are you able to accept blows without retaliating?" "Are you able to endure the ordeal of jail?" We decided to schedule our direct-action program for the Easter season, realizing that except for Christmas, this is the main shopping period of the year. Knowing that a strong economic-withdrawal program would be the by-product of direct action, we felt that this would be the best time to bring pressure to bear on the merchants for the needed change.

9   Then it occurred to us that Birmingham's mayoral election was coming up in March, and we speedily decided to postpone action until after election day. When we discovered that the Commissioner of Public Safety, Eugene "Bull" Connor, had piled up enough votes to be in the run-off, we decided again to postpone action until the day after the run-off so that the demonstrations could not be used to cloud the issues. Like many others, we waited to see Mr. Connor defeated, and to this end we endured postponement after postponement. Having aided in this community need, we felt that our direct-action program could be delayed no longer.

10   You may well ask: "Why direct action? Why sit-ins, marches and so forth? Isn't negotiation a better path?" You are quite right in calling for negotiation. Indeed, this is the very purpose of direct action. Nonviolent direct action seeks to create such a crisis and foster such a tension that a community which has constantly refused to negotiate is forced to confront the issue. It seeks so to dramatize the issue that it can no longer be ignored. My citing the creation of tension as part of the work of the nonviolent-resister may sound rather shocking. But I must confess that I am not afraid of the word "tension." I have earnestly opposed violent tension, but there is a type of constructive, nonviolent tension which is necessary for growth. Just as Socrates felt that it was necessary to create a tension in the mind so that individuals could rise from the bondage of myths and half-truths to the unfettered realm of creative analysis and objective appraisal, so must we see the need for nonviolent gadflies to create the kind of tension in society that will help men rise

from the dark depths of prejudice and racism to the majestic heights of understanding and brotherhood.

The purpose of our direct-action program is to create a situation so crisis-packed that it will inevitably open the door to negotiation. I therefore concur with you in your call for negotiation. Too long has our beloved Southland been bogged down in a tragic effort to live in monologue rather than dialogue.

11

One of the basic points in your statement is that the action that I and my associates have taken in Birmingham is untimely. Some have asked: "Why didn't you give the new city administration time to act?" The only answer that I can give to this query is that the new Birmingham administration must be prodded about as much as the outgoing one, before it will act. We are sadly mistaken if we feel that the election of Albert Boutwell as mayor will bring the millennium to Birmingham. While Mr. Boutwell is a much more gentle person than Mr. Connor, they are both segregationists, dedicated to maintenance of the status quo. I have hope that Mr. Boutwell will be reasonable enough to see the futility of massive resistance to desegregation. But he will not see this without pressure from devotees of civil rights. My friends, I must say to you that we have not made a single gain in civil rights without determined legal and nonviolent pressure. Lamentably, it is an historical fact that privileged groups seldom give up their privileges voluntarily. Individuals may see the moral light and voluntarily give up their unjust posture; but, as Reinhold Niebuhr has reminded us, groups tend to be more immoral than individuals.

12

We know through painful experience that freedom is never voluntarily given by the oppressor; it must be demanded by the oppressed. Frankly, I have yet to engage in a direct-action campaign that was "well timed" in the view of those who have not suffered unduly from the disease of segregation. For years now I have heard the word "Wait!" It rings in the ear of every Negro with piercing familiarity. This "Wait" has almost always meant "Never." We must come to see, with one of our distinguished jurists, that "justice too long delayed is justice denied."

13

We have waited for more than 340 years for our constitutional God-given rights. The nations of Asia and Africa are moving with jetlike speed toward gaining political independence, but we still creep at horse-and-buggy pace toward gaining a cup of coffee at a lunch counter. Perhaps it is easy for those who have never felt the stinging darts of segregation to say, "Wait." But when you have seen vicious mobs lynch your mothers and fathers at will and drown your sisters and brothers at whim; when you have seen hate-filled policemen curse, kick, and even kill your black brothers and sisters; when you see the vast majority of your twenty million Negro brothers smothering in an airtight cage of poverty in the midst of an affluent society; when you suddenly find your tongue twisted and your speech stammering as you seek to explain to your six-year-old daughter why she can't go to the public amusement park that has just been advertised on television, and see tears welling up in her eyes when she is told that Funtown is closed to colored children, and see ominous clouds of inferiority beginning to form in her little mental sky, and see her beginning to distort her personality by developing an unconscious bitterness toward white people; when you have to concoct an answer for a five-year-old son who is asking: "Daddy, why do white people treat colored people so mean?"; when you take a cross-country drive and find it necessary

14

to sleep night after night in the uncomfortable corners of your automobile because no motel will accept you; when you are humiliated day in and day out by nagging signs reading "white" and "colored"; when your first name becomes "nigger," your middle name becomes "boy" (however old you are) and your last name becomes "John," and your wife and mother are never given the respected title "Mrs."; when you are harried by day and haunted by night by the fact that you are a Negro, living constantly at tiptoe stance, never quite knowing what to expect next, and are plagued with inner fears and outer resentments; when you are forever fighting a degenerating sense of "nobodiness"—then you will understand why we find it difficult to wait. There comes a time when the cup of endurance runs over, and men are no longer willing to be plunged into the abyss of despair. I hope, sirs, you can understand our legitimate and unavoidable impatience.

15   You express a great deal of anxiety over our willingness to break laws. This is certainly a legitimate concern. Since we so diligently urge people to obey the Supreme Court's decision of 1954 outlawing segregation in the public schools, at first glance it may seem rather paradoxical for us consciously to break laws. One may well ask: "How can you advocate breaking some laws and obeying others?" The answer lies in the fact that there are two types of laws: just and unjust. I would be the first to advocate obeying just laws. One has not only a legal but a moral responsibility to obey just laws. Conversely, one has a moral responsibility to disobey unjust laws. I would agree with St. Augustine that "an unjust law is no law at all."

16   Now, what is the difference between the two? How does one determine whether a law is just or unjust? A just law is a man-made code that squares with the moral law or the law of God. An unjust law is a code that is out of harmony with the moral law. To put it in the terms of St. Thomas Aquinas: An unjust law is a human law that is not rooted in eternal law and natural law. Any law that uplifts human personality is just. Any law that degrades human personality is unjust. All segregation statutes are unjust because segregation distorts the soul and damages the personality. It gives the segregator a false sense of superiority and the segregated a false sense of inferiority. Segregation, to use the terminology of the Jewish philosopher Martin Buber, substitutes an "I–it" relationship for an "I–thou" relationship and ends up relegating persons to the status of things. Hence, segregation is not only politically, economically and sociologically unsound, it is morally wrong and sinful. Paul Tillich has said that sin is separation. Is not segregation an existential expression of man's tragic separation, his awful estrangement, his terrible sinfulness? Thus it is that I can urge men to obey the 1954 decision of the Supreme Court, for it is morally right; and I can urge them to disobey segregation ordinances, for they are morally wrong.

17   Let us consider a more concrete example of just and unjust laws. An unjust law is a code that a numerical or power majority group compels a minority group to obey but does not make binding on itself. This is *difference* made legal. By the same token, a just law is a code that a majority compels a minority to follow and that it is willing to follow itself. This is *sameness* made legal.

18   Let me give another explanation. A law is unjust if it is inflicted on a minority that, as a result of being denied the right to vote, had no part in enacting or devising the law. Who can say that the legislature of Alabama which set up that state's segregation laws was dem-

ocratically elected? Throughout Alabama all sorts of devious methods are used to prevent Negroes from becoming registered voters, and there are some counties in which, even though Negroes constitute a majority of the population, not a single Negro is registered. Can any law enacted under such circumstances be considered democratically structured?

Sometimes a law is just on its face and unjust in its application. For instance, I have been arrested on a charge of parading without a permit. Now, there is nothing wrong in having an ordinance which requires a permit for a parade. But such an ordinance becomes unjust when it is used to maintain segregation and to deny citizens the First-Amendment privilege of peaceful assembly and protest.   19

I hope you are able to see the distinction I am trying to point out. In no sense do I advocate evading or defying the law, as would the rabid segregationist. That would lead to anarchy. One who breaks an unjust law must do so openly, lovingly, and with a willingness to accept the penalty. I submit that an individual who breaks a law that conscience tells him is unjust, and who willingly accepts the penalty of imprisonment in order to arouse the conscience of the community over its injustice, is in reality expressing the highest respect for law.   20

Of course, there is nothing new about this kind of civil disobedience. It was evidenced sublimely in the refusal of Shadrach, Meshach and Abednego to obey the laws of Nebuchadnezzar, on the ground that a higher moral law was at stake. It was practiced superbly by the early Christians, who were willing to face hungry lions and the excruciating pain of chopping blocks rather than submit to certain unjust laws of the Roman Empire. To a degree, academic freedom is a reality today because Socrates practiced civil disobedience. In our own nation, the Boston Tea Party represented a massive act of civil disobedience.   21

We should never forget that everything Adolf Hitler did in Germany was "legal" and everything the Hungarian freedom fighters did in Hungary was "illegal." It was "illegal" to aid and comfort a Jew in Hitler's Germany. Even so, I am sure that, had I lived in Germany at the time, I would have aided and comforted my Jewish brothers. If today I lived in a Communist country where certain principles dear to the Christian faith are suppressed I would openly advocate disobeying that country's antireligious laws.   22

I must make two honest confessions to you, my Christian and Jewish brothers. First, I must confess that over the past few years I have been gravely disappointed with the white moderate. I have almost reached the regrettable conclusion that the Negro's great stumbling block in his stride toward freedom is not the White Citizen's Counciler or the Ku Klux Klanner, but the white moderate, who is more devoted to "order" than to justice; who prefers a negative peace which is the presence of tension to a positive peace which is the presence of justice; who constantly says, "I agree with you in the goal you seek, but I cannot agree with your methods of direct action"; who paternalistically believes he can set the timetable for another man's freedom; who lives by a mythical concept of time and who constantly advises the Negro to wait for a "more convenient season." Shallow understanding from people of good will is more frustrating than absolute misunderstanding from people of ill will. Lukewarm acceptance is much more bewildering than outright rejection.   23

I had hoped that the white moderate would understand that law and order exist for the purpose of establishing justice and that when they fail in this purpose they become the   24 dangerously structured dams that block the flow of social progress. I had hoped that the white moderate would understand that the present tension in the South is a necessary phase of the transition from an obnoxious negative peace, in which the Negro passively accepted his unjust plight, to a substantive and positive peace, in which all men will respect the dignity and worth of human personality. Actually, we who engage in nonviolent direct action are not the creators of tension. We merely bring to the surface the hidden tension that is already alive. We bring it out in the open, where it can be seen and dealt with. Like a boil that can never be cured so long as it is covered up but must be opened with all its ugliness to the natural medicines of air and light, injustice must be exposed, with all the tension its exposure creates, to the light of human conscience and the air of national opinion before it can be cured.

25   In your statement you assert that our actions, even though peaceful, must be condemned because they precipitate violence. But is this a logical assertion? Isn't this like condemning a robbed man because his possession of money precipitated the evil act of robbery? Isn't this like condemning Socrates because his unswerving commitment to truth and his philosophical inquiries precipitated the act by the misguided populace in which they made him drink hemlock? Isn't this like condemning Jesus because his unique God-consciousness and never-ceasing devotion to God's will precipitated the evil act of crucifixion? We must come to see that, as the federal courts have consistently affirmed, it is wrong to urge an individual to cease his efforts to gain his basic constitutional rights because the quest may precipitate violence. Society must protect the robbed and punish the robber.

26   I had also hoped that the white moderate would reject the myth concerning time in relation to the struggle for freedom. I have just received a letter from a white brother in Texas. He writes: "All Christians know that the colored people will receive equal rights eventually, but it is possible that you are in too great a religious hurry. It has taken Christianity almost two thousand years to accomplish what it has. The teachings of Christ take time to come to earth." Such an attitude stems from a tragic misconception of time, from the strangely irrational notion that there is something in the very flow of time that will inevitably cure all ills. Actually, time itself is neutral; it can be used either destructively or constructively. More and more I feel that the people of ill will have used time much more effectively than have the people of good will. We will have to repent in this generation not merely for the hateful words and actions of the bad people but for the appalling silence of the good people. Human progress never rolls in on wheels of inevitability; it comes through the tireless efforts of men willing to be co-workers with God, and without this hard work, time itself becomes an ally of the forces of social stagnation. We must use time creatively, in the knowledge that the time is always ripe to do right. Now is the time to make real the promise of democracy and transform our pending national elegy into a creative psalm of brotherhood. Now is the time to lift our national policy from the quicksand of racial injustice to the solid rock of human dignity.

27   You speak of our activity in Birmingham as extreme. At first I was rather disappointed that fellow clergymen would see my nonviolent efforts as those of an extremist. I began thinking about the fact that I stand in the middle of two opposing forces in the Negro community. One is a force of complacency, made up in part of Negroes who, as a result of long

years of oppression, are so drained of self-respect and a sense of "somebodiness" that they have adjusted to segregation; and in part of a few middle-class Negroes who, because of a degree of academic and economic security and because in some ways they profit by segregation, have become insensitive to the problems of the masses. The other force is one of bitterness and hatred, and it comes perilously close to advocating violence. It is expressed in the various black nationalists groups that are springing up across the nation, the largest and best-known being Elijah Muhammad's Muslim movement. Nourished by the Negro's frustration over the continued existence of racial discrimination, this movement is made up of people who have lost faith in America, who have absolutely repudiated Christianity, and who have concluded that the white man is an incorrigible "devil."

I have tried to stand between these two forces, saying that we need emulate neither   28
the "do-nothingism" of the complacent nor the hatred and despair of the black nationalist. For there is the more excellent way of love and nonviolent protest. I am grateful to God that, through the influence of the Negro church, the way of nonviolence became an integral part of our struggle.

If this philosophy had not emerged, by now many streets of the South would, I am con-   29
vinced, be flowing with blood. And I am further convinced that if our white brothers dismiss as "rabble-rousers" and "outside agitators" those of us who employ nonviolent direct action, and if they refuse to support our nonviolent efforts, millions of the Negroes will, out of frustration and despair, seek solace and security in black-nationalist ideologies—a development that would inevitably lead to a frightening racial nightmare.

Oppressed people cannot remain oppressed forever. The yearning for freedom eventu-   30
ally manifests itself, and that is what has happened to the American Negro. Something within has reminded him of his birthright of freedom, and something without has reminded him that it can be gained. Consciously or unconsciously, he has been caught up by the *Zeitgeist,* and with his black brothers of Africa and his brown and yellow brothers of Asia, South America and the Caribbean, the United States Negro is moving with a sense of great urgency toward the promised land of racial justice. If one recognizes this vital urge that has engulfed the Negro community, one should readily understand why public demonstrations are taking place. The Negro has many pent-up resentments and latent frustrations, and he must release them. So let him march; let him make prayer pilgrimages to the city hall; let him go on freedom rides—and try to understand why he must do so. If his repressed emotions are not released in nonviolent ways, they will seek expression through violence; this is not a threat but a fact of history. So I have not said to my people: "Get rid of your discontent." Rather, I have tried to say that this normal and healthy discontent can be channeled into the creative outlet of nonviolent direct action. And now this approach is being termed extremist.

But though I was initially disappointed at being categorized as an extremist, as I con-   31
tinued to think about the matter I gradually gained a measure of satisfaction from the label. Was not Jesus an extremist for love: "Love your enemies, bless them that curse you, and persecute you." Was not Amos an extremist for justice: "Let justice roll down like waters and righteousness like an ever-flowing stream." Was not Paul an extremist for the Christian gospel: "I bear in my body the marks of the Lord Jesus." Was not Martin Luther an

extremist: "Here I stand; I cannot do otherwise, so help me God." And John Bunyan: "I will stay in jail to the end of my days before I make a butchery of my conscience." And Abraham Lincoln: "This nation cannot survive half slave and half free." And Thomas Jefferson: "We hold these truths to be self-evident, that all men are created equal. . . ." So the question is not whether we will be extremists, but what kind of extremists we will be. Will we be extremists for hate or for love? Will we be extremists for the preservation of injustice or for the extension of justice? In that dramatic scene on Calvary's hill three men were crucified. We must never forget that all three were crucified for the same crime—the crime of extremism. Two were extremists for immorality, and thus fell below their environment. The other, Jesus Christ, was an extremist for love, truth and goodness, and thereby rose above his environment. Perhaps the South, the nation and the world are in dire need of creative extremists.

32   I had hoped that the white moderate would see this need. Perhaps I was too optimistic; perhaps I expected too much. I suppose I should have realized that few members of the oppressor race can understand the deep groans and passionate yearnings of the oppressed race, and still fewer have the vision to see that injustice must be rooted out by strong, persistent and determined action. I am thankful, however, that some of our white brothers in the South have grasped the meaning of this social revolution and committed themselves to it. They are still all too few in quantity, but they are big in quality. Some—such as Ralph McGill, Lillian Smith, Harry Golden, James McBride Dabbs, Ann Braden and Sarah Patton Boyle—have written about our struggle in eloquent and prophetic terms. Others have marched with us down nameless streets of the South. They have languished in filthy, roach-infested jails, suffering the abuse and brutality of policemen who view them as "dirty nigger-lovers." Unlike so many of their moderate brothers and sisters, they have recognized the urgency of the moment and sensed the need for powerful "action" antidotes to combat the disease of segregation.

33   Let me take note of my other major disappointment. I have been so greatly disappointed with the white church and its leadership. Of course, there are some notable exceptions. I am not unmindful of the fact that each of you has taken some significant stands on this issue. I commend you, Reverend Stallings, for your Christian stand on this past Sunday, in welcoming Negroes to your worship service on a nonsegregated basis. I commend the Catholic leaders of this state for integrating Spring Hill College several years ago.

34   But despite these notable exceptions, I must honestly reiterate that I have been disappointed with the church. I do not say this as one of those negative critics who can always find something wrong with the church. I say this as a minister of the gospel, who loves the church; who was nurtured in its bosom; who has been sustained by its spiritual blessings and who will remain true to it as long as the cord of life shall lengthen.

35   When I was suddenly catapulted into the leadership of the bus protest in Montgomery, Alabama, a few years ago, I felt we would be supported by the white church. I felt that the white ministers, priests and rabbis of the South would be among our strongest allies. Instead, some have been outright opponents, refusing to understand the freedom movement and misrepresenting its leaders; all too many others have been more cautious than courageous and have remained silent behind the anesthetizing security of stained-glass windows.

In spite of my shattered dreams, I came to Birmingham with the hope that the white re-   36
ligious leadership of this community would see the justice of our cause and, with deep moral
concern, would serve as the channel through which our just grievances could reach the power
structure. I had hoped that each of you would understand. But again I have been disappointed.

I have heard numerous southern religious leaders admonish their worshipers to com-   37
ply with a desegregation decision because it is the law, but I have longed to hear white ministers declare: "Follow this decree because integration is morally right and because the
Negro is your brother." In the midst of blatant injustices inflicted upon the Negro, I have
watched white churchmen stand on the sideline and mouth pious irrelevancies and sanc-
timonious trivialities. In the midst of a mighty struggle to rid our nation of racial and economic injustice, I have heard many ministers say: "Those are social issues, with which the
gospel has no real concern." And I have watched many churches commit themselves to a
completely otherworldly religion which makes a strange, un-Biblical distinction between
body and soul, between the sacred and the secular.

I have traveled the length and breadth of Alabama, Mississippi and all the other south-   38
ern states. On sweltering summer days and crisp autumn mornings I have looked at the
South's beautiful churches with their lofty spires pointing heavenward. I have beheld the
impressive outlines of her massive religious-education buildings. Over and over I have
found myself asking: "What kind of people worship here? Who is their God? Where were
their voices when the lips of Governor Barnett dripped with words of interposition and nul-
lification? Where were they when Governor Wallace gave a clarion call for defiance and hatred? Where were their voices of support when bruised and weary Negro men and women
decided to rise from the dark dungeons of complacency to the bright hills of creative
protest?"

Yes, these questions are still in my mind. In deep disappointment I have wept over   39
the laxity of the church. But be assured that my tears have been tears of love. There can
be no deep disappointment where there is not deep love. Yes, I love the church. How
could I do otherwise? I am in the rather unique position of being the son, the grandson,
and the great-grandson of preachers. Yes, I see the church as the body of Christ. But, oh!
How we have blemished and scarred that body through social neglect and through fear
of being nonconformists.

There was a time when the church was very powerful—in the time when the early   40
Christians rejoiced at being deemed worthy to suffer for what they believed. In those days
the church was not merely a thermometer that recorded the ideas and principles of popular opinion; it was a thermostat that transformed the mores of society. Whenever the early
Christians entered a town, the people in power became disturbed and immediately sought
to convict the Christians for being "disturbers of the peace" and "outside agitators." But
the Christians pressed on, in the conviction that they were "a colony of heaven," called to
obey God rather than man. Small in number, they were big in commitment. They were too
God-intoxicated to be "astronomically intimidated." By their effort and example they
brought an end to such ancient evils as infanticide and gladiatorial contests.

Things are different now. So often the contemporary church is a weak, ineffectual voice   41
with an uncertain sound. So often it is an archdefender of the status quo. Far from being

disturbed by the presence of the church, the power structure of the average community is consoled by the church's silent—and often even vocal—sanction of things as they are.

42   But the judgment of God is upon the church as never before. If today's church does not recapture the sacrificial spirit of the early church, it will lose its authenticity, forfeit the loyalty of millions, and be dismissed as an irrelevant social club with no meaning for the twentieth century. Every day I meet young people whose disappointment with the church has turned into outright disgust.

43   Perhaps I have once again been too optimistic. Is organized religion too inextricably bound to the status quo to save our nation and the world? Perhaps I must turn my faith to the inner spiritual church, the church within the church, as the true *ekklesia* and the hope of the world. But again I am thankful to God that some noble souls from the ranks of organized religion have broken loose from the paralyzing chains of conformity and joined us as active partners in the struggle for freedom. They have left their secure congregations and walked the streets of Albany, Georgia, with us. They have gone down the highways of the South on tortuous rides for freedom. Yes, they have gone to jail with us. Some have been dismissed from their churches, have lost the support of their bishops and fellow ministers. But they have acted in the faith that right defeated is stronger than evil triumphant. Their witness has been the spiritual salt that has preserved the true meaning of the gospel in these troubled times. They have carved a tunnel of hope through the dark mountain of disappointment.

44   I hope the church as a whole will meet the challenge of this decisive hour. But even if the church does not come to the aid of justice, I have no despair about the future. I have no fear about the outcome of our struggle in Birmingham, even if our motives are at present misunderstood. We will reach the goal of freedom in Birmingham and all over the nation, because the goal of America is freedom. Abused and scorned though we may be, our destiny is tied up with America's destiny. Before the pilgrims landed at Plymouth, we were here. Before the pen of Jefferson etched the majestic words of the Declaration of Independence across the pages of history, we were here. For more than two centuries our forebears labored in this country without wages; they made cotton king; they built the homes of their masters while suffering gross injustice and shameful humiliation—and yet out of a bottomless vitality they continued to thrive and develop. If the inexpressible cruelties of slavery could not stop us, the opposition we now face will surely fail. We will win our freedom because the sacred heritage of our nation and the eternal will of God are embodied in our echoing demands.

45   Before closing I feel impelled to mention one other point in your statement that has troubled me profoundly. You warmly commended the Birmingham police force for keeping "order" and "preventing violence." I doubt that you would have so warmly commended the police force if you had seen its dogs sinking their teeth into unarmed, nonviolent Negroes. I doubt that you would so quickly commend the policemen if you were to observe their ugly and inhumane treatment of Negroes here in the city jail; if you were to watch them push and curse old Negro women and young Negro girls; if you were to see them slap and kick old Negro men and young boys; if you were to observe them, as they did on two occasions, refuse to give us food because we wanted to sing our grace together. I cannot join you in your praise of the Birmingham police department.

It is true that police have exercised a degree of discipline in handling the demonstrators. In this sense they have conducted themselves rather "nonviolently" in public. But for what purpose? To preserve the evil system of segregation. Over the past few years I have consistently preached that nonviolence demands that the means we use must be as pure as the ends we seek. I have tried to make clear that it is wrong to use immoral means to attain moral ends. But now I must affirm that it is just as wrong, or perhaps even more so, to use moral means to preserve immoral ends. Perhaps Mr. Connor and his policemen have been rather nonviolent in public, as was Chief Pritchett in Albany, Georgia, but they have used the moral means of nonviolence to maintain the immoral end of racial injustice. As T. S. Eliot has said: "The last temptation is the greatest treason: To do the right deed for the wrong reason." 46

I wish you had commended the Negro sit-inners and demonstrators of Birmingham for their sublime courage, their willingness to suffer and their amazing discipline in the midst of great provocation. One day the South will recognize its real heroes. They will be the James Merediths, with the noble sense of purpose that enables them to face jeering and hostile mobs, and with the agonizing loneliness that characterizes the life of the pioneer. They will be old, oppressed, battered Negro women, symbolized in a seventy-two-year-old woman in Montgomery, Alabama, who rose up with a sense of dignity and with her people decided not to ride segregated buses, and who responded with ungrammatical profundity to one who inquired about her weariness: "My feets is tired, but my soul is at rest." They will be the young high school and college students, the young ministers of the gospel and a host of their elders, courageously and nonviolently sitting in at lunch counters and willingly going to jail for conscience' sake. One day the South will know that when these disinherited children of God sat down at lunch counters, they were in reality standing up for what is best in the American dream and for the most sacred values in our Judaeo-Christian heritage, thereby bringing our nation back to those great wells of democracy which were dug deep by the founding fathers in their formulation of the Constitution and the Declaration of Independence. 47

Never before have I written so long a letter. I'm afraid it is much too long to take your precious time. I can assure you that it would have been much shorter if I had been writing from a comfortable desk, but what else can one do when he is alone in a narrow jail cell, other than write long letters, think long thoughts and pray long prayers? 48

If I have said anything in this letter that overstates the truth and indicates an unreasonable impatience, I beg you to forgive me. If I have said anything that understates the truth and indicates my having a patience that allows me to settle for anything less than brotherhood, I beg God to forgive me. 49

I hope this letter finds you strong in faith. I also hope that circumstances will soon make it possible for me to meet each of you, not as an integrationist or a civil-rights leader but as a fellow clergyman and a Christian brother. Let us all hope that the dark clouds of racial prejudice will soon pass away and the deep fog of misunderstanding will be lifted from our fear-drenched communities, and in some not too distant tomorrow the radiant stars of love and brotherhood will shine over our great nation with all their scintillating beauty. 50

Yours for the cause of Peace and Brotherhood
Martin Luther King, Jr.

Civil Disobedience: Destroyer of Democracy

Lewis H. Van Dusen, Jr.

1   As Charles E. Wyzanski, Chief Judge of the United States District Court in Boston, wrote in the February, 1968, *Atlantic:* "Disobedience is a long step from dissent. Civil disobedience involves a deliberate and punishable breach of legal duty." Protesters might prefer a different definition. They would rather say that civil disobedience is the peaceable resistance of conscience.

2   The philosophy of civil disobedience was not developed in our American democracy, but in the very first democracy of Athens. It was expressed by the poet Sophocles and the philosopher Socrates. In Sophocles's tragedy, Antigone chose to obey her conscience and violate the state edict against providing burial for her brother, who had been decreed a traitor. When the dictator Creon found out that Antigone had buried her fallen brother, he confronted her and reminded her that there was a mandatory death penalty for this deliberate disobedience of the state law. Antigone nobly replied, "Nor did I think your orders were so strong that you, a mortal man, could overrun the gods' unwritten and unfailing laws."

3   Conscience motivated Antigone. She was not testing the validity of the law in the hope that eventually she would be sustained. Appealing to the judgment of the community, she explained her action to the chorus. She was not secret and surreptitious—the interment of her brother was open and public. She was not violent; she did not trespass on another citizen's rights. And finally, she accepted without resistance the death sentence—the penalty for violation. By voluntarily accepting the law's sanctions, she was not a revolutionary denying the authority of the state. Antigone's behavior exemplifies the classic case of civil disobedience.

4   Socrates believed that reason could dictate a conscientious disobedience of state law, but he also believed that he had to accept the legal sanctions of the state. In Plato's *Crito,* Socrates from his hanging basket accepted the death penalty for his teaching of religion to youths contrary to state laws.

5   The sage of Walden, Henry David Thoreau, took this philosophy of nonviolence and developed it into a strategy for solving society's injustices. First enunciating it in protest against the Mexican War, he then turned it to use against slavery. For refusing to pay taxes that would help pay the enforcers of the fugitive slave law, he went to prison. In Thoreau's words, "If the alternative is to keep all just men in prison or to give up slavery, the state will not hesitate which to choose."

6   Sixty years later, Gandhi took Thoreau's civil disobedience as his strategy to wrest Indian independence from England. The famous salt march against a British imperial tax is his best-known example of protest.

7   But the conscientious law breaking of Socrates, Gandhi and Thoreau is to be distinguished from the conscientious law testing of Martin Luther King, Jr., who was not a civil disobedient. The civil disobedient withholds taxes or violates state laws knowing he is legally wrong, but believing he is morally right. While he wrapped himself in the mantle of Gandhi and Thoreau, Dr. King led his followers in violation of state laws he believed were

contrary to the Federal Constitution. But since Supreme Court decisions in the end generally upheld his many actions, he should not be considered a true civil disobedient.

The civil disobedience of Antigone is like that of the pacifist who withholds paying the percentage of his taxes that goes to the Defense Department, or the Quaker who travels against State Department regulations to Hanoi to distribute medical supplies, or the Vietnam war protester who tears up his draft card. This civil disobedient has been nonviolent in his defiance of the law; he has been unfurtive in his violation; he has been submissive to the penalties of the law. He has neither evaded the law nor interfered with another's rights. He has been neither a rioter nor a revolutionary. The thrust of his cause has not been the might of coercion but the martyrdom of conscience.   8

WAS THE BOSTON TEA PARTY CIVIL DISOBEDIENCE?

Those who justify violence and radical action as being in the tradition of our Revolution show a misunderstanding of the philosophy of democracy.   9

James Farmer, former head of the Congress of Racial Equality, in defense of the mass action confrontation method, has told of a famous organized demonstration that took place in opposition to political and economic discrimination. The protesters beat back and scattered the law enforcers and then proceeded to loot and destroy private property. Mr. Farmer then said he was talking about the Boston Tea Party and implied that violence as a method for redress of grievances was an American tradition and a legacy of our revolutionary heritage. While it is true that there is no more sacred document than our Declaration of Independence, Jefferson's "inherent right of rebellion" was predicated on the tyrannical denial of democratic means. If there is no popular assembly to provide an adjustment of ills, and if there is no court system to dispose of injustices, then there is, indeed, a right to rebel.   10

The seventeenth century's John Locke, the philosophical father of the Declaration of Independence, wrote in his *Second Treatise on Civil Government:* "Wherever law ends, tyranny begins . . . and the people are absolved from any further obedience. Governments are dissolved from within when the legislative [chamber] is altered. When the government [becomes] . . . arbitrary disposers of lives, liberties and fortunes of the people, such revolutions happen. . . ."   11

But there are some sophisticated proponents of the revolutionary redress of grievances who say that the test of the need for radical action is not the unavailability of democratic institutions but the ineffectuality of those institutions to remove blatant social inequalities. If social injustice exists, they say, concerted disobedience is required against the constituted government, whether it be totalitarian or democratic in structure.   12

Of course, only the most bigoted chauvinist would claim that America is without some glaring faults. But there has never been a utopian society on earth and there never will be unless human nature is remade. Since inequities will mar even the best-framed democracies, the injustice rationale would allow a free right of civil resistance to be available always as a shortcut alternative to the democratic way of petition, debate and assembly. The lesson of history is that civil insurgency spawns far more injustices than it removes. The Jeffersons, Washingtons and Adamses resisted tyranny with the aim of promoting the procedures of democracy. They would never have resisted a democratic government with the risk of promoting the techniques of tyranny.   13

LEGITIMATE PRESSURES AND ILLEGITIMATE RESULTS

14   There are many civil leaders who show impatience with the process of democracy. They rely on the sit-in, boycott or mass picketing to gain speedier solutions to the problems that face every citizen. But we must realize that the legitimate pressures that won concessions in the past can easily escalate into the illegitimate power plays that might extort demands in the future. The victories of these civil rights leaders must not shake our confidence in the democratic procedures, as the pressures of demonstration are desirable only if they take place within the limits allowed by law. Civil rights gains should continue to be won by the persuasion of Congress and other legislative bodies and by the decision of courts. Any illegal entreaty for the rights of some can be an injury to the rights of others, for mass demonstrations often trigger violence.

15   Those who advocate taking the law into their own hands should reflect that when they are disobeying what they consider to be an immoral law, they are deciding on a possibly immoral course. Their answer is that the process for democratic relief is too slow, that only mass confrontation can bring immediate action, and that any injuries are the inevitable cost of the pursuit of justice. Their answer is, simply put, that the end justifies the means. It is this justification of any form of demonstration as a form of dissent that threatens to destroy a society built on the rule of law.

16   Our Bill of Rights guarantees wide opportunities to use mass meetings, public parades and organized demonstrations to stimulate sentiment, to dramatize issues and to cause change. The Washington freedom march of 1963 was such a call for action. But the rights of free expression cannot be mere force cloaked in the garb of free speech. As the courts have decreed in labor cases, free assembly does not mean mass picketing or sit-down strikes. These rights are subject to limitations of time and place so as to secure the rights of others. When militant students storm a college president's office to achieve demands, when certain groups plan rush-hour car stalling to protest discrimination in employment, these are not dissent, but a denial of rights to others. Neither is it the lawful use of mass protest, but rather the unlawful use of mob power.

17   Justice Black, one of the foremost advocates and defenders of the right of protest and dissent, has said:

> Experience demonstrates that it is not a far step from what to many seems to be the earnest, honest, patriotic, kind-spirited multitude of today, to the fanatical, threatening, lawless mob of tomorrow. And the crowds that press in the streets for noble goals today can be supplanted tomorrow by street mobs pressuring the courts for precisely opposite ends.

18   Society must censure those demonstrators who would trespass on the public peace, as it must condemn those rioters whose pillage would destroy the public peace. But more ambivalent is society's posture toward the civil disobedient. Unlike the rioter, the true civil disobedient commits no violence. Unlike the mob demonstrator, he commits no trespass on others' rights. The civil disobedient, while deliberately violating a law, shows an oblique respect for the law by voluntarily submitting to its sanctions. He neither resists arrest nor evades punishment. Thus, he breaches the law but not the peace.

19   But civil disobedience, whatever the ethical rationalization, is still an assault on our democratic society, an affront to our legal order and an attack on our constitutional gov-

ernment. To indulge civil disobedience is to invite anarchy, and the permissive arbitrariness of anarchy is hardly less tolerable than the repressive arbitrariness of tyranny. Too often the license of liberty is followed by the loss of liberty, because into the desert of anarchy comes the man on horseback, a Mussolini or a Hitler.

Violations of Law Subvert Democracy. Law violations, even for ends recognized as laudable, are not only assaults on the rule of law, but subversions of the democratic process. The disobedient act of conscience does not ennoble democracy; it erodes it.   20

First, it courts violence, and even the most careful and limited use of nonviolent acts of disobedience may help sow the dragon-teeth of civil riot. Civil disobedience is the progenitor of disorder, and disorder is the sire of violence.   21

Second, the concept of civil disobedience does not invite principles of general applicability. If the children of light are morally privileged to resist particular laws on grounds of conscience, so are the children of darkness. Former Deputy Attorney General Burke Marshall said: "If the decision to break the law really turned on individual conscience, it is hard to see in law how [the civil rights leader] is better off than former Governor Ross Barnett of Mississippi who also believed deeply in his cause and was willing to go to jail."   22

Third, even the most noble act of civil disobedience assaults the rule of law. Although limited as to method, motive and objective, it has the effect of inducing others to engage in different forms of law breaking characterized by methods unsanctioned and condemned by classic theories of law violation. Unfortunately, the most patent lesson of civil disobedience is not so much nonviolence of action as defiance of authority.   23

Finally, the greatest danger in condoning civil disobedience as a permissible strategy for hastening change is that it undermines our democratic processes. To adopt the techniques of civil disobedience is to assume that representative government does not work. To resist the decisions of courts and the laws of elected assemblies is to say that democracy has failed.   24

There is no man who is above the law, and there is no man who has a right to break the law. Civil disobedience is not above the law, but against the law. When the civil disobedient disobeys one law, he invariably subverts all law. When the civil disobedient says that he is above the law, he is saying that democracy is beneath him. His disobedience shows a distrust for the democratic system. He is merely saying that since democracy does not work, why should he help make it work. Thoreau expressed well the civil disobedient's disdain for democracy: 25

> As for adopting the ways which the state has provided for remedying the evil, I know not of such ways. They take too much time and a man's life will be gone. I have other affairs to attend to. I came into this world not chiefly to make this a good place to live in, but to live in it, be it good or bad.

Thoreau's position is not only morally irresponsible but politically reprehensible. When citizens in a democracy are called on to make a profession of faith, the civil disobedients offer only a confession of failure. Tragically, when civil disobedients for lack of faith abstain from democratic involvement, they help attain their own gloomy prediction. They help create the social and political basis for their own despair. By foreseeing failure, they help forge it. If citizens rely on antidemocratic means of protest, they will help bring about the undemocratic result of an authoritarian or anarchic state.   26

27   How far demonstrations properly can be employed to produce political and social change is a pressing question, particularly in view of the provocations accompanying the National Democratic Convention in Chicago last August and the reaction of the police to them. A line must be drawn by the judiciary between the demands of those who seek absolute order, which can lead only to a dictatorship, and those who seek absolute freedom, which can lead only to anarchy. The line, wherever it is drawn by our courts, should be respected on the college campus, on the streets and elsewhere.

28   Undue provocation will inevitably result in overreaction, human emotions being what they are. Violence will follow. This cycle undermines the very democracy it is designed to preserve. The lesson of the past is that democracies will fall if violence, including the intentional provocations that will lead to violence, replaces democratic procedures, as in Athens, Rome and the Weimar Republic. This lesson must be constantly explained by the legal profession.

29   We should heed the words of William James:

> Democracy is still upon its trial. The civic genius of our people is its only bulwark and . . . neither battleships nor public libraries nor great newspapers nor booming stocks: neither mechanical invention nor political adroitness, nor churches nor universities nor civil service examinations can save us from degeneration if the inner mystery be lost.
>
> That mystery, at once the secret and the glory of our English-speaking race, consists of nothing but two habits. . . . One of them is habit of trained and disciplined good temper towards the opposite party when it fairly wins its innings. The other is that of fierce and merciless resentment toward every man or set of men who break the public peace. (James, *Pragmatism,* 127–28)

From The Crito

Plato

1   SOCRATES: . . . Ought a man to do what he admits to be right, or ought he to betray the right?

2   CRITO: He ought to do what he thinks right.

3   SOCRATES: But if this is true, what is the application? In leaving the prison against the will of the Athenians, do I wrong any? Or rather do I not wrong those whom I ought least to wrong? Do I not desert the principles which are acknowledged by us to be just—what do you say?

4   CRITO: I cannot tell, Socrates; for I do not know.

5   SOCRATES: Then consider the matter in this way:—Imagine that I am about to play truant (you may call the proceeding by any name which you like), and the laws of the government come and interrogate me: "Tell us, Socrates," they say: "what are you about? Are you not going by an act of yours to overturn us—the laws, and the whole state, as far as in you lies? Do you imagine that a state can subsist and not be overthrown, in which the decisions of

law have no power, but are set aside and trampled upon by individuals?" What will be our answer, Crito, to these and the like words? Any one, and especially a rhetorician, will have a good deal to say on behalf of the law which requires a sentence to be carried out. He will argue that this law should not be set aside; and shall we reply, "Yes, but the state has injured us and given an unjust sentence." Suppose I say that?

CRITO: Very good, Socrates.   6

SOCRATES: "And was that our agreement with you?" the law would answer; "or were you   7
to abide by the sentence of the state?" And if I were to express my astonishment at their words, the law would probably add: "Answer, Socrates, instead of opening your eyes—you are in the habit of asking and answering questions. Tell us,—What complaint have you to make against us which justifies you in attempting to destroy us and the state? In the first place did we not bring you into existence? Your father married your mother by our aid and begat you. Say whether you have any objection to urge against those of us who regulate marriage?" None, I should reply. "Or against those of us who after birth regulate the nurture and education of children, in which you also were trained? Were not the laws, which have the charge of education, right in commanding your father to train you in music and gymnastics?" Right, I should reply. "Well then, since you were brought into the world and nurtured and educated by us, can you deny in the first place that you are our child and slave, as your fathers were before you? And if this is true you are not on equal terms with us; nor can you think that you have a right to do to us what we are doing to you. Would you have any right to strike or revile or do any other evil to your father or your master, if you had one, because you have been struck or reviled by him, or received some other evil at his hands?—you would not say this? And because we think right to destroy you, do you think that you have any right to destroy us in return, and your country as far as in you lies? Will you, O professor of true virtue, pretend that you are justified in this? Has a philosopher like you failed to discover that our country is more to be valued and higher and holier far than mother or father or any ancestor, and more to be regarded in the eyes of the gods and of men of understanding? Also to be soothed, and gently and reverently entreated when angry, even more than a father, and either to be persuaded, or if not persuaded, to be obeyed? And when we are punished by her, whether with imprisonment or stripes, the punishment is to be endured in silence, and if she leads us to wounds or death in battle, thither we follow as is right; neither may any one yield or retreat or leave his rank, but whether in battle or in a court of law, or in any other place, he must do what his city and his country order him; or he must change their view of what is just: and if he may do no violence to his father or mother, much less may he do violence to his country." What answer shall we make to this, Crito? Do the laws speak truly, or do they not?

CRITO: I think that they do.   8

SOCRATES: Then the laws will say, "Consider, Socrates, if we are speaking truly that in your   9
present attempt you are going to do us an injury. For, having brought you into the world, and nurtured and educated you, and given you and every other citizen a share in every good which we had to give, we further proclaim to any Athenian by the liberty which we allow him, that if he does not like us when he has become of age and has seen the ways of the

city, and made our acquaintance, he may go where he pleases and take his goods with him. None of our laws will forbid him or interfere with him. Any one who does not like us and the city, and who wants to emigrate to a colony or to any other city, may go where he likes, retaining his property. But he who has experience of the manner in which we order justice and administer the state, and still remains, has entered into an implied contract that he will do as we command him. And he who disobeys us is, as we maintain, thrice wrong; first, because in disobeying us he is disobeying his parents; secondly, because we are the authors of his education; thirdly, because he has made an agreement with us that he will duly obey our commands; and he neither obeys them nor convinces us that our commands are unjust; and we do not rudely impose them, but give him the alternative of obeying or convincing us;—that is what we offer, and he does neither.

10   "These are the sort of accusations to which, as we were saying, you, Socrates, will be exposed if you accomplish your intentions; you, above all other Athenians." Suppose now I ask, why I rather than anybody else? They will justly retort upon me that I above all other men have acknowledged the agreement. "There is clear proof," they will say, "Socrates, that we and the city were not displeasing to you. Of all Athenians you have been the most constant resident in the city, which, as you never leave, you may be supposed to love. For you never went out of the city either to see the games, except once when you went to the Isthmus, or to any other place unless when you were on military service; nor did you travel as other men do. Nor had you any curiosity to know other states or their laws: your affections did not go beyond us and our state; we were your special favourites, and you acquiesced in our government of you; and here in this city you begat your children, which is a proof of your satisfaction. Moreover, you might in the course of the trial, if you had liked, have fixed the penalty at banishment; the state which refuses to let you go now would have let you go then. But you pretended that you preferred death to exile, and that you were not unwilling to die. And now you have forgotten these fine sentiments, and pay no respect to us the laws, of whom you are the destroyer; and are doing what only a miserable slave would do, running away and turning your back upon the compacts and agreements which you made as a citizen. And first of all answer this very question: Are we right in saying that you agreed to be governed according to us in deed, and not in word only? Is that true or not?" How shall we answer, Crito? Must we not assent?

11   CRITO: We cannot help it, Socrates.

12   CRITO: Then will they not say: "You, Socrates, are breaking the covenants and agreements which you made with us at your leisure, not in any haste or under any compulsion or deception, but after you have had seventy years to think of them, during which time you were at liberty to leave the city, if we were not to your mind, or if our covenants appeared to you to be unfair. You had your choice, and might have gone either to Lacedaemon or Crete, both which states are often praised by you for their good government, or to some other Hellenic or foreign state. Whereas you, above all other Athenians, seemed to be so fond of the state, or, in other words, of us her laws (and who would care about a state which has no laws?), that you never stirred out of her; the halt, the blind, the maimed were not more stationary in her than you were. And now you run away and forsake your

agreements. Not so, Socrates, if you will take our advice; do not make yourself ridiculous by escaping out of the city.

"For just consider, if you transgress and err in this sort of way, what good will you 13 do either to yourself or to your friends? That your friends will be driven into exile and deprived of citizenship, or will lose their property, is tolerably certain; and you yourself, if you fly to one of the neighboring cities, as, for example, Thebes or Megara, both of which are well governed, will come to them as an enemy, Socrates, and their government will be against you, and all patriotic citizens will cast an evil eye upon you as a subverter of the laws, and you will confirm in the minds of the judges the justice of their own condemnation of you. For he who is a corrupter of the laws is more than likely to be a corrupter of the young and foolish portion of mankind. Will you then flee from well-ordered citizens and virtuous men? and is existence worth having on these terms? Or will you go to them without shame, and talk to them, Socrates? And what will you say to them? What you say here about virtue and justice and institutions and laws being the best things among men? Would that be decent of you? Surely not. But if you go away from well-governed states to Crito's friends in Thessaly, where there is a great disorder and licence, they will be charmed to hear the tale of your escape from prison, set off with ludicrous particulars of the manner in which you were wrapped in a goatskin or some other disguise, and metamorphosed as the manner is of runaways; but will there be no one to remind you that in your old age you were not ashamed to violate the most sacred laws from a miserable desire of a little more life? Perhaps not, if you keep them in a good temper; but if they are out of temper you will hear many degrading things; you will live, but how?—as the flatterer of all men, and the servant of all men; and doing what?—eating and drinking in Thessaly, having gone abroad in order that you may get a dinner. And where will be your fine sentiments about justice and virtue? Say that you wish to live for the sake of your children—you want to bring them up and educate them—will you take them into Thessaly and deprive them of Athenian citizenship? Is this the benefit which you will confer upon them? Or are you under the impression that they will be better cared for and educated here if you are still alive, although absent from them: for your friends will take care of them? Do you fancy that if you are an inhabitant of Thessaly they will take care of them, and if you are an inhabitant of the other world that they will not take of them? Nay: but if they who call themselves friends are good for anything, they will—to be sure they will.

"Listen, then Socrates, to us who have brought you up. Think not of life and children 14 first, and of justice afterwards, but of justice first, that you may be justified before the princes of the world below. For neither will you nor any that belong to you be happier or holier or juster in this life, or happier in another, if you do as Crito bids. Now you depart in innocence, a sufferer and not a doer of evil; a victim, not of the laws of men. But if you go forth, returning evil for evil, and injury for injury, breaking the covenants and agreements which you have made with us, and wronging those whom you ought least of all to wrong, that is to say, yourself, your friends, your country, and us, we shall be angry with you while you live, and our brethren, the laws in the world below, will receive you as an enemy; for they will know that you have done your best to destroy us. Listen, then, to us and not to Crito."

15   This, dear Crito, is the voice which I seem to hear murmuring in my ears, like the sound of the flute in the ears of the mystic; that voice, I say, is humming in my ears, and prevents me from hearing any other. And I know that anything more which you may say will be vain. Yet speak, if you have anything to say.

16   CRITO: I have nothing to say, Socrates.

17   SOCRATES: Leave me then, Crito, to fulfill the will of God, and to follow whither he leads.

FOR CLASS DISCUSSION

1. Analyze and evaluate the disagreement between Martin Luther King, Jr., and Lewis Van Dusen, Jr., over the ethics of civil disobedience by applying the first set of guide questions from page 455. How do you account for their disagreement?

2. To what extent do you think that Van Dusen and Socrates agree on their reasons for disapproving civil disobedience?

3. Choose one of the arguments for closer analysis, applying the second set of guide questions on page 455–456.

Optional Writing Assignments

1. You are a successful civil rights attorney. The principal of your child's junior high school has approached you with a concern. It seems that none of the social studies textbooks discusses the concept of civil disobedience. He wants to provide the social studies teachers with a statement on civil disobedience.

Drawing on the preceding essays, personal experience, and any other research you may have done, write a brief explanation of the role of civil disobedience in a democracy. Before you start writing, believe/doubt the following statement: "There is no place for civil disobedience in a modern democracy." Whatever you decide about that statement, construct a brief explanation of your view that would be appropriate for use in an eighth grade textbook.

2. The aerial bombardment of Iraq at the start of the 1991 war set off waves of student protests on college campuses reminiscent of the Vietnam antiwar movement. Several students at one college missed a midterm exam to join a protest march at the start of the war. When the students showed up the next day asking to take the midterm, the professor refused. He explained that his syllabus specifically stated that students could make up an exam only in cases of illness or personal emergency. Write a letter to the professor either supporting or opposing his decision that political protests do not constitute grounds for missing an exam.

CENSORSHIP ON THE INTERNET

In Defense of Decency

Mike Romano

Sometime in the more recent course of human events, these truths have become self-evident: that we are endowed with certain unalienable rights and that among these are Life, Liberty, and the unfettered pursuit of prurience over the Internet. In turn, an anti-censorship crusade has swept through with such frenzy that nearly every pundit and political activist of repute has encouraged swift action by the Supreme Court to overturn the now infamous Communications Decency Act of 1996—a law that seeks to shield children from obscene material on the Internet.

Lying somewhere between libertarianism and neo-progressivism, and literally banking on a wired future of mass interactivity, an important socio-political movement has blossomed. The fight against Internet censorship is its primary rallying point. The movement is snowballing fast, teaming Netizens with Microsoft, *Time* magazine, and the ACLU. Strange allies. Maybe a strange idea?

Let's look first at the legal issues. In May, a three-judge panel of the Third Circuit Court held a special session in Philadelphia to consider objections to the CDA in *ACLU v. Janet Reno.* On June 11, the court struck down the CDA in no uncertain terms, calling the law "profoundly repugnant" and "unconstitutional on its face." Writing for the court, Judge Stewart Dalzell explained, "As the most participatory form of mass speech yet developed, the Internet deserves the highest protection from government intrusion."

The most contentious, and constitutionally questionable, portion of the CDA bans the use of "any interactive computer service to display in a manner available to a person under 18 years of age, any comment, request, suggestion, proposal, image, or other communication that, in context, depicts or describes, in terms patently offensive as measured by contemporary community standards, sexual or excretory activities or organs."

CDA critics launched a three-pronged attack. First, they argued that the very nature of the Internet makes all postings equally available to minors as to adults. Therefore, prohibition of all such material—a circumstance found unconstitutional in 1957 when the Supreme Court found in *Butler v. Michigan* that an obscenity law meant to protect minors effectively "reduce[d] the adult population of Michigan to reading only what is fit for children."

Next, anti-censors decried the CDA's vague definition of "patently offensive." Relying heavily on slippery-slope arguments throughout the debate, many critics of censorship worry that governments could ban a depiction on the Internet of the Sistine Chapel or instructions for preventing transmission of AIDS. Accordingly, among the co-plaintiffs in *Reno* are the American Library Association, which represents public providers of on-line access to "famous nude works by Botticelli, Manet, Matisse, Cezanne, and others" (according to the Plaintiff's brief), and the Internet-based AIDS Global Information Service, whose mission is self-explanatory.

7   Finally, *Reno* plaintiffs object that "community standards," which mean to measure indecency levels for the CDA, vary considerably from state to state, but the statute applies to the boundary-less Internet. Case in point, *United States v. Thomas* where Californians Robert and Carleen Thomas were convicted for breaking Tennessee's conservative community standards for decency when a postal worker downloaded "obscene" material from a computer which happened to be sitting in Memphis. (Note: The Thomases violated Tennessee obscenity law which applies to all media, not the CDA.)

8   All is not so simple. There are reasonable, non-fundamentalist, Internet-savvy responses to each of the anti-censor objections. Furthermore, important questions are raised by their absence from public debate.

9   Start by reading past the CDA's controversial paragraph, quoted above. It continues: "... It is a defense to a prosecution ... that a person has taken, in good faith, reasonable, effective, and appropriate actions under the circumstances to restrict or prevent access by minors to a[n obscene] communication." Meaning, Web sites, servers or providers can freely publish e-smut if access to those sites is restricted to adults by simply "requiring the use of a verified credit card, debit account, adult access code," or by any other "method which is feasible under available technology," according to the CDA.

10   These good-faith defenses avoid the strictures of the *Butler* decision by allowing access to adults, albeit restricted access, while at the same time excluding access to minors. Many people still want to run straight for the First Amendment as soon as any fetter to published material is allowed, but in one of the most important Supreme Court rulings of this era, *FCC v. Pacifica* (1978), a ban on indecent broadcast programming was upheld "when children are undoubtedly in the audience." In *Pacifica,* that permitted a remedy such as restricting offensive material from George Carlin's "Filthy Words" routine to late-night broadcasts. In the CDA case, requiring a credit card limits the audience of minors, just as access to X-rated films or pornographic telephone services are limited.

11   The second objection of CDA critics suggests that the phrase "patently offensive" is overly vague and could even encompass popular art that metropolitans may take for granted but which puritanical hicks (with e-mail) may seek to ban. Such reasoning not only runs contrary to *Pacifica,* which speaks approvingly and at length to the contextual nature of "patently offensive references," but also to the CDA's own Conference Agreement, authored in congressional conference committee while hammering out the final version of the bill. Published as an addendum to the law for judges to read in determining legislative intent, the CDA Agreement notes that the law shall not apply to "material with serious redeeming value ... intended to edify and educate, not to offend." The committee defined "patently offensive" as material *intended* to be such. Without demonstrable intent to offend, therefore, neither AIDS material nor works of art face serious threat from the CDA.

12   The third objection to the CDA contends that geographically defined "community standards" are incongruent with the ubiquitous nature of cyberspace. In *Pacifica,* measures are allowed to shield "patently offensive" material from children, and the CDA does the same

with its prescriptions for "good faith" exceptions. Personally, I fail to see how the Internet is substantively more ubiquitous than radio or television. The Internet may not be time-dependent like broadcast media which limits adult language to time slots past most children's bedtimes, so the CDA shield children with the same age-verifying measures used by dial-a-porn companies.

Writing for Reno, Judge Dalzell argues: "The Internet is a far more speech-enhancing   13
medium than print, the village green, or the mails. . . . Some of the dialogue on the Internet surely tests the limits of conventional discourse. Speech on the Internet can be unfettered, unpolished, and unconventional, even emotionally charged, sexually explicit, and vulgar. . . . But we should expect such speech to occur in a medium in which all walks of life have a voice. We should also protect the autonomy that such a medium confers to ordinary people as well as media magnates."

Such language reminds me of Microsoft's television commercials—and neither corre-   14
spond to any actual experience on-line. Measuring media solely by "interactive" volume would lead us to believe that Rush Limbaugh's call-in radio show is the most democratic event in history. According to a very supportive *Time* magazine article on *Reno,* the judges based their decisions on "a kind of Socratic on-line safari," led by Internet experts. It's incredible that with such limited (and possibly slanted) experience, a responsible court could draw such romantic notions of the Internet and grant such sweeping Constitutional protections.

Dalzell's judicial decree could lead many to think that the Internet has become a last,   15
best chance for democracy. But how many people do you know who actually use the Internet regularly? How many people you know have personal Web sites? Let me guess: all of your poor, black, lesbian friends, right? In fact, the Internet is dominated by young, white men. And access to the Web is essentially controlled by two mega-companies: Microsoft and Netscape. The Internet is not cheap. Computers and ISDN lines cost lots of money (and the two terminals with Web access at the library don't make any difference whatsoever). This newspaper is cheap, truly accessible to all walks of life; it's way more demographically representative than the Internet, yet I'm not about to call it a democracy.

Moreover, despite our loaded relationship with "censorship," government regulation   16
may not be such a bad thing in some situations. We have a vested interest, moral responsibility, *and* constitutional mandate to protect children from degrading and lascivious pornography. When we are forced into a back room to rent pornographic videos, we surely sacrifice some liberties, but we do so without complaint—and the world isn't coming to an end. It's no worse than presenting some sort of age verification, as is asked for in the CDA. Furthermore, Internet providers already know that porn-free environments draw investors. Companies like America Online proudly advertise their product as a clean and safe electronic service. In every other medium and industry a stamp of governmental approval is an incentive for economic investment. Why not for the Internet?

Conventional wisdom has *Reno* on fast track to the Supreme Court. It's being driven   17
there by an overwhelming juggernaut of cyberhype. Microsoft, America Online, Prodigy, CompuServe, Nintendo, and others are proud co-plaintiffs in *Reno,* along with the ACLU, American Library Association, and the Society of Professional Journalists. Shouldn't that constellation give us pause? Remember, the computer industry is in midstride of the biggest marketing campaign in world history. Intended or not, their expedient embrace of the First Amendment tracks perfectly with that marketing scheme—but our courts must be no party to it.

Net Benefit

Kathleen Durkan

1   When a federal district court recently held that the Congressional Decency Act amounts to censorship of free speech, the judges dropped their normally restrained language and defended the Internet with purple prose. The Net, they argued, is different from other media because it is a participatory democracy deserving special protection.

2   Their ruling may not withstand further judicial scrutiny, but they grasped several points correctly. The Internet is a democracy. Freedoms of expression and access are essential to its success. Stamping out smut on the Internet is a lousy way to deal with the larger issues raised by this new medium. And we will be better off allowing the Internet industry to police itself before inviting in the government as its regulator.

3   More important than the problems of pornography on the Net (a serious problem, to be sure) are questions about the developing structure of the Web itself, and access to it. If we guarantee First Amendment rights to the Net, we still may lose the wider war if the Internet evolves into a structure that accommodates only a few huge corporate voices and cost and technology lock out the small home page in Dallas or voices of dissent in China.

4   One central point about the Internet is that it is an international medium. Opposition voices in undemocratic nations use the Net as one of their few tools of free speech. These dissidents often have no First Amendment–style rights; they can't get CNN. But they can access the new and democratic technology, learn about the broader world, and tell their own stories.

5   The dictators are busy figuring out how to control access to this dangerous new medium. They may not need to worry if the corporations make the new tools too expensive, or if they stamp out the niche programming that ties together micro-communities.

6   Let me give an example of a recent program I produced for Progressive Networks of Seattle. We broadcast the audio of a joint speech by President Clinton and Israeli Prime Minister Peres before an audience of Jewish activists in Washington, DC, followed by interviews with experts on the peace process and international terrorism. An interactive page encouraged listener feedback. Some of the audience was in Middle Eastern countries whose state-run media don't air speeches by Israeli leaders or permit debate about terrorism. When we asked the participants, 30 percent said they were unable to access events like this in their nation's media.

7   Many forces work against such programming: dictators, the profit motive in broadcast media, national cultures afraid of modernism. The United States, as a primary purveyor of democracy and technology, has a special responsibility to keep the Net as a force for such programming. The threats are many. For instance, we need to be wary of asking dictators to police the economic interests of our technological industries. What might China expect as payment for its promise to fight software piracy?

8   Moreover, there are enormous challenges within the existing American media cultures, which feel threatened and defensive about the new medium. Take the example of television news, fearful about the loss of audiences for network news. NBC and Microsoft

have formed a partnership that may amount to putting much the same product, complete with anchors and sets and star correspondents, into the new medium. But that overlooks the network's main problem: its current product. That product is relentlessly secular, contemptuous of spiritual aspects, prizing of cynicism, and fond of treating politics as a sport that feeds off conflict and tactics. Television has abandoned any pretension to public service, once a federally mandated obligation.

My fear, then, is that these big corporate ventures into cyberspace will sustain the present media monopolies on serious information. They have the brand names and the money to reduce the multiplicity of voices on the Net to the 13 depressingly imitative channels on commercial television.   9

Possibly the bigger players will be forced to adapt to the Web culture, rather than imposing their old culture on the Web. Perhaps the Internet will be left free enough to evolve on its own into a more substantive version of the democracy it already has created. Perhaps the old media will recommit itself to public service programming. But we will never encourage these good things to happen, developments that could transform and revitalize American media, if we allow a concern about smut on the Net to upstage these far more basic issues.   10

The Net Doesn't Need Thought Police

Marc Rothenberg

A copy of *The Naked Society* sits in my office. Some people might think it is a collection of dirty pictures. Not at all.   1

It's a book written by Vance Packard, the author of three national best-sellers, about the growth of surveillance and the loss of personal freedom. Packard used "naked society" to describe how new technology strips us of our privacy. The book begins with a quote from a famous judge and ends with the Bill of Rights.   2

Now give some politician the ability to do a global search and delete, and I have little doubt that all electronic copies of books such as *The Naked Society* would be erased overnight from the Internet.   3

Think I'm exaggerating? Here's what happened when Bavarian prosecutors told CompuServe, Inc. to pull the plug on newsgroups with "sex" in the title. The fan club for Patrick Stewart, the actor who plays Capt. Jean-Luc Picard on *Star Trek* and does an excellent one-man performance of *A Christmas Carol* at holiday time, got zapped. The reason? The newsgroup is alt.sexy.bald.captains. Also knocked off the 'net by zealous thought police was a support group for disabled people (alt.support.disabled.sexuality) and a parody of an annoying children's television character (alt.sex.bestiality.barney).   4

Of course, censorship isn't just about sex. The Chinese government recently told Reuters and the Dow Jones News Service that they could no longer provide economic information to   5 the country without government approval. Why? To protect economic security. And the government of Singapore continues its campaign to ensure that speech is sanitized before it reaches the minds or hearts of its citizens.

6   The U.S. is getting drawn into this craziness because religious zealots and their allies in Congress have decided they know what is good for us and our children. Telling others what they should read, think or believe is about as un-American as it gets. But through the Exon-Coats Communications Decency Act, which recently passed as part of the Telecommunications Deregulation and Reform Bill, such nonsense has become the law.

7   Supporters of this act say it's nothing more than old-fashioned regulation of TV and radio. Anyone who uses the 'net knows that's completely wrong. (Not surprisingly, a sponsor of the Communications Decency Act proudly proclaims he doesn't use the 'net.)

8   Regulating the Internet isn't like regulating radio or television. No World Wide Web site operator is licensed. No scarce spectrum is used. Regulating speech on the Internet is like telling bookstore owners, newsstand operators and librarians which books to stock and which magazines to sell. It's like the government telling people who use the telephone which words they can use.

9   Supporters of the legislation say it will protect children from the evils of dirty pictures. That's crazy, too. Young kids aren't interested in dirty pictures. Like all campaigners against sexuality, all the publicity-seeking moralists have accomplished is to splash the stuff they most fear across the front pages of the nation's newspapers. They might as well put a blinking arrow on top of the *Playboy* home page and say, "Don't look here!"

10   Of course, parents should be free to select materials that are appropriate for their children, and Internet users should be able to reject material that is objectionable. If you really don't like an on-line service's policy or content, cancel your membership.

11   But be careful when people tell you which words you can speak and which books you can read. Once they start drawing lines, they rarely stop. Parody, criticism, satire, adult conversation, literature and art all would become suspect.

12   The legislation gives federal investigators the right to comb through Web sites, newsgroup posts and even private electronic mail to find evidence of indecent speech. Use a word that someone doesn't like, and you could get thrown in jail. The bill even threatens the right to use privacy technologies, such as encryption, because the government now will have the right to open private E-mail if it suspects the message contains offensive language. Flaming becomes a criminal offense.

13   The supporters of government censorship will say they don't intend to eliminate the acceptable stuff, just the bad stuff. And that's exactly the problem the First Amendment was designed to avoid. It gives us the right and the responsibility to decide for ourselves what is objectionable and what isn't. It forces us to make choices when we are confronted with controversial ideas and new viewpoints. We don't need the First Amendment to protect greeting card prose. We need it to protect the openness and diversity of a free society.

14   The timing for this congressional nonsense couldn't be worse. The U.S. has a vital role to play in the new on-line environment as defender of free speech and open debate. Many countries will be tempted to impose restrictions because of culture, for economic security, for national security or simply to intimidate opponents. Political leaders in the U.S. should stand up against the thought police, not join their ranks.

We all have an interest in opposing censorship. No matter what your views, they may   15
be illegal somewhere. If each country imposes a filter on information, there may be little
content left.

Vance Packard wrote in *The Naked Society,* "the Bill of Rights represents a magnifi-   16
cent vision for assuring the Blessings of Liberty." Those are important words. Kids should
have a chance to read them before the high-tech moralists sweep the books off the shelves
of cyberspace.

Only the Force of Law Can Deter Pornographers

James Exon

Children and families won an important victory in Congress on February 1.   1

The Telecommunications Deregulation and Reform Bill, which includes the Exon-Coats   2
Communications Decency Act, was passed by the Senate and House. Congress agreed that
we need to take reasonable steps to protect children on the information superhighway instead of simply handing the keys of our homes to pornographers.

Some basic rules of the road are necessary to make the information superhighway safer   3
and more useful for children and families.

Because our legislation follows previous court rulings, it won't violate the First   4
Amendment. It makes clear that current obscenity laws apply to computers. It protects
users from on-line harassment and prohibits the use of a computer to lure children into illegal sexual activity.

The legislation also provides for compliance through the good-faith use of "reason-   5
able, effective and appropriate means" to restrict children's access to indecent or pornographic material.

The Communications Decency Act could help to ensure that our kids have a chance   6
to travel safely through cyberspace and would still let adults access whatever legal material they choose. It would apply to computers the same antipornography laws that exist
for U.S. mail, broadcast and telephone communications. The legislation focuses clearly
on wrongdoers.

If someone let a child browse freely through an adult bookstore or an X-rated video ar-   7
cade, I suspect and hope that most people would call the police to arrest that person. Yet
these very offenses occur every day in America's electronic neighborhoods. A child can get
on the information superhighway and freely ride to on-line "red light districts" that contain
some of the most perverse and depraved pornographic material available.

The Supreme Court has said repeatedly that Congress may act to protect kids from   8
indecency.

A recent FBI sting operation resulted in the arrest of several people nationwide for   9
distributing child pornography over computers, which shows that some of our child

pornography laws also work in the world of cyberspace. But we need more legal tools to deal with this type of problem before more child victims are lured into pornography. Our law will shield children from pornography that is only a few clicks away on their computers and will make it illegal to engage children in sexual conversations on-line.

10   It will impose penalties on people who transmit pornographic material via computer networks that are accessible to children. The maximum penalty for such an offense would be up to two years in jail and a fine of up to $250,000.

11   Don't let opponents of the legislation fool you: Nothing in it applies to constitutionally protected speech between consenting adults. It simply says a person can't use a computer to transmit or display indecent material in a way that is openly accessible to a person under 18 years of age.

12   This law will be enforced the same way as our existing pornography laws: If someone files a complaint, law enforcement will investigate. Federal privacy laws haven't been repealed. "Cybercops" won't surf the 'net to look for violators. Indecent communications simply must be conducted in a place that is out of reach for children.

13   Access for children can be restricted in several ways, including requiring use of a verified credit card, debit account, adult access code or adult personal identification number. The Supreme Court already has approved such means for limiting child access to telephone "dial-a-porn" services.

14   Parents, schools and a responsible industry still must be involved in the effort to make the Internet safer. But does anyone really think that parents can monitor their children all of their waking hours? We need the added deterrent of law so that those who would pervert the network will think twice.

15   Our legislation has steered the industry toward developing possible blocking devices, and we applaud those efforts. Unfortunately, expensive and complicated screening devices alone don't hold enough hope of adequate success.

16   Opponents forsake reason when they say they want to protect children from indecency, seduction and harassment but maintain that the overriding issue is freedom of access to anything by anybody. Tell that to a parent who has had a child lured away by a deviant on a computer network. Hardly a day goes by without another story about the mix of depravity and children on the 'net. How many more are never reported?

'Net Protection

17   We have laws against murder, and we have laws against speeding. We still have murder, and we still have speeding. But I think most reasonable people would agree that we very likely would have more murders and more speeders if we didn't have laws as deterrents.

18   This measure won't make the Internet pristine, but it will help protect our children.

19   There is too much of the self-serving philosophy of the hands-off elite. They seem to rationalize that the framers of the Constitution plotted to make certain that the profiteering pornographer, the pervert and the pedophile be free to practice their pursuits in the presence of children on a taxpayer-created and subsidized computer network.

20   That is nonsense.

This Is Safe Sex?

James Gleick

At first glance, there's a lot of sex on the Internet. Or, not at *first* glance—nobody can find anything on the Internet at first glance. But if you have time on your hands, if you're comfortable with computing, and if you have an unflagging curiosity about sex—in other words, if you're a teen-ager—you may think you've suddenly landed in pornography heaven. Nude pictures! Foul language! Weird bathroom humor! No wonder the Christian Coalition thinks the Internet is turning into a red-light district. There's even a "Red Light District" World Wide Web page.

So we explore. Some sites make you promise to be a grown-up. (O.K.: you promise.) You try "Girls," a link leading to a computer at the University of Bordeaux, France. The message flashes back: *Document Contains No Data.* "Girls" at Funet, Finland, seems to offer lots of pictures (Dolly Parton! Ivana Trump!)—*Connect Timed Out.* "Girls," courtesy of Liberac University of Technology, Czech Republic, does finally, with painful slowness, delivery itself of a 112,696-byte image of Madchen Amick. You could watch it spread across your screen, pixel by tantalizing pixel, but instead you go have lunch during the download, and when you return, there she is—in black-and-white and wearing clothes.

These pictures, by the way, are obviously scanned from magazines. And magazines are the ideal medium for them. Clearly the battle cry of the on-line voyeur is "Host Contacted—Waiting for Reply."

With old Internet technology, retrieving and viewing any graphic image on a PC at home could be laborious. New Internet technology, like browsers for the Web, makes all this easier, though it still takes minutes for the typical picture to squeeze its way through your modem. Meanwhile, though, ease of use has killed off the typical purveyor of dirty pictures, capable of serving hundreds of users a day but uninterested in handling hundreds of thousands. The Conservatoire National des Arts et Métiers has turned off its "Femmes femmes femmes je vous aime" Web page. The good news for erotica fans is that users are redirected to a new site where "You can find *naked women,* including *topless* and *total nudity*"; the bad news is that this new site is the Louvre.

The Internet does offer access to hundreds of sex "newsgroups," forums for discussion encompassing an amazing spectrum of interests. They're easy to find—in the newsgroup hierarchy "alt.sex" ("alt" for alternative) comes right after "alt.sewing." And yes, alt.sex is busier than alt.sewing. But quite a few of them turn out to be sham and self-parody. Look at alt.sex.fish—practically nothing. Alt.sex.bestiality—aha! just what Jesse Helms fears most—gives way to alt.sex.bestiality.hamster.duct-tape, and fascinating as this sounds, when you call it up you find it's empty, presumably the vestige of a short-lived joke. Alt.sex.bondage.particle-physics is followed by alt.sex.sheep.baaa.baaa.baaa.moo—help!

6   Still, if you look hard enough, there is grotesque stuff available. If pornography doesn't bother you, your stomach may be curdled by the vulgar commentary and clinical how-to's in the militia and gun newsgroups. Your local newsstand is a far more user-friendly source of obscenity than the on-line world, but it's also true that, if you work at it, you can find plenty on line that will disgust you, and possibly even disgust your children.

7   This is the justification for an effort in Congress to give the Federal Government tools to control the content available on the Internet. The Communications Decency Act, making its way through Congress, aims to transform the obscene-phone-call laws into a vehicle for prosecuting any Internet user, bulletin-board operator, or on-line service that knowingly makes obscene material available.

8   As originally written, the bill would not only have made it a crime to write lewd E-mail to your lover; it would also have made it a crime for your Internet provider to transmit it. After a round of lobbying from the large on-line services, the bill's authors have added "defenses" that could exempt mere unwitting carriers of data, and they say it is children, not consenting adults, they aim to protect. Nevertheless, the legislation is a historically far-reaching attempt at censorship on a national scale.

9   The Senate authors of this language do not use E-mail themselves, or browse the Web, or chat in newsgroups, and their legislation reflects a mental picture of how the on-line world works that does not match the reality. The existing models for Federal regulation of otherwise protected speech—for example, censorship of broadcast television and prohibition of harassing telephone calls—come from a world that is already vanishing over the horizon. There aren't three big television networks now, serving a unified mass market; there are thousands of television broadcasters serving ever-narrower special interests. And on the Internet, the number of broadcasters is rapidly approaching the number of users: uncountable.

10   With Internet use spreading globally, most live sources of erotic images already seem to be overseas. The sad reality for Federal authorities is that they cannot cut those off without forcing the middlemen—on-line services in the United States—to do the work of censorship, and that work is a practical impossibility. Any teen-ager with an account on Prodigy can use its new Web browser to search for the work "pornography" and click his way to "Femmes femmes femmes" (oh, well, better luck next time). Policing discussion groups presents the would-be censor with an even more hopeless set of choices. A typical Internet provider carries more than 10,000 groups. As many as 100 million new words flow through them every day. The actual technology of these discussion groups is hard to fathom at first. They are utterly decentralized. Every new message begins on one person's computer and propagates outward in waves, like a chain letter that could eventually reach every mailbox in the world. Legislators would like to cut off a group like alt.sex.bondage.particle-physics at the source, or at its home—but it has no source and no home, or rather, it has as many homes as there are computers carrying newsgroups.

11   This is the town-square speech the First Amendment was for: often rancorous, sometimes harsh and occasionally obscene. Voices do carry farther now. The world has never been this global and this intimate at once. Even seasoned Internet users sometimes forget

that, lurking just behind the dozen visible participants in an out-of-the-way newsgroup, tens of millions of potential readers can examine every word they post.

If a handful of people wish to share their private experiences with like-minded peo- 12
ple in alt.sex.fetish.hair, they can do so, efficiently—the most fervent wishes of Congress notwithstanding—and for better or worse, they'll have to learn that children can listen in. Meanwhile, if gun-wielding extremists wish to discuss the vulnerable points in the anatomy of F.B.I. agents, they too can do so. At least the rest of us can listen in on them, too. Perhaps there is a grain of consolation there—instead of censorship, exposure to the light. Anyway, the only real alternative now would be to unwire the Information Super-highway altogether.

FOR CLASS DISCUSSION

1. Analyze and evaluate disagreements among these writers about the value and utility of trying to censor the Internet by applying the first set of guide questions from page 455. How do you account for the differing points of view?

2. Choose one of the arguments for closer analysis, applying the second set of guide questions on page 455–456.

Optional Writing Assignment   A bombing incident in your city has leveled a local church, injuring several people. Two suspects are subsequently captured, tried, and convicted of the bombing. During the course of that trial, it is learned that the two young men who planted the bomb got the "recipe" for their device off the Internet. They are, it turns out, subscribers to a list called "alt.Nazi.pranks" that calls for a return to "the mastery of the white race" through such strategies as hate speech against minorities, sharing intelligence about those federal office buildings with lax security, and explaining how to make explosive devices out of ordinary household items like lawn fertilizer.

The members of your quiet little community are outraged to learn about the ready availability of such dangerous information, not to mention the vile and of-fensive language used by subscribers to support their widely discredited theories of racial superiority. Many of these people are equally outraged by the easy avail-ability of pornography on the Net. Letters begin flooding in to the paper calling for censorship of the Internet, including removal of the Nazi list. Some go so far as to demand the criminal prosecution of the list's subscribers.

Having just read all about this issue in your college writing course, you feel like you have something to add to the debate. So you repair to your word proces-sor and begin writing two responses. The first is a letter to the editor, aimed at the outraged citizenry of your town; the second is directed to Congressman Ralph Pangloss, your district's congressional representative and longtime foe of censor-ship of any sort. Whichever side in the debate you support, your letters should be responsive to your two different audiences.

THE LEGALIZATION OF DRUGS

The Federal Drugstore

An Interview with Michael S. Gazzaniga

1   **Q:**   Professor Gazzaniga, as you know, there are those who have recommended the decriminalization of drugs. Before we take up a concrete proposal coming in from that quarter, we want to ask you a question or two, the answers to which will shed light on any such proposal. The first question is this:

2   It is said that the drug crack is substantively different from its parent drug, cocaine, in that it is, to use the term of Professor van den Haag, "crimogenic." In other words a certain (unspecified) percentage of those who take crack are prompted to—well, to go out and commit mayhem of some kind. Is that correct?

3   **A:**   No, not in the way you put it. What you are asking is, Is there something about how crack acts on the brain that makes people who take it likelier to commit crime?

4   Let's begin by making it clear what crack is. It is simply cocaine that has been mixed with baking soda, water, and then boiled. What this procedure does is to permit cocaine to be smoked. Now any drug ingested in that way—i.e., absorbed by the lungs—goes more efficiently to the brain, and the result is a quicker, more intense experience. That is what crack gives the consumer. But its impact on the brain is the same as with plain cocaine and, as a matter of fact, amphetamines. No one has ever maintained that these drugs are "crimogenic."

5   The only study I know about that inquires into the question of crack breeding crime reports that most homicides involving crack were the result not of the use of crack, but of dealer disputes. Crack did not induce users to commit crimes. Do some crack users commit crimes? Of course. After all, involvement in proscribed drug traffic is dangerous. Moreover, people who commit crimes tend to use drugs at a high rate, though which drug they prefer varies from one year to the next.

6   **Q:**   You are telling us that an increase in the use of crack would not mean an increase in crime?

7   **A:**   I am saying that what increase there would be in crime would not be simply the result of the pharmacology of that drug. Look, let's say there are 200,000 users/abusers of crack in New York City—a number that reflects one of the current estimates. If so, and if the drug produced violent tendencies in all crack users, the health-care system would have come to a screeching halt. It hasn't. In fact, in 1988 the hospitals in New York City (the crack capital of the world) averaged only seven crack-related admissions, citywide, a day. The perception of crack-based misbehavior is exaggerated because it is the cases that show up in the emergency rooms that receive public notice, and the whole picture begins to look very bleak. All of this is to say: when considering any aspect of the drug problem, keep in mind the matter of selection of the evidence.

It is prudent to recall that, in the past, dangerous and criminal behavior has been said   8
to have been generated by other drugs, for instance marijuana (you remember *Reefer Madness?*). And bear it in mind that since cocaine is available everywhere, so is crack available everywhere, since the means of converting the one into the other are easy, and easily learned. It is important to note that only a small percentage of cocaine users actually convert their stuff to crack. Roughly one in six.

Q: Then would it follow that even if there were an increase in the use of crack, the le-   9
galization of it would actually result in a decrease in crime?
A: That is correct.   10

Q: Isn't crack a drug whose addictive power exceeds that of many other drugs? If that is   11
the case, one assumes that people who opt to take crack do so because it yields the faster and more exhilarating satisfactions to which you make reference.
A: That is certainly the current understanding, but there are no solid data on the ques-   12
tion. Current observations are confounded by certain economic variables. Crack is cheap—

Q: Why? If cocaine is expensive, how can crack be cheap?   13
A: Cocaine costs $1,000 per ounce if bought in quantity. One ounce can produce one   14
thousand vials of crack, each of which sells for $5. The drug abuser is able to experience more drug episodes. Crack being cheap, the next high can come a lot more quickly and since there is a down to every up, or high, the cycle can become intense.

So yes, crack is addictive. So is cocaine. So are amphetamines. The special punch of crack,   15
as the result of going quickly via the lungs to the brain, may prompt some abusers to want more. By the way, it is the public knowledge that crack acts in this way that, as several studies document, causes most regular cocaine users to be cautious about crack. The casual-to-moderate user very clearly wants to stay in that category. So, all you can say is that there is a *perception,* widely shared, that crack is more addictive. Whether it is, isn't really known. One thing we do know is that crack does not begin to approach tobacco as a nationwide health hazard. For every crack-related death, there are three hundred tobacco-related deaths.

Q: You are confusing us. You say that because of the especially quick effects that come   16
from taking crack, there is a disposition on the part of the user to want more. Isn't that a way of saying that it is more addictive? If someone, after smoking, say, ten cigarettes, begins to want cigarettes every day, isn't tobacco "addictive," as you say it is? Or are you saying that crack finds most users indifferent to the highs it brings on, and for *that* reason it can't be said to be more addictive than cocaine?
A: The current, official definition of an addict is someone who compulsively seeks psy-   17
choactive drugs. The definition, you will note, focuses on human behavior, not on pharmacologic action on the brain. In respect of crack, there are factors that might lead to a higher rate of addiction. Some of these factors are certainly social in nature and some may be pharmacologic. The purported higher rate of addiction among crack users could be due to social values, for instance the low cost of crack. We simply don't know as yet.

Keep in mind our experience with LSD. When it was fashionable to take it, droves did   18
so. But LSD has unpleasant side-effects, and eventually the use of it greatly diminished. In drugs, as in much else, there is a strong tendency to follow the herd. Sorting out the real threat from the hyperbole takes time.

19   Another example of hyperbole is the recent claim that there were 375,000 "crack babies" born last year; how could that possibly be, when the government (the National Institutes on Drug Abuse) informs us that there were only 500,000 crack *users* last year? Exaggeration and misinformation run rampant on this subject.

20   **Q:**   Well, if crack were legally available alongside cocaine and, say, marijuana, what could be the reason for a consumer to take crack?

21   **A:**   You need to keep your drug classifications straight. If your goal were, pure and simple, to get high, you might try crack or cocaine, or some amphetamine. You wouldn't go for marijuana, which is a mild hallucinogen and tranquilizer. So, if you wanted to be up and you didn't have much time, you might go to crack. But then if it were absolutely established that there was a higher addiction rate with crack, legalization could, paradoxically, diminish its use. This is so because if cocaine were reduced to the same price as crack, the abuser, acknowledging the higher rate of addiction, might forgo the more intensive high of crack, opting for the slower high of cocaine. Crack was introduced years ago as offering an alluring new psychoactive experience. But its special hold on the ghetto is the result of its price. Remember that—on another front—we know that 120-proof alcohol doesn't sell as readily as the 86 proof, not by a long shot, even though the higher the proof, the faster the psychological effect that alcohol users are seeking.

22   **Q:**   The basic question, we take it, has got to be this: It is everywhere assumed that if drugs were legal, their consumption would increase. That guess is based on empirical observations of a past phenomenon. Mr. Bennett, for instance, has said that when Prohibition ended, the consumption of alcohol increased by 400 percent. What are your comments on that?

23   **A:**   Books and even careers have been built around studies of the Eighteenth Amendment. Arguments about its meaning continue to rage in the scientific journals. Arguments always continue when available data are inconclusive.

24   Most experts insist that the rate of alcohol use before Prohibition was the same as after. Some qualify that assertion by pointing out that the pre-Prohibition rate of consumption was not realized again until years after Prohibition was over. From this we are invited to conclude that, in that sense, Prohibition was really successful—i.e., it interrupted many potential drinkers on their way to the saloon. And then some point out that although alcohol was freely available during Prohibition, it was harder to get in some parts of America. Even so overall consumption was rising (some say to pre-Prohibition levels) toward the middle and end of Prohibition.

25   Frankly, here is what's important: *There is a base rate of drug abuse, and it is achieved one way or another.* This is so even though there are researchers who point to different rates of abuse in different cultures. The trouble with that generality is that it is usually made without taking into account correlative factors, such as national traditions, the extent of education programs available, and so on. In which connection, I think the Federal Government should establish a study group to collect drug information from different cultures in an effort to get useful leads.

26   **Q:**   Is there evidence that the current consumption of drugs is restrained by their illegality? We have read that ninety million Americans have experimented, at one time or another, with illegal drugs. Would more than ninety million have experimented with them if drugs had been legal?

A: I think illegality has little if anything to do with drug consumption—and, incidentally,   27
I am certain that far more than ninety million Americans have at some point or other experimented with an illegal drug.

This gets to the issue of actual availability. Drugs are everywhere, simply everywhere.   28
In terms of availability, drugs might just as well be legal as illegal. Now it has been argued
that legalization will create a different social climate, a more permissive, more indulgent
climate. It is certainly conceivable, primarily for that reason, that there would be greater
initial use—the result of curiosity. But the central point is that human beings in all cultures
tend to seek out means of altering their mental state, and that although some will shop
around and lose the powers of self-discipline, most will settle down to a base rate of use,
and a much smaller rate of abuse, and those rates are pretty much what we have in the
United States right now.

Q: Then the factor of illegality, in your opinion, does not weigh heavily? But, we come to   29
the critical question, if ninety million (or more) Americans have experimented with the use
of drugs, why is drug abuse at such a (relatively) low level?

A: If you exclude tobacco, in the whole nation less than 10 percent of the adult popula-   30
tion abuses drugs. That is, 9 to 12 million adult Americans abuse drugs. That figure includes
alcohol, by the way, and the figure remains fairly constant.

Consider alcohol. In our culture alone, 70 to 80 percent of us use alcohol, and the   31
abuse rate is now estimated at 5 to 6 percent. We see at work here a major feature of the
human response to drug availability, namely, the inclination to moderation. Most people are
adjusted and are intent on living productive lives. While most of us, pursuing that goal,
enjoy the sensations of euphoria, or anxiety reduction, or (at times) social dis-inhibition or
even anaesthesia, we don't let the desire for these sensations dominate our behavior. Alcohol fills these needs for many people and its use is managed intelligently.

It is worth noting that the largest proportion of this drug is sold to the social drinker,   32
not the drunk, just as most cocaine is sold to the casual user, not the addict. Now, early exposure to alcohol is common and inevitable, and youthful drinking can be extreme. Yet studies have shown that it is difficult to determine which drunk at the college party will evolve
into a serious alcoholic. What is known is that the vast majority of early drinkers stop ex-
cessive drinking all by themselves. In fact, drug use of all types drops off radically with age.

Q: Wait a minute. Are you telling us that there is only a 10 percent chance that any user   33
will become addicted to a drug, having experimented with it?

A: The 10 percent figure includes all drugs except tobacco. The actual risk for abuse of some   34
drugs is much lower. Consider last year's National Household Survey (NHS), which was carried out by the National Institutes on Drug Abuse. It is estimated that some 21 million people tried cocaine in 1988. But according to the NHS only three million defined themselves as
having used the drug at least once during the month preceding their interview. Most of the
three million were casual users. Now think about it. *All* the cocaine users make up 2 percent
of the adult population, and the addicts make up less than one-quarter of 1 percent of the total
population. These are the government's own figures. Does that sound like an epidemic to you?

Q: But surely an epidemic has to do with the rate at which an undesirable occurrence is   35
increasing. How many more cocaine users were there than the year before? Or the year before that?

36   **A:**   The real question is whether or not more and more Americans are becoming addicted to something. Is the rate of addiction to psychoactive substances going up? The answer to that is a flat no. Are there fads during which one drug becomes more popular than another as the drug of abuse? Sure. But, when one drug goes up in consumption, others go down. Heroin use is down, and so is marijuana use. That is why the opiate and marijuana pushers are trying to improve their purity—so they can grab back some of their market share, which apparently they have done for heroin in New York City.

37   But, having said that, you should know that the actual use of cocaine and all other illicit drugs is on the decline, according to the NHS. The just-published National High School Survey carried out by the University of Michigan reports that the same is true among high-school students. Crack is used at such a low rate throughout the country that its use can hardly be measured in most areas.

38   **Q:**   Well, if a low addiction rate is the rule, how do we come to terms with the assertion, which has been made in reputable circles, that over 40 percent of Americans fighting in Vietnam were using heroin and 80 percent marijuana?

39   **A:**   Stressful situations provoke a greater use of drugs. Vietnam was one of them. But what happens when the soldiers come home?

40   That point was examined in a large study by Dr. Lee Robins at Washington University. During the Vietnam War, President Nixon ordered a study on the returning vets who seemed to have a drug problem. (Nixon didn't know what he was looking for, but he was getting a lot of flak on the point that the war was producing a generation of addicts.) Dr. Robins chose to study those soldiers returning to the United States in 1971. Of the 13,760 Army enlisted men who returned and were included in her sample, 1,400 had a positive urine test for drugs (narcotics, amphetamines, or barbiturates). She was able to re-test 495 men from this sample a few months later. The results were crystal clear: Only 8 percent of the men who had been drug positive in their first urine tests remained so. In short, over 90 percent of them, now that they were back home, walked away from drug use. And all of them knew how to get hold of drugs, if they had wanted them. Incidentally, Dr. Robins did a follow-up study a couple of years later on the same soldiers. She reported there had not been an increase in drug use.

41   **Q:**   Aha! You are saying that under special circumstances, the use of drugs increases. Well, granted there was stress in Vietnam. Isn't there stress also in American ghettos?

42   **A:**   Floyd Bloom of the Scripps Medical Institute—one of the foremost brain scientists in the country—has posited that most psychoactive drugs work on the brain's reward systems. There is good neurobiologic research to support this idea. It is an idea that can easily be understood and applied to everyday life.

43   What it tells you is that some people want artificial ways of getting their kicks out of life, but also that some people need those artificial crutches. If you live in poverty and frustration, and see few rewards available to you, you are likelier than your better-satisfied counterpart to seek the escape of drugs, although the higher rate of consumption does not result in a higher rate of addiction. Virtually every study finds this to be the case with one possibly interesting twist. A recent Department of Defense study showed that drug use in the military was lower for blacks than for whites, the reverse of civilian life. (It is generally

agreed that the military is the only institution in our country that is successfully integrated.) In short, environmental factors play an important role in the incidence of drug use.

Q: So you are saying that there are social circumstances that will raise the rate of consumption, but that raising the rate of consumption doesn't in fact raise the rate of addiction. In other words, if 50 percent of the troops in Vietnam had been using crack, this would not have affected the rate at which, on returning to the United States, they became addicted. They would have kicked the habit on reaching home?   44

A: That's the idea. Drug consumption can go up in a particular population, fueled by stress, but the rate of addiction doesn't go up no matter what the degree of stress. Most people can walk away from high drug use if their lives become more normal. Of course, the stress of the ghetto isn't the only situation that fuels high drug consumption. Plenty of affluent people who for some reason or another do not find their lives rewarding also escape into drugs.   45

Q: If it is true, then, that only a small percentage of those who take crack will end up addicted, and that that is no different from the small percentage who, taking one beer every Saturday night, will become alcoholics, what is the correct way in which to describe the relative intensity of the addictive element in a particular drug?   46

A: That is an interesting question and one that can't satisfactorily be answered until much more research is done. There are conundrums. Again, it is estimated that 21 million people tried cocaine in 1988. Yet, of those, only 3 million currently use it, and only a small percentage are addicted. As for crack, it is estimated that 2.5 million have used it, while only a half million say they still do, and *that* figure includes the addicted and the casual user. Some reports claim that as many as one half of crack users are addicted. As I have said, crack is cheap, and for that reason may be especially attractive to the poor. That is a non-pharmacological, non-biological factor, the weight of which we have not come to any conclusions about. We don't even have reliable data to tell us that crack creates a greater rate of addiction than, say, cocaine. My own guess is it doesn't. Remember that the drug acts on the same brain systems that cocaine and amphetamines do.   47

What is needed, in order to answer your question, is a science of comparative pharmacology where the various psychoactive drugs could be compared against some kind of common physiological/psychological measure. Doing that would be difficult, which is one of the reasons why those data don't exist. How do you capture fluctuating moods and motivations? There are times when the smallest dose of a drug can have a sublime effect on someone, while at another time it takes ten times the dose to have any noticeable effect. These are tough problems to quantify and study, even in the laboratory.   48

Q: To what extent is the addictive factor affected by education? Here is what I mean by this: Taking a drug, say heroin or cocaine or crack—or, for that matter, alcohol—is a form of Russian roulette, using a ten-cartridge revolver. Now, presumably, an educated person, concerned for his livelihood, wouldn't take a revolver with nine empty cartridges and one full cartridge, aim it at his head, and pull the trigger. But granted, decisions of that kind are based on ratiocinative skills. And we have to assume these skills don't exist even among college students. If they did, there would be no drinking in college, let alone drug taking. Comments?   49

50   **A:**   Most people perceive themselves as in control of their destiny. They do not think the initial exposure will ruin their lives, because of their perceived self-control, and they are right. Take the most difficult case, tobacco—the most highly addictive substance around. In a now classic study, Stanley Schachter of Columbia University formally surveyed his highly educated colleagues at Columbia. At the same time, he polled the working residents of Amagansett, a community on Long Island where he summered. He first determined who were ongoing smokers, and who had been smokers. He took into account how long they had smoked, what they had smoked, and all other variables he could think of.

51   It wasn't long before the picture began to crystallize. Inform a normally intelligent group of people about the tangible hazards of using a particular substance and the vast majority of them simply stop. It wasn't easy for some, but in general they stopped, and they didn't need treatment programs, support programs, and all the rest. Dr. Schachter concluded, after this study, that it is only the thorny cases that show up at the treatment centers, people who have developed a true addiction. For those people, psychological prophylactics, including education, are of little or no value. Yet it is these people that are held up as examples of what happens when one uses drugs. This is misleading. It creates an unworkable framework for thinking about the problem. Most people can voluntarily stop using a psychoactive substance, and those people who do continue to use it can moderate their intake to reduce the possibility of health hazards. This is true, as I say, for most substances, but I repeat, less true for tobacco because of its distinctively addictive nature. The people who unwisely continue to use tobacco tend to smoke themselves into major illness even though they are amply warned that this is likely to happen.

52   **Q:**   So no matter how widely you spread the message, it is in fact going to be ignored, both by PhDs and by illiterates?

53   **A:**   If they are real abusers, yes. That is the reason for the high recidivism rate among graduates of drug treatment centers. Here we are talking about the true addicts. Education appears not to help the recalcitrant abusers, who are the ones that keep showing up at health centers.

54   Yet, manifestly, education contributes to keeping the abuse rate as low as it is. I think the message gets to the ghetto, but where there are other problems—the need for an artificial reward—drugs are going to be taken by many people because the excruciating pain of a current condition overrides long-term reason. In short, the ghetto citizen or the psychologically isolated person might well decide that the probability of living a better life is low, so grab some rewards while you can.

55   **Q:**   At what level of intelligence is a potential drug user influenced to take a less dangerous, rather than a more dangerous, drug? I mean, if it were known to all PhDs that crack was more dangerous than marijuana, that the small percentage who became addicted to crack would suffer greater biological change from it, up to and including death, in contrast to comparatively lenient sentences from addiction to marijuana, what percentage of PhDs would be influenced to stay away from the hard stuff, compared to illiterate 17-year-old ghetto dwellers?

56   **A:**   Again, this is difficult to answer because the educational message interacts with innumerable social problems. For example, drug abuse is three times greater among the unemployed. Someone who is unemployed on Monday might be re-employed on Friday, and

this may stop, or reduce, his use of drugs. Gainful employment has a bigger effect in a case like this than education does. But in general, education plays a big role, and this is established. Remember, we are a health-oriented society, and we do care about our bodies and minds, by and large. Marijuana is a mild drug, compared to crack, for a variety of biological and psychological reasons. There are studies showing that casual-to-moderate cocaine users will not go the crack route because of fear of a greater chance of addiction or of an immediate physiological crisis. A recent issue of the *New England Journal of Medicine* reports that cocaine use contributes to heart disease in a rather muted way. However, crack may have a far greater impact and be responsible for a much more serious increase in drug-related heart failures. Does that kind of thing influence a kid in the ghetto? I think the message does get there. It certainly gets to Park Avenue first, however.

Q:　In that case, education, even in the popular media, is likely to influence primarily the　57
educated classes. That has to mean that the uneducated class will suffer more addiction than the educated class.

A:　Well, again, people in the lowest socio-economic status will continue to consume more　58
drugs, but that doesn't change the addiction rate. Still, legalization shouldn't change the current figures, since drugs are literally available everywhere in the ghetto. They are also available on every college campus. They are available in prisons! I suppose if one wants to conjure up fresh problems brought on by legalization, they will center on the folks living on Park Avenue, where drugs are less easily secured, not the ghetto. Legalization of drugs would reduce crime in the ghetto, and much that is positive would follow.

Q:　If the number of addicts would be increased by decriminalization, is the trade-off　59
worth it? Is it wise to decriminalize, even if by doing so: we a) abort the $150-billion per-year drug-crime business; b) release $10 billion in federal money now going to the pursuit of drug merchants; c) end the corruption of government subsidized by drug dealers; and d) come upon a huge sum of money available to give treatment to addicts? Is this, in your judgment, a moral recommendation to make, given our knowledge of the psychological problems we are talking about?

A:　Are you asking me to commit myself at this point to the question of whether that trade-　60
off is wise?

Q:　Well, no, not quite yet. Let me describe a situation, the concrete situation I spoke of　61
a while ago, and ask you to comment on it in the light of the questions put to you above.

Suppose that drugs were made available. All of them, legally, in a Federal Drugstore.　62
But above each of the common drugs—crack, cocaine, heroin, hash, marijuana, amphetamines, LSD, etc.—there was a graphic description of what addiction to that drug would do to you. Suppose a situation in which, for instance, over the punch bowl at the far left of the counter that contained crack were written: "This drug will create an appetite to take another dose. That appetite is very strong. If you become an addict, you will want to take as many as twenty of these every day, and the results of doing so will be serious for your health. With overuse, you may suffer a heart attack and die."

By contrast, let's say that the placard directly above the punch bowl that houses mari-　63
juana were to say: "Not addictive, but chronic use may lead to cancer, chromosome damage, birth deformities in future children, memory loss, paranoia, and depression." Is there

any reason to suppose that this kind of merchandising will have the effect of propelling the majority of consumers either to taking no drugs at all, or to taking the less dangerous drugs? For example, marijuana over, say, cocaine?

64   **A:**   For those not intent on self-abuse, yes. After all, as I said, we are a health-oriented society. Hard-liquor sales are down, and, for that matter, so are wine sales. You can now buy low-cholesterol popcorn and so on. We want our kicks, but within a knowledgeable health-safety framework. On the other hand, for those intent on self-abuse, drug consumption will continue. Self-abuse occurs at all levels of our society, not only in the ghetto. Remember, most people in America are not living in ghettos, and a certain percentage of them are addicted to something. I think we as a society ought to focus attention on addiction groups and see if some factors can be isolated that might help out. Currently, drug treatment programs, which should more accurately be called drug management programs, need a lot of help. Treatment is not a reality for most of these centers. As I have already indicated, the recidivism rate is high at drug centers and this in part reflects the fact the drug centers get only the tough cases, the hard-core abusers that can not stop abuse themselves. Much more research is key.

65   **Q:**   All right then, presumably the price of the drugs available for sale at the Federal Drugstore will be low enough to discourage black-market activity. Would such Federal Drugstores eliminate black-market activity altogether?

66   **A:**   No, of course not. The criminal mind is ever inventive. Special services will be supplied, like home-delivery services, and the inevitable (and positively illegal) pushing to children. There will be new drugs dreamed up, and they will have their own market until they are isolated, and then will be sold legally. But, the vast majority of the crime network ought to crumble. The importance of that cannot be underestimated.

67   **Q:**   So, the Federal Drugstores would obviously charge the cost of providing the drugs and the overhead of retailing them. Let's suppose that they could then double the acquisition cost without activating black-market competition; if double proved too much, they would simply lower the price. Whatever; profits would go to the treatment centers and toward more advertising of the dangers of drug abuse, and indeed of drug consumption. Do you have any difficulty with that?

68   **A:**   No, but I would caution against setting up a plan that found the government playing the role of pusher. If the drug-treatment centers were dependent on income from the Drugstore, the bureaucrats running the store might be tempted to increase profits. Once Congress comes around to thoughtfully considering legalization, the actual mechanisms will have to be carefully thought out.

69   **Q:**   What would be your prediction, as a scientist, of what the advent of the Federal Drugstore, combined with a program of intensified education, would accomplish in the next ten years?

70   **A:**   Drug-consumption rates will bounce around, related as they are to environmental factors, fads, and a host of other factors. Drug-abuse rates will not change much, if at all. Yet many of the negative social consequences of keeping drugs illegal will be neutralized. The health costs of drug abuse will always be with us. We should try to focus on those problems with more serious neurobiologic and neurobehavioral research and help where we can to reduce the percentage that fall victim. I am an experimental scientist, and like most people can see that the present system doesn't work. We need to try another approach. If for whatever reason, legalization doesn't improve the situation, it would take five minutes to reverse it.

Biting the Bullet: The Case for Legalizing Drugs

Walter Wink

The drug war is over. We lost it long before the latest declaration of war by President Bush. Whatever the other factors, we lost primarily for spiritual reasons. We merely repeated the mistake of Prohibition: the harder we tried to stamp out the evil, the more lucrative we made it. We should know that prohibition doesn't work. Forcible resistance to evil simply makes it more profitable.

Our attempts to stamp out drugs violate a fundamental principle that Jesus articulated in the Sermon on the Mount: "Resist not evil." The Greek term translated "resist" is *antistenai.* When it is used by the Greek Old Testament or by the first-century Jewish historian Josephus, however, the word is usually translated, "to be engaged in a revolt, rebellion, riot, insurrection." It is virtually a synonym for war. It means to stand up against an enemy and fight. So Jesus' words should be translated, "Do not resist evil by violent means. Do not fight evil with evil. Do not mirror evil, do not let evil set the terms of your response." Applied to the drug issue, this means, "Do not resist drugs by violent methods."

When we oppose evil with the same weapons that evil employs, we commit the same atrocities, violate the same civil liberties and break the same laws as do those whom we oppose. We become what we hate. Evil makes us over into its mimetic double. If one side prevails, the evil continues by virtue of having been established through the means used. More often, however, both sides grow, fed by their mutual resistance, as in the arms race, the Vietnam war, the Salvadoran civil war and Lebanon. This principle of mimetic opposition is illustrated abundantly in the drug war.

Bush's drug-war strategy has three elements. First, it requires cutting off the drug source in Colombia, Peru and Bolivia. Yet this appears to be impossible. Already we see signs that Colombia is collapsing into civil war. Officials and journalists are being gunned down on the streets, civilian homes are being raided and seized, civilian government is increasingly being taken over by the military—and so far the drug lords have only engaged in selective terrorism.

Moreover, the Colombian army has seldom confronted the 140 paramilitary private armies of the drug lords, or raided their training bases. For in certain areas of the country the military has formed a marriage of convenience with drug traffickers and landowners in a common front against a 30-year-old leftist guerrilla insurgency. With an income in the billions of dollars, drug leaders are able to buy generals, judges and police. In one week last fall, the Colombian national police fired 2,075 officers for having links with the cartels. The drug lords have also bought limited public acceptance by sponsoring the national soccer league, diversifying into legitimate businesses, supporting charities and offering to pay off the government's $10 billion external debt.

To test public reaction, the Bush administration may talk about sending in U.S. troops. But even if only military advisers are sent, they will soon discover in the field what our advisers found in Vietnam: an army not really committed to a fight. And even if those producing countries could be rid of coca tomorrow, production would simply be moved somewhere else, and the eradication effort would have to be started all over again in Southeast Asia, Turkey, Afghanistan and other countries far less likely to let us call the shots. So far, cocaine cultivation uses only 700 square miles of the 2.5 million square miles suitable for its growth in South America. There is simply no way the U.S. can police so vast an area.

7   Second, the Bush strategy calls for interdicting cocaine at our borders. We have been trying that for years, and it simply cannot be done short of militarizing the borders. According to a Government Accounting Office study, the U.S. Air Force spent $3.3 million on drug interdiction, using sophisticated AWACS surveillance planes over a 15-month period ending in 1987. The grand total of drug seizures from that effort was eight. During the same period, the combined efforts of the U.S. Coast Guard and Navy, sailing for 2,512 ship days at a cost of $40 million, resulted in the seizure of a mere 20 drug-carrying vessels. Drugs are easy to smuggle. The entire country's current annual import of cocaine would fit into a single C-5A cargo plane.

8   Even when interdiction works, it does nothing to reduce drug availability. On September 29, 1989, 21.4 tons of cocaine was seized in Los Angeles; within a week nine tons was taken in Harlingen, Texas, and five more at sea off Mexico's Yucatan Peninsula. The almost 36 tons netted in the three seizures was valued at $11 billion. Yet ten days later undercover agents were able to buy cocaine in bulk at the same price as before the seizures.

9   William Bennett, director of the National Office of Drug Control Policy, hopes that interdiction will raise drug prices. In fact, however, cocaine has become more available, while its wholesale price has dropped by 80 percent during the past decade. Increased prices would not deter addicts anyway; it would simply increase their rate of criminal acts. In Dade County, Florida, a mere 254 young addicts accounted for 223,000 crimes in a single year—almost 2.5 per youth per day. Multiply that by a nation and you see why the drug war was lost before it began.

10   As Senator John Kerry's subcommittee on narcotics reported in December 1988, increased cooperation with foreign governments has neither cut the amount of cocaine entering the U.S. nor led to the destruction of the major smuggling organizations. Fifteen percent of the drugs entering this country are being confiscated, but "for the drug cartels, whose production capacities stagger the imagination, a 15 percent loss rate is more than acceptable."

11   Third, the Bush plan calls for arresting drug dealers and casual users. There are already 750,000 drug arrests per year, and the current prison population is overtaxing facilities. At an average of $51,000 per inmate per year, just to incarcerate the 750,000 arrested annually would cost $38 billion. There are 35 to 40 million Americans who have used illegal drugs within the past year. To jail all users would run a tidy $1.785 trillion.

12   As for using the death penalty for deterrence, it seems unlikely that this country is ready to execute drug dealers by the hundreds of thousands. If so many millions are flouting the law, Prohibition style, is there really a political will for harsh enforcement? And how sincere is our antidrug effort going to be when the financial community realizes that the cash flow from the drug trade is the only thing preventing a default by some of the heavily indebted Latin American nations or major money-laundering banks? Cocaine trade brings Bolivia's economy about $600 million per year, a figure equal to the country's total legal ex-

port income. Revenues from drug trafficking in Miami are greater than those from tourism, exports, health care and all other legitimate businesses combined.

It is not drugs but rather drug laws that have made drug dealing profitable. Drug laws   13
have also fostered drug-related murders and an estimated 40 percent of all property crime in the U.S. Ethan A. Nadelmann, whose article "Drug Prohibition in the United States" in the September 1, 1989, issue of *Science* has been a major catalyst for public discussion of legalization, argues that "the greatest beneficiaries of the drug laws are organized and unorganized drug traffickers. The criminalization of the drug market effectively imposes a de facto value-added tax that is enforced and occasionally augmented by the law enforcement establishment and collected by the drug traffickers." Rather than collecting taxes on the sale of drugs, governments at all levels expend billions of dollars in what amounts to a subsidy of organized criminals.

The war on drugs creates casualties beyond those arrested. There are those killed in   14
fights over turf, innocents caught in cross fire, citizens terrified of city streets, escalating robberies, children fed free crack to get them addicted and then enlisted as runners and dealers, mothers so crazed for a fix that they abandon their babies, prostitute themselves and their daughters, and addict their unborn. Much of that, too, is the result of the drug laws. Cocaine, after all, has been around a long time and was once sold over the counter in tablet form and consumed in *Coca*-Cola. What makes it so irresistible today is its lucrativeness. And it is lucrative only because it is illegal.

The media usually portray cocaine and crack use as a black ghetto phenomenon. This   15
is a racist caricature. The *New York Times* reported on October 1, 1989, that there are more crack addicts among the white middle and upper class than any other segment of the population and far more such occasional cocaine users. The typical user is a single white male 20 to 40 years old who generally obtains his drugs from black dealers. The white demand makes the drugs flow. Americans consume 60 percent of the world's illegal drugs—too profitable a market for dealers to ignore.

In the drug war, we are blindly fighting what we have become as a nation. Some ob-   16
servers say that drugs are the ultimate consumer product for people who want to feel good now without benefit of hard work, social interaction, or making a productive contribution to society. Drug dealers are living out the rags-to-riches American dream as private entrepreneurs trying desperately to become upwardly mobile. That is why we cannot win the war on drugs. We Americans are the enemy, and we cannot face that fact. So we launch a half-hearted, half-funded, half-baked war against a menace that only mirrors what we have ourselves become as a nation.

The uproar about drugs is itself odd. In 1987, according to the Kerry subcommittee,   17
there were 1,400 deaths from cocaine; in 1988, that figure had increased to 3,308. Deaths from *all* forms of illegal drugs total under 6,000. By contrast, 320,000 to 390,000 people die prematurely each year from tobacco and 100,000 to 200,000 from misuse of alcohol. Alcohol is associated with 40 percent of all suicide attempts, 40 percent of all traffic deaths, 54 percent of all violent crimes and 10 percent of all work-related injuries.

18   None of the illegal drugs are as lethal as tobacco or alcohol. If anyone has ever died as a direct result of a marijuana overdose, no one seems to know about it. Many people can be addicted to heroin for most of their lives without serious consequences. Cocaine in powder form is not as addictive as nicotine; Nadelmann points out that only 3 percent of those who try it become addicted. Crack is terribly addictive, but its use is a direct consequence of the high cost of powdered cocaine. Crack was a cheap ghetto alternative, and its spread to the middle and upper classes has in part been a function of its low price. Severely addicted humans may in some ways resemble those experimental monkeys who will starve themselves to death if supplied with unlimited cocaine, but the vast majority of users are not in such danger (and alcoholic humans also will drink themselves to death).

19   We must be honest about these facts, because much of the hysteria about illegal drugs has been based on misinformation. All addiction is a serious matter, and the churches are right to be concerned about the human costs. But many of these costs are a consequence of a wrong-headed approach to eradication. Our tolerance of the real killer drugs and our abhorrence of the drugs which are far less lethal is hypocritical, or at best a selective moralism reflecting fashions of indignation.

20   Drug addiction is singled out as evil, yet we are a society of addicts living in an addictive society. We project on the black drug subculture profound anxieties about our own addictions (to wealth, power, sex, food, work, religion, alcohol and tobacco) and attack addiction in others without having to gain insight about ourselves. New York City Councilman Wendell Foster illustrated this scapegoating attitude when he suggested chaining addicts to trees so people could spit on them.

21   I'm not advocating giving up the war on drugs because we cannot win. I am saying that we cannot win as long as we let drugs dictate the means we use to oppose them. The only way to win is to ruin the world market price of drugs by legalizing them. When drug prices plummet, drug profits will collapse—and with them, the drug empire.

22   Some people have called for decriminalization, but they probably mean legalization. Decriminalization would mean no more laws regulating drugs, no governmental restraints on sales to minors, no quality controls to curtail overdose and no prosecution of the inevitable bootleggers. Legalization, however, means that the government would maintain regulatory control over drug sales, possibly through state clinics or stores. Advertising would be strictly prohibited, selling drugs to children would continue to be a criminal offense, and other evasions of government regulation would be prosecuted. Driving, flying or piloting a vessel under the influence would still be punished. Taxes on drugs would pay for enforcement, education, rehabilitation and research (Nadelmann estimates a net benefit of at least $10 billion from reduced expenditures on enforcement and new tax revenues). Street users would be picked up and taken to hospitals, like drunks, instead of arrested.

23   Legalization would lead to an immediate decrease in murders, burglaries and robberies, paralleling the end of alcohol prohibition in 1933. Cheap drugs would mean that most addicts would not be driven to crime to support their habit, and that drug lords would no longer have a turf to fight over. Legalization would be a blow to South American peasants, who would need support in switching back to less lucrative crops, but that would be less devastating than destruction of their crops altogether by aerial spraying or

biological warfare. Legalization would enable countries like Peru to regularize the cocaine sector and absorb its money-making capacity in the taxable, legal, unionized economic world. Legalization would be a blow to ghetto dealers, who would be deprived of their ticket to riches. It would remove glamorous, Al Capone–type traffickers who are role models for the young, and it would destroy the "cool" status of drug use. It would cancel the corrupting role of the drug cartels in South American politics, a powerful incentive to corruption at all levels of our own government and a dangerous threat to our civil liberties through mistaken enforcement and property confiscation. It would free law-enforcement agencies to focus on other crimes and reduce the strain on the court and prison systems. It would nip in the bud a multibillion-dollar bureaucracy whose prosperity depends on *not* solving the drug probe. It would remove a major cause of public cynicism about obeying the laws of the land.

Legalization would also free up money wasted on interdiction of supplies that are needed desperately for treatment, education and research. Clinics in New York have room for only 48,000 of the state's estimated half-million addicts. Only $700 million has been earmarked by the Bush administration for treatment, out of a total expenditure of $8 billion for the drug war. Yet nationally, approximately 90 percent of the addicts who apply to drug treatment and rehabilitation centers are turned away for lack of space, resources and personnel. For those who do persist, the waiting period is six to 18 months. Even then, one-third to one-half of drug abusers turned away do reapply after waiting the extended time.   24

The worst prospect of legalization is that it might lead to a short-term increase in the use of drugs, due to availability, lower prices and the sudden freedom from prosecution. The repeal of Prohibition had that result. Drugs cheap enough to destroy their profitability would also be in the range of any child's allowance, just like beer and cigarettes. Cocaine is easily concealable and its effects less overt than alcohol. The possibility of increased teenage use is admittedly frightening.   25

On the other hand, ending the drug war would free drug control officers to concentrate on protecting children from exploitation, and here stiff penalties would continue to be in effect. The alarmist prediction that cheap available drugs could lead to an addiction rate of 75 percent of regular users simply ignores the fact that 35 to 40 million Americans are already using some drugs and that only 3 percent become addicts. Most people have strong reasons *not* to become addicts. A major educational program would need to be in effect well before drug legalization took effect.   26

Fighting the drug war may appear to hold the high moral ground, but this is only an illusion. And while some have argued that legalization would place the state's moral imprimatur on drugs, we have already legalized the most lethal drugs—and no one argues that this constitutes governmental endorsement. But legalizing would indeed imply that drugs are no longer being satanized like "demon rum." It's time we bit the bullet. Addicts will be healed by care and compassion, not condemnation. Dealers will be cured by a ruined world drug market, not by enforcement that simply escalates the profitability of drugs. Legalization offers a nonviolent, nonreactive, creative alternative that will let the drug menace collapse of its own deadly weight.   27

The Economics of Legalizing Drugs

Richard J. Dennis

1   Last year federal agents in southern California broke the six-dollar lock on a warehouse and discovered twenty tons of cocaine. The raid was reported to be the largest seizure of illegal narcotics ever. Politicians and law-enforcement officials heralded it as proof not only of the severity of our drug problem but also of the success of our interdiction efforts, and the need for more of the same. However, in reality the California raid was evidence of nothing but the futility and irrationality of our current approach to illegal drugs. It is questionable whether the raid prevented a single person from buying cocaine. Addicts were not driven to seek treatment. No drug lord or street dealer was put out of business. The event had no perceptible impact on the public's attitude toward drug use. People who wanted cocaine still wanted it—and got it.

2   If the raid had any effect at all, it was perverse. The street price of cocaine in southern California probably rose temporarily, further enriching the criminal network now terrorizing the nation's inner cities. William Bennett, the director of national drug-control policy, and his fellow moral authoritarians were offered another opportunity to alarm an already overwrought public with a fresh gust of rhetoric. New support was given to a Bush Administration plan that is meant to reduce supply but in fact guarantees more money to foreign drug lords, who will soon become the richest private individuals in history.

3   Indeed, Americans have grown so hysterical about the drug problem that few public figures dare appear soft on drugs or say anything dispassionate about the situation. In a 1989 poll 54 percent of Americans cited drugs as the nation's greatest threat. Four percent named unemployment. It is time, long past time, to take a clear-eyed look at illegal drugs and ask what government and law enforcement can really be expected to do.

4   Drug illegality has the same effect as a regressive tax: its chief aim is to save relatively wealthy potential users of drugs like marijuana and cocaine from self-destruction, at tremendous cost to the residents of inner cities. For this reason alone, people interested in policies that help America's poor should embrace drug legalization. It would dethrone drug dealers in the ghettos and release inner-city residents from their status as hostages.

5   Once the drug war is considered in rational terms, the solution becomes obvious: declare peace. Legalize the stuff. Tax it and regulate its distribution, as liquor is now taxed and regulated. Educate those who will listen. Help those who need help.

6   Arguments for the benefits of drug legalization have appeared frequently in the press, most of them making the point that crime and other social hazards might be reduced as a result. This article presents an economic analysis of the benefits of legalizing drugs.

SOME WRONG WAYS TO DISCUSS THE DRUG PROBLEM

7   In order to make any sort of sane argument about drugs, of course, we have to decide what the problem is. That isn't as simple as it might seem, Bennett's thirty-second sound bites notwithstanding. It's easier to say what the drug problem is not.

8   The drug problem is not a moral issue. There's a streak of puritanism in the national soul, true, but most Americans are not morally opposed to substances that alter one's mind

and mood. That issue was resolved in 1933, with the repeal of Prohibition. There is no question that drugs used to excess are harmful; so is alcohol. Americans seem to have no moral difficulty with the notion that adults should be allowed to use alcohol as they see fit, as long as others are not harmed.

The drug problem is not the country's most important health issue. The use of heroin   9
and cocaine can result in addiction and death; so can the use of alcohol and tobacco. In fact, some researchers estimate the yearly per capita mortality rate of tobacco among smokers at more than a hundred times that of cocaine among cocaine users. If the drug-policy director is worried about the effect on public health of substance abuse, he should spend most of his time talking about cigarettes and whiskey.

The drug problem is not entirely a societal issue—at least not in the sense that it is   10
portrayed as one by politicians and the media. Drug dealing is a chance for people without legitimate opportunity. The problem of the underclass will never be solved by attacking it with force of arms.

So what is the problem? The heart of it is money. What most Americans want is less   11
crime and less profit for inner-city thugs and Colombian drug lords. Less self-destruction by drug users would be nice, but what people increasingly demand is an end to the foreign and domestic terrorism—financed by vast amounts of our own money—associated with the illegal drug trade.

This, as it happens, is a problem that can be solved in quick and pragmatic fashion, by   12
legalizing the sale of most drugs to adults. Virtually overnight crime and corruption would be reduced. The drug cartels would be shattered. Public resources could be diverted to meaningful education and treatment programs.

The alternative—driving up drug prices and increasing public costs with an accelerated   13
drug war—inevitably will fail to solve anything. Instead of making holy war on the drug barons, the President's plan subsidizes them.

Laws protecting children should obviously be retained. Some might question the ef-   14
fectiveness of combining legal drug use by adults with harsh penalties for the sale of drugs to minors. But effective statutory-rape laws demonstrate that society can maintain a distinction between the behavior of adults and that of minors when it truly believes such a distinction is warranted.

Legalization would require us to make some critical distinctions among drugs and drug   15
users, of course. The Administration's plan approaches the drug problem as a seamless whole. But in fact crack and heroin are harmful in ways that marijuana is not. This failure to distinguish among different drugs and their consequences serves only to discredit the anti-drug effort, especially among young people. It also disperses law-enforcement efforts, rendering them hopelessly ineffective. Instead of investing immense resources in a vain attempt to control the behavior of adults, we should put our money where the crisis is. Why spend anything to prosecute marijuana users in a college dormitory when the focus should be on the crack pusher in the Bronx schoolyard?

The appropriate standard in deciding if a drug should be made legal for adults ought to   16
be whether it is more likely than alcohol to cause harm to an innocent party. If not, banning it cannot be justified while alcohol remains legal. For example, a sensible legalization plan would allow users of marijuana to buy it legally. Small dealers could sell it legally but would

be regulated, as beer dealers are now in states where beer is sold in grocery stores. Their suppliers would be licensed and regulated. Selling marijuana to minors would be criminal.

17   Users of cocaine should be able to buy it through centers akin to state liquor stores. It is critical to remove the black-market profit from cocaine in order to destabilize organized crime and impoverish pushers. Selling cocaine to minors would be criminal, as it is now, but infractions could be better policed if effort were concentrated on them. Any black market that might remain would be in sales of crack or sales to minors, transactions that are now estimated to account for 20 percent of drug sales.

18   Cocaine runs the spectrum from coca leaf to powder to smokable crack; it's the way people take it that makes the difference. Crack's effects on individual behavior and its addictive potential place it in a category apart from other forms of cocaine. The actual degree of harm it does to those who use it is still to be discovered, but for the sake of argument let's assume that it presents a clear danger to people who come in contact with the users. A crack user, therefore, should be subject to a civil fine, and mandatory treatment after multiple violations. Small dealers should have their supplies seized and be subject to moderate punishment for repeat offenses. Major dealers, however, should be subject to the kinds of sentences that are now given. And any adult convicted of selling crack to children should face the harshest prison sentence our criminal-justice system can mete out.

19   The same rules should apply to any drug that presents a substantial threat to others.

20   A serious objection to legalizing cocaine while crack remains illegal is that cocaine could be bought, turned into crack, and sold. But those who now buy powder cocaine could take it home and make it into crack, and very few do so. Moreover, legal cocaine would most likely be consumed in different settings and under different circumstances than still-illegal crack would be. Researchers believe that more-benign settings reduce the probability of addiction. Legalization could make it less likely that cocaine users will become crack users. In addition, an effective dose of crack is already so cheap that price is not much of a deterrent to those who want to try it. No price reduction as a result of the legalization of cocaine, then, should lead to a significant increase in the number of crack users.

21   As for heroin, the advent of methadone clinics shows that society has realized that addicts require maintenance. But there is little practical difference between methadone and heroin, and methadone clinics don't get people off methadone. Heroin addicts should receive what they require, so that they don't have to steal to support their habit. This would make heroin unprofitable for its pushers. And providing addicts with access to uninfected needles would help stop the spread of AIDS and help lure them into treatment programs.

WHAT THE DRUG WAR COSTS AND WHAT WE COULD SAVE

22   The major argument against legalization, and one that deserves to be taken seriously, is a possible increase in drug use and addiction. But it can be shown that if reasonable costs are assigned to all aspects of the drug problem, the benefits of drug peace would be large enough to offset even a doubling in the number of addicts.

23   Any numerical cost-benefit analysis of drug legalization versus the current drug war rests on assumptions that are difficult to substantiate. The figures for the costs of drug use must be estimates, and so the following analysis is by necessity illustrative rather than de-

finitive. But the numbers used in the analysis below are at least of the right magnitude; most are based on government data. These assumptions, moreover, give the benefit of the doubt to the drug warriors and shortchange proponents of drug legalization.

The statistical assumptions that form the basis of this cost-benefit analysis are as follows: 24

The social cost of all drug use at all levels can be estimated by assuming that America   25
now has two million illicit-drug addicts. Slightly more than one million addicts use cocaine (including crack) about four times a week; 500,000 addicts use heroin at about the same rate. This means that there are about 1.5 million hardcore addicts. Some experts argue that the figures for addiction should be higher. An estimate of the social cost of drug use should also take into account casual use, even if the social cost of it is arguable; 10 million people, at most, use cocaine and other dangerous drugs monthly. To ensure a fair estimate of social cost, let's assume that America now has two million drug addicts.

Legalization would result in an immediate and permanent 25 percent increase in the   26
number of addicts and the costs associated with them. This projection is derived by esti-mating the number of people who would try hard drugs if they were legalized and then es-timating how many of them would end up addicted. In past years—during a time when marijuana was more or less decriminalized—approximately 60 million Americans tried marijuana and almost 30 million tried cocaine, America's most popular hard drug. (It is fair to assume that nearly all of those who tried cocaine also tried marijuana and that those who haven't tried marijuana in the past twenty-five years will not decide to try decriminalized cocaine.) This leaves 30 million people who have tried marijuana but not cocaine, and who might be at risk to try legal, inexpensive cocaine.

In a 1985 survey of people who voluntarily stopped using cocaine, 21 percent claimed   27
they did so because they feared for their health, 12 percent because they were pressured by friends and family, and 12 percent because the drug was too expensive. The reasons of the other half of those surveyed were unspecified, but for the purpose of this exercise we will as-sume that they stopped for the same reasons in the same proportions as the other respondents. (Interestingly, the survey did not mention users who said they had stopped because cocaine is illegal or out of fear of law enforcement.) It seems reasonable to assume that many people would decide not to use legalized drugs for the same reasons that these experimenters quit. Therefore, of the 30 million people estimated to be at risk of trying legal cocaine, only about a quarter might actually try it—the quarter that is price-sensitive, because the price of cocaine, once the drug was legalized, would plummet. This leaves us with approximately 7.5 million new cocaine users. How many of them could we expect to become cocaine addicts? The esti-mate that there are now one million cocaine addicts suggests a one-in-thirty chance of addic-tion through experimentation. Thus from the 7.5 million new users we could expect about 250,000 new addicts, or an increase of 25 percent over the number of cocaine addicts that we now have. We can assume about the same increase in the number of users of other hard drugs.

Those who argue that wide availability must mean significantly higher usage overlook   28
the fact that there is no economic incentive for dealers to push dirt-cheap drugs. Legaliza-tion might thus lead to less rather than more drug use, particularly by children and teenagers. Also, the public evinces little interest in trying legalized drugs. Last year, at the

direction of the author, the polling firm Targeting Systems Inc., in Arlington, Virginia, asked a nationwide sample of 600 adults, "If cocaine were legalized, would you personally consider purchasing it or not?" Only one percent said they would.

29   *The drug war will result in a 25 percent decrease in drug use.* That's the midpoint in William Bennett's ten-year plan to cut drug use by 50 percent by the year 2000. Since this figure is based on Bennett's official prediction, we might expect it to be highly optimistic. But to demonstrate the enormous benefits of legalization, let's accept his rosy scenario.

30   *The drug war will cost government at all levels $30 billion a year.* Keeping drugs illegal costs state and local law-enforcement agencies approximately $10 billion a year—a conservative figure derived from the costs of arresting, prosecuting, and imprisoning several hundred thousand people a year for drug violations. Bennett recently implied before Congress that state governments will need to spend as much as $10 billion in new money when he was asked about what it will cost to keep in prison a higher proportion of the country's 20 million or more users of hard and soft drugs. The drug war will also cost the federal government about $10 billion a year, mostly in law enforcement—about what Congress has agreed to spend in the next fiscal year.

31   If marijuana and cocaine were legalized and crack and all drugs for children remained illegal, about 80 percent of current illegal drug use would become legal. This would permit savings of 80 percent—or $8 billion—of the current costs of state and local law enforcement. By rolling back the war on drugs, we could save up to all $20 billion of projected new federal and state expenditures.

32   *The current dollar volume of the drug trade is approximately $100 billion a year.* If Bennett's prediction is accurate and drug consumption is cut by half over the next ten years, Colombian drug lords will still receive, on average, $3.75 billion a year, assuming that they net five percent of gross receipts—a conservative estimate. The money reaped by drug lords can be used for weapons, planes, and bombs, which could necessitate U.S. expenditures of at least one dollar to combat every dollar of drug profits if a drug war turned into real fighting.

33   If legalized, taxed drugs were sold for a seventh or an eighth of their current price—a level low enough for illegal dealing to be financially unattractive—the taxes could bring in at least $10 billion at the current level of usage.

34   *The most important—and most loosely defined—variable is the social cost of drug use.* The term "social cost" is used indiscriminately. A narrow definition includes only health costs and taxes lost to the government through loss of income, and a broad definition counts other factors, such as the loss of personal income itself and the value of stolen property associated with drug use. The Alcohol, Drug Abuse, and Mental Health Administration has estimated that drug and alcohol abuse cost the nation as much as $175 billion a year, of which alcohol abuse alone accounts for at least $115 billion. These figures probably include costs not really related to drug use, as a result of the Administration's zeal to dramatize the drug crisis. We will assume that $50 billion a year is a realistic estimate of the share for drug use.

Once these usually qualitative factors have been assigned numbers, it is possible to es- 35
timate how much the drug war costs in an average year and how much drug peace might
save us. Again, this assumes that 25 percent fewer people in a mid-point year will use drugs
owing to a successful drug war and 25 percent more people will use drugs with the establishment of drug peace.

If we choose drug peace as opposed to drug war, we'll save $10 billion a year in fed- 36
eral law enforcement, $10 billion a year in new state and local prosecution, about $8 billion a year in other law-enforcement costs (80 percent of the current $10 billion a year),
about $6 billion a year in the value of stolen property associated with drug use (80 percent
of the current $7.5 billion), and $3.75 billion a year by eliminating the need to match the
Colombians' drug profits dollar for dollar. We'll also benefit from taxes of $12.5 billion.
These social gains amount to $50.25 billion.

If use rises 25 percent, instead of declining by that amount, it will result in a social 37
cost of $25 billion (50 percent of $50 billion). Therefore, the net social gain of drug peace
is $25.25 billion. If legalization resulted in an immediate and permanent increase in use of
more than 25 percent, the benefits of drug peace would narrow. But additional tax revenue
would partly make up for the shrinkage. For example, if the increase in use was 50 percent
instead of 25 percent, that would add another $12.5 billion in social costs per year but
would contribute another $2.5 billion in tax revenue.

At the rate at which those numbers converge, almost a 100 percent increase in the num- 38
ber of addicts would be required before the net benefits of drug peace equaled zero. This
would seem to be a worst-case scenario. But to the drug warriors, any uncertainty is an opportunity to fan the flames of fear. Last year Bennett wrote, in *The Wall Street Journal,* "Of
course, no one . . . can say with certainty what would happen in the U.S. if drugs were suddenly to become a readily purchased product. We do know, however, that whenever drugs
have been cheaper and more easily obtained, drug use—and addiction—have skyrocketed."
Bennett cited two examples to prove his thesis: a fortyfold increase in the number of heroin
addicts in Great Britain since the drug began to be legally prescribed there, and a 350 percent increase in alcohol consumption in the United States after Prohibition.

In fact experts are far from certain about the outcome of the British experiment. The 39
statistics on the increase in the number of drug abusers are unreliable. All that is known is
that a significant rise in the number of addicts seeking treatment took place. Moreover, according to some estimates, Britain has approximately sixty-two addicts or regular users of
heroin per 100,000 population (for a total of 30,000 to 35,000), while the United States
has 209 heroin addicts or users per 100,000 population, for a total of 500,000. And very
few British heroin addicts engage in serious crime, unlike heroin addicts in America. Bennett's criticism notwithstanding, the British apparently have broken the link between
heroin addiction and violent crime.

As for Prohibition, its effects were hardly as dramatic as Bennett implied. During 40
1916–1919 per capita consumption of pure alcohol among the U.S. drinking-age population was 1.96 gallons a year; during Prohibition it dropped to 0.90 gallons; after Repeal,
during 1936–1941, it went up about 70 percent, to 1.54 gallons.

And how does Bennett explain the experience of the Netherlands, where the decrim- 41
inalization of drugs has resulted in decreased use? Does he think that what made all the

difference in Holland is the fact that it has a smaller underclass than we do? In essence, the Dutch policy involves vigorous enforcement against dealers of hard drugs, official tolerance of soft drugs such as marijuana and hashish, and decriminalization of all users. The number of marijuana users began decreasing shortly after the Dutch government decriminalized marijuana, in 1976. In 1984 about four percent of Dutch young people age ten to eighteen reported having smoked marijuana—roughly a third the rate among minors in the United States. In Amsterdam the number of heroin addicts has declined from 9,000 in 1984 to fewer than 6,000 today. Over that same period the average age of addicts has risen from twenty-six to thirty-one, indicating that few new users have taken up the habit. And there is no evidence that crack has made inroads among Dutch addicts, in contrast to its prevalence in America.

42   Amsterdam is a capital city close in size (population 695,000), if not in culture and economic demographics, to Washington, D.C. (population 604,000). Amsterdam had forty-six homicides last year, of which perhaps 30 percent were related to the drug trade. Washington had 438 homicides, 60 to 80 percent of which were drug related. The rate of homicides per 100,000 population was 6.6 in Amsterdam, less than a tenth the rate of 72.5 in Washington.

43   Holland's strategy is one of only two that have been shown to cause a real decline in drug use. The other is Singapore's, which consists of imposing the death penalty on people caught in possession of as little as fifteen grams of heroin. If this is Bennett's fallback position, perhaps he should say so explicitly.

SOME OBJECTIONS CONSIDERED

44   The fear that legalization would lead to increased drug use and addiction is not, of course, the only basis on which legalization is opposed. We should address other frequently heard objections here.

45   *Crack is our No. 1 drug problem. Legalizing other drugs while crack remains illegal won't solve the problem.* Although crack has captured the lion's share of public attention, marijuana has always commanded the bulk of law-enforcement interest. Despite de facto urban decriminalization, more than a third of all drug arrests occur in connection with marijuana—mostly for mere possession. Three fourths of all violations of drug laws relate to marijuana, and two thirds of all people charged with violation of federal marijuana laws are sentenced to prison (state figures are not available).

46   Crack appears to account for about 10 percent of the total dollar volume of the drug trade, according to National Institute on Drug Abuse estimates of the number of regular crack users. Legalizing other drugs would free up most of the law-enforcement resources currently focused on less dangerous substances and their users. It's true that as long as crack remains illegal, there will be a black market and associated crime. But we would still reap most of the benefits of legalization outlined above.

47   *Legalization would result in a huge loss in productivity and in higher health-care costs.* In truth, productivity lost to drugs is minor compared with productivity lost to alcohol and cigarettes, which remain legal. Hundreds of variables affect a person's job performance, ranging from the consumption of whiskey and cigarettes to obesity and family problems. On a purely statistical level it can be demonstrated that marital status affects productivity, yet we do not allow employers to dismiss workers on the basis of that factor.

If legal drug use resulted in higher social costs, the government could levy a tax on the   48
sale of drugs in some rough proportion to the monetary value of those costs—as it does now
for alcohol and cigarettes. This wouldn't provide the government with a financial stake in
addiction. Rather, the government would be making sure that users of socially costly items
paid those social costs. Funds from the tax on decriminalized drugs could be used for anti-
drug advertising, which could be made more effective by a total ban on drug advertising. A
government that licenses the sale of drugs must actively educate its citizens about their dangers, as Holland does in discouraging young people from using marijuana.

Drug legalization implies approval. One of the glories of American life is that many things   49
that are not condoned by society at large, such as atheism, offensive speech, and heavy-metal
music, are legal. The well-publicized death of Len Bias and other harrowing stories have carried the message far and wide that drugs are dangerous. In arguing that legalization would
persuade people that drug use is safe, drug warriors underestimate our intelligence.

Any restriction on total legalization would lead to continuing, substantial corruption.   50
Under the plan proposed here, restrictions would continue on the sale of crack and on the
sale of all drugs to children. Even if black-market corruption continued in those areas, we
would experience an immediate 80 percent reduction in corruption overall.

Legalization is too unpredictable and sweeping an action to be undertaken all at   51
once. It would be better to establish several test areas first, and evaluate the results. The
results of such a trial would probably not further the case of either side. If use went up
in the test area, it could be argued that this was caused by an influx of people from areas
where drugs were still illegal; if use went down, it could be argued that the area chosen
was unrepresentative.

Even if current drugs are legalized, much more destructive drugs will be developed in   52
the future. The most destructive current drug is crack, which would remain illegal. Many analysts believe that the development of crack was a marketing strategy, since powder cocaine
was too expensive for many users. If cocaine had been legal, crack might never have been
marketed. In any case, if a drug presents a clear danger to bystanders, it should not be legal.

No matter how the government distributes drugs, users will continue to seek greater   53
quantities and higher potency on the black market. If the government restricts the amount
of a drug that can be distributed legally, legalization will fail. It must make drugs available
at all levels of quantity and potency. The government should regulate the distribution but
not the product itself. The model should be the distribution of alcohol through state-regu-
lated liquor stores.

Legalizing drugs would ensure that America's inner cities remain places of hopeless-   54
ness and despair. If drugs disappeared tomorrow from America's ghettos, the ghettos would
remain places of hopelessness and despair. But legalization would put most drug dealers out
of business and remove the main source of financing for violent gangs. At the least, legalization would spare the inner cities from drug-driven terrorism.

Marijuana in itself may be relatively harmless, but it is a "gateway drug." Legalization   55
would lead its users to more harmful and addictive drugs. While government studies show
some correlation between marijuana use and cocaine addiction, they also show that tobacco
and alcohol use correlate with drug addiction. Moreover, keeping marijuana illegal forces
buyers into an illegal market, where they are likely to be offered other drugs. Finally,   60

million Americans have tried marijuana, and there are one million cocaine addicts. If marijuana is a gateway drug, the gate is narrow.

56   *Legalizing drugs would aggravate the growing problem of "crack babies."* The sale of crack would remain illegal. Even so, it is difficult to believe that anyone ignorant or desperate enough to use crack while pregnant would be deterred by a law. Laws against drug use are more likely to deter users from seeking treatment. Crack babies probably would have a better chance in a less censorious environment, in which their mothers had less to fear from seeking treatment.

57   Drug use in the United States can be seen as a symptom of recent cultural changes that have led to an erosion of traditional values and an inability to replace them. There are those who are willing to pay the price to try to save people from themselves. But there are surely just as many who would pay to preserve a person's right to be wrong. To the pragmatist, the choice is clear: legalization is the best bet.

Against the Legalization of Drugs

James Q. Wilson

1   In 1972, the President appointed me chairman of the National Advisory Council for Drug Abuse Prevention. Created by Congress, the Council was charged with providing guidance on how best to coordinate the national war on drugs. (Yes, we called it a war then, too.) In those days, the drug we were chiefly concerned with was heroin. When I took office, heroin use had been increasing dramatically. Everybody was worried that this increase would continue. Such phrases as "heroin epidemic" were commonplace.

2   That same year, the eminent economist Milton Friedman published an essay in *Newsweek* in which he called for legalizing heroin. His argument was on two grounds: as a matter of ethics, the government has no right to tell people not to use heroin (or to drink or to commit suicide); as a matter of economics, the prohibition of drug use imposes costs on society that far exceed the benefits. Others, such as the psychoanalyst Thomas Szasz, made the same argument.

3   We did not take Friedman's advice. (Government commissions rarely do.) I do not recall that we even discussed legalizing heroin, though we did discuss (but did not take action on) legalizing a drug, cocaine, that many people then argued was benign. Our marching orders were to figure out how to win the war on heroin, not to run up the white flag of surrender.

4   That was 1972. Today, we have the same number of heroin addicts that we had then—half a million, give or take a few thousand. Having that many heroin addicts is no trivial matter; these people deserve our attention. But not having had an increase in that number for over fifteen years is also something that deserves our attention. What happened to the "heroin epidemic" that many people once thought would overwhelm us?

5   The facts are clear: a more or less stable pool of heroin addicts has been getting older, with relatively few new recruits. In 1976 the average age of heroin users who appeared in hospital emergency rooms was about twenty-seven; ten years later it was thirty-two. More than two-thirds of all heroin users appearing in emergency rooms are now over the age of

thirty. Back in the early 1970's, when heroin got onto the national political agenda, the typical heroin addict was much younger, often a teenager. Household surveys show the same thing—the rate of opiate use (which includes heroin) has been flat for the better part of two decades. More fine-grained studies of inner-city neighborhoods confirm this. John Boyle and Ann Brunswick found that the percentage of young blacks in Harlem who used heroin fell from 8 percent in 1970–71 to about 3 percent in 1975–76.

Why did heroin lose its appeal for young people? When the young blacks in Harlem   6
were asked why they stopped, more than half mentioned "trouble with the law" or "high cost" (and high cost is, of course, directly the result of law enforcement). Two-thirds said that heroin hurt their health; nearly all said they had had a bad experience with it. We need not rely, however, simply on what they said. In New York City in 1973–75, the street price of heroin rose dramatically and its purity sharply declined, probably as a result of the heroin shortage caused by the success of the Turkish government in reducing the supply of opium base and of the French government in closing down heroin-processing laboratories located in and around Marseilles. These were short-lived gains for, just as Friedman predicted, alternative sources of supply—mostly in Mexico—quickly emerged. But the three-year heroin shortage interrupted the easy recruitment of new users.

Health and related problems were no doubt part of the reason for the reduced flow of   7
recruits. Over the preceding years, Harlem youth had watched as more and more heroin users died of overdoses, were poisoned by adulterated doses, or acquired hepatitis from dirty needles. The word got around: heroin can kill you. By 1974 new hepatitis cases and drug-overdose deaths had dropped to a fraction of what they had been in 1970.

Alas, treatment did not seem to explain much of the cessation in drug use. Treatment   8
programs can and do help heroin addicts, but treatment did not explain the drop in the number of *new* users (who by definition had never been in treatment) or even much of the reduction in the number of experienced users.

No one knows how much of the decline to attribute to personal observation as opposed   9
to high prices or reduced supply. But other evidence suggests strongly that price and supply played a large role. In 1972 the National Advisory Council was especially worried by the prospect that U.S. servicemen returning to this country from Vietnam would bring their heroin habits with them. Fortunately, a brilliant study by Lee Robins of Washington University in St. Louis put that fear to rest. She measured drug use of Vietnam veterans shortly after they had returned home. Though many had used heroin regularly while in Southeast Asia, most gave up the habit when back in the United States. The reason: here, heroin was less available and sanctions on its use were more pronounced. Of course, if a veteran had been willing to pay enough—which might have meant traveling to another city and would certainly have meant making an illegal contact with a disreputable dealer in a threatening neighborhood in order to acquire a (possibly) dangerous dose—he could have sustained his drug habit. Most veterans were unwilling to pay this price, and so their drug use declined or disappeared.

RELIVING THE PAST

Suppose we had taken Friedman's advice in 1972. What would have happened? We   10
cannot be entirely certain, but at a minimum we would have placed the young heroin addicts (and, above all, the prospective addicts) in a very different position from the one in

which they actually found themselves. Heroin would have been legal. Its price would have been reduced by 95 percent (minus whatever we chose to recover in taxes). Now that it could be sold by the same people who make aspirin, its quality would have been assured—no poisons, no adulterants. Sterile hypodermic needles would have been readily available at the neighborhood drugstore, probably at the same counter where the heroin was sold. No need to travel to big cities or unfamiliar neighborhoods—heroin could have been purchased anywhere, perhaps by mail order.

11   There would no longer have been any financial or medical reason to avoid heroin use. Anybody could have afforded it. We might have tried to prevent children from buying it, but as we have learned from our efforts to prevent minors from buying alcohol and tobacco, young people have a way of penetrating markets theoretically reserved for adults. Returning Vietnam veterans would have discovered that Omaha and Raleigh had been converted into the pharmaceutical equivalent of Saigon.

12   Under these circumstances, can we doubt for a moment that heroin use would have grown exponentially? Or that a vastly larger supply of new users would have been recruited? Professor Friedman is a Nobel Prize–winning economist whose understanding of market forces is profound. What did he think would happen to consumption under his legalized regime? Here are his words: "Legalizing drugs might increase the number of addicts, but it is not clear that it would. Forbidden fruit is attractive, particularly to the young."

13   Really? I suppose that we should expect no increase in Porsche sales if we cut the price by 95 percent, no increase in whiskey sales if we cut the price by a comparable amount—because young people only want fast cars and strong liquor when they are "forbidden." Perhaps Friedman's uncharacteristic lapse from the obvious implications of price theory can be explained by a misunderstanding of how drug users are recruited. In his 1972 essay he said that "drug addicts are deliberately made by pushers, who give likely prospects their first few doses free." If drugs were legal it would not pay anybody to produce addicts, because everybody would buy from the cheapest source. But as every drug expert knows, pushers do not produce addicts. Friends or acquaintances do. In fact, pushers are usually reluctant to deal with nonusers because a non-user could be an undercover cop. Drug use spreads in the same way any fad or fashion spreads: somebody who is already a user urges his friend to try, or simply shows already-eager friends how to do it.

14   But we need not rely on speculation, however plausible, that lowered prices and more abundant supplies would have increased heroin usage. Great Britain once followed such a policy and with almost exactly those results. Until the mid-1960's, British physicians were allowed to prescribe heroin to certain classes of addicts. (Possessing these drugs without a doctor's prescription remained a criminal offense.) For many years this policy worked well enough because the addict patients were typically middle-class people who had become dependent on opiate painkillers while undergoing hospital treatment. There was no drug culture. The British system worked for many years, not because it prevented drug abuse, but because there was no problem of drug abuse that would test the system.

15   All that changed in the 1960's. A few unscrupulous doctors began passing out heroin in wholesale amounts. One doctor prescribed almost 600,000 heroin tablets—that is, over

thirteen pounds—in just one year. A youthful drug culture emerged with a demand for drugs far different from that of the older addicts. As a result, the British government required doctors to refer users to government-run clinics to receive their heroin.

But the shift to clinics did not curtail the growth in heroin use. Throughout the 1960's the number of addicts increased—the late John Kaplan of Stanford estimated by fivefold—in part as a result of the diversion of heroin from clinic patients to new users on the streets. An addict would bargain with the clinic doctor over how big a dose he would receive. The patient wanted as much as he could get, the doctor wanted to give as little as needed. The patient had an advantage in this conflict because the doctor could not be certain how much was really needed. Many patients would use some of their "maintenance" dose and sell the remaining part to friends, thereby recruiting new addicts. As the clinics learned of this, they began to shift their treatment away from heroin and toward methadone, an addictive drug that, when taken orally, does not produce a "high" but will block the withdrawal pains associated with heroin abstinence.

Whether what happened in England in the 1960's was a mini-epidemic or an epidemic depends on whether one looks at numbers or at rates of change. Compared to the United States, the numbers were small. In 1960 there were 68 heroin addicts known to the British government; by 1968 there were 2,000 in treatment and many more who refused treatment. (They would refuse in part because they did not want to get methadone at a clinic if they could get heroin on the street.) Richard Hartnoll estimates that the actual number of addicts in England is five times the number officially registered. At a minimum, the number of British addicts increased by thirtyfold in ten years; the actual increase may have been much larger.

In the early 1980's the numbers began to rise again, and this time nobody doubted that a real epidemic was at hand. The increase was estimated to be 40 percent a year. By 1982 there were thought to be 20,000 heroin users in London alone. Geoffrey Pearson reports that many cities—Glasgow, Liverpool, Manchester, and Sheffield among them—are now experiencing a drug problem that once had been largely confined to London. The problem, again, was supply. The country was being flooded with cheap, high-quality heroin, first from Iran and then from Southeast Asia.

The United States began the 1960's with a much larger number of heroin addicts and probably a bigger at-risk population than was the case in Great Britain. Even though it would be foolhardy to suppose that the British system, if installed here, would have worked the same way or with the same results, it would be equally foolhardy to suppose that a combination of heroin available from leaky clinics and from street dealers who faced only minimal law-enforcement risks would not have produced a much greater increase in heroin use than we actually experienced. My guess is that if we had allowed either doctors or clinics to prescribe heroin, we would have had far worse results than were produced in Britain, if for no other reason than the vastly larger number of addicts with which we began. We would have had to find some way to police thousands (not scores) of physicians and hundreds (not dozens) of clinics. If the British civil service found it difficult to keep heroin in the hands of addicts and out of the hands of recruits when it was dealing with a few hundred people, how well would the American civil service have accomplished the same tasks when dealing with tens of thousands of people?

BACK TO THE FUTURE

20   Now cocaine, especially in its potent form, crack, is the focus of attention. Now as in 1972 the government is trying to reduce its use. Now as then some people are advocating legalization. Is there any more reason to yield to those arguments today than there was almost two decades ago?[1]

21   I think not. If we had yielded in 1972 we almost certainly would have had today a permanent population of several million, not several hundred thousand, heroin addicts. If we yield now we will have a far more serious problem with cocaine.

22   Crack is worse than heroin by almost any measure. Heroin produces a pleasant drowsiness and, if hygienically administered, has only the physical side effects of constipation and sexual impotence. Regular heroin use incapacitates many users, especially poor ones, for any productive work or social responsibility. They will sit nodding on a street corner, helpless but at least harmless. By contrast, regular cocaine use leaves the user neither helpless nor harmless. When smoked (as with crack) or injected, cocaine produces instant, intense, and short-lived euphoria. The experience generates a powerful desire to repeat it. If the drug is readily available, repeat use will occur. Those people who progress to "bingeing" on cocaine become devoted to the drug and its effects to the exclusion of almost all other considerations—job, family, children, sleep, food, even sex. Dr. Frank Gawin at Yale and Dr. Everett Ellinwood at Duke report that a substantial percentage of all high-dose, binge users become uninhibited, impulsive, hypersexual, compulsive, irritable, and hyperactive. Their moods vacillate dramatically, leading at times to violence and homicide.

23   Women are much more likely to use crack than heroin, and if they are pregnant, the effects on their babies are tragic. Douglas Besharov, who has been following the effects of drugs on infants for twenty years, writes that nothing he learned about heroin prepared him for the devastation of cocaine. Cocaine harms the fetus and can lead to physical deformities or neurological damage. Some crack babies have for all practical purposes suffered a disabling stroke while still in the womb. The long-term consequences of this brain damage are lowered cognitive ability and the onset of mood disorders. Besharov estimates that about 30,000 to 50,000 such babies are born every year, about 7,000 in New York City alone. There may be ways to treat such infants, but from everything we now know the treatment will be long, difficult, and expensive. Worse, the mothers who are most likely to produce crack babies are precisely the ones who, because of poverty or temperament, are least able and willing to obtain such treatment. In fact, anecdotal evidence suggests that crack mothers are likely to abuse their infants.

24   The notion that abusing drugs such as cocaine is a "victimless crime" is not only absurd but dangerous. Even ignoring the fetal drug syndrome, crack-dependent people are, like heroin addicts, individuals who regularly victimize their children by neglect, their spouses by improvidence, their employers by lethargy, and their coworkers by carelessness.

---

[1] I do not here take up the question of marijuana. For a variety of reasons—its widespread use and its lesser tendency to addict—it presents a different problem from cocaine or heroin. For a penetrating analysis, see Mark Kleiman, *Marijuana: Costs of Abuse, Costs of Control* (Greenwood Press, 217 pp., $37.95).

Society is not and could never be a collection of autonomous individuals. We have a stake in ensuring that each of us displays a minimal level of dignity, responsibility, and empathy. We cannot, of course, coerce people into goodness, but we can and should insist that some standards must be met if society itself—on which the very existence of the human personality depends—is to persist. Drawing the line that defines those standards is difficult and contentious, but if crack and heroin use do not fall below it, what does?

The advocates of legalization will respond by suggesting that my picture is overdrawn.   25
Ethan Nadelmann of Princeton argues that the risk of legalization is less than most people suppose. Over 20 million Americans between the ages of eighteen and twenty-five have tried cocaine (according to a government survey), but only a quarter million use it daily. From this Nadelmann concludes that at most 3 percent of all young people who try cocaine develop a problem with it. The implication is clear: make the drug legal and we only have to worry about 3 percent of our youth.

The implication rests on a logical fallacy and a factual error. The fallacy is this: the per-   26
centage of occasional cocaine users who become binge users *when the drug is illegal* (and thus expensive and hard to find) tells us nothing about the percentage who will become dependent when the drug is legal (and thus cheap and abundant). Drs. Gawin and Ellinwood report, in common with several other researchers, that controlled or occasional use of cocaine changes to compulsive and frequent use "when access to the drug increases" or when the user switches from snorting to smoking. More cocaine more potently administered alters, perhaps sharply, the proportion of "controlled" users who become heavy users.

The factual error is this: the federal survey Nadelmann quotes was done in 1985, *be-*   27
fore crack had become common. Thus the probability of becoming dependent on cocaine was derived from the responses of users who snorted the drug. The speed and potency of cocaine's action increases dramatically when it is smoked. We do not yet know how greatly the advent of crack increases the risk of dependency, but all the clinical evidence suggests that the increase is likely to be large.

It is possible that some people will not become heavy users even when the drug is   28
readily available in its most potent form. So far there are no scientific grounds for predicting who will and who will not become dependent. Neither socio-economic background nor personality traits differentiate between casual and intensive users. Thus, the only way to settle the question of who is correct about the effect of easy availability on drug use, Nadelmann or Gawin and Ellinwood, is to try it and see. But that social experiment is so risky as to be no experiment at all, for if cocaine is legalized and if the rate of its abusive use increases dramatically, there is no way to put the genie back in the bottle, and it is not a kindly genie.

HAVE WE LOST?

Many people who agree that there are risks in legalizing cocaine or heroin still favor   29
it because, they think, we have lost the war on drugs. "Nothing we have done has worked" and the current federal policy is just "more of the same." Whatever the costs of greater drug use, surely they would be less than the costs of our present, failed efforts.

30   That is exactly what I was told in 1972—and heroin is not quite as bad a drug as cocaine. We did not surrender and we did not lose. We did not win, either. What the nation accomplished then was what most efforts to save people from themselves accomplish: the problem was contained and the number of victims minimized, all at a considerable cost in law enforcement and increased crime. Was the cost worth it? I think so, but others may disagree. What are the lives of would-be addicts worth? I recall some people saying to me then, "Let them kill themselves." I was appalled. Happily, such views did not prevail.

31   Have we lost today? Not at all. High-rate cocaine use is not commonplace. The National Institute of Drug Abuse (NIDA) reports that less than 5 percent of high-school seniors used cocaine within the last thirty days. Of course this survey misses young people who have dropped out of school and miscounts those who lie on the questionnaire, but even if we inflate the NIDA estimate by some plausible percentage, it is still not much above 5 percent. Medical examiners reported in 1987 that about 1,500 died from cocaine use; hospital emergency rooms reported about 30,000 admissions related to cocaine abuse.

32   These are not small numbers, but neither are they evidence of a nationwide plague that threatens to engulf us all. Moreover, cities vary greatly in the proportion of people who are involved with cocaine. To get city-level data we need to turn to drug tests carried out on arrested persons, who obviously are more likely to be drug users than the average citizen. The National Institute of Justice, through its Drug Use Forecasting (DUF) project, collects urinalysis data on arrestees in 22 cities. As we have already seen, opiate (chiefly heroin) use has been flat or declining in most of these cities over the last decade. Cocaine use has gone up sharply, but with great variation among cities. New York, Philadelphia, and Washington, D.C., all report that two-thirds or more of their arrestees tested positive for cocaine, but in Portland, San Antonio, and Indianapolis the percentage was one-third or less.

33   In some neighborhoods, of course, matters have reached crisis proportions. Gangs control the streets, shootings terrorize residents, and drug-dealing occurs in plain view. The police seem barely able to contain matters. But in these neighborhoods—unlike at Palo Alto cocktail parties—the people are not calling for legalization, they are calling for help. And often not much help has come. Many cities are willing to do almost anything about the drug problem except spend more money on it. The federal government cannot change that; only local voters and politicians can. It is not clear that they will.

34   It took about ten years to contain heroin. We have had experience with crack for only about three or four years. Each year we spend perhaps $11 billion on law enforcement (and some of that goes to deal with marijuana) and perhaps $2 billion on treatment. Large sums, but not sums that should lead anyone to say, "We just can't afford this any more."

35   The illegality of drugs increases crime, partly because some users turn to crime to pay for their habits, partly because some users are stimulated by certain drugs (such as crack or PCP) to act more violently or ruthlessly than they otherwise would, and partly because criminal organizations seeking to control drug supplies use force to manage their markets. These also are serious costs, but no one knows how much they would be reduced if drugs were legalized. Addicts would no longer steal to pay black-market prices for drugs, a real gain. But some, perhaps a great deal, of that gain would be offset by the great increase in the number of addicts. These people, nodding on heroin or living in the delusion-ridden high of cocaine, would hardly be ideal employees. Many would steal simply to support themselves, since snatch-and-grab, opportunistic crime can be managed even by people unable

to hold a regular job or plan an elaborate crime. Those British addicts who get their supplies from government clinics are not models of law-abiding decency. Most are in crime, and though their per-capita rate of criminality may be lower thanks to the cheapness of their drugs, the total volume of crime they produce may be quite large. Of course, society could decide to support all unemployable addicts on welfare, but that would mean that gains from lowered rates of crime would have to be offset by large increases in welfare budgets.

Proponents of legalization claim that the costs of having more addicts around would be largely if not entirely offset by having more money available with which to treat and care for them. The money would come from taxes levied on the sale of heroin and cocaine.   36

To obtain this fiscal dividend, however, legalization's supporters must first solve an economic dilemma. If they want to raise a lot of money to pay for welfare and treatment, the tax rate on the drugs will have to be quite high. Even if they themselves do not want a high rate, the politicians' love of "sin taxes" would probably guarantee that it would be high anyway. But the higher the tax, the higher the price of the drug, and the higher the price the greater the likelihood that addicts will turn to crime to find the money for it and that criminal organizations will be formed to sell tax-free drugs at below-market rates. If we managed to keep taxes (and thus prices) low, we would get that much less money to pay for welfare and treatment and more people could afford to become addicts. There may be an optimal tax rate for drugs that maximizes revenue while minimizing crime, bootlegging, and the recruitment of new addicts, but our experience with alcohol does not suggest that we know how to find it.   37

THE BENEFITS OF ILLEGALITY

The advocates of legalization find nothing to be said in favor of the current system except, possibly, that it keeps the number of addicts smaller than it would otherwise be. In fact, the benefits are more substantial than that.   38

First, treatment. All the talk about providing "treatment on demand" implies that there is a demand for treatment. That is not quite right. There are some drug-dependent people who genuinely want treatment and will remain in it if offered; they should receive it. But there are far more who want only short-term help after a bad crash: once stabilized and bathed, they are back on the street again, hustling. And even many of the addicts who enroll in a program honestly wanting help drop out after a short while when they discover that help takes time and commitment. Drug-dependent people have very short time horizons and a weak capacity for commitment. These two groups—those looking for a quick fix and those unable to stick with a long-term fix—are not easily helped. Even if we increase the number of treatment slots—as we should—we would have to do something to make treatment more effective.   39

One thing that can often make it more effective is compulsion. Douglas Anglin of UCLA, in common with many other researchers, has found that the longer one stays in a treatment program, the better the chances of a reduction in drug dependency. But he, again like most other researchers, has found that drop-out rates are high. He has also found, however, that patients who enter treatment under legal compulsion stay in the program longer than those not subject to such pressure. His research on the California civil-commitment program, for example, found that heroin users involved with its required drug-testing program had over the long term a lower rate of heroin use than similar addicts who were free   40 of such constraints. If for many addicts compulsion is a useful component of treatment, it is not clear how compulsion could be achieved in a society in which purchasing, possessing, and using the drug were legal. It could be managed, I suppose, but I would not want to have to answer the challenge from the American Civil Liberties Union that it is wrong to compel a person to undergo treatment for consuming a legal commodity.

41   Next, education. We are now investing substantially in drug-education programs in the schools. Though we do not yet know for certain what will work, there are some promising leads. But I wonder how credible such programs would be if they were aimed at dissuading children from doing something perfectly legal. We could, of course, treat drug education like smoking education: inhaling crack and inhaling tobacco are both legal, but you should not do it because it is bad for you. That tobacco is bad for you is easily shown; the Surgeon General has seen to that. But what do we say about crack? It is pleasurable, but devoting yourself to so much pleasure is not a good idea (though perfectly legal)? Unlike tobacco, cocaine will not give you cancer or emphysema, but it will lead you to neglect your duties to family, job, and neighborhood? Everybody is doing cocaine, but you should not?

42   Again, it might be possible under a legalized regime to have effective drug-prevention programs, but their effectiveness would depend heavily, I think, on first having decided that cocaine use, like tobacco use, is purely a matter of practical consequences; no fundamental moral significance attaches to either. But if we believe—as I do—that dependency on certain mind-altering drugs *is* a moral issue and that their illegality rests in part on their immorality, then legalizing them undercuts, if it does not eliminate altogether, the moral message.

43   That message is at the root of the distinction we now make between nicotine and cocaine. Both are highly addictive; both have harmful physical effects. But we treat the two drugs differently, not simply because nicotine is so widely used as to be beyond the reach of effective prohibition, but because its use does not destroy the user's essential humanity. Tobacco shortens one's life, cocaine debases it. Nicotine alters one's habits, cocaine alters one's soul. The heavy use of crack, unlike the heavy use of tobacco, corrodes those natural sentiments of sympathy and duty that constitute our human nature and make possible our social life. To say, as does Nadelmann, that distinguishing morally between tobacco and cocaine is "little more than a transient prejudice" is close to saying that morality itself is but a prejudice.

THE ALCOHOL PROBLEM

44   Now we have arrived where many arguments about legalizing drugs begin: is there any reason to treat heroin and cocaine differently from the way we treat alcohol?

45   There is no easy answer to that question because, as with so many human problems, one cannot decide simply on the basis either of moral principle or of individual consequences; one has to temper any policy by a common-sense judgment of what is possible. Alcohol, like heroin, cocaine, PCP, and marijuana, is a drug—that is, a mood-altering substance—and consumed to excess it certainly has harmful consequences: auto accidents, barroom fights, bedroom shootings. It is also, for some people, addictive. We cannot confidently compare the addictive powers of these drugs, but the best evidence suggests that crack and heroin are much more addictive than alcohol.

46   Many people, Nadelmann included, argue that since the health and financial costs of alcohol abuse are so much higher than those of cocaine or heroin abuse, it is hypocritical folly

to devote our efforts to preventing cocaine or drug use. But as Mark Kleiman of Harvard has pointed out, this comparison is quite misleading. What Nadelmann is doing is showing that a *legalized* drug (alcohol) produces greater social harm than *illegal* ones (cocaine and heroin). But of course. Suppose that in the 1920's we had made heroin and cocaine legal and alcohol illegal. Can anyone doubt that Nadelmann would not be writing that it is folly to continue our ban on alcohol because cocaine and heroin are so much more harmful?

And let there be no doubt about it—widespread heroin and cocaine use are associated with all manner of ills. Thomas Bewley found that the mortality rate of British heroin addicts in 1968 was 28 times as high as the death rate of the same age group of non-addicts, even though in England at the time an addict could obtain free or low-cost heroin and clean needles from British clinics. Perform the following mental experiment: suppose we legalized heroin and cocaine in this country. In what proportion of auto fatalities would the state police report that the driver was nodding off on heroin or recklessly driving on a coke high? In what proportion of spouse-assault and child-abuse cases would the local police report that crack was involved? In what proportion of industrial accidents would safety investigators report that the forklift or drill-press operator was in a drug-induced stupor or frenzy? We do not know exactly what the proportion would be, but anyone who asserts that it would not be much higher than it is now would have to believe that these drugs have little appeal except when they are illegal. And that is nonsense.   47

An advocate of legalization might concede that social harm—perhaps harm equivalent to that already produced by alcohol—would follow from making cocaine and heroin generally available. But at least, he might add, we would have the problem "out in the open" where it could be treated as a matter of "public health." That is well and good, *if* we knew how to treat—that is, cure—heroin and cocaine abuse. But we do not know how to do it for all the people who would need such help. We are having only limited success in coping with chronic alcoholics. Addictive behavior is immensely difficult to change, and the best methods for changing it—living in drug-free therapeutic communities, becoming faithful members of Alcoholics Anonymous or Narcotics Anonymous—require great personal commitment, a quality that is, alas, in short supply among the very persons—young people, disadvantaged people—who are often most at risk for addiction.   48

Suppose that today we had, not 15 million alcohol abusers, but half a million. Suppose that we already knew what we have learned from our long experience with the widespread use of alcohol. Would we make whiskey legal? I do not know, but I suspect there would be a lively debate. The Surgeon General would remind us of the risks alcohol poses to pregnant women. The National Highway Traffic Safety Administration would point to the likelihood of more highway fatalities caused by drunk drivers. The Food and Drug Administration might find that there is a non-trivial increase in cancer associated with alcohol consumption. At the same time the police would report great difficulty in keeping illegal whiskey out of our cities, officers being corrupted by bootleggers, and alcohol addicts often resorting to crime to feed their habit. Libertarians, for their part, would argue that every citizen has a right to drink anything he wishes and that drinking is, in any event, a "victimless crime."   49

However the debate might turn out, the central fact would be that the problem was still, at that point, a small one. The government cannot legislate away the addictive tendencies in all of us, nor can it remove completely even the most dangerous addictive substances. But it can cope with harms when the harms are still manageable.   50

SCIENCE AND ADDICTION

51   One advantage of containing a problem while it is still containable is that it buys time for science to learn more about it and perhaps to discover a cure. Almost unnoticed in the current debate over legalizing drugs is that basic science has made rapid strides in identifying the underlying neurological process involved in some forms of addiction. Stimulants such as cocaine and amphetamines alter the way certain brain cells communicate with one another. That alteration is complex and not entirely understood, but in simplified form it involves modifying the way in which a neurotransmitter called dopamine sends signals from one cell to another.

52   When dopamine crosses the synapse between two cells, it is in effect carrying a message from the first cell to activate the second one. In certain parts of the brain that message is experienced as pleasure. After the message is delivered, the dopamine returns to the first cell. Cocaine apparently blocks this return, or "reuptake," so that the excited cell and others nearby continue to send pleasure messages. When the exaggerated high produced by cocaine-influenced dopamine finally ends, the brain cells may (in ways that are still a matter of dispute) suffer from an extreme lack of dopamine, thereby making the individual unable to experience any pleasure at all. This would explain why cocaine users often feel so depressed after enjoying the drug. Stimulants may also affect the way in which other neurotransmitters, such as serotonin and noradrenaline, operate.

53   Whatever the exact mechanism may be, once it is identified it becomes possible to use drugs to block either the effect of cocaine or its tendency to produce dependency. There have already been experiments using desipramine, imipramine, bromocriptine, carbamazepine, and other chemicals. There are some promising results.

54   Tragically, we spend very little on such research, and the agencies funding it have not in the past occupied very influential or visible posts in the federal bureaucracy. If there is one aspect of the "war on drugs" metaphor that I dislike, it is its tendency to focus attention almost exclusively on the troops in the trenches, whether engaged in enforcement or treatment, and away from the research-and-development efforts back on the home front where the war may ultimately be decided.

55   I believe that the prospects of scientists in controlling addiction will be strongly influenced by the size and character of the problem they face. If the problem is a few hundred thousand chronic, high-dose users of an illegal product, the chances of making a difference at a reasonable cost will be much greater than if the problem is a few million chronic users of legal substances. Once a drug is legal, not only will its use increase but many of those who then use it will prefer the drug to the treatment: they will want the pleasure, whatever the cost to themselves or their families, and they will resist—probably successfully—any effort to wean them away from experiencing the high that comes from inhaling a legal substance.

IF I AM WRONG . . .

56   No one can know what our society would be like if we changed the law to make access to cocaine, heroin, and PCP easier. I believe, for reasons given, that the result would be a sharp increase in use, a more widespread degradation of the human personality, and a greater rate of accidents and violence.

I may be wrong. If I am, then we will needlessly have incurred heavy costs in law enforcement and some forms of criminality. But if I am right, and the legalizers prevail anyway, then we will have consigned millions of people, hundreds of thousands of infants, and hundreds of neighborhoods to a life of oblivion and disease. To the lives and families destroyed by alcohol we will have added countless more destroyed by cocaine, heroin, PCP, and whatever else a basement scientist can invent.   57

Human character is formed by society; indeed, human character is inconceivable without society, and good character is less likely in a bad society. Will we, in the name of an abstract doctrine of radical individualism, and with the false comfort of suspect predictions, decide to take the chance that somehow individual decency can survive amid a more general level of degradation?   58

I think not. The American people are too wise for that, whatever the academic essayists and cocktail-party pundits may say. But if Americans today are less wise than I suppose, then Americans at some future time will look back on us now and wonder, what kind of people were they that they could have done such a thing?   59

Drug Use by U.S. Army Enlisted Men in Vietnam: A Follow-Up on Their Return Home

Lee N. Robins, Darlene H. Davis, and Donald W. Goodwin

Abstract

Between May and September 1972, 943 men who had returned to the United States from Vietnam in September 1971 as Army enlisted men were sought for interview and collection of urine specimens. Of these men, 470 represented the general population of Army enlisted men returning at that time; 495 represented those whose urine had been positive for opiates at time of departure from Vietnam. At interview 8–12 months after their return, 83 percent were civilians and 17 percent still in service. Nine hundred were personally interviewed and urine specimens collected for 876. Almost half of the "general" sample tried heroin or opium while in Vietnam and one-fifth developed physical or psychological dependence. In the 8- to 12-month period since their return, about 10 percent had some experience with opiates, but less than 1 percent had shown signs of opiate dependence. In the "drug positive" sample, three-quarters felt they had been addicted to narcotics in Vietnam. After return, one-third had some experience with opiates, but only 7 percent showed signs of dependence. Rather than giving up drugs altogether, many had shifted from heroin to amphetamines or barbiturates. Nevertheless, almost none expressed a desire for treatment. Pre-service use of drugs and extent of use in Vietnam were the strongest predictors of continued use after Vietnam. The results indicate that, contrary to conventional belief, the occasional use of narcotics without becoming addicted appears possible even for men who have previously been dependent on narcotics.

INTRODUCTION

1   During the summer and fall of 1971, drug use by United States servicemen in Vietnam had, by all estimates, reached epidemic proportions. Starting in June 1971, the military screened urines of servicemen for drugs just before scheduled departure from Vietnam. In September 1971, the Department of Defense estimated that 5 percent of all urines of Army servicemen tested indicated drug use in the immediately preceding period, despite common knowledge that testing would be done and if positive, would result in a six- or seven-day delay in departure from Vietnam.

2   At this time, troop strength in Vietnam was being reduced rapidly, returning to the United States each month thousands of men, of whom about 40 percent were due for immediate release from service. The Armed Forces, the Veterans Administration, and civilian drug treatment facilities were concerned that the arrival of these men might tax existing drug treatment programs. There was also concern about how drug use might affect veterans' ability to get and hold jobs and their chances of becoming involved in criminal activities if they continued heroin use in the United States, where the price of heroin was many times its price in Vietnam. If the men designated as "drug positives" at DEROS (Date Eligible for Return from Overseas) were actually heroin addicts and if heroin addiction among these soldiers was as chronic and unresponsive to treatment as it had been found to be in the heroin addicts seen in the Public Health Hospitals of Lexington and Fort Worth (1–3), there was reason for concern.

3   To evaluate these concerns and to learn how many men would require treatment, the kinds of treatment and social services they might need, and how to identify which men needed services, the White House Special Action Office for Drug Abuse Prevention arranged for and assisted in a follow-up study of Army enlisted men who returned from Vietnam to the United States in September 1971. This study promised not only to answer questions relevant to planning programs for these soldiers, but also to teach us something about the natural history of drug utilization and abuse when drugs were readily available to young men from all over the United States and from all kinds of social backgrounds.

4   Specifically, the study was designed to answer, among other questions, the following:

1. What proportion of Army enlisted men who departed Vietnam for the United States in September 1971, had used drugs in Vietnam? What drugs did they use and how much? What were the distinguishing characteristics of the drug users in terms of demographic variables, civilian history, and prior military record?

2. What proportion of these men had used narcotics or other illicit drugs (marijuana, amphetamines, barbiturates) since their return eight to 12 months previously? How many had been "dependent" on these drugs after return to the United States?

3. How many of them had been treated for drug use since returning? What was the nature of the treatment? Where was it received, and what was its duration? Was there a desire for drug treatment among these veterans that present facilities were not meeting?

4. Among men detected as using narcotics in Vietnam, what factors predicted continued use upon return to the United States?

METHOD

Study design.   Military programs to counter drug abuse among troops in Vietnam have   5
grown and changed over time. As a result, men leaving Vietnam at different dates were exposed to different programs. Because different military programs might lead to different
post-Vietnam adjustments, and because comparisons of outcomes since Vietnam for men
who had been detected as drug positive with outcomes for the general run of soldiers would
be valid only if the two groups had had equal periods in which to get jobs, begin drug use,
or whatever, we decided to study only a single month's departures and to interview the men
selected within as circumscribed a time period as possible.

We chose a month of departures, September 1971, thought to represent the period in   6
which use of heroin by soldiers was at its height. And among the military departing Vietnam during that month, we chose the group with the highest rate of positive urines: male
Army enlisted personnel. We studied only those who returned to the United States, including all the continental United States plus Hawaii, Puerto Rico and the Virgin Islands.
The population we selected for study, Army enlisted men, not only had a high rate of positive urines at departure from Vietnam but also constituted the largest group of returnees
to the United States. Thus we were studying the population that should contribute most to
veteran candidates for drug treatment. A "general" sample of approximately 500 was to be
drawn from this population.

Within the general population of Army enlisted men returning to the United States in   7
September from Vietnam, there was a subpopulation of men who had been detected as drug
positive at the time they left Vietnam. From this subpopulation of drug positives we wanted
to take a "drug positive" sample of approximately 500 persons. The "general" sample would
serve to provide us with estimates of the proportion of Army enlisted men who used drugs
in Vietnam, the proportion detected as drug positive at DEROS, the proportion who used
drugs after their return to the United States, and the proportion who wanted treatment.
Using the "drug positive" sample, we hoped to distinguish between drug users in Vietnam
who were likely to be drug users in the United States after their return and those who
would use little or no drugs after returning to the United States.

Each man was to be interviewed and asked to contribute a urine specimen. The urine   8
specimens were analyzed for morphine, codeine, methadone, quinine, amphetamines, and
barbiturates. Army records were also analyzed to test the validity of the interview data and
to provide additional information.

Sample selection.   A full description of how the two samples were selected appears   9
elsewhere (4).

The population from which the general sample was drawn—Army enlisted men who   10
left Vietnam in September 1971 to return to the United States—totaled approximately
13,760, according to Department of Defense statistics. Names of approximately 11,000 of
these eligible men were made available to us by the military on a tape derived from the
master tape of Enlisted Record Briefs for all men on active duty within 120 days of November 30, 1971. (The missing 2760 probably resulted largely from failure to correct departure dates for men leaving Vietnam at dates other than originally scheduled.) From this
tape we selected a simple random sample of 470.

11   From approximately 1000 eligible names and/or service numbers provided by the Surgeon General of men who had been identified as "drug positive" at DEROS, we selected a simple random sample of 495. There was an overlap between the "general" and "drug positive" samples of 22 men.

12   For each name chosen, the hard copy of the military record was sought to verify the departure date from Vietnam (and thus confirm eligibility for the sample) and to obtain the address of record and the names and addresses of next of kin. Difficulties in locating the military records prolonged sample selection into the interviewing period, greatly reducing the efficiency of travel schedules.

13   *The interview.*   The interview (also available in reference 4) was a product of repeated revision during pretests with approximately 50 Vietnam veterans who had returned at dates other than September, some recruited through active drug programs.

14   The interview form provided principally precoded answers, plus verbatim answers to open-ended questions. The results in the current report come only from the precoded sections.

15   Questions about drug use referred to five time periods: 1) before service; 2) in service, before Vietnam; 3) in Vietnam; 4) in service, after Vietnam; and 5) after release from active duty. Questions were also asked about deviance of other kinds during these five time periods, about the nature of the man's experience in Vietnam, his opinion as to how the Army and the Veterans Administration should combat drug abuse, and about his adjustment since his return from Vietnam. At the end of the interview, he was asked to give a urine sample.

16   Interviewing was conducted by the National Opinion Research Center. Interviewers received five days of training, which encompassed not only interviewing techniques but also military terminology, the nature of the Vietnam experience, drug language, facts about drug abuse, and the maintenance of confidentiality. A faculty of social scientists and psychiatrists experienced in drug research, a representative of the Veterans Administration, and members of the Armed Forces with Vietnam experience provided the training, along with the staff of supervisors and field directors from the National Opinion Research Center. During training, each interviewer carried out and observed several interviews with veterans currently in drug programs. There were both black and white interviewers, male and female; most but not all were young. Puerto Rican subjects were interviewed by a Puerto Rican interviewer in Spanish.

17   Interviews were conducted in person and in private. They lasted an average of one hour and 40 minutes, and ranged from 30 minutes to more than three and one-half hours.

18   The first contact with the subject was via a letter, signed by the Veterans Administration, asking the subject's cooperation with the project as a person who better than anyone else knew the concerns of men returning from Vietnam. The letter mentioned that the subject would be paid for his cooperation, and invited him to call the National Opinion Research Center to set up an appointment. If the letter was returned as undeliverable, efforts were made to contact a relative to inquire about the man's current address. Interviewers made every possible attempt to contact each man, because other research had indicated that men hard to find at home are much more likely to show social deviance than men readily found at home (5). The subjects constituted a young population in the process of mov-

ing to new jobs or getting married, and, therefore, locating them sometimes took great persistence and ingenuity. Because of difficulties in choosing the sample, interviewers had to return to various locations repeatedly. Despite this, they interviewed 97 percent of the general sample that survived until the time of interview and 96 percent of the drug positive sample, a completed total of 900 interviews.

Among the 43 men not interviewed, there were six deaths (two auto accidents, one death in a fire, one electrocution on the job, one shot while burglarizing a home, and one overdose of drugs), three refusals, 15 unlocated with no further leads, and 19 still in process of location or arrangement for interview at time of terminating the field work.   19

Urinalysis.   Of the 900 men interviewed, only 1 percent refused to provide a urine sample. An additional two were unable to urinate on request, one man was too ill to be asked, and a few urines were lost by leakage in transit. In all, urinalyses were obtained for 98 percent of the general sample and 96 percent of the drug positives interviewed.   20

Urine specimens were sent airmail in sealed containers to the Addiction Research Foundation in Toronto for urinalysis. Barbiturates, morphine, codeine, quinine and methadone were screened initially by thin layer chromatography, and positive morphines were confirmed by gas liquid chromatography. Amphetamines and methamphetamines were screened by gas liquid chromatography. Details are described elsewhere (4).   21

Confidentiality.   Confidentiality was maintained to prevent bias on the part of interviewers and to protect the men's privacy. To avoid bias the interviewers had to be ignorant about whether a subject had been identified as a drug abuser. To be certain that interviewers had no such information, the names composing the two samples were scrambled by giving each a random number. When the interview was complete, it was mailed to the Addiction Research Foundation, Toronto, Canada, in an envelope showing the random number assigned but with no identifying data on the interview and neither name nor address of the subject on the envelope. Waiting for its arrival in Canada was a list showing that random number associated with a single digit which identified the sample from which the case came ("general," "drug" or both) and, for cases in only one of the two samples, whether or not the case appeared in the population from which the other sample had been selected. The possible categories were: 1) in both general and drug samples; 2) in general sample only, also on Surgeon General's list of drug positives; 3) in general sample only, not on Surgeon General's list; 4) in drug sample only, also on Army tape of September returnees; 5) in drug sample only, not on Army tape of September returnees.   22

In Canada, the random number was removed and a new number was selected for the interview, the first digit of which was the digit indicating to which sample the case belonged. The only list linking the random number to this newly assigned number was kept in Canada. Therefore, it was impossible for anyone in the United States to link an interview's contents to any individual. Nor was there danger to confidentiality in Canada since nothing was kept there except a list of paired numbers. This method closely follows the recommendations of Astin and Boruch (6). The same technique was used for maintaining the confidentiality of urinalysis reports and abstracts of military records. Because the same new number was assigned to all data pertaining to the same individual, data from various sources could be connected without endangering confidentiality.   23

24   *Validity.*   Most information in this report comes from interviews. This information is valuable to the extent that the interview is accurate. One way of checking accuracy is to look at the rate of admitted drug use by men known to be drug positive by the Surgeon General. In interviews with the drug positive sample, 97 percent reported having used narcotics in Vietnam. This level of honesty is particularly impressive when we remember that the interviewer had no idea whether the man was, in fact, a member of the drug positive sample.

25   Men were also asked whether their urines had been drug positive at DEROS. Among the men in the "drug positive" sample, only 7 percent denied ever having been detected as drug positive while in Vietnam. Eighty-one percent said they had been positive at DEROS; 7 percent said they had turned themselves in as users at DEROS rather than go through the DEROS screen; 5 percent said they were negative at DEROS but had been in a drug treatment program earlier. It seems improbable that men would try to hide having had a positive urine at DEROS if they were willing to reveal other detection as drug positive in Vietnam. Thus it seems likely that 93 percent of the men identified by the Surgeon General's office gave honest answers, and that the list of "DEROS-positives" provided by the Surgeon General's office actually included some men who had been identified by procedures other than the DEROS screen.

RESULTS

Drug Use in Vietnam

26   We will present results for the general sample, keeping in mind that this is a random sample of Army enlisted men leaving Vietnam at the height of public concern over drug abuse. If we had included women officers, personnel from the other services, and Army enlisted men departing Vietnam at other dates, lower rates of drug use would probably have been found.

27   *Narcotic use.*   Almost half the Army enlisted men who left Vietnam in September 1971 had tried one or more of the narcotic drugs listed in Table 1 while there. About one-third tried heroin and one-third tried opium, and most who tried either, tried both. Only a few tried forms of narcotics such as morphine, codeine, and Dilaudid.

28   Because the heroin in Vietnam was very pure, it was effective when used in a number of ways: mixed with tobacco and smoked, sniffed, eaten, injected under the skin or into a muscle, or injected into a vein. However, the "kick" or "flash" associated with injection was more intense and preferred by a few.

29   Most of the use of narcotics in Vietnam was by smoking. Two-thirds of those who used any narcotics more than a few times said their preferred method in Vietnam was smoking. The next most common method was sniffing, preferred by 24 percent of those who used narcotics. Injection by needle was tried by 18 percent of users but was the preferred method for 9 percent.

30   Most of those who used narcotics in Vietnam used them repeatedly and over a considerable period. Almost half the users (20 percent of the whole general sample) used narcotics more than weekly for six months to a year. Only one-fourth of the users (11 percent of the sample) were "experimenters," that is, tried a narcotic but used it less than five times.

TABLE 1 Nature of narcotic use in Vietnam (interviewed general sample of Army enlisted men returning to the USA in September 1971: No. = 451)

	%
Tried any narcotic	**43**
Narcotic tried:	
Heroin	34
Opium	38
Morphine	3
Codeine	2
Methadone	2
Each of the others*	1 or less
No. of different narcotic drugs tried:	
1	15
2	23
3 or more	6
Frequency and duration of use:	
Less than 5 times	10
5+ times, not more than once a week	4
More than weekly:	
For less than 6 months	9
For 6–8 months	10
For 9 months or more	10
Consider themselves to have been addicted	20
Ever injected	8
Usual route of administration for those using	
5 times or more (No. = 149):	
Smoking	67
Sniffing	24
Injection	9

*Demerol, Dilaudid, paregoric, Robitussin A/C.

About half (46 percent) of those who used narcotics at all in Vietnam felt that they had been addicted or "strung out." Over all, one out of five (20 percent) of all Army enlisted men returning in September 1971, said that they felt that they had been "strung out" on heroin while in Vietnam. While we cannot be certain that all who said they were addicted actually were so, all had used narcotics regularly for more than one month, and 83 percent for more than six months, suggesting that the figure of 20 percent is realistic. 31

Amphetamines and barbiturates. One-fourth said that they had used amphetamines while they were in Vietnam (Table 2). Barbiturates were used by 23 percent. A few used these drugs heavily; 7 percent used amphetamines at least 25 times and 9 percent used barbiturates at least 25 times. 32

TABLE 2   Drugs used in Vietnam

	Interviewed general sample (No. = 451) %	Interviewed drug positive sample (No. = 469) %
Any drug: narcotics, amphetamines, or barbiturates	45	97
Narcotics	43	96
Amphetamines	25	59
Barbiturates	23	77
Combinations of drug types:		
All 3: narcotics, amphetamines, and barbiturates	18	54
Narcotics and amphetamines	6	4
Narcotics and barbiturates	5	23
Narcotics only	15	15
Amphetamines only	2	0
Barbiturates only	*	*

*Less than .5%.

33   If men used any drug in Vietnam, the most common pattern was to use all three types: narcotics, barbiturates, and amphetamines. Eighteen percent followed this pattern. The next most common pattern was to use only narcotics; 15 percent followed this pattern. A combination of narcotics with either amphetamines or barbiturates, but not both, was used by 11 percent. Two percent used only amphetamines and less than 1 percent used only barbiturates. No man told us that he had used both amphetamines and barbiturates but not narcotics.

34   The Vietnam soldier who restricted his use of dangerous drugs to heroin was atypical—constituting only 23 percent of drug users. The more common pattern (54 percent of drug users) was to use at least two types of narcotics plus amphetamines or barbiturates. This multiple drug use is similar to the use patterns of heroin addicts in the United States (7). What was unusual about drug use in Vietnam as compared with use in the United States was the infrequency with which amphetamines and barbiturates were used without the use of narcotics as well. Thus in Vietnam the terms "dangerous-drug user" and "narcotics user" were virtually synonymous.

35   Multiple drug use was especially common among men detected as drug positive at DEROS. Almost all (85 percent) reported use of amphetamines and barbiturates as well as narcotics, and more than half (54 percent) reported having used all three types of drugs, even though the drug detected at DEROS was almost always a narcotic. Only 18 percent of the men detected as positive had not used either amphetamines or barbiturates in Vietnam.

36   *Distinguishing characteristics of the drug users.*   As compared with soldiers who used no drugs or only marijuana, drug users tended to be younger, less well educated, to come from

larger cities, to be single, and more often reared in broken homes (Table 3). Race was not significantly related to drug use, although blacks were more likely to be detected as positive at DEROS. The majority of users were Regular Army, while the majority of non-users were draftees. Before entering service, more users had had civilian arrests, and somewhat more had had military disciplinary actions before arrival in Vietnam. The most striking difference between users and non-users was in their drug experience before Vietnam. Two-thirds of users in Vietnam had tried marijuana before Vietnam compared with less than one-fifth of non-users, and almost half had tried amphetamines, compared with less than one out of 10 non-users. While more users of drugs in Vietnam than non-users had previously tried barbiturates and narcotics, only a minority had done so. Most of their narcotic experience had been with mild forms: codeine cough syrups, predominantly. Very few had tried heroin.

While pre-Vietnam histories of drug users and non-users differed, it would be a mistake to think of the Vietnam drug user as a highly deviant soldier with prior drug experience who could have been expected to get into trouble. While each type of prior deviance was more common in drug users than in non-users, each except marijuana use occurred in only a minority of the drug users.

37

TABLE 3   How men who used drugs in Vietnam differed from non-users at arrival in Vietnam (interviewed general sample of Army enlisted men returning to the USA in September 1971: No. = 451)*

	Users of narcotics, amphetamines, or barbiturates (interviewed: No. = 205) %	No drugs or marijuana only (interviewed: No. = 246) %
Demographic differences:		
Under 20 years of age	25	7
Less than 12 years education	39	23
Core city residence	23	14
Never married	81	57
Broken home	36	23
Prior civilian history:		
Civilian arrest	44	20
Drugs ever used—		
Marijuana	69	18
Amphetamines	42	9
Barbiturates	29	1
Narcotics	22	2
Military status:		
Regular Army	65	44
Prior disciplinary history	30	17

*All differences are statistically significant at $p < .05$ or better.

DRUG USE SINCE RETURN FROM VIETNAM

38   *Narcotics.*   In the general sample, 9.5 percent reported that they had used some narcotics since their return, 2.5 percent only while they were still in the service and 7 percent since they had been veterans.

39   How many of these prospective narcotics users after Vietnam had the Army identified through the DEROS screen program? Of the 43 men in the general sample who reported having used narcotics since their return from Vietnam, 19 (less than half) had any indication in records or interview of having been detected as drug positive at DEROS. Therefore, even if treatment could have deterred every man detected in DEROS from future use, half the number who would be narcotics users after return from Vietnam would not have been reached.

40   While 9.5 percent had used narcotics since their return and 3 percent had used them heavily (more than once a week for more than a month), only 0.7 percent (three) said that they had been addicted at any time during the eight to 12 months since their return (Table 4). Among the 91 men in the general sample who said they were addicted in Vietnam, only two (2 percent) reported continuation of that addiction after their return to the United States. Among 348 men in the drug positive sample who said they were addicted in Vietnam, only 9 percent reported continuation of their addiction in the United States. These are much lower rates of recidivism than one would have predicted based on readdiction rates among treated civilian addicts.

41   Interview reports may, of course, be unreliable. But urinalyses confirmed the low rate of current use. In the general sample, 0.7 percent of the urines collected at interview were positive for morphine or codeine, and in the drug positive sample, urines were positive for morphine or codeine in 2 percent. While there may have been some abstention from drug use because of the interview appointment, urinalysis results certainly suggest a relatively low level of current addiction.

42   To find enough users since return to study patterns of post-Vietnam narcotic usage, we turn to the drug positive sample, a third of whom reported having used narcotics since their return (Table 4). Returnees were now using the heroin they were introduced to in Vietnam, rather than the codeine and milder narcotics some were familiar with before Vietnam. Of those using any narcotic since their return, 84 percent had used heroin (28 percent of the total drug positive sample). Methadone use had also entered the picture, but it was still much less common than the use of heroin. One striking change in patterns of narcotic use since Vietnam was the shift to injection as the usual mode of administration. Seventy-seven percent of the frequent users in the United States usually injected, compared to the 18 percent of the frequent users among drug positives who usually injected in Vietnam. This, of course, reflects the lower strength and higher price of heroin in this country. Smoking narcotics, the most common mode of administration in Vietnam, was hardly used at all after return to the United States.

43   Initiation of use in the United States occurred almost immediately on return for about one-fourth of the users, but another one-fourth began more than four months after their re-

TABLE 4   Narcotic use since Vietnam

	General sample (No. = 451) %	Drug positives (No. = 469) %
Any narcotic use since return	9.5	33
Type of narcotic used		
Heroin	7	28
Opium	2	7
Codeine	1	6
Methadone	1	5
Morphine	1	3
Robitussin A/C	*	4
Demerol	*	3
Dilaudid	*	2
Paregoric	0	1
Used narcotics heavily (more than once a week for more than one month)	3	15
Felt addicted	0.7	7.2
Current use		
By interview	2	8
By urinalysis	0.7	2.4
Usual method (for those who used 5 times or more)	(No. = 19)	(No. = 82)
Smoking	11	5
Sniffing	21	13
Injection	63	77
Swallowing	5	5
Interval between return and first use, for users	(No. = 43)	(No. = 157)
Less than one week	12	20
Less than one month	23	43
Less than two months	47	57
Less than four months	65	78

*Less than 0.5%.

turn. Because the return to narcotics occurred throughout the post-Vietnam period, we cannot be sure that those who had not used narcotics by the time of interview would not use them later.

Most of the men who reported having taken narcotics since their return to the United States denied having used them regularly (defined as more than weekly for at least a month), and only about one-fifth of the users felt they had been addicted since their return.

45   *Marijuana, amphetamines, and barbiturates.*   Marijuana use was widespread among these veterans after their return, whether or not they had been detected as drug positive at DEROS. Half of the general sample and four-fifths of the drug positive sample reported using marijuana since their return to the United States (Table 5). However, less than a quarter of the users had smoked marijuana heavily (three days or more a week for more than a month) since their return. A small minority of both the general sample and of the drug positives reported that they have been using marijuana "too much" since their return (5 and 9 percent, respectively). The drug positive sample was almost twice as likely as the general sample to have used marijuana, to have used it heavily, and to have felt they had problems with it.

46   The drug positive sample was also twice as likely as the general sample to have used amphetamines. Since their return, use of amphetamines created a problem in terms of tolerance, hallucinations, or paranoia for 8 percent of the drug positives and 3 percent of the general sample. The drug positive sample reported as much dependence on or problems with amphetamines as with narcotics since their return, while there have been more amphetamine than narcotic problems among members of the general sample.

47   Among the drug positive sample, 30 percent had taken barbiturates since their return, as had 12 percent of the general sample. Tolerance to barbiturates or withdrawal symptoms since their return were reported by 4 percent of the drug positives and 2 percent of the general sample.

TABLE 5   Use of marijuana, amphetamines and barbiturates since Vietnam

	General sample (No. = 451) %	Drug positives (No. = 469) %
Any use:		
Marijuana	45	81
Amphetamines	19	38
Barbiturates	12	30
Heavy use:		
Marijuana	7	18
Amphetamines	5	8*
Barbiturates	2	6
Tolerance or problems:		
Marijuana	5	9
Amphetamines	3	8
Barbiturates	2	4
Current use (shown by urinalysis):		
Amphetamines	11	11*
Barbiturates	2	6

*Not significantly different from general sample. All other differences are significant, $p < .05$.

The analysis of urines collected at interview showed considerably higher rates of amphetamines and barbiturates than of narcotics. In the general sample, 11 percent of urines were positive for amphetamines, 2 percent for barbiturates, and 0.7 percent for narcotics. In the sample of men detected as positive for drugs at DEROS, amphetamines were found in the urines collected at interview of 11 percent, barbiturates in the urines of 6 percent, and narcotics in 2 percent. (Surprisingly, the two samples showed equally high rates of urines positive for amphetamines.) These urinalysis results would indicate that use of both amphetamines and barbiturates was more common at time of interview among returnees than was the use of narcotics, even among men who had been narcotic-dependent in Vietnam.

Use of dangerous drugs in the first 10 months after Vietnam was about half as common as in Vietnam (compare Tables 6 and 2). The dropoff in use was greatest for narcotics (78 percent less common) and least for amphetamines (24 percent less common).

Whereas in Vietnam the user of only a single drug type was usually a narcotics user, after Vietnam he was usually an amphetamine user. Use of multiple drug types was common in both periods, with half of all users trying more than one type since Vietnam.

While men detected as drug positive at DEROS were especially likely to use each type of drug after Vietnam, the same changes in rate of use and choice of drugs had occurred; the rate of use of one or more of these drugs since Vietnam was half the rate in Vietnam (49 vs. 97 percent); the decrease in use was greatest with respect to narcotics (a 66 percent drop) and least for amphetamines (a 36 percent drop). The drug most commonly used alone had changed from narcotics in Vietnam to amphetamines since Vietnam, and about half the drug positives who used a drug since Vietnam have used more than one type of drug.

48

49

50

51

TABLE 6   Dangerous drugs used since Vietnam

	General sample (No. = 451) %	Drug positive sample (No. = 469) %
Any drugs: narcotics, amphetamines, barbiturates	23	49
Narcotics	10	33
Amphetamines	19	38
Barbiturates	12	30
Combinations of drug types		
All 3: narcotics, amphetamines, barbiturates	6	14
Amphetamines and barbiturates	3	6
Narcotics and amphetamines	2	7
Narcotics and barbiturates	1	6
Narcotics only	1	7
Amphetamines only	9	10
Barbiturates only	2	5

Post-Vietnam Treatment for Drug Problems

52   Five percent of returnees had some treatment for drug use in the eight to 12 months since they returned to the United States. Almost all of that treatment was while still in service. Among men detected as drug positive in Vietnam, 46 percent had had some drug treatment since their return to the United States, again almost all while still in service, although 4 percent got treatment through the Veterans Administration, 3 percent had been inpatients in other hospitals, 1 percent attended drug clinics, and 2 percent entered some nonmedically oriented program. The treatment was usually brief, averaging about two weeks. Entering methadone maintenance programs was rare—only 0.4 percent of the general sample and 5 percent of the drug positive sample reported it.

53   Reporting at time of interview that they were in treatment were: none of the general sample, 3 percent of all drug positives, 8 percent of the drug positives still on active duty, and 2.5 percent of those released from service. Two men reported being currently in a methadone maintenance program, a low rate confirmed by urinalysis: only two men showed methadone in their urines.

54   Asked whether they were interested in continuing or beginning drug treatment, 0.7 percent of the general sample and 5.2 percent of the drug positive sample showed interest. To learn whether those showing interest could be expected to have difficulty finding a treatment facility that would accept them, men were asked whether they had asked for treatment at any place where they failed to get it. Among the general sample 0.4 percent, and among drug positives 4 percent had sought treatment and not received it. These few failures to receive treatment resulted as often from the applicant's changing his mind as from rejection by the agency. Thus the low rate of treatment received after leaving service did not seem to reflect a lack of treatment opportunities.

55   Since civilian treatment facilities typically get histories of addiction of several years' duration from men admitted for the first time, it is possible that a demand for treatment may emerge later among veterans now drug dependent but not yet ready to seek help.

Predictors of Post-Vietnam Drug Use

56   The man most likely to be detected as drug positive in Vietnam was a young, single, black, low-ranking member of the Regular Army who had little education, came from a broken home, had an arrest history before service, and had used drugs before service.

57   None of the demographic characteristics which had forecast detection as drug positive at DEROS were of any use in forecasting continuing narcotic use after return to the United States among those detected as positive by the DEROS screen. Blacks and whites had about the same risk of using narcotics once they returned to the United States. Men under 22 had the same risk as older men. Single men and married men had equal risks. It made no difference whether the man had grown up in a large city or a small town. Neither did low military rank nor being in the Regular Army predict use on return.

The only pre-service factors that predicted continuing use were delinquency, high school [58] dropout, and drug experience (Table 7). The strongest of these predictors was pre-service narcotic use. Men with such a history had two and one-half times the risk of continuing narcotic use as did men first introduced to narcotics in Vietnam. The only pre-Vietnam military indicator was disciplinary action.

Use of barbiturates or amphetamines in Vietnam, and particularly frequent use of either [59] drug, was associated with use of narcotics after return. About half of those reporting taking amphetamines or barbiturates 25 times or more while in Vietnam continued their narcotic use after returning to the United States.

TABLE 7 Significant predictors of narcotic use after return to the USA for men detected positive at DEROS*

Predictors of narcotic use after return by drug positives	% using a narcotic after return			
	Of men with this characteristic		Of men without this characteristic	
	No.	%	No.	%
Prior to Vietnam:				
Civilian arrest	168	45	301	27
Did not finish high school	216	40	253	27
Tried marijuana	170	54	299	22
Tried a narcotic	106	63	363	25
Disciplinary action	166	42	255	28
In Vietnam:				
Used any amphetamines	275	43	192	19
25+ times	75	52	394	20
Used any barbiturates	363	38	104	16
25+ times	144	53	325	19
No drinking or less than weekly	351	38	117	21
Narcotic used:				
Opium	331	41	138	15
Codeine	50	50	419	32
Methadone	63	59	406	30
Morphine	63	71	406	28
Used narcotics heavily 6+ months	319	43	150	13
Usually injected narcotics	84	54	385	27
Usually "sniffed" narcotics	210	51	259	19
Felt addicted to narcotics	349	40	118	14

*Date eligible for return from overseas.

60   The heavy use of alcohol in Vietnam was negatively related to narcotic use after return. Among men drug positive at DEROS who drank at least weekly in Vietnam, only 21 percent used narcotics after return to the United States, as compared with 36 percent of those who drank less than once a week.

61   Furthermore, the type of narcotic used in Vietnam was a predictor of continued use. Heroin had been used in Vietnam by almost every man detected as drug positive, and one-third of heroin users used narcotics in the United States after their return. Addition of the less common narcotics to the use of heroin was associated with a greater likelihood of using some narcotic after return. Rates of use after return were especially high for morphine users (71 percent) and methadone users (59 percent). Even the addition of codeine, a less addicting narcotic than heroin, was associated with a greater risk of continuing narcotics (50 vs. 35 percent).

62   Prolonged narcotic usage in Vietnam increased the chance that a man would continue use after leaving Vietnam. Only 13 percent of the men who confined their use to less than a six-month period used any narcotic after return, while use for more than six months was followed by use in the United States for 43 percent.

63   Asked their usual method of administration of narcotics in Vietnam, one-sixth of the drug positives said the needle was the preferred method, one-quarter preferred sniffing, and half preferred smoking. Those who preferred sniffing or injecting were more likely to use on return. There was little difference in later use between those who sniffed or injected.

64   Drug positives who said they were addicted or "strung out" in Vietnam were more likely to continue use than those denying addiction (40 vs. 14 percent), but more than half of the drug positives who considered themselves addicted in Vietnam never tried narcotics after their return from overseas.

65   In summary, patterns of drug use, both before and in Vietnam, were the best predictors of narcotics use after return to the United States by the drug positives. Social status and military status indicators were not helpful. Pre-service delinquency and failure to complete high school were reasonably good predictors, although less powerful than drug use patterns.

66   There are many ways in which these correlates of drug use after return to the United States could be combined to serve as a predictive tool. One successful combination we discovered was regular narcotic use in Vietnam for more than a month, plus two of the three following correlates: a) use of narcotics before service, b) frequent use of amphetamines or barbiturates in Vietnam, and c) little use of alcohol in Vietnam. This combination identified 67 percent of the drug positives who did use narcotics on return, while selecting only 28 percent of the drug positives who did not use narcotics on return. An index similar to this one may prove useful for selecting those men most in need of intervention.

67   It would be of much greater interest, of course, to predict *heavy or addictive* use on return to the United States rather than predicting *any* use of narcotics. We discovered no information that would have been obtainable before their departure from Vietnam that could have predicted which of the men likely to continue narcotic use in the States would be heavy or addictive users here. The degree of use after return, if a man uses at all, either is determined more by the local scene than by his history prior to his return, or it is determined by factors our interview has not tapped.

DISCUSSION

The Vietnam experience has been a natural experiment in the exposure of masses of   68
young men to narcotic drugs. In Vietnam, in 1970, almost every enlisted man was approached by someone offering him heroin, usually within the first month of his arrival. This "natural experiment" provides an opportunity to learn what happens when first exposure to heroin occurs in a foreign and for many a frightening setting, without the deterrents of high prices, impure drugs, or the presence of disapproving family.

What happened in this population of young Army enlisted men returning from Vietnam in September 1971 was that almost half of them did try heroin or opium or both while   69
in Vietnam and that about one-fifth of them used narcotics there with sufficient regularity to develop some signs of physical or psychological dependence. Men who came to Vietnam with a history of deviant behavior (crime, drug use, or high school dropout) were more likely than others to use drugs in Vietnam.

Surprisingly, in the light of the common belief that dependence on narcotics is easily   70
acquired and virtually impossible to rid oneself of, most of the men who used narcotics heavily in Vietnam stopped when they left Vietnam and had not begun again eight to 12 months later. Demographic variables and military rank did not predict which men would continue use after Vietnam. Pre-service use of drugs and extent of use in Vietnam were powerful predictors of continued use after Vietnam.

Of those who continued narcotic use after their return to the United States, most re-   71
ported that they had not become addicted or readdicted. Contrary to conventional belief, the occasional use of narcotics without becoming addicted appears to be possible even for men who have previously been dependent on narcotics. The returnees' lack of interest in obtaining treatment for drug use perhaps reflects this experience with successful voluntary abstinence and light use. The small percentage who did become readdicted on return were not detectably different in terms of prior history; none of the indicators of social or military status or even of deviant behavior and drug use before or in Vietnam predicted which men could use narcotics occasionally in the United States without readdiction, and which men would become addicted if they used narcotics after return.

Public concern about drugs in both the Vietnam and post-Vietnam periods has centered   72
on narcotics, and heroin in particular. While heroin was very commonly used in Vietnam, so was opium. Nor was there a lack of use in Vietnam of dangerous nonnarcotic drugs, both stimulants and sedatives. In Vietnam, the latter drugs were used almost exclusively by men also using narcotics. Since Vietnam, stimulants and sedatives are playing a larger role than narcotics in the drug behavior of veterans. In the light of the wider use of barbiturates and amphetamines than of narcotics and the small number of veterans who feel they need treatment for narcotic addiction, there should be little pressure on the capacities of existing narcotic treatment programs from these veterans at the present time. However, those using narcotics occasionally since return have usually injected heroin rather than smoking or sniffing heroin and opium as they did in Vietnam, or drinking codeine cough syrups as a few did before Vietnam. This choice of method and substance may be associated with increasing addiction rates in the next few years.

73   The high completion rates for interviews and urinalyses in these large, carefully selected random samples, plus the willingness of the subjects to talk freely about their drug
experiences, gives us some confidence that the results reported accurately describe the experience of the population studied: Army enlisted men who returned to the United States
from Vietnam in September 1971 and who had been in the United States for eight to 12
months. To what extent our findings can be extrapolated to the drug experiences of civilians or other servicemen is not known.

REFERENCES

1. Hunt GH, Odoroff ME: Follow-up study of narcotic drug addicts after hospitalization. Public
    Health Rep 77:41–54, 1962
2. O'Donnell JA: Narcotic addicts in Kentucky. PHS Publ No. 1881, Washington DC, US GPO, 1969
3. Vaillant GE: Twelve year follow-up of New York narcotic addicts. Am J Psychiatry 122:727–737,
    1966
4. Robins LN: A follow-up of Vietnam drug users. Special Action Office Monograph, Series A:1,
    April, 1973
5. Robins LN: Deviant Children Grown Up. Baltimore, The Williams & Wilkins Company, 1966
6. Astin AW, Boruch RF: A "link" system for assuring confidentiality of research data in longitudi-
    nal studies. Am Educational Research J 7:615–624, 1970
7. Drug use in America: problem in perspective. Second report of the National Commission on Mar-
    ihuana and Drug Abuse. Washington, DC, US GPO, 1973

 FOR CLASS DISCUSSION

1. Analyze and evaluate the dispute on the legalization of drugs by applying the
    first set of guide question from page 455. How do you account for the enor-
    mous disagreements between Wilson and those arguing that drugs should be
    legalized?

2. Choose one of the arguments for closer analysis, applying the second set of
    guide questions on page 455–456.

Optional Writing Assignment   Your state has an initiative on the ballot to legalize
all drugs. Because you are a well-known writer of book blurbs, celebrated for your
ability to summarize seven-hundred-page tomes in a few paragraphs, you have
been asked by both sides to write up their side of the case for the voters' pamphlet.
You can't help yourself. You're broke. You take on both clients. Now the day of
truth has arrived. Your deadline is tomorrow. Drawing on the preceding essays,
personal experience, and any other research you may have done, write two-hun-
dred-fifty-word arguments for and against drug legalization suitable for use in a
voting pamphlet.

SEXUAL HARASSMENT: WHEN IS OFFENSIVENESS A CIVIL OFFENSE?

Gender Dilemmas in Sexual Harassment Policies and Procedures

Stephanie Riger

Sexual harassment—unwanted sexually oriented behavior in a work context—is the most recent form of victimization of women to be redefined as a social rather than a personal problem, following rape and wife abuse. A sizeable proportion of women surveyed in a wide variety of work settings reported being subject to unwanted sexual attention, sexual comments or jokes, offensive touching, or attempts to coerce compliance with or punish rejection of sexual advances. In 1980 the U.S. Merit Systems Protection Board (1981) conducted the first comprehensive national survey of sexual harassment among federal employees: About 4 out of 10 of the 10,648 women surveyed reported having been the target of sexual harassment during the previous 24 months. A recent update of this survey found that the frequency of harassment in 1988 was identical to that reported earlier: 42% of all women surveyed in 1988 reported that they had experienced some form of unwanted and uninvited sexual attention compared to exactly the same percentage of women in 1980 (U.S. Merit Systems Protection Board, 1988).

Women ranging from blue-collar workers (LaFontaine & Tredeau, 1986; Maypole & Skaine, 1982) to lawyers (Burleigh & Goldberg, 1989) to airline personnel (Littler-Bishop, Seidler-Feller, & Opaluch, 1982) have reported considerable amounts of sexual harassment in surveys. Among a random sample of private sector workers in the Los Angeles area, more than one half of the women surveyed by telephone reported experiencing at least one incident that they considered sexual harassment during their working lives (Gutek, 1985). Some estimate that up to about one third of women in educational institutions have experienced some form of harassment (Kenig & Ryan, 1986). Indeed, Garvey (1986) stated that "Unwanted sexual attention may be the single most widespread occupational hazard in the workplace today" (p. 75).

It is a hazard faced much more frequently by women than men. About 40% of the women in the original U.S. Merit Systems Protection Board survey reported having experienced sexual harassment, compared with only 15% of the men (U.S. Merit Systems Protection Board, 1981). Among working people surveyed in Los Angeles, women were nine times more likely than men to report having quit a job because of sexual harassment, five times more likely to have transferred, and three times more likely to have lost a job (Konrad

& Gutek, 1986). Women with low power and status, whether due to lower age, being single or divorced, or being in a marginal position in the organization, are more likely to be harassed (Fain & Anderton, 1987; LaFontaine & Tredeau, 1986; Robinson & Reid, 1985).

4   Sex differences in the frequency of harassment also prevail in educational environments (Fitzgerald et al., 1988). A mailed survey of more than 900 women and men at the University of Rhode Island asked about a wide range of behavior, including the frequency of respondents' experience of sexual insult, defined as an "uninvited sexually suggestive, obscene or offensive remark, stare, or gesture" (Lott, Reilly, & Howard, 1982, p. 309). Of the female respondents, 40% reported being sexually insulted occasionally or often while on campus, compared with 17% of the men. Both men and women reported that women are rarely the source of such insults. Similar differences were found in a survey of social workers, with 2½ times as many women as men reporting harassment (Maypole, 1986).

5   Despite the high rates found in surveys of sexual harassment of women, few complaints are pursued through official grievance procedures. Dzeich and Weiner (1984) concluded, after reviewing survey findings, that 20% to 30% of female college students experience sexual harassment. Yet academic institutions averaged only 4.3 complaints each during the 1982–1983 academic year (Robertson, Dyer, & Campbell, 1988), a period roughly consecutive with the surveys cited by Dzeich and Weiner. In another study conducted at a university in 1984, of 38 women who reported harassment, only 1 reported the behavior to the offender's supervisor and 2 reported the behavior to an adviser, another professor, or employer (Reilly, Lott, & Gallogly, 1986). Similar findings have been reported on other college campuses (Adams, Kottke, & Padgitt, 1983; Benson & Thompson, 1982; Brandenburg, 1982; Cammaert, 1985; Meek & Lynch, 1983; Schneider, 1987).

6   Low numbers of complaints appear in other work settings as well. In a survey of federal workers, only about 11% of victims reported the harassment to a higher authority, and only 2.5% used formal complaint channels (Livingston, 1982). Similarly, female social workers reacted to harassment by avoiding or delaying the conflict or attempting to defuse the situation rather than by adopting any form of recourse such as filing a grievance (Maypole, 1986). The number of complaints alleging sexual harassment filed with the Equal Employment Opportunity Commission in Washington, DC, has declined since 1984, despite an increase in the number of women in the workforce during that time (Morgenson, 1989), and surveys suggest that the rate of sexual harassment has remained relatively stable (U.S. Merit Systems Protection Board, 1981, 1988).

7   It is the contention of this article that the low rate of utilization of grievance procedures is due to gender bias in sexual harassment policies that discourages their use by women. Policies are written in gender-neutral language and are intended to apply equally to men and women. However, these policies are experienced differently by women than men because of gender differences in perceptions of harassment and orientation toward conflict. Although victims of all forms of discrimination are reluctant to pursue grievances (Bumiller, 1987), women, who are most likely to be the victims of sexual harassment, are especially disinclined to pursue sexual harassment grievances for at least two reasons. First, the interpretation in policies of what constitutes harassment may not reflect women's viewpoints, and their complaints may not be seen as valid. Second, the procedures in some poli-

cies that are designed to resolve disputes may be inimical to women because they are not compatible with the way that many women view conflict resolution. Gender bias in policies, rather than an absence of harassment or lack of assertiveness on the part of victims, produces low numbers of complaints.

GENDER BIAS IN THE DEFINITION OF SEXUAL HARASSMENT

The first way that gender bias affects sexual harassment policies stems from differences   8
between men and women in the interpretation of the definition of harassment. Those writing sexual harassment policies for organizations typically look to the courts for the distinction between illegal sexual harassment and permissible (although perhaps unwanted) social interaction (see Cohen, 1987, for a discussion of this distinction in legal cases). The definition of harassment in policies typically is that provided by the U.S. Equal Employment Opportunity Commission (1980) guidelines:

> Unwelcome sexual advances, requests for sexual favors, and other verbal or physical conduct of a sexual nature constitute sexual harassment when (1) submission to such conduct is made either explicitly or implicitly a term or condition of an individual's employment, (2) submission to or rejection of such conduct by an individual is used as the basis for employment decisions affecting such individual, or (3) such conduct has the purpose or effect of unreasonably interfering with an individual's work performance or creating an intimidating, hostile, or offensive working environment. (p. 74677)

The first two parts of the definition refer to a quid pro quo relationship involving people in positions of unequal status, as superior status is usually necessary to have control over another's employment. In such cases bribes, threats, or punishments are used. Incidents of this type need happen only once to fall under the definition of sexual harassment. However, courts have required that incidents falling into the third category, "an intimidating, hostile, or offensive working environment," must be repeated in order to establish that such an environment exists (Terpstra & Baker, 1988); these incidents must be both pervasive and so severe that they affect the victim's psychological well-being (Trager, 1988). Harassment of this type can come from peers or even subordinates as well as superiors.

In all three of these categories, harassment is judged on the basis of conduct and its ef-   9
fects on the recipient, not the intentions of the harasser. Thus, two typical defenses given by accused harassers—"I was just being friendly," or "I touch everyone, I'm that kind of person"—do not hold up in court. Yet behavior may have an intimidating or offensive effect on some people but be inoffensive or even welcome to others. In deciding whose standards should be used, the courts employ what is called the *reasonable person rule,* asking whether a reasonable person would be offended by the conduct in question. The dilemma in applying this to sexual harassment is that a reasonable woman and a reasonable man are likely to differ in their judgments of what is offensive.

Definitions of sexual harassment are socially constructed, varying not only with char-   10
acteristics of perceiver but also those of the situational context and actors involved. Behavior is more likely to be labelled harassment when it is done by someone with greater

power than the victim (Gutek, Morasch, & Cohen, 1983; Kenig & Ryan, 1986; Lester et al., 1986; Popovich, Licata, Nokovich, Martelli, & Zoloty, 1987); when it involves physical advances accompanied by threats of punishment for noncompliance (Rossi & Weber-Burdin, 1983); when the response to it is negative (T. S. Jones, Remland, & Brunner, 1987); when the behavior reflects persistent negative intentions toward a woman (Pryor & Day, 1988); the more inappropriate it is for the actor's social role (Pryor, 1985); and the more flagrant and frequent the harasser's actions (Thomann & Wiener, 1987). Among women, professionals are more likely than those in secretarial-clerical positions to report the more subtle behaviors as harassment (McIntyre & Renick, 1982).

11   The variable that most consistently predicts variation in people's definition of sexual harassment is the sex of the rater. Men label fewer behaviors at work as sexual harassment (Kenig & Ryan, 1986; Konrad & Gutek, 1986; Lester et al., 1986; Powell, 1986; Rossi & Weber-Burdin, 1983). Men tend to find sexual overtures from women at work to be flattering, whereas women find similar approaches from men to be insulting (Gutek, 1985). Both men and women agree that certain blatant behaviors, such as sexual assault or sexual bribery, constitute harassment, but women are more likely to see as harassment more subtle behavior such as sexual teasing or looks or gestures (Adams et al., 1983; Collins & Blodgett, 1981; Kenig & Ryan, 1986; U.S. Merit Systems Protection Board, 1981). Even when they do identify behavior as harassment, men are more likely to think that women will be flattered by it (Kirk, 1988). Men are also more likely than women to blame women for being sexually harassed (Kenig & Ryan, 1986; Jensen & Gutek, 1982).

12   These gender differences make it difficult to apply the reasonable person rule. Linenberger (1983) proposed 10 factors that permit an "objective" assessment of whether behavior constitutes sexual harassment, regardless of the perception of the victim and the intent of the perpetrator. These factors range from the severity of the conduct to the number and frequency of encounters, and the relationship of the parties involved. For example, behavior is less likely to be categorized as harassment if it is seen as a response to provocation from the victim. But is an objective rating of provocation possible? When gender differences are as clear-cut and persistent as they are in the perception of what behavior constitutes sexual harassment, the question is not one of objectivity, but rather of which sex's definition of the situation will prevail. Becker (1967) asserted that there is a "hierarchy of credibility" in organizations, and that credibility and the right to be heard are differentially distributed: "In any system of ranked groups, participants take it as given that members of the highest group have the right to define the way things really are" (p. 241). Because men typically have more power in organizations (Kanter, 1977), Becker's analysis suggests that in most situations the male definition of harassment is likely to predominate. As MacKinnon (1987) put it, "objectivity—the nonsituated, universal standpoint, whether claimed or aspired to—is a denial of the existence or potency of sex inequality that tacitly participates in constructing reality from the dominant point of view" (p. 136). "The law sees and treats women the way men see and treat women" (p. 140). This means that men's judgments about what behavior constitutes harassment, and who is to blame, are likely to prevail. Linenberger's 10 factors thus may not be an objective measure, but rather a codification of the male perspective on harassment. This is likely to discourage women who want to bring complaints about more subtle forms of harassment.

SEX DIFFERENCES IN THE ATTRIBUTION OF HARASSMENT

Attribution theory provides an explanation for the wider range of behaviors that women define as harassment and for men's tendency to find women at fault (Kenig & Ryan, 1986; Pryor, 1985; Pryor & Day, 1988). Attribution theory suggests that people tend to see their own behaviors as situationally determined, whereas they attribute the behaviors of others to personality characteristics or other internal causes (E. E. Jones & Nisbett, 1971). Those who see sexual harassment through the eyes of the actor are likely to be male. As actors are wont to do, they will attribute their behaviors to situational causes, including the "provocations" of the women involved. They will then not perceive their own behaviors as harassment. In fact, those who take the perspective of the victim do see specific behaviors as more harassing than those who take the perspective of the actor (Pryor & Day, 1988). Women are more likely to view harassment through the eyes of the victim; therefore they will label more behaviors as harassment because they attribute them to men's disposition or personality traits. Another possibility is that men, as potential harassers, want to avoid blame in the future, and so shift the blame to women (Jensen & Gutek, 1982) and restrict the range of behaviors that they define as harassment (Kenig & Ryan, 1986). Whatever the cause, a reasonable man and a reasonable woman are likely to differ in their judgments of whether a particular behavior constitutes sexual harassment.   13

Men tend to misinterpret women's friendliness as an indication of sexual interest (Abbey, 1982; Abbey & Melby, 1986; Saal, Johnson, & Weber, 1989; Shotland & Craig, 1988). Acting on this misperception may result in behavior that is harassing to women. Tangri, Burt, and Johnson (1982) stated that "Some sexual harassment may indeed be clumsy or insensitive expressions of attraction, while some is the classic abuse of organizational power" (p. 52). Gender differences in attributional processes help explain the first type of harassment, partially accounting for the overwhelming preponderance of sexual harassment incidents that involve a male offender and a female victim.   14

GENDER BIAS IN GRIEVANCE PROCEDURES

Typically, procedures for resolving disputes about sexual harassment are written in gender-neutral terms so that they may apply to both women and men. However, men and women may react quite differently to the same procedures.   15

Analyzing this problem requires looking at specific policies and procedures. Educational institutions will serve as the context for this discussion for three reasons. First, they are the most frequent site of surveys about the problem, and the pervasive nature of harassment on campuses has been well documented (Dzeich & Weiner, 1984). Second, although sexual harassment is harmful to women in all occupations, it can be particularly devastating to those in educational institutions, in which the goal of the organization is to nurture and promote development. The violation of relationships based on trust, such as those between faculty and students, can leave long-lasting and deep wounds, yet many surveys find that those in positions of authority in educational settings are often the sources of the problem (Benson & Thomson, 1982; Fitzgerald et al., 1988; Glaser & Thorpe, 1986; Kenig & Ryan, 1986; Maihoff & Forrest, 1983; Metha & Nigg, 1983; Robinson & Reid, 1985;   16

K. R. Wilson & Kraus, 1983). Third, educational institutions have been leaders in the development of sexual harassment policies, in part because of concern about litigation. In *Alexander v. Yale University* (1977) the court decided that sexual harassment constitutes a form of sex discrimination that denies equal access to educational opportunities, and falls under Title IX of the Educational Amendments of 1972. The Office of Civil Rights in the U.S. Department of Education now requires institutions that receive Title IX funds to maintain grievance procedures to resolve complaints involving sexual discrimination or harassment (M. Wilson, 1988). Consequently, academic institutions may have had more experience than other work settings in developing procedures to combat this problem. A survey of U.S. institutions of higher learning conducted in 1984 (Robertson et al., 1988) found that 66% of all responding institutions had sexual harassment policies, and 46% had grievance procedures specifically designed to deal with sexual harassment complaints, with large public schools more likely to have them than small private ones. These percentages have unquestionably increased in recent years, given the government funding regulations. Although the discussion here is focused on educational contexts, the problems identified in sexual harassment policies exist in other work settings as well.

17   Many educational institutions, following guidelines put forward by the American Council on Education (1986) and the American Association of University Professors (1983), have established policies that prohibit sexual harassment and create grievance procedures. Some use a formal board or hearing, and others use informal mechanisms that protect confidentiality and seek to resolve the complaint rather than punish the offender (see, e.g., Brandenburg, 1982; Meek & Lynch, 1983). Still others use both types of procedures. The type of procedure specified by the policy may have a great impact on victims' willingness to report complaints.

Comparison of Informal and Formal Grievance Procedures

18   Informal attempts to resolve disputes differ from formal procedures in important ways (for a general discussion of dispute resolution systems, see Brett, Goldberg, & Ury, 1990). First, their goal is to solve a problem, rather than to judge the harasser's guilt or innocence. The assumptions underlying these processes are that both parties in a dispute perceive a problem (although they may define that problem differently); that both share a common interest in solving that problem; and that together they can negotiate an agreement that will be satisfactory to everyone involved. Typically, the goal of informal processes is to end the harassment of the complainant rather than judge (and punish, if appropriate) the offender. The focus is on what will happen in the future between the disputing parties, rather than on what has happened in the past. Often policies do not specify the format of informal problem solving, but accept a wide variety of strategies of reconciliation. For example, a complainant might write a letter to the offender (Rowe, 1981), or someone might talk to the offender on the complainant's behalf. The offender and victim might participate in mediation, in which a third party helps them negotiate an agreement. Many policies accept a wide array of strategies as good-faith attempts to solve the problem informally.

19   In contrast, formal procedures generally require a written complaint and have a specified procedure for handling cases, usually by bringing the complaint to a group officially designated to hear the case, such as a hearing board. The informal process typically ends when

the complainant is satisfied (or decides to drop the complaint); the formal procedure ends when the hearing board decides on the guilt or innocence of the alleged harasser. Thus, control over the outcome usually rests with the complainant in the case of informal mechanisms, and with the official governance body in the case of a hearing. Compliance with a decision is usually voluntary in informal procedures, whereas the decision in a formal procedure is binding unless appealed to a higher authority. Formal procedures are adversarial in nature, with the complainant and defendant competing to see whose position will prevail.

A typical case might proceed as follows: A student with a complaint writes a letter to   20
the harasser (an informal procedure). If not satisfied with the response, she submits a written complaint to the sexual harassment hearing board, which then hears both sides of the case, reviews available evidence, and decides on the guilt or innocence of the accused (a formal procedure). If the accused is found guilty, the appropriate officer of the institution decides on punishment.

Gender Differences in Orientation to Conflict

Women and men may differ in their reactions to dispute resolution procedures for at   21
least two reasons. First, women typically have less power than men in organizations (Kanter, 1977). Using a grievance procedure, such as appearing before a hearing board, may be inimical because of the possibility of retaliation for a complaint. Miller (1976) suggested that differences in status and power affect the way that people handle conflict:

> As soon as a group attains dominance it tends inevitably to produce a situation of conflict and . . . it also, simultaneously, seeks to suppress conflict. Moreover, subordinates who accept the dominant's conception of them as passive and malleable do not openly engage in conflict. Conflict . . . is forced underground (p. 127).

This may explain why some women do not report complaints at all. When they do com-   22
plain, however, their relative lack of power or their values may predispose women to prefer informal rather than formal procedures. Beliefs about the appropriate way to handle disputes vary among social groups (Merry & Silbey, 1984). Gilligan's (1982) distinction between an orientation toward rights and justice compared with an emphasis on responsibilities to others and caring is likely to be reflected in people's preferences for ways of handling disputes (Kolb & Coolidge, 1988). Neither of these orientations is exclusive to one sex, but according to Gilligan, women are more likely to emphasize caring. Women's orientation to caring may be due to their subordinate status (Miller, 1976). Empirical support for Gilligan's theories is inconclusive (see, e.g., Mednick, 1989, for a summary of criticisms). Yet the fact that most victims of sexual harassment state that they simply want an end to the offending behavior rather than punishment of the offender (Robertson et al., 1988) suggests a "caring" rather than "justice" perspective (or possibly, a fear of reprisals).

In the context of dispute resolution, an emphasis on responsibilities and caring is com-   23
patible with the goals of informal procedures to restore harmony or at least peaceful coexistence among the parties involved, whereas that of justice is compatible with formal procedures that attempt to judge guilt or innocence of the offender. Thus women may prefer to use informal procedures to resolve conflicts, and indeed most cases in educational

institutions are handled through informal mechanisms (Robertson et al., 1988). Policies that do not include an informal dispute resolution option are likely to discourage many women from bringing complaints.

Problems with Informal Dispute-Resolution Procedures

24   Although women may prefer informal mechanisms, they are problematic for several reasons (Rifkin, 1984). Because they do not result in punishment, offenders suffer few negative consequences of their actions and may not be deterred from harassing again. In institutions of higher learning, the most common form of punishment reported is a verbal warning by a supervisor, which is given only "sometimes" (Robertson et al., 1988). Dismissal and litigation are almost never used. It seems likely, then, that sexual harassment may be viewed by potential harassers as low-risk behavior, and that victims see few incentives for bringing official complaints.

25   The confidentiality usually required by informal procedures prevents other victims from knowing that a complaint has been lodged against a multiple offender. If a woman knows that another woman is bringing a complaint against a particular man who has harassed both of them, then she might be more willing to complain also. The secrecy surrounding informal complaint processes precludes this information from becoming public and makes it more difficult to identify repeat offenders. Also, complaints settled informally may not be included in reports of the frequency of sexual harassment claims, making these statistics underestimate the scope of the problem. Yet confidentiality is needed to protect the rights of the accused and may be preferred by those bringing complaints.

26   These problems in informal procedures could discourage male as well as female victims from bringing complaints. Most problematic for women, however, is the assumption in informal procedures that the complainant and accused have equal power in the process of resolving the dispute. This assumption is likely to put women at a disadvantage. Parties involved in sexual harassment disputes may not be equal either in the sense of formal position within the organization (e.g., student versus faculty) or status (e.g., female versus male students), and position and status characteristics that reflect levels of power do not disappear simply because they are irrelevant to the informal process. External status characteristics that indicate macrolevel social stratification (e.g., sex and age) help explain the patterns of distribution of sexual harassment in the workplace (Fain & Anderton, 1987). It seems likely that these external statuses will influence the interpersonal dynamics within a dispute-resolution procedure as well. Because women are typically lower than men in both formal and informal status and power in organizations, they will have less power in the dispute resolution process.

27   When the accused has more power than the complainant (e.g., a male faculty member accused by a female student), the complainant is more vulnerable to retaliation. Complainants may be reluctant to use grievance procedures because they fear retaliation should the charge be made public. For example, students may fear that a faculty member will punish them for bringing a complaint by lowering their grades or withholding recommendations. The person appointed to act as a guide to the informal resolution process is usually expected

to act as a neutral third party rather than advocate for the complainant, and may hold little formal power over faculty: "Relatively few institutions have persons empowered to be (non-legal) advocates for the complainants; a student bringing a complaint has little assurance of stopping the harassment and avoiding retaliation" (Robertson et al., 1988, p. 801). The victim then is left without an advocate to face an opponent whose formal position, age, and experience with verbal argument is often considerably beyond her own. The more vulnerable a woman's position is in her organization, the more likely it is that she will be harassed (Robinson & Reid, 1985); therefore sexual harassment, like rape, involves dynamics of power and domination as well as sexuality. The lack of an advocate for the complainant who might equalize power between the disputing parties is particularly troubling. However, if an advocate is provided for the complainant in an informal process, fairness and due process require that the defendant have an advocate as well. The dilemma is that this seems likely to transform an informal, problem-solving process into a formal, adversarial one.

OTHER OBSTACLES TO REPORTING COMPLAINTS

Belief that Sexual Harassment of Women is Normative

Because of differences in perception of behavior, men and women involved in a sexual harassment case are likely to have sharply divergent interpretations of that case, particularly when a hostile environment claim is involved. To women, the behavior in question is offensive, and they are likely to see themselves as victims of male actions. The requirement that an attempt be made to mediate the dispute or solve it through informal processes may violate their perception of the situation and of themselves as victims of a crime. By comparison, a victim of a mugging is not required to solve the problem with the mugger through mediation (B. Sandler, personal communication, 1988). To many men, the behavior is not offensive, but normative. In their eyes, no crime has been committed, and there is no problem to be solved. [28]

Some women may also consider sexual harassment to be normative. Women may believe that these sorts of behaviors are simply routine, a commonplace part of everyday life, and thus not something that can be challenged. Younger women—who are more likely to be victims (Fain & Anderton, 1987; LaFontaine & Tredeau, 1986; McIntyre & Renick, 1982)—are more tolerant of harassment than are older women (Lott et al., 1982; Reilly et al., 1986). Indeed, Lott et al. concluded that "younger women in particular have accepted the idea that prowling men are a 'fact of life'" (p. 318). This attitude might prevent women from labelling a negative experience as harassment. Surveys that ask women about sexual harassment and about the frequency of experiencing specific sexually harassing behaviors find discrepancies in responses to these questions (Fitzgerald et al., 1988). Women report higher rates when asked if they have been the target of specific harassing behaviors than when asked a general question about whether they have been harassed. Women are also more willing to report negative reactions to offensive behaviors than they are to label those behaviors as sexual harassment (Brewer, 1982). [29]

Normative beliefs may deter some male victims of harassment from reporting complaints also, because men are expected to welcome sexual advances if those advances are from women. [30]

Negative Outcome for Victims Who Bring Complaints

31   The outcome of grievance procedures does not appear to provide much satisfaction to victims who bring complaints. In academic settings, despite considerable publicity given to a few isolated cases in which tenured faculty have been fired, punishments are rarely inflicted on harassers, and the punishments that are given are mild, such as verbal warnings (Robertson et al., 1988). Among federal workers, 33% of those who used formal grievance procedures to protest sexual harassment found that it "made things worse" (Livingston, 1982). More than 65% of the cases of formal charges of sexual harassment filed with the Illinois Department of Human Rights involved job discharge of the complainant (Terpstra & Cook, 1985). Less than one third of those cases resulted in a favorable settlement for the complainant, and those who received financial compensation got an average settlement of $3,234 (Terpstra & Baker, 1988). Similar findings in California were reported by Coles (1986), with the average cash settlement there of $973, representing approximately one month's pay. Although a few legal cases have resulted in large settlements (Garvey, 1986), these studies suggest that typical settlements are low. Formal actions may take years to complete, and in legal suits the victim usually must hire legal counsel at considerable expense (Livingston, 1982). These small settlements seem unlikely to compensate victims for the emotional stress, notoriety, and financial costs involved in filing a public complaint. Given the consistency with which victimization falls more often to women than men, it is ironic that one of the largest settlements awarded to an individual in a sexual harassment case ($196,500 in damages) was made to a man who brought suit against his female supervisor (Brewer & Berk, 1982), perhaps because sexual aggression by a woman is seen as especially egregious.

Emotional Consequences of Harassment

32   In academic settings, harassment can adversely affect students' learning, and therefore their academic standing. It can deprive them of educational and career opportunities because they wish to avoid threatening situations. Students who have been harassed report that they consequently avoid taking a class from or working with a particular faculty member, change their major, or leave a threatening situation (Adams et al., 1983; Lott et al., 1982). Lowered self-esteem follows the conclusion that rewards, such as a high grade, may have been based on sexual attraction rather than one's abilities (McCormack, 1985). Decreased feelings of competence and confidence and increased feelings of anger, frustration, depression, and anxiety all can result from harassment (Cammaert, 1985; Crull, 1982; Hamilton, Alagna, King & Lloyd, 1987; Livingston, 1982; Schneider, 1987). The psychological stress produced by harassment is compounded when women are fired or quit their jobs in fear or frustration (Coles, 1986).

33   Meek and Lynch (1983) proposed that victims of harassment typically go through several stages of reaction, at first questioning the offender's true intentions and then blaming themselves for the offender's behavior. Women with traditional sex-role beliefs are more likely to blame themselves for being harassed (Jensen & Gutek, 1982). Victims then worry about being believed by others and about possible retaliation if they take formal steps to protest the behavior. A victim may be too frightened or confused to assert herself or pun-

ish the offender. Psychologists who work with victims of harassment would do well to recognize that not only victims' emotional reactions but also the nature of the grievance process as discussed in this article may discourage women from bringing formal complaints.

PREVENTION OF SEXUAL HARASSMENT

Some writers have argued that sexual harassment does not occur with great frequency, or if it once was a problem, it has been eliminated in recent years. Indeed, Morgenson (1989), writing in the business publication *Forbes,* suggested that the whole issue had been drummed up by professional sexual harassment counselors in order to sell their services. Yet the studies cited in this article have documented that sexual harassment is a widespread problem with serious consequences.   34

Feminists and union activists have succeeded in gaining recognition of sexual harassment as a form of sex discrimination (MacKinnon, 1979). The law now views sexual harassment not as the idiosyncratic actions of a few inconsiderate males but as part of a pattern of behaviors that reflect the imbalance of power between women and men in society. Women in various occupations and educational settings have sought legal redress for actions of supervisors or coworkers, and sexual harassment has become the focus of numerous organizational policies and grievance procedures (Brewer & Berk, 1982).   35

Well-publicized policies that use an inclusive definition of sexual harassment, include an informal dispute resolution option, provide an advocate for the victim (if desired), and permit multiple offenders to be identified seem likely to be the most effective way of addressing claims of sexual harassment. However, even these modifications will not eliminate all of the problems in policies. The severity of the consequences of harassment for the victim, coupled with the problematic nature of grievance procedures and the mildness of punishments for offenders, makes retribution less effective than prevention of sexual harassment. Organizational leaders should not assume that their job is completed when they have established a sexual harassment policy. Extensive efforts at prevention need to be mounted at the individual, situational, and organizational level.   36

In prevention efforts aimed at the individual, education about harassment should be provided (e.g., Beauvais, 1986). In particular, policymakers and others need to learn to "think like a woman" to define which behaviors constitute harassment and recognize that these behaviors are unacceptable. Understanding that many women find offensive more subtle forms of behavior such as sexual jokes or comments may help reduce the kinds of interactions that create a hostile environment. Educating personnel about the punishments involved for offensive behavior also may have a deterring effect.   37

However, education alone is not sufficient. Sexual harassment is the product not only of individual attitudes and beliefs, but also of organizational practices. Dzeich and Weiner (1984, pp. 39–58) described aspects of educational institutions that facilitate sexual harassment, including the autonomy afforded the faculty, the diffusion of authority that permits lack of accountability, and the shortage of women in positions of authority. Researchers are beginning to identify the practices in other work settings that facilitate or support sexual harassment, and suggest that sexual harassment may be part of a pattern of unprofessional and disrespectful attitudes and behaviors that characterizes some workplaces (Gutek, 1985).   38

39   Perhaps the most important factor in reducing sexual harassment is an organizational culture that promotes equal opportunities for women. There is a strong negative relationship between the level of perceived equal employment opportunity for women in a company and the level of harassment reported (LaFontaine & Tredeau, 1986): Workplaces low in perceived equality are the site of more frequent incidents of harassment. This finding suggests that sexual harassment both reflects and reinforces the underlying sexual inequality that produces a sex-segregated and sex-stratified occupational structure (Hoffman, 1986). The implementation of sexual harassment policies demonstrates the seriousness of those in authority; the language of the policies provides some measure of clarity about the types of behavior that are not acceptable; and grievance procedures may provide relief and legitimacy to those with complaints (Schneider, 1987). But neither policies nor procedures do much to weaken the structural roots of gender inequalities in organizations.

40   Reforms intended to ameliorate women's position sometimes have unintended negative consequences (see Kirp, Yudof, & Franks, 1986). The presence of sexual harassment policies and the absence of formal complaints might promote the illusion that this problem has been solved. Assessment of whether organizational policies and practices promote or hinder equality for women is required to insure that this belief does not prevail. A long-range strategy for organizational reform in academia would thus attack the chilly climate for women in classrooms and laboratories (Project on the Status and Education of Women, 1982), the inferior quality of athletic programs for women, differential treatment of women applicants, the acceptance of the masculine as normative, and a knowledge base uninfluenced by women's values or experience (Fuehrer & Schilling, 1985). In other work settings, such a long-range approach would attack both sex-segregation of occupations and sex-stratification within authority hierarchies. Sexual harassment grievance procedures alone are not sufficient to insure that sexual harassment will be eliminated. An end to this problem requires gender equity within organizations.

REFERENCES

Abbey, A. (1982). Sex differences in attributions for friendly behavior: Do males misperceive females' friendliness? *Journal of Personality and Social Psychology, 42,* 830–838.

Abbey, A., & Melby, C. (1986). The effects of nonverbal cues on gender differences in perceptions of sexual intent. *Sex Roles, 15,* 283–298.

Adams, J. W., Kottke, J. L., & Padgitt, J. S. (1983). Sexual harassment of university students. *Journal of College Student Personnel, 23,* 484–490.

Alexander et al. v. Yale University, 459 F. Supp. 1 (D. Conn. 1977), affirmed 631 F. 2d 178 (2nd Cir. 1980).

American Association of University Professors. (1983). Sexual harassment: Suggested policy and procedures for handling complaints. *Academe, 69,* 15a–16a.

American Council on Education. (1986). *Sexual harassment on campus: Suggestions for reviewing campus policy and educational programs.* Washington, DC: Author.

Beauvais, K. (1986). Workshops to combat sexual harassment: A case study of changing attitudes. *Signs: Journal of Women in Culture and Society, 12,* 130–145.

Becker, H. S. (1967). Whose side are we on? *Social Problems, 14,* 239–247.

Benson, D. J., & Thomson, G. (1982). Sexual harassment on a university campus: The confluence of authority relations, sexual interest and gender stratification. *Social Problems, 29,* 236–251.

Brandenburg, J. B. (1982). Sexual harassment in the university: Guidelines for establishing a grievance procedure. *Signs: Journal of Women in Culture and Society, 8,* 320–336.

Brett, J. M., Goldberg, S. B., & Ury, W. L. (1990). Designing systems for resolving disputes in organizations. *American Psychologist, 45,* 162–170.

Brewer, M. (1982). Further beyond nine to five: An integration and future directions. *Journal of Social Issues, 38,* 149–157.

Brewer, M. B., & Berk, R. A. (1982). Beyond nine to five: Introduction. *Journal of Social Issues, 38,* 1–4.

Bumiller, K. (1987). Victims in the shadow of the law: A critique of the model of legal protection. *Signs: Journal of Women in Culture and Society, 12,* 421–439.

Burleigh, N., & Goldberg, S. (1989). Breaking the silence: Sexual harassment in law firms. *ABA Journal, 75,* 46–52.

Cammaert, L. P. (1985). How widespread is sexual harassment on campus? *International Journal of Women's Studies, 8,* 388–397.

Cohen, C. F. (1987, November). Legal dilemmas in sexual harassment cases. *Labor Law Journal,* 681–689.

Coles, F. S. (1986). Forced to quit: Sexual harassment complaints and agency response. *Sex Roles, 14,* 81–95.

Collins, E. G. C., & Blodgett, T. B. (1981). Some see it . . . some won't. *Harvard Business Review, 59,* 76–95.

Crull, P. (1982). The stress effects of sexual harassment on the job. *American Journal of Orthopsychiatry, 52,* 539–543.

Dzeich, B., & Weiner, L. (1984). *The lecherous professor.* Boston: Beacon Press.

Fain, T. C., & Anderton, D. L. (1987). Sexual harassment: Organizational context and diffuse status. *Sex Roles, 5/6,* 291–311.

Fitzgerald, L. F., Schullman, S. L., Bailey, N., Richards, M., Swecker, J., Gold, Y., Ormerod, M., & Weitzman, L. (1988). The incidence and dimensions of sexual harassment in academia and the workplace. *Journal of Vocational Behavior, 32,* 152–175.

Fuehrer, A., & Schilling, K. M. (1985). The values of academe: Sexism as a natural consequence. *Journal of Social Issues, 41,* 29–42.

Garvey, M. S. (1986). The high cost of sexual harassment suits. *Labor Relations, 65,* 75–79.

Gilligan, C. (1982). *In a different voice: Psychological theory and women's development.* Cambridge, MA: Harvard University Press.

Glaser, R. D., & Thorpe, J. S. (1986). Unethical intimacy: A survey of sexual contact and advances between psychology educators and female graduate students. *American Psychologist, 41,* 43–51.

Gutek, B. A. (1985). *Sex and the workplace.* San Francisco: Jossey-Bass.

Gutek, B. A., Morasch, B., & Cohen, A. G. (1983). Interpreting social-sexual behavior in a work setting. *Journal of Vocational Behavior, 22,* 30–48.

Hamilton, J. A., Alagna, S. W., King, L. S., & Lloyd, C. (1987). The emotional consequences of gender-based abuse in the workplace: New counseling programs for sex discrimination. *Women and Therapy, 6,* 155–182.

Hoffman, F. L. (1986). Sexual harassment in academia: Feminist theory and institutional practice. *Harvard Educational Review, 56*(2), 107–121.

Jensen, I. W., & Gutek, B. A. (1982). Attributions and assignment of responsibility in sexual harassment. *Journal of Social Issues, 38,* 121–136.

Jones, E. E., & Nisbett, R. E. (1971). *The actor and the observer: Divergent perceptions of the causes of behavior.* Morristown, N.J.: General Learning Press.

Jones, T. S., Remland, M. S., & Brunner, C. C. (1987). Effects of employment relationship, response of recipient and sex of rater on perceptions of sexual harassment. *Perceptual and Motor Skills, 65,* 55–63.

Kanter, R. M. (1977). *Men and women of the corporation.* New York: Basic Books.

Kenig, S., & Ryan, J. (1986). Sex differences in levels of tolerance and attribution of blame for sexual harassment on a university campus. *Sex Roles, 15,* 535–549.

Kirk, D. (1988, August). *Gender differences in the perception of sexual harassment.* Paper presented at the Academy of Management National Meeting, Anaheim, CA.

Kirp, D. L., Yudof, M. G., & Franks, M. S. (1986). *Gender justice.* Chicago: University of Chicago Press.

Kolb, D. M., & Coolidge, G. G. (1988). *Her place at the table: A consideration of gender issues in negotiation* (Working paper series 88-5). Harvard Law School, Program on Negotiation.

Konrad, A. M., & Gutek, B. A. (1986). Impact of work experiences on attitudes toward sexual harassment. *Administrative Science Quarterly, 31,* 422–438.

LaFontaine, E., & Tredeau, L. (1986). The frequency, sources, and correlates of sexual harassment among women in traditional male occupations. *Sex Roles, 15,* 433–442.

Lester, D., Banta, B., Barton, J., Elian, N., Mackiewicz, L., & Winkelried, J. (1986). Judgments about sexual harassment: Effects of the power of the harasser. *Perceptual and Motor Skills, 63,* 990.

Linenberger, P. (1983, April). What behavior constitutes sexual harassment? *Labor Law Journal,* 238–247.

Littler-Bishop, S., Seidler-Feller, D., & Opaluch, R. E. (1982). Sexual harassment in the workplace as a function of initiator's status: The case of airline personnel. *Journal of Social Issues, 38,* 137–148.

Livingston, J. A. (1982). Responses to sexual harassment on the job: Legal, organizational, and individual actions. *Journal of Social Issues, 38*(4), 5–22.

Lott, B., Reilly, M. E., & Howard, D. R. (1982). Sexual assault and harassment: A campus community case study. *Signs: Journal of Women in Culture and Society, 8,* 296–319.

MacKinnon, C. A. (1979). *Sexual harassment of working women: A case of sex discrimination.* New Haven, CT: Yale University Press.

MacKinnon, C. A. (1987). Feminism, Marxism, method and the state: Toward feminist jurisprudence. In S. Harding (Ed.), *Feminism and methodology: Social science issues.* Bloomington: Indiana University Press.

Maihoff, N., & Forrest, L. (1983). Sexual harassment in higher education: An assessment study. *Journal of the National Association for Women Deans, Administrators, and Counselors, 46,* 3–8.

Maypole, D. E. (1986). Sexual harassment of social workers at work: Injustice within? *Social Work, 31,* 29–34.

Maypole, D. E., & Skaine, R. (1982). Sexual harassment of blue-collar workers. *Journal of Sociology and Social Welfare, 9,* 682–695.

McCormack, A. (1985). The sexual harassment of students by teachers: The case of students in science. *Sex Roles, 13,* 21–32.

McIntyre, D. I., & Renick, J. C. (1982). Protecting public employees and employers from sexual harassment. *Public Personnel Management Journal, 11,* 282–292.

Mednick, M. T. (1989). On the politics of psychological constructs: Stop the bandwagon, I want to get off. *American Psychologist, 44,* 1118–1123.

Meek, P. M., & Lynch, A. Q. (1983). Establishing an informal grievance procedure for cases of sexual harassment of students. *Journal of the National Association for Women Deans, Administrators, & Counselors, 46,* 30–33.

Merry, S. E., & Silbey, S. S. (1984). What do plaintiffs want? Reexamining the concept of dispute. *Justice System Journal, 9,* 151–178.

Metha, J., & Nigg, A. (1983). Sexual harassment on campus: An institutional response. *Journal of the National Association for Women Deans, Administrators, & Counselors, 46,* 9–15.

Miller, J. B. (1976). *Toward a new psychology of women.* Boston: Beacon Press.

Morgenson, G. (1989, May). Watch that leer, stifle that joke. *Forbes,* 69–72.

Popovich, P. M., Licata, B. J., Nokovich, D., Martelli, T., & Zoloty, S. (1987). Assessing the incidence and perceptions of sexual harassment behaviors among American undergraduates. *Journal of Psychology, 120,* 387–396.

Powell, G. N. (1986). Effects of sex role identity and sex on definitions of sexual harassment. *Sex Roles, 14,* 9–19.

Project on the Status and Education of Women. (1982). The campus climate: A chilly one for women? Washington, DC: Association of American Colleges.

Pryor, J. B. (1985). The lay person's understanding of sexual harassment. *Sex Roles, 13,* 273–286.

Pryor, J. B., & Day, J. D. (1988). Interpretations of sexual harassment: An attributional analysis. *Sex Roles, 18,* 405–417.

Reilly, M. E., Lott, B., & Gallogly, S. (1986). Sexual harassment of university students. *Sex Roles, 15,* 333–358.

Rifkin, J. (1984). Mediation from a feminist perspective: Promise and problems. *Mediation, 2,* 21–31.

Robertson, C., Dyer, C. E., & Campbell, D. (1988). Campus harassment: Sexual harassment policies and procedures at institutions of higher learning. *Signs: Journal of Women in Culture and Society, 13,* 792–812.

Robinson, W. L., & Reid, P. T. (1985). Sexual intimacy in psychology revisited. *Professional Psychology: Research and Practice, 16,* 512–520.

Rossi, P. H., & Weber-Burdin, E. (1983). Sexual harassment on the campus. *Social Science Research, 12,* 131–158.

Rowe, M. P. (1981, May–June). Dealing with sexual harassment. *Harvard Business Review,* 42–46.

Saal, F. E., Johnson, C. B., & Weber, N. (1989). Friendly or sexy? It may depend on whom you ask. *Psychology of Women Quarterly, 13,* 263–276.

Schneider, B. E. (1987). Graduate women, sexual harassment, and university policy. *Journal of Higher Education, 58,* 46–65.

Shotland, R. L., & Craig, J. M. (1988). Can men and women differentiate between friendly and sexually interested behavior? *Social Psychology Quarterly, 51,* 66–73.

Tangri, S. S., Burt, M. R., & Johnson, L. B. (1982). Sexual harassment at work: Three explanatory models. *Journal of Social Issues, 38,* 33–54.

Terpstra, D. E., & Baker, D. D. (1988). Outcomes of sexual harassment charges. *Academy of Management Journal, 31,* 185–194.

Terpstra, D. E., & Cook, S. E. (1985). Complainant characteristics and reported behaviors and consequences associated with formal sexual harassment charges. *Personnel Psychology, 38,* 559–574.

Thomann, D. A., & Wiener, R. L. (1987). Physical and psychological causality as determinants of culpability in sexual harassment cases. *Sex Roles, 17,* 573–591.

Trager, T. B. (1988). Legal considerations in drafting sexual harassment policies. In J. Van Tol (Ed.), *Sexual harassment on campus: A legal compendium* (pp. 181–190). Washington, DC: National Association of College and University Attorneys.

U.S. Equal Employment Opportunity Commission. (1980, November 10). Final amendment to guidelines on discrimination because of sex under Title VII of the Civil Rights Act of 1964, as amended. 29 CFR Part 1604. *Federal Register, 45,* 74675–74677.

U.S. Merit Systems Protection Board. (1981). *Sexual harassment in the federal workplace: Is it a problem?* Washington, DC: U.S. Government Printing Office.

U.S. Merit Systems Protection Board. (1988). *Sexual harassment in the federal government: An update.* Washington, DC: U.S. Government Printing Office.

Wilson, K. R., & Krause, L. A. (1983). Sexual harassment in the university. *Journal of College Student Personnel, 24,* 219–224.

Wilson, M. (1988). Sexual harassment and the law. *The Community Psychologist, 21,* 16–17.

Harassment Blues

Naomi Munson

1   When I was graduated from college in the early '70s, I had the good fortune to land a job at a weekly newsmagazine. It was a wonderful place to work, financially lucrative, intellectually demanding but not overwhelming, and, above all, fun.

2   There was, actually, a sort of hierarchy of fun at the office. Ranking lowest were the hard-news departments; although (or perhaps because) they offered the excitement of late-breaking news and fast-developing stories, both the national- and the foreign-affairs sections were socially rather staid. Next up the scale came the business section, where the people were lively enough but where the general tone nevertheless reflected the serious nature of the subject matter. Then there was the culture department, a barrel of laughs in its own way, though the staff did seem to spend a certain amount of time at the opera. At the top of the scale stood the department where I wound up, which included science, sports, education, religion, and the like. Though there might be the occasional breaking news, these sections generally called more for long thought and thorough research, which led to a very laidback atmosphere and a lot of down time. Drinking at nearby bars, dining at the finest restaurants, and dancing at local discos occupied a great deal of that time. And sex played a major role in all of this. (It did throughout the magazine, of course, but nowhere so openly and unselfconsciously as here.)

3   The men were a randy lot, dedicated philanderers, and foul-mouthed to boot; the women, having vociferously demanded—and been granted—absolutely equal status, were considered fair game (though there were a couple of secretaries whose advancing age and delicate sensibilities consigned them to the sidelines).

4   Imagine my surprise, then, when one day a young woman who worked with me flounced into my office, cheeks flushed, eyes flashing, to announce that she had just been subjected to sexual harassment. (It was a fairly new concept back then, at the end of the '70's, but being in the vanguard of social trends, we had heard of it.) When she explained that the offense had occurred not in our own neck of the woods but in the national-affairs section, I was truly shocked. When she identified the offender, however—sexually, one of the least lively types on the premises—I began to be skeptical. And when she described his crime—which was having said something to the effect that he longed for the good old days of miniskirts when a fellow had a real chance to see great legs like hers—I scoffed. "Oh, come on," I said. "That's not sexual harassment; that's just D. trying to pay you a compliment." To myself, after she had calmed down and left, I said, "She's even dimmer than I thought. She thinks *that's* what they mean by sexual harassment."

5   If I was convinced that this woman's experience did not constitute sexual harassment, I, like the vast majority of people at that time, had rather vague notions of what did. Whatever it was, however, it already seemed clear that the charge of sexual harassment would serve as a perfect instrument of revenge for disgruntled female employees. This was borne out by the story I came to know, years later, about a man at another office who had had several formal harassment charges brought against him by women who worked for him. The man was someone who would, as his coworkers saw it, "nail" anything that moved. He

had, in fact, had longstanding affairs—which he had ended in order to move on to fresh conquests—with the women now accusing him of having offered financial inducements in exchange for sexual favors. The women claimed to have declined the offers and consequently suffered the loss of promotions.

Disgruntlement aside, however, it still seemed obvious to me that in a case of sexual harassment, something *sexual* might be supposed to have occurred. That quaint notion of mine was finally laid to rest during the Clarence Thomas–Anita Hill debacle. Professor Hill's performance convinced me of nothing save that if she told me the sun was shining, I would head straight for my umbrella and galoshes. The vast outpouring of feminist outrage that accompanied the event did, however, succeed in opening my eyes to the sad fact that it was I, way back when, who had been the dim one; my erstwhile colleague had merely been a bit ahead of her time. For, it now turns out, what she described is precisely what they *do* mean by sexual harassment.

During the course of the hearing, story after story appeared in the media supporting the claim that men out there are abusive to their female employees. It was declared, over and over, that virtually every woman in the country had either suffered sexual harassment herself or knew someone who had (I myself, I realize, figure in that assessment). The abuse, it appeared, had been going on since time immemorial and was so painful to some of the women involved that they had repressed it for decades.

It became clear amid all the hand-wringing that we were not talking here about bosses exacting sexual favors in exchange for promotions, raises, or the like. Even Professor Hill never claimed that Judge Thomas promised to promote her if she succumbed to his charms, or that he threatened to fire her if she failed to do so. What she said, as all the world now knows, was that he pestered her for dates; that he boasted of his natural endowments and of his sexual prowess; that he used obscene language in her presence; that he regaled her with the details of porno flicks; and that he discussed the joys of, as Miss Hill so expressively put it, "(gulp) oral sex." The closest anyone at the hearing came to revealing anything like direct action was a Washington woman who was horrified when a member of Congress played footsie with her under the table at an official function, and a friend of Anita Hill who announced that she had been "touched in the workplace."

What we—or, to be more precise, they—were talking about was sexual innuendo, ogling, obscenity, unwelcome importuning, nude pin-ups; about an "unpleasant atmosphere in the workplace"; about male "insensitivity." One columnist offered behavioral guidelines to men who had been reduced to "whining" that they no longer knew what was appropriate—something to the effect that though it is OK to say, "Gee, I bet you make the best blackened redfish in town," it is not OK to say, "Wow, I bet you're really hot between the sheets." Even Judge Thomas himself declared that if he *had* said the things the good professor was accusing him of, it *would* have constituted sexual harassment.

Yet in response to all of this it also emerged very plainly that the American public just was not buying it. Single women were heard to worry that putting a lid on sex at the office might hurt their chances of finding a husband; one forthright woman was even quoted by a newspaper as saying that office sex was the spice of life. Rather more definitively, polls showed that most people, black and white, male and female, thought Judge Thomas should be confirmed, *even if the charges against him were true.*

11   How can it be that the majority of Americans were dismissing the significance of sexual harassment (as now defined) even as their elected representatives were declaring it just the most hideous, heinous, gosh-awful stuff they had ever heard of? How is it possible that, at the very moment newspapers and TV were proclaiming that American women were mad as hell and weren't going to take it any more, most of these women themselves—and their husbands—were responding with a raised eyebrow and a small shrug of the shoulders?

12   For one thing, most Americans—unlike the ideologues who brought us sexual harassment in the first place, and who have worked a special magic on pundits and politicos for more than two decades now—have a keen understanding of life's realities. Having had no choice but to work, in order to feed and clothe and doctor and educate their children, they have always known that, while work has its rewards, financial and otherwise, "an unpleasant atmosphere in the workplace" is something they may well have to put up with. That, where women are concerned, the unpleasantness might take on sexual overtones gives it no more weight than the uncertainties, the frustrations, and the humiliations, petty and grand, encountered by men.

13   Most people, furthermore, have a healthy respect for the ability of women to hold their own in the battle of the sexes. They know that women have always managed to deal perfectly well with male lust: to evade it, to quash it, even to be flattered by it. The bepaunched and puffing boss, chasing his buxom secretary around the desk, is, after all, a figure of fun—because we realize that he will never catch her, and that even if he did, she would know very well how to put him in his place.

14   The women's movement and its fellow travelers, on the other hand, have never had any such understanding or any such respect. On the contrary, rage against life's imperfections, and a consequent revulsion against men, has been the bone and sinew of that movement.

15   The feminists came barreling into the workforce, some twenty years ago, not out of necessity, but with the loud assertion that here was to be found something called fulfillment. Men, they claimed, had denied them access to this fulfillment out of sheer power-hungry selfishness. Women, they insisted, were no different from men in their talents or their dispositions; any apparent differences had simply been manufactured, as a device to deprive mothers, wives, and sisters of the excitement and pleasure to which men had had exclusive title for so long, and which they had come to view as their sole privilege.

16   No sooner had these liberated ladies taken their rightful place alongside men at work, however, than it began to dawn on them that the experience was not quite living up to their expectations. They quickly discovered, for example, what their fathers, husbands, and brothers had always known: that talent is not always appreciated, that promotions are not so easy to come by, that often those most meritorious are inexplicably passed over in favor of others. But rather than recognizing this as a universal experience, they descried a "glass ceiling," especially constructed to keep them in their place, and they called for the hammers.

17   Feminists had insisted that child-bearing held no more allure for them than it did for men. That insistence quickly began to crumble in the face of a passionate desire for babies.

But rather than recognizing that life had presented them with a choice, they demanded special treatment. They reserved the right to take leave from their work each time the urge to procreate came upon them. And they insisted that husbands, employers, and even the government take equal responsibility with them for the care and upbringing of the little bundles of joy resulting from that urge.

And as for sex in the workplace, well, that was pretty much what it had always been everywhere: an ongoing battle involving, on the one side, attentions both unwelcome and welcome, propositions both unappealing and appealing, and compliments both unpleasing and pleasing, and on the other, evasive action, outright rejection, or happy capitulation. Having long ago decided that the terms of this age-old battle were unacceptable to them, the women of the movement might have been expected to try to eliminate them. With the invention of sexual harassment, they have met that expectation, and with a vengeance. Laws have been made, cases have been tried and, in the Clarence Thomas affair, a decent man was pilloried.   18

Having, in other words, finally been permitted to play with the big boys, these women have found the game not to their liking. But rather than retiring from the field, they have called for a continuous and open-ended reformation of the rules. Indeed, like children in a temper, who respond to maternal placating with a rise in fury, they have met every accommodating act of the men in their lives with a further escalation of demand. The new insistence that traditional male expressions of sexual interest be declared taboo, besides being the purest revelation of feminist rage, is the latest arc in that vicious cycle.   19

Fear of Flirting

Erica Jong

I have never worked on Capital Hill with Sen. Bob Packwood and his many merry colleagues, so maybe I am not to be considered an expert on sexual harassment. But in 20 years as a professional author, I've had my share of midnight phone calls from obscure publishers at the Frankfurt Book Fair and, as a young miniskirted poet, of being groped at the Algonquin Round Table by old goats who didn't seem to know whether they wanted my next folio or my next something-else-that-starts-with-"f"-that-you-can't-write-in-a-family-newspaper.   1

In my callow youth, there were no grievance committees to combat sexual harassment. The very term had not yet been invented. You simply ran around the desk, smiled sweetly and told the old goat that though he was devastatingly attractive, you had: a) a boyfriend, b) your period (that generation saw this as a deterrent) or c) a communicable disease (pre-AIDS, this was less daunting than it would be today). You assumed you had to flatter him. After all, he had the power and you didn't. It never occurred to you to call in the Rape Crisis Commandoes. There were none to call.   2

Now I admit this makes me sound like a fossil. My daughter accuses me of being "from the '70s" in a way that makes '70s sound like "old Stone Age." But few of us got raped by old goats (some did, to be sure) and some of us managed to keep our careers and our values.   3

We hated the condescension of being treated like objects, but we also liked having sexual power over men; above all, we assumed that men were men—i.e., less evolved than we were—and that given the topsy-turvy state of the world—i.e., the less evolved had more power—we had to figure out how to survive and thrive.

4   We also wanted to change the world, but realizing that might not come soon enough for us to benefit as our daughters will, we evolved various strategies to stay alive. We might not find these strategies ideologically pure, but ideological purity was a luxury we could not afford. Survival was. Survival and the best use of our talents. Look, even Gloria Steinem dressed up as a bunny and got a brilliant piece out of it. That's what you did then: turned second sexdom into intelligence, wit, a glittering piece of prose.

5   Times change. Generations change. Sen. Packwood can't make the connection between the legislation he votes for and the pretty young things he chases around his desk when drunk (or even when sober). Like Woody Allen, he has a moral blind spot the size of Oregon. He may be pro-choice in his votes, pro-woman in his hiring, but he just doesn't understand that the times they are a-changing. Too bad for him. And too bad for the 15 or so women he harassed. But what is the price he should pay? He did vote for women's rights while he perpetrated these wrongs. His public stance was as enlightened as his private stance was benighted. In a party that had thrown itself fiercely to the right, he stayed with women on women's issues. Meanwhile, he played out a kind of parody of *droit de seigneur* in the back office. Like Woody Allen, he couldn't bring his intellect and his emotions into the same century.

6   What to do about men like that? They are a vanishing breed, but alas, they aren't vanishing fast enough. They don't know the new rules of male-female interaction. They don't understand that what's wrong with sexual harassment is that it's an abuse of power. They don't see the unfairness of the power they have and they don't understand that with power comes weighty responsibility. They are fiduciaries of female trust—Woody as stepfather, Packwood as senator. We expect more of them, not less. As with Clarence Thomas, we expect exemplary behavior. When we get something less—much less—we are very disappointed.

7   The Packwood ethics probe is a clash of generations. A man of 30 would know better than to do what Packwood did. But even men of 30 are confused. "What's the line between flirtation and harassment?" they often ask. Terrified of rejection by women they fancy, they now have to face court-martial by the sexual harassment commandoes. It will be surprising if any erection ever survives this scrutiny. One suspects that the sexual harassment commandoes will be happy with this outcome because sex is insufficiently P.C. anyway. Puritans that they are, they want to rule out even the possibility of the messiness of sex. Babies by artificial insemination are much neater, not to mention ideologically pure.

8   While I am glad that sexual harassment is now recognized as a phenomenon and glad that Sen. Packwood's and Woody Allen's generation are inevitably being replaced by younger, more empathetic males, the question remains: How should we treat these old guys—as antiques or as rapists? It's a tough question because these dirty old men grew up in another world, a world where standards were different. They must feel baffled by being judged the way we would judge younger men, and yet we cannot allow them to act like

Louis XIV in the halls of Versailles—or even in the halls of Congress, not to mention the Astoria Studios. In a clockwork-orange world they would be reprogrammed: locked in a room with Andrea Dworkin until they came to understand the many errors of their ways. Perhaps that *is* the path they *voluntarily* should take. Or else we should invent a 12-step program designed especially for men who abuse power over women: "I discovered I was powerless over my abuse of power and my life had become unmanageable. . . ." But until such therapy exists, shall we simply call for their ouster?

9   I, for one, would have loved to see Les AuCoin elected for his support for the National Endowment for the Arts, if nothing else, but I also recognize that Packwood stood up for women in a dark time. We do not excuse his egregious blindness to women's needs as autonomous individuals, but should there be a grandfather clause for some of these ideologically impure people who helped us along the way? Who is so ideologically pure that she has never done a non-P.C. thing in her life? Not me.

10   I am for working to change the system, but I am also for mercy and rehabilitation. A just goddess would make Packwood into a pretty young aide on Capital Hill for a day. Then he'd understand. But failing the reappearance of Juno in Washington, how to retrain him? More to the point, shall we allow feminism to become a reign of terror? We are all—men and women both—stumbling human beings. If we can't forgive each other, how can we ever forgive ourselves? Above all, how can we eradicate sexism without eradicating sex?

11   In some curious way, I feel more able to deal with old goats chasing me around the desk than with the ideology commandoes who want to scrutinize my writing to make sure I never say a non-P.C. thing as long as I live. I can trip the old goat or I can call his wife, but the P.C. brigade will never be satisfied with anything as ambivalent or murky as human nature. Under their stern care, art will turn to agitprop and humor will be banned for having double vision. Love songs will be silenced for abetting sex, wine for dissolving the superego and miniskirts for provoking lasciviousness. Hollywood will close down—for what happens both on the screen and behind the screens. Broadway will go dark. Novels will all have to be rewritten for political correctness and no one will ever dare make a dirty joke. Apparently, Cotton Mather still rules America.

12   Much as I loathe the Packwoods and Allens of this world, I *fear* the P.C. commandoes. Packwood and Allen are motivated by lust and power, but the sexual harassment squads claim benevolence and feminism as their only motives. Hah! When people prate of their purity, I reach for my gun.

13   Something about the sexual harassment hysteria is starting to remind me of the adolescent girls in *The Crucible* or the raving nuns in *The Devils of Loudun*. Just as men can use sexuality for political power, women can use anti-sexuality for political power. It has happened before in this country: The Women's Christian Temperance Union arose out of the same social forces that produced the first wave of feminism.

14   If we get rid of Packwood, what message are we sending to other men who voted for women's legislation? Women will get you no matter what you do? I dare to ask the forbidden

question because as a feminist I always worry about feminism when it moves from legislating public issues to legislating private ones. America is a Puritan country and feminists
can be just as puritanical as male chauvinists. It is the American disease to want to tell people how to behave in bed, but I am one who thinks feminists should be immune to this disease. When we become infected, I fear we are setting up the next backlash. When we
become infected, I fear we have fallen into a right-wing trap. Sexual hot-button issues like
harassment serve to distract us from focusing, for instance, on the fact that women continue to be underpaid. But take away economic inequity, and I believe that sexual inequity
will eventually wither too.

15   Yes, I do expect greater enlightenment from women than from men. Call me a female
chauvinist, but I believe that women are the more spiritually advanced sex. If we take our
power and use it as badly as men have used theirs throughout the centuries, we will not
have brought about the world of equality we seek.

16   I want a feminist movement that allows for singing, dancing, humor, sex and free
speech. Punish the villains, but punish them fairly. Reprogram the abusers and get them to
use their seniority to make the world safe for women. If we demand a feminism so pure
that no human being is good enough, we won't be able to join our own movement.

Watch That Leer, Stifle That Joke

Gretchen Morgenson

1   It's been almost ten years since the Equal Employment Opportunity Commission wrote
its guidelines defining sexual harassment as a form of sex discrimination and, therefore, illegal under Title VII of the Civil Rights Act of 1964.

2   During that time, women have transformed the workplace, taken on untraditional jobs,
excelled in male-oriented businesses, started their own firms and garnered new power on
corporate boards.

3   Have women been harassed every inch of the way by leering, lascivious male chauvinists? It sometimes sounds that way. Following the Equal Employment Opportunity Commission's lead, an estimated three out of four companies nationwide have instituted strict
policies against harassment; millions of dollars are dutifully spent each year educating employees in Title VII etiquette.

4   What are the boundaries? Where does good-humored kidding cease and harassment
begin? How deeply should the courts concern themselves with personal behavior and good
manners? Requests or demands for sexual favors are clear-cut cases of behavior that lie beyond the pale. Sleep-with-me-and-you'll-get-promoted propositions are clearly illegal. Where
the law gets hazy and goes beyond where some reasonable people think the law should go
is in what is known as hostile environment harassment—the hazing, joking, sexually suggestive talk between men and the women who work alongside them.

5   Both types of behavior are increasing? That's the story you get from the media, which
loves a salacious issue, and from employee relations consultants who make money telling

corporations how to protect themselves from costly harassment claims. These are the loudest voices in the din. Loud but not persuasive.

The peddlers of sex harassment advice have, of course, their own moneymaking 6
agenda. Equally suspect are those extremists who would politicize all of American life and seek to regulate human behavior to suit their private prejudices. These people want to impose stringently moralistic standards on private industry that are not met in any other environment. It's all part of the transformation taking place today in employment law in which employers' responsibilities to their workers seem to grow just as workers' responsibilities to the bosses seem to diminish.

A growth industry has sprung up to dispense harassment advice to worried companies 7
in the form of seminars, videos and group gropes.

The deeper *Forbes* delved, the more we became convinced that the alleged increase in 8
sexual harassment was more a product of propaganda from self-interested parties. "At least 35% and as many as 90% of women get harassed," contends Linda Krystal Doran, president of Krystal & Kalan Associates, a sex harassment consultant in Issaquah, Wash. Doran conjures up images of a major portion of the work force wolfishly and lustfully abused by another portion. If her figures are taken seriously, as many as 49 million women are getting pinched, propositioned or annoyed on the job.

But why then is the number of federal cases alleging harassment on the job actually de- 9
clining? This, in spite of a growing female work force. According to the EEOC, where anyone bringing a federal sex harassment case must first file a complaint, the number of Title VII complaints in which sexual harassment was mentioned peaked at 6,342 five years ago; last year there were 4,984 cases.

Sound like a lot? It's not. It's 0.0091% of the female work force—one in every 11,000. 10
And that's cases filed, not cases proven. Furthermore, these cases may primarily involve other forms of discrimination: race, national origin, color and religion.

Forbes consulted human rights commissions that compile such figures in four populous, 11
regionally diverse states: California, Michigan, New York and Texas. Excepting California, where there has been a modest increase, sex harassment cases in these states are down.

Yet the money to be made these days advising corporations on the issue of harassment 12
is not insubstantial. Susan Webb, president of Pacific Resource Development Group, a Seattle consultant, says she spends 95% of her time advising on sex harassment. Like most of the consultants, Webb acts as an expert witness in harassment cases, conducts investigations for companies or municipalities and teaches seminars. She charges clients $1,495 to buy her 60-minute sex harassment video program and handbooks. Webb, who's worked for 350 companies or municipalities, is one of a dozen such consultants, and her prices are typical. Solving the problem is supposed to be their business, but hyping the problem is very much in their personal interests.

Michael Connolly, former general counsel to the EEOC, and now a partner at Cross 13
Wrock in Detroit, says: "There are a lot of bad consultants taking advantage of the fact that harassment is in vogue." There are even consultants who act as agents for other consultants. Jennifer Coplon of Resource Group-Videolearning in Boston represents some 15 sex harassment video producers, connecting them with corporations, universities and government agencies. "Among all employment issues, sexual harassment is the biggest concern among companies," she reports happily.

14   Sexual harassment became a serious legal issue in the early 1980s, just after the Equal Employment Opportunity Commission published its first guidelines. But it was Mentor Savings Bank v. Vinson, a harassment case that made it to the Supreme Court in 1986, that really acted as a full employment act for sex harassment consultants. In Vinson, the Supreme Court conveyed the idea that employers could limit their liability to harassment claims by implementing antiharassment policies and procedures in the workplace. And so the antiharassment industry was born. Even today corporate attorneys are sometimes the best salespeople for the sexual harassment prevention industry. They tell their bosses that the existence of a corporate program should be part of a company's legal defenses.

15   No surprise then that sexual harassment consultants like to claim the problem is getting worse, not better.

16   What about those bothersome EEOC numbers? The consultants say that there is a more than offsetting increase in private suits. Really? There's simply no proof that huge or increasing numbers of private actions are being filed and litigated. The San Francisco law firm of Orrick, Herrington & Sutcliffe has monitored private sex harassment cases filed in California since 1984. From 1984 to March 1989, the number of sexual harassment cases in California that were litigated through to a verdict totaled 15. That's in a litigation-happy state with 5.8 million working women.

17   Those sex harassment actions that do get to a jury are the ones that really grab headlines. A few scary awards have been granted recently—five plaintiffs were awarded $3.8 million by a jury in a North Carolina case against a Texas S&L, Murray Savings Association—but mammoth awards are often reduced in subsequent court proceedings. In California the median jury verdict for all sex harassment cases litigated since 1984 is $183,000. The top verdict in the state was just under $500,000, the lowest was $45,000. California, known for its sympathetic jurors, probably produces higher awards than most states.

18   Paul Tobias, a partner at the Cincinnati law firm of Tobias & Kraus and executive director of the Plaintiffs Employment Lawyers Association, for the past decade has focused on individual employees' problems, including sex harassment. His experience? "During a year, 10 or 15 people may come in and complain; maybe one of those cases is winnable."

19   Of the dozen or so labor lawyers *Forbes* interviewed—from both plaintiffs' and defendants' bars—most feel that job-related harassment, though not gone, occurs much less frequently now than it did ten years ago.

20   Well, maybe, the sex harassment industry replies, but that's only because women are afraid or ashamed to complain. Bringing a sex harassment case is similar to filing a rape case, consultants and lawyers say; both are nasty proceedings that involve defamation, possible job loss and threats to family harmony. "More people are experiencing harassment, but they may not want to bring a case," says Webb, the Seattle trainer.

21   Maybe so, but there is no evidence of this. After reading cases and talking to the lawyers who litigate them, it becomes clear that women have become much more aggressive in filing sex harassment claims.

22   According to the New York State Division of Human Rights, more than half of the complaint outcomes from 1980 through 1986 were dismissed for lack of probable cause. Actual number: 521, or 52%. Compare this with the cases in which probable cause was found and a conciliation was reached: 39, or 4% of the total.

One explanation for the large percentage of dismissed cases is that hostile environ-   23
ment harassment is difficult to define. Asking a subordinate to perform sexual favors in
exchange for a raise is clearly illegal. But a dirty joke? Behavior that one woman may consider harassment could be seen by another as a nonthreatening gag. Whose standards
should be used?

Under tort law, the standard that must be met is called the reasonable person rule. This   24
means that the behavior that has resulted in a case—such as an assault or the intent to
cause emotional distress—must be considered objectionable by a "reasonable person." The
EEOC follows this lead and in its guidelines defines environmental harassment as that
which "unreasonably interferes with an individual's job performance."

How to define that? Says Freada Klein of Klein Associates, a Boston consulting firm: 25
"My goal is to create a corporate climate where every employee feels free to object to behavior, where people are clear about their boundaries and can ask that objectionable behavior stop." Objectionable to whom? By what standards?

Can rudeness and annoying behavior really be legislated out of existence? Can women   26
really think they have the right to a pristine work environment free of rude behavior? These
are permissive times: Mrs. Grundy has been laughed out of most areas of our life. Should
she be allowed to flourish in the workplace alone? Says Susan Hartzoge Gray, an employment lawyer at Haworth, Riggs, Kuhn & Haworth in High Point, N.C.: "We condone sexual jokes and innuendo in the media—a movie might get a PG rating—yet an employer can
be called on the carpet because the same thing bothers someone in an office."

In a curious way, the news stories, the harassment seminars, the showing of video-   27
tapes—even if educational—can act to perpetuate the woman-as-victim mentality. There is
even a kind of backlash at work. Increasing numbers of wrongful discharge cases are
brought by men who believe they were fired because of a false harassment claim.

Yet the noise will probably continue for a long time to come. The demand by some   28
women for a perfect work climate is part of a larger trend in society. Many people feel they
are entitled not only to jobs but to work conditions that suit their tastes.

Some of those higher standards, as far as sex harassment is concerned, are approach-   29
ing the unreasonable. To combat incidents of hostile environment harassment, management
is effectively being told to shoulder two new and onerous responsibilities. First, provide a
pristine work environment, and second, police it as well.

But if women want a level corporate playing field on which they can compete with   30
men, should they expect to be coddled and protected from rudeness or boors? Why can't
they be expected to take care of themselves?

Women do themselves and their careers no favors by playing victim. Sexual harassment   31
is not about sex, it is about power. If women act powerless at work, they'll almost certainly
be taken advantage of. Women are more powerful than the sex harassment peddlers will
have you believe. A woman's power is not in her ability to bring a harassment claim, it's in
her ability to succeed on her merits. And to be able to say, "Back off, bub."

As more and more women recognize this, sex harassment will likely become even less   32
of a real problem in the years ahead than it is today. But don't expect the sex harassment
specialists to go out of business. They'll only stop levying their special tax on U.S. business
and consumers when demand for their services dries up.

A Wink Here, a Leer There: It's Costly

Susan Crawford

1   Did the Anita Hill–Clarence Thomas hearings serve as a cautionary tale? For many employers, yes; for many others, regrettably, no. Sexual harassment in the workplace continues to be an insidious problem, as well as a degrading and career-limiting experience for many women. Research indicates that 50 to 85 percent of all female employees experience some form of harassment during their careers, and 15 percent in any given year. Similarly, 90 percent of Fortune 500 companies have received complaints of sexual harassment, more than a third have been sued and nearly a quarter have been sued repeatedly.

2   It is unrealistic to think we can eradicate harassment in a single generation. But huge strides can be made if it is viewed as an *economic* problem.

3   With more women in the workplace, we must realize that their abilities—and productivity—are critical to our nation's economic health. It is imperative that companies grasp an essential fact: sexual harassment damages the bottom line.

4   As we evolve from an industrial economy toward one based on information and services, human resources are becoming the true engine of added value. Skilled, experienced and committed employees frequently provide a company its competitive edge. But many companies fail to understand that valuable human capital can be squandered by tolerance of harassment.

5   A 1988 study of 160 Fortune 500 companies reached a striking conclusion: harassment costs the average big company, with 23,750 employees, $6.7 million a year. The study calculated losses linked to absenteeism, low productivity and turnover; it did not count the hard-to-measure costs of legal defense, time lost and tarnished public image. Recent research by the author, Freada Klein, a Cambridge, Mass., analyst, confirmed that the data are still valid; anecdotal evidence suggests the costs may be even higher now.

6   How can a company lose $6.7 million a year?

7   First, sexual harassment results in a costly tax on employee performance. At the least, the victim is forced to waste time parrying unwanted attention or enduring improper comments. At the same time, the transgressor is devoting work time to activities that are in no way good for business.

8   Typically, victims retreat into a passive or even sullen acceptance: 12 percent of women who face harassment report stress-related health problems, 27 percent report undermined self-confidence and 13 percent see long-term career damage.

9   Second, harassment breeds resentment and mistrust. Tension can spread to others, breeding widespread cynicism—and limiting productivity.

10   Third, harassment contributes to costly turnover. Women are nine times as likely as men to quit because of harassment, five times as likely to transfer and three times as likely to lose jobs. Fully 25 percent of women who believe they have been harassed have been dismissed or have quit.

11   Every woman who leaves because of harassment represents a large loss of investment, which is compounded by employee replacement costs.

To attack the problem, many forward-thinking companies are using awareness-training 12
programs to help employees understand the pain and indignity of harassment. Such programs, if they are comprehensive and used aggressively, can be highly effective. The cost ranges from $5,000 for a small company to $200,000 for a large one.

Thus, for that Fortune 500 company facing a $6.7 million liability, it is 34 times as 13
costly to ignore the problem as to take steps to eradicate it. Looked at another way, a sexual-harassment program can be cost-effective if it averts the loss of one key employee—or prevents one lawsuit.

We are failing to exploit the full potential of half the nation's work force. And the cost 14
to business is increasingly burdensome. As competition intensifies, managers and directors cannot afford sexual harassment. Corporations—indeed, all organizations—should take aggressive action to eliminate it. Not just to avoid litigation, not just because it is "politically correct" or "the right thing to do," but also because such programs can yield a startlingly positive return on investment.

It's an opportunity we can't afford to miss. 15

Universal Truth and Multiple Perspectives:
Controversies on Sexual Harassment

Martha Chamallas

The question I wish to pose has to do with whether the Constitution and the Bill of Rights 1
will prove up to the challenge of a postmodern world. The term "postmodern" is an overused but nonetheless useful way of describing contemporary society—a society that is marked by diversity, contradiction, and complicated interrelationships. In such a postmodern world, invocations of shared values and fundamental rights are not likely to go unchallenged—in almost every conversation, someone will first want to know just who shares these values and who considers these interests to be fundamental? In a postmodern world it makes sense to speak in the plural—to talk about truths rather than a single truth and to think in terms of American cultures rather than the American culture.

In a variety of disciplines, feminist and postmodern scholars have changed their fields 2
by their persistence in investigating the relationship between knowledge and power. There is now a rich body of scholarship demonstrating how particular views of the world come to dominate the discourse, how our knowledge is far less diverse than our people. A central feature of these new critical inquiries is their skepticism about claims of "objectivity" and "neutrality" and of statements that purport to have "universal" applicability. The take home message of much of this work is that frequently what passes for the whole truth is instead a representation of events from the perspective of those who possess the power to have their version of reality accepted. The search is on for multiple meanings and multiple perspectives, whether attached to language, texts, or human events.

3   One area of the law in which the postmodern challenge to objectivity is the most visible is anti-discrimination law and discourse. I am using anti-discrimination law and discourse here broadly to include specific constitutional protections such as the fifth and fourteenth amendment protections of equality; specific statutory provisions, including the various civil rights legislation prohibiting discrimination based on race, ethnicity, sex, religion, disability and age; as well as public debate on matters such as race and gender equality which highlight the legal dimension of the issues.

4   These days even law professors must of necessity go beyond the cases decided by appellate courts and become conversant in what is sometimes referred to as "cultural politics." It has occurred to me that the most celebrated sexual harassment case of our time—Professor Anita Hill's accusation of sexual harassment by Clarence Thomas—was not a lawsuit at all. However, Hill's statements generated the most thorough and diverse public discussion of the intersection of gender and race and of the harms caused by sexual harassment that I have ever witnessed. What was most striking for me was the variety of viewpoints from which the controversy was viewed. Opinion about the Thomas matter did not break down neatly along gender lines, nor along racial lines. The response to the hearings dramatically demonstrated that women are not a monolithic group who think alike, nor are African-Americans all of the same mindset.

5   But this acknowledgment of diversity of opinion among women and among African-American men and women does not mean that perspective was not important to one's understanding of the Thomas hearings. Instead I regard the voluminous commentary generated by the Thomas hearing to be an excellent example of multiple realities and multiple perspectives operating in public debate. It was not just a matter of how inclined a person was to believe that either Hill or Thomas was telling the truth. Rather it seemed that for many people what Hill described as her experience readily fit into a coherent and familiar pattern of behavior for them. There was an immediate sense of recognition. Other people had great difficulty making sense of Hill's story. For them, it just did not seem to add up.

6   Hill's revelations prompted many women to tell about their own encounters with sexually harassing behavior—both in private and in public. The day after the hearings ended I sat at a public hearing in Des Moines as a member of a statewide taskforce investigating racial and gender bias in the Iowa judicial system. One of the witnesses that day was a woman who is now a United States Magistrate. She told about an incident that happened to her many years before when she was a young attorney. A man who then served as bailiff for the local courthouse had known this young woman since she was in grade school—in fact, he had been the bus driver for her elementary school. At the end of one day, the woman attorney asked the bailiff to get her a file. He walked over to her, put his arm around her, said he'd do anything for her, and kissed her on the lips. The woman attorney was stunned and humiliated and rushed out of the courtroom. She never reported the incident, never told her friends or family, and spent considerable emotional energy trying to avoid the bailiff while she worked in that area. As she told her experiences to the taskforce, she expressed her empathy for Anita Hill. In her assessment, Hill's account had no holes in it.

Hill was not simply a credible witness (or, as one of the Senators on the Judiciary Committee put it, Hill did not just "present" herself well). Instead, she shared a similar "victim's perspective" with Anita Hill. For this woman, Hill's story possessed an internal logic and expressed a reality about the working lives of women.

In some feminist groups I have participated in, we talk about being "of the experience." This means being part of a group who has experienced a certain type of discrimination first-hand or supporting close friends through such a period of victimization. And I think it is experiences like these that give people a certain perspective on the world. Only some women and some men share a victim's perspective on sexual harassment.   7

When those in a position to judge insist that the victim respond as they imagine they would in such circumstances, the perspective of the victim most often is erased.   8

If anti-discrimination law and discourse is to respond to a postmodern world, we need to find ways to reach out for and to give weight to suppressed perspectives in the decisional rules that structure legal definitions of equality. We seldom find victim's perspectives embraced in the law. For example, the leading equal protection case—*Washington v. Davis* (1)—requires that plaintiff prove that defendant intended to discriminate. This means that the perspective that determines whether a constitutional violation has occurred is the perspective of the defendant. Although like all legal standards, the intent requirement is highly manipulable, it symbolizes that the viewpoint of the defendant—not the victim—is the one that should control. It is not surprising that critical race scholars such as Charles Lawrence have renewed their criticism of *Washington v. Davis* and have urged the courts in constitutional cases to go beyond the motivations of lawmakers and judge the race-based nature of an action by its "cultural meaning." (2) For Lawrence, the cultural meaning of an action is more likely to take into account the perspectives of suppressed minorities than would the intent of those elected to Congress or state legislatures.   9

One area of the law in which we can begin to glimpse the victim's perspective being taken into account is in Title VII sexual harassment cases involving claims of a hostile or intimidating work environment—the kind of claim Anita Hill might have brought against EEOC had she filed suit. In these cases the plaintiff must prove that the harassing conduct "had the purpose or effect of unreasonably interfering with an individual's work performance or creating an intimidating, hostile or offensive working environment." (3) This standard is more victim-friendly than the current constitutional standard. Because there is no requirement to prove bad intent on the part of the defendant, the perpetrator's perspective is not necessarily determinative.   10

Recently, courts have recognized that events can look very different from the standpoint of plaintiff or defendant—and a few courts have opted to credit plaintiff's version of reality in an effort to uncover and validate a formerly suppressed perspective. An important recent case is *Ellison v. Brady* (4), decided by a panel of the Ninth Circuit in 1991. Depending on your perspective you could call this case either the "love letters" case or the "delusional romance" case. The plaintiff in the case, Kerry Ellison, received two letters from Sterling Gray, a man in her office with whom she had had only casual contact as a co-employee. They both worked as trainees for the IRS. The letters described Gray's intense feelings for Ellison. In   11 one note, for example, he wrote: "I cried over you last night and I'm totally drained today. I've never been in such constant term oil [sic]." They also contained several statements that seemed to assume that the two had formed a genuine and mutual relationship. In one single-spaced, three-page letter, Gray wrote to Ellison "I know you are worth knowing with or without sex . . . Leaving aside the hassles and disasters of recent weeks. I have enjoyed you so much over these past months. Watching you. Experiencing you from O so far away. Admiring your style and your elan . . . Don't you think it odd that two people who have never even talked together alone are striking off such intense sparks . . . I will write another letter in the near future." (5)

12   This pursuit frightened Ellison because as far as she was concerned there was no such relationship: she had rejected several of Gray's invitations to lunch and had asked a male colleague to inform Gray that she had no interest in him and to leave her alone. Ellison then complained about Gray's conduct to her supervisor and insisted that something be done to make Gray stop.

13   Ellison's perspective was that this was a case of "delusional romance." She saw Gray's actions as a nontrivial threat of sexual coercion. From Ellison's perspective, through no action of her own, she had been made the object of a man's fantasies who had ignored her clear requests to stop his aggressive behavior towards her. This victim's perspective differed sharply from the perspective expressed by the district court which dismissed Ellison's claim as stating no cause of action under Title VII. The district court saw Gray's letters as harmless love letters designed to win over Ellison's affections, and stressed that there had been no explicit threats or physically aggressive conduct.

14   On appeal to the Ninth Circuit, Ellison won. The plurality consisting of Judge Beezer and Judge Kozinsky held that Ellison had stated a cause of action and that the case ought to be judged from the perspective of a "reasonable woman" in the position of plaintiff who had received such letters. I'll save for another day the very interesting discussion of whether it is best to describe the victim perspective in sexual harassment litigation in terms of the "reasonable woman." What I think is most important about *Ellison* is the adoption of a perspective other than the perspective of either the accused or the administrators who handled the complaint.

15   I applaud the result in *Ellison* because it validates my own perspective on such matters. On more than one occasion I have been consulted by women students who have received similar, one-sided "love" notes from men in their class. In those cases, the men refused to stop their pursuit of these women, despite warnings from administrators. These "delusional romances" interfered with the women's education. They were afraid to go to class, to go to the library, and they worried when the phone rang when they were alone in their apartments. In my view these were not harmless love letters; they were forms of sexual harassment.

16   Taking the victim's perspective in anti-discrimination law would mean a profound change and I do not expect the courts to go far in this direction until I am way too old to teach employment discrimination. I do believe, however, that suppressed perspectives are now being publicly expressed with greater clarity and with greater frequency. The days of universal truth are numbered.

NOTES

I have explored some of the ideas in this essay in greater depth in Martha Chamallas, "Feminist Constructions of Objectivity: Multiple Perspectives in Sexual and Racial Harassment Litigation," 1. *Texas Journal of Women & the Law* 95 (1992).

1. 426 U.S. 229 (1976).
2. Charles Lawrence, "The Id, the Ego and Equal Protection: Reckoning with Unconscious Racism," 39. *Stan. Law Review* 317 (1987).
3. EEOC Guidelines on Discrimination Because of Sex, 29. C.F.R., §1604.11(a)(3) (1982).
4. 924 F.2d 872 (9th Cir. 1991).
5. Id. at 874.

 FOR CLASS DISCUSSION

1. Analyze and evaluate the disagreements among these writers concerning sexual harassment by applying the first set of guide questions from page 455. How do you account for the differing points of view?

2. Choose one of the arguments for closer analysis, applying the second set of guide questions on page 455–456.

Optional Writing Assignment   The following story recently appeared in a local newspaper. It was told originally by a former high federal official at a meeting of bankers:

> There was a woman, an old maid, who was looking for some adventure in her life and decided to take a cruise. These are her journal entries.
>
> Day 1:   Glorious morning. It's great to be alive.
>
> Day 2:   Perfect weather. Having a wonderful time.
>
> Day 3:   Sat at the captain's table at dinner. Captain propositioned me. Turned him down.
>
> Day 4:   Captain insisted I sleep with him and said that if I didn't, he'd run the ship into rocks and drown all the passengers.
>
> Day 5:   Saved 600 lives last night.

A columnist who reprinted the story called two sexual harassment consultants and asked them if telling the story in the workplace would constitute sexual harassment. They gave the columnist markedly different answers. Drawing on your reading of the preceding arguments, write your own response to the question: "Does telling this story constitute an act of sexual harassment?"

RECYCLING AND GARBAGE

America's 'Garbage Crisis': A Toxic Myth

Patricia Poore

1   Let us recall, for a moment, the *Mobro*—the infamous garbage barge that, in 1987, laden with an increasingly ripe pile of waste, wandered from port to port in search of a home. The *Mobro,* which was carrying plain old municipal solid waste—household garbage—occasioned headlines about the nation's looming "garbage crisis": we were throwing away too much, our landfills were running out of space, and soon the seas would be full of *Mobros,* all looking for a place to dump our trash. And yet here we are, seven years later, and our landfills are not overflowing; our waterways are not crowded with wandering barges. What happened to the garbage crisis?

2   The environmental movement continues to focus its attention on garbage and recycling, as if household garbage were the single most important issue we face and recycling the only solution. Of course, garbage does have an environmental impact; so does almost everything, from prairie-grass fires to the breath you just took. But, contrary to the rhetoric of some environmentalists, garbage is not a serious environmental hazard. True hazards are ones that threaten human lives and health. There are plenty of these, including toxic waste (which is quite distinct from household garbage), groundwater pollution, and urban smog. Compared with these real crises, the problems of municipal garbage disposal pale. There are times and places when household garbage *can* cause environmental problems—like when toxic runoff leaches into drinking water—but these are increasingly rare. Newer landfills are double-lined, piped, vented, leachate-tested, and eventually capped. These new standards have made current American waste management safer by far than ever before.

3   Some critics argue that we shouldn't downplay the threat of garbage because of its symbolic value to the environmentalist agenda. Environmental organizations are well aware of the emotional power of garbage: nothing can trigger a bounteous direct-mail response or inspire a powerful grass-roots campaign like the threat of a new landfill or incineration plant. But when symbols like the *Mobro* barge are used to divert attention and money from more pressing environmental and social problems, the symbol itself becomes a threat.

4   If there is a garbage crisis, it is that we are treating garbage as an environmental threat and not as what it is: a manageable—though admittedly complex—civic issue. Although many old urban landfills are reaching their capacity, the reality is that there is—and always will be—plenty of room in this country for safe landfill. We've chosen to look at garbage not as a management issue, however, but as a moral crisis. The result is that recycling is

now seen as an irreproachable virtue, beyond the scrutiny of cost-benefit analysis. But in the real world, the money municipalities spend on recycling is money that can't be spent on schools, libraries, health clinics, and police. In the real world, the sort of gigantic recycling programs that many cities and towns have embarked upon may not be the best use of scarce government funds.

These programs were often sold to local taxpayers as money-saving ventures. In fact, the costs associated with consumer education, separate pickup (often in newly purchased trucks), hand- and machine-sorting, transfer stations, trucking, cleaning, and reprocessing are considerably higher than initial estimates, far higher than receipts from buyers of recyclables, and, in many areas, higher than disposal costs. 5

Putting aside financial concerns, let's consider other justifications for the recycling-above-all-else movement. Do we need recycling to extend the life of landfills? No. Landfill sites, in fact, are not scarce, and incineration remains a reasonable and safe option. The most ambitious collection programs still leave well over half of municipal waste to be disposed of, so recycling cannot completely replace disposal facilities, even if we needed it to. 6

Do we need recycling to save resources? No, not in the real world. The reason recycling is unprofitable is that most of the materials being recycled are either renewable (paper from tree farms) or cheap and plentiful (glass from silica). Aluminum *is* profitable to recycle—and private concerns were already recycling it before the legislated mandates. 7

Recycling is beginning to lose its halo as its costs become apparent and its effect on the volume of waste is found to be smaller than anticipated. Quotas and fines may force people to separate their trash, but they can't create industrial markets for the waste we recycle. Recycling can work, very effectively, on a region-by-region and commodity-by-commodity basis. But recycling as a government-mandated garbage-management option has largely failed. 8

Although the special attention we pay to garbage, to the exclusion of more serious environmental threats, may be irrational, it does make a certain emotional sense. We as individuals are intimate with our trash, which makes it a more tangible issue than, say, groundwater contamination. Nobody particularly likes garbage; nobody likes taking it out or paying to have it hauled away. We feel we should be able to control it. Furthermore, controlling it—whether by banning plastics or sorting materials neatly at curbside—alleviates consumer guilt. "There," we say, tossing our bundled newspapers on the curb, "I've done my part for the environment." 9

But for all the psychological benefit that approach may confer, it is distracting us from much more pressing national problems. Trash-handling issues should be debated and decided regionally, and those decisions have to be based, at least in part, on economics. That can't happen when one option—recycling—is elevated by environmentalist rhetoric into a national moral imperative. We have real environmental problems to worry about: We have to protect the water supply. We must improve the quality of the air we breathe. We need a better plan for energy management. And we have to monitor toxic waste more effectively. In that context, it is foolish and extremely wasteful to expend so much effort wringing our hands (and spending our money) on garbage. 10

Time to Dump Recycling?

Chris Hendrickson, Lester Lave, and Francis McMichael

1   After decades of lobbying by environmentalists and extensive experience with voluntary programs, municipal solid waste recycling has recently received widespread official acceptance. The U.S. Environmental Protection Agency (EPA) has set a national goal that 25 percent of municipal solid waste (MSW) be recycled. Forty-one states plus the District of Columbia have set recycling goals that range up to 70 percent. Twenty-nine states require municipalities or counties to enact recycling ordinances or develop recycling programs. Before celebrating this achievement, however, we need to take a hard look at the price of victory and the value of the spoils.

2   No one seeing the overflowing trash containers in front of each house on collection day can deny that MSW is a serious concern. Valuable resources are apparently being squandered with potentially serious environmental consequences. The popular media have carried numerous warnings that landfills are close to capacity, and we expect to find vehement local opposition to the siting of any new landfills. At first glance, recycling seems to be the perfect antidote, and it does have widespread public support.

3   Because it seemed to be the right thing to do, we have tolerated numerous glitches in establishing recycling programs. The supply of recycled materials has grown much faster than the capacity for converting them to useful products. Prices for materials have fluctuated wildly, making planning difficult. It takes time to develop efficient collection and processing systems. But the public and policymakers have been willing to be patient as the kinks in the system are worked out. The self-evident wisdom of recycling reassured everyone that all these problems could be solved.

4   But as these difficulties are being resolved, we are developing a much clearer picture of the economics of recycling. Beneath the debates about markets and infrastructure lurk two fundamental questions: Is it cost effective? Does it actually preserve resources and benefit the environment? What "obviously" makes sense sometimes does not stand up to careful scrutiny.

UNDERSTANDING THE PROBLEM

5   The U.S. gross domestic product (GDP) of $6 trillion entails a lot of "getting and spending." From short-lived items such as food and newspapers to clothing, computers, cars, household furnishings, and the buildings we live and work in, everything eventually becomes municipal solid waste. The average U.S. citizen produces 1,600 pounds of solid waste a year.

6   For most of our history, waste was carted to an open site outside of town and dumped there. When the public became unhappy with the smell, the appearance, and the threat to public health of these traditional dumps, EPA ruled that waste would have to be placed in engineered landfills. These sophisticated capital-intensive facilities must have liners to

keep the leachate from spreading, collection and treatment systems for leachate, and covers to keep away pests and to inhibit blowing dust and debris. EPA's regulations resulted in the closure of most dumps and the elimination of the most serious environmental problems caused by MSW. Still, most people objected if their neighborhood was picked as the site of a landfill. Some analysts erred in interpreting the closure of dumps and siting difficulties as signs that the country was running short of landfills. Although a few cities, notably New York and Philadelphia, are indeed having trouble finding nearby landfills, there is no national shortage of landfills. Thus, lack of space for disposing of waste is not a rationale for recycling.

But even without a pressing need to find a new way to manage MSW, many people   7
would promote recycling as an economically and environmentally superior strategy. Recycling is portrayed as a public-spirited activity that will generate income and conserve valuable resources. These claims need to be examined critically.

THE PITTSBURGH STORY

To get a detailed picture of how current recycling programs work, we focus on Pitts-   8
burgh—an example of an older Northeastern city where one would expect waste disposal to be an expensive problem. In response to a state mandate, Pittsburgh introduced MSW recycling in selected districts in 1990 and gradually increased coverage of the municipality and the number of products accepted for recycling.

After studying numerous alternatives, Pittsburgh implemented a system by which re-   9
cyclable trash was commingled in distinctive blue bags, separately collected at curbside, and delivered to a privately operated municipal recovery facility (MRF) for separation and eventual marketing to recyclers. The contract for operating the facility is awarded on the basis of competitive bidding. Recyclable trash is collected weekly by municipal employees using standard MSW trucks and equipment owned by the city. In addition, special leaf collections are made in the fall for composting purposes.

In 1991, the last year for which complete data are available, Pittsburgh collected   10
167,000 tons of curbside MSW. This represents roughly two-thirds of the city's total MSW; the other third included retail, industrial, office, and park wastes. Curbside pickup of glass, plastic, and metal produced 5,100 tons (3.1 percent of curbside MSW) for recycling. In 1993, newsprint collection was added, and the total curbside pickup of recyclable material was 6,700 tons of newsprint and 5,300 tons of glass, plastic, and metal.

When Pittsburgh started its recycling program in 1989, it sought bids from MRF op-   11
erators. The best bid was an offer to pay the city $2.18 per ton of glass, metal, and plastic delivered to the MRF facility and to charge the city $8.39 per ton to take the material if newsprint was included. The tipping fee at the landfill at the time was $24 per ton. Either option was therefore less expensive than landfilling if—and as we will see, this is a very big "if"—one does not take collection costs into account.

In the second round of bidding in 1992, the city was committed to recycling newsprint,   12
so it solicited only bids that included newsprint. The best bid was a cost to the city of $31.60 per ton. Meanwhile, the fee for landfilling had fallen to $16.15 per ton. The city

therefore had to pay almost twice as much per ton to get rid of its recyclable MSW—again, without accounting for collection costs.

13   The increased tipping fees for recyclable materials reflects recognition of the sorting costs associated with the Pittsburgh blue bags and the difficulties of marketing MSW recyclables. A study by Waste Management, Inc. found that the price of a typical set of recyclable MSW materials had fallen from $107 per ton (in 1992 dollars) in 1988 to $44 per ton in 1992. Prices have continued to fluctuate widely since then. Although they are high at the moment, there is no guarantee about the future.

COLLECTOR'S ITEM

14   The price instability of recycled material has darkened the economic prospects for recycling and received extensive public attention. But an even more troubling problem—the cost of collecting recyclable material—has been largely overlooked. Pittsburgh's experience is particularly eye-opening. The city uses the same employees and type of equipment as it uses for regular MSW, but the trucks on the recycling collection routes use a crew of two instead of three. Using the city's own accounting figures and dividing the costs between recycling and regular collection in proportion to employee hours worked and time of truck use, we calculated total collection costs. In 1991, it cost Pittsburgh $94 per ton to collect regular MSW and $470 per ton to collect recyclable MSW. With tipping fees for recyclables now higher than those for regular MSW, the total cost of disposing of recyclable MSW is more than four times the cost for regular MSW.

15   Several factors account for the very large difference. First is the lower density of recyclables; a full truck will hold fewer tons of recyclables. A second reason is that the amount of material picked up at each house is much smaller (recyclable material is less than 10 percent of the total MSW in Pittsburgh) so that the truck has to travel farther and make more stops to collect each ton of recyclable MSW. Because the purpose of recycling is to preserve resources and protect the environment, it should be noted that collecting recyclable MSW results in a significant increase in fuel use and combustion emissions.

16   Care must be taken in generalizing from Pittsburgh, where the narrow streets and hilly terrain make collection difficult, to other cities. The cost of collecting recyclable MSW is not that high in most cities. Waste Management, Inc., reports an average collection and sorting cost of $175 per ton for recycled material, based on its experience with 5.2 million households in more than 600 communities. However, the cost of collecting regular MSW is also significantly lower elsewhere, so that the difference in the costs of collecting recyclable and regular MSW is very large everywhere. Data available for other municipalities suggests that Pittsburgh's experience is not atypical. For example, San Jose reports costs of $28 per ton to landfill versus $147 per ton to recycle.

17   Although the cost estimates cited above are a very rough estimate of actual costs, the difference between landfilling and recycling is so large that we are convinced that more finely tuned financial data would not have any significant effect on the bottom-line conclusion that most recycling is too expensive. City officials are apparently beginning to reach the same conclusion. After some years of experience, Pennsylvania's cities have begun to scale back their recycling program as a result of the unforeseen additional costs.

DISAPPOINTING ALTERNATIVES

Because collection accounts for such a large share of the cost of recycling, we need to look at alternatives to Pittsburgh's system of separate curbside pickup. One option would be to improve the efficiency of the current pickup system. In Pittsburgh, collection routes are determined by tradition, with little attention paid to minimizing cost. However, research by graduate students at Carnegie Mellon found that savings from improved routing and other improvements in the current collections system would be small. Although any reduction in cost would be desirable, the savings are available to regular as well as recyclable MSW collection so there should be no change in the relative costs.

A related strategy would be to decrease the frequency of collection. For example, under pressure from the city council to reduce costs, Pittsburgh adopted in mid-1994 a biweekly schedule for collecting recyclable MSW. By increasing the amount of recyclables at each residence, the density of collection has increased somewhat, but it still does not approach the density of regular MSW. Also, residences now have to store recyclable materials longer, which could weaken their willingness to participate. This might explain why Pittsburgh's 1994 collection of recyclables was 25 percent less by weight than it had been in 1993.

A second alternative for cost savings is to use a private firm for collection. This might result in marginal savings but could hardly be expected to make a significant difference. A third possibility is to use the same truck for collecting MSW and recyclables. The efficiency of this system depends on how much additional time is lost in collecting the recyclables and then dropping them off at the MRF on the way to emptying the MSW at a landfill. A few cities have adopted this approach, but no reliable economic evaluation has been done. For Pittsburgh, we estimate that combined collection would actually increase costs by 10 percent.

Fourth, collection of recycled MSW might be abandoned in favor of distributed dropoff stations. Households would reap the benefits of lower taxes at the expense of dropping off their recyclables. The efficiency of this system depends on the amount of recyclables to be dropped off and the number of additional miles driven. To obtain a rough estimate, assume that each household drives three extra miles (30 percent of an average shopping trip) every two weeks. The household generates 150 pounds of MSW every two weeks, of which 8 percent (12 pounds) is recyclable. Thus, the $0.90 additional driving cost amounts to $0.075 per pound or $150 per ton. Costs of dropoff center implementation and maintenance should also be added. In Wellesley, Massachusetts, the operating cost of a dropoff center is reported as $16 per ton of recycled material in 1988–1989 or roughly $18 in 1992 dollars. Thus, an estimate of the total direct cost of recycling in dropoff stations is $168 per ton. This does not include the value of volunteer labor such as sorting recyclable material and driving to the dropoff center. At $5 per hour, the labor cost is more than the vehicle costs, with a total of about $400 per ton. Having more dropoff centers would lower driving costs but add a neighborhood nuisance and increase center costs. Another consideration is that the total volume of recycled material might be much smaller because people would not want to do the extra work. Smaller volume would make it more difficult to establish a market for the recycled material and to benefit from economies of scale in processing the material.

22   Because the value of recycled material varies so much, efficiency might be increased by limiting collection to the most valuable materials. For example, assuming that typical MRF processing costs $150 per ton, that collecting recyclable MSW costs $75 per ton more than collecting regular MSW, and that tipping fees are about $35 per ton, the recyclable material would have to sell for at least $190 per ton to be worth separating from MSW. Only aluminum, which was selling for about $750 per ton in 1993, qualifies on this criteria. At that time, plastic was $100–$130 per ton, steel and bimetal from cans was $80 per ton, clear glass was $50 per ton, and newsprint was $30 per ton. By limiting collection to aluminum and other metal cans, plastic, and plastic containers, one could lower the separation costs at the MRF, but the unit collection cost would increase so much that it would probably dwarf the savings at the MRF. In addition, collecting only high-value materials contradicts the EPA goal of recycling 25 percent of all MSW.

23   A major problem with recycling is the low demand for recycled materials. For example, Germany instituted a packaging recycling program that collected essentially all used packaging, but now Europe is swamped with inexpensive (and subsidized) recycled plastic. One possible policy prescription for reducing the imposed costs of recycling is to stimulate the demand for recycled materials. For example, the federal government has changed its procurement policy to insure that 20 percent of paper purchases are of recycled pulp. In some cases, there is needless discrimination against recycled materials. However, at our estimated cost of $190 per ton for additional collection and separation costs, not many materials would be worth recycling even if demand for them surged.

24   Finally, we could move to a completely different arrangement such as the "take-back" system being tried in Germany in which the manufacturer is responsible for getting packaging material back from the consumer and recycling it. Germany is even considering legislation that would require manufacturers to take back and recycle their own products. In this system, firms would be required to arrange "reverse logistics" systems for collecting and eventually recycling their discarded products. For example, newspaper delivery services would have to collect used newspapers. The United States already has take-back regulation for a few particularly hazardous products such as the lead acid batteries used in automobiles. Although this approach creates strong incentives for manufacturers to reduce waste, the costs are likely to be much higher than those of the present system, because it will almost certainly require numerous collection systems.

WHAT ABOUT THE ENVIRONMENT?

25   Our analysis convinces us that recycling is substantially more expensive than landfilling MSW. But the primary motivation for recycling laws is not to save money; it is to save the environment. As it happens, saving the environment is not so different from saving money in this case. The greater costs stem from additional trucks, fuel, and sorting facilities. Every truck mile adds carcinogenic diesel particles, carbon monoxide, organic compounds, oxides of nitrogen, and rubber particles to the environment, just as building and maintaining each truck does. Collection in urban areas also increases traffic congestion and noise. Constructing, heating, and lighting for an MRF similarly use energy and other scarce

resources. The variety of activities associated with the two- to fourfold increase in costs associated with recycling is almost certain to result in a net increase in resource use and environmental discharges.

For Pittsburgh and similar cities, the social cost of MSW recycling is far greater than   26
the cost of placing the waste in landfills. No minor modifications in collection programs or prices of recycled materials are likely to change this conclusion. Approaches such as dropoff stations that attempt to hide the cost by removing it from the city ledger are likely to have the highest social cost.

Although many people object to landfill disposal, modern landfills are designed and operated to have minimal discharges to the environment. Current regulations are sufficient   27
to minimize the environmental impacts of landfills for several decades. Nevertheless, landfills are unlikely to be the optimum long-term solutions.

The fundamental problem remains: A society in which each individual produces 1,600   28
pounds of MSW a year is consuming too much of our natural resources and is diminishing environmental quality. Today's MSW recycling systems are analogous to the "end-of-the-pipe" emission controls enacted 25 years ago. Air and water discharge standards were designed to stop pollution. They do so, but at a cost of about $150 billion per year. Recycling MSW lowers the amount going into landfills but at too high a cost.

EPA and some progressive companies have stressed "pollution prevention" and "green   29
design" as the only real solution to pollution problems. Just cleaning up Superfund waste sites has proven extraordinarily expensive. Less expensive but still inefficient is the cost of preventing environmental discharges through better management of hazardous waste. The ideal solution is to redesign production processes so that no hazardous waste is created in the first place and no money is needed for discharge control and remediation.

For MSW, this approach would mean designing consumer products to reduce waste and   30
to facilitate recycling. The potential hazards associated with toxic materials in landfills could be reduced by eliminating the toxic components in many products. For example, stop adding cadmium to plastics to give them a shiny appearance and stop using lead pigments in paints and ink. Another example is choosing packaging to minimize the volume of waste. Finally, products can be designed so that at disposal time the high-value recyclable materials can be easily removed.

Producers and consumers don't have good information to help them make choices   31
among materials. And even when they have the information, they are not sufficiently motivated to use it. Most consumers know that they shouldn't dump used motor oil down the drain and shouldn't put old smoke detectors or half-empty pesticide containers in their trash. If they were charged the social cost of these practices, they would find more environmentally satisfactory ways of handling these unwanted products. In some cases it may be cost effective for manufacturers to include prepaid shipping vouchers to encourage consumers to return highly toxic components such as radioactive materials in smoke detectors before disposing of a product.

The best way to inform consumers and producers and to motivate them to act in socially   32
desirable ways is to establish a pricing mechanism for materials and products that reflects their full social cost, including resource depletion and environmental damage. Full-cost pricing of

raw materials would lead producers to make more socially desirable choices of materials and lead them to designs that are easier to reuse or recycle. A major problem with the current system is that product wastes in MSW arrive at the MRF having been manufactured with little or no thought for making them easy to recycle. Full-cost pricing would change the choice of materials and design so that the MRF was an integrated part of a product's design.

33   Unfortunately, more research is required to determine the full cost of materials, and after that is done, it will be necessary to develop a means of implementing the concept. Neither task will be easy, but the alternative is to neglect environmental problems or to attempt to regulate every decision.

34   Even under the best of conditions, improved design and recycling will not eliminate the need for disposal. The waste stream will be smaller and less hazardous, but the total volume will still be daunting. We will have to come back to comparing the merits of landfills, recycling, and incineration. Changes in the waste stream will force us to examine each option with fresh eyes. At present, this might mean reserving recycling for metals, using the plastic and wood product portions of MSW as fuel for energy-producing incineration, and landfilling the rest.

35   MSW is a systems problem. Any one-dimensional solution, be it mandated recycling, incineration, or something else, is likely to do more harm than good. An assumed preference for recycling flies in the face of economic reality unless mechanisms can be found to greatly lower the costs of collection and sorting. The long-term answer to managing MSW is likely to include green design, materials choice, component reuse, and incineration, as well as recycling. Finding a way to use full-cost pricing so that decisions are decentralized and quickly adaptable will be the key to achieving thoughtful use of resources and improvements in environmental quality.

Don't Dump Recycling

Robert Steuteville

1   I take strong exception to the shaky facts and conclusions presented in "Time to Dump Recycling?" by Chris Hendrickson, Lester Lave, and Francis McMichael (*Issues,* Spring 1995). The authors show considerable ignorance of both the economic and environmental impacts of recycling.

2   The authors assume that typical materials recovery facility (MRF) processing costs are $150 per ton. Whoa. They missed that by a factor of three. One study, sponsored by the National Solid Waste Management Association, found average MRF costs of about $50 per ton. Waste Management Inc. has stated that its MRF processing costs are $40 per ton. Based on my own discussions with MRF operators, costs are generally $30 to $50 per ton.

3   Although the authors may be right about recycling collection running $75 per ton more than refuse collection, their absurd processing cost throws their subsequent calculation out the window. They state that it would take recyclable commodity prices of about $190 per ton to make recycling worthwhile, but if their own equation and real MRF costs are used,

the breakeven commodity prices drop down to $80 or $90 per ton. It just so happens that the current value of curbside materials averages $100 or more per ton nationally.

The article mentions that "the public and policymakers have been willing to be patient as   4
the kinks in the system are worked out." But not the authors. They pick as their primary example Pittsburgh, using figures for 1991, the city's first full year of recycling. In fact, the program was still being implemented in various neighborhoods that year. They compare those costs with those of a refuse system that has been in place for a half century or more. Not exactly fair.

If they couldn't get more recent figures (which I find hard to believe, because Pittsburgh's   5
budget is public), why not pick another city? In any case, as the authors themselves note, the costs cited ($470 per ton) are not representative of average recycling expenses. In fact, an examination of recycling costs in eight Pennsylvania municipalities funded by the National Soft Drink Association (published in 1993, also using 1991 figures) showed that Pittsburgh, for a variety of reasons, was way off the scale. The next highest cost cited was $150 per ton.

The authors state that prices for recyclable commodities have "fluctuated wildly" since   6
1992, when they were $44 per ton. Wrong. Average prices stayed fairly constant, maybe rising a little, in 1993 and early 1994, and in the past 12 months they have increased dramatically. The authors dismiss the recent rise offhandedly, but in fact prices are pretty much in line (in constant dollars) with what they were in 1988. They dropped between 1988 and 1992, in part because of the rapid increase in recycling programs, which increased supplies of materials at a pace that is not likely to occur again.

There are other errors in analysis: The authors cite Waste Management's recycling   7
costs without factoring in the offsetting revenues, and San Jose's landfill tipping fee costs are compared with total recycling costs, as if garbage gets to the disposal facility by magic.

The authors dismiss any environmental benefits of recycling. "The two- to fourfold in-   8
crease in costs associated with recycling is almost certain to result in a net increase in resource use and environmental discharges." Even if the cost figures were correct (which they are not), the logic boggles the mind. If low-cost systems equate to the least environmental damage, why do we treat sewage when we could just dump it in a stream? In fact, the authors' statement comes out of left field, with no data to support it. Every reputable study that has looked at energy, resources, and pollution discharge shows a considerable overall advantage for recycling (recent studies include reports by Keep America Beautiful and the U.S. Department of Energy).

Finally, the authors lump all recycling together. When the curbside programs began, so   9
did thousands of business recycling programs and dropoff systems. These various forms of recycling have been driven by the same factors, such as environmental concerns and the general popularity of recycling. Moreover, the curbside programs have prompted the construction of MRFs, which have enabled more dropoff and commercial programs to get started. Commercial recycling often saves huge amounts of money and resources.

Even if the authors only mean to criticize curbside recycling, there are almost as many   10
different varieties as there are programs (7,200 at last count). Some are highly cost effective, some are less so, but most are constantly evolving. Even in the past five years we've seen new types of collection and equipment, more materials added, and more efficient systems. Some cities are contracting out services for collection and processing of curbside materials for $60 per ton or less. Try to collect, haul, and dump garbage for that price.

Response to Hendrickson et al.

Reid Lifset and John Schall

1   It has become fashionable of late to debunk recycling. Unlike many of the self-interested groups attacking the economic feasibility and environmental benefits of recycling, Hendrickson, Lave, and McMichael are knowledgeable and responsible scholars. Nonetheless, contrary to their analysis, recycling can be both cost effective and environmentally beneficial.

2   The best data on this issue come from a 25-year solid waste management plan prepared for the Region Plan Association (RPA) by the Tellus Institute of Boston. RPA is a nonprofit association that works to facilitate regionwide planning in the greater New York City area. The 31-county, 20-million-person RPA Region includes not only New York City proper but large portions of northern New Jersey, western Connecticut, and southern New York. As such, it includes urban, suburban, and semirural communities and accounts for 8 percent of the U.S. population and 10 percent of its trash.

3   The RPA study is particularly valuable in that it assessed waste management costs by 1) comparing systemwide costs of competing approaches to trash management (thereby capturing the many interactive effects of recycling and trash collection and disposal services alluded to by Hendrickson et al.) and 2) relying on current rather than projected innovations in waste collection and processing practices. The RPA study found that when two regionwide systems are compared at the end of the planning period (one with no source reduction but realizing the state-mandated recycling and composting goals and another that simply collects all waste as garbage and buried or burned it), the disposal-only system and the recycling-intensive approach are roughly equal in cost.

4   Even given the historically low prices available from the sale of recyclables in 1990, recycling and composting nearly half of the region's waste stream is therefore essentially no more expensive (but also no less so) than burying or burning this same material. However, if those same figures are recalculated using the higher prices available in 1994 and 1995 for recyclables, the recycling-intensive system is more than $20 per ton less expensive than the disposal-only approach. Note here that Hendrickson and his colleagues use $30 per ton as their benchmark for strong prices for old newsprint. That commodity is now selling for $210. While some of the very high prices currently being paid for recyclables are likely to wane, the prices for paper have undergone a structural change. The paper industry has made investments of over $10 billion in recycled production capacity—10,000 tons/day worth of capacity—that has permanently altered demand for waste paper.

5   On the environmental front, the prospects for recycling are equally good. The findings from the RPA study emphasize that the benefits from recycling do not come primarily from the avoidance of disposal-related threats. Instead, the environmental payoff from recycling arises because it allows us to reduce resource extraction damages and to manufacture more cleanly. Think here of the benefits of recycling steel or aluminum. When recovered metals from the municipal waste stream are used in place of virgin materials, the demand for mining declines with commensurate decreases in acid mine drainage, ecosystem disturbance, and so on. Further, manufacturing is less polluting when recy-

clables are used in place of virgin materials, in part because manufacturing using recyclables typically consumes less energy.

The RPA findings underscore the importance of viewing solid waste management in the larger context of resource extraction, production, consumption, and disposal in our economy. Combined with the recent improvements in end markets for recyclables, these findings show that it is most definitely not time to dump recycling. 6

Response to Hendrickson et al.

Brenda Platt and Neil Seldman

Chris Hendrickson, Lester Lave, and Francis McMichael's article, which argues against recycling as too costly and too polluting, contains many errors and arrives at wrong conclusions. The authors make four important errors. 1

1) They rely on 1991 data for costs, tonnages, and market prices. Since 1991, prices have increased from zero to $60 per ton for mixed paper and from $5 to $110 per ton for newspaper. The authors claim that demand for recycled materials is low, when in fact demand is at an all-time high. 2

2) The authors use the experience of only one city, Pittsburgh, to conclude that "most recycling is too expensive." Not only does this represent a poor scientific sample, but Pittsburgh's program is a poor choice. At only 7 percent, its recycling rate is far below the national average. When cities recycle this little, they invariably treat recycling as an add-on to their existing collection systems. That raises costs. Cities with higher recycling rates can redesign their equipment and pickup schedules to lower or eliminate additional costs. Consider Loveland, Colorado, which recovers 51 percent of its residential waste, using the same vehicles to simultaneously collect trash and segregated recyclables. Costs (per household) did not rise with the new system. Takoma Park, Maryland, which recycles 50 percent of its residential wastes, split collection crews between recycling and trash collection, thereby integrating recycling and avoiding the need to hire additional workers. Plano, Texas, replaced one of its two weekly trash collection days with collection of recyclables and yard waste at no additional cost. Richmond, Virginia, eliminated one of its trash collection routes by adding mixed paper to its recycling program. 3

In general, cities that reach recycling levels of 40 percent or more see their per-ton recycling costs drop (this is well documented in the Institute for Local Self-Reliance's report *Beyond 40 Percent: Record-Setting Recycling and Composting Programs,* which the authors include on their recommended reading list). Pittsburgh could raise its recycling levels to 30 to 50 percent by imitating the actions of other cities. 4

3) The authors' analysis of the environmental consequences of recycling is inadequate as it overlooks the industrial pollution, water, and energy saved by recycling materials rather than extracting raw materials. Collection and disposal of trash uses more fuel than recycling because trash trucks are heavier than recycling vehicles. Further, unlike recyclables, trash must be hauled long distances to landfills. 5

6   4) The authors don't consider the economic benefits of recycling. We should examine not only the impact of recycling on city budgets but also its overall impact on the local economy. Just sorting recyclables sustains five to nine times more jobs per ton than does disposal. However, it is making new products from old that offers the largest economic payoff. Recycling-based manufacturers employ more people and at higher wages. Some mills employ 60 times more workers than do landfills. With a metropolitan population of 2 million, the Pittsburgh region would generate enough material to sustain 3,000 to 4,000 manufacturing jobs (plus 4,500 to 6,000 indirect jobs) if it recycled 50 percent of its waste. Today, most of the materials are exported from the region, virtually precluding such job creation potential. Contrary to the authors' assertions, the economic benefits from recycling can be quite significant. Baltimore, Maryland, is now saving $550,000 a year as a result of its recycling program.

7   It would be tragic if the *Issues* article led cities like Pittsburgh that are just climbing up the recycling curve to cut back their programs, especially when industry is crying for recycled materials and when many municipal programs are hitting their stride in terms of efficiency and effectiveness.

Recycling: Asking the Right Questions

Lynn Scarlett

1   There it was on my desk. Fresh off the press, a copy of *New York Times Magazine.* "What a Waste," announced bold letters on the cover imposed atop pictures of neatly stacked bottles, cans, paper, and mills jugs. Inside, the cover story title told the rest of the tale, "Recycling is Garbage."

2   I dug into my files. There they were. Stacks of articles from the early 1990s bearing a different theme, "Garbage is Gold" or "Trash is Treasure."

3   What's going on here? A bit of eyecatching media hyperbole, yes. But these polar headlines reflect a deeper problem in discussions about recycling—an insistence on casting recycling as all virtue or all villain.

4   Neither combatant in this war of words is asking (or answering) the right question. The right question is not, "Is recycling good or bad?" The right question is, "How do we best ensure efficient (conserving) use of resources?"

5   Recycling has a role to play in resource conservation. But the extent of that role varies by material, product and production process. And costs associated with collecting, processing and remanufacturing of recyclables vary depending on location and situation. There is, in short, no one-size-fits-all solution.

6   Recycling is not a new phenomenon. Basic economics spawned the scrap industry a century ago. Economics shaped the ups and downs of recycling. And it still does.

7   Making a new soda can out of recycled aluminum takes 95 percent less energy than to make new cans from basic bauxite. Less energy translates into lower costs, helping the aluminum can compete in the container marketplace.

8   Glass manufacturers also benefit by using recycled clear glass. For each 10 percent of recycled glass they incorporate into their bottles, they reduce energy consumption by 2 to

3 percent. And using recycled content helps extend the life of their glass furnaces, another economic benefit.

But reality is complex, a point too many recycling advocates overlook. Location, for example, can be a constraint. Transporting recycled glass to far-off factories can be so costly that it can undo any economic benefits achieved at the plant site.

Or take paper. Whether paper recycling makes economic and environmental sense depends on the type of paper. Newsprint recycles well; old tissue and wet paper towels may have little or no reuse value.

The value of paper recycling also varies by end use. A cereal box commonly contains 100 percent recycled content. But high-performance paperboard, which has strict strength requirements, won't perform properly with too much recycled content. To compensate for lost performance, manufacturers need to add more virgin pulp to the product, reducing environmental benefits and increasing costs.

At a recent wastepaper conference, one speaker summarized the matter this way: "The multitude of factors influencing the behavior of recycled pulps during papermaking makes it difficult to make predictable sense from existing information."

Combatants in the recycling debate could learn a lot from Seattle and the state of Washington, though the lessons are not those usually pronounced by Seattle's recycling champions. Too often, those champions fall into the "more is better no matter what" syndrome. They spend a lot of time counting recycling rates; they spend too little time asking "big picture" questions about economy, environment and the complexities of resource conservation.

What then, are the lessons of the state and its biggest city? First of all, Seattle's pay-as-you-throw fee system reminds us that prices give information to consumers—and that information creates incentives for conservation. Just about all Seattle residents can tell you ways that they limit trash generation so that they can limit their trash bill. They recycle, they compost, they make sure to take old clothes to the thrift store, they eliminate "resident-only" mail delivery, they feed scraps to the pet pig.

Second, flexibility and competition are important. Seattle uses a competitive contracting process to determine who will provide curbside recycling service. In that process, they don't micromanage how contractors must provide the curbside service. Contractors can experiment figuring out the most efficient ways to serve the city. And the competitive process keeps them focused on efficient service over time. The result is lower costs to residents.

Third, the state's recycling market development program—the Clean Washington Center—recognizes that economics matter. Sustainable recycling must be built on non-subsidized markets for end products that use recycled materials. That means working with manufacturers to identify promising opportunities and then nudging the process along with technical assistance where needed. It means avoiding one-size-fits-all prescriptions that would require all products—regardless of the devilish details that determine what really saves resources—to use recycled materials as feedstocks.

Nearly one hundred years ago, Colonel George E. Waring, New York's first "crusader for cleanliness," warned that to regain value from the rejectamenta of human life "is a matter of minute detail." That's another way of saying what makes sense depends on the material, the product, the process and local circumstance.

Recycling: The Other Coast, the Other Story

Nancy Glaser

1   Is recycling a money saver or a boondoggle, a planet saver or environmental overkill?

2   A recent *New York Times* story*. . . questions the value, cost and motivation of recycling. The story lists complaints and problems associated with New York City's recycling program and, by extension, with recycling everywhere. In Seattle and the Northwest, recycling is a proven, cost-effective part of the solid waste system and, increasingly, of the regional economy.

3   Seattle and other parts of the country have always recycled. Materials have been rescued from the garbage to be made into something new, worn again or sold to the salvage yard. When it was recognized that some reusable materials could be kept out of the garbage and returned to manufacturers who could make them into new cans, bottles, and newspapers, a new market niche of small recycling collectors was spawned.

4   By the mid-1980s Seattle businesses and residents were recycling 24 percent of their solid waste, mostly at privately owned drop sites in supermarket parking lots or, for businesses, through private collection.

5   Then local events put a spotlight on recycling. Seattle's landfills—Midway and Kent highlands—had already been closed and declared federal Superfund sites. We were sending our garbage to the King County-owned Cedar Hills landfill, where rates were high. We had to find another way to dispose of our garbage or face serious budget problems.

6   City officials and residents decided that recycling might be part of the answer to our garbage problem. If we recycled more, we could send less waste to a landfill.

7   In 1988 Seattle began a revolution that made us the nation's leader in recycling, bringing in officials from around the world to learn from our experience and solutions.

8   Policy-makers and residents decided to make recycling a cornerstone of Seattle's Solid Waste Utility. In 1988 the city adopted a recycling goal of 60 percent and offered voluntary, city-sponsored, curbside recycling collection to every single-family household. Since then collection services for apartments, condominiums and businesses have been expanded and made more convenient. Today more than 90 percent of residents and 80 percent of businesses recycle.

9   Equally impressive is the amount of residential solid waste that goes into the recycling bins instead of the garbage—48 percent, or nearly half. By the end of 1994, Seattle ratepayers had saved $9.6 million by recycling instead of sending those materials to the landfill. By the end of 1995, up to $2.5 million more had been saved.

10   While Seattle still sends just over half its solid waste to a state-of-the-art landfill in Eastern Oregon, recycling has made a huge difference in our solid-waste system. It has not only saved money but also created jobs, grown new businesses and industries and encouraged innovative product design. Recyclable materials are resources now, just like trees, minerals and other natural resources that go into making the products we use every day. Of course we still have garbage, but it's just what's left over after we recycle.

---

*John Tierney, "Recycling Is Garbage." *The New York Times Magazine,* June 30, 1996, 247.

Recycling has always attracted myths and criticisms, often from industries and think   11
tanks that benefit from consuming natural resources or investing in the various segments
of the garbage collection and disposal business. The *New York Times* story didn't make up
the myths surrounding recycling, but it did embellish and pass them on. What are the truths
about recycling here in Seattle and the Pacific Northwest?

Myth: Recycling isn't cost-effective.   12

Truth: In Seattle recycling is a part of our solid-waste system that saves us money.   13

"Every time a sanitation department crew picks up a load of bottles and cans from the
curb, New York City loses money."—*The New York Times*

Every time a collection crew picks up a load of bottles, cans and other recyclables from   14
the curb, the city of Seattle saves money. This remains true even though market prices for
recycled materials have dropped significantly over the past several months.

Recycling does cost money, but today it still costs about $10 less to collect a ton of re-   15
cyclable materials than to collect and dispose of a ton of garbage from Seattle residents ($95
per ton for recyclables versus $105 per ton for garbage). Last year, when the market prices
were much stronger, the price gap between collecting recyclables and garbage was far more
dramatic—$50 per ton for recyclables vs. $100 per ton for garbage.

Unlike New York, Seattle has contracts with private companies to collect the recyclables   16
that residents set out at the curb. We also share the risk with contractors for recyclable material market prices. When the market prices for recyclable materials go up, we pay less to
our contractors, and when prices go down, we pay more.

But according to *The New York Times* article, the study conducted by the Solid Waste   17
Association of North America indicated that Seattle's curbside program was only one-tenth
of 1 percent cheaper than putting garbage into a landfill. That just isn't true.

What the article failed to mention was that the study was flawed in design. For exam-   18
ple, it only looked at data from one year (1992—the worst year for recycling markets to date)
rather than more accurately evaluating costs and benefits over several years. This longer period is necessary to evaluate the return on investment and diminishing costs over time.

The New York Times article also states that environmental groups are pressuring local   19
governments to expand their recycling programs to meet the goals set in law, but that there
aren't many more materials in the garbage worth recycling.

Seattle doesn't recycle for the sake of recycling. On the contrary, we do economic analy-   20
ses of all our programs before starting them to make sure the long-term benefits exceed
costs. As with any new business—and recycling is a business—some parts of the business
may lose money in the short term. What's important are the long-run economic and environmental benefits. Right now, the city is concentrating on several materials that still make
up a big part of the waste stream. Some of the items we're working on are food waste, construction debris, and self-haul waste.

Because Seattleites have been so successful at recycling, isn't it true that there's a glut   21
of unwanted materials? It's true that the markets for recyclable materials are still developing. Our success has assured investors that a consistent, quality-controlled volume of recyclables is available for manufacturing. Businesses have upgraded their factories and
plants to use recyclable materials in manufacturing new products. They are finally starting
to recognize the value of recyclable materials as a resource and are realizing a competitive
advantage from recycling—recycling has become good business. In fact, with leadership

from the Clean Washington Center and local recycling experts such as Jeff Morris and Don Kneass, the value of recyclable materials has been recognized and they are being traded on the Chicago Board of Trade.

22   In addition to adding value to manufactured products, recycling has also created jobs. According to a May 1996 report by the King County Solid Waste Division, total recycling employment in Washington state has increased by about 29 percent since 1992. Part of that job growth occurred in firms that make recycled-content products, during a time in which thousands of other manufacturing jobs were lost in the state.

23   **Myth:** We must recycle because we're running out of landfill space.

24   **Truth:** The landfill myth is a tricky one. Landfill space is still available in some parts of the country, but siting a new landfill is costly and politically difficult.

25   Seattle did choose to recycle, in part, because of the scarcity and expense of landfill space. There is no landfill crisis in this area now, but space in individual landfills is not un-limited and they eventually fill up. At current disposal rates, Washington has an estimated 40 years of landfill capacity, according to the state Department of Ecology in a 1994 report. The majority of the capacity is privately owned, with about 69 percent of the total statewide capacity being at Roosevelt Regional Landfill in Klickitat County.

26   Landfills are expensive and they're becoming more and more difficult to site, especially with the regulations designed to protect ratepayers and neighbors from repeating previous mistakes in landfill management. Minimizing the amount and toxicity of waste Seattle sends to landfills is in the best interests of residents and businesses as it reduces current costs and future liability. It is short-sighted and expensive to consider only the effects on the current generation when making decisions about managing solid waste.

27   **Myth:** Recycling doesn't do much to help the environment.

28   **Truth:** Using recycled materials in manufacturing is easier on the environment than using virgin materials. It conserves energy and results in less air and water pollution.

29   "Recycling is a messy way to try to help the environment."—*The New York Times*

30   There's no denying that recycling can be a messy business. As with garbage, money is spent and natural resources are used to collect and handle recyclable material. In fact, a study by John Schall at Tellus Institute shows that the overall environmental effects of re-cycling collection and handling are no greater (or no less) than disposing of that same ma-terial as garbage. The environmental effects are just different.

31   The most significant environmental benefits of recycling come from using recycled ma-terials instead of virgin materials in manufacturing new products.

32   Life-cycle studies comparing the environmental effects of recycled materials and virgin materials have found that, for 18 of 18 categories of air and water pollutants, recycling re-sulted in a net reduction in the release of pollutants compared with burying or burning the same material.

33   It's obvious that if you make paper from recycled feedstock rather than trees you would be causing a lot less habitat destruction and stream siltation, both of which are documented effects of logging.

34   We're not running out of wood so why do we worry so much about recycling paper?

35   Environmental benefits aside, some still question the need to recycle if we're not re-ally "running out" of natural resources such as trees or fossil fuel.

There's no arguing that trees are renewable but they may take a long time to renew. Most trees can be harvested in 25 to 50 years. What's not as readily renewable are the habitat diversity and aesthetic values provided by a mature or maturing forest.

Tree farms are creating their own environmental problems: soil depletion, new breeds of insects and pests that are resistant to control. Many tree farms are located in the Southeast United States, increasing costs of moving the forest products to where they are used. Recycling regionally lessens the need for single-species tree farms and mitigates some transportation costs.

People don't recycle just because it makes them feel good. For most of us, recycling means added hassle. People recycle to save money and, importantly, they recycle out of a sense of stewardship for the envrionment . . . a fundamental belief in using resources wisely.

Myth: The environmental costs of a product are included in its purchase price.

Truth: Environmental costs are broader than anything included in price. Check where corporate subsidies and tax breaks go.

"When consumers follow their preferences, they are guided by the simplest, and often the best, measure of a product's environmental impact: its price."—*The New York Times*

If this statement were true, when you go out and buy a can of beans or a packet of envelopes, you would be paying not only for the direct cost of growing, packaging and transporting cans of beans or of making paper envelopes, but also for any environmental "costs" of these activities.

The price of a U.S. product usually reflects the cost of complying with strict environmental regulations. Growing beans generally involves the use of chemical fertilizers and pesticides, which has been documented to cause ground-water contamination, human exposure and illness and destruction of beneficial insects.

What is the cost of these consequences? When ground water is contaminated to the point it is undrinkable, a new supply must be found. When people are exposed, they have medical costs and, in some cases, long-term disabilities. When pesticides kill bees, local honey production is impaired. These costs are not borne by the producer and, therefore, are not included in the price of the product.

Imagine how much greater are the environmental effects and costs resulting from agriculture in many countries overseas, to which we export chemicals whose use is banned in the United States and where regulations governing application may be nonexistent. Is this included in the price of the product?

To the extent that the environmental regulations require activities and investments that reduce these effects—like proper disposal of toxic residues or scrubbers for air emissions—they are included in the price of the product. But even a reduced effect has a cost, and you are not paying for these effects when you shop.

You are paying—through your federal taxes—to keep the price of the can even lower than the direct cost of producing it. Federal "depletion allowances" compensate corporations for every ton of raw material they mine, thereby artificially subsidizing the price of products made with depletable raw materials.

After you've eaten the beans, you rinse out the can and throw it away, or recycle it. Both activities have a cost. It costs less to recycle the can than put it into a landfill. But it still costs something. Is the price of managing the discarded can included in the product price? No, it's included on your monthly garbage bill.

49   In the end we all pay the price. We, or our children and grandchildren. *The New York Times* may not want to consider future generations, but the majority of the American public does, as evidenced by consistent support for environmental regulations.

50   Theoretically we learn from our experience. As we have become aware of human effects on the environment and the importance of protecting the world that supports us, we have slowly started to change—and the changes have been for the good. Recycling is a small but important part of these changes.

51   **Myth:** We've done all we can do with recycling . . . mission accomplished.

52   **Truth:** Some cities have done a lot; others have barely started.

53   In Seattle it's true we've done a lot. We recycle nearly half our residential and commercial solid waste. But a lot of material that could be recycled is still going to the landfill. For example, half the cardboard from residents and one-quarter of cardboard from businesses is being thrown away. And cardboard is a material that's worth $75 per ton in today's recycling market.

54   In fact, about 40 percent of what Seattle residents put in the garbage could be recycled.

55   It is true that national trends show that, despite a much higher level of recycling, per capita generation of solid waste continues to increase. While we will continue to look for cost-effective ways to recycle materials that have value rather than throw them away, it is time to look for ways to reduce the total amount of waste each of us generates.

56   *The New York Times* says we recycle because we're "racked with garbage guilt." A little guilt is probably OK if it makes us think about the way we consume. In a Solid Waste Utility survey last fall, 94 percent of respondents said it was important to them that the city encourage people and businesses to reduce waste.

57   Maybe it's some sort of New York attitude that sorting waste is suited only to "the most destitute members of society." In Seattle, residents and the city have a mutually beneficial partnership in which people from every neighborhood sort out their recyclables and take them to the curb to save money and resources. In last fall's survey, 84 percent of respondents said they would recycle more if they could—fabric, food waste and more plastics.

58   "The public's obsession with recycling wouldn't have lasted this long unless recycling met some emotional need," *The New York Times* says.

59   Our respondents told us that recycling and waste reduction save them money. While it should be no surprise that there's some emotion attached to conserving natural resources and treading a little more lightly on the Earth, money seems to be a motivator, too.

60   Why train children to be garbage sorters? Well, why not? Environmental education doesn't create little eco-guerrillas who go home and bully their parents into environmental correctness. It does teach kids about the inter-relatedness of the human species with other species on this planet. It teaches about energy, ecosystems, habitats, animal and plant species and weather. In the process, kids learn the basics of measuring, graphing, weighing, tabulating, writing, analyzing and logic. They also learn more about their place in the world and about personal responsibility and citizenship. Environmental stewardship is a fun and rewarding activity children can share with their families.

61   In Seattle and the Northwest, recycling works. It saves money, energy and natural resources. It grows new businesses and product lines, helps old industries expand in new ways and creates jobs. Recycling is here to stay—as part of our solid waste system, part of our economy and even part of our mythology.

FOR CLASS DISCUSSION

1. Analyze and evaluate disagreements among these writers about the value of recycling by applying the first set of guide questions from page 455. How do you account for the differing points of view?

2. Choose one of the arguments for closer analysis, applying the second set of guide questions on page 455–456.

Optional Writing Assignment   The city of Medelia is a blue-collar town adjacent to a large industrial city. Like many municipalities it has had budget problems over the past decade that have tested everyone's ingenuity. The latest crisis looks like it will result in a substantial deficit. The city council could raise the money by approving a half-percent increase in the city sales tax. But they know that they would all be thrown out of office if they raise taxes. So they have to come up with program cuts; given that city services have been stripped down to the minimum over the years, none of their choices will be politically popular. So, shrewd political thinkers that they are, they have decided to throw it back in the voters' laps.

They will ask voters to decide whether to dismantle their recycling program—which costs the city a substantial outlay of tax dollars in the form of subsidies to the recycling industry that converts glass, plastic, tires, and newspapers to salable commodities—or to substantially reduce the Parks and Recreation Summer Program.

As soon as the vote is announced, supporters of each side begin lining up their arguments. On the Parks and Recreation side are the 1,500 members of the various summer sports leagues (softball, baseball, basketball, and soccer) along with their families and fans. School and police officials like the program because it keeps kids busy and off the streets in the summer; parents like the program because it keeps their kids happy and out of their hair. The two city swimming pools are centers of social activity, particularly for twenty-something parents of young children. On the other side are the environmental groups who have fought hard over the years to reclaim local land areas damaged by years of industrial abuse and who view the recycling program as a sort of spiritual center to the environmental movement.

As a prominent member of the community, you have been asked to participate in the local League of Women Voters debate. One of these debates will take place in a local school in a neighborhood that overwhelmingly supports the continued support of the recreation program. The other debate will take place in the local headquarters of the Nature Conservancy. Before the debate, you have been asked to submit an opening statement that is "responsive" to each of the two highly partisan audiences. Choosing whichever side of the parks versus recycling debate that you prefer, and based on the readings in this section of the anthology, prepare two statements of about 500 words, one for each audience, that "nutshell" your view on the issue.

SOCIAL POLICY TOWARD
THE MENTALLY ILL HOMELESS*

Crazy in the Streets

Paul S. Appelbaum

I

1   They are an inescapable presence in urban America. In New York City they live in sub-way tunnels and on steam grates, and die in cardboard boxes on windswept street corners. The Los Angeles City Council has opened its chambers to them, allowing them to seek refuge from the Southern California winter on its hard marble floors. Pioneer Square in Seattle, Lafayette Park in Washington, the old downtown in Atlanta have all become places of refuge for these pitiable figures, so hard to tell apart: clothes tattered, skins stained by the streets, backs bent in a perpetual search for something edible, smokable, or tradable that may have found its way to the pavement below.

2   Riddled by psychotic illnesses, abandoned by the systems that once pledged to care for them as long as they needed care, they are the deinstitutionalized mentally ill, the detritus of the latest fashion in mental-health policy. The lucky ones live in board-and-care homes where they can be assured of their next meal; perhaps they have a place to go a few hours a week for support, coffee, even an effort at restoring their productive capacity. Those less fortunate live in our public places, existing on the beneficence of their fellow men and God. It is extraordinary how quickly we have become immune to their presence. Where we might once have felt compassion, revulsion, or fear, now we feel almost nothing at all.

3   There are times, of course, when the reality of the deinstitutionalized breaks through our defenses. Three days after the Statue of Liberty extravaganza in New York harbor last July, in the shadow of the icon of huddled masses, a psychotic man ran amok on the Staten Island ferry, slashing at enemies in a war entirely of his own imagining. Two victims died. Investigations ensued. For a moment we became aware of the world of shelters and emergency rooms, a world where even those willing to accept help and clearly in need of it are turned away because the state has deliberately dismantled the system where they might once have received care. Briefly, the curious wondered, how did this come to be?

4   Like its victims, the policy of deinstitutionalization has been taken for granted. It is difficult to recall that mentally ill persons ever were treated differently. Yet the process that came to be called deinstitutionalization (no one knows when the term was coined) only began in the mid-1950's, and did not move into high gear until a decade later. Although

---

*For two additional arguments on the mentally ill homeless, see Charles Krauthammer's "How to Save the Homeless Mentally Ill" (pp. 221–227) and student essay "What Should Be Done about the Mentally Ill Homeless?" (pp. 330–338).

the term itself suggests a unitary policy, deinstitutionalization has had complex roots, and at different times has sought diverse goals. Its failure, however, was all but preordained by several of the forces that gave it birth. Any attempt to correct the debacle that has attended the contraction—some might say implosion—of our public mental-health systems will require an understanding of those forces.

II

The idea that the states bear some responsibility for the care of the mentally ill was not   5
immediately obvious to the founders of this country. Through the colonial and federalist periods, care of psychotic and other dependent persons was the responsibility of local communities. They responded then as many of them do today. Almshouses and jails were overrun with the mentally ill, who, though thrown together with the criminal, tubercular, and mendicant, were often treated with a cruelty visited on none of the others.

Change came in the second quarter of the 19th century. New interest was stimulated   6
among a small number of physicians in a system of treatment of the mentally ill begun in a Quaker hospital in England and called "moral" care. The name—with its ironic allusion to the immorality that had governed most other efforts to deal with the mentally ill—denoted a therapeutic system based on the radical idea that the mentally ill were more like us than unlike. If they were treated with kindness, encouraged to establish order in their lives, given the opportunity to work at productive trades, and provided with models of behavior, their mental illnesses might dissipate.

The belief that the mentally ill could be treated, and thus need not be relegated to the   7
cellars of local jails, was championed by Dorothea Dix, a spinster Sunday-school teacher from Massachusetts, who traversed the country, cataloguing the barbarities inflicted on mentally ill persons and petitioning legislatures to establish facilities where moral treatment might be applied. Her efforts and those of others resulted in the creation of a network of state-operated hospitals. As the states assumed ever wider responsibility for the mentally ill, the hospitals grew in size, absorbing the denizens of the jails and poorhouses.

In the wake of the Civil War, as the burdens created by waves of immigration stood   8
unrelieved by increases in funding, the public hospitals surrendered the goal of active treatment. They continued to expand, but changed into enormous holding units, to which the mentally ill were sent and from which many never emerged. Once again sliding to the bottom of the list of social priorities, the mentally ill were often treated with brutality. At best, they suffered from benign indifference to anything more than their needs for shelter and food.

Such had been the condition of public mental hospitals for nearly eighty years as World   9
War II came to a close. Periodic efforts at reform had left them largely untouched. Over one-half million patients languished in their wards, accounting for half of all the occupants of hospital beds in the country. The state hospitals had swelled to bloated proportions. Pilgrim State Hospital on Long Island, New York's largest, held nearly 20,000 patients. St. Elizabeths in Washington, D.C., the only mental hospital operated directly by the federal government, had its own railroad and post office. Most facilities, located away from major population centers, used patients to work large farms on their grounds, thus defraying a good part of the costs of running the institution.

10   A new generation of psychiatrists, returning from the war, began to express their disquiet with the system as it was. They had seen how rapid-treatment models in hospitals close to the front and the introduction of group therapy had drastically cut the morbidity of psychiatric conditions evident earlier in World War I. With the belief that patients need not spend their lives sitting idly in smoky, locked wards, they determined to tackle a situation which Albert Deutsch had described as the "shame of the states."

11   These psychiatrists and their disciples, emphasizing the desirability of preparing patients for return to the community, began to introduce reforms into the state systems. Wards that had been locked for nearly a century were opened; male and female patients were allowed to mix. Active treatment programs were begun, and many patients, particularly elderly ones, were screened prior to admission, with efforts made to divert them where possible to more appropriate settings. The effects soon became evident. More than a century of inexorable growth in state-hospital populations began to reverse itself in 1955, when the number of residents peaked at just over 558,000. The first phase of deinstitutionalization was under way.

12   A second factor was introduced at this point. In 1952, French scientists searching for a better antihistamine discovered chlorpromazine, the first medication with the power to mute and even reverse the symptoms of psychosis. Introduced in this country in 1954 under the trade name Thorazine (elsewhere the medication was called Largactil, a name that better conveys the enormous hope that accompanied its debut), the drug rapidly and permanently altered the treatment of severe mental illness. The ineffective treatment of the past, from bleedings and purgings, cold baths and whirling chairs, to barbiturates and lobotomies, were supplanted by a genuinely effective medication. Thorazine's limitations and side-effects would become better known in the future; for now the emphasis was on its ability to suppress the most flagrant symptoms of psychosis.

13   Patients bedeviled by hallucinatory voices and ridden by irrational fears, who previously could have been managed only in inpatient units, now became tractable. They still suffered from schizophrenia, still manifested the blunted emotions, confused thinking, odd postures that the disease inflicts. But the symptoms which had made it impossible for them to live outside the hospital could, in many cases, be controlled.

14   Psychiatrists still argue over whether the new ideas of hospital and community treatment or the introduction of Thorazine provided the initial push that lowered state-hospital censuses. The truth is that both factors probably played a role, with the medications allowing the new psychiatric enthusiasm for community-based care to be applied to a larger group of patients than might otherwise have been the case. The effects of the first stage of deinstitutionalization can be seen in the figures for patients resident in state psychiatric facilities. By 1965 that number had decreased gradually but steadily to 475,000.

III

15   Until the mid-1960's, deinstitutionalization had been a pragmatic innovation; its driving force was the conviction that some patients could be treated and maintained in the community. Although large-scale studies supporting this belief were lacking, psychiatrists' everyday experiences confirmed its validity. Further, control of the process of discharging patients

was solidly in the hands of mental-health professionals. By the end of the first decade of de-institutionalization, however, the process was in the midst of being transformed.

What had begun as an empirical venture was now about to become a movement. De-institutionalization was captured by the proponents of a variety of ideologies, who sensed its value for their causes. Although their underlying philosophies were often at odds, they agreed on what seemed a simple statement of mission: all patients should be treated in the community or in short-term facilities. The state hospitals should be closed.   16

Some of the earliest advocates of this position were themselves psychiatrists. Unlike their predecessors, who first let light and air into the back wards, these practitioners were not content to whittle away at the number of patients in state hospitals. They sought systemic changes. The pragmatism of the psychiatrists, persuaded on their return from the war that many patients could be treated without long-term hospitalization, was transmuted into a rigid credo. No patient should be confined in a massive state facility, it was now declared. All treatment should take place in the community.   17

These advocates, who saw themselves as part of a new subspecialty of community psychiatry, were heavily influenced by the sociologists of institutional life, notable Erving Goffman, the author of *Asylums.* That book, based on a year of observing patients and staff at St. Elizabeths Hospital in Washington, D.C., catalogued the ways, subtle and blatant, in which patients were forced by the demands of a large institution into an unthinking conformity of behavior and thought. The rules that constrained their behavior, Goffman wrote, derived not from a consideration of therapeutic needs, but from the desires of hospital staff members to simplify their own tasks. From Goffman's work a new syndrome was defined— "institutionalism": the progressive loss of functional abilities caused by the denial of opportunities to make choices for oneself, and leading to a state of chronic dependency. Robbed of their ability to function on their own, state-hospital patients had no alternative but to remain in an environment in which their lives were directed by others.   18

Community psychiatry embellished Goffman's charges. Articles in professional journals began to allege that the chronic disability accompanying psychiatric illnesses, particularly schizophrenia, was not a result of the disease process itself, but an effect of archaic treatment methods in which patients were uprooted from their own communities. With the attachments of a lifetime severed, often irretrievably, patients lost the incentive and then the will to maintain their abilities to relate to others and function in social environments. Thus, state hospitals, in addition to subjecting patients to abominable physical conditions—the stuff of exposés since the 1860's—were exacerbating and embedding the very symptoms they purported to treat. The only way to prevent the development of a new generation of dysfunctional chronic patients was to close the hospitals.   19

Of course, alternative places of treatment would have to be created. In 1963, the new community psychiatrists persuaded a President already interested in mental-health issues and a receptive Congress that, with a new approach, chronicity could be averted. The consensus that emerged was embodied in the Community Mental Health Center Act of 1963. With seed money from the federal government, the law encouraged the development of outpatient clinics in every area of the country. Ultimately, it was hoped, no citizen would live outside one of the 2,000 designated "catchment areas" in which community-based treatment could be provided.   20

21   Psychiatric proponents of closing the state hospitals found unlikely allies in a group of civil-libertarian attorneys who were now turning their attention to the mentally ill. Fresh from victories in the civil-rights movement, and armed with potent new constitutional interpretations that restricted the power of the state to infringe personal liberties, these lawyers sought the dismantling of state hospitals as the first step in eliminating all coercive treatment of the mentally ill. They sought this end not simply because they believed that encouraging autonomy reduced chronicity, as the community psychiatrists claimed, but because in their own hierarchy of values individual autonomy was paramount.

22   Mentally ill persons seemed particularly appropriate targets for a crusade against governmental power, for the state was depriving them of liberty—with ostensibly benevolent aims, yet in conditions that belied the goal of treatment. It appeared to these critics that ultimately the state was concerned most with maintaining imbalances of power that favored the privileged classes and with suppressing dissent. By confining and discrediting the more obstreperous members of the lower classes, the mental-health system served as a pillar of the ruling elite.

23   Critiques of this sort were not rare in the late 1960's, when skepticism of established power was, for many, a prerequisite of intellectual discourse. Its application to psychiatry was encouraged, however, by the writings of iconoclastic psychiatrists like Thomas Szasz, who maintained that mental illness was a "myth," perpetuated only as a mechanism for social control, and R. D. Laing, whose books touted the value of the psychotic experience for elevating one's perceptions of the meaning of life. Additional academic support for Szasz's views came from sociologists known as labeling theorists who believed that deviance was a creation of the person with the power so to name it.

24   Whereas the community psychiatrists initially sought to achieve their ends through a legislative reconstruction of the mental-health system, the civil-libertarian attorneys favored the judicial route. They attacked the major mechanism for entry into the public mental-health system, the statutes governing involuntary commitment. These laws, they charged, were unconstitutionally broad in allowing any mentally ill person in need of treatment to be hospitalized against his will. Surely individual liberty could not legitimately be abridged in the absence of a substantial threat to a person's life or to the life of others. In addition, they alleged that the wording of the statutes, many little changed for one hundred years, was impermissibly vague; particularly problematic for the civil libertarians were the definitions of mental illness and the circumstances that rendered one committable.

25   In an era of judicial activism, many courts, both federal and state, agreed. Involuntary commitment came to be limited to persons exhibiting danger to themselves or others; strict, criminal-law-style procedures came to be required, including judicial hearings with legal representation. As the trend in the courts became apparent, many legislatures altered their statutes in anticipation of decisions in their own jurisdictions, or in emulation of California, where civil libertarians won legislative approval of a tightened statute even without the threat of court action.

26   The final common pathway of this complex set of interests led through the state legislatures. Although concerns about better treatment for chronic patients and the enhancement of individual liberty were not foreign here, more mundane concerns made themselves felt as well. The old state mental hospitals took up a significant proportion of most state

budgets, in some jurisdictions the largest single allocation. Advocates of closing the old facilities were not reticent in claiming enormous cost savings if patients were transferred to community-based care. And even if real costs remained constant, the availability of new federal entitlement programs such as Supplemental Security Income and Medicaid, to which outpatients but not inpatients would have access, promised a shift in the cost of supporting these people from the states to the federal government.

In many states, this was the final straw. The possibility that patients could be cared for   27
in the community at less expense, perhaps with better results, and certainly with greater liberty, was an irresistible attraction. Deinstitutionalization was too valuable a tool of social policy to remain a discretionary option of state-hospital psychiatrists. It now became an avowed goal of the states. Quotas were set for reductions in state-hospital populations; timetables were drawn up for the closure of facilities. Individual discretion in the release of patients was overridden by legislative and administrative fiat. Patients were to be released at all costs. New admissions were to be discouraged, in some cases prohibited. In the words of Joseph Morrissey, if the first phase of deinstitutionalization reflected an opening of the back wards, the second phase was marked by a closing of the front door.[1]

Thus did deinstitutionalization assume the form in which we know it today.   28

IV

If a decrease in patient population is the sole measure for gauging the outcome of de-   29
institutionalization, the success of the policy is unquestionable. From 1965 to 1975, inpatient populations in state hospitals fell from 475,000 to 193,000. By 1980, the figure was 137,000, and today all indications are that the number is even smaller. Relatively few of the state hospitals closed. The majority shrank from bustling colonies with thousands of patients to enclaves of a few hundred patients, clustered in a few buildings in largely abandoned campuses.

Yet by the mid-1970's professionals in the field and policy analysts had begun to ask   30
whether the underlying goals espoused by the advocates of deinstitutionalization were really being met. Are the majority of the mentally ill, by whatever measure one chooses to apply, better off now than before the depopulation of the state hospitals? The inescapable answer is that they are not.

A large part of the reason for the movement's failure stems from its overly optimistic be-   31
lief in the ability of many mentally ill persons to function on their own, without the much-maligned structure of state-hospital care. Rather than liberating patients from the constraints of institutional life, the movement to reduce the role of state hospitals merely shifted the locus of their regimented existences. Indeed, *trans*institutionalization may be a better term to describe the process that occurred. It is estimated that 750,000 chronic mentally ill persons now live in nursing homes, a figure nearly 50 percent higher than the state-hospital

---

[1] A good comprehensive history of deinstitutionalizaton has yet to be written. The best of the existing, essay-length works is Joseph Morrissey's "Deinstitutionalizing the Mentally Ill: Process, Outcomes, and New Directions," in W. R. Gove, ed., *Deviance and Mental Illness* (Sage Publications, 1982). Morrissey focuses in particular on the experiences in Massachusetts, New York, and California.

population at its 1955 apogee. Additional hundreds of thousands live in board-and-care homes or other group residences. Many of these facilities, particularly the nursing homes, have locked wards nearly indistinguishable from the old state hospitals. They are, in psychiatrist H. Richard Lamb's evocative phrase, the asylums in the community.

32   Many of the mentally ill, of course, have drifted away entirely from any form of care. Given the freedom to choose, they have chosen to live on the streets; according to various estimates they comprise between 40 and 60 percent of homeless persons. They filter into overcrowded shelters—as Juan Gonzalez did before becoming the agent of his fantasies on the Staten Island ferry—where they may experience fleeting contact with mental-health personnel. The lack of external structure is reflected in their internal disorganization. Whatever chance they had to wire together their shattered egos has been lost.

33   What of the hopes of the community psychiatrists that liberating patients from state hospitals would prevent the development of the chronic dependency which stigmatizes the mentally ill and inhibits their reintegration into the community? They learned a sad lesson suspected by many of their colleagues all along. The withdrawal, apathy, bizarre thinking, and oddities of behavior which Goffman and his students attributed to "institutionalism" appear even in populations maintained outside of institutions. They are the effects of the underlying psychiatric illnesses, usually schizophrenia, not of the efforts to treat those conditions. And contrary to the claims of the labeling theorists, it is the peculiar behavior of severely psychotic persons, not the fact that they were once hospitalized and "labeled" ill, that stigmatizes and isolates them in the community. Studies of discharged patients demonstrate that those who continue to display the signs of their illnesses and disrupt the lives of others are the ones who suffer social discrimination.

34   To some extent, the community psychiatrists never had a chance to test their theories. The community mental-health centers in which they envisioned care taking place were, for the most part, never built. Fewer than half of the projected 2,000 centers reached operation. Of those that did, many turned from the severely ill to more desirable patients, less disturbed, easier to treat, more gratifying, and above all, as federal subsidies were phased out, able to pay for their own care. A few model programs, working with a selected group of cooperative patients, are all the community psychiatrists have to show for their dreams. But the evidence suggests that even optimal levels of community care cannot enable many mentally ill persons to live on their own.

35   The goals of the civil libertarians, except in the narrowest sense, have fared little better. If one conceives that liberty is enhanced merely by the release of patients from the hospitals to the streets, then perhaps one might glean some satisfaction from the course of deinstitutionalization to date. But if individual autonomy implies the ability to make reasoned choices in the context of a coherent plan for one's life, then one must conclude that few of the deinstitutionalized have achieved autonomy. One study found fewer than half the residents of a large board-and-care home with a desire to change anything at all about their lives, no matter how unrealistic their objectives might be. If the façade of autonomy has been expanded, the reality has suffered.

36   Finally, and with fitting irony, not even the hope that deinstitutionalization would save money has been realized. It was originally anticipated that the closing of state hospitals would allow the transfer of their budgetary allocations to community facilities. But state

hospitals proved difficult to close. As many hospitals existed in 1980 as in 1955, despite a fourfold reduction in patients. Even with current, broad definitions of who can survive in the community, tens of thousands of patients nationwide continue to require institutional care, often long-term. They are so regressed, self-destructive, violent, or otherwise disruptive that no community can tolerate them in its midst. Moreover, the communities that derive jobs from the facilities have fought hard to preserve them. As censuses have fallen, per-capita costs of care have increased, pushed up even further by pressure to improve the level of care for those who remain. Many costs for the treatment of outpatients have been redistributed, with the federal and local governments bearing heavier burdens; but no one has ever demonstrated overall savings. Even as the quality of life for many mentally ill persons has fallen, state mental-health budgets have continued to expand.

V

Both the failure of deinstitutionalization and our seeming paralysis in correcting it stem 37 from the same source: the transformation of deinstitutionalization from a pragmatic enterprise to an ideological crusade. The goal of the first phase of the process—to treat in the community all mentally ill persons who did not require full-time supervision and might do equally well or better in alternate settings—was hardly objectionable. Had state-hospital populations been reduced in a deliberate manner, with patients released no faster than treatment, housing, and rehabilitative facilities became available in the community, the visions of psychiatry's Young Turks of the 1950's might well have been realized.

Once the release of state-hospital patients became a matter of faith, however, this in- 38 dividualized approach was thrown to the winds. In the Manichean view that soon predominated, confinement in state hospitals came to be seen as invariably bad. Freedom was always to be preferred, both for its own sake and because it had a desirable, albeit mysterious therapeutic value. Further, we came to doubt our own benevolent impulses, yielding *Rebuttal* to those who claimed that any effort to act for the welfare of others was illegitimate and doomed to end with their oppression. Thus, although we may now recognize the failure of deinstitutionalization, we as a society have been unable to reverse course; these same ideologies continue to dominate our policies not by the power of logic but by the force of habit.

It is time to rethink these presuppositions. That freedom *per se* will not cure mental 39 illness is evident from the abject condition of so many of the deinstitutionalized. More difficult to deal with is the belief that, even if the lives of hundreds of thousands of mentally ill persons have been made objectively more miserable by the emptying of our state hospitals, we have no right to deprive people of liberty, even for their own benefit. In the currently fashionable jargon of bioethics, the value of autonomy always trumps the value of beneficence.

Interestingly, this position is now being challenged by a number of our leading public 40 philosophers, who have called attention to its neglected costs. Robert Burt of the Yale Law School and Daniel Callahan of the Hastings Center, for example, have taken aim at the belief that the freedom to do as we please should be our primary societal value. This emphasis on individual autonomy, they point out, has come to mean that in making our choices, as long as we do not actively infringe on the prerogatives of others, we face no obligation to consider them and their needs. The result has been the creation of an atomistic community in which, relieved of the duty to care for others, we pursue our goals in disregard of the suffering that surrounds us. This lack of an obligation to care for others has been transmuted in some cases into an actual duty to ignore their suffering, lest we act in such a way as to limit their autonomy.

41   Although Burt and Callahan have not addressed themselves to mental-health policy *per se,* there is no better illustration of their thesis. The right to liberty has become an excuse for failing to address, even failing to recognize, the needs of the thousands of abandoned men and women we sweep by in our streets, in our parks, and in the train and bus stations where they gather for warmth. We have persuaded ourselves that it is better to ignore them—that we have an obligation to ignore them—because their autonomy would be endangered by our concern.

42   But the impulse to act for the benefit of others is the adhesive substance that binds human communities together. A value system that looses those bonds by glorifying individual autonomy threatens the cohesion of the polity. Nobody wants to live in a society characterized by unrestrained intervention (even with benevolent intent), but that does not mean we must reject altogether the notion that doing good for others, despite their reluctance, is morally appropriate under some conditions.

43   Meaningful autonomy does not consist merely in the ability to make choices for oneself. Witness the psychotic ex-patients on the streets, who withdraw into rarely used doorways, rigidly still for hours at a time, hoping, like chameleons on the forest floor, that immobility will help them fade into the grimy urban background, bringing safety and temporary peace from a world which they envision as a terrifying series of threats. Can the choices they make, limited as they are to the selection of a doorway for the day, be called a significant embodiment of human autonomy? Or is their behavior rather to be understood on the level of a simple reflex—autonomous only in a strictly formal sense?

44   Far from impinging on their autonomy, treatment of such psychotics, even coercive treatment, would not only hold out some hope of mitigating their condition but might simultaneously increase their capacity for more sophisticated autonomous choices. To adopt the typological scheme of the philosopher Bruce Miller, patients might thereby be enabled to move from mere freedom of action to choices that reflect congruence with personal values, effective rational deliberation, and moral reflection. Our intervention, though depriving them of the right to autonomy in the short term, may enhance that quality in the long run. In such circumstances, benevolence and autonomy are no longer antagonistic principles.

VI

45   Deinstitutionalization is a remnant of a different era in our political life, one in which we sought broadly-framed solutions to human problems that have defied man's creativity for millennia. In the 1960's and 70's we declared war on poverty, and we determined to wipe out injustice and bigotry; government, we believed, had the tools and resources to accomplish these ends; all that was needed was the will.

46   This set of beliefs, applied to the mentally ill, allowed us to ignore the failure of a century-and-a-half of mental-health reform in this country, in the conviction that this time

we had the answer. The problem, as it was defined, was the system of large state hospitals. Like a cancer, it could be easily excised. And the will was there.

Unfortunately, the analysis was wrong. The problems of severe mental illness have   47
proved resistant to unitary solutions. For some patients, discharge from the state hospitals was a blessing. For all too many others, it was the ultimate curse. Far from a panacea, the policy created as many problems as it solved, perhaps more. To be sure, it is never easy to admit that massive social initiatives have been misconceived. The time has come, however, to lay deinstitutionalization to rest.

It would not be difficult to outline a reasonable program to restore some sense to the   48
care of the mentally ill: moderate expansion of beds in state facilities, especially for the most severely ill patients; good community-based services for those patients—and their number is not small—who could prosper outside of an institution with proper supports; and greater authority for the state to detain and treat the severely mentally ill for their own benefit, even if they pose no immediate threat to their lives or those of others.

Deinstitutionalization has been a tragedy, but it need not be an irreversible one.   49

Are the Homeless Crazy?

Jonathan Kozol

It is commonly believed by many journalists and politicians that the homeless of Amer-   1
ica are, in large part, former patients of large mental hospitals who were deinstitutionalized in the 1970s—the consequence, it is sometimes said, of misguided liberal opinion that favored the treatment of such persons in community-based centers. It is argued that this policy, and the subsequent failure of society to build such centers or to provide them in sufficient number, is the primary cause of homelessness in the United States.

Those who work among the homeless do not find that explanation satisfactory. While   2
conceding that a certain number of the homeless are or have been mentally unwell, they believe that, in the case of most unsheltered people, the primary reason is economic rather than clinical. The cause of homelessness, they say with disarming logic, is the lack of homes and of income with which to rent or acquire them.

They point to the loss of traditional jobs in industry (2 million every year since 1980)   3
and to the fact that half of those who are laid off end up in work that pays a poverty-level wage. They point out that since 1968 the number of children living in poverty has grown by 3 million, while welfare benefits to families with children have declined by 35 percent.

And they note, too, that these developments have occurred during a time in which the   4
shortage of low-income housing has intensified as the gentrification of our major cities has accelerated. Half a million units of low-income housing are lost each year to condominium conversion as well as to arson, demolition, or abandonment. Between 1978 and 1980, median rents climbed 30 percent for people in the lowest income sector, driving many of these families into the streets. Since 1980, rents have risen at even faster rates.

5   Hard numbers, in this instance, would appear to be of greater help than psychiatric labels in telling us why so many people become homeless. Eight million American families now use half or more of their income to pay their rent or mortgage. At the same time, federal support for low-income housing dropped from $30 billion (1980) to $7.5 billion (1988). Under Presidents Ford and Carter, 500,000 subsidized private housing units were constructed. By President Reagan's second term, the number had dropped to 25,000.

6   In our rush to explain the homeless as a psychiatric problem even the words of medical practitioners who care for homeless people have been curiously ignored. A study published by the Massachusetts Medical Society, for instance, has noted that, with the exceptions of alcohol and drug use, the most frequent illnesses among a sample of the homeless population were trauma (31 percent), upper-respiratory disorders (28 percent), limb disorders (19 percent), mental illness (16 percent), skin diseases (15 percent), hypertension (14 percent), and neurological illnesses (12 percent). Why, we may ask, of all these calamities, does mental illness command so much political and press attention? The answer may be that the label of mental illness places the destitute outside the sphere of ordinary life. It personalizes an anguish that is public in its genesis; it individualizes a misery that is both general in cause and general in application.

7   There is another reason to assign labels to the destitute and single out mental illness from among their many afflictions. All these other problems—tuberculosis, asthma, scabies, diarrhea, bleeding gums, impacted teeth, etc.—bear no stigma, and mental illness does. It conveys a stigma in the United States. It conveys a stigma in the Soviet Union as well. In both nations the label is used, whether as a matter of deliberate policy or not, to isolate and treat as special cases those who, by deed or word or by sheer presence, represent a threat to national complacence. The two situations are obviously not identical, but they are enough alike to give Americans reason for concern.

8   The notion that the homeless are largely psychotics who belong in institutions, rather than victims of displacement at the hands of enterprising realtors, spares us from the need to offer realistic solutions to the deep and widening extremes of wealth and poverty in the United States. It also enables us to tell ourselves that the despair of homeless people bears no intimate connection to the privileged existence we enjoy—when, for example, we rent or purchase one of those restored town houses that once provided shelter for people now huddled in the street.

9   What is to be made, then, of the supposition that the homeless are primarily the former residents of mental hospitals, persons who were carelessly released during the 1970s? Many of them are, to be sure. Among the older men and women in the streets and shelters, as many as one-third (some believe as many as one-half) may be chronically disturbed, and a number of these people were deinstitutionalized during the 1970s. But to operate on that assumption in a city such as New York—where nearly half the homeless are small children whose average age is six—makes no sense. Their parents, with an average age of twenty-seven, are not likely to have been hospitalized in the 1970s, either.

10   A frequently cited set of figures tells us that in 1955 the average daily census of non-federal psychiatric institutions was 677,000, and that by 1984 the number had dropped to 151,000. But these people didn't go directly from a hospital room to the street. The bulk of those who had been psychiatric patients and were released from hospitals during

the 1960s and early 1970s had been living in low-income housing, many in skid-row hotels or boardinghouses. Such housing—commonly known as SRO (single-room occupancy) units—was drastically diminished by the gentrification of our cities that began in the early '70s. Almost 50 percent of SRO housing was replaced by luxury apartments or office buildings between 1970 and 1980, and the remaining units have been disappearing even more rapidly.

Even for those persons who are ill and were deinstitutionalized during the decades be-   11
fore 1980, the precipitating cause of homelessness in 1987 is not illness but loss of housing. SRO housing offered low-cost sanctuaries for the homeless, providing a degree of safety and mutual support for those who lived within them. They were a demeaning version of the community health centers that society had promised; they were the de facto "halfway houses" of the 1970s. For these people too—at most half of the homeless single persons in America—the cause of homelessness is lack of housing.

Even in those cases where mental instability is apparent, homelessness itself is often   12
the precipitating factor. For example, many pregnant women without homes are denied prenatal care because they constantly travel from one shelter to another. Many are anemic. Many are denied essential dietary supplements by recent federal cuts. As a consequence, some of their children do not live to see their second year of life. Do these mothers sometimes show signs of stress? Do they appear disorganized, depressed, disordered? Frequently. They are immobilized by pain, traumatized by fear. So it is no surprise that when researchers enter the scene to ask them how they "feel," the resulting reports tell us that the homeless are emotionally unwell. The reports do not tell us that we have *made* these people ill. They do not tell us that illness is a natural response to intolerable conditions. Nor do they tell us of the strength and the resilience that so many of these people retain despite the miseries they must endure.

A writer in the *New York Times* describes a homeless woman standing on a traffic is-   13
land in Manhattan. "She was evicted from her small room in the hotel just across the street," and she is determined to get revenge. Until she does, "nothing will move her from that spot. . . . Her argumentativeness and her angry fixation on revenge, along with the apparent absence of hallucinations, mark her as a paranoid." Most physicians, I imagine, would be more reserved in passing judgment with so little evidence, but this reporter makes his diagnosis without hesitation. "The paranoids of the street," he says, "are among the most difficult to help."

Perhaps so. But does it depend on who is offering the help? Is anyone offering to help   14
this woman get back her home? Is it crazy to seek vengeance for being thrown into the street? The absence of anger, some psychiatrists believe, might indicate much greater illness.

"No one will be turned away," says the mayor of New York City, as hundreds of young   15
mothers with their infants are turned from the doors of shelters season after season. That may sound to some like a denial of reality. "Now you're hearing all kinds of horror stories," says the President of the United States as he denies that anyone is cold or hungry or unhoused. On another occasion he says that the unsheltered "are homeless, you might say, by choice." That sounds every bit as self-deceiving.

The woman standing on the traffic island screaming for revenge until her room has   16
been restored to her sounds relatively healthy by comparison. If 3 million homeless people did the same, and all at the same time, we might finally be forced to listen.

The Homeless Mentally Ill

Steven Vanderstaay

1   More of the mentally ill now live on our streets than in our public health hospitals.[1] This number—which does not include alcoholics or drug addicts—appears to be increasing, as is the fear of such people, and the number of voices raised to demand to "do" something about them.

2   This is not to say that most homeless people are mentally ill. They are not. Nor did the much debated deinstitutionalization of mentally ill patients create homelessness—though homelessness would be much easier to understand if it had.

3   Rather, and like all segments of the homeless population, the homeless mentally ill are a diverse group, more varied than alike. Understanding their situation is a delicate matter of avoiding these and other generalizations, and of accepting multiple truths: truths that may at best yield a pastiche—rather than a single tidy portrait—of the problem and its causes.

4   The argument that deinstitutionalization created homelessness goes like this:[2] psychiatric institutions released more than half a million patients between 1955 and 1984. The Community Mental Health Centers (CMHCs), originally designed to provide outpatient care for such people, failed to do so.[3] Adrift from their institutional moorings, and unable or unwilling to take the medications they need, hundreds of thousands of these people now live in our streets.

5   But the crisis in homelessness did not immediately follow deinstitutionalization. State hospitals released most of their patients before 1978, the greatest percentage of patients having been released in the 1960s. Homelessness did not begin to be recognized as a national crisis until the early 1980s, when families and the working poor—as well as the seriously mentally ill—began to overrun shelters and social services heretofore dominated by street alcoholics and transients. As Jonathan Kozol has remarked, if a significant number of the homeless were institutionalized "before they reappeared in subway stations and in public shelters," one might wonder "where they were and what they were doing from 1972 to 1980."[4]

6   Furthermore, formerly deinstitutionalized patients constitute but a small portion of the present population of homeless people. In fact, while deinstitutionalization did remove more than half a million patients from state hospitals, the bulk of these people ended up in nursing homes—not the street.[5] This is documented in numerous studies, all of which show a direct correlation between deinstitutionalization and nursing home admissions.[6] Reporting on data from across the country, for example, the U.S. General Accounting Office (GAO) announced in 1977 that deinstitutionalization would be more accurately described as "reinstitutionalization," because the nursing home had replaced the state hospital as the "largest single place of care for the mentally ill."[7]

7   Finally, up to one-fourth of the homeless people in our nation may be children,[8] and the median age for homeless adults is 36—still too young to have been released from state hospitals in the 1960s and 1970s.[9]

8   Certainly, some deinstitutionalized patients were discharged to homeless shelters and did end up homeless. Others may have become homeless after being pushed out of low-

income housing, or tenuous situations where they lived with and were cared for by a relative, during the more significant current of homelessness that struck in the early 1980s. But while deinstitutionalization and the subsequent failure of the CMHCs contributed to homelessness, these factors can hardly be considered the precipitating cause of such a widespread, national crisis.

Nevertheless, it is true that rates of mental illness among homeless people are extremely   9
high, many times that of the general population.[10] A portion of that figure can be attributed to the deinstitutionalization of ex-patients,[11] and another can be ascribed to the fact that some of the homeless mentally ill would have been hospitalized under the previous system. This would account for the many homeless schizophrenics who can be shown to have been genetically predisposed to mental illness. But even these considerations do not account for the roughly 30 percent of homeless people who appear mentally ill—especially those who demonstrate no sign of mental illness until after they become homeless.[12] Hence, if the so-called myth of deinstitutionalization is dismissed, one is left with the question of where so many homeless, mentally ill people come from.

One approach to this question is to examine the role homelessness may play in men-   10
tal illness. This is the approach that most homeless people themselves take when considering the issue. Simply put, they think homelessness can drive you insane. In contrast, the great bulk of the psychiatric literature on homelessness assumes only the converse: that insanity can drive you to homelessness.

This occurs because the present psychiatric view considers most serious mental illness   11
as the result of biological rather than environmental factors. According to this view, schizophrenia and manic-depressive psychoses, among others, are genetic illnesses—more like diabetes than emotional stress or the residual effects of traumatic childhood experiences. The underlying theory is that serious mental illness is located in the individual, rather than in the social context of the individual's experience. Accordingly, mental illness is seen as preceding (and thereby causing) homelessness for the mentally ill of our streets and shelters.

Homeless people tend to disagree. While acknowledging that many mentally ill people   12
do become homeless, they stress the debilitating effects of their situations as a chief cause of mental illness among them. "When you're homeless your mind kind of wags," says Tanya, a homeless, college-educated woman who was hospitalized for depression and schizophrenia after losing her children to the state. Cyrell, a homeless man working to create a cooperative survival center in Philadelphia, explains it this way:

> People become self-absorbed in their own minds when they're homeless. People say they're insane or psychotic, but a lot of people are neither. What happens is they become absorbed in theirselves and their problems. I call it "mental inwardness," because nothing on the outside matters to them.
>
> If you don't have decent clothing, or you're dirty and have no money, you're looked down upon. People turn their heads, say "Get away from me, scum!" So you don't fit in. Society rejects you, doesn't care for you, and you begin to lose hope. When that happens you just sit alone, thinking about your problems. Dejected. And with no human contact you just totally block everything out. The outer world gets canceled out. You get up off the grate, look this way and that. Self-absorbed.

13   This rather commonsense point of view is frequently corroborated by mental health clinicians like Dr. Anne Braden Johnson, a clinical social worker who oversees mental health services for women in New York City's Rikers Island Jail. As she notes in her widely respected book, *Out of Bedlam: The Truth about Deinstitutionalization:*

> Something that has not been studied to any appreciable degree, surprisingly, is the relationship between life without a home and mental status. Living on the street or in a shelter, as many homeless people do, cannot possibly have a positive effect on one's self-esteem or provide much in the way of gratifying experience; and homelessness itself is a state of such unremitting crisis that one would expect it to provoke some kind of emotional or mental disorder, in and of itself. For the most part, though, the detachment prized by science has allowed researchers to look at specimen homeless people so objectively that the possibility of their having been driven mad by worry, fear, grief, guilt, or shame has not seriously entered the observers' minds.[13]

14   The lack of research on this question is particularly egregious because documentation to support it has existed for years. Examining whether mental illness might be best understood as a "response to conditions in the social environment," Johns Hopkins sociologist and epidemiologist M. Harvey Brenner studied the relationship between economic conditions and admissions to mental hospitals in New York State. He found that "instabilities in the national economy have been the single most important source of fluctuation in mental-hospital admission rates" for the last 127 years. This effect of economic conditions on rates of mental illness, Brenner notes, has been particularly strong "in the last two decades."[14]

15   Not surprisingly, rates of homicides, suicides, and deaths from alcohol-related illnesses also correlate with some periods of economic decline.[15] Similarly, unemployment among men has been associated with a myriad of emotional difficulties and psychiatric symptoms, while women in unemployed families have been shown to be inordinately depressed, anxious, and phobic.[16] Homeless people have also been shown to be significantly more "demoralized" than the general population.[17]

16   This research does not deny that factors predisposing certain people to mental illness exist. Rather, it demonstrates that economic stress correlates with the appearance of mental illness. Thus while mental illness in a dormant or mild form may precede homelessness, the stresses of poverty and homelessness activate or accelerate the disease. As Brenner puts it, "the appearance of mental illness is seen as *the* maladaptive response to the precipitating stress situation."[18]

17   The ramifications of these findings are startling. First, rates of mental illness would naturally be expected to be higher among those for whom the stress of economic change has been greatest. This would certainly include people who have lost their jobs, homes, friends, and families. Second, the stress of homelessness explains why many of the homeless mentally ill demonstrate no sign of mental illness until after the onset of their homelessness. Third, to the extent that this view is accurate, such rates of mental illness among homeless people must be understood in societal terms, for it is in response to conditions in the larger society that homelessness has occurred. Finally, it follows that any treatment of the mentally ill must address the socioeconomic sources of the stress responsible for the rise in mental illness among those affected. For homeless people such "sources" would include the

unavailability of low-income housing, cuts in disability and assistance benefits, unemployment, low wages, and their acute isolation.

Homeless people also question whether the conditions of homelessness could generate responses that may be mistaken as symptoms of mental illness. That is, while the conditions of homelessness might elicit or exacerbate mental illnesses, is it not also likely that any "normal" response to such experiences would be apt to include depression, phobias, rage, and other behaviors symptomatic of mental illness?   18

People who work with homeless people find this a rather obvious assertion. In fact, one counselor has commented that she has learned to treat the displaced rural homeless she sees just as she treats East Asian refugees suffering from cultural displacement and post-traumatic stress syndrome. "Their conditions are surprisingly similar," she remarked.[19]   19

Common sense deems that one should be cautious in designating a Cambodian refugee as mentally ill for behavior that seems out of place or odd. Adjustment and behavioral difficulties would be expected in such a situation. Similarly, one should be cautious when interpreting the behavior of homeless people. In point of fact, however, the exigencies of homeless life are rarely considered in examinations of mental illness among homeless people. In this way, psychiatrists and other researchers can misinterpret symptoms and misdiagnose the disease.   20

Alcoholism, drug abuse, and other medical problems also confuse psychiatric profiles. Homeless diabetics, for example, often lose their insulin, have syringes stolen, or fail to find the proper balance of food they need. Unable to control their disease, such diabetics can appear drunk and severely mentally ill.[20] The same is true of lesser maladies. Soiling oneself may indicate mental illness, or it may indicate a lack of toilets. It may even indicate an attempt to fend off rapists. Sleep deprivation, another common effect of homelessness, also manifests itself in symptoms identical to those of mental illness.   21

But even if it were accepted that the treatment most needed by homeless people—the mentally ill included—is an income, a community, and stable housing, the question of what to do with those who do need greater psychiatric care would remain unresolved.   22

Lithium and antipsychotic medications, for instance, control many of the symptoms of mental illness. Regular treatment with such medication could enable some of the homeless mentally ill to hold down jobs and gain greater control of their minds and bodies.[21] But a large proportion of the people who could benefit from medication will not take it. Typically, they are either not aware of their illness (people who are paranoid, for example, do not believe their fears to be delusions), or they fear the medication itself, some of which causes drowsiness, confusion, and tardive dyskinesia, a condition marked by tics and facial contortions.[22]   23

[The case of] Joshua . . . is a good example. Joshua's problems may be endemic to the trauma of his experience in Vietnam, or he may have acquired them through physical injury or inherited family traits. Regardless of cause, the debilitating conditions of homelessness and unemployment, and the rejection he has suffered as a poor, black veteran exacerbate his frustration and anger. Brenner's research would suggest that the stress of these factors triggered or activated the symptoms of his illness. Homeless people might say the stress caused them. In any case, Joshua is demonstrably violent, having been convicted of murder, and says that he is apt to "hurt somebody" again. For Joshua's good, as well as that of society at large, some kind of assistance is urgently needed.   24

25   Fortunately, Joshua is eligible for health care through the Veterans Administration. But he will not accept the treatment (read "medication") they offer. Whether such medication would help him is beside the point—too many of the other "treated" veterans "walk around like zombies" and he refuses to.

26   The question of whether Joshua should be forced to accept medication occupies much of the debate surrounding the homeless mentally ill. The issue is largely moot, however, as the facilities and funding needed to (re)institutionalize such people do not exist. Even homeless people who seek psychiatric hospitalization are routinely denied it.[23] Nor would forced medication create affordable housing, cure substance abuse, or provide education, counseling, a supportive community, and job skills—most likely the "treatment" Joshua actually needs.

27   Ultimately, helping the homeless mentally ill means understanding both their homelessness and their illnesses. While not a mental illness in itself, homelessness is complicated by mental illness and the manifestations of homelessness frequently mirror those of schizophrenia and other psychoses. As the following testimonies make clear, solutions to the difficulties faced by homeless people who are mentally ill must address both issues and acknowledge the extent to which mental illnesses are triggered and exacerbated—perhaps even caused—by the conditions of homelessness itself. One step toward this end is to do what has not yet been done: to consider the mental illness of homeless people in the context of their lives, as well as their genes.

NANCY

Washington, D.C.

28   I am taking notes at a table when Nancy sits down and begins talking. She speaks for nearly an hour, rambling, crying, exclaiming. While the names, facts, and details of her narrative cannot all be real, the pain clearly is. So are the photos of her daughters she shows me. It strikes me that the stories, when delusional, are metaphorically true—true to the experience of her suffering.

29   Nancy says she will soon be 38, which seems reasonable. She is tall, white, blond, and must once have been thought very beautiful.

30   Nancy lives in the House of Ruth, a women's shelter. A staff member tells me she was released from a state mental hospital some time ago. Nowhere to go; no family to claim her. Luckily, the shelter took her in.

31   When I was four years old Jesus gave me God. That's nothing to lie about. My morning star of David came two years ago, in Indiana, he baptized two of my daughters. Right now what I'm going to do is in Ecclesiastes 3:1. A time for getting into heaven, a time to forewarn, a time to die, a time to tear down, a time to rebuild—you have time for all this? I tell you, you could write a book about my life.

32   I woke up on the delivery table three years ago and my twins were gone. Two children. I have one daughter that's been murdered. I've been paid off by courts, lawyers, judges, and psychiatrists from Elk Heat, Indiana, to the Pacific Ocean. I was blackmailed by this girl that works in Senator Byrd's office. I had to put my two oldest daughters—my very miserable and very unhappy . . . this is my Tammy, she'll be seventeen [she hands me a photograph of the young woman]. She's in the Indiana Soldiers and Sailors Home.

I cannot keep track of all of it, but Jesus came to Harvard University, and when the 33
Lord comes to the earth he comes out from the heavens in a white cloud. . . . There's a
right, a wrong, a true and a false, and I cannot deal with anything else, with anything but
truth and righteousness, it makes me mad! [she pounds the table in her anger]. I cannot
deal with drugs and abortions, I cannot deal with this kind of stuff, with these whores, Las
Vegas tramps, Jim and Tammi Bakker—and if you knew . . . they took me, and I'm angry
about it. I'm not going to kill them. But I'm going to kill the murderer of one of my children, I'm going to kill two psychiatrists. . . .

I was in Indianapolis, with a doctor Joyce. She says I'm schizophrenia, paranoid, men- 34
tally ill, and crazy. But like I told her when she gave me my commitment papers, I told her
she would have to go before God to take her papers, take 'em before God.

I lost three children. Do you know what a mother would do, what in hell would she 35
do? If you woke up and your kids—I mean my children . . . they were gone from me! My
three, I don't know where they're at—and President Reagan flew into Indiana—remember?
Brakes went out on Air Force One. Do unto others as they do unto you.

But Jesus Christ this is no way for a woman to live: to wind up in sanitariums, and in 36
and out of hospitals, lose the kids . . . I have an underground filming of all this. I also have
the filming of Satan the serpent. In the end the girl in Senator Byrd's office is Satan. She
followed me when I was twelve, after I went to the inaugural dance of John Kennedy.

This is real, this is not fantasy. And I'm going into the Congress and Senate shortly 37
and I'm gonna kill—I've got a sword from Bush. In the Bible you know God asks for
twelve swords. I don't know how many they've gotten, but I do know Bush has a sword
for me.

But I'm love, too. I love Iowa, Oregon, Wyoming, Colorado, and like if I could do the 38
whole world with God I would want it all perfect, like Tom Sawyer . . . I love Mark Twain,
and hats, and fishing pools, not dumpy chlorine pools. What's the name of that song Johnny
Cash sings, "Little Baby Ducks." I love that record, and I love "Sunday Morning I was Drinking Beer" [laughs]. That reminds me of one of my brothers that was in Vietnam. He got
messed up over there.

See a psychiatrist gets a hold of a woman—instead of a minister or a priest—gets her 39
on Medicare, Medicaid. You know the money they rake off on each one of us people? They
take our kids, stick us here, put us on welfare, food stamps, we're a burden to taxpayers.
My bills were a hundred and thirty thousand. They sent the bills to the state. Hell yes, they
pick that up. And I'm just one patient.

DUANE

Washington, D.C.

"People treat homeless people like they idiots, they treat 'em just like trash. I mean if 40
you think about it, you gotta realize that homeless people are not stupid. Nobody stupid
gonna survive the street. And maybe if you think about it . . . maybe it was a loved one or
somethin' that put 'em there . . . My mother is deceased now. We were real tight. When
she died my mind just zapped out."

Duane is 27 and an African American. 41

42   Mom had it hard. She was a social worker, had to quit her job 'cause things got too out of hand. She used to always tell me to keep the family together. She was everything . . . without her there I wouldn't of survived.

43   My father wasn't . . . he'd beat on ya, punch on ya. And then the things he did to my mother . . . so there was all that, all that inside of me. . . .

44   But what really put me uneasy was the way she died. They pulled the plug and all I could smell was her waste comin' through her bottom, comin' through her mouth and nose. I couldn't believe it was happin'. . . .

45   I guess it was just too much pressure. Half the time I didn't even know who I was. Then it got worse, where I never knew who I was. I used to go to the park after she died, just sit back, rock back and forth. My girlfriend used to call me by name. I didn't know who I was, didn't even think about my boy. My mind had just snapped. . . . You stand there and see somebody die, see them pull the plug out and all you smell . . . that's enough . . . push you over the hill.

46   The night of my mother's funeral I slept in the street. I had on my suit and I layed across the bench with a fifth of liquor on my chest. My mother had a place but after she died my sister, she just threw all of us out. My baby brother, he was sleepin' in the hallway of an apartment. And the look he had in his face . . . oh man, that look could of killed me.

47   I kept feelin' like I was reachin' out for help, but I didn't know how to reach out for help. It was like I sometimes knew what was happenin', but I couldn't do nothin' about it. I was out of it—that lasted a long time, lasted to the point where I became mean, violent, so violent that I was punching my girlfriend. Here I was in jail one day, didn't even know I'd done it. They said I was mentally disturbed. I got myself back together but . . . then, like I was goin' to say, these are things that really put people where they are.

48   There came time when I slept in a box. I had two quilts, two blankets, the snow was knee deep. I wrapped it up with trash bags, anything to keep myself warm. One time it was rainin' and snowin', I was so cold my brain started to ache like a popsicle. Cold, my clothes all wet, shivering, wishing that I had some place to go, somebody to come say, "Hi, you're wet. Come on, I'll take you home, dry your clothes." And I said, "Wow, is this the way it's gonna end? Am I gonna die? Am I gonna freeze up?" I really didn't know.

49   I slept down by the State Department. I'd take a bath right on in the street 'cause they had a big ol' pool. I'd wait until about 1:00, when I knew the place was closed, take a bath, wash my clothes. And you know, people stop and look at you. Stuff like that really knocks over a man, or woman, or whoever it may be.

50   I was 19 when the girl got pregnant, 20 when my boy was born, 24 when my mother died. Now I'm almost 30 years old. And I wish that . . . I was an honor roll student, and I always dreamt that I could have half of what I wanted by the time I was thirty. I always dreamt that when I had my son—when I was a father—my boy would want for nothin'. So far I've felt like I haven't givin' him nothin'. He says, "Daddy, you take me home tonight?" I say, "I can't son, Daddy got to work tonight." 'Cause I'd give anything in the world for him not to ever know I live here. But I don't want to make him think I don't want to be around him.

51   It was my old man. If he'd a treated us like somebody, not abusin' ya all the time. . . . He used to make you sit in the middle of the floor—if you moved, if you scratched, he'd

knock your head off. We were so scared. . . . It got to the point where I said, "What the hell, he done beat me up so much I don't have no reason to be scared no more." It just don't matter no more.

But being here [a shelter] . . . it's like it kills me. You can't concentrate, the lights go out at a certain time. If you read, you know, you don't have an outlet or anything. You go to the TV room you still can't concentrate because of all the noise. I'm stayin' here to get a little money, keep my body clean—I didn't like to be dirty and stinky. But it's somewhere I don't want to be, somewhere I don't belong. And the drugs here, man: acid, snort, the pipe, lovely—that's PCP—herb, anything. They're here. I just wish, if you were—I'm not prejudiced or anything you know—but if you were black I could get you a cot and you could stay here a few nights. You could see exactly what I'm sayin'. You don't have to go through it you won't understand. 52

A couple people have died. One guy got drunk and layed down on his back, threw up and it just went back down into his lungs, and he was smothered. Another guy OD'd in here. People have been found dead—killed, stabbed, shot . . . people dyin' around me, I can't take that. 53

All I want is a piece of this crummy world—a piece for me and a piece for my boy. 'Cause that's what it is, a crummy world. When you're not workin' you have to go out and hustle to get money, this and that. I'm so tired of it. See people don't understand the things a homeless man has to do just to keep things together. Me, I don't know what's going to happen from day to day; I don't know if I'm going to be alive. 54

My mother danced with us, she participated in everything we did. She was a father and a mother. Sometimes all I can hear is her talkin'. I hear her sayin', "I'll be back Monday morning, Dingy"—that was her nickname for me. She never come back. And the way she died. . . . 55

I got no money in my pockets right now, I got nothin'. I'm working with a food service, washin' dishes. Last paycheck I put half in the bank and took care of my kid. Now I'm two weeks behind in child support. The court don't have nothin' to do with that, I do it 'cause he's my son and I know I'm supposed to. I don't need nobody to tell me to take care of my boy, my baby—my only baby. He's six years old. His mother, my ex-lady, she grew up a lot, she quite mature now. 56

I know what must be done. Right now I eat out in the street to save money, and I work as much as possible. I figure maybe on my off days, Saturday, Sunday, I might be able to find another job. I need the money. I keep only what I have to keep. I take care of my son, I pay for my mother's cemetery plaque, the rest I put away. That way I can get out of here. 57

1. See E. Fuller Torrey, *Nowhere to Go: The Tragic Odyssey of the Homeless Mentally Ill* (New York: Harper and Row, 1988), p. 35.

2. See Torrey (note 1); also Michael J. Dear and Jennifer R. Wolch, *Landscapes of Despair: From Deinstitutionalization to Homelessness* (Princeton: Princeton University Press, 1987); and Rael Jean Isaac and Virginia C. Armat, *Madness in the Streets: How Psychiatry and the Law Abandoned the Mentally Ill* (New York: The Free Press, 1990).

3. Documenting the preference of psychiatrists for the suburban "worried well," and their general reluctance to treat the seriously mentally ill, Torrey (note 1) implicates the psychiatric community in this situation.

4. Jonathan Kozol, "Distancing the Homeless," *Yale Review,* Winter 1988, p. 153.

5. Johnson (1990), p. 118.

6. Jonathon O. Cole, George Gardos, and Michael Nelson, "Alternatives to Chronic Hospitalization—The Boston State Hospital Experience," in Leonard I. Stein and Mary Ann Test, eds., *Alternatives to Mental Hospital Treatment* (New York: Plenum, 1978), p. 221. See also Carol A. B. Warren, "New Forms of Social Control: The Myth of Deinstitutionalization," *American Behavioral Scientist* 24 (1981), p. 727.

7. U.S. General Accounting Office, *Returning the Mentally Disabled to the Community: Government Needs to Do More* (Washington, D.C.: U.S. Government Printing Office, 1977), pp. 10–11, as cited in Johnson (note 5), p. 275.

8. See Kozol (note 4), p. 158.

9. Rossi (note 1, chap. 1), p. 121.

10. Rossi (note 1, chap. 1), combining twenty-five studies, finds 26.8 percent of homeless people have had "mental hospital experience." This compares with a less than 5 percent rate for the general population (pp. 146–47). A larger discussion of mental illness rates among homeless people appears below.

11. One study found fewer than 5 percent of homeless people treated in a 19-city health-care demonstration project were deinstitutionalized patients (*U.S. News and World Report* 106, March 20, 1989), p. 28.

12. Data regarding mental illness among homeless people remain contradictory and inconclusive. Nevertheless, there is value in an estimate. To my view, the most persuasive figures are those presented by Torrey (note 1) and the National Conference of Mayors, both of whom estimate that the homeless mentally ill represent 30 percent of the larger population. Assuming that a small percentage of the homeless mentally ill have never received "mental hospital experience," this figure would corroborate Rossi's estimate. For its part, the Department of Health and Human Services has said 33 to 66 percent of all shelter residents are severely mentally ill, while the National Institute of Mental Health has estimated the figure to be as high as 50 percent (*Washington Post,* April 20, 1985). Other studies have found yet greater rates of mental illness among the homeless. One psychiatric study of homeless people staying at an emergency shelter in Boston found that 46 percent suffered "major mental illness," with an additional 21 percent suffering "severe personality or character disorders" (Ellen L. Bassuk et al., "Is Homelessness a Mental Health Problem?" *American Journal of Psychiatry* 141, 12 Dec. 1984, pp. 1546–50). Greater rates of mental illness have also been found among runaway and homeless youth (Paul G. Shane, "Changing Patterns among Homeless and Runaway Youth," *American Journal of Orthopsychiatry* 59.2, April 1989, p. 208). In contrast, a study by the University of Chicago's School of Social Service Administration concluded that homelessness among their subjects stemmed largely from poverty, rather than from preexisting illnesses or disabilities. The study, which surveyed participants of free-meal programs (rather than those staying in shelters), found the homeless largely similar to other very poor people (Rossi, note 1, chap. 1, p. 288). The differences in the conclusions reached by the Chicago study most likely lie in the populations studied. By surveying meal participants, the Chicago study broadened its survey beyond shelter inhabitants who, after all, represent but a small percentage of the larger population of homeless people. Homeless people who are neither mentally ill nor substance abusers tend to avoid inner-city shelters due to poor conditions and the same high concentration of mentally ill and substance-abusing patrons.

13. Johnson (note 6), p. 150.

14. M. Harvey Brenner, *Mental Illness and the Economy* (Cambridge: Harvard University Press, 1973), p. ix.

15. M. Harvey Brenner, "Estimating the Effects of Economic Changes on National Health and Social Well-Being," a study prepared for the use of the subcommittee on Economic Goals and Inter-governmental Policy of the Joint Economic Committee (Washington, D.C.: U.S. Government Printing Office, 1984), as cited in Ruth Sidel, *Women and Children Last: The Plight of Poor Women in Affluent America* (New York: Viking, 1986).

16. Ramsay Liem and Paula Raymen, "Health and Social Costs of Unemployment," *American Psychologist* 37, October 1982, pp. 1116–23. More recent research supports such conclusions. See, for example, J. L. Hagen and A. M. Ivanoff, "Homeless Women: A High-risk Population," *Affilia: Journal of Women and Social Work,* Vol. 3, number 1, 1988, pp. 19–33.

17. As determined by the CES-D scale developed by the Center for Epidemiologic Studies at the National Institute of Mental Health (Rossi, note 1, chap. 1, pp. 147–149).

18. Brenner, note 14.

19. Conversation with Reggie Goldman, manager of the Alfred Benjamin Counseling Service, Jewish Family and Children Services, Overland Park, Kansas.

20. See Alan R. Sutherland, "Health Care for the Homeless," *Issues in Science and Technology* 5, Fall 1988, p. 79.

21. E. Fuller Torrey, "Forced Medication is Part of the Cure," *The New Physician* 35.9, December 1986, pp. 34–37 (reprinted from *Washington Monthly*).

22. Susan Stefan, "The Psychiatric Cure for Homelessness: Wrong Diagnosis, Wrong Treatment," *The New Physician* 35.9, December 1986, pp. 44–45.

23. Stories abound of homeless people who commit atrocious acts to get themselves admitted for psychiatric treatment. Alice K. Johnson and Larry W. Krueger tell the story of a woman who reportedly "drew a razor from her pocket and slashed it across the eyes of a small child" reasoning, "maybe if I hurt someone else I will get the help I need" ("Toward a Better Understanding of Homeless Women," *Social Work* 34.6, November 1989, p. 537).

Who Goes Homeless?

E. Fuller Torrey

Should the homeless be included in the statement, "Ye have the poor always with you"? Given the array of individuals who have become permanent fixtures on the streets of every American city in the last decade, the answer would appear to be yes. In fact, however, homelessness has evolved from being a homogeneous, sphinx-like problem to being a heterogeneous cluster of interrelated problems for which many of the solutions are known. The mystery no longer is what to do, but rather why do we not do it.

One change in homelessness has been the perceived magnitude of the problem. Until 1987 some advocates were claiming that more than two million Americans were homeless. A 1987 study by the Urban Institute initially estimated the number to be between 567,000 and 600,000; the primary author later revised this downward to between 355,000 and 445,000. Peter H. Rossi, in his 1989 book, *Down and Out in America,* concluded that "the most believable national estimate is that at least 300,000 people are homeless each night in this country, and possibly as many as 400,000 to 500,000." In 1990, Census takers claimed to have found 228,621 homeless on the night of March 20, including 49,793 persons "visible at preidentified street locations." If it is assumed that only one-third of those actually living on the streets were counted by the Census, the total number of homeless persons would be 328,207, a number consistent with the estimates by both the Urban Institute and Rossi.

CHANGING CLIMATES

3   Another change is a decrease in the public's tolerance for the homeless. In New York City, labeled by one newspaper as "Calcutta on the Hudson," police evicted the homeless from Penn Station and razed their temporary shelters in Tompkins Square Park. In Washington, D.C., a right-to-shelter law was rescinded in a 1990 referendum, and local police began enforcing a city ordinance against begging. Atlanta's Mayor Maynard Jackson in 1991 asked the City Council to impose stiff penalties, including up to sixty days in jail, for aggressive begging or sleeping in vacant buildings.

4   Perhaps most surprising has been the decreased sympathy for the homeless in towns and cities traditionally thought of as bastions of liberalism. In Santa Monica, which serves free meals daily on the City Hall lawn, a 1990 poll showed voters favoring tougher law enforcement against the homeless. In Berkeley, police regularly make sweeps of People's Park, and across the Bay, San Franciscans overwhelmingly picked homelessness as the city's biggest problem—bigger than drugs, crime, or AIDS—in a newspaper poll. Indeed, according to *San Francisco Chronicle* columnist Cyra McFadden, "You could get rich in this town right now by selling T-shirts reading, 'Eat the homeless.' " Decreasing public tolerance does not by itself produce any more solutions to the homelessness problem than did the earlier indulgences of public guilt, but it does tend to force harder thinking about solutions. Shelters and soup kitchens provide short-term respite from serious thinking about long-term solutions.

5   Probably the most significant shift in debates about the homeless has been a growing consensus that they are not a monolithic group, but rather composed of three distinct groups. Eliciting the most sympathy from the public are the down-on-my-luck individuals and families, especially children. Economic recession, shrinking availability of low-income housing, and marginal job skills have affected this group. Eliciting somewhat less sympathy are homeless individuals with serious mental illnesses, especially schizophrenia, because many people are frightened of them and do not realize that they have a brain disease that places them in the same category as people with Alzheimer's disease. It has been estimated that there are now twice as many schizophrenics living in public shelters and on the streets as there are in all state and county psychiatric hospitals. Eliciting by far the least public sympathy are the alcoholics and drug abusers. Many of them use public shelters and soup kitchens in order to save their money to feed their addiction, and they panhandle the most aggressively.

6   It is widely agreed that approximately half of all the homeless have an alcohol and/or drug problem; some of these are also mentally ill and/or have marginal job skills. The mentally ill account for approximately one-third; this percentage is lower in cities with relatively good public psychiatric services (e.g., Salt Lake City) and higher in cities where such ser-

vices are abysmal (e.g., Los Angeles, Houston, Miami). The pure down-on-my-luck group is relatively small (about 15 per cent) although very visible in stories about the homeless; advocates learned long ago that this group most effectively elicits support for their cause.

SEPARATING THE STRANDS

Henry J. Kaiser once wrote that "problems are only opportunities in work clothes." This is certainly true for homelessness, which is really three separate problems corresponding to these three groups.   7

The easiest of the three problems is what to do with the mentally ill. Their homelessness is a consequence of deinstitutionalization and the subsequent breakdown of public psychiatric services. A 1983 study of discharges from Metropolitan State Hospital in Boston, for example, found that 27 per cent of all discharged patients became at least intermittently homeless within six months of discharge. A similar study in 1986 of discharges from Columbus State Hospital in Ohio reported that 36 per cent were homeless within six months. Furthermore, the number of beds in state mental hospitals was reduced from 552,000 in 1955 to 108,000 in 1986. As was pointed out in *The 1990 Annual Report of the Interagency Council on the Homeless,* given the 41 per cent increase in the population of the United States since 1955, if there had been no deinstitutionalization there would be 800,000 state psychiatric beds today, nearly eight times the actual number.   8

The major reason for the failure of public psychiatric services has been a fiscal one. It is not, however, a question of *how much* is being spent, as is commonly supposed; the approximately $20 billion in public funds currently being spent each year is probably sufficient to buy first-class services if it were utilized properly. Rather, the problem is *how these services are funded.* Until the early 1960s, approximately 96 per cent of public psychiatric services were funded by the states, with the other 4 percent split between federal and local sources. As deinstitutionalization got under way, the released patients were made eligible for federal Supplemental Security Income (SSI), Social Security Disability Income (SSDI), Medicaid, Medicare, food stamps, and other federal subsidies. By 1985 it was estimated that the states' share of the cost for the mentally ill had fallen to 53 per cent of the total, while the federal share had risen to 38 per cent (it is undoubtedly several percentage points higher by now).   9

The shift of the fiscal burden from the states to the Federal Government was not, by itself, a disaster. The problems arose out of how the various fiscal supports were related to each other. For example, the patients in Metropolitan State Hospital and Columbus State Hospital mentioned above were primarily the fiscal responsibilities of the states of Massachusetts and Ohio as long as they were in the hospitals. Once discharged, they became primarily the responsibility of the Federal Government. If such patients relapse and need rehospitalization, as most of them do, they typically are sent to the psychiatric ward of a general hospital, where Medicaid pays most of the bill. Elderly psychiatric patients were similarly transferred from state hospitals to nursing homes not because the care was necessarily better (often it was worse) but rather because such a transfer made them eligible for Medicare and Medicaid. Even with the states coming up with Medicaid matching funds, it was extremely cost-effective, from the point of view of state government, to shift the fiscal burden to the Federal Government.   10

11   The fiscal organization of public psychiatric services in the United States is more thought-disordered than most of their patients. The incentives all lead to discharging psychiatric patients from state facilities as quickly as possible; there is no incentive to worry about where they go, whether they get aftercare, or whether they become homeless. Indeed, if you tried to set up a system for funding public psychiatric services in a way which would guarantee its failure, you would set up just such a system as we have created.

12   The solution is to meld federal and state funding streams into a single stream with responsibility placed at the state level, unless states wish to delegate to the county level (as do California, Minnesota, and Wisconsin). All incentives to shift the fiscal burden to the Federal Government must be removed. States would rapidly learn that it is cost-effective to provide good psychiatric aftercare, because the costs of repeated rehospitalizations are very high. Continuity of care between inpatient and outpatient programs would become the rule rather than the exception. Existing model programs for the homeless mentally ill such as Seattle's El Rey Residential Treatment Facility or the widely praised Weingart Center in Los Angeles, which combine treatment, housing, and rehabilitation, would spread quickly. State laws making it difficult to hospitalize obviously impaired individuals would be amended as it became apparent that good psychiatric care does not cost more in the long run than not-so-benign neglect. And the homeless mentally ill, including the emblematic bag ladies, would become a thing of the past.

NOW FOR THE HARDER ONES

13   The problem of the homeless mentally ill is easy to solve compared with the problems of the other groups. Alcoholics have always made up a significant percentage of the homeless population, from the days of the early American almshouses to the hobos who rode the rails in the years before World War II. When one is addicted to alcohol or drugs the highest priority is to save as much money as possible to feed that addiction. Present homeless policies, which in some cities have guaranteed free beds and food for everyone who asks, have probably exacerbated rather than relieved the problem of homeless substance abusers.

14   Although there is no policy which can force a person to help himself, it stands to reason that public programs should not make alcohol and drug problems worse. All substance abusers who have any income should be required to pay a certain proportion of it for shelter and food and should also be required to attend regular meetings of Alcoholics Anonymous or Narcotics Anonymous. Rehabilitation programs including vocational training should be readily available, but abstinence should be a requirement for participation. For those who refuse to meet minimal requirements for such publicly funded programs, there is a network of private and church-run shelters (such as the Salvation Army's) which have provided exemplary care for alcoholics and drug abusers for many years.

15   Solutions to the down-on-my-luck homeless are both easy and difficult at the same time. Many of them are victims of reduced stocks of low-income housing. It does not take a PhD to realize that when single-room-occupancy (SRO) hotel units were reduced from 127,000 to 14,000, as happened in New York City between 1970 and 1983, or from 1,680 to 15, as happened in Nashville between 1970 and 1990, some people would be left with nowhere to live.

But housing is the easy half of solving the down-on-my-luck problem. Many of these   16
people have a poor education and marginal job skills. As the workplace demands increasing technological skills for even entry-level positions, this group is likely to continue to grow.
Solutions require the whole panoply of often discussed but rarely available services from re-
medial education to vocational training, job coaching, transitional employment, supported
employment, and counseling. This is certainly the most difficult and most expensive segment
of the homeless population to rehabilitate, but not rehabilitating them is also expensive.

As long as programs for the mentally ill, substance abusers, and consumers of low-income   17
housing are part of the ongoing political tug-of-war between federal and state governments,
solutions to the problems of the homeless will be elusive. The homeless are, in one sense,
daily reminders of the lack of resolution of this issue.

In the area of public psychiatric and substance-abuse services, the Federal Government   18
has a miserable record of achievement. Exhibit A is the federally funded Community Mental
Health Centers program, which wasted over $3 billion setting up 769 centers, most of which
never did what they were intended to do. It seems likely that service programs conceived by
federal officials, who are too far removed from the real world, will almost inevitably fail.

What, then, should be the Federal Government's role? The setting of minimal standards   19
and enforcement of such standards through fiscal incentives and disincentives is necessary,
e.g., expecting states to reduce the mentally ill homeless to a specified level and reducing
federal subsidies if they fail. The enforcement function should probably be vested in the Office of Inspector General in departments such as Health and Human Services (HHS) or Housing and Urban Development (HUD). Model programs such as those under the McKinney
Act, the HHS-HUD collaborative program to improve housing and services for the homeless
mentally ill, or Senator Pete Domenici's recently introduced "Projects to Aid the Transition
from Homelessness" bill, should be encouraged. The problem is that from most states' point
of view, such programs are not regarded merely as models, but rather as an ongoing federal
commitment to replace the efforts of the states themselves.

The homeless, then, will be with us until we are able to resolve the issue of federal   20
versus state responsibility for social programs. Hallucinating quietly next to vacant buildings, lying under bushes in the park, or aggressively accosting strangers on the street, the
homeless represent not only a failure of social programs, but more broadly a failure of government at all levels.

❧ FOR CLASS DISCUSSION

1. Analyze and evaluate the debate on the mentally ill homeless by applying the
   first set of guide questions from page 455. How do you account for the disagreements among the disputants? This is a particularly good controversy for
   examining disagreements based on disputes about facts as well as values.
   Also, many of these arguments turn on knotty definitional questions: When is
   a person mentally ill? When is a person homeless? At what point does a person lose his or her rights as a free, autonomous individual?

2. Choose one of the arguments for closer analysis, applying the second set of
   guide questions on page 455–456.

Optional Writing Assignment   You are a newly hired research assistant to Senator Sarah Goodperson. For the past several weeks Senator Goodperson has been lobbied extensively by the National Coalition for the Homeless. The lobbyists are urging Senator Goodperson to support new legislation calling for the construction of 2.5 million low-cost, subsidized housing units in major cities across the United States. However, she has been lobbied with almost equal force by organizations devoted to reducing federal taxes and trimming what they see as a huge welfare bureaucracy. To add to her confusion, a coalition of big-city mayors, in partnership with an association of psychiatrists, has been calling for the rebuilding of state mental hospitals to provide treatment for the mentally ill homeless. These persons have sent Senator Goodperson copies of Charles Krauthammer's "How to Save the Homeless Mentally Ill" (pp. 221–227 in this text) and are urging her to support Krauthammer's proposal.

Sarah Goodperson throws up her hands in confusion. "What is the truth about homelessness?" she asks herself. "What ought we to do?" That night she sits at her word processor and writes you the following memo:

To: [Your name goes here]
From: Sarah Goodperson
Re: A national policy on the homeless

I'm being lobbied every which way but loose on the homeless issue, and frankly I'm confused about it. I've spent so much of my time recently focusing on national health care and reduction of the deficit that I haven't devoted much attention to what our country should be doing about the homeless. I want to start again from ground zero and rethink my entire position on the homeless. I want to develop a consistent position for myself, something that I believe in ethically and that I can support with appropriate reasons and data. My long-range goal is to help forge a coalition of legislators to create a long-range national policy on the homeless. But before I can do that I need time to think—and also I need to surround myself with a team of well-informed research assistants to bat around ideas with me.

This is where you come in. I would like you to examine the problem of the mentally ill homeless in light of the attached article by Charles Krauthammer [pp. 221–227 in this text], which is being avidly supported by a group of psychiatrists and big-city mayors. Read what the current literature is saying about the mentally ill homeless and get back to me with your analysis and advice. Should I support Krauthammer's proposal? What alternative approaches are suggested by the literature? Based on your first pass through the literature, which approach do you most recommend and why?

Because I will be using your document for my preliminary planning, all I need at this time is a basic overview of the literature on the mentally ill. I want to know what the alternatives are to Krauthammer's approach and get your recommendation of which approach is best and why. A reasonably short document ought to do the trick—say, four or five double-spaced pages.

Your task: Write the document called for by Senator Goodperson.

SAME-SEX MARRIAGE*

Here Comes the Groom:
A (Conservative) Case for Gay Marriage

Andrew Sullivan

Last month in New York, a court ruled that a gay lover had the right to stay in his deceased partner's rent-control apartment because the lover qualified as a member of the deceased's family. The ruling deftly annoyed almost everybody. Conservatives saw judicial activism in favor of gay rent control: three reasons to be appalled. Chastened liberals (such as the *New York Times* editorial page), while endorsing the recognition of gay relationships, also worried about the abuse of already stretched entitlements that the ruling threatened. What neither side quite contemplated is that they both might be right, and that the way to tackle the issue of unconventional relationships in conventional society is to try something both more radical and more conservative than putting courts in the business of deciding what is and is not a family. That alternative is the legalization of civil gay marriage.

The New York rent-control case did not go anywhere near that far, which is the problem. The rent-control regulations merely stipulated that a "family" member had the right to remain in the apartment. The judge ruled that to all intents and purposes a gay lover is part of his lover's family, inasmuch as a "family" merely means an interwoven social life, emotional commitment, and some level of financial interdependence.

It's a principle now well established around the country. Several cities have "domestic partnership" laws, which allow relationships that do not fit into the category of heterosexual marriage to be registered with the city and qualify for benefits that up till now have been reserved for straight married couples. San Francisco, Berkeley, Madison, and Los Angeles all have legislation, as does the politically correct Washington, D.C., suburb, Takoma Park. In these cities, a variety of interpersonal arrangements qualify for health insurance, bereavement leave, insurance, annuity and pension rights, housing rights (such as rent-control apartments), adoption and inheritance rights. Eventually, according to gay lobby groups, the aim is to include federal income tax and veterans' benefits as well. A recent case even involved the right to use a family member's accumulated frequent-flier points. Gays are not the only beneficiaries; heterosexual "live-togethers" also qualify.

There's an argument, of course, that the current legal advantages extended to married people unfairly discriminate against people who've shaped their lives in less conventional arrangements. But it doesn't take a genius to see that enshrining in the law a vague principle like "domestic partnership" is an invitation to qualify at little personal cost for a vast array of entitlements otherwise kept crudely under control.

---

*For an additional argument on this issue, see student writer Sam Isaacson's essay on pages 300–301.

5   To be sure, potential DPs have to prove financial interdependence, shared living arrangements, and a commitment to mutual caring. But they don't need to have a sexual relationship or even closely mirror old-style marriage. In principle, an elderly woman and her live-in nurse could qualify. A couple of uneuphemistically confirmed bachelors could be DPs. So could two close college students, a pair of seminarians, or a couple of frat buddies. Left as it is, the concept of domestic partnership could open a Pandora's box of litigation and subjective judicial decision-making about who qualifies. You either are or are not married; it's not a complex question. Whether you are in a "domestic partnership" is not so clear.

6   More important, the concept of domestic partnership chips away at the prestige of traditional relationships and undermines the priority we give them. This priority is not necessarily a product of heterosexism. Consider heterosexual couples. Society has good reason to extend legal advantages to heterosexuals who choose the formal sanction of marriage over simply living together. They make a deeper commitment to one another and to society; in exchange, society extends certain benefits to them. Marriage provides an anchor, if an arbitrary and weak one, in the chaos of sex and relationships to which we are all prone. It provides a mechanism for emotional stability, economic security, and the healthy rearing of the next generation. We rig the law in its favor not because we disparage all forms of relationship other than the nuclear family, but because we recognize that not to promote marriage would be to ask too much of human virtue. In the context of the weakened family's effect upon the poor, it might also invite social disintegration. One of the worst products of the New Right's "family values" campaign is that its extremism and hatred of diversity has disguised this more measured and more convincing case for the importance of the marital bond.

7   The concept of domestic partnership ignores these concerns, indeed directly attacks them. This is a pity, since one of its most important objectives—providing some civil recognition for gay relationships—is a noble cause and one completely compatible with the defense of the family. But the decision to go about it is not to undermine straight marriage; it is to legalize old-style marriage for gays.

8   The gay movement has ducked this issue primarily out of fear of division. Much of the gay leadership clings to notions of gay life as essentially outsider, anti-bourgeois, radical. Marriage, for them, is co-optation into straight society. For the Stonewall generation, it is hard to see how this vision of conflict will ever fundamentally change. But for many other gays—my guess, a majority—while they don't deny the importance of rebellion 20 years ago and are grateful for what was done, there's now the sense of a new opportunity. A need to rebel has quietly ceded to a desire to belong. To be gay and to be bourgeois no longer seems such an absurd proposition. Certainly, since AIDS, to be gay and to be responsible has become a necessity.

9   Gay marriage squares several circles at the heart of the domestic partnership debate. Unlike domestic partnership, it allows for recognition of gay relationships, while casting no aspersions on traditional marriage. It merely asks that gays be allowed to join in. Unlike domestic partnership, it doesn't open up avenues for heterosexuals to get benefits without the responsibilities of marriage, or a nightmare of definitional litigation. And unlike domestic partnership, it harnesses to an already established social convention the yearnings for stability and acceptance among a fast-maturing gay community.

Gay marriage also places more responsibilities upon gays: it says for the first time that gay relationships are not better or worse than straight relationships, and that the same is expected of them. And it's clear and dignified. There's a legal benefit to a clear, common symbol of commitment. There's also a personal benefit. One of the ironies of domestic partnership is that it's not only more complicated than marriage, it's more demanding, requiring an elaborate statement of intent to qualify. It amounts to a substantial invasion of privacy. Why, after all, should gays be required to prove commitment before they get married in a way we would never dream of asking of straights? **10**

Legalizing gay marriage would offer homosexuals the same deal society now offers heterosexuals: general social approval and specific legal advantages in exchange for a deeper and harder-to-extract-yourself-from commitment to another human being. Like straight marriage, it would foster social cohesion, emotional security, and economic prudence. Since there's no reason gays should not be allowed to adopt or be foster parents, it could also help nurture children. And its introduction would not be some sort of radical break with social custom. As it has become more acceptable for gay people to acknowledge their loves publicly, more and more have committed themselves to one another for life in full view of their families and their friends. A law institutionalizing gay marriage would merely reinforce a healthy social trend. It would also, in the wake of AIDS, qualify as a genuine public health measure. Those conservatives who deplore promiscuity among some homosexuals should be among the first to support it. Burke could have written a powerful case for it. **11**

The argument that gay marriage would subtly undermine the unique legitimacy of straight marriage is based upon a fallacy. For heterosexuals, straight marriage would remain the most significant—and only legal—social bond. Gay marriage could only delegitimize straight marriage if it were a real alternative to it, and this is clearly not true. To put it bluntly, there's precious little evidence that straights could be persuaded by any law to have sex with—let alone marry—someone of their own sex. The only possible effect of this sort would be to persuade gay men and women who force themselves into heterosexual marriage (often at appalling cost to themselves and their families) to find a focus for their family instincts in a more personally positive environment. But this is clearly a plus, not a minus: gay marriage could both avoid a lot of tortured families and create the possibility for many happier ones. It is not, in short, a denial of family values. It's an extension of them. **12**

Of course, some would claim that any legal recognition of homosexuality is a de facto attack upon heterosexuality. But even the most hardened conservatives recognize that gays are a permanent minority and aren't likely to go away. Since persecution is not an option in a civilized society, why not coax gays into traditional values rather than rail incoherently against them? **13**

There's a less elaborate argument for gay marriage: it's good for gays. It provides role models for young gay people who, after the exhilaration of coming out, can easily lapse into short-term relationships and insecurity with no tangible goal in sight. My own guess is that most gays would embrace such a goal with as much (if not more) commitment as straights. Even in our society as it is, many lesbian relationships are virtual textbook cases of monogamous commitment. Legal gay marriage could also help bridge the gulf often found between gays and their parents. It could bring the essence of gay life—a gay couple—into the heart **14** of the traditional straight family in a way the family can most understand and the gay off-spring can most easily acknowledge. It could do as much to heal the gay-straight rift as any amount of gay rights legislation.

15   If these arguments sound socially conservative, that's no accident. It's one of the rich-est ironies of our society's blind spot toward gays that essentially conservative social goals should have the appearance of being so radical. But gay marriage is not a radical step. It avoids the mess of domestic partnership; it is humane; it is conservative in the best sense of the word. It's also practical. Given the fact that we already allow legal gay relationships, what possible social goal is advanced by framing the law to encourage those relationships to be unfaithful, undeveloped, and insecure?

Against Gay Marriage—
I: What Heterosexuality Means

Dennis O'Brien

1   My firmest conviction on this debate is that it will end with no conviction. To reach some common view would require an agreement on the meaning of *marriage*—no easy sub-ject; an agreement on whether homosexuality has a meaning—or is it just a natural fact; fi-nally, we would have to find a tone of "sexual wisdom" for the discussion—we are usually too passionate about our passions for wise dispassion.

2   The very day that *Commonweal* asked me to comment on the subject, I happened to read a personality squib in the local paper about the movie actors Kurt Russell and Goldie Hawn. It seems that they are "together" after previous unhappy marriages. They now have a four-year-old son and they would consider marriage if their current arrangement proved difficult to the youngster. Since Hollywood is usually the avant-garde of the culture, it may be that marriage of any kind is a charming anachronism. I assume that the reluctance to enter marriage is that it destroys the honesty and commitment of "true love." Genuine com-mitment does not need the sanctions of judge or priest. In fact, it shows a weakening of ardor to rest fidelity on formality.

3   I have no doubt that there are deep and abiding homosexual commitments. What would formal marriage add? Legal marriages do help in divorce proceedings because there is a known system for dissolution and disposition of claims. If legal rights are an issue, they can, of course, be settled by (non-marriage) civil contracts. Should Kurt and Goldie break up this side of marriage, there are "palimony" settlements and similar suits have been brought for homosexual partnerships.

4   If the sole meaning of "marriage" is legal, then marriage of any sex may become a mat-ter of "indifference." Perhaps truly loving couples should be as "indifferent" to marriage as our Hollywood pair. That there have been homosexual palimony cases would suggest that the law already brings homosexual partners into some sort of "coupled" network of legal restriction. It seems a short step from palimony to matrimony.

If there is an *issue* regarding homosexual marriage, it must rest on some deeper political or "religious" concerns. I do not mean what the newspapers think of as "political": who has the clout to carry the day. I am interested in the basic values of the American *polis.* What does our society express about itself and the human condition through its sanctioned institutions?   5

One might believe that the American *polis* avoids deep value issues; America is a debating society of opposing philosophies and life styles. Arguments are settled, if necessary or at all, by clout not cultural commitment. On the other hand, it is doubtful that any *polis* can exist at all without a cultural sense, however suppressed. American democracy rests on a powerful set of assumptions about human nature and society which legitimate the character of its institutions. Would homosexual marriage harmonize with our underlying values? I am not certain I can answer that question, but it is worth pointing out that "nonnormal" marriages have previously received constitutional scrutiny. The most famous are "the Mormon cases" which ruled on the legitimacy of polygamy (as a religiously protected right). The Supreme Court struck down polygamous marriage in part on *democratic* grounds. "Polygamy leads to the patriarchal principle . . . which, when applied to large communities, fetters the people in stationary despotism, while that principle cannot long exist in connection with monogamy" *Reynolds* v. *United States* 98 US 145 (1879).   6

I am not overwhelmed by the sociology of the Court's opinion, but the justices were correct in attempting to connect marriage customs with the deeper values of the society. If homosexual marriage were to be seriously advanced, similar large concepts should be brought into play.   7

Are there potential problems for the *polis* if homosexual marriage becomes a legally sanctioned institution? There are some obvious social concerns. Heterosexual arrangements remain the mainstay for creating the next generation—which is not an incidental issue for any continuing social body. Surrounding heterosexual arrangements with political blessing and legal structures could be judged to have special social utility on that ground alone. Giving heterosexual marriage a positive place in the legal structure does not, however, imply that homosexual relations need suffer from negative legal stricture. What consenting adults do, and so forth—but the state is not obliged to bless every bedroom. (The Athenian *polis,* while it practiced a form of sanctioned homosexuality, did not amalgamate that practice to marriage.)   8

A *religious* position on homosexual marriage would go beyond the merely legal and the larger political values. (I believe that homosexuality should not be discussed as a straightforward *moral* issue; *moral* issues generally deal with specific acts but the concern here is a life choice. The church has thought traditionally that a religiously celibate life choice was more exalted than marriage. For all that, marriage did not thus become "immoral.")   9

Is the *meaning of marriage* (as religious sacrament) consonant with the *meaning of homosexuality*? The latter meaning may be even less recoverable than the former. To the extent that superficial accounts of homosexuality treat it as a direct expression of a biologically determined appetite, they displace it from the web of cultural development that would assay the worth of homosexual life patterns. If all there is to homosexuality (or heterosexuality) is natural determinism, we could remove it from the human spiritual agenda.   10

11   I would like to believe that sex is a human artifact for all that it has a biological base. (Human eating habits are not just feeding behavior. The prevalence of fantasy in sex certainly suggests heavy human seasoning of an essential appetite.) Assuming that sex has a human meaning, it seems plausible that homosexual life patterns differ from heterosexual if for no other reason than that male bodies and female bodies are different. If we were only accidentally related to our bodies (angels in disguise, ghosts in a machine), then how these mechanisms got sexual kicks might not *fundamentally* invade our sense of person and human value. *Playboy* and Puritanism both assume the triviality of bodies; they are for playful/sinful distraction only. Catholics seem more stuck with incarnation—and somewhere along that line would be a Catholic answer to the question posed.

12   I am no fan at all of the "natural law" arguments about procreative sexuality as presented in *Humanae vitae.* These arguments assume that one can read the moral law off the book of nature. Social Darwinists argued that because humans are naturally aggressive, war was morally desirable. (The same mistake occurs when someone argues from a natural urge for hetero/homosexuality to the moral obligation to carry forward the urge.) But for all that nature gives no dogmas, nature presents an ur-text for human meaning. Heterosexual marriage is a deep story developed from the ur-text of genital biology.

13   What difference could there possibly be in homosexual relations? Well, perhaps homosexual relations are better sex. After all, one knows one's own sex's response better than the heterosexual response. "It takes one to know one!" (As Oscar Wilde said about masturbation: "cleaner, more efficient, and you meet a better class of people.") The sexiness of homosexuality may or may not be the case, but I believe that reflection on hetero/homosexual embodiments would reveal quite different erotic story lines. It seems eminently plausible that bedding with an other (strange?) sex is as different as travel abroad can be from staying at home.

14   One could conclude that the homosexual story line was valuable—perhaps more valuable than the heterosexual. But not all things are possible in either variation. There are distinct spiritual problems with homosexual "marriage" in the Jewish and Christian traditions. Franz Rosenzweig states a deep truth when he attempts to explicate Jewish "faith": "the belief of the Jew is not the content of a testimony, but rather the product of reproduction. The Jew, engendered a Jew, attests his belief by continuing to procreate the Jewish people."

15   Underneath all the heated argument about artificial contraception, abortion, population control, family planning and the lot, the traditional Jewish *mitzvah* for procreation expresses human solidarity with a Creator God. The Christian claim for an embodied God moves in the same spiritual territory. (I do not imply that family size scales one up in blessedness.)

16   Kierkegaard regarded marriage as spirit's proper synthesis of recollection and hope. Without getting into deep theological water, it is certainly the case that heterosexual marriage normally carries with it the meaning of recollection and hope. Normative heterosexual marriage recollects parents in the act of parenting and literally embodies hope in the bringing forth of children. Homosexuals may, of course, recall parents and be hopeful for the future but they do not, of course, embody a family history. In so far as these Judaic faiths are not finally enacted in the realm of attitudes, they seem destined to give a special place to embodiment. Procreative "marriage" seems to me to be a special and irreplaceable central symbol of the tradition.

Gay Rights, Gay Marriages

John Leo

The next big gay controversy is here, touched off by the state supreme court of Hawaii. The court opened the door to legal gay marriage. It ruled that Hawaii's ban on same-sex marriages "is presumed to be unconstitutional" unless the state can show, in a lower-court trial, that the prohibition is "justified by compelling state interests." 1

The issue has been bubbling toward the surface for years, mostly in the churches, partly in campaigns around the country for city "domestic partners" legislation that offers gays some spousal benefits of married couples. 2

During the week of the gay march on Washington, gay marriage was the centerpiece of a long article in the *New Republic* by its editor, Andrew Sullivan, a gay, conservative Catholic. He called it "the critical measure necessary for full gay equality." 3

There's a traditionalist argument in favor: Society ought to sanction almost any arrangement that promotes personal commitment and social stability. But the most common argument, like most advanced by interest groups these days, is a charge of bias, inequality and "privileging." If gays are the social equals of straights, why can't they marry too? 4

This is a potent argument. Egalitarian arguments seem strong: privileging seems unfair. But all societies privilege certain activities and practices and discourage others. Because of family disintegration, we are finally trying to privilege two-parent families and discourage one-parent families. 5

We privilege parents over nonparents in some ways because we know that parenting is difficult and expensive and essential to society. Marriage is privileged for the same reason. Society has a crucial stake in protecting the connection between sex, procreation and a commitment to raise children. If it didn't, why would the state be involved with marriage at all? All couplings, gay or straight, would be merely private matters, settled by contract or handshake, not licenses. 6

TRUE PARTNERS

Are gays entitled to many benefits that married couples get? I think so. Committed couples should have the same health-plan coverage as straights, for instance. When a lover dies, a gay or lesbian shouldn't lose an apartment, or the right to control the funeral. 7

But this can come about through domestic-partner legislation or registered bonding ceremonies. The insistence on calling these arrangements marriages is quite another matter. It's an attempt to overhaul tradition, language and common sense for perhaps one tenth of one percent of the population interested in appropriating heterosexual practice and ceremony. 8

Many gays, like Andrew Sullivan, favor marriage because they honor it, but another motive is at work, too. Some gay activists are frankly interested in diluting or breaking down heterosexual norms and downgrading the nuclear family to one lifestyle choice among many. 9

But marriage isn't just about lifestyle or personal fulfillment. It's also about children and the continuation of the human project. Popping loose the connection between marriage and procreation (or at least the possibility of procreation) seems like an extraordinary step, profoundly altering a conception of marriage that goes back thousands of years. 10

11   We don't even know what the immediate effects would be. Would it effectively convert the emerging policy of tolerance for gays into one of de facto approval? For instance, at some public schools, 8- and 9-year-olds are currently being taught about gay sex. Parents are protesting, but if the state says gay and straight marriages are equal, apart from "age appropriateness," what grounds for protest would be left?

12   Polls show that large majorities of Americans approve of some spousal rights for gays but reject the idea of gay marriage. That seems to point to a compromise based on domestic-partner laws. But large majorities do not always count for much in the age of litigation.

13   It's worth noting that the apparent victory for gay marriage in Hawaii turned on the word "sex" in the state's equal-protection law forbidding discrimination "because of race, religion, sex, or ancestry." (The state law doesn't protect sexual orientation.)

14   This seems to mean that prohibitions against sex discrimination, which most states have, can be contorted into justifications for gay marriage. Julian Eule, a constitutional-law expert at the University of California at Los Angeles, said the court's reasoning "converts all homosexuality issues into gender issues." Quite a trick.

15   The court itself found that a right to same-sex marriage "is not so rooted in the traditions and collective conscience of Hawaii's people that failure to recognize it would violate the fundamental principles of liberty and justice. . . ." But it managed to conjure up the right anyway by stretching the meaning of sex discrimination.

16   This is yet another example of our judicial problem. We vote for one thing; relentless litigation and imaginative judges turn it into something wildly different. In this case, it may amount to a fundamental reordering of society, all done without any input from the people.

For Better or Worse?
The Case for Gay (and Straight) Marriage

Jonathan Rauch

1   Whatever else marriage may or may not be, it is certainly falling apart. Half of today's marriages end in divorce, and, far more costly, many never begin—leaving mothers poor, children fatherless and neighborhoods chaotic. With timing worthy of Neville Chamberlain, homosexuals have chosen this moment to press for the right to marry. What's more, Hawaii's courts are moving toward letting them do so. I'll believe in gay marriage in America when I see it, but if Hawaii legalizes it, even temporarily, the uproar over this final insult to a besieged institution will be deafening.

2   Whether gay marriage makes sense—and whether straight marriage makes sense—depends on what marriage is actually for. Current secular thinking on this question is shockingly sketchy. Gay activists say: marriage is for love, and we love each other, therefore we should be able to marry. Traditionalists say marriage is for children, and homosexuals do not (or should not) have children, therefore you should not be able to marry. That, unfortunately, pretty well covers the spectrum. I say 'unfortunately' because both views are wrong. They misunderstand and impoverish the social meaning of marriage.

So what is marriage for? Modern marriage is, of course, based upon traditions that religion helped to codify and enforce. But religious doctrine has no special standing in the world of secular law and policy (the "Christian nation" crowd notwithstanding). If we want to know what and whom marriage is for in modern America, we need a sensible secular doctrine.   3

At one point, marriage in secular society was largely a matter of business: cementing family ties, providing social status for men and economic support for women, conferring dowries, and so on. Marriages were typically arranged, and "love" in the modern sense was no prerequisite. In Japan, remnants of this system remain, and it works surprisingly well. Couples stay together because they view their marriage as a partnership: an investment in social stability for themselves and their children. Because Japanese couples don't expect as much emotional fulfillment as we do, they are less inclined to break up. They also take a somewhat more relaxed attitude toward adultery. What's a little extracurricular love provided that each partner is fulfilling his or her many other marital duties?   4

In the West, of course, love is a defining element. The notion of lifelong love is charming, if ambitious, and certainly love is a desirable element of marriage. In society's eyes, however, it cannot be the defining element. You may or may not love your husband, but the two of you are just as married either way. You may love your mistress, but that certainly doesn't make her your spouse. Love helps make sense of marriage emotionally, but it is not terribly important in making sense of marriage from the point of view of social policy.   5

If love does not define the purpose of secular marriage, what does? Neither the law nor secular thinking provides a clear answer. Today marriage is almost entirely a voluntary arrangement whose contents are up to the people making the deal. There are few if any behaviors that automatically end a marriage. If a man beats his wife, which is about the worst thing he can do to her, he may be convicted of assault, but his marriage is not automatically dissolved. Couples can be adulterous ("open") yet remain married. They can be celibate, too; consummation is not required. All in all, it is an impressive and also rather astonishing victory for modern individualism that so important an institution should be so bereft of formal social instruction as to what should go on inside of it.   6

Secular society tells us only a few things about marriage. First, marriage depends on the consent of the parties. Second, the parties are not children. Third, the number of parties is two. Fourth, one is a man and the other a woman. Within those rules a marriage is whatever anyone says it is.   7

Perhaps it is enough simply to say that marriage is as it is and should not be tampered with. This sounds like a crudely reactionary position. In fact, however, of all the arguments against reforming marriage, it is probably the most powerful.   8

Call it a Hayekian argument, after the great libertarian economist F. A. Hayek, who developed this line of thinking in his book *The Fatal Conceit.* In a market system, the prices generated by impersonal forces may not make sense from any one person's point of view, but they encode far more information than even the cleverest person could ever gather. In a similar fashion, human societies evolve rich and complicated webs of nonlegal rules in the form of customs, traditions and institutions. Like prices, they may seem irrational or arbitrary. But the very fact that they are the customs that have evolved implies that they embody a practical logic that may not be apparent to even a sophisticated analyst. And the web of custom cannot be torn apart and reordered at will because once its internal logic is   9 violated it falls apart. Intellectuals, such as Marxists or feminists, who seek to deconstruct and rationally rebuild social traditions, will produce not better order but chaos.

10   So the Hayekian view argues strongly against gay marriage. It says that the current rules may not be best and may even be unfair. But they are all we have, and, once you say that marriage need not be male-female, soon marriage will stop being anything at all. You can't mess with the formula without causing unforeseen consequences, possibly including the implosion of the institution of marriage itself.

11   However, there are problems with the Hayekian position. It is untenable in its extreme form and unhelpful in its milder version. In its extreme form, it implies that no social reforms should ever be undertaken. Indeed, no laws should be passed, because they interfere with the natural evolution of social mores. How could Hayekians abolish slavery? They would probably note that slavery violates fundamental moral principles. But in so doing they would establish a moral platform from which to judge social rules, and thus acknowledge that abstracting social debate from moral concerns is not possible.

12   If the ban on gay marriage were only mildly unfair, and if the costs of changing it were certain to be enormous, then the ban could stand on Hayekian grounds. But, if there is any social policy today that has a fair claim to be scaldingly inhumane, it is the ban on gay marriage. As conservatives tirelessly and rightly point out, marriage is society's most fundamental institution. To bar any class of people from marrying as they choose is an extraordinary deprivation. When not so long ago it was illegal in parts of America for blacks to marry whites, no one could claim that this was a trivial disenfranchisement. Granted, gay marriage raises issues that interracial marriage does not; but no one can argue that the deprivation is a minor one.

13   To outweigh such a serious claim it is not enough to say that gay marriage might lead to bad things. Bad things happened as a result of legalizing contraception, but that did not make it the wrong thing to do. Besides, it seems doubtful that extending marriage to, say, another 3 or 5 percent of the population would have anything like the effects that no-fault divorce has had, to say nothing of contraception. By now, the "traditional" understanding of marriage has been sullied in all kinds of ways. It is hard to think of a bigger affront to tradition, for instance, than allowing married women to own property independently of their husbands or allowing them to charge their husbands with rape. Surely it is unfair to say that marriage may be reformed for the sake of anyone and everyone except homosexuals, who must respect the dictates of tradition.

14   Faced with these problems, the milder version of the Hayekian argument says not that social traditions shouldn't be tampered with at all, but that they shouldn't be tampered with lightly. Fine. In this case, no one is talking about casual messing around; both sides have marshaled their arguments with deadly seriousness. Hayekians surely have to recognize that appeals to blind tradition and to the risks inherent in social change do not, a priori, settle anything in this instance. They merely warn against frivolous change.

15   So we turn to what has become the standard view of marriage's purpose. Its proponents would probably like to call it a child-centered view, but it is actually an anti-gay view, as will become clear. Whatever you call it, it is the view of marriage that is heard most often, and in the context of the debate over gay marriage it is heard almost exclusively. In its most straightforward form it goes as follows (I quote from James Q. Wilson's fine book *The Moral Sense*):

A family is not an association of independent people; it is a human commitment designed to make possible the rearing of moral and healthy children. Governments care—or ought to care—about families for this reason, and scarcely for any other.

Wilson speaks about "family" rather than "marriage" as such, but one may, I think, read him as speaking of marriage without doing any injustice to his meaning. The resulting proposition—government ought to care about marriage almost entirely because of children—seems reasonable. But there are problems. The first, obviously, is that gay couples may have children, whether through adoption, prior marriage or (for lesbians) artificial insemination. Leaving aside the thorny issue of gay adoption, the point is that if the mere presence of children is the test, then homosexual relationships can certainly pass it.

16

You might note, correctly, that heterosexual marriages are more likely to produce children than homosexual ones. When granting marriage licenses to heterosexuals, however, we do not ask how likely the couple is to have children. We assume that they are entitled to get married whether or not they end up with children. Understanding this, conservatives often make an interesting move. In seeking to justify the state's interest in marriage, they shift from the actual presence of children to the anatomical possibility of making them. Hadley Arkes, a political science professor and prominent opponent of homosexual marriage, makes the case this way:

17

> The traditional understanding of marriage is grounded in the "natural teleology of the body"—in the inescapable fact that only a man and a woman, and only two people, not three, can generate a child. Once marriage is detached from that natural teleology of the body, what ground of principle would thereafter confine marriage to two people rather than some larger grouping? That is, on what ground of principle would the law reject the claim of a gay couple that their love is not confined to a coupling of two, but that they are woven into a larger ensemble with yet another person or two?

What he seems to be saying is that, where the possibility of natural children is nil, the meaning of marriage is nil. If marriage is allowed between members of the same sex, then the concept of marriage has been emptied of content except to ask whether the parties love each other. Then anything goes, including polygamy. This reasoning presumably is what those opposed to gay marriage have in mind when they claim that, once gay marriage is legal, marriage to pets will follow close behind.

18

But Arkes and his sympathizers make two mistakes. To see them, break down the claim into two components: (1) Two-person marriage derives its special status from the anatomical possibility that the partners can create natural children; and (2) Apart from (1), two-person marriage has no purpose sufficiently strong to justify its special status. That is, absent justification (1), anything goes.

19

The first proposition is wholly at odds with the way society actually views marriage. Leave aside the insistence that natural, as opposed to adopted, children define the importance of marriage. The deeper problem, apparent right away, is the issue of sterile heterosexual couples. Here the "anatomical possibility" crowd has a problem, for a homosexual union is, anatomically speaking, nothing but one variety of sterile union and no different even in principle: a woman without a uterus has no more potential for giving birth than a man without a vagina.

20

21   It may sound like carping to stress the case of barren heterosexual marriage: the vast majority of newlywed heterosexual couples, after all, can have children and probably will. But the point here is fundamental. There are far more sterile heterosexual unions in America than homosexual ones. The "anatomical possibility" crowd cannot have it both ways. If the possibility of children is what gives meaning to marriage, then a post-menopausal woman who applies for a marriage license should be turned away at the courthouse door. What's more, she should be hooted at and condemned for stretching the meaning of marriage beyond its natural basis and so reducing the institution to frivolity. People at the Family Research Council or Concerned Women for America should point at her and say, "If she can marry, why not polygamy?"

22   Obviously, the "anatomical" conservatives do not say this, because they are sane. They instead flail around, saying that sterile men and women were at least born with the right-shaped parts for making children, and so on. Their position is really a nonposition. It says that the "natural children" rationale defines marriage when homosexuals are involved but not when heterosexuals are involved. When the parties to union are sterile heterosexuals, the justification for marriage must be something else. But what?

23   Now arises the oddest part of the "anatomical" argument. Look at proposition (2) above. It says that, absent the anatomical justification for marriage, anything goes. In other words, it dismisses the idea that there might be other good reasons for society to sanctify marriage above other kinds of relationships. Why would anybody make this move? I'll hazard a guess: to exclude homosexuals. Any rationale that justifies sterile heterosexual marriages can also apply to homosexual ones. For instance, marriage makes women more financially secure. Very nice, say the conservatives. But that rationale could be applied to lesbians, so it's definitely out.

24   The end result of this stratagem is perverse to the point of being funny. The attempt to ground marriage in children (or the anatomical possibility thereof) falls flat. But, having lost that reason for marriage, the antigay people can offer no other. In their fixation on excluding homosexuals, they leave themselves no consistent justification for the privileged status of *heterosexual* marriage. They thus tear away any coherent foundation that secular marriage might have, which is precisely the opposite of what they claim they want to do. If they have to undercut marriage to save it from homosexuals, so be it!

25   For the record, I would be the last to deny that children are one central reason for the privileged status of marriage. When men and women get together, children are a likely outcome; and, as we are learning in ever more unpleasant ways, when children grow up without two parents, trouble ensues. Children are not a trivial reason for marriage; they just cannot be the only reason.

26   What are the others? It seems to me that the two strongest candidates are these: domesticating men and providing reliable caregivers. Both purposes are critical to the functioning of a humane and stable society, and both are much better served by marriage—that is, by one-to-one lifelong commitment—than by any other institution.

27   Civilizing young males is one of any society's biggest problems. Wherever unattached males gather in packs, you see no end of trouble: wildings in Central Park, gangs in Los Angeles, soccer hooligans in Britain, skinheads in Germany, fraternity hazings in universities,

grope-lines in the military and, in a different but ultimately no less tragic way, the bath-houses and wanton sex of gay San Francisco or New York in the 1970s.

For taming men, marriage is unmatched. "Of all the institutions through which men may   28
pass—schools, factories, the military—marriage has the largest effect," Wilson writes in *The Moral Sense.* (A token of the casualness of current thinking about marriage is that the man who wrote those words could, later in the very same book, say that government should care about fostering families for "scarcely any other" reason than children.) If marriage—that is, the binding of men into couples—did nothing else, its power to settle men, to keep them at home and out of trouble, would be ample justification for its special status.

Of course, women and older men don't generally travel in marauding or orgiastic packs.   29
But in their case the second rationale comes into play. A second enormous problem for so-ciety is what to do when someone is beset by some sort of burdensome contingency. It could be cancer, a broken back, unemployment or depression; it could be exhaustion from work or stress under pressure. If marriage has any meaning at all, it is that, when you collapse from a stroke, there will be at least one other person whose "job" is to drop everything and come to your aid; or that when you come home after being fired by the postal service there will be someone to persuade you not to kill the supervisor.

Obviously, both rationales—the need to settle males and the need to have people   30
looked after—apply to sterile people as well as fertile ones, and apply to childless couples as well as to ones with children. The first explains why everybody feels relieved when the town delinquent gets married, and the second explains why everybody feels happy when an aging widow takes a second husband. From a social point of view, it seems to me, both rationales are far more compelling as justifications of marriage's special status than, say, love. And both of them apply to homosexuals as well as to heterosexuals.

Take the matter of settling men. It is probably true that women and children, more than   31
just the fact of marriage, help civilize men. But that hardly means that this settling effect of marriage on homosexual men is negligible. To the contrary, being tied to a committed rela-tionship plainly helps stabilize gay men. Even without marriage, coupled gay men have steady sex partners and relationships that they value and therefore tend to be less wanton. Add mar-riage, and you bring a further array of stabilizing influences. One of the main benefits of pub-licly recognized marriage is that it binds couples together not only in their own eyes but also in the eyes of society at large. Around the partners is woven a web of expectations that they will spend nights together, go to parties together, take out mortgages together, buy furniture at Ikea together, and so on—all of which helps tie them together and keep them off the streets and at home. Surely that is a very good thing, especially as compared to the closet-gay cul-ture of furtive sex with innumerable partners in parks and bathhouses.

The other benefit of marriage—caretaking—clearly applies to homosexuals. One of the   32
first things many people worry about when coming to terms with their homosexuality is: Who will take care of me when I'm ailing or old? Society needs to care about this, too, as the AIDS crisis has made horribly clear. If that crisis has shown anything, it is that homosexuals can and will take care of each other, sometimes with breathtaking devotion—and that no institu-tion can begin to match the care of a devoted partner. Legally speaking, marriage creates kin. Surely society's interest in kin-creation is strongest of all for people who are unlikely to be supported by children in old age and who may well be rejected by their own parents in youth.

33   Gay marriage, then, is far from being a mere exercise in political point-making or rights-mongering. On the contrary, it serves two of the three social purposes that make marriage so indispensable and irreplaceable for heterosexuals. Two out of three may not be the whole ball of wax, but it is more than enough to give society a compelling interest in marrying off homosexuals.

34   There is no substitute. Marriage is the *only* institution that adequately serves these purposes. The power of marriage is not just legal but social. It seals its promise with the smiles and tears of family, friends and neighbors. It shrewdly exploits ceremony (big, public weddings) and money (expensive gifts, dowries) to deter casual commitment and to make bailing out embarrassing. Stag parties and bridal showers signal that what is beginning is not just a legal arrangement but a whole new stage of life. "Domestic partner" laws do none of these things.

35   I'll go further: far from being a substitute for the real thing, marriage-lite may undermine it. Marriage is a deal between a couple and society, not just between two people: society recognizes the sanctity and autonomy of the pair-bond, and in exchange each spouse commits to being the other's nurse, social worker and policeman of first resort. Each marriage is its own little society within society. Any step that weakens the deal by granting the legal benefits of marriage without also requiring the public commitment is begging for trouble.

36   So gay marriage makes sense for several of the same reasons that straight marriage makes sense. That would seem a natural place to stop. But the logic of the argument compels one to go a twist further. If it is good for society to have people attached, then it is not enough just to make marriage available. Marriage should also be *expected.* This, too, is just as true for homosexuals as for heterosexuals. So, if homosexuals are justified in expecting access to marriage, society is equally justified in expecting them to use it. I'm not saying that out-of-wedlock sex should be scandalous or that people should be coerced into marrying. The mechanisms of expectation are more subtle. When grandma cluck-clucks over a still-unmarried young man, or when mom says she wishes her little girl would settle down, she is expressing a strong and well-justified preference: one that is quietly echoed in a thousand ways throughout society and that produces subtle but important pressure to form and sustain unions. This is a good and necessary thing, and it will be as necessary for homosexuals as heterosexuals. If gay marriage is recognized, single gay people over a certain age should not be surprised when they are disapproved of or pitied. That is a vital part of what makes marriage work. It's stigma as social policy.

37   If marriage is to work it cannot be merely a "lifestyle option." It must be privileged. That is, it must be understood to be better, on average, than other ways of living. Not mandatory, not good where everything else is bad, but better: a general norm, rather than a personal taste. The biggest worry about gay marriage, I think, is that homosexuals might get it but then mostly not use it. Gay neglect of marriage wouldn't greatly erode the bonding power of heterosexual marriage (remember, homosexuals are only a tiny fraction of the population)—but it would certainly not help. And heterosexual society would rightly feel betrayed if, after legalization, homosexuals treated marriage as a minority taste rather than as a core institution of life. It is not enough, I think, for gay people to say we want the right to marry. If we do not use it, shame on us.

FOR CLASS DISCUSSION

1. Analyze and evaluate disagreements among these writers about the social value and legitimacy of same-sex marriage by applying the first set of guide questions from page 455. How do you account for the differing points of view?

2. Choose one of the arguments for closer analysis, applying the second set of guide questions on page 455–456.

Optional Writing Assignment   Imagine that you have to deliver a speech on the subject of same-sex marriage to a strongly resistant audience. (For example, imagine speaking in favor of same-sex marriage to a older, conservative audience; conversely, imagine speaking against same-sex marriage at a meeting of PFLAG [Parents and Friends of Lesbians and Gays].) Using the strategies of delayed thesis or Rogerian argument (see pages 182–185), develop a speech that attempts to lower the level of hostility to your ideas, reduce threat, highlight common ground, and promote a slight movement toward your position.

FAMILY VALUES, SINGLE PARENTHOOD, AND WELFARE REFORM*

Why I Hate "Family Values"
(Let Me Count the Ways)

Katha Pollitt

Unlike many of the commentators who have made Murphy Brown the most famous   1
unmarried mother since Ingrid Bergman ran off with Roberto Rossellini,† I actually watched the notorious childbirth episode. After reading my sleep-resistant 4-year-old her entire collection of Berenstain Bears books, television was all I was fit for. And that is how I know that I belong to the cultural elite: Not only can I spell "potato" correctly, and many other

---

*For additional arguments on these issues, see Charles Murray's "The Coming White Underclass" on pages 27–31 and Dorothy Gilliam's "Wrong Way to Reform Welfare" on pages 48–50.

†Primarily a reference to a speech delivered by then Vice President Dan Quayle during his last year in office. Quayle criticized sitcom heroine Murphy Brown's decision to have a child out of wedlock as an example of the dissolution of Judeo-Christian family values.

vegetables as well, I thought the show was a veritable riot of family values. First of all, Murph is smart, warm, playful, decent and rich: She'll be a great mom. Second, the dad is her ex-husband: The kid is as close to legitimate as the scriptwriters could manage, given that Murph is divorced. Third, her ex spurned *her*, not, as Dan Quayle implies, the other way around. Fourth, she rejected abortion. On TV, women have abortions only in docudramas, usually after being raped, drugged with birth-defect-inducing chemicals or put into a coma. Finally, what does Murph sing to the newborn? "You make me feel like a natural woman"! Even on the most feminist sitcom in TV history (if you take points off *Kate and Allie* for never so much as mentioning the word "gay"), anatomy is destiny.

2   That a show as fluffy and genial as *Murphy Brown* has touched off a national debate about "family values" speaks volumes—and not just about the apparent inability of Dan Quayle to distinguish real life from a sitcom. (And since when are TV writers part of the cultural elite, anyway? I thought they were the crowd-pleasing lowbrows, and *intellectuals* were the cultural elite.) The *Murphy Brown* debate, it turns out, isn't really about Murphy Brown; it's about inner-city women, who will be encouraged to produce fatherless babies by Murph's example—the trickle-down theory of values. (Do welfare moms watch *Murphy Brown*? I thought it was supposed to be soap operas, as in "they just sit around all day watching the soaps." Marriage is a major obsession on the soaps—but never mind.) Everybody, it seems, understood this substitution immediately. After all, why get upset about Baby Boy Brown? Is there any doubt that he will be safe, loved, well schooled, taken for checkups, taught to respect the rights and feelings of others and treated to *The Berenstain Bears Visit the Dentist* as often as his little heart desires? Unlike millions of kids who live with both parents, he will never be physically or sexually abused, watch his father beat his mother (domestic assault is the leading cause of injury to women) or cower beneath the blankets while his parents scream at each other. And chances are excellent that he won't sexually assault a retarded girl with a miniature baseball bat, like those high school athletes in posh Glen Ridge, New Jersey; or shoot his lover's spouse, like Amy Fisher; or find himself on trial for rape, like William Kennedy Smith—children of intact and prosperous families every one of them. He'll probably go to Harvard and major in semiotics. Maybe that's the problem. Just think, if Murph were married, like Dan Quayle's mom, he could go to DePauw University and major in golf.

3   That there is something called "the family"—Papa Bear, Mama Bear, Brother Bear and Sister Bear—that is the best setting for raising children, and that it is in trouble because of a decline in "values," are bromides accepted by commentators of all political stripes. The right blames a left-wing cultural conspiracy: obscene rock lyrics, sex ed, abortion, prayerless schools, working mothers, promiscuity, homosexuality, decline of respect for authority and hard work, welfare and, of course, feminism. (On the *Chicago Tribune* Op-Ed page, Allan Carlson, president of the ultraconservative Rockford Institute, found a previously overlooked villain: federal housing subsidies. With all that square footage lying around, singles and unhappy spouses could afford to live on their own.) The left blames the ideology of postindustrial capitalism: consumerism, individualism, selfishness, alienation, lack of social supports for parents and children, atrophied communities, welfare and feminism. The center agonizes over teen sex, welfare moms, crime and divorce, unsure what the causes are beyond some sort of moral failure—probably related to feminism. Interesting how that word keeps coming up.

I used to wonder what family values are. As a matter of fact, I still do. If abortion, according to the right, undermines family values, then single motherhood (as the producers of *Murphy Brown* were quick to point out) must be in accord with them, no? Over on the left, if gender equality, love and sexual expressivity are desirable features of contemporary marriage, then isn't marriage bound to be unstable, given how hard those things are to achieve and maintain? Not really.

4

Just say no, says the right. Try counseling, says the left. Don't be so lazy, says the center. Indeed, in its guilt-mongering cover story "Legacy of Divorce: How the Fear of Failure Haunts the Children of Broken Marriages," *Newsweek* was unable to come up with any explanation for the high American divorce rate except that people just didn't try hard enough to stay married.

5

When left, right and center agree, watch out. They probably don't know what they're talking about. And so it is with "the family" and "family values." In the first place, these terms lump together distinct social phenomena that in reality have virtually nothing to do with one another. The handful of fortysomething professionals like Murphy Brown who elect to have a child without a male partner have little in common with the millions of middle- and working-class divorced mothers who find themselves in desperate financial straits because their husbands fail to pay court-awarded child support. And neither category has much in common with inner-city girls like those a teacher friend of mine told me about the other day: a 13-year-old and a 12-year-old, impregnated by boyfriends twice their age and determined to bear and keep the babies—to spite abusive parents, to confirm their parents' low opinion of them, to have someone to love who loves them in return.

6

Beyond that, appeals to "the family" and its "values" frame the discussion as one about morals instead of consequences. In real life, for example, teen sex—the subject of endless sermons—has little relation with teen childbearing. That sounds counterfactual, but it's true. Western European teens have sex about as early and as often as American ones, but are much less likely to have babies. Partly it's because there are far fewer European girls whose lives are as marked by hopelessness and brutality as those of my friend's students. And partly it's because European youth have much better access to sexual information, birth control and abortion. Or consider divorce. In real life, parents divorce for all kinds of reasons, not because they lack moral fiber and are heedless of their children's needs. Indeed, many divorce because they *do* consider their kids, and the poisonous effects of growing up in a household marked by violence, craziness, open verbal warfare or simple lovelessness.

7

Perhaps this is the place to say that I come to the family-values debate with a personal bias. I am recently separated myself. I think my husband and I would fall under *Newsweek*'s "didn't try harder" rubric, although we thought about splitting up for years, discussed it for almost a whole additional year and consulted no fewer than four therapists, including a marital counselor who advised us that marriage was one of modern mankind's only means of self-transcendence (religion and psychoanalysis were the others, which should have warned me) and admonished us that we risked a future of shallow relationships if we shirked our spiritual mission, not to mention the damage we would "certainly" inflict on our daughter. I thought he was a jackass—shallow relationships? *moi?* But he got to me. Because our marriage wasn't some flaming disaster—with broken dishes and hitting and strange hotel

8

charges showing up on the MasterCard bill. It was just unhappy, in ways that weren't going to change. Still, I think both of us would have been willing to trudge on to spare our child suffering. That's what couples do in women's magazines; that's what the Clintons say they did. But we saw it wouldn't work: As our daughter got older, she would see right through us, the way kids do. And, worse, no matter how hard I tried to put on a happy face, I would wordlessly communicate to her—whose favorite fairy tale is "Cinderella," and whose favorite game is Wedding, complete with bath-towel bridal veil—my resentment and depression and cynicism about relations between the sexes.

9   The family-values types would doubtless say that my husband and I made a selfish choice, which society should have impeded or even prevented. There's a growing sentiment in policy land to make divorce more difficult. In *When the Bough Breaks,* Sylvia Ann Hewlett argues that couples should be forced into therapy (funny how ready people are to believe that counseling, which even when voluntary takes years to modify garden-variety neuroses, can work wonders in months with resistant patients who hate each other). Christopher Lasch briefly supported a constitutional amendment forbidding divorce to couples with minor children, as if lack of a separation agreement would keep people living together (he's backed off that position, he told me recently). The Communitarians, who flood *The Nation*'s mailboxes with self-promoting worryfests, furrow their brows wondering "How can the family be saved without forcing women to stay at home or otherwise violating their rights?" (Good luck.) But I am still waiting for someone to explain why it would be better for my daughter to grow up in a joyless household than for her to live as she does now, with two reasonably cheerful parents living around the corner from each other, both committed to her support and cooperating, as they say on *Sesame Street,* in her care. We may not love each other, but we both love her. Maybe that's as much as parents can do for their children, and all that should be asked of them.

10   But, of course, civilized cooperation is exactly what many divorced parents find they cannot manage. The statistics on deadbeat and vanishing dads are shocking—less than half pay child support promptly and in full, and around half seldom or never see their kids within a few years of marital breakup. Surely, some of this male abdication can be explained by the very thinness of the traditional paternal role worshiped by the preachers of "values"; it's little more than bread-winning, discipline and fishing trips. How many diapers, after all, has Dan Quayle changed? A large percentage of American fathers have never changed a single one. Maybe the reason so many fathers fade away after divorce is that they were never really there to begin with.

11   It is true that people's ideas about marriage are not what they were in the 1950s—although those who look back at the fifties nostalgically forget both that many of those marriages were miserable and that the fifties were an atypical decade in more than a century of social change. Married women have been moving steadily into the work force since 1890; beginning even earlier, families have been getting smaller; divorce has been rising; sexual activity has been initiated even earlier and marriage delayed; companionate marriage has been increasingly accepted as desirable by all social classes and both sexes. It may be that these trends have reached a tipping point, at which they come to define a new norm. Few men expect to marry virgins, and children are hardly "stigmatized" by divorce, as they might

have been a mere fifteen or twenty years ago. But if people want different things from family life—if women, as Arlie Hochschild pointed out in *The Second Shift,* cite as a major reason for separation the failure of their husbands to share domestic labor; if both sexes are less willing to resign themselves to a marriage devoid of sexual pleasure, intimacy or shared goals; if single women decide they want to be mothers; if teenagers want to sleep together—why shouldn't society adapt? Society is, after all, just us. Nor are these developments unique to the United States. All over the industrialized world, divorce rates are high, single women are having babies by choice, homosexuals are coming out of the closet and infidelity, always much more common than anyone wanted to recognize, is on the rise. Indeed, in some ways America is behind the rest of the West: We still go to church, unlike the British, the French and, now that Franco is out of the way, the Spanish. More religious than Spain! Imagine.

I'm not saying that these changes are without cost—in poverty, loneliness, insecurity and stress. The reasons for this suffering, however, lie not in moral collapse but in our failure to acknowledge and adjust to changing social relations. 12

We still act as if mothers stayed home with children, wives didn't need to work, and men earned a "family wage." We'd rather preach about teenage "promiscuity" than teach young people—especially young women—how to negotiate sexual issues responsibly. If my friend's students had been prepared for puberty by schools and discussion groups and health centers, the way Dutch young people are, they might not have ended up pregnant, victims of what is, after all, statutory rape. And if women earned a dollar for every dollar earned by men, divorce and single parenthood would not mean poverty. Nobody worries about single fathers raising children, after all; indeed, paternal custody is the latest legal fad. 13

What is the point of trying to put the new wine of modern personal relations in the old bottles of the sexual double standard and indissoluble marriage? For that is what most of the current discourse on "family issues" amounts to. No matter how fallacious, the culture greets moralistic approaches to these subjects with instant agreement. Judith Wallerstein's travesty of social science, *Second Chances,* asserts that children are emotionally traumatized by divorce, and the fact that she had no control group is simply ignored by an ecstatic press. As it happens, a recent study in *Science* did use a control group. By following 17,000 children for four years, and comparing those whose parents split with those whose parents stayed in troubled marriages, the researchers found that the "divorce effect" disappeared entirely for boys and was very small for girls. Not surprisingly, this study attracted absolutely no attention. 14

Similarly, we are quick to blame poor unmarried mothers for all manner of social problems—crime, unemployment, drops in reading scores, teen suicide. The solution? Cut off all welfare for additional children. Force teen mothers to live with their parents. Push women to marry in order to attach them to a male income. (So much for love—talk about marriage as legalized prostitution!) 15

New Jersey's new welfare reform law gives economic coercion a particularly bizarre twist. Welfare moms who marry can keep part of their dole, but only if the man is *not* the father of their children. The logic is that, married or not, Dad has a financial obligation to his kids, but Mr. Just Got Into Town does not. If the law's inventors are right that welfare policy can micromanage marital and reproductive choice, they have just guaranteed that no poor woman will marry her children's father. This is strengthening the family? 16

17   Charles Murray, of the American Enterprise Institute, thinks New Jersey does not go far enough. Get rid of welfare entirely, he argued in *The New York Times:* Mothers should marry or starve, and if they are foolish enough to prefer the latter, their kids should be put up for adoption or into orphanages. Mickey Kaus, who favors compulsory low-wage employment for the poor, likes orphanages too.

18   None of those punitive approaches will work. There is no evidence that increased poverty decreases family size, and welfare moms aren't likely to meet many men with family-sized incomes, or they'd probably be married already, though maybe not for long. The men who impregnated those seventh graders, for example, are much more likely to turn them out as prostitutes than to lead them to the altar. For one thing, those men may well be married themselves.

19   The fact is, the harm connected with the dissolution of "the family" is not a problem of values—at least not individual values—it's a problem of money. When the poor are abandoned to their fates, when there are no jobs, people don't get to display "work ethic," don't feel good about themselves and don't marry or stay married. The girls don't have anything to postpone motherhood for; the boys have no economic prospects that would make them reasonable marriage partners. This was as true in the slums of eighteenth-century London as it is today in the urban slums of Latin America and Africa, as well as the United States. Or take divorce: The real harm of divorce is that it makes lots of women, and their children, poor. One reason, which has got a fair amount of attention recently, is the scandalously low level of child support, plus the tendency of courts to award a disproportionate share of the marital assets to the man. The other reason is that women earn much less than men, thanks to gender discrimination and the failure of the workplace to adapt to the needs of working mothers. Instead of moaning about "family values" we should be thinking about how to provide the poor with decent jobs and social services, and about how to insure economic justice for working women. And let marriage take care of itself.

20   Family values and the cult of the nuclear family is, at bottom, just another way to bash women, especially poor women. If only they would get married and stay married, society's ills would vanish. Inner-city crime would disappear because fathers would communicate manly values to their sons, which would cause jobs to spring up like mushrooms after rain. Welfare would fade away. Children would do well in school. (Irene Impellizeri, anti-condom vice president of the New York City Board of Education, recently gave a speech attributing inner-city children's poor grades and high dropout rates to the failure of their families to provide "moral models," the way immigrant parents did in the good old days—a dangerous argument for her, in particular, to make; doesn't she know that Italian-American kids have dropout and failure rates only slightly lower than black and Latino teens?)

21   When pundits preach morality, I often find myself thinking of Samuel Johnson, literature's greatest enemy of cant and fatuity. What would the eighteenth-century moralist make of our current obsession with marriage? "Sir," he replied to Boswell, who held that marriage was a natural state, "it is so far from being natural for a man and woman to live in the state of marriage that we find all the motives which they have for remaining in that connection, and the restraints which civilized society imposes to prevent separation, are hardly sufficient to keep them together." Dr. Johnson knew what he was talking about: He and his wife lived apart. And what would he think of our confusion of moral preachments with prac-

tical solutions to social problems? Remember his response to Mrs. Thrale's long and flowery speech on the cost of children's clothes. "Nay, madam," he said, "when you are declaiming, declaim; and when you are calculating, calculate."

Which is it going to be? Declamation, which feeds no children, employs no jobless and   22
reduces gender relations to an economic bargain? Or calculation, which accepts the fact that the Berenstain Bears, like Murphy Brown, are fiction. The people seem to be voting with their feet on "the family." It's time for our "values" to catch up.

Abolishing Welfare Won't
Stop Poverty, Illegitimacy

Elija Anderson

Those who have been calling recently for an end to welfare, seeing this as a way of   1
solving poverty and illegitimacy, are wrong. Eliminating the program would only make things much worse. As an ethnographer and sociologist who has worked in poor, inner-city neighborhoods, I welcome the debate and the search for solutions to these problems. But the proposals to abolish welfare outright espoused by such people as syndicated columnist Charles Krauthammer and Charles Murray are dangerously shortsighted.

Krauthammer, in fact, cites my research in one inner-city neighborhood in support of his   2
thinking. Since welfare provides economic support to illegitimate babies and their mothers—a fact of inner-city life my research has indeed shown to be one consideration in the sexual game that leads to illegitimate births—he argues that eliminating welfare will eliminate the interest in having babies. This reasoning is seriously flawed precisely because it ignores all the other considerations bearing down on inner-city adolescents, thereby exaggerating the role played by welfare.

In "Sex Codes and Family Life Among Poor Inner-City Youths," a chapter in my book   3
"Streetwise," I describe ethnographically the perspectives and experiences of young black men and women in one community.

I found that the lack of family-sustaining jobs denies many young men the possibility   4
of forming an economically self-reliant family, the traditional American mark of manhood. Partially in response, the young men's peer groups emphasize sexual prowess as a sign of manhood, with babies as evidence. A sexual game emerges as girls are lured by the (usually older) boys' vague but convincing promises of love and marriage. When the girls submit, they often end up pregnant and abandoned. I also noted that these new mothers become eligible for a limited but steady welfare income that may allow them to establish their own households and at times attract other men who need money. But it is simplistic and wrongheaded to suggest that if you stop welfare, you will stop this behavior. A fundamental question is: Why do people behave in the ways I have described?

A significant part of the answer is: because of the unraveling of the economy in their   5
communities, which results in hopelessness. The lack of responsibility shown by the men, the "wantonness," is exacerbated by the very bad economic conditions—the exodus of jobs

and the inability of people to get the jobs still available because of a lack of education, skills and training.

6   Illegitimacy is not caused by welfare, but it is, in part, an outgrowth of the failure of the welfare system to achieve its purpose—to alleviate the human problems inherent in the vicissitudes of capitalism, enabling people temporarily (according to theory) displaced by changes in the economic marketplace to survive. Yet I see that what so many people in the inner city are up against are, in fact, the vicissitudes of the economy and an economy now global in scope that has left them behind.

7   The situation I describe in the "Sex Codes" chapter springs from alienation and despair—which then creates nihilism. This is born of a lack of hope and the inability to form a positive view of the future. So many of the young men I got to know don't get married because they don't feel they can "play house." What they mean is they can't play the roles of men in families in the way they would like.

8   Their assumption is that men in middle- and upper-class families that they see as models control their households. To be that upstanding husband and father, you need resources, you need money. Facing persistent discrimination, a lot of the men I interviewed believe they can't get the money, can't get the family-sustaining jobs. This has a profound impact on how they see their future.

9   As we move from a manufacturing to a service and high-tech economy, great numbers of inner-city poor people are not making an effective adjustment to the change. The service jobs they are able to obtain often don't pay them enough money to live, and so some of the most enterprising young people have opted for the underground economy of drugs and crime. One of the results is the social disorganization that contributes not only to increasing violence and alienation but also to a syndrome of abuse, in which people are bent on getting what they can out of other people—including sex and money—without any real concern for those they victimize.

10   Buffeted by the global economy, communities such as this one find themselves with fewer and fewer dependable sources of capital. Welfare is one relatively small but reliable source. To eliminate welfare is to destroy an important source of capital in the community. If welfare suddenly ceased to exist, many people would be forced to look elsewhere for resources. Some would seek the low-paying jobs available, but the hard reality is that others would be driven to more desperate measures. The nihilism that you now see among inner-city people would only increase and spread further beyond the bounds of ghetto communities. Cities would become almost unlivable. Blacks would continue to be the primary victims, though; illegitimacy rates would rise, not diminish.

11   The welfare system is in need of an overhaul, but it does not follow that we should throw meager income supports overboard. We need to maintain the support at the same time that we create opportunity for independent income. The way to make real headway is to create jobs and job opportunities and build hope through education and job training.

12   When a sense of the future exists, we will see more responsible behavior, sexual and otherwise. To take welfare away without replacing it with such opportunities would effectively remove a lifeline for the very poor but also what has become a safety valve protecting both inner-city communities and the rest of society from the consequences of steadily escalating frustration.

Dan Quayle Was Right

Barbara Dafoe Whitehead

Divorce and out-of-wedlock childbirth are transforming the lives of American children.   1
In the postwar generation more than 80 percent of children grew up in a family with two
biological parents who were married to each other. By 1980 only 50 percent could expect
to spend their entire childhood in an intact family. If current trends continue, less than half
of all children born today will live continuously with their own mother and father throughout childhood. Most American children will spend several years in a single-mother family.
Some will eventually live in stepparent families, but because stepfamilies are more likely to
break up than intact (by which I mean two-biological-parent) families, an increasing number of children will experience family breakup two or even three times during childhood.

According to a growing body of social-scientific evidence, children in families disrupted   2
by divorce and out-of-wedlock birth do worse than children in intact families on several
measures of well-being. Children in single-parent families are six times as likely to be poor.
They are also likely to stay poor longer. Twenty-two percent of children in one-parent families will experience poverty during childhood for seven years or more, as compared with
only two percent of children in two-parent families. A 1988 survey by the National Center
for Health Statistics found that children in single-parent families are two to three times as
likely as children in two-parent families to have emotional and behavioral problems. They
are also more likely to drop out of high school, to get pregnant as teenagers, to abuse drugs,
and to be in trouble with the law. Compared with children in intact families, children from
disrupted families are at a much higher risk for physical or sexual abuse.

Contrary to popular belief, many children do not "bounce back" after divorce or re-   3
marriage. Difficulties that are associated with family breakup often persist into adulthood.
Children who grow up in single-parent or stepparent families are less successful as adults,
particularly in the two domains of life—love and work—that are most essential to happiness. Needless to say, not all children experience such negative effects. However, research
shows that many children from disrupted families have a harder time achieving intimacy in
a relationship, forming a stable marriage, or even holding a steady job.

Despite this growing body of evidence, it is nearly impossible to discuss changes in   4
family structure without provoking angry protest. Many people see the discussion as no
more than an attack on struggling single mothers and their children: Why blame single
mothers when they are doing the very best they can? After all, the decision to end a marriage or a relationship is wrenching, and few parents are indifferent to the painful burden
this decision imposes on their children. Many take the perilous step toward single parenthood as a last resort, after their best efforts to hold a marriage together have failed. Consequently, it can seem particularly cruel and unfeeling to remind parents of the hardships
their children might suffer as a result of family breakup. Other people believe that the dramatic changes in family structure, though regrettable, are impossible to reverse. Family
breakup is an inevitable feature of American life, and anyone who thinks otherwise is in-
dulging in nostalgia or trying to turn back the clock. Since these new family forms are here

to stay, the reasoning goes, we must accord respect to single parents, not criticize them. Typical is the view expressed by a Brooklyn woman in a recent letter to *The New York Times:* "Let's stop moralizing or blaming single parents and unwed mothers, and give them the respect they have earned and the support they deserve."

5   Such views are not to be dismissed. Indeed, they help to explain why family structure is such an explosive issue for Americans. The debate about it is not simply about the social-scientific evidence, although that is surely an important part of the discussion. It is also a debate over deeply held and often conflicting values. How do we begin to reconcile our long-standing belief in equality and diversity with an impressive body of evidence that suggests that not all family structures produce equal outcomes for children? How can we square traditional notions of public support for dependent women and children with a belief in women's right to pursue autonomy and independence in childbearing and child-rearing? How do we uphold the freedom of adults to pursue individual happiness in their private relationships and at the same time respond to the needs of children for stability, security, and permanence in their family lives? What do we do when the interests of adults and children conflict? These are the difficult issues at stake in the debate over family structure.

6   In the past these issues have turned out to be too difficult and too politically risky for debate. In the mid-1960s Daniel Patrick Moynihan, then an assistant secretary of labor, was denounced as a racist for calling attention to the relationship between the prevalence of black single-mother families and the lower socioeconomic standing of black children. For nearly twenty years the policy and research communities backed away from the entire issue. In 1980 the Carter Administration convened a historic White House Conference on Families, designed to address the growing problems of children and families in America. The result was a prolonged, publicly subsidized quarrel over the definition of "family." No President since has tried to hold a national family conference. Last year, at a time when the rate of out-of-wedlock births had reached a historic high, Vice President Dan Quayle was ridiculed for criticizing Murphy Brown. In short, every time the issue of family structure has been raised, the response has been first controversy, then retreat, and finally silence.

7   Yet it is also risky to ignore the issue of changing family structure. In recent years the problems associated with family disruption have grown. Overall child well-being has declined, despite a decrease in the number of children per family, an increase in the educational level of parents, and historically high levels of public spending. After dropping in the 1960s and 1970s, the proportion of children in poverty has increased dramatically, from 15 percent in 1970 to 20 percent in 1990, while the percentage of adult Americans in poverty has remained roughly constant. The teen suicide rate has more than tripled. Juvenile crime has increased and become more violent. School performance has continued to decline. There are no signs that these trends are about to reverse themselves.

8   If we fail to come to terms with the relationship between family structure and declining child well-being, then it will be increasingly difficult to improve children's life prospects, no matter how many new programs the federal government funds. Nor will we be able to make progress in bettering school performance or reducing crime or improving the quality of the nation's future work force—all domestic problems closely connected to family break up. Worse, we may contribute to the problem by pursuing policies that actually increase family instability and breakup.

FROM DEATH TO DIVORCE

Across time and across cultures, family disruption has been regarded as an event that 9
threatens a child's well-being and even survival. This view is rooted in a fundamental biological fact: unlike the young of almost any other species, the human child is born in an ab-
jectly helpless and immature state. Years of nurture and protection are needed before the
child can achieve physical independence. Similarly, it takes years of interaction with at least
one but ideally two or more adults for a child to develop into a socially competent adult.
Children raised in virtual isolation from human beings, though physically intact, display few
recognizably human behaviors. The social arrangement that has proved most successful in
ensuring the physical survival and promoting the social development of the child is the family unit of the biological mother and father. Consequently, any event that permanently denies a child the presence and protection of a parent jeopardizes the life of the child.

The classic form of family disruption is the death of a parent. Throughout history this 10
has been one of the risks of childhood. Mothers frequently died in childbirth, and it was
not unusual for both parents to die before the child was grown. As recently as the early
decades of this century children commonly suffered the death of at least one parent. Almost
a quarter of the children born in this country in 1900 lost one parent by the time they were
fifteen years old. Many of these children lived with their widowed parent, often in a household with other close relatives. Others grew up in orphanages and foster homes.

The meaning of parental death, as it has been transmitted over time and faithfully 11
recorded in world literature and lore, is unambiguous and essentially unchanging. It is universally regarded as an untimely and tragic event. Death permanently severs the parent-
child bond, disrupting forever one of the child's earliest and deepest human attachments.
It also deprives a child of the presence and protection of an adult who has a biological stake
in, as well as an emotional commitment to, the child's survival and well-being. In short, the
death of a parent is the most extreme and severe loss a child can suffer.

Because a child is so vulnerable in a parent's absence, there has been a common cultural 12
response to the death of a parent: an outpouring of support from family, friends, and strangers
alike. The surviving parent and child are united in their grief as well as their loss. Relatives
and friends share in the loss and provide valuable emotional and financial assistance to the
bereaved family. Other members of the community show sympathy for the child, and public assistance is available for those who need it. This cultural understanding of parental
death has formed the basis for a tradition of public support to widows and their children.
Indeed, as recently as the beginning of this century widows were the only mothers eligible
for pensions in many states, and today widows with children receive more-generous welfare benefits from Survivors Insurance than do other single mothers with children who depend on Aid to Families With Dependent Children.

It has taken thousands upon thousands of years to reduce the threat of parental death. 13
Not until the middle of the twentieth century did parental death cease to be a commonplace event for children in the United States. By then advances in medicine had dramatically reduced mortality rates for men and women.

At the same time, other forms of family disruption—separation, divorce, out-of-wedlock 14
birth—were held in check by powerful religious, social, and legal sanctions. Divorce was

widely regarded both as a deviant behavior, especially threatening to mothers and children, and as a personal lapse: "Divorce is the public acknowledgment of failure," a 1940s sociology textbook noted. Out-of-wedlock birth was stigmatized, and stigmatization is a powerful means of regulating behavior, as any smoker or overeater will testify. Sanctions against nonmarital childbirth discouraged behavior that hurt children and exacted compensatory behavior that helped them. Shotgun marriages and adoption, two common responses to nonmarital birth, carried a strong message about the risks of premarital sex and created an intact family for the child.

15   Consequently, children did not have to worry much about losing a parent through divorce or never having had one because of nonmarital birth. After a surge in divorces following the Second World War, the rate leveled off. Only 11 percent of children born in the 1950s would by the time they turned eighteen see their parents separate or divorce. Out-of-wedlock childbirth barely figured as a cause of family disruption. In the 1950s and early 1960s, five percent of the nation's births were out of wedlock. Blacks were more likely than whites to bear children outside marriage, but the majority of black children born in the twenty years after the Second World War were born to married couples. The rate of family disruption reached a historic low point during those years.

16   A new standard of family security and stability was established in postwar America. For the first time in history the vast majority of the nation's children could expect to live with married biological parents throughout childhood. Children might still suffer other forms of adversity—poverty, racial discrimination, lack of educational opportunity—but only a few would be deprived of the nurture and protection of a mother and a father. No longer did children have to be haunted by the classic fears vividly dramatized in folklore and fable— that their parents would die, that they would have to live with a stepparent and stepsiblings, or that they would be abandoned. These were the years when the nation confidently boarded up orphanages and closed foundling hospitals, certain that such institutions would never again be needed. In movie theaters across the country parents and children could watch the drama of parental separation and death in the great Disney classics, secure in the knowledge that such nightmare visions as the death of Bambi's mother and the wrenching separation of Dumbo from his mother were only make-believe.

17   In the 1960s the rate of family disruption suddenly began to rise. After inching up over the course of a century, the divorce rate soared. Throughout the 1950s and early 1960s the divorce rate held steady at fewer than ten divorces a year per 1,000 married couples. Then, beginning in about 1965, the rate increased sharply, peaking at twenty-three divorces per 1,000 marriages by 1979. (In 1974 divorce passed death as the leading cause of family breakup.) The rate has leveled off at about twenty-one divorces per 1,000 marriages—the figure for 1991. The out-of-wedlock birth rate also jumped. It went from five percent in 1960 to 27 percent in 1990. In 1990 close to 57 percent of births among black mothers were nonmarital, and about 17 percent among white mothers. Altogether, about one out of every four women who had a child in 1990 was not married. With rates of divorce and nonmarital birth so high, family disruption is at its peak. Never before have so many children experienced family breakup caused by events other than death. Each year a million children go through divorce or separation and almost as many more are born out of wedlock.

Half of all marriages now end in divorce. Following divorce, many people enter new relationships. Some begin living together. Nearly half of all cohabiting couples have children in the household. Fifteen percent have new children together. Many cohabiting couples eventually get married. However, both cohabiting and remarried couples are more likely to break up than couples in first marriages. Even social scientists find it hard to keep pace with the complexity and velocity of such patterns. In the revised edition (1992) of his book *Marriage, Divorce, Remarriage,* the sociologist Andrew Cherlin ruefully comments: "If there were a truth-in-labeling law for books, the title of this edition should be something long and unwieldy like *Cohabitation, Marriage, Divorce, More Cohabitation, and Probably Remarriage.*"   18

Under such conditions growing up can be a turbulent experience. In many single-parent families children must come to terms with the parent's love life and romantic partners. Some children live with cohabiting couples, either their own unmarried parents or a biological parent and a live-in partner. Some children born to cohabiting parents see their parents break up. Others see their parents marry, but 56 percent of them (as compared with 31 percent of the children born to married parents) later see their parents' marriages fall apart. All told, about three quarters of children born to cohabiting couples will live in a single-parent home at least briefly. One of every four children growing up in the 1990s will eventually enter a stepfamily. According to one survey, nearly half of all children in stepparent families will see their parents divorce again by the time they reach their late teens. Since 80 percent of divorced fathers remarry, things get even more complicated when the romantic or marital history of the noncustodial parent, usually the father, is taken into account. Consequently, as it affects a significant number of children, family disruption is best understood not as a single event but as a string of disruptive events: separation, divorce, life in a single-parent family, life with a parent and live-in lover, the remarriage of one or both parents, life in one stepparent family combined with visits to another stepparent family; the breakup of one or both stepparent families. And so on. This is one reason why public schools have a hard time knowing whom to call in an emergency.   19

Given its dramatic impact on children's lives, one might reasonably expect that this historic level of family disruption would be viewed with alarm, even regarded as a national crisis. Yet this has not been the case. In recent years some people have argued that these trends pose a serious threat to children and to the nation as a whole, but they are dismissed as declinists, pessimists, or nostalgists, unwilling or unable to accept the new facts of life. The dominant view is that the changes in family structure are, on balance, positive.   20

There are several reasons why this is so, but the fundamental reason is that at some point in the 1970s Americans changed their minds about the meaning of these disruptive behaviors. What had once been regarded as hostile to children's best interests was now considered essential to adults' happiness. In the 1950s most Americans believed that parents should stay in an unhappy marriage for the sake of the children. The assumption was that a divorce would damage the children, and the prospect of such damage gave divorce its meaning. By the mid-1970s a majority of Americans rejected that view. Popular advice literature reflected the shift. A book on divorce published in the mid-1940s tersely asserted: "Children are entitled to the affection and *association* of two parents, not one." Thirty years later another popular divorce   21 book proclaimed just the opposite: "A two-parent home is not the only emotional structure within which a child can be happy and healthy. . . . The parents who take care of themselves will be best able to take care of their children." At about the same time, the long-standing taboo against out-of-wedlock childbirth also collapsed. By the mid-1970s three fourths of Americans said that it was not morally wrong for a woman to have a child outside marriage.

22   Once the social metric shifts from child well-being to adult well-being, it is hard to see divorce and nonmarital birth in anything but a positive light. However distressing and difficult they may be, both of these behaviors can hold out the promise of greater adult choice, freedom, and happiness. For unhappy spouses, divorce offers a way to escape a troubled or even abusive relationship and make a fresh start. For single parents, remarriage is a second try at marital happiness as well as a chance for relief from the stress, loneliness, and economic hardship of raising a child alone. For some unmarried women, nonmarital birth is a way to beat the biological clock, avoid marrying the wrong man, and experience the pleasures of motherhood. Moreover, divorce and out-of-wedlock birth involve a measure of agency and choice; they are man- and woman-made events. To be sure, not everyone exercises choice in divorce or nonmarital birth. Men leave wives for younger women, teenage girls get pregnant accidentally—yet even these unhappy events reflect the expansion of the boundaries of freedom and choice.

23   This cultural shift helps explain what otherwise would be inexplicable: the failure to see the rise in family disruption as a severe and troubling national problem. It explains why there is virtually no widespread public sentiment for restigmatizing either of these classically disruptive behaviors and no sense—no public consensus—that they can or should be avoided in the future. On the contrary, the prevailing opinion is that we should accept the changes in family structure as inevitable and devise new forms of public and private support for single-parent families.

24   With its affirmation of the liberating effects of divorce and nonmarital childbirth, this opinion is a fixture of American popular culture today. Madison Avenue and Hollywood did not invent these behaviors, as their highly paid publicists are quick to point out, but they have played an influential role in defending and even celebrating divorce and unwed motherhood. More precisely, they have taken the raw material of demography and fashioned it into a powerful fantasy of individual renewal and rebirth. Consider, for example, the teaser for *People* magazine's cover story on Joan Lunden's divorce: "After the painful end of her 13-year marriage, the *Good Morning America* cohost is discovering a new life as a single mother—and as her own woman." *People* does not dwell on the anguish Lunden and her children might have experienced over the breakup of their family, or the difficulties of single motherhood, even for celebrity mothers. Instead, it celebrates Joan Lunden's steps toward independence and a better life. *People,* characteristically, focuses on her shopping: in the first weeks after her breakup Lunden leased "a brand-new six-bedroom, 8,000 square foot" house and then went to Bloomingdale's, where she scooped up sheets, pillows, a toaster, dishes, seven televisions, and roomfuls of fun furniture that was "totally unlike the serious traditional pieces she was giving up."

25   This is not just the view taken in supermarket magazines. Even the conservative bastion of the greeting-card industry, Hallmark, offers a line of cards commemorating divorce

as liberation. "Think of your former marriage as a record album," says one Contemporary card. "It was full of music—both happy and sad. But what's important now is . . . YOU! the recently released HOT, NEW, SINGLE! You're going to be at the TOP OF THE CHARTS!" Another card reads: "Getting divorced can be very healthy! Watch how it improves your circulation! Best of luck! . . ." Hallmark's hip Shoebox Greetings division depicts two female praying mantises. Mantis One: "It's tough being a single parent." Mantis Two: "Yeah . . . Maybe we shouldn't have eaten our husbands."

Divorce is a tired convention in Hollywood, but unwed parenthood is very much in fashion: in the past year or so babies were born to Warren Beatty and Annette Bening, Jack Nicholson and Rebecca Broussard, and Eddie Murphy and Nicole Mitchell. *Vanity Fair* celebrated Jack Nicholson's fatherhood with a cover story (April, 1992) called "Happy Jack." What made Jack happy, it turned out, was no-fault fatherhood. He and Broussard, the twenty-nine-year-old mother of his children, lived in separate houses. Nicholson said, "It's an unusual arrangement, but the last twenty-five years or so have shown me that I'm not good at cohabitation. . . . I see Rebecca as much as any other person who is cohabiting. And *she* prefers it. I think most people would in a more honest and truthful world." As for more-permanent commitments, the man who is not good at cohabitation said: "I don't discuss marriage much with Rebecca. Those discussions are the very thing I'm trying to avoid. I'm after this immediate real thing. That's all I believe in." (Perhaps Nicholson should have had the discussion. Not long after the story appeared, Broussard broke off the relationship.)   26

As this story shows, unwed parenthood is thought of not only as a way to find happiness but also as a way to exhibit such virtues as honesty and courage. A similar argument was offered in defense of Murphy Brown's unwed motherhood. Many of Murphy's fans were quick to point out that Murphy suffered over her decision to bear a child out of wedlock. Faced with an accidental pregnancy and a faithless love, she agonized over her plight and, after much mental anguish, bravely decided to go ahead. In short, having a baby without a husband represented a higher level of maternal devotion and sacrifice than having a baby with a husband. Murphy was not just exercising her rights as a woman; she was exhibiting true moral heroism.   27

On the night Murphy Brown became an unwed mother, 34 million Americans tuned in, and CBS posted a 35 percent share of the audience. The show did not stir significant protest at the grass roots and lost none of its advertisers. The actress Candice Bergen subsequently appeared on the cover of nearly every women's and news magazine in the country and received an honorary degree at the University of Pennsylvania as well as an Emmy award. The show's creator, Diane English, popped up in Hanes stocking ads. Judged by conventional measures of approval, Murphy Brown's motherhood was a hit at the box office.   28

Increasingly, the media depicts the married two-parent family as a source of pathology. According to a spate of celebrity memoirs and interviews, the married-parent family harbors terrible secrets of abuse, violence, and incest. A bumper sticker I saw in Amherst, Massachusetts, read UNSPOKEN TRADITIONAL FAMILY VALUES: ABUSE, ALCOHOLISM, INCEST. The pop therapist John Bradshaw explains away this generation's problems with the dictum that 96 percent of families are dysfunctional, made that way by the addicted society we live in. David Lynch creates a new aesthetic of creepiness by juxtaposing scenes of traditional family life with images of seduction and perversion. A Boston-area museum puts on an exhibit   29 called "Goodbye to Apple Pie," featuring several artists' visions of child abuse, including one mixed-media piece with knives poking through a little girl's skirt. The piece is titled *Father Knows Best.*

30   No one would claim that two-parent families are free from conflict, violence, or abuse. However, the attempt to discredit the two-parent family can be understood as part of what Daniel Patrick Moynihan has described as a larger effort to accommodate higher levels of social deviance. "The amount of deviant behavior in American society has increased beyond the levels the community can 'afford to recognize,' " Moynihan argues. One response has been to normalize what was once considered deviant behavior, such as out-of-wedlock birth. An accompanying response has been to detect deviance in what once stood as a social norm, such as the married-couple family. Together these responses reduce the acknowledged levels of deviance by eroding earlier distinctions between the normal and the deviant.

31   Several recent studies describe family life in its postwar heyday as the seedbed of alcoholism and abuse. According to Stephanie Coontz, the author of the book *The Way We Never Were: American Families and the Nostalgia Trap,* family life for married mothers in the 1950s consisted of "booze, bowling, bridge, and boredom." Coontz writes: "Few would have guessed that radiant Marilyn Van Derbur, crowned Miss America in 1958, had been sexually violated by her wealthy, respectable father from the time she was five until she was eighteen, when she moved away to college." Even the budget-stretching casserole comes under attack as a sign of culinary dysfunction. According to one food writer, this homely staple of postwar family life brings back images of "the good mother of the 50's . . . locked in Ozzie and Harriet land, unable to move past the canvas of a Corning Ware dish, the palette of a can of Campbell's soup, the mushy dominion of which she was queen."

32   Nevertheless, the popular portrait of family life does not simply reflect the views of a cultural elite, as some have argued. There is strong support at the grass roots for much of this view of family change. Survey after survey shows that Americans are less inclined than they were a generation ago to value sexual fidelity, lifelong marriage, and parenthood as worthwhile personal goals. Motherhood no longer defines adult womanhood, as everyone knows; equally important is the fact that fatherhood has declined as a norm for men. In 1976 less than half as many fathers as in 1957 said that providing for children was a life goal. The proportion of working men who found marriage and children burdensome and restrictive more than doubled in the same period. Fewer than half of all adult Americans today regard the idea of sacrifice for others as a positive moral virtue.

33   It is true that many adults benefit from divorce or remarriage. According to one study, nearly 80 percent of divorced women and 50 percent of divorced men say they are better off out of the marriage. Half of divorced adults in the same study report greater happiness. A competent self-help book called *Divorce and New Beginnings* notes the advantages of single parenthood: single parents can "develop their own interests, fulfill their own needs, choose their own friends and engage in social activities of their choice. Money, even if limited, can be spent as they see fit." Apparently, some women appreciate the opportunity to have children out of wedlock. "The real world, however, does not always allow women who are dedicated to their careers to devote the time and energy it takes to find— or be found by—the perfect husband and father wanna-be," one woman said in a letter to

The Washington Post. A mother and chiropractor from Avon, Connecticut, explained her unwed maternity to an interviewer this way: "It is selfish, but this was something I needed to do for me."

There is very little in contemporary popular culture to contradict this optimistic view. But in a few small places another perspective may be found. Several racks down from its divorce cards, Hallmark offers a line of cards for children—To Kids With Love. These cards come six to a pack. Each card in the pack has a slightly different message. According to the package, the "thinking of you" messages will let a special kid "know how much you care." Though Hallmark doesn't quite say so, it's clear these cards are aimed at divorced parents. "I'm sorry I'm not always there when you need me but I hope you know I'm always just a phone call away." Another card reads: "Even though your dad and I don't live together anymore, I know he's still a very special part of your life. And as much as I miss you when you're not with me, I'm still happy that you two can spend time together." 34

Hallmark's messages are grounded in a substantial body of well-funded market research. Therefore it is worth reflecting on the divergence in sentiment between the divorce cards for adults and the divorce cards for kids. For grown-ups, divorce heralds new beginnings (A HOT NEW SINGLE). For children, divorce brings separation and loss ("I'm sorry I'm not always there when you need me"). 35

An even more telling glimpse into the meaning of family disruption can be found in the growing children's literature on family dissolution. Take, for example, the popular children's book *Dinosaurs Divorce: A Guide for Changing Families* (1986), by Laurene Krasny Brown and Marc Brown. This is a picture book, written for very young children. The book begins with a short glossary of "divorce words" and encourages children to "see if you can find them" in the story. The words include "family counselor," "separation agreement," "alimony," and "child custody." The book is illustrated with cartoonish drawings of green dinosaur parents who fight, drink too much, and break up. One panel shows the father dinosaur, suitcase in hand, getting into a yellow car. 36

The dinosaur children are offered simple, straightforward advice on what to do about the divorce. *On custody decisions:* "When parents can't agree, lawyers and judges decide. Try to be honest if they ask you questions; it will help them make better decisions." *On selling the house:* "If you move, you may have to say good-bye to friends and familiar places. But soon your new home will feel like the place you really belong." *On the economic impact of divorce:* "Living with one parent almost always means there will be less money. Be prepared to give up some things." *On holidays:* "Divorce may mean twice as much celebrating at holiday times, but you may feel pulled apart." *On parents' new lovers:* "You may sometimes feel jealous and want your parent to yourself. Be polite to your parents' new friends, even if you don't like them at first." *On parents' remarriage:* "Not everyone loves his or her stepparents, but showing them respect is important." 37

These cards and books point to an uncomfortable and generally unacknowledged fact: what contributes to a parent's happiness may detract from a child's happiness. All too often the adult quest for freedom, independence, and choice in family relationships conflicts with a child's developmental needs for stability, constancy, harmony, and permanence in family life. In short, family disruption creates a deep division between parents' interests and the interests of children. 38

39   One of the worst consequences of these divided interests is a withdrawal of parental investment in children's well-being. As the Stanford economist Victor Fuchs has pointed out, the main source of social investment in children is private. The investment comes from the children's parents. But parents in disrupted families have less time, attention, and money to devote to their children. The single most important source of disinvestment has been the widespread withdrawal of financial support and involvement by fathers. Maternal investment, too, has declined, as women try to raise families on their own and work outside the home. Moreover, both mothers and fathers commonly respond to family breakup by investing more heavily in themselves and in their own personal and romantic lives.

40   Sometimes the tables are completely turned. Children are called upon to invest in the emotional well-being of their parents. Indeed, this seems to be the larger message of many of the children's books on divorce and remarriage. *Dinosaurs Divorce* asks children to be sympathetic, understanding, respectful, and polite to confused, unhappy parents. The sacrifice comes from the children: "Be prepared to give up some things." In the world of divorcing dinosaurs, the children rather than the grown-ups are the exemplars of patience, restraint, and good sense.

THREE SEVENTIES ASSUMPTIONS

41   As it first took shape in the 1970s, the optimistic view of family change rested on three bold new assumptions. At that time, because the emergence of the changes in family life was so recent, there was little hard evidence to confirm or dispute these assumptions. But this was an expansive moment in American life.

42   The first assumption was an economic one: that a woman could now afford to be a mother without also being a wife. There were ample grounds for believing this. Women's work-force participation had been gradually increasing in the postwar period, and by the beginning of the 1970s women were a strong presence in the workplace. What's more, even though there was still a substantial wage gap between men and women, women had made considerable progress in a relatively short time toward better-paying jobs and greater employment opportunities. More women than ever before could aspire to serious careers as business executives, doctors, lawyers, airline pilots, and politicians. This circumstance, combined with the increased availability of child care, meant that women could take on the responsibilities of a breadwinner, perhaps even a sole breadwinner. This was particularly true for middle-class women. According to a highly regarded 1977 study by the Carnegie Council on Children, "The greater availability of jobs for women means that more middle-class children today survive their parents' divorce without a catastrophic plunge into poverty."

43   Feminists, who had long argued that the path to greater equality for women lay in the world of work outside the home, endorsed this assumption. In fact, for many, economic independence was a stepping-stone toward freedom from both men and marriage. As women began to earn their own money, they were less dependent on men or marriage, and marriage diminished in importance. In Gloria Steinem's memorable words, "A woman without a man is like a fish without a bicycle."

This assumption also gained momentum as the meaning of work changed for women. 44
Increasingly, work had an expressive as well as an economic dimension: being a working
mother not only gave you an income but also made you more interesting and fulfilled than
a stay-at-home mother. Consequently, the optimistic economic scenario was driven by a cultural imperative. Women would achieve financial independence because, culturally as well
as economically, it was the right thing to do.

The second assumption was that family disruption would not cause lasting harm to chil- 45
dren and could actually enrich their lives. *Creative Divorce: A New Opportunity for Personal Growth,* a popular book of the seventies, spoke confidently to this point: "Children
can survive any family crisis without permanent damage—and grow as human beings in
the process. . . ." Moreover, single-parent and stepparent families created a more extensive
kinship network than the nuclear family. This network would envelop children in a web of
warm and supportive relationships. "Belonging to a stepfamily means there are more people in your life," a children's book published in 1982 notes. "More sisters and brothers, including the step ones. More people you think of as grandparents and aunts and uncles. More
cousins. More neighbors and friends. . . . Getting to know and like so many people (and
having them like you) is one of the best parts of what being in a stepfamily . . . is all about."

The third assumption was that the new diversity in family structure would make Amer- 46
ica a better place. Just as the nation has been strengthened by the diversity of its ethnic and
racial groups, so it would be strengthened by diverse family forms. The emergence of these
brave new families was but the latest chapter in the saga of American pluralism.

Another version of the diversity argument stated that the real problem was not family 47
disruption itself but the stigma still attached to these emergent family forms. This lingering
stigma placed children at psychological risk, making them feel ashamed or different; as the
ranks of single-parent and stepparent families grew, children would feel normal and good
about themselves.

These assumptions continue to be appealing, because they accord with strongly held 48
American beliefs in social progress. Americans see progress in the expansion of individual
opportunities for choice, freedom, and self-expression. Moreover, Americans identify progress with growing tolerance of diversity. Over the past half century, the pollster Daniel
Yankelovich writes, the United States has steadily grown more open-minded and accepting
of groups that were previously perceived as alien, untrustworthy, or unsuitable for public
leadership or social esteem. One such group is the burgeoning number of single-parent and
stepparent families.

In 1981 Sara McLanahan, now a sociologist at Princeton University's Woodrow Wilson 49
School, read a three-part series by Ken Auletta in *The New Yorker.* Later published as a book
titled *The Underclass,* the series presented a vivid portrait of the drug addicts, welfare
mothers, and school dropouts who took part in an education-and-training program in New
York City. Many were the children of single mothers, and it was Auletta's clear implication
that single-mother families were contributing to the growth of an underclass. McLanahan
was taken aback by this notion. "It struck me as strange that he would be viewing single
mothers at that level of pathology."

50   "I'd gone to graduate school in the days when the politically correct argument was that single-parent families were just another alternative family form, and it was fine," McLanahan explains, as she recalls the state of social-scientific thinking in the 1970s. Several empirical studies that were then current supported an optimistic view of family change. (They used tiny samples, however, and did not track the well-being of children over time.)

51   One, *All Our Kin,* by Carol Stack, was required reading for thousands of university students. It said that single mothers had strengths that had gone undetected and unappreciated by earlier researchers. The single-mother family, it suggested, is an economically resourceful and socially embedded institution. In the late 1970s McLanahan wrote a similar study that looked at a small sample of white single mothers and how they coped. "So I was very much of that tradition."

52   By the early 1980s, however, nearly two decades had passed since the changes in family life had begun. During the intervening years a fuller body of empirical research had emerged: studies that used large samples, or followed families through time, or did both. Moreover, several of the studies offered a child's-eye view of family disruption. The National Survey on Children, conducted by the psychologist Nicholas Zill, had set out in 1976 to track a large sample of children aged seven to eleven. It also interviewed the children's parents and teachers. It surveyed its subjects again in 1981 and 1987. By the time of its third round of interviews the eleven-year-olds of 1976 were the twenty-two-year-olds of 1987. The California Children of Divorce Study, directed by Judith Wallerstein, a clinical psychologist, had also been going on for a decade. E. Mavis Hetherington, of the University of Virginia, was conducting a similar study of children from both intact and divorced families. For the first time it was possible to test the optimistic view against a large and longitudinal body of evidence.

53   It was to this body of evidence that Sara McLanahan turned. When she did, she found little to support the optimistic view of single motherhood. On the contrary. When she published her findings with Irwin Garfinkel in a 1986 book, *Single Mothers and Their Children,* her portrait of single motherhood proved to be as troubling in its own way as Auletta's.

54   One of the leading assumptions of the time was that single motherhood was economically viable. Even if single mothers did face economic trials, they wouldn't face them for long, it was argued, because they wouldn't remain single for long: single motherhood would be a brief phase of three to five years, followed by marriage. Single mothers would be economically resilient: if they experienced setbacks, they would recover quickly. It was also said that single mothers would be supported by informal networks of family, friends, neighbors, and other single mothers. As McLanahan shows in her study, the evidence demolishes all these claims.

55   For the vast majority of single mothers, the economic spectrum turns out to be narrow, running between precarious and desperate. Half the single mothers in the United States live below the poverty line. (Currently, one out of ten married couples with children is poor.) Many others live on the edge of poverty. Even single mothers who are far from poor are likely to experience persistent economic insecurity. Divorce almost always brings a decline in the standard of living for the mother and children.

56   Moreover, the poverty experienced by single mothers is no more brief than it is mild. A significant number of all single mothers never marry or remarry. Those who do, do so only after spending roughly six years, on average, as single parents. For black mothers the dura-

tion is much longer. Only 33 percent of African-American mothers had remarried within ten years of separation. Consequently, single motherhood is hardly a fleeting event for the mother, and it is likely to occupy a third of the child's childhood. Even the notion that single mothers are knit together in economically supportive networks is not borne out by the evidence. On the contrary, single parenthood forces many women to be on the move, in search of cheaper housing and better jobs. This need-driven restless mobility makes it more difficult for them to sustain supportive ties to family and friends, let alone other single mothers.

Single-mother families are vulnerable not just to poverty but to a particularly debilitat- 57 ing form of poverty: welfare dependency. The dependency takes two forms: First, single mothers, particularly unwed mothers, stay on welfare longer than other welfare recipients. Of those never-married mothers who receive welfare benefits, almost 40 percent remain on the rolls for ten years or longer. Second, welfare dependency tends to be passed on from one generation to the next. McLanahan says, "Evidence on intergenerational poverty indicates that, indeed, offspring from [single-mother] families are far more likely to be poor and to form mother-only families than are offspring who live with two parents most of their preadult life." Nor is the intergenerational impact of single motherhood limited to African-Americans, as many people seem to believe. Among white families, daughters of single parents are 53 percent more likely to marry as teenagers, 111 percent more likely to have children as teenagers, 164 percent more likely to have a premarital birth, and 92 percent more likely to dissolve their own marriages. All these intergenerational consequences of single motherhood increase the likelihood of chronic welfare dependency.

McLanahan cites three reasons why single-mother families are so vulnerable econom- 58 ically. For one thing, their earnings are low. Second, unless the mothers are widowed, they don't receive public subsidies large enough to lift them out of poverty. And finally, they do not get much support from family members—especially the fathers of their children. In 1982 single white mothers received an average of $1,246 in alimony and child support, black mothers an average of $322. Such payments accounted for about 10 percent of the income of single white mothers and for about 3.5 percent of the income of single black mothers. These amounts were dramatically smaller than the income of the father in a two-parent family and also smaller than the income from a second earner in a two-parent family. Roughly 60 percent of single white mothers and 80 percent of single black mothers received no support at all.

Until the mid-1980s, when stricter standards were put in place, child-support awards 59 were only about half to two-thirds what the current guidelines require. Accordingly, there is often a big difference in the living standards of divorced fathers and of divorced mothers with children. After divorce the average annual income of mothers and children is $13,500 for whites and $9,000 for nonwhites, as compared with $25,000 for white nonresident fathers and $13,600 for nonwhite nonresident fathers. Moreover, since child-support awards account for a smaller portion of the income of a high-earning father, the drop in living standards can be especially sharp for mothers who were married to upper-level managers and professionals.

Unwed mothers are unlikely to be awarded any child support at all, partly because the 60 paternity of their children may not have been established. According to one recent study, only 20 percent of unmarried mothers receive child support.

61   Even if single mothers escape poverty, economic uncertainty remains a condition of life. Divorce brings a reduction in income and standard of living for the vast majority of single mothers. One study, for example, found that income for mothers and children declines on average about 30 percent, while fathers experience a 10 to 15 percent increase in income in the year following a separation. Things get even more difficult when fathers fail to meet their child-support obligations. As a result, many divorced mothers experience a wearing uncertainty about the family budget; whether the check will come in or not; whether new sneakers can be bought this month or not; whether the electric bill will be paid on time or not. Uncertainty about money triggers other kinds of uncertainty. Mothers and children often have to move to cheaper housing after a divorce. One study shows that about 38 percent of divorced mothers and their children move during the first year after a divorce. Even several years later the rate of moves for single mothers is about a third higher than the rate for two-parent families. It is also common for a mother to change her job or increase her working hours or both following a divorce. Even the composition of the household is likely to change, with other adults, such as boyfriends or babysitters, moving in and out.

62   All this uncertainty can be devastating to children. Anyone who knows children knows that they are deeply conservative creatures. They like things to stay the same. So pronounced is this tendency that certain children have been known to request the same peanut-butter-and-jelly sandwich for lunch for years on end. Children are particularly set in their ways when it comes to family, friends, neighborhoods, and schools. Yet when a family breaks up, all these things may change. The novelist Pat Conroy has observed that "each divorce is the death of a small civilization." No one feels this more acutely than children.

63   Sara McLanahan's investigation and others like it have helped to establish a broad consensus on the economic impact of family disruption on children. Most social scientists now agree that single motherhood is an important and growing cause of poverty, and that children suffer as a result. (They continue to argue, however, about the relationship between family structure and such economic factors as income inequality, the loss of jobs in the inner city, and the growth of low-wage jobs.) By the mid-1980s, however, it was clear that the problem of family disruption was not confined to the urban underclass, nor was its sole impact economic. Divorce and out-of-wedlock childbirth were affecting middle- and upper-class children, and these more privileged children were suffering negative consequences as well. It appeared that the problems associated with family breakup were far deeper and far more widespread than anyone had previously imagined.

64   Judith Wallerstein is one of the pioneers in research on the long-term psychological impact of family disruption on children. The California Children of Divorce Study, which she directs, remains the most enduring study of the long-term effects of divorce on children and their parents. Moreover, it represents the best-known effort to look at the impact of divorce on middle-class children. The California children entered the study without pathological family histories. Before divorce they lived in stable, protected homes. And although some of the children did experience economic insecurity as the result of divorce, they were generally free from the most severe forms of poverty associated with family breakup. Thus the

study and the resulting book (which Wallerstein wrote with Sandra Blakeslee), *Second Chances: Men, Women, and Children a Decade after Divorce* (1989), provide new insight into the consequences of divorce which are not associated with extreme forms of economic or emotional deprivation.

When, in 1971, Wallerstein and her colleagues set out to conduct clinical interviews with 131 children from the San Francisco area, they thought they were embarking on a short-term study. Most experts believed that divorce was like a bad cold. There was a phase of acute discomfort, and then a short recovery phase. According to the conventional wisdom, kids would be back on their feet in no time at all. Yet when Wallerstein met these children for a second interview more than a year later, she was amazed to discover that there had been no miraculous recovery. In fact, the children seemed to be doing worse.   65

The news that children did not "get over" divorce was not particularly welcome at the time. Wallerstein recalls, "We got angry letters from therapists, parents, and lawyers saying we were undoubtedly wrong. They said children are really much better off being released from an unhappy marriage. Divorce, they said, is a liberating experience." One of the main results of the California study was to overturn this optimistic view. In Wallerstein's cautionary words, "Divorce is deceptive. Legally it is a single event, but psychologically it is a chain—sometimes a never-ending chain—of events, relocations, and radically shifting relationships strung through time, a process that forever changes the lives of the people involved."   66

Five years after divorce more than a third of the children experienced moderate or severe depression. At ten years a significant number of the now young men and women appeared to be troubled, drifting, and underachieving. At fifteen years many of the thirty-ish adults were struggling to establish strong love relationships of their own. In short, far from recovering from their parents' divorce, a significant percentage of these grownups were still suffering from its effects. In fact, according to Wallerstein, the long-term effects of divorce emerge at a time when young adults are trying to make their own decisions about love, marriage, and family. Not all children in the study suffered negative consequences. But Wallerstein's research presents a sobering picture of divorce. "The child of divorce faces many additional psychological burdens in addition to the normative tasks of growing up," she says.   67

Divorce not only makes it more difficult for young adults to establish new relationships. It also weakens the oldest primary relationship: that between parent and child. According to Wallerstein, "Parent-child relationships are permanently altered by divorce in ways that our society has not anticipated." Not only do children experience a loss of parental attention at the onset of divorce, but they soon find that at every stage of their development their parents are not available in the same way they once were. "In a reasonably happy intact family," Wallerstein observes, "the child gravitates first to one parent and then to the other, using skills and attributes from each in climbing the developmental ladder." In a divorced family, children find it "harder to find the needed parent at needed times." This may help explain why very young children suffer the most as the result of family disruption. Their opportunities to engage in this kind of ongoing process are the most truncated and compromised.   68

69   The father-child bond is severely, often irreparably, damaged in disrupted families. In a situation without historical precedent, an astonishing and disheartening number of American fathers are failing to provide financial support to their children. Often, more than the father's support check is missing. Increasingly, children are bereft of any contact with their fathers. According to the National Survey of Children, in disrupted families only one child in six, on average, saw his or her father as often as once a week in the past year. Close to half did not see their father at all in the past year. As time goes on, contact becomes even more infrequent. Ten years after a marriage breaks up, more than two thirds of children report not having seen their father for a year. Not surprisingly, when asked to name the "adults you look up to and admire," only 20 percent of children in single-parent families named their father, as compared with 52 percent of children in two-parent families. A favorite complaint among Baby Boom Americans is that their fathers were emotionally remote guys who worked hard, came home at night to eat supper, and didn't have much to say to or do with the kids. But the current generation has a far worse father problem: many of their fathers are vanishing entirely.

70   Even for fathers who maintain regular contact, the pattern of father-child relationships changes. The sociologists Andrew Cherlin and Frank Furstenberg, who have studied broken families, write that the fathers behave more like other relatives than like parents. Rather than helping with homework or carrying out a project with their children, nonresidential fathers are likely to take the kids shopping, to the movies, or out to dinner. Instead of providing steady advice and guidance, divorced fathers become "treat" dads.

71   Apparently—and paradoxically—it is the visiting relationship itself, rather than the frequency of visits, that is the real source of the problem. According to Wallerstein, the few children in the California study who reported visiting with their fathers once or twice a week over a ten-year period still felt rejected. The need to schedule a special time to be with the child, the repeated leave-takings, and the lack of connection to the child's regular, daily schedule leaves many fathers adrift, frustrated, and confused. Wallerstein calls the visiting father a parent without portfolio.

72   The deterioration in father-child bonds is most severe among children who experience divorce at an early age, according to a recent study. Nearly three quarters of the respondents, now young men and women, report having poor relationships with their fathers. Close to half have received psychological help, nearly a third have dropped out of high school, and about a quarter report having experienced high levels of problem behavior or emotional distress by the time they became young adults.

LONG-TERM EFFECTS

73   Since most children live with their mothers after divorce, one might expect that the mother-child bond would remain unaltered and might even be strengthened. Yet research shows that the mother-child bond is also weakened as the result of divorce. Only half of the children who were close to their mothers before a divorce remained equally close after the divorce. Boys, particularly, had difficulties with their mothers. Moreover, mother-child relationships deteriorated over time. Whereas teenagers in disrupted families were no more

likely than teenagers in intact families to report poor relationships with their mothers, 30 percent of young adults from disrupted families have poor relationships with their mothers, as compared with 16 percent of young adults from intact families. Mother-daughter relationships often deteriorate as the daughter reaches young adulthood. The only group in society that derives any benefit from these weakened parent-child ties is the therapeutic community. Young adults from disrupted families are nearly twice as likely as those from intact families to receive psychological help.

Some social scientists have criticized Judith Wallerstein's research because her study 74 is based on a small clinical sample and does not include a control group of children from intact families. However, other studies generally support and strengthen her findings. Nicholas Zill has found similar long-term effects on children of divorce, reporting that "effects of marital discord and family disruption are visible twelve to twenty-two years later in poor relationships with parents, high levels of problem behavior, and an increased likelihood of dropping out of high school and receiving psychological help." Moreover, Zill's research also found signs of distress in young women who seemed relatively well adjusted in middle childhood and adolescence. Girls in single-parent families are also at much greater risk for precocious sexuality, teenage marriage, teenage pregnancy, nonmarital birth, and divorce than are girls in two-parent families.

Zill's research shows that family disruption strongly affects school achievement as well. 75 Children in disrupted families are nearly twice as likely as those in intact families to drop out of high school; among children who do drop out, those from disrupted families are less likely eventually to earn a diploma or a GED. Boys are at greater risk for dropping out than girls, and are also more likely to exhibit aggressive, acting-out behaviors. Other research confirms these findings. According to a study by the National Association of Elementary School Principals, 33 percent of two-parent elementary school students are ranked as high achievers, as compared with 17 percent of single-parent students. The children in single-parent families are also more likely to be truant or late or to have disciplinary action taken against them. Even after controlling for race, income, and religion, scholars find significant differences in educational attainment between children who grow up in intact families and children who do not. In his 1992 study *America's Smallest School: The Family,* Paul Barton shows that the proportion of two-parent families varies widely from state to state and is related to variations in academic achievement. North Dakota, for example, scores highest on the math-proficiency test and second highest on the two-parent-family scale. The District of Columbia is second lowest on the math test and lowest in the nation on the two-parent-family scale.

Zill notes that "while coming from a disrupted family significantly increases a young 76 adult's risks of experiencing social, emotional or academic difficulties, it does not foreordain such difficulties. The majority of young people from disrupted families have successfully completed high school, do not currently display high levels of emotional distress or problem behavior, and enjoy reasonable relationships with their mothers." Nevertheless, a majority of these young adults do show maladjustment in their relationships with their fathers.

These findings underscore the importance of both a mother and a father in fostering 77 the emotional well-being of children. Obviously, not all children in two-parent families are free from emotional turmoil, but few are burdened with the troubles that accompany family breakup. Moreover, as the sociologist Amitai Etzioni explains in a new book, *The Spirit of Community,* two parents in an intact family make up what might be called a mutually supportive education coalition. When both parents are present, they can play different, even contradictory, roles. One parent may goad the child to achieve, while the other may encourage the child to take time out to daydream or toss a football around. One may emphasize taking intellectual risks, while the other may insist on following the teacher's guidelines. At the same time, the parents regularly exchange information about the child's school problems and achievements, and have a sense of the overall educational mission. However, Etzioni writes,

> The sequence of divorce followed by a succession of boy or girlfriends, a second marriage, and frequently another divorce and another turnover of partners often means a repeatedly disrupted educational coalition. Each change in participants involves a change in the educational agenda for the child. Each new partner cannot be expected to pick up the previous one's educational post and program. . . . As a result, changes in parenting partners mean, at best, a deep disruption in a child's education, though of course several disruptions cut deeper into the effectiveness of the educational coalition than just one.

THE BAD NEWS ABOUT STEPPARENTS

78   Perhaps the most striking, and potentially disturbing, new research has to do with children in stepparent families. Until quite recently the optimistic assumption was that children saw their lives improve when they became part of a stepfamily. When Nicholas Zill and his colleagues began to study the effects of remarriage on children, their working hypothesis was that stepparent families would make up for the shortcomings of the single-parent family. Clearly, most children are better off economically when they are able to share in the income of two adults. When a second adult joins the household, there may be a reduction in the time and work pressures on the single parent.

79   The research overturns this optimistic assumption, however. In general the evidence suggests that remarriage neither reproduces nor restores the intact family structure, even when it brings more income and a second adult into the household. Quite the contrary. Indeed, children living with stepparents appear to be even more disadvantaged than children living in a stable single-parent family. Other difficulties seem to offset the advantages of extra income and an extra pair of hands. However much our modern sympathies reject the fairy-tale portrait of stepparents, the latest research confirms that the old stories are anthropologically quite accurate. Stepfamilies disrupt established loyalties, create new uncertainties, provoke deep anxieties, and sometimes threaten a child's physical safety as well as emotional security.

80   Parents and children have dramatically different interests in and expectations for a new marriage. For a single parent, remarriage brings new commitments, the hope of enduring love and happiness, and relief from stress and loneliness. For a child, the same event often provokes confused feelings of sadness, anger, and rejection. Nearly half the children in Wallerstein's study said they felt left out in their stepfamilies. The National Commission on

Children, a bipartisan group headed by Senator John D. Rockefeller, of West Virginia, reported that children from stepfamilies were more likely to say they often felt lonely or blue than children from either single-parent or intact families. Children in stepfamilies were the most likely to report that they wanted more time with their mothers. When mothers remarry, daughters tend to have a harder time adjusting than sons. Evidently, boys often respond positively to a male presence in the household, while girls who have established close ties to their mother in a single-parent family often see the stepfather as a rival and an intruder. According to one study, boys in remarried families are less likely to drop out of school than boys in single-parent families, while the opposite is true for girls.

A large percentage of children do not even consider stepparents to be part of their families, according to the National Survey on Children. The NSC asked children, "When you think of your family, who do you include?" Only 10 percent of the children failed to mention a biological parent, but a third left out a stepparent. Even children who rarely saw their noncustodial parents almost always named them as family members. The weak sense of attachment is mutual. When parents were asked the same question, only one percent failed to mention a biological child, while 15 percent left out a stepchild. In the same study stepparents with both natural children and stepchildren said that it was harder for them to love their stepchildren than their biological children and that their children would have been better off if they had grown up with two biological parents.   81

One of the most severe risks associated with stepparent-child ties is the risk of sexual abuse. As Judith Wallerstein explains, "The presence of a stepfather can raise the difficult issue of a thinner incest barrier." The incest taboo is strongly reinforced, Wallerstein says, by knowledge of paternity and by the experience of caring for a child since birth. A stepfather enters the family without either credential and plays a sexual role as the mother's husband. As a result, stepfathers can pose a sexual risk to the children, especially to daughters. According to a study by the Canadian researchers Martin Daly and Margo Wilson, preschool children in stepfamilies are forty times as likely as children in intact families to suffer physical or sexual abuse. (Most of the sexual abuse was committed by a third party, such as a neighbor, a stepfather's male friend, or another nonrelative.) Stepfathers discriminate in their abuse: they are far more likely to assault nonbiological children than their own natural children.   82

Sexual abuse represents the most extreme threat to children's well-being. Stepfamilies also seem less likely to make the kind of ordinary investments in the children that other families do. Although it is true that the stepfamily household has a higher income than the single-parent household, it does not follow that the additional income is reliably available to the children. To begin with, children's claim on stepparents' resources is shaky. Stepparents are not legally required to support stepchildren, so their financial support of these children is entirely voluntary. Moreover, since stepfamilies are far more likely to break up than intact families, particularly in the first five years, there is always the risk—far greater than the risk of unemployment in an intact family—that the second income will vanish with another divorce. The financial commitment to a child's education appears weaker in stepparent families, perhaps because the stepparent believes that the responsibility for educating the child rests with the biological parent.   83

84   Similarly, studies suggest that even though they may have the time, the parents in step-families do not invest as much of it in their children as the parents in intact families or even single parents do. A 1991 survey by the National Commission on Children showed that the parents in stepfamilies were less likely to be involved in a child's school life, including involvement in extracurricular activities, than either intact-family parents or single parents. They were the least likely to report being involved in such time-consuming activities as coaching a child's team, accompanying class trips, or helping with school projects. According to McLanahan's research, children in stepparent families report lower educational aspirations on the part of their parents and lower levels of parental involvement with schoolwork. In short, it appears that family income and the number of adults in the household are not the only factors affecting children's well-being.

DIMINISHING INVESTMENTS

85   There are several reasons for this diminished interest and investment. In the law, as in the children's eyes, stepparents are shadowy figures. According to the legal scholar David Chambers, family law has pretty much ignored stepparents. Chambers writes, "In the substantial majority of states, stepparents, even when they live with a child, have no legal obligation to contribute to the child's support; nor does a stepparent's presence in the home alter the support obligations of a noncustodial parent. The stepparent also has . . . no authority to approve emergency medical treatment or even to sign a permission slip. . . ." When a marriage breaks up, the stepparent has no continuing obligation to provide for a stepchild, no matter how long or how much he or she has been contributing to the support of the child. In short, Chambers says, stepparent relationships are based wholly on consent, subject to the inclination of the adult and the child. The only way a stepparent can acquire the legal status of a parent is through adoption. Some researchers also point to the cultural ambiguity of the stepparent's role as a source of diminished interest, while others insist that it is the absence of a blood tie that weakens the bond between stepparent and child.

86   Whatever its causes, the diminished investment in children in both single-parent and stepparent families has a significant impact on their life chances. Take parental help with college costs. The parents in intact families are far more likely to contribute to children's college costs than are those in disrupted families. Moreover, they are usually able to arrive at a shared understanding of which children will go to college, where they will go, how much the parents will contribute, and how much the children will contribute. But when families break up, these informal understandings can vanish. The issue of college tuition remains one of the most contested areas of parental support, especially for higher-income parents.

87   The law does not step in even when familial understandings break down. In the 1980s many states lowered the age covered by child-support agreements from twenty-one to eighteen, thus eliminating college as a cost associated with support for a minor child. Consequently, the question of college tuition is typically not addressed in child-custody agreements. Even in states where the courts do require parents to contribute to college costs, the requirement may be in jeopardy. In a recent decision in Pennsylvania the court overturned an earlier de-

cision ordering divorced parents to contribute to college tuition. This decision is likely to inspire challenges in other states where courts have required parents to pay for college. Increasingly, help in paying for college is entirely voluntary.

Judith Wallerstein has been analyzing the educational decisions of the college-age men and women in her study. She reports that "a full 42 percent of these men and women from middle class families appeared to have ended their educations without attempting college or had left college before achieving a degree at either the two-year or the four-year level." A significant percentage of these young people have the ability to attend college. Typical of this group are Nick and Terry, sons of a college professor. They had been close to their father before the divorce, but their father remarried soon after the divorce and saw his sons only occasionally, even though he lived nearby. At age nineteen Nick had completed a few junior-college courses and was earning a living as a salesman. Terry, twenty-one, who had been tested as a gifted student, was doing blue-collar work irregularly. 88

Sixty-seven percent of the college-age students from disrupted families attended college, as compared with 85 percent of other students who attended the same high schools. Of those attending college, several had fathers who were financially capable of contributing to college costs but did not. 89

The withdrawal of support for college suggests that other customary forms of parental help-giving, too, may decline as the result of family breakup. For example, nearly a quarter of first-home purchases since 1980 have involved help from relatives, usually parents. The median amount of help is $5,000. It is hard to imagine that parents who refuse to contribute to college costs will offer help in buying first homes, or help in buying cars or health insurance for young adult family members. And although it is too soon to tell, family disruption may affect the generational transmission of wealth. Baby Boomers will inherit their parents' estates, some substantial, accumulated over a lifetime by parents who lived and saved together. To be sure, the postwar generation benefited from an expanding economy and a rising standard of living, but its ability to accumulate wealth also owed something to family stability. The lifetime assets, like the marriage itself, remained intact. It is unlikely that the children of disrupted families will be in so favorable a position. 90

Moreover, children from disrupted families may be less likely to help their aging parents. The sociologist Alice Rossi, who has studied intergenerational patterns of help-giving, says that adult obligation has its roots in early-childhood experience. Children who grow up in intact families experience higher levels of obligation to kin than children from broken families. Children's sense of obligation to a nonresidential father is particularly weak. Among adults with both parents living, those separated from their father during childhood are less likely than others to see the father regularly. Half of them see their father more than once a year, as compared with nine out of ten of those whose parents are still married. Apparently a kind of bitter justice is at work here. Fathers who do not support or see their young children may not be able to count on their adult children's support when they are old and need money, love, and attention. 91

In short, as Andrew Cherlin and Frank Furstenburg put it, "Through divorce and remarriage, individuals are related to more and more people, to each of whom they owe less and less." Moreover, as Nicholas Zill argues, weaker parent-child attachments leave many 92 children more strongly exposed to influences outside the family, such as peers, boyfriends or girlfriends, and the media. Although these outside forces can sometimes be helpful, common sense and research opinion argue against putting too much faith in peer groups or the media as surrogates for Mom and Dad.

POVERTY, CRIME, EDUCATION

93   Family disruption would be a serious problem even if it affected only individual children and families. But its impact is far broader. Indeed, it is not an exaggeration to characterize it as a central cause of many of our most vexing social problems. Consider three problems that most Americans believe rank among the nation's pressing concerns: poverty, crime, and declining school performance.

94   More than half of the increase in child poverty in the 1980s is attributable to changes in family structure, according to David Eggebeen and Daniel Lichter, of Pennsylvania State University. In fact, if family structure in the United States had remained relatively constant since 1960, the rate of child poverty would be a third lower than it is today. This does not bode well for the future. With more than half of today's children likely to live in single-parent families, poverty and associated welfare costs threaten to become even heavier burdens on the nation.

95   Crime in American cities has increased dramatically and grown more violent over recent decades. Much of this can be attributed to the rise in disrupted families. Nationally, more than 70 percent of all juveniles in state reform institutions come from fatherless homes. A number of scholarly studies find that even after the groups of subjects are controlled for income, boys from single-mother homes are significantly more likely than others to commit crimes and to wind up in the juvenile justice, court, and penitentiary systems. One such study summarizes the relationship between crime and one-parent families in this way: "The relationship is so strong that controlling for family configuration erases the relationship between race and crime and between low income and crime. This conclusion shows up time and again in the literature." The nation's mayors, as well as police officers, social workers, probation officers, and court officials, consistently point to family breakup as the most important source of rising rates of crime.

96   Terrible as poverty and crime are, they tend to be concentrated in inner cities and isolated from the everyday experience of many Americans. The same cannot be said of the problem of declining school performance. Nowhere has the impact of family breakup been more profound or widespread than in the nation's public schools. There is a strong consensus that the schools are failing in their historic mission to prepare every American child to be a good worker and a good citizen. And nearly everyone agrees that the schools must undergo dramatic reform in order to reach that goal. In pursuit of that goal, moreover, we have suffered no shortage of bright ideas or pilot projects or bold experiments in school reform. But there is little evidence that measures such as curricular reform, school-based management, and school choice will address, let alone solve, the biggest problem schools face: the rising number of children who come from disrupted families.

97   The great educational tragedy of our time is that many American children are failing in school not because they are intellectually or physically impaired but because they are emotionally incapacitated. In schools across the nation principals report a dramatic rise in the ag-

gressive, acting-out behavior characteristic of children, especially boys, who are living in single-parent families. The discipline problems in today's suburban schools—assaults on teachers, unprovoked attacks on other students, screaming outbursts in class—outstrip the problems that were evident in the toughest city schools a generation ago. Moreover, teachers find many children emotionally distracted, so upset and preoccupied by the explosive drama of their own family lives that they are unable to concentrate on such mundane matters as multiplication tables.

In response, many schools have turned to therapeutic remediation. A growing proportion of many school budgets is devoted to counseling and other psychological services. The curriculum is becoming more therapeutic: children are taking courses in self-esteem, conflict resolution, and aggression management. Parental advisory groups are conscientiously debating alternative approaches to traditional school discipline, ranging from teacher training in mediation to the introduction of metal detectors and security guards in the schools. Schools are increasingly becoming emergency rooms of the emotions, devoted not only to developing minds but also to repairing hearts. As a result, the mission of the school, along with the culture of the classroom, is slowly changing. What we are seeing, largely as a result of the new burdens of family disruption, is the psychologization of American education. 98

Taken together, the research presents a powerful challenge to the prevailing view of family change as social progress. Not a single one of the assumptions underlying that view can be sustained against the empirical evidence. Single-parent families are not able to do well economically on a mother's income. In fact, most teeter on the economic brink, and many fall into poverty and welfare dependency. Growing up in a disrupted family does not enrich a child's life or expand the number of adults committed to the child's well-being. In fact, disrupted families threaten the psychological well-being of children and diminish the investment of adult time and money in them. Family diversity in the form of increasing numbers of single-parent and stepparent families does not strengthen the social fabric. It dramatically weakens and undermines society, placing new burdens on schools, courts, prisons, and the welfare system. These new families are not an improvement on the nuclear family, nor are they even just as good, whether you look at outcomes for children or outcomes for society as a whole. In short, far from representing social progress, family change represents a stunning example of social regress. 99

THE TWO-PARENT ADVANTAGE

All this evidence gives rise to an obvious conclusion: growing up in an intact two-parent family is an important source of advantage for American children. Though far from perfect as a social institution, the intact family offers children greater security and better outcomes than its fast-growing alternatives: single-parent and stepparent families. Not only does the intact family protect the child from poverty and economic insecurity; it also provides greater noneconomic investments of parental time, attention, and emotional support over the entire life course. This does not mean that all two-parent families are better for children than all single-parent families. But in the face of the evidence it becomes increasingly difficult to sustain the proposition that all family structures produce equally good outcomes for children. 100

101   Curiously, many in the research community are hesitant to say that two-parent families generally promote better outcomes for children than single-parent families. Some argue that we need finer measures of the extent of the family-structure effect. As one scholar has noted, it is possible, by disaggregating the data in certain ways, to make family structure "go away" as an independent variable. Other researchers point to studies that show that children suffer psychological effects as a result of family conflict preceding family breakup. Consequently, they reason, it is the conflict rather than the structure of the family that is responsible for many of the problems associated with family disruption. Others, including Judith Wallerstein, caution against treating children in divorced families and children in intact families as separate populations, because doing so tends to exaggerate the differences between the two groups. "We have to take this family by family," Wallerstein says.

102   Some of the caution among researchers can also be attributed to ideological pressures. Privately, social scientists worry that their research may serve ideological causes that they themselves do not support, or that their work may be misinterpreted as an attempt to "tell people what to do." Some are fearful that they will be attacked by feminist colleagues, or, more generally, that their comments will be regarded as an effort to turn back the clock to the 1950s—a goal that has almost no constituency in the academy. Even more fundamental, it has become risky for anyone—scholar, politician, religious leader—to make normative statements today. This reflects not only the persistent drive toward "value neutrality" in the professions but also a deep confusion about the purposes of public discourse. The dominant view appears to be that social criticism, like criticism of individuals, is psychologically damaging. The worst thing you can do is to make people feel guilty or bad about themselves.

103   When one sets aside these constraints, however, the case against the two-parent family is remarkably weak. It is true that disaggregating data can make family structure less significant as a factor, just as disaggregating Hurricane Andrew into wind, rain, and tides can make it disappear as a meteorological phenomenon. Nonetheless, research opinion as well as common sense suggests that the effects of changes in family structure are great enough to cause concern. Nicholas Zill argues that many of the risk factors for children are doubled or more than doubled as the result of family disruption. "In epidemiological terms," he writes, "the doubling of a hazard is a substantial increase. . . . the increase in risk that dietary cholesterol poses for cardiovascular disease, for example, is far less than double, yet millions of Americans have altered their diets because of the perceived hazard."

104   The argument that family conflict, rather than the breakup of parents, is the cause of children's psychological distress is persuasive on its face. Children who grow up in high-conflict families, whether the families stay together or eventually split up, are undoubtedly at great psychological risk. And surely no one would dispute that there must be societal measures available, including divorce, to remove children from families where they are in danger. Yet only a minority of divorces grow out of pathological situations; much more common are divorces in families unscarred by physical assault. Moreover, an equally compelling hypothesis is that family breakup generates its own conflict. Certainly, many families exhibit more conflictual and even violent behavior as a consequence of divorce than they did before divorce.

Finally, it is important to note that clinical insights are different from sociological find-   105
ings. Clinicians work with individual families, who cannot and should not be defined by
statistical aggregates. Appropriate to a clinical approach, moreover, is a focus on the internal dynamics of family functioning and on the immense variability in human behavior. Nevertheless, there is enough empirical evidence to justify sociological statements about the
causes of declining child well-being and to demonstrate that despite the plasticity of human
response, there are some useful rules of thumb to guide our thinking about and policies affecting the family.

For example, Sara McLanahan says, three structural constants are commonly associated   106
with intact families, even intact families who would not win any "Family of the Year"
awards. The first is economic. In intact families, children share in the income of two adults.
Indeed, as a number of analysts have pointed out, the two-parent family is becoming more
rather than less necessary, because more and more families need two incomes to sustain a
middle-class standard of living.

McLanahan believes that most intact families also provide a stable authority structure.   107
Family breakup commonly upsets the established boundaries of authority in a family. Children are often required to make decisions or accept responsibilities once considered the
province of parents. Moreover, children, even very young children, are often expected to behave like mature adults, so that the grown-ups in the family can be free to deal with the emotional fallout of the failed relationship. In some instances family disruption creates a complete
vacuum in authority; everyone invents his or her own rules. With lines of authority disrupted
or absent, children find it much more difficult to engage in the normal kinds of testing behavior, the trial and error, the failing and succeeding, that define the developmental pathway
toward character and competence. McLanahan says, "Children need to be the ones to challenge the rules. The parents need to set the boundaries and let the kids push the boundaries.
The children shouldn't have to walk the straight and narrow at all times."

Finally, McLanahan holds that children in intact families benefit from stability in what   108
she neutrally terms "household personnel." Family disruption frequently brings new adults
into the family, including stepparents, live-in boyfriends or girlfriends, and casual sexual
partners. Like stepfathers, boyfriends can present a real threat to children's, particularly to
daughters', security and well-being. But physical or sexual abuse represents only the most
extreme such threat. Even the very best of boyfriends can disrupt and undermine a child's
sense of peace and security, McLanahan says. "It's not as though you're going from an unhappy marriage to peacefulness. There can be a constant changing until the mother finds a
suitable partner."

McLanahan's argument helps explain why children of widows tend to do better than   109
children of divorced or unmarried mothers. Widows differ from other single mothers in all
three respects. They are economically more secure, because they receive more public assistance through Survivors Insurance, and possibly private insurance or other kinds of support from family members. Thus widows are less likely to leave the neighborhood in search
of a new or better job and a cheaper house or apartment. Moreover, the death of a father
is not likely to disrupt the authority structure radically. When a father dies, he is no longer
physically present, but his death does not dethrone him as an authority figure in the child's
life. On the contrary, his authority may be magnified through death. The mother can draw

on the powerful memory of the departed father as a way of intensifying her parental authority: "Your father would have wanted it this way." Finally, since widows tend to be older than divorced mothers, their love life may be less distracting.

110   Regarding the two-parent family, the sociologist David Popenoe, who has devoted much of his career to the study of families, both in the United States and in Scandinavia, makes this straightforward assertion:

> Social science research is almost never conclusive. There are always methodological difficulties and stones left unturned. Yet in three decades of work as a social scientist, I know of few other bodies of data in which the weight of evidence is so decisively on one side of the issue: on the whole, for children, two-parent families are preferable to single-parent and stepfamilies.

THE REGIME EFFECT

111   The rise in family disruption is not unique to American society. It is evident in virtually all advanced nations, including Japan, where it is also shaped by the growing participation of women in the work force. Yet the United States has made divorce easier and quicker than in any other Western nation with the sole exception of Sweden—and the trend toward solo motherhood has also been more pronounced in America. (Sweden has an equally high rate of out-of-wedlock birth, but the majority of such births are to cohabiting couples, a long-established pattern in Swedish society.) More to the point, nowhere has family breakup been greeted by a more triumphant rhetoric of renewal than in America.

112   What is striking about this rhetoric is how deeply it reflects classic themes in American public life. It draws its language and imagery from the nation's founding myth. It depicts family breakup as a drama of revolution and rebirth. The nuclear family represents the corrupt past, an institution guilty of the abuse of power and the suppression of individual freedom. Breaking up the family is like breaking away from Old World tyranny. Liberated from the bonds of the family, the individual can achieve independence and experience a new beginning, a fresh start, a new birth of freedom. In short, family breakup recapitulates the American experience.

113   This rhetoric is an example of what the University of Maryland political philosopher William Galston has called the "regime effect." The founding of the United States set in motion a new political order based to an unprecedented degree on individual rights, personal choice, and egalitarian relationships. Since then these values have spread beyond their original domain of political relationships to define social relationships as well. During the past twenty-five years these values have had a particularly profound impact on the family.

114   Increasingly, political principles of individual rights and choice shape our understanding of family commitment and solidarity. Family relationships are viewed not as permanent or binding but as voluntary and easily terminable. Moreover, under the sway of the regime effect the family loses its central importance as an institution in the civil society, accomplishing certain social goals such as raising children and caring for its members, and becomes a means to achieving greater individual happiness—a lifestyle choice. Thus, Galston says, what is happening to the American family reflects the "unfolding logic of authoritative, deeply American moral-political principles."

One benefit of the regime effect is to create greater equality in adult family relationships. Husbands and wives, mothers and fathers, enjoy relationships far more egalitarian than past relationships were, and most Americans prefer it that way. But the political principles of the regime effect can threaten another kind of family relationship—that between parent and child. Owing to their biological and developmental immaturity, children are needy dependents. They are not able to express their choices according to limited, easily terminable, voluntary agreements. They are not able to act as negotiators in family decisions, even those that most affect their own interests. As one writer has put it, "a newborn does not make a good 'partner.'" Correspondingly, the parental role is antithetical to the spirit of the regime. Parental investment in children involves a diminished investment in self, a willing deference to the needs and claims of the dependent child. Perhaps more than any other family relationship, the parent-child relationship—shaped as it is by patterns of dependency and deference—can be undermined and weakened by the principles of the regime.   115

More than a century and a half ago Alexis de Tocqueville made the striking observation that an individualistic society depends on a communitarian institution like the family for its continued existence. The family cannot be constituted like the liberal state, nor can it be governed entirely by that state's principles. Yet the family serves as the seedbed for the virtues required by a liberal state. The family is responsible for teaching lessons of independence, self-restraint, responsibility, and right conduct, which are essential to a free, democratic society. If the family fails in these tasks, then the entire experiment in democratic self-rule is jeopardized.   116

To take one example: independence is basic to successful functioning in American life. We assume that most people in America will be able to work, care for themselves and their families, think for themselves, and inculcate the same traits of independence and initiative in their children. We depend on families to teach people to do these things. The erosion of the two-parent family undermines the capacity of families to impart this knowledge; children of long-term welfare-dependent single parents are far more likely than others to be dependent themselves. Similarly, the children in disrupted families have a harder time forging bonds of trust with others and giving and getting help across the generations. This, too, may lead to greater dependency on the resources of the state.   117

Over the past two and a half decades Americans have been conducting what is tantamount to a vast natural experiment in family life. Many would argue that this experiment was necessary, worthwhile, and long overdue. The results of the experiment are coming in, and they are clear. Adults have benefited from the changes in family life in important ways, but the same cannot be said for children. Indeed, this is the first generation in the nation's history to do worse psychologically, socially, and economically than its parents. Most poignantly, in survey after survey the children of broken families confess deep longings for an intact family.   118

Nonetheless, as Galston is quick to point out, the regime effect is not an irresistible undertow that will carry away the family. It is more like a swift current, against which it is possible to swim. People learn; societies can change, particularly when it becomes apparent that certain behaviors damage the social ecology, threaten the public order, and impose new burdens on core institutions. Whether Americans will act to overcome the legacy of family disruption is a crucial but as yet unanswered question.   119

FOR CLASS DISCUSSION

1. Analyze and evaluate the disagreements among these writers concerning issues of family values, single parenthood, and welfare by applying the first set of guide questions from page 455. How do you account for the differing points of view?

2. Choose one of the arguments for closer analysis, applying the second set of guide questions on page 455–456.

Optional Writing Assignment   As the junior staffer for Senator Murk, you've been asked to help the Senator determine an appropriate response to Charles Murray's proposal that welfare benefits be eliminated for unwed mothers (see pages 27–31 for Murray's argument). In particular, the Senator has asked you to prepare a working paper that summarizes the arguments for and against Murray's proposal, evaluates these arguments, and sets forth recommendations for the stand that Senator Murk should take. Drawing on your reading of the Murray and Gilliam arguments (Gilliam's argument is on pp. 48–50) as well as the arguments in this section, write your working paper for Senator Murk.

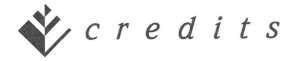 *credits*

Gordon F. Adams, "Petition to Waive the University Math Requirement." Reprinted with the permission of the author.

Elijah Anderson, "Abolishing Welfare Won't Stop Poverty" from *The Seattle Times* (January 6, 1994). Copyright © 1994 by Elijah Anderson. Reprinted with the permission of the author.

Anonymous, "Reading, Writing and (Ugh!) You Know What" from *Science '86* (May 1986): 7–8. Copyright © 1986 by American Association for the Advancement of Science. Reprinted by permission.

Paul Applebaum, "Crazy in the Streets" from *Commentary* (May 1987). Copyright © 1987 by Paul Applebaum. Reprinted with the permission of the author and *Commentary*.

Stephen Bean, "What Should Be Done about the Mentally Ill Homeless?." Reprinted with the permission of the author.

Susan Brownmiller, "Pornography Hurts Women" from *Against Our Will: Men, Women and Rape*. Copyright © 1975 by Susan Brownmiller. Reprinted with the permission of Simon & Schuster, Inc.

Patricia Bucalo, "Letter to the Editor in Response to Charles Murray". Reprinted by permission of the author.

Martha Chamallas, "Universal Truth and Multiple Perspectives: Controversies on Sexual Harassment" from *Et Cetera* (Fall 1992). Copyright © 1992. Reprinted with the permission of International Society for General Semantics, Box 728, Concord, CA 94522.

Lynnea Clark, "Women Police Officers: Should Size and Strength Be a Criteria for Patrol Duty?" Reprinted by permission of the author.

Susan Crawford, "A Wink Here, A Leer There: It's Costly" from *The New York Times* (March 28, 1993). Copyright © 1993 by The New York Times Company. Reprinted with the permission of *The New York Times*.

Dao Do, "Choose Life!" Reprinted by permission of the author.

Richard J. Dennis, "The Economics of Legalizing Drugs" from *The Atlantic Monthly* (November 1990). Copyright © 1990 by Richard J. Dennis. Reprinted with the permission of the author.

Kathleen Durkan, "Net Benefit" from *Seattle Weekly* (July 31, 1996). Copyright © 1996 by Kathleen Durkan. Reprinted with the permission of the author.

James Exon, "On the Force of Law Can Deter Pornographers" from *Computer World* (February 19, 1996). Copyright 1996.

Victor Fuchs, "Why Married Mothers Work" from *How We Live*. Copyright © 1983 by the President and Fellows of Harvard College. Reprinted with the permission of Harvard University Press.

Michael S. Gazzaniga, "The Federal Drugstore," an interview with Dr. Michael S. Gazzaniga, from *National Review* (February 5, 1990). Copyright © 1990 by National Review, Inc. Reprinted with the permission of *National Review*, 150 East 35th Street, New York, NY 10016.

Dorothy Gilliam, "Wrong Way to Reform Welfare" from *The Washington Post* (December 12, 1993). Copyright © 1993 by *The Washington Post*. Reprinted with the permission of The Washington Post Writers Group.

index

Absolute obligation, 345
Abstracts, 31
Accidental criteria, 207
Accommodating your audience, 166–188
Adams, Gordon (student), 22, 158
Ad hominem fallacy, 425–427
Adjusted numbers, 128
Alphabetization rules, 367
Analogies. *See also* Precedents
  in causal arguments, 243–244, 252
  evoking *pathos* with, 158–159
  extended, 269–270
  faulty, 244, 432
  refuting arguments based on, 274–276
  in resemblance arguments, 268–271
  undeveloped, 268–269
  writing assignment on, 267–268
Annotations
  reading-to-believe, 33
  reading-to-doubt, 40
APA (American Psychological Association) documentation system, 397–410
  examples of, 413, 420
  style sheet for, 413
Appeal to false authority fallacy, 425
Appeal to ignorance fallacy, 424
Appeal to irrational premises fallacy, 424
Argumentation, 83
Arguments
  accommodating your audience with, 166–188

causal, 195, 228–263
committee model for, 17–22
consequentialist, 195, 348–349
defining features of, 7–12
definitional, 194–195, 198–227
ethical, 339–353
evaluation, 281–303
evidence in, 113–144
explicit vs. implicit, 4–6
five-category schema for, 191–197
genuine vs. pseudo, 85–88
logical fallacies in, 421–434
logical structure of, 88–91, 95–112
misconceptions about, 3–4
moving your audience with, 145–165
origin of, 83–85
problem of truth and, 12–15
proposal, 304–338
reading, 24–51
resemblance, 195–196, 264–280
social context for, 81–83
writing, 52–77
Argument to the people fallacy, 423–424
Aristotelian definitions
  effect of rhetorical context on, 208–209
  explained, 206–207
Aristotle, 97
Arizona State University (ASU), 17
Assumptions
  disagreement about, 42–48
  lack of shared, 86–87
Attributive tags, 37, 394–395
Audience accommodation, 166–188

determining audience resistance, 170–172
neutral or undecided audiences and, 173–182
resistant audiences and, 182–186
supportive audiences and, 172–173
Audience-based reasons
  beliefs and emotions, 154–159
  credibility, 153–154
  finding, 149–150
  writer-based reasons vs., 146–149

Backing, 100, 101
  conditions of rebuttal and, 102–106
Bandwagon fallacy, 424
Bar graphs, 122–124
Bean, Stephen (student), 330
Because clauses
  brainstorming pro and con, 61–62
  causal arguments and, 233–236
  expressing reasons in, 90–91
Begging the question fallacy, 428
Beliefs
  appealing to, 82, 154–159
  disagreement about, 42–48
Believing and doubting game, 58, 60–61
Bibliographic list, 397–398
Block quotations, 390
Book citations, 400–404
Bookmarks of Internet sites, 376
Book Review Digest, 378
Brackets, 392

Brainstorming
  networks of related issues,
    62–63
  pro and con "because"
    clauses, 61–62
Branch diagram, 36
Brownmiller, Susan, 268, 278

Cain, Jeffrey (student), 323
Callicles, 12–13
Card catalog, 367–369
Casual chain, 231, 237–238,
  240, 250
Causal arguments, 195, 228–263
  conditions of rebuttal for,
    250–252
  essay assignment on, 236–237
  examples of, 228–229, 253–263
  frequency of, 229–230
  glossary of terms encountered
    in, 244–245
  logical structure of, 233–236
  methodologies of, 237–244
  nature of, 230–232
  organizing, 248–250
  writing, 247–250
Causality
  described, 230–232
  directly explaining, 237–239,
    240
  idea map illustrating, 246
  inductive methods for
    establishing, 239, 241–242
CD-ROM database searches, 375
Chain of reasons, 110–112
Charts, pie, 124, 125
Chats, Internet, 364–366
Churchill, Winston, 17
Circular arguments, 428
Citations. See also Documenting
    sources
  end of text, 397–398
  examples of, 37–38, 338, 383
  formats for, 397, 400–410
  style sheets for, 412, 413
  in text, 398–400
  when to use, 396–397

Claims, 88
  qualifying, 103–106
Clark, Lynnea (student),
  380–382, 414
Classical arguments, 63–66
  delayed thesis arguments vs.,
    160–164, 182–183
  diagram of, 65
  Rogerian arguments vs.,
    183–185
  self-announcing structure in,
    92–93
  writing assignment on, 188
Clonethink, 436
Collaborative learning, 435
Committee model for argument,
  17–22
Communities, writing. See
    Writing communities
Complex question fallacy, 429
Composition process, 54–55
Concession strategy, 181–182
Conclusiveness in arguments,
  421–422
Concrete language, 155
Conditions of rebuttal, 102–106.
    See also Refuting opposing
    views
  for causal arguments, 250–252
  for definitional arguments,
    217–219
  for evaluation arguments,
    295–296
  for proposal arguments,
    320–322
  for resemblance arguments,
    274–276
Confirmatio, 64
Confutatio, 64
Congressional Abstracts, 378
Connotations, 158–159
Consequences. See also
    Principles
  arguments based on, 195,
    348–349
  ethical systems grounded in,
    343, 345

  evaluating, 309
  predicting future, 308
Consequentialist arguments,
  345, 348–349
Conservatism, 308
Constraints, 245
Context for arguments, 81–83,
  208–209
Contributing cause, 245
Controversy
  definitional, 210–211
  exploring areas of, 71–72
Convictions. See Beliefs; Value
Cooked data, 119
Correlation, 241–242, 252
Correlation for cause fallacy,
  239, 430
Cost-benefit analysis, 309
Cost issues
  in evaluation arguments, 288
  in proposal arguments, 321
Counteranalogy, 276
Counterproposals, 322
Courtroom model. See Toulmin
    system
Credibility, 153–154
Criteria for evaluation
    arguments
  category determinations and,
    288–291
  evaluation of X against,
    291–293
  judgment criteria and, 290
  purpose/function of class
    and, 289–290
  relative weightings and,
    291, 295
Criteria-match structure
  conditions of rebuttal and,
    217–219
  conducting an argument
    using, 206
  of definitional arguments,
    201–202
  of evaluation arguments,
    284–286, 296
Current affairs indexes, 370

Data. *See also* Numerical data;
Personal experience data;
Research data
discriminating use of, 135
manipulating, 118–119,
125, 126
recency, representativeness,
and sufficiency of, 134–135
selecting from reliable sources,
133–134
"Data dumps," 357
Debate
essay format for, 76–77
misconception of argument
as, 4
Declaration of Independence, 17
Definitional arguments, 194–195,
198–227
conceptual problems of,
203–205
conditions of rebuttal for,
217–219
conducting the match part of,
209–210
criteria-match structure of,
201–202, 206, 214–215
definitional issues and,
199–200
essay assignment on, 200–201
establishing criteria for Y in,
206–209, 212–214
examples of, 198–199, 219–227
organizational structure for,
215, 216
resemblance arguments
compared to, 265–267
writing, 210–217
Definitions
arguments from, 194–195
Aristotelian, 206–209
difficulties inherent in,
203–205
operational, 209
rule of justice and, 204–205
Delayed thesis arguments
classical arguments vs.,
160–164

for resistant audiences, 182
Dependent variable, 123
Dewey Decimal System, 367, 368
Dictionary definitions, 203–204
Disagreement
among experts, 128–133
analyzing sources of, 42–48
writing an analysis of, 48–50
Disanalogies, 275–276
Discovering and exploring
ideas, 56–63
Discovery draft
for causal arguments, 248–250
for definitional arguments,
215, 216
for evaluation arguments, 94
for proposal arguments,
319–320
Do, Dao (student), 142
Documenting sources, 396–410.
See also Citations
examples of, 38, 338, 383
general guidelines for, 396–397
style sheets for, 412, 413
systems of, 397–410
Does/says analysis, 32–34
Double quotation marks,
392–393
Doubt
reading-to-doubt process, 39–41
suspending, 38–39
Doubting game, 60, 61

Egothink, 436
Electronic sources
accessing, 372–373, 375
citing information from,
407–409
Ellipses, 392
Emotional appeals, 82, 154–159
Empathic listening, 26, 183
Empirical measures, 287–288, 296
Encyclopedias, 377
End-of-text citation, 397–398
Enthymeme, 97–98, 99, 103–106
Equivocation fallacy, 429
Ethical appeals, 81, 153–154

Ethical arguments, 339–353
developing, 346–347
ethical systems and, 340–346
examples of, 349–353
special difficulties of, 339–340
testing, 348–349
Ethical systems, 340–346
comparing, 344–345
naive egoism, 341–343
principle-based, 344
Utilitarianism, 343, 344, 347
Ethos, 81, 145
creating an effective, 153–154
fallacies of, 425–427
persuasive appeals and,
151–153
proposal arguments and, 308
thesis placement and, 159–164
Evaluating
conflicting positions, 50–51
consequences, 309
Evaluation arguments, 281–303
conditions of rebuttal for,
295–296
criteria-match structure of,
284–286
determining criteria for,
288–291
essay assignment on, 283
evaluating X against criteria
of, 291–293
examples of, 281–282, 297–303
general strategy for, 286–288
writing, 294–295
Evidence, 113–144
disagreement among experts
and, 128–133
effective positioning of,
136–137
from interviews, 115
numerical data and statistics
as, 118–128
from personal experience,
113–114
persuasive use of, 133–137
from reading and research,
117–118

Evidence *continued*
   strategies for rebutting,
     178–179
   as support strategy, 107–110
   from surveys or
     questionnaires, 116–117
Examples
   as evidence, 117
   evoking *pathos* with, 155–156
Exordium, 64
Expert opinion, 118
Explication, 83
Explicit arguments, 4–6
Exploration and rehearsal stage,
   73–74
Exploring ideas, 56–63
   believing and doubting game
     for, 58–61
   brainstorming methods for,
     61–63
   expressive writing tasks for,
     71–73
   freewriting for, 56–57
   idea mapping for, 58, 59
Expressive writing
   exploring ideas through,
     56–63
   generating ideas through,
     71–74
Extended analogies, 269–270

Facts
   defined, 135
   disagreement about, 42,
     131–132
   distinguishing from inference
     or opinion, 135
   as evidence, 117
Facts on File, 378
Fair summary, 174
Fallacies of logic. *See* Informal
   fallacies
False authority fallacy, 425
False dilemma fallacy, 429
Fanatics, 85–86
Faulty analogies, 244, 432
Feminist theories of
   argument, 184

Fight misconception, 3–4
Footnotes, 397
Formal fallacies, 422
Formal logic, 95–96
Freewriting, 56–57, 318, 359–360
Frequently asked questions
   (FAQs), 361, 364
Fuchs, Victor, 242, 249, 259

Gilliam, Dorothy, 46
Goodman, Ellen, 160
Goodwin, Debra (student), 302
Gopher, 375–377
Gorgias, The (Plato), 12–13
Grapes of Wrath (Steinbeck), 4
Graphically enhancing
   presentations, 124–127
Graphs
   bar, 122–124
   line, 121–121
Grounds, 100–101
   conditions of rebuttal and,
     102–106
Groups
   avoiding bad habits in, 436
   classroom debate exercise for,
     451–452
   five-to-seven person, 438–440
   "good argumentative writing"
     project for, 442–451
   skills and roles in, 437–440
   value of working in, 436–437
   working in pairs in, 440–441
Guarantees, 100

Hasty generalization fallacy, 241,
   431–432
Hotlists of Internet sites, 376
Hume, David, 230

Idea mapping, 58, 59
   for causal arguments, 246, 248
Imaginative impact, 82
Immediate cause, 244
Implicit arguments, 4–6
Independent variable, 123
Indexed numbers, 128
Inductive methods

   correlation, 241–242
   informal induction, 239, 241
   scientific experimentation, 241
Inference
   defined, 135
   distinguishing fact from, 135
Informal fallacies, 422–433. *See
   also names of specific fallacies*
   of *ethos*, 425–427
   of *logos*, 427–433
   of *pathos*, 423–425
Informal induction, 239, 241
Information questions, 83–85
INFOTRAC, 375
Inserted quotations, 391
Internet Relay Chat (IRC), 365
Internet resources, 360–366
   Gopher, 375–377
   listserv discussions, 360–362
   real-time discussions, 364–366
   usenet newsgroups, 362–364
   World Wide Web, 375–377
Interview data, 115
In-text citation, 398–400
Invention, 54
Inventory of topics, 71
Irrational premises, 424
Isaacson, Sam (student), 300
Issue questions, 83–85, 88
Issues, problematic, 72

James, William, 203
Jefferson, Thomas, 17
Johnson, Lyndon, 272, 275
Journal articles
   citation formats for, 404–405
   indexes of, 369–372, 373, 374
Judeo-Christian ethics, 346–347
Justification of claims, 7–9

Kant, Immanuel, 344, 346
Krauthammer, Charles, 58,
   219, 221

Language
   evoking *pathos* with, 158–159
   ordering the world
     through, 203

Leader role in groups, 438
Lecture citations, 410
Legends on bar graphs, 122, 123
Le Guin, Ursula, 349
Leo, John, 26, 46
Levin, Michael, 387
Library of Congress System, 367, 369
Library resources, 366–378
    card catalog, 367–369
    electronic databases, 375
    Gopher, 375–377
    online catalogs, 372–373, 375
    periodical and newspaper indexes, 369–372, 373, 374
    reference books, 377–378
    World Wide Web, 375–377
Likes/dislikes list, 247
Line graphs
    manipulating data with, 125, 126
    presenting numerical data with, 121–122
Listserv discussions, 360–362
Logic, formal, 95–96
Logical appeals, 81
Logical fallacies, 421–434
Logical structure of arguments, 88–91, 95–112
    causal arguments and, 233–236
    explained, 95–98
    strategies of support for, 106–112
    Toulmin system for articulating, 99–106
Logos, 81, 145
    fallacies of, 427–433
    overview of, 95–98
    persuasive appeals and, 151–153
    thesis placement and, 159–164
Lycos search engine, 376

Magazine articles
    citation formats for, 404–405
    indexes of, 369–372, 373, 374

Manipulating data, 118–119, 125, 126
Mapplethorpe, Robert, 193
Marginal notations
    reading-to-believe, 33
    reading-to-doubt, 40
Marx, Karl, 269
Massaging data, 118
Match argument. See Criteria-match structure
Meaning of Meaning, The (Richards & Ogden), 203
Memory, data collected from, 113–114
Metaphors. See also Analogies
    evoking pathos with, 158–159
Microtheme exercises, 138–142, 267–268
Mill, John Stuart, 343, 344
Minot, Walter S., 249, 252, 262
Mitigating circumstances, 287
MLA (Modern Language Association) documentation system, 37, 322, 397–410
    examples of, 38, 338, 412
    style sheet for, 412
MLA Handbook for Writers of Research Papers, 400, 410
Modifying quotations, 391–392
Moral arguments. See Ethical arguments
Moving your audience, 145–165
Multisided arguments
    exercise on, 166–169
    one-sided arguments vs., 169, 186–187
Murray, Charles, 26, 27

Naive egoism, 341–343
Naming process, 203
Narratio, 64
Narratives, 156–158
Necessary cause, 245
Necessary criteria, 207
Neutral audiences, 173–182
    conceding to opposing views for, 181–182

refuting opposing views for, 174–181
    summarizing opposing views for, 173–174
Newsgroups, Usenet, 362–364
Newspaper articles
    citation formats for, 406
    indexes of, 369–372, 373, 374
    microtheme exercise using, 140–141
    simulation game using, 15–17
New York Times Index, 370, 378
Non sequitur fallacy, 432–433
Note taking
    article summaries as tool for, 386
    developing a system of, 382
    plagiarism and, 396
Numerical data. See also Research data
    bar graphs for presenting, 122–124
    graphics for effect with, 124–127
    line graphs for presenting, 121–122
    manipulation of, 118–119, 125, 126
    pie charts for presenting, 124, 125
    strategic use of, 127–128
    tables for presenting, 119–121

Observational data, 114
Ogden, C. K., 203
100-word argument summary, 35
One-sentence argument summary, 35
One-sided arguments
    exercise on, 166–169
    multisided arguments vs., 169, 186–187
    supportive audiences and, 172–173
Online information sources
    accessing, 372–373, 375
    citing information from, 407–409

Opinion vs. fact, 135
Opposing arguments
    conceding to, 181–182
    evaluation of, 50–51
    refuting, 174–181
    summarizing, 173–174
Opposing counsel, 99
Organizing arguments. *See*
    Shaping arguments
Origins of argument, 83–85
"Ought" arguments. *See*
    Proposal arguments
Outlines, 66–70
Oversimplified cause fallacy, 244
Owen, Wilfred, 5

Paraphrasing arguments, 386, 390
Parenthetical citations, 398–400
Pars pro toto fallacy, 432
Partitio, 64
Pathos, 82, 145
    evoking, 154–159
    fallacies of, 423–425
    persuasive appeals and,
        151–153
    proposal arguments and, 307
    thesis placement and, 159–164
Periodical articles
    citation formats for, 404–405
    indexes of, 369–372, 373, 374
Peroratio, 64
Personal experience data. *See
    also* Research data
    from memory, 113–114
    from observations, 114
    writing assignment using,
        138–139
Persuasion
    appealing to beliefs and
        emotions in, 154–159
    audience-based reasons and,
        146–151
    credibility and, 153–154
    truth seeking and, 10–12
    using evidence for, 133–137
Pie charts, 124, 125
Plagiarism, 395–396
Plato, 12–13

Pluralist culture, 15
Poincaré, Jules Henri, 192
Policy proposals
    explained, 305–306
    writing assignments on, 310
Positioning of evidence, 136–137
Post hoc, ergo propter hoc fallacy,
    239, 430
Practical proposals
    explained, 305–306
    writing assignment on,
        309–310
Precedents. *See also* Analogies
    in causal arguments, 243–244
    refuting arguments based
        on, 274
    in resemblance arguments,
        271–273
    writing assignment on, 268
Precipitating cause, 245
Precis, 31
Predicting future
    consequences, 308
Premises. *See* Reasons
"Presence" in arguments, 124,
    307–308
Prima facie obligation, 345–346
Principles. *See also* Consequences
    arguments based on, 194–195,
        348–349
    ethical systems grounded in,
        344, 345–346
Problematic issues, 72
Process, argument as, 9–10
Pro-con debate, 4
Product, argument as, 9–10
Proposal arguments, 304–338
    conditions of rebuttal for,
        320–322
    developing, 311–314
    essay assignments on, 309–310
    examples of, 304–305, 323–338
    nature of, 305–306
    special requirements of,
        306–309
    stock issues strategy for,
        314–315
    structure and strategy of, 306

Toulmin system and, 315–317
    writing, 318–320
Propositio, 64
Provincialism fallacy, 424
Pseudo-arguments, 85–88
*Publication Manual of the
    American Psychological
    Association*, 410

Qualifiers, 103–106
Quarrel misconception, 3–4
Questionnaire data, 116–117
Questions
    formulating for research
        papers, 358–360
    information, 83–85
    issue, 83–85, 88
    trigger, 71, 73
Quotations, 386–387, 390–393
    block quotations, 390
    citing, 400
    example of using, 393
    inserted quotations, 391
    shortening or modifying,
        391–392
    using quotations within,
        392–393

Ray, Dixie Lee, 134
*Readers' Guide to Periodical
    Literature*, 370, 373, 375
Reading arguments, 24–51
    branch diagram for, 36
    evaluating conflicting
        positions in, 50–51
    importance of, 24
    improving reading process for,
        24–25
    reading as a believer, 26–39
    reading as a doubter, 39–41
    sources of disagreement in,
        42–48
    strategies for, 26
    summary writing and, 31–37
    suspending doubt in, 38–39
    unfolding structure and, 93–94
    written analysis of a
        disagreement and, 48–50

Real-time discussions, 364–366

Reasons
audience-based, 146–151
chain of, 110–112
conditions of rebuttal and, 102–106
as core of argument, 88–91
defined, 88
expressed in "because" clauses, 90–91
support strategies for, 106–112
Toulmin system for articulating, 99–106

Rebuttal. *See also* Conditions of rebuttal; Refuting opposing strategies for rebutting evidence, 178–179

Recency of factual data, 134

Recorder role, 439

Red herring fallacy, 424–425

Reference books, 377–378

"References" list, 397–398, 400–410

Refuting opposing views, 174–181. *See also* Conditions of rebuttal
example of refutation strategy, 179–181
strategies for rebutting evidence, 178–179
writing assignment on, 187

Remote cause, 244–245

Representativeness of factual data, 134

Research data. *See also* Personal experience data
discriminating use of, 135
documentation systems for, 397–410, 412, 413
facts and examples as, 117–118
incorporating into arguments, 382–395
from the Internet, 360–366
from interviews, 115
from libraries, 366–378
numerical and statistical, 118–128

recency, representativeness, and sufficiency of, 134–135
selecting from reliable sources, 133–134
summaries of, 118, 384–385, 389
from surveys and questionnaires, 116–117
from testimonies, 118

Research papers, 357–379
attributive tags in, 394–395
citing information in, 383, 397–410, 412, 413
clarifying your thinking for, 380–382
developing a note-taking system for, 382
documenting your sources in, 396–397
formulating questions for, 358–360
Internet resources for, 360–366
library resources for, 366–378
paraphrasing arguments in, 386, 390
plagiarism and, 395–396
quoting passages in, 386–387, 390–393
summarizing arguments in, 384–385, 389

Resemblance arguments, 195–196, 264–280
analogies in, 268–271
conditions of rebuttal for, 274–276
definitional arguments compared to, 265–267
essay assignments on, 267–268
examples of, 264–265, 277, 278–280
precedents in, 271–273
writing, 274

Resistant audiences, 182–186
delayed thesis argument for, 182–183
determining level of resistance in, 170–172
Rogerian argument for, 183–186

Revision
of causal arguments, 250
of definitional arguments, 215–217
of evaluation arguments, 295
of proposal arguments, 320

Rhetorical context, 208–209

Rhetorical effects, 125

Rhetorical triangle, 81–83, 151

Richards, I. A., 203

Rogerian argument, 183–186
example of, 185–186
writing assignment on, 188

Rogers, Carl, 26, 183

Rule of justice, 204–205

Sagan, Carl, 134, 238, 250, 253

Scale of resistance, 170, 172

Scientific experimentation, 241, 251

Search engines, 375–376

Self-announcing structures, 92–93

Shaping arguments, 63–70
classical argument structure for, 63–66
power of tree diagrams for, 66–70

Shared assumptions, 86–87

Shared values, 150

Shortening quotations, 391–392

"Should" arguments. *See* Proposal arguments

Simulation game, 15

Single quotation marks, 392–393

Skeptics, 85–86

Slanted language, 158–159

Slippery-slope arguments, 348, 430–431

Social context for arguments, 81–83

Social Sciences Index, 370, 374, 375

Socrates, 12–13

Sophistry, 13, 341

Specialized indexes, 370–372

Standards in evaluation arguments, 286–287, 296

Statistical Abstracts of the United States, 378
Statistics. *See also* Numerical data
    manipulating, 118–119, 125, 126
    presenting as evidence, 118–128
    writing assignment using,
        142, 143
Steinbeck, John, 4
Stock issues strategy, 314–315
Strawperson fallacy, 427
Style sheets for citing sources,
    412, 413
Sufficiency of factual data,
    134–135
Sufficient cause, 245
Sufficient criteria, 207
Sullivan, Kathy (student), 220
Summarizing
    arguments, 384–385, 389
    opposing views, 173–174, 187
Summary writing
    as note-taking tool, 386
    reading-to-believe process
        and, 31–37
    of research data, 118,
        384–385, 389
    in your own written
        arguments, 37–38
Supportive audiences, 172–173
Support strategy, 106–112
    chain of reasons as, 110–112
    evidence as, 107–110
Suppressed evidence, 432
Survey data, 116–117
Suspending doubt, 38–39

Tables, 119–121
Tang, Terry, 298
Teasing data, 118
Television program citations, 410
Ten Commandments, 344
Testimony as evidence, 118
Thesis placement, 159–164
Tierney, John, 176
Topics inventory, 71
Torpey, Mary Lou (student), 239,
    249, 257

Toulmin, Stephen, 99
Toulmin system, 99–112
    causal arguments and,
        233–236
    definitional arguments and,
        201–202, 215–217
    determining strategies of
        support with, 106–112
    evaluation arguments and,
        284–285, 292–293
    explained, 99–106
    proposal arguments and,
        315–317
    refuting opposing views with,
        175, 176–177
    resemblance arguments and,
        267, 272–273, 275
Tree diagrams, 66–70
Trends list, 247–248
Trigger questions, 71, 73, 318
Truth. *See also* Values
    disagreement about, 42
    problem of, 12–15
    seeking for, 10–12
Truth arguments, 191–192
Tweaking data, 118
250-word argument summary,
    35, 37

Uncertainty, coping with, 131–133
Undecided audiences, 173–182
    conceding to opposing views
        for, 181–182
    refuting opposing views for,
        174–181
    summarizing opposing views
        for, 173–174
Undeveloped analogies, 268–269
Unfair summary, 173
Unfolding structures, 92, 93–94
Uniform Resource Locator
    (URL), 360
U.S. Supreme Court, 17
University Standards
    Committee, 17–22
Usenet newsgroups, 362–364
Utilitarianism, 343, 344, 347

Values. *See also* Truth
    disagreement about, 42–48,
        132–133
    shared, 150
Values arguments
    explained, 192–193
    strategy for developing,
        193–196
Veronica search engine, 375
Videocassette citations, 409

Wall Street Journal, 26
Warrants, 99, 100
    conditions of rebuttal and,
        102–106
    problem of, 340
Webcrawler search engine, 376
Weidenbaum, Murray, 297
Weighting of criteria, 291, 295
Word choice, 158–159
Working thesis statement, 91
"Works Cited" list, 397–398,
    400–410
World Wide Web. *See also*
    Internet resources
    searching for resources on,
        375–377
    Uniform Resource
        Locators, 360
Writing arguments, 52–77
    argument summaries, 31–38,
        118, 384–385, 389
    causal arguments, 247–250
    definitional arguments,
        210–217
    discovery and exploration
        strategies, 56–63
    evaluation arguments,
        294–295
    expressive writing and, 56–63,
        71–74
    improving your writing
        processes, 54–55
    organization and shaping
        strategies, 63–70
    proposal arguments, 318–320
    resemblance arguments, 274

stages in writing process and, 52–53
structures for stating your claim in, 92–93
Writing assignments
analogy microtheme, 267–268
analyzing disagreements, 48–50, 76
argument summary, 76
causal arguments, 236–237
classical arguments, 188
debate essay, 76
definitional arguments, 200–201
evaluation arguments, 283
evidence from research, 139–140

letter to instructor, 75–76
multi-reasoned formal argument, 142
newspaper data, 140–141
personal experience data, 138–139
precedence microtheme, 268
project proposal, 77
proposal arguments, 309–310
resemblance arguments, 267–268
Rogerian strategy, 188
statistical data, 142, 143
summarizing and refuting opposing views, 187–188
Writing communities, 435–452
avoiding bad habits of, 436

classroom debate exercise for, 451–452
"good argumentative writing" project for, 442–451
skills and roles in, 437–441
value of, 436–437

Yahoo search engine, 376
Y terms
defining, 206–209
developing criteria for, 212–214

Zinn, Howard, 275

Checklist for Peer Reviewers

Understanding the Writer's Intentions

- What is the issue being addressed in this essay?
- What is the writer's major thesis/claim?
- Where does the writer present this thesis/claim? (See pp. 159–64.)
- Who disagrees with this claim and why?
- Who is the primary audience for this argument? Does the writer regard this audience as friendly to the writer's position? As neutral or undecided? As hostile? (See pp. 170–87.)

Reconstructing the Writer's Argument

- Summarize the writer's main reason for making this claim in the form of because clauses. (See pp. 90–93.)
- Make a tree diagram, flow chart, or outline of the writer's argument.

Identifying the Argument's Claim Type

- Does the writer's claim fit one of the argument types (strategies) discussed in Part III (definition, cause, resemblance, evaluation, or proposal)?
- If so, does the writer use argumentative strategies appropriate to that claim type?
- How well does the argument address possible conditions of rebuttal for its major claim assuming that it is a claim of:
    - —Definition (see pp. 217–19)
    - —Cause (see pp. 250–52)
    - —Resemblance (see pp. 274–76)
    - —Evaluation (see pp. 295–96)
    - —Proposal (see pp. 320–22)

Critiquing the Main Lines of the Argument

- Is each supporting reason clearly relevant to the argument's major claim? Can you offer any supporting reasons or lines of argument that the writer may have overlooked?
- Is each supporting reason in turn supported with sufficient evidence or chains of reasons (grounds)? Identify at least one place where a skeptical reader might require more substantial support for a reason.